An
Empire
of
Their
Own

An Empire of Their Own

HOW THE JEWS INVENTED HOLLYWOOD

BY NEAL GABLER

ANCHOR BOOKS
DOUBLEDAY
NEW YORK LONDON TORONTO SYDNEY AUCKLAND

To my beloved daughters, Laurel and Tanne,

*And to all those who stand outside
the corridors of power and privilege*

AN ANCHOR BOOK
PUBLISHED BY DOUBLEDAY
a division of Bantam Doubleday Dell Publishing Group, Inc.
1540 Broadway, New York, New York 10036

ANCHOR BOOKS, DOUBLEDAY, and the portrayal
of an anchor are trademarks of Doubleday, a division of
Bantam Doubleday Dell Publishing Group, Inc.

An Empire of Their Own was originally published
in hardcover by Crown Publishers, Inc. in 1988.
The Anchor Books edition is published by arrangement
with Crown Publishers, Inc.

Acknowledgments for permission to use copyrighted material
begin on page 488.

Library of Congress Cataloging-in-Publication Data
Gabler, Neal.
    An empire of their own: how the Jews invented
    Hollywood / by Neal Gabler. — 1st Anchor books ed.
        p.   cm.
    "This book was originally published in hardcover by
    Crown Publishers, Inc." — T.p. verso.
    Bibliography: p.
    Includes index.
    1. Motion picture industry—California—Los
    Angeles—History.   2. Jews in the motion
    picture industry—United States.   3. Jewish
    motion picture producers and directors—United
    States—Biography.   I. Title.
    [PN1993.5.U65G28   1989]   89-32940
    384′.8′0979494—dc20   CIP
    ISBN 0-385-26557-3

Contents

I want to give an all-fireworks illumination of the intense passion in Stahr's soul, his love of life, his love for the great thing he's built out here, his, perhaps not exactly satisfaction, but his feeling certainly of coming home to an empire of his own—an empire he has made.

F. SCOTT FITZGERALD,
THE LAST TYCOON

Introduction

Russian-Jewish immigrants came from the *shtetls* and ghettos out to Hollywood.... In this magical place that had no relationship to any reality they had ever seen before in their lives, or that anyone else had ever seen, they decided to create their idea of an eastern aristocracy....The American Dream—is a Jewish invention.

JILL ROBINSON

They [the Jews of Hollywood] not only believed in the American Dream, rather than see it fail, they tried desperately and successfully to manufacture the evidence for its survival...and for its existence.

HY KRAFT, SCREENWRITER

THIS BOOK BEGINS, AS HOLLY-wood itself did, with something of a paradox. The paradox is that the American film industry, which Will Hays, president of the original Motion Picture Producers and Distributors of America, called "the quintessence of what we mean by 'America,'" was founded and for more than thirty years operated by Eastern European Jews who themselves seemed to be anything *but* the quintessence of America. The much-vaunted "studio system," which provided a prodigious supply of films during the movies' heyday, was supervised by a second generation of Jews, many of whom also regarded themselves as marginal

1

men trying to punch into the American mainstream. The storefront theaters of the late teens were transformed into the movie palaces of the twenties by Jewish exhibitors. And when sound movies commandeered the industry, Hollywood was invaded by a battalion of Jewish writers, mostly from the East. The most powerful talent agencies were run by Jews. Jewish lawyers transacted most of the industry's business and Jewish doctors ministered to the industry's sick. Above all, Jews produced the movies. "Of 85 names engaged in production," a 1936 study noted, "53 are Jews. And the Jewish advantage holds in prestige as well as numbers." All of which led F. Scott Fitzgerald to characterize Hollywood carpingly as "a Jewish holiday, a gentiles [sic] tragedy."

The real tragedy, however, was certainly the Jews'. Their dominance became a target for wave after wave of vicious anti-Semites— from fire-and-brimstone evangelicals in the teens and early twenties who demanded the movies' liberation from "the hands of the devil and 500 un-Christian Jews" to Red-baiters in the forties for whom Judaism was really a variety of communism and the movies their chief form of propaganda. The sum of this anti-Semitic demonology was that the Jews, by design or sheer ignorance, had used the movies to undermine traditional American values. As one antagonist put it, "It is only because they [the Hollywood Jews] are outside the moral sphere of American culture that they blunder so badly that they require periodic campaigns such as that of the Legion of Decency [a Catholic reform group] to set them right." Ducking from these assaults, the Jews became the phantoms of the film history they had created, haunting it but never really able to inhabit it.

What deepened the pathos was that while the Hollywood Jews were being assailed by know-nothings for conspiring against traditional American values and the power structure that maintained them, they were desperately embracing those values and working to enter the power structure. Above all things, they wanted to be regarded as Americans, not Jews; they wanted to reinvent themselves here as new men. The movie Jews were acting out what Isaiah Berlin, in a similar context, had described as "an over-intense admiration or indeed worship" for the majority, a reverence that, Berlin also noted, sometimes oscillated with a latent resentment too, creating what he sympathetically called a "neurotic distortion of the facts." Hollywood became both the vehicle for and the product of their distortions.

The Hollywood Jews, at least the first generation that built the industry and form the core of this book, were a remarkably homogeneous group with remarkably similar childhood experiences. The eldest, Carl Laemmle, was born in 1867 in Laupheim, a small village in southwestern Germany. His beloved mother died shortly after his thirteenth birthday, and he prevailed upon his father, a penurious land speculator, to let him come to America to seek his fortune. He would eventually found Universal Pictures.

Adolph Zukor was born in a small Hungarian village in the Tokay grape district. His father died while Adolph was in infancy, his mother a few years later, and Adolph was bundled off to an uncle nearby, a steely, bloodless rabbinical scholar. Lonely, independent, and unloved, Zukor, like Laemmle, petitioned to leave for America and a new life. He would later build Paramount Pictures.

William Fox was another Hungarian. In his case his parents were the emigrés, but his father was shiftless and irresponsible (William would spit on his coffin during the funeral), and the boy was forced to become an entrepreneur, hawking soda pop, sandwiches, and chimney black. He would parlay these experiences into the Fox Film Corporation.

Louis B. Mayer said that he had forgotten exactly where in Russia he had been born and on what day. (He would later appropriate the Fourth of July for his birthday.) He settled with his parents in maritime Canada, where his father established a junkyard and salvage operation. By his teens, Louis was bridling at his father's authority, and he left for Boston, where he tried setting up a junk and salvage operation of his own. He would, of course, head the greatest studio of them all, Metro-Goldwyn-Mayer.

Benjamin Warner left his wife, son, and infant daughter in Poland while he followed relatives who had sought their fortune in America. After two years as a cobbler in Baltimore, he had earned enough to send for his family and promptly began increasing their number. For years, he roamed the East and Canada, peddling notions from a wagon, before finally settling in Youngstown, Ohio, and it was there his sons, Harry, Sam, Albert, and Jack, decided to pool their resources and buy a broken movie projector. The result was the eponymous company, Warner Brothers.

The most striking similarity among the Hollywood Jews, however, wasn't their Eastern European origins. What united them in deep spiritual kinship was their utter and absolute rejection of their pasts and their equally absolute devotion to their new country. For immigrant Jews to want to assimilate, particularly when they had been victimized in their home countries, was nothing exceptional. But something drove the young Hollywood Jews to a ferocious, even pathological, embrace of America. Something drove them to deny whatever they had been before settling here.

One common, undeniable factor was a patrimony of failure. All had grown up in destitution. All, with the exception of Zukor, who had no father at all, had *luftmenshen* for fathers, men who shuttled from one job to another, from one place to another. Those fathers who emigrated found themselves unable to adjust to America. Some, like Jacob Mayer, sought solace and stability in religion, becoming a *macher* at the new synagogue in St. John, New Brunswick. Others, like William Fox's father, sought refuge in women, drink, and cards. Judging from the children's lives and words, this failure had a profound effect on them. The sons, who speak so lovingly of their doting mothers, are pointedly silent or even hostile toward their fathers. At best, the men are adjudged to have been kind—a left-handed compliment from individuals who venerated mettle.

One hesitates getting too Oedipal here, but the evidence certainly supports the view that the sons, embittered by their fathers' failures, launched a war against their own pasts—a patricide, one could say, against everything their fathers represented. To escape their fathers' fate meant escaping the past: the European roots, the language and accents, the customs and the religion. The past exerted a hold, fashioned a style. One had to erase it, as Mayer erased his birthdate, and adopt a new style—a style for America. America was the baptism to cleanse and renew.

The Hollywood Jews embarked on an assimilation so ruthless and complete that they cut their lives to the pattern of American respectability as they interpreted it. To enter America and be accepted there as Americans, however, was a formidable challenge in the early part of this century when nativism and xenophobia were rampant. The same impulse that drove the Jews to assimilate drove self-appointed defenders of America to prevent Jews from assimilating and, in their view, tainting the country. Beyond the barricades erected by America's guardians, the Jews saw an America of gentility, respectability, and status, but they were prohibited from entering those precincts. "That's the important thing," said one Jewish producer who knew the so-called moguls. "The motion picture hierarchy felt that they were on the outside of the real power source of the country. They were not members of the power elite. They were outside of that New England-Wall Street-Middle West money." And that is where the movies came in.

The movie industry held out a number of blandishments to these Jews, not the least of which was that it admitted them. There were no social barriers in a business as new and faintly disreputable as the movies were in the early years of this century. There were none of the impediments imposed by loftier professions and more firmly entrenched businesses to keep Jews and other undesirables out. Financial barriers were lower too, and that attracted Jews and other immigrant entrepreneurs. In fact, one could conceivably open a theater for less than four hundred dollars.

The Jews also had a special compatibility with the industry, one that gave them certain advantages over their competitors. For one thing, having come primarily from fashion and retail, they understood public taste and were masters at gauging market swings, at merchandising, at pirating away customers and beating the competition. For another, as immigrants themselves, they had a peculiar sensitivity to the dreams and aspirations of other immigrants and working-class families, two overlapping groups that made up a significant portion of the early moviegoing audience. The Jews were their own best appraisers of entertainment. "They *were* the audience," a producer told me. "They were the same people. They were not too far removed from those primitive feelings and attitudes."

But in order to understand what may have been the chief appeal of the movies to these Jews, one must understand their hunger for assimilation and the way in which the movies could uniquely satisfy that hunger. If the Jews were proscribed from entering the real corridors of gentility and status in America, the movies offered an ingenious option. Within the studios and on the screen, the Jews could simply create a new country—an empire of their own, so to speak—

one where they would not only be admitted, but would govern as well. They would fabricate their empire in the image of America as they would fabricate themselves in the image of prosperous Americans. They would create its values and myths, its traditions and archetypes. It would be an America where fathers were strong, families stable, people attractive, resilient, resourceful, and decent. This was *their* America, and its invention may be their most enduring legacy.

It was also, if one examined it, a fictive rehabilitation of the moguls' own lives—lives where fathers had been weak, families destabilized, people unattractive, doomed, impractical, and indifferent. But the rehabilitation wasn't only fictive. While they were mythologizing America on the screen, the Hollywood Jews also set about redesigning themselves. Their own lives became a kind of art, and the process affected every aspect of Hollywood. They lived in large, palatial homes that imitated (some would say "vulgarized") the estates of the eastern establishment. They became members of a lavish new country club called Hillcrest that mimicked the gentile clubs that barred them. They subscribed to a cultural life, centered around the Hollywood Bowl, that simulated the cultural life of the eastern aristocracy. For their social life, they organized a system of estates, a rigid hierarchy, that could easily have been modeled after the court of Louis XIV. For their politics they forsook the Democrats, for whom the overwhelming majority of their coreligionists voted, and swore fealty instead to the Republicans as American aristocrats did. Guilt ran too deep for them to disavow Judaism entirely, but the religious community to which they contributed came awfully close; by its lights, Jews were to be seen and not heard. As the rabbi who guided the Hollywood Jews put it, "For God's sakes, I'm living in America. I have to be part of my environment. I don't want any ghettos here for myself."

In short, like Disraeli, another Jew who felt alienated from and patronized by a class-conscious society, the Hollywood Jews would cope through "a sustained attempt to live a fiction, and to cast its spell over the minds of others." What is amazing is the extent to which they succeeded in promulgating this fiction throughout the world. By making a "shadow" America, one which idealized every old glorifying bromide about the country, the Hollywood Jews created a powerful

cluster of images and ideas—so powerful that, in a sense, they colo-
nized the American imagination. No one could think about this
country without thinking about the movies. As a result, the paradox
—that the movies were quintessentially American while the men who
made them were not—doubled back on itself. Ultimately, American
values came to be *defined* largely by the movies the Jews made. Ultimately, by creating their idealized America on the screen, the Jews
reinvented the country in the image of their fiction.

How they did so, why they did so, and what they gained and lost by
doing so is the story of this book.

PART ONE

The Men

1

The Killer

With the power, he wanted the recognition. There was a big ego here: that he was the biggest man in the whole damn motion picture industry, that he was bigger than Fox, and he was bigger than Mayer, and he was bigger than the Warner brothers, and he was bigger than the Cohns.... I know one thing. He expected as a result of what he had done and the enormity of the power which he had achieved, that that's the way it [film history] would be written. He almost took it for granted. When it was written, it would start [with him].

MAX YOUNGSTEIN, FILM EXECUTIVE

ADOLPH ZUKOR HATED TWO things. One was losing. It didn't matter what the stakes were. A friendly bridge game with his associate Marcus Loew could suddenly erupt, as one witness noted, into a shouting match followed by the crash of the table. "Loew came out, followed by Zukor, who was trembling with rage. After some discussion the host cleared up a point about a certain club lead," but the antagonists still refused to speak to one another. On another occasion Jesse Lasky, a rival producer, tried to lure away one of Zukor's stars. Zukor topped Lasky's initial offer, and a bidding war ensued, with Zukor upping the ante by one or two thousand dollars each time, until Lasky finally folded. Then Zukor promptly turned around and lent Lasky the star for his next production. The victory was all.

The second thing Zukor hated was being lied to. Once, he invited a new member of his company's sales staff to one of his famous bridge games. The man had claimed some expertise in cards, but after the first bid Zukor could see he had been bluffing to win favor. After the third deal, remembered Zukor's son, Eugene, "my father took the deck of cards and threw them on the floor. He said, 'I can tolerate a person who will admit he doesn't know. . . . But you said you are a bridge player, and you don't know the first goddamn thing about it, and you spoiled our whole evening, and this I won't tolerate. . . . As far as I'm concerned, you can leave right now.' And the guy packed up and went home."

Almost everyone found him unbending, puritanical, and even chilling. "Mr. Zukor always remained *Mister* Zukor," said William de Mille, a writer and the brother of Zukor's most important director, Cecil B. De Mille. "The rest of us were 'Cecil' and 'Jesse,' 'Sam' and 'Bill,' but only on rare and completely informal occasions have I ever heard the soft-voiced little man addressed as 'Adolph,' although he was not much older than we were." Some employees nicknamed him "Creepy" because of the way he had of icily staring at them with his "long eyes like an Indian chief's." Even Jesse Lasky, with whom he formed a fifteen-year alliance, treated him with a mixture of "formality and reverence." Lasky was so terrified of Zukor's moral rigidity that when, during a business trip, he returned to his hotel after an evening's dalliance and found Zukor waiting for him, he felt compelled to pretend that he was actually dressing for the day rather than undressing to sleep.

To his detractors—and there were many—Zukor's will to win and his dogmatism were symptoms of megalomania. That may have been so, but Zukor had profound reasons for wanting to impose his will on the world. His is really the story of a man who had been emptied out in childhood, who had lost or been deprived of love and security, and who then set about to fill himself back up again, even if that meant appropriating everything around him. He was born in Risce, Hungary, a tiny farming village in the famous Tokay grape district. His father, who both farmed and ran a dry goods store, died in a freak accident when Adolph was barely a year old; he had burst a vein lifting a box. His mother remarried, but, at least as young Adolph remembered it, she never fully recovered from her husband's death and died herself seven years later. When Adolph's stepfather refused to care for him and his older brother, Arthur, the two were shuffled off to an uncle in a nearby village.

The uncle, Kalman Lieberman, was a stern, dedicated, argumentative Judaic scholar who believed that studying religion was one's chief moral obligation, and he took the boys in primarily to honor his sister's dying wish that her sons commit their lives to Judaism. Arthur, who was gregarious and bright, did. (He eventually became the rabbi at a large temple in Berlin.) Adolph, who was far more withdrawn than his brother, couldn't help but study Judaism. His family was steeped in it. Judaism was "a question that was always in the minds of the principal people in the family." But, by his own admission, he wasn't very good at arcane disquisitions on the Talmud, the Jewish law, and entering the rabbinate didn't interest him in the slightest. "What I was interested in," he said later, "was the Bible . . . the story and the individuals—their lives fascinated me."

Unfortunately, in a family where religious fervor was a prerequisite for approval, Adolph apparently paid for his lack of interest in things Jewish with loneliness and lovelessness. His uncle eventually adopted Arthur. Whether Hungarian law prevented him from also adopting Adolph or whether he chose not to, Zukor never knew. He only knew he wasn't chosen. Adolph did, however, find a father surrogate in his school's impoverished young headmaster, Samuel Rosenberg, and it was Rosenberg who taught him the Bible and explained what it meant, who gave him private lessons and generally showed the concern that no one else had shown. "I am sure that he looked upon this man as a living god," Eugene Zukor recalled. Many years later, Eugene discovered an old doctor's bag in his father's closet containing t'fillin, Jewish prayer boxes, and a prayer shawl. He assumed his father had carried these from Risce and that he had kept them out of devotion to his mentor. "That was his secret self," Eugene said, believing his father never quite relinquished it or his attachment to Rosenberg.

It was one of the few positive associations to Judaism he had. If Judaism had become Zukor's secret self, as his son suggested, Eugene also speculated it was because Zukor perceived neither his God nor his religion as having been particularly beneficent, and his identification with his faith was at best tenuous even then. "I didn't believe in a whole deep Orthodox Jew," Zukor said later. If the Hungarian Jews had been more assimilated, as American Jews were, "I'd have been a very devout Jew." But he admitted that, as it was, he didn't "sympathize" with his coreligionists. This obviously made it impossible for him to fulfill his uncle's expectations and become a rabbi, and he asked Rosenberg to break the news to Kalman Lieberman. Lieberman was shattered by the decision. He felt betrayed but nevertheless arranged for Adolph to take an apprenticeship in another nearby village with a family friend who owned a large dry goods store.

Zukor's family had been poor; "a new pair of shoes was an event," he recalled. But they had also been enlightened and educated, and from their enlightenment and education Zukor assumed an air of superiority that he never lost. Suffering the taunts of his fellow apprentices, he "felt as though someone had dipped me into a sewer." He quickly became the favored apprentice, and the Blau family, for whom he worked, took him in, treating him as one of their own. It was from the American dime novels Blau's children devoured that Zukor learned about America. When his three-year apprenticeship neared its end, he began to ask himself, "'What's next? What future can I look forward to?' I didn't see much of a prospect. I then decided that I'd like to go to America." In petitioning the Orphans' Board, which exercised guardianship over the parentless, for ship's passage to the United States, Zukor said, "I had no father and no mother, and I had nobody that lay awake at night to figure out how to educate me. . . . I was alone." Moved by this sincere Dickensian plea, the board advanced him the money, and with forty dollars sewed in his vest to secure it from thieves on the ship, sixteen-year-old Adolph Zukor set out for America.

Zukor had come, he had said, to learn a trade and construct a future, but in America he also began the process of filling himself back up after his childhood deprivations. Hungary was a void; his own refrain about his years there was that no one, except for Samuel Rosenberg, took any particular interest in him. No one cared. So in leaving Hungary, Zukor decided to banish his youth and exile his secret self. In America he felt he was starting from scratch. As he wrote years later, "No sooner did I put my foot on American soil than I was a newborn person."

Zukor plunged into assimilation. He attended night school. He took up boxing, buying gloves, practicing, and taking part in impromptu bouts at New York's Tompkins Square on the Lower East Side. (He had a cauliflower left ear as a souvenir.) Within a few years he became a baseball enthusiast and played regularly. And he left any vestige of his Judaism, anything that might brand him as different, behind. He worked on the Sabbath, and he remembered a fellow worker at lunchtime pulling a lobster out of a bag and offering to share it. He had never seen a lobster before; in Jewish dietary law, which his family had observed, lobster was regarded as *trayf*, or taboo. But Zukor gladly indulged. He was an American now.

Like most young immigrants, he began modestly. When he first landed in New York, he stayed with a friend of his mother's, then with a cousin who was a prosperous doctor, then moved to the Lower East Side after getting a job tacking batting over springs in an upholstery shop. A few weeks later he ran into another apprentice from the Blaus who had emigrated. The friend's brother was a foreman at a furrier's, and he got Zukor a job as an apprentice. Zukor stayed for two years. When he left to become a "contract" worker, sewing fur pieces and selling them himself, he was nineteen years old and an accomplished designer. He had also opened his first bank account.

Contracting himself out this way, he was "fairly successful. I got work and a little money." But he was young and adventuresome, and the 1892 Columbian Exposition in Chicago, commemorating Columbus's discovery of America, drew him to the Midwest. Once there, he looked up a friend who had worked with him at the furrier's. The friend insisted there was a better opportunity in Chicago than in New York for novelty fur items like scarves, capes, and hats, so Zukor, with no deeper commitments in New York than he had had in Hungary, decided to stay and form a partnership.

The way the collaboration worked, his friend would solicit the orders, and Zukor would fill them. The first season, relying chiefly on a fox scarf with a clasp in the fox's mouth, the partners each cleared $1,000. The next season, despite a national business slump, Zukor's Novelty Fur Company expanded to twenty-five men and opened a branch in Peoria, some 125 miles southwest of Chicago. That year they each cleared $8,000.

But if Zukor was achieving success, he was also learning its capriciousness. His partner, Max Schosberg, also a Hungarian immigrant, decided to return home for a visit and was promptly conscripted into the Hungarian army. Zukor, usually remote and diffident, had to take over as "outside man," soliciting orders, and he discovered that he liked the work. When Schosberg returned in 1896, the partners agreed to dissolve their business; Schosberg took the Peoria branch, Zukor took Chicago. Zukor almost immediately sank all his money into a voguish fur cape, but this time his instinct failed him. The cape was a disaster.

He averted bankruptcy only because he had impressed another Chicago fur trader, Morris Kohn. Kohn, a Hungarian immigrant like Zukor, had learned the fur business from the bottom up, having traded for pelts with the Indians in the Dakotas. He knew all the angles—where to pick up small contracts, how to liquidate stock, how to drive a bargain. With Kohn's help, Zukor managed to pay off his creditors, but for Kohn it wasn't all altruism. He admired Zukor's ambition, and he proposed another partnership. He would provide the capital and sales. Zukor would be responsible for design and manufacture. Zukor agreed, and Kohn & Company opened its doors in December 1896. Within weeks Zukor had also married Kohn's niece, Lottie Kaufman.

Kohn & Company lasted nearly a decade, and it made Adolph Zukor a relatively wealthy young man. By 1899 it had opened a New York branch, and when the partners decided that they themselves needed to be closer to the fashion centers in New York, they moved the headquarters and resettled. Three years later they achieved their real breakthrough. Zukor guessed that red fox was going to be the fashionable fur of the season, and this time his prophecy proved correct. The company's profits soared. Zukor, barely thirty years old, estimated his own windfall at somewhere between $100,000 and $200,000.

One of the stubborn fallacies of movie history is that the men who created the film industry were all impoverished young vulgarians whose motives were purely mercenary. Zukor clearly didn't fit this profile. By 1903 he already looked and lived like a wealthy young burgher, and he certainly earned the income of one. He had a commodious apartment at 111th Street and Seventh Avenue (which, his son claimed, nevertheless stank of fur) in a wealthy German-Jewish section, and he dressed like a gentleman in perfectly tailored suits. It was entirely likely that he could have continued in furs and continued to do well. His life's course seemed set.

But there was something in Zukor that went unsatisfied, though he never defined what it was and may not have known himself. It could have been that he felt his social mobility was blocked by the fur business; no matter how much wealth he accumulated, he would still be associated with something unmistakably Jewish, as the fur trade was, and slightly declassé, as all the garment trades were. It could have been that he was bored. Zukor gave a hint of this, years later, when he discussed the appeal of the movies. "It's not like making shoes or automobiles, where you have a model and you follow through for the year. Every picture is an enterprise by itself. There are certain ingredients you have to study, and certain ingredients that you have to say, 'I don't think I'll take that story, I don't think I'll make it, I don't think it's what the public will take.' All of that is a very pleasant occupation." It could have been that the reserved, enigmatic Zukor simply wanted another challenge, another world to conquer and appropriate.

Whatever the motive, Zukor was obviously restless in 1903 when a cousin, Max Goldstein, approached him for a loan. Goldstein had just returned from the Pan-American Exposition in Buffalo, New York, where he had met an impresario named Mitchell Mark. Mark operated what he called Edsonia Hall, an arcade that featured Thomas Edison's marvels: phonographs, electric lights, peep shows, and moving pictures. He was also Edison's Buffalo sales representative. Now Mark had decided to open an arcade on 125th Street in New York City, and he offered a partnership to Goldstein for $3,000. Goldstein didn't have the money, but he had a wealthy cousin who did—Zukor.

Zukor not only gave Goldstein the money—which was an uncharacteristic gesture for someone as cautious as Zukor—but he visited the arcade and within a short time convinced Kohn they should set up one of their own on Fourteenth Street, which at that time was New York's tenderloin, crammed with dance halls, saloons, and arcades and teeming with immigrants looking for inexpensive thrills. As he later recounted his inspiration to Michael Korda, "I looked around and said, 'A Jew could make a lot of money at this.'" The partners rented a deserted restaurant, ripped out the seats, and installed over one hundred "peep" machines. Jesse Lasky remembered it as "filled with automatic fortune tellers, strength testers, and other fascinating gadgets. . . . But a row of peep-box dispensers of thirty-second dramas was collecting the steadiest stream of coins."

Even as a young man Zukor always tried to hedge his bets, and he never intended the arcade, called Automatic Vaudeville, to be a full-time occupation. It was a diversion, a sideline to the fur business, and in any case Kohn was to be its chief operative. But to Zukor the pull was irresistible. "Our fur offices were nearby on Twelfth Street," he wrote, "and, though handling the main end there, I couldn't keep away from the arcade." Finally he asked Kohn to switch positions with him, and Kohn complied. By this time, though, both men were smitten. They were rapidly losing interest in furs, and Kohn & Company was rapidly becoming a satellite to Automatic Vaudeville. Its success astonished even its owners. It took in between $500 and $700 each day and more than $100,000 in the first year. It had also spawned a subsidiary through which they opened arcades in Newark, Boston, and Philadelphia. By year's end, with so much of their attention now focused on Automatic Vaudeville, Kohn and Zukor, not surprisingly, decided to liquidate their fur business and concentrate exclusively on their arcades.

This was one of the scenarios for the Jews who had maneuvered into entertainment, and Kohn and Zukor were fairly typical representatives of it—middle-aged men of some means seeking new outlets for their investments and energies. But once the Jews began expanding their operations, as Kohn and Zukor did, they needed new sources of capital. What really created a Jewish "network" and populated the amusements with Jews were the friends and relatives who came aboard as investors and employees and then used their experience to embark on their own ventures. Such was the case with Marcus Loew.

Morris Kohn had first met Loew at the St. Paul Hotel in Minnesota when both were "drummers" making the rounds for their respective clothing companies. Loew was wearing an ostentatious fur-lined overcoat and a top hat, and when he caught Kohn staring at his getup, he winked and said, "I wear 'em to impress 'em." Loew had a face like a silent-screen comedian. Every feature seemed slightly oversized. He had a long, bulbous nose, a bushy mustache, and large, spaniel eyes. One theatrical producer described him upon their first meeting as "an undersized and slightly pathetic figure in an overcoat that was none too new and a walk that reminded me of some of David Warfield's stage characters." Loew was well aware of the impression he made, and he was frequently the target of his own gibes. He once told a reporter, "I'm another Napoleon," then added, "I'm just a little more than five feet tall, and I don't weigh much."

He had been born on May 7, 1870, on New York's Lower East Side, the son of a Viennese waiter and a German widow with two sons from her previous marriage. The Loews were desperately poor. As a child Marcus sold lemons and newspapers, and his mother used the unsold papers as tablecloths. But he always regarded his poverty as an opportunity. "I was poor," he once told a reporter, "but so was everyone around me. . . . It's an advantage to be poor in one sense. That's why so many successes come from the East Side. The ones with talent for better things have every incentive there to exercise them."

Small and sickly as a child, Loew compensated with a natural gregariousness. At nine he quit school to color maps at a printing company, then lost the job when he convinced his co-workers to demand a raise. A year later he was running an eight-page weekly newspaper, bustling from store to store to solicit ads, then racing back to write and edit, until an older partner nudged him aside. Like the majority of young men on the Lower East Side, he eventually went to work in the garment industry, and after seven years at a wholesale fur company, he scraped together enough capital to go into business for himself. Unfortunately the business collapsed after the first season, leaving him $1,800 in debt. To pay his creditors, he went to work as a salesman and later became a partner in his employer's new venture— golf caps. Once again disaster struck, this time leaving Loew with seven dollars in assets. "It is pretty sentiment to think industry always brings success," he said shortly before his death, possibly remembering this period of his life, "but it is a fallacy."

When Loew met Morris Kohn in St. Paul, he was probably drumming up business for a company making velveteen capes, but he had already begun rebounding from his financial doldrums and back in New York he had forged an important connection that would secure his economic position. Standing outside his apartment building one day, he struck up a conversation with a neighbor. The neighbor turned out to be the famous stage actor David Warfield. Warfield and Loew quickly became fast friends, and the two apparently began speculating in some real estate together. It was also around this time that Kohn introduced Zukor to Loew, and when Zukor moved to New York in 1900, Loew suggested he take an available apartment across the street.

Though they were friends, after a fashion, two men could not have had more dissimilar temperaments. Zukor was quiet, grave, measured, and private. Loew was garrulous, chipper, impulsive, and extroverted. Zukor had extraordinary foresight but moved with extreme caution and deliberation. Loew had less foresight but was far more apt to take chances. About the only characteristic they shared was their almost pathological desire to win—a common trait that made them especially fierce antagonists. "Ambition!" Loew told an interviewer. "You must want a big success and then beat it into submission; you must be as ravenous to reach it as the wolf who licks his teeth behind a fleeing rabbit; you must be as mad to win as the man who, with one hand growing cold on the revolver in his pocket, with the other hand pushes his last gold piece on the 'Double-O' at Monte Carlo."

When Zukor opened the Automatic Vaudeville in 1903 and then formed his subsidiary to spread it to other cities, it was inevitable, given their rivalry, that Loew would want a share, too, and he petitioned Zukor to let him invest. Zukor, possibly exhibiting his own competitive streak, seemed reluctant, but he finally relented when Warfield and Loew agreed to split a single share at $20,000 apiece. How magnanimous a gesture this really was is uncertain, since Zukor himself, concerned that the company was expanding too rapidly, was already preparing to divest his own shares of the arcade subsidiary while holding on to his piece of the original Automatic Vaudeville on

Fourteenth Street. In any case, after Zukor left, Loew and Warfield didn't last long. According to one version, they were forced out by Kohn and the remaining partners. According to a more charitable version, they left voluntarily when they decided to open an arcade of their own and felt it was unethical to retain their holdings.

Loew, unlike Zukor, never dallied. By November 1904 he and Warfield had formed the People's Vaudeville Company (a suggestive title) to operate an arcade on Twenty-third Street. Within months they had added four others in New York and a fifth in Cincinnati called the Penny Hippodrome. It was while he was setting up in Cincinnati that Loew heard about a phenomenon just across the Ohio River in Covington, Kentucky. An old hermit had opened a moving picture theater there, and Loew paid a visit. "We were surprised to see the people literally fight to get inside the place," Loew recalled. "It gave me my inspiration, and pretty soon I found myself devoting my entire attention to the development of the motion picture theater."

Loew wasn't being entirely truthful about his commitment to the movies; he was never the advocate that Zukor would become. But he did recognize opportunity. After his experience in Covington, he installed a 110-seat theater above the Hippodrome and attracted five thousand patrons on his first Sunday. Soon after that he began converting his New York arcades into movie houses. Within six months the arcades and nickelodeons had returned all of the partners' initial $100,000 investment. Within a year they had a score of storefront theaters scattered throughout New York City. Loew may have been right that success was more a function of chance than industry, but this time chance had smiled upon him. Marcus Loew had arrived.

———

Adolph Zukor remembered an evening in 1897, just before his wedding, when he took his intended to Chicago's Hopkins Theater and saw a brief film of May Irwin kissing John C. Rice in a scene from the Broadway hit *The Widow Jones*. "The next night he went back to the [fur] shop after dinner," wrote his biographer, "intending to spend the evening over a design. But toward nine o'clock he closed up and went again to the theatre—drawn irresistibly by that fascinating marvel." That was how Zukor claimed he first got interested in the movies. "It ran maybe a minute . . . but it made an indelible impression on my mind."

With the movies a coming thing, Zukor, who had learned a good deal about public taste from his years in the fur business, decided to convert the top floor of Automatic Vaudeville into a small theater, as Loew had done. "We had this empty floor over the arcade," he remembered,

> about forty feet by two hundred and fifty feet. We put in two hundred seats and then began to worry because it seemed like an awful lot, especially as most of our customers didn't know what moving pictures were and were used to paying one cent, not five. So we put in a wonderful glass staircase. Under the glass was a metal trough of running water, like a waterfall, with red, green, and blue lights shining through. We called it Crystal Hall, and people paid their five cents mainly on account of the staircase, not the movies. It was a big success.

With the success of Crystal Hall, sometime in 1906 Zukor took a trip to Pittsburgh to see Harry Davis's Nickelodeon. The Nickelodeon, which was a converted billiard hall dedicated exclusively to showing movies, had been packing in patrons ever since it opened, and it had become something of a national shrine for arcade owners like Zukor. When Zukor visited, he was already feeling uncertain about the long-term prospects of the penny arcade, and he was doing his usual groundwork to determine whether the "store shows" or nickelodeons would be financially viable. He returned convinced they would and rented the vacant store next to Automatic Vaudeville for his first movie theater.

Zukor's activities over the next year, however, indicated that he was more interested in getting involved with movies than he was in determining just what that involvement should be. He had no sooner rented the store than a former prizefight promoter and vaudeville entrepreneur named William Brady convinced him to form a partnership and operate the new storefront theater together. Brady's life was the stuff inferior Victorian melodramas were made of. As a child, Brady, a ruddy Irish-Catholic from San Francisco, had been spirited away from his mother by his deranged derelict father and then abandoned in New York. After years of odd jobs he finally became an actor and then a fight promoter, and though he was hardly in the first rank of entertainment figures, he was solidly in the second, having produced a number of successful vaudeville shows.

One thing Brady knew from years in vaudeville and prizefighting was the scent of money. In 1906, when he first met Zukor, that scent had brought him to the movies, and he had secured the New York franchise of Hale's Tours—a theater rigged up to look like a train car and showing short, filmed travelogues to give the impression of movement. "This is a big thing, and this is going to be much bigger than opening and putting chairs into a building," he insisted.

Zukor agreed with him, and for a while business was so good that the partners expanded to Philadelphia, Pittsburgh, Boston, Newark, and Coney Island. In each city Hale's Tours did smashingly for roughly six weeks. Then the novelty wore off, and the number of patrons plummeted. Grabbing for an expedient, they kept the theaters afloat for six months by obtaining *The Great Train Robbery*. This eight-minute drama with its self-explanatory title was among the very first fictional narratives on screen when it was made in 1903. It was also among the most accomplished, and it energized the movies the way the nickelodeon would later energize movie theaters. But the train cars had cost between $6,000 and $8,000 apiece to outfit, and in less than a year, even with *The Great Train Robbery*, Zukor's company had gone $160,000 in debt.

"I can hardly remember an occasion when the four of us—my father and mother and sister and I—didn't sit down to dinner together," said Zukor's son, Eugene. "My father would discuss all the events of the day, good and bad. And if disaster was ahead we would know it and be prepared for it. And if he had made a mistake in judgment, we would know it. We were always moving from an apartment with an elevator and servants to an apartment over a candy store, from Riverside Drive to Broadway." Zukor's wife was stalwart. She would say, "'Well, so we move again. I'll find a place. Now how much can we afford?' So Pa said, 'As little as possible and still be near a good school.'... This is the way our life appeared to be: a hop, skip, and jump, up and down and back and forth."

Zukor's nerve and confidence were remarkable. "With each crash that occurred," said his son, "he always sat with a cigar in his mouth as though nothing had happened." After the Hale's Tours debacle, Brady suggested they declare bankruptcy. "It was as though I'd touched him with a live wire. He bounced up from his chair and came at me with his hands out. I never dreamed he had such a temper. And he yelled, 'I won't go into bankruptcy! I won't!'" For Zukor, who had the sternest and least forgiving of moral codes, bankruptcy was not so much an admission of defeat as the breaking of an obligation. To break an obligation was tantamount to lying—one of Zukor's cardinal sins. Instead, Zukor sent Brady back to Broadway and took complete charge of the theaters, this time following the policy he had set at the Crystal Hall. He ripped out the train cars, reinstalled seats, and kept the theaters open from nine until midnight each evening. At the end of two years he had retired the debt and was even showing a profit.

Aside from vindicating himself once again, Zukor had learned a lesson from his Hale's Tours experience that was to determine the course of his life. He came to realize that the movies only seemed like novelties because they had been treated like novelties. He sensed that their potential was much greater. How he arrived at this conclusion he never really said; like most things in Zukor's life, it was probably less the result of inspiration than of rumination. But by 1908 he perceived "that these short films, one-reelers or less, didn't give me the feeling that this was something that was going to be permanent." Permanence would come only by attracting the middle-class as well as the working-class audience, and one could attract the middle-class audience only by exhibiting longer and better films—by, in a sense, imitating the middle-class forms of the novel and legitimate theater. That was precisely what Zukor was now recommending.

However obvious it might have seemed in hindsight, at the time what Zukor was proposing was a radical change in the basic conception of motion pictures (which is not to say that he was the only one who proposed it, only one of the first and most vehement). Zukor never acted impulsively, but when he did set his mind on something he was a zealot, and now he became almost messianic on the subject of longer, better films. "You couldn't head him," recalled William Brady. "Presently he was in my office bubbling over with grandiose ideas about the future of the movie racket. Some sixth sense had convinced him that the day of mere shorts was drawing to a close and full-length features, like *The Great Train Robbery*, only far longer and far better, could be the coming thing. . . . It didn't make sense to me then. . . . Zukor was about the only living human being who could guess what would happen."

Brady wasn't alone. Zukor lectured the regulars at Shanley's Grill —Loew, Brady, the Shubert brothers, who owned several legitimate theaters, and Nick and Joe Schenck, associates of Loew—on the untold possibilities of the feature film. Even Jesse Lasky, who shared Zukor's conviction about quality films, received his impassioned plea for features.

Since his Comedy Theater on Fourteenth Street was still doing standing-room business, the motive for Zukor's sudden obsession seemed far less mercenary than psychological. He must have known or at least sensed that the idea of quality feature films comported perfectly with his ongoing re-creation of himself. "Every Hungarian is either a peasant or an artist; sometimes both," he once said, but the regal, guarded Zukor of America clearly aspired to art. Changing the tone and the status of movies was a more direct route to the higher echelons of legitimate, genteel America—which Zukor had always regarded as his rightful place—and the means he would later use to effect this change indicated that raising his station and gaining acceptance from artists already accepted in literature and theater was an important consideration for him. Finally, while other movie Jews were exploiting the "democratic" possibilities of the movies, Zukor had always been vaguely uncomfortable with these possibilities and distrustful of anything even remotely demagogic; he claimed he became a Republican after hearing William Jennings Bryan's rabble-rousing "Cross of Gold" speech at the Democratic convention in Chicago, calling it "bunk." The others could secure the movies with the working-class and immigrant audiences. Zukor, whose ties to these groups were purposely tenuous, would bring them to "the better class."

Whether or not there was a specifically Jewish component in Zukor's sudden preoccupation, it was true that many if not most of the producers who would take up the banner of feature films were

Jewish, and the idea was certainly compatible with the deepest strains in Jewish life where culture had always been held in special esteem. In America, where ambitious Jews could conceivably ride culture into higher social strata, this esteem carried an even greater force. It was the Jews, like Zukor, who were most sensitive to the movies' low esteem, and the Jews who had most to gain by raising it.

Acting on this idea, in 1910 Zukor took his family to see an hour-and-a-half film of the Passion play, photographed on location in Oberammergau, Germany, where the pageant had been performed once each decade since 1634, and then promptly bought the right to exhibit the film in New York and New Jersey. The cost was $40,000. "Everybody thought I was crazy," he remembered, "and told my wife I'll lose all my money—made all kinds of predictions why I'll 'go to the wall.' Nobody believed that people would sit through a picture for hours as they would a play. There were all sorts of reasons why the thing would not succeed." That was why Marcus Loew shied away from the movies.

Zukor obviously disagreed, but he proceeded cautiously nonetheless, fearing that the Catholic church might organize opposition to a film depicting Christ. According to one version, he booked the film into Newark first to test reaction, and when a priest strenuously objected that Zukor was usurping the role of the Church, Zukor begged for mercy, claiming that he would be broke if the film failed. The ploy, if it was a ploy, worked. When the film opened in New York, it did very well, justifying Zukor's faith that audiences would sit through movies just as they sat through stage plays.

Zukor next did an extraordinary thing. While he had been evangelizing for feature films, Marcus Loew had gradually been accumulating theaters and had become a power in popular entertainment. Now Zukor proposed to pool their holdings in a new company, to be called Loew's Consolidated Enterprises. But Zukor had a proviso. "I made a condition that I would put my interest in, but that I would not take any active part in the business," he said later, "because it was not the thing I had in mind. My mind was made up on these pictures." Loew agreed, and in 1910 Zukor, released from all his obligations, left the entertainment industry to conduct what he said would be a three-year study of the movies—a personal investigation into their prospects.

Among those who remained unconvinced about those prospects was Loew himself. Zukor attributed his partner's skepticism to the 1907 national depression, when several of Loew's theaters slumped along with the rest of the economy. (Zukor had suffered, too.) Whatever the source, his confidence had been shaken. Many years later he enjoyed telling the story of opening night at one of his movie theaters where only a single patron came. Thinking quickly, he had the usher tell the fellow that this was really a dry run and he had been sold the ticket by mistake, but the man was undeterred and insisted on seeing a show. Loew wandered glumly back to Shanley's, seeking commiseration from his friends.

Since almost everywhere else the movies were prospering, it is hard to tell how much of this was apocryphal and revisionist, Loew's way of justifying his lack of vision, and how much was truth. But if Loew was less sanguine about the movies than Zukor, he did share one thing with him—the aspiration to graduate from working-class to middle-class audiences—and together the two men came to represent the two basic strategies of the movie Jews. Zukor concentrated on improving the movies themselves. Loew chose to concentrate on improving the theaters, and he was soon refurbishing old burlesque houses and reopening them as "popularly priced" combination movie and vaudeville houses. His first, in 1908, was called The Royal, formerly the Cozy Corner, and if one needed any evidence of Loew's ambition, The Royal premiered with an Italian tragedian named Antonio Moro appearing live in scenes from Shakespeare.

Loew's scheme was class by association, mixing live acts with films and doing so at reasonable prices so that he would be adding the middle class without leaving the working class behind. "I don't offer widely advertised top liners," he said, explaining his economical policy. "I do not need Mrs. Thaw [a famous beauty whose jealous husband murdered a rival] or Jim Corbett [former boxing champion] or performers of that class, whom an audience may want to see for curiosity's sake, but through whose act they are likely to yawn. Just the same, I find girls who can dance with the best, and the writers of jokes turn out as good stuff for my artists as for anybody else."

The proof was in the profits. In 1909 Loew rented two large theaters from the Shuberts. The year after that he consolidated with

Zukor. And the next year, 1911, he purchased the vaudeville circuit of one of the largest entrepreneurs, William Morris, and moved his office to Morris's old flagship, the swanky American Music Hall on Forty-second Street. When his company reorganized later that same year, under the banner of Loew's Theatrical Enterprises, it was capitalized at $5 million. For Loew, who was now more a vaudeville promoter than a movie exhibitor, that was vindication enough.

Meanwhile Zukor, "well taken care of" by his Loew dividends, continued his firsthand examination of the movies. "I traveled all through Europe and this country, watched the audiences, and was interested in any picture that had a subject that I felt would appeal to the public." Zukor wasn't only observing. He was also stumping. In 1910 he had even gone to Weisbaden, where Carl Laemmle, a major producer and distributor, was vacationing, to convince Laemmle to make features. Laemmle declined. But roughly a year later, back in New York, Laemmle introduced Zukor to Edwin Porter, the projectionist-turned-director who had made *The Great Train Robbery.* Porter, subjected to Zukor's sermon on feature films, mentioned that Joseph Engel of the Rex Film Company had just secured the American rights to a French film of Sarah Bernhardt starring in *Queen Elizabeth.* Zukor promptly contacted Engel and without even dickering agreed to buy the rights for $35,000.

Zukor didn't care about negotiations. He realized *Queen Elizabeth* was the fulfillment of a dream. On the subway not long before, Zukor had hit upon a formula for the advancement of the movies to the middle class. "Famous Players in Famous Plays," he scrawled on the back of an envelope. His intention was that the movies would become a kind of "canned" theater, that the diversions of the middle and upper classes could be popularized, attracting a new audience while elevating the old one. With *Queen Elizabeth,* Zukor now had a test case handed to him—one of the world's greatest stage actresses in a bona fide theatrical hit—and he immediately set up an office in the Times Building, overlooking the theater district. Using his own slogan for the title of his new enterprise, he incorporated as the Famous Players Company.

Zukor was fully conscious that he was now engaged in prestige building—for the movies and for himself. His plan was to capitalize on the material's theatrical antecedents by mounting *Queen Elizabeth* as if it were a stage production; he would make its presentation an event as he had once, on a much smaller scale, made the presentation of one-reelers an event at Crystal Hall. For the opening he rented the Lyceum Theater, a legitimate stage house, and he invited leading lights from the theater and genteel culture, using Bernhardt as the draw. By almost any standard the film itself was crude, with none of the visual dexterity that innovative directors would soon be bringing to the screen. But Zukor realized that *Queen Elizabeth* was a cultural event, not an aesthetic one. When it premiered on July 12, 1912, the response was enthusiastic, and the occasion—in retrospect, at least—was historic. It proved, to Zukor's satisfaction, at any rate, that feature films were economically viable, as long as they were the right films. No one complained of boredom or restlessness watching the great Bernhardt.

But far more significant, Zukor felt that it "had gone a long way toward breaking down the prejudice of theatrical people toward the screen." Culturally, this meant the movies had edged away from novelty and toward art and had opened exhibitors' eyes "to the possibility of a higher class of trade with feature pictures." Personally, it meant Zukor might now be admitted to their aerie. He might be regarded as a man of refinement and culture, which, for the Jewish and orphaned Zukor, would be apt compensation for all he had been denied.

The extent to which this personal elevation might have animated him was evident in his ardent pursuit of a theater connection during and shortly after the *Queen Elizabeth* affair. "In order to give himself validity," Eugene Zukor said, "he needed [someone of stature] to put a stamp on it and say, 'This man is on the right track. He's going to use the screen for a purpose beyond anyone's conception. He's going to take the library shelves and open them up to the world visually.'" Brady had already refused, though Zukor had offered him extremely favorable terms—25 percent of the stock in Famous Players and a guarantee of $25,000 per year for the use of his name. "You're out of your head," he told Zukor. "These pictures are just a fad."

Through Marcus Loew, Zukor had met Elek Ludvigh, an aristocratic, goateed attorney who represented many of the major theatrical producers. Sympathetic to Zukor's mission, Ludvigh offered to sound out Daniel Frohman, one of the leading showmen on Broadway. Frohman agreed to meet with Zukor, but like almost every other theatrical figure, he was still apprehensive, and Zukor remembered the meeting as more interrogation than interview. Would the enterprise be high-minded? Would the actors be well compensated? Though Zukor was never especially articulate ("He talks the English he learned on the fur bench," wrote one observer), he could be quite impassioned when it came to the movies, and he did finally convince Frohman to give Famous Players his imprimatur—though not without also giving him a large share of the proceeds. This, and Frohman's feeling that he might be gaining some advantage over his more famous brother, Charles, probably tipped the scales.

Zukor was not at war with the establishment; on the contrary, he wanted its sanction—which professionally meant the approval of a motion picture trust formed by Thomas Alva Edison.* Now, with his theatrical connection in place, he asked Frohman to approach Edison for a license to produce films. Edison gladly consented to a meeting with the prestigious Broadway producer, but he insisted that his interests in the Motion Picture Patents Company were limited, and that he would likely be outvoted. Frohman, infected by Zukor's fervor, stressed that Famous Players "would improve the character of the entire industry, and its activities would not be confined alone to Famous Players. Others would follow in our footsteps in bringing great plays and great stage stars to the screen." Edison, softened more by some reminiscences with Frohman than by the possibilities of the movies, wrote two letters to the chief officers of the Patents Company, instructing them to give Zukor a license. Zukor was so elated that he had the letters photographed and framed.

The joy, however, proved premature. J. J. Kennedy, the former engineer and loan collector who now headed the Edison Trust, kept him waiting for three hours, and when Zukor finally got in to see him, Kennedy sat behind his imposing desk and said the "time is not ripe for feature pictures, if it ever will be." It was the same resistance that many of the renegade movie Jews were meeting from the intransigent, bull-headed Trust. "What they were making belonged entirely to technicians," Zukor said sometime later in a concise analysis of what distinguished the older movie gentiles from the Jews. "What I was talking about—that was show business."

*See chapter 2.

Determined to make movies anyway, with or without the Trust's authorization, Zukor liquidated all his holdings in Loew's Theatrical Enterprises and funneled the money into Famous Players. Loew was dismayed—for Zukor's sake and for his own, since Zukor was a considerable stockholder. He even enlisted Zukor's wife to express his concern, but Zukor was adamant. He had invested enormous psychological capital in being the one man who would elevate the movies, and within months he had begun preparation for the film of the swashbuckling melodrama *The Prisoner of Zenda*, which Frohman had produced on stage.*

For the director, he hired the droopy, lugubrious Edwin Porter. For a set, he rented an old armory and stationed his brother-in-law outside to scout for Trust goons enforcing Edison's patent rights. For a star, he hoped to snare James K. Hackett, who, after years of appearing in the stage version of *Zenda*, had practically become synonymous with the role. But Zukor knew that "if I talked to an actor about pictures, he'd think, well, I'm out of my mind. . . . They wouldn't know where I came from, whether I was a shoemaker or what." That's where Frohman came in. "All Dan Frohman had to do was to say to each one [actor], 'Mr. Zukor would like to see you. I've set an appointment.' Zoom. They'd come over there on their own."

But it was then up to Zukor to convince them, and the appeal he usually used was the one he had used on himself: art. When Hackett came to visit Zukor, he was the very picture of the faded matinee idol. He wore a fur-collared coat with frayed sleeves and carried a gold-headed cane. He had come only as a favor to Frohman, and his attitude was calculatedly disdainful—until he caught sight of a poster of Bernhardt in *Queen Elizabeth*. His resistance began to melt. "My father had a great way of romanticizing the vehicle [*Prisoner of Zenda*], the story and the possibilities of it and what it means to posterity," recalled Eugene Zukor. As Zukor himself later recounted it, Hackett "realized that this was an art that was going to amount to something and thought he might as well have the honor of being the

---

*Actually, Zukor first produced a film version of *The Count of Monte Cristo* starring James O'Neill, Eugene's father, but *The Prisoner of Zenda* was Famous Players' first film by dint of being released before *Monte Cristo*.

first American star." Within weeks Hackett was making his claims on posterity in the movies.

Of course, Zukor was also not unmindful about his own claims. He had even hired the critic of the *New York Evening Journal* to act as his evangelist. In a very short time—a matter of months, really, after *Queen Elizabeth*—he was being regarded precisely the way he wanted to be—as the man who brought distinction to motion pictures. "The most notable figure in the moving picture field today," rhapsodized the *Evening Journal* in December 1912, "is Adolph Zukor, a young man of medium size, slender build, clean-cut face, keen eyes, of Hungarian birth, who speaks the English language with a marked accent, but whose mind works with all the swiftness and certainty of the mind of a Napoleon." "Adolph Zukor, president of the Famous Players, is one of the seven wonders of the motion picture business," said the *New York Clipper*. "The very first to recognize the possibilities of producing famous plays and introducing famous players cinematographically, Mr. Zukor added a tone and a dignity to the film game that it had not possessed before his entrance." Another article simply called the formation of Famous Players "perhaps the greatest single phase of the entire advancement of the art of the silent drama."

But Zukor was always one to press an advantage. In 1913 he had Frohman approach a brilliant young director who was already gaining notice as the most innovative and exciting filmmaker in America and offer him a $50,000 contract. "I dropped into my seat amazed," Frohman wrote, "for we, as a young and growing company, were not achieving at that time any very large income, although we were making money." Nevertheless, he dined with D. W. Griffith and tendered Zukor's offer. Griffith refused, saying coolly, "I think I can earn more."

Zukor had more success with Frohman's older brother, Charles, also a prestigious Broadway producer. Zukor wanted badly to gain the film rights to Charles's plays, but despite his brother's participation or possibly because of it, the producer "looked upon this new plan for adapting plays to the motion picture screen as a ridiculous quixotic dream." Daniel happened to be in Charles's office one day when he heard that his brother urgently needed $25,000 for a new production. The next day Daniel returned with a $25,000 check from Zukor for the rights to Frohman's plays and half the movie profits. Skeptical about the ultimate value of the deal but needing the money, Charles quickly agreed, and Famous Players gained a windfall. (In time, Zukor would buy the elder Frohman's company.)

By the summer of 1913 Zukor had completed five feature films, including *The Count of Monte Cristo*, *Tess of the D'Urbervilles*, and *The Prisoner of Zenda*, and had decided to invade the European markets. "I must say I am getting on nicely here," he wrote his wife from London. "It seems everybody heard of us and I don't have to introduce myself. Wherever I send my card they receive me very cordially." With this kind of recognition in America and now in Europe, Zukor was very close to being the man he wanted to become, but he would never settle for anything less than full satisfaction. There was still one more sphere to conquer.

"Mr. Zukor enjoys power," wrote director Cecil B. De Mille, and he could be a master of intimidation. "There would come a time when he would put his two clenched fists together and, slowly separating them, say to me, 'Cecil, I can break you like that.'" "When he meets a new acquaintance," wrote another observer,

> he has the air of waiting for him to say something pleasant; of expecting it. Then, as the stranger begins to do business with him, impression of that comely, quietly engaging personality begins to fade; wiped out by perception of that round, full skull, that close mouth with the tight grip over the short, close-biting teeth of a fighter, that radiation of power.

De Mille regarded it as a vestige of Zukor's boxing days on the Lower East Side. But power wasn't simply a relic of Zukor's adolescence, nor had it been a means to an end. For Zukor power was an end in itself—a way of turning the tables on a world that had rendered him powerless in childhood. In elevating the movies as he did, Zukor had quickly accrued a kind of cultural power. Now he was about to repeat the process. Everything he did artistically from 1912 to 1915, he would replicate financially from 1915 to 1919. The aim this time seemed, quite simply, to appropriate the entire motion picture industry.

Zukor loved to take long constitutionals, and, according to De Mille, he had hatched his plan of conquest during a walk from the Battery, at the tip of Manhattan, to Central Park and back. The target of his takeover plot was Paramount, a company most appropriately named for Zukor's purposes. Paramount, the brainchild of a former correspondence school salesman from Utah named W. W. Hodkinson, had been formed in 1914 by five exchangemen to distribute films on a reliable and national basis. Producers got $35,000 per film, in advance, and 65 percent of the profits of each film. Its symbol was a snow-capped mountain from Hodkinson's native Wasatch Range. Zukor had reluctantly agreed to distribute Famous Players' films through Paramount, but within two years the terms began to rankle him, and he would even pound around the golf course grousing about having completed 65 percent of the holes, in reference to what he regarded as Paramount's extortionate percentage.

Whether or not he was already scheming to take over the company, Zukor had proposed a merger with the Lasky Feature Play Company, the second largest producer distributing through Paramount. Jesse Lasky, president of the company, had succeeded the same way Zukor had—by purchasing stage properties and putting them on screen— but he was a very different sort of man. "Jesse Lasky in no way resembled the stock Hollywood tycoon," said one screenwriter. "He was a gentle, considerate man, blessed with a gracious wife ... endowed with an almost childlike enthusiasm for his work, and cursed with a total lack of either interest or expertise in financial matters."

A San Francisco Jew, Lasky was so assimilated he was barely aware that he was Jewish and was much more a product of the civic religion of America than of any older faith. "He did not crawl out of a ghetto in Europe or the East Side of New York where you had to fight, to scrape to stay alive," said his daughter, Betty. "That accounted for his gentle disposition and the fact that he was never a killer. He was never ruthless. I don't think he would have climbed to the heights he did had he not hitched his wagon to a star: Adolph Zukor. And Adolph Zukor was the shark, the killer."

After a series of ill-fated get-rich-quick schemes—an at-home maple syrup confectioner, a contraption said to "magnetize" gold out of sand—Lasky teamed up with his demure sister Blanche playing cornet duets in a vaudeville act. By 1903 they were playing the very best vaudeville houses in New York, but Blanche didn't have the temperament for show business, and Jesse was weary of traveling the vaudeville circuit. He decided to open an agency of his own, booking acts. Lasky, a diplomatic man who legitimately appreciated talent, built the agency into a profitable concern, sending out forty acts each year and finally becoming a Broadway entrepreneur himself.

"I yearned to trespass on Quality Street," he once said in what could have been the anthem for nearly all the Hollywood Jews. "I realized that no matter how many headwaiters and bartenders knew my name, there was no theatrical prestige in producing musical acts for vaudeville—not the kind of prestige, say, that clung to the name of Charles Frohman." Lasky's grand stab at prestige was to create on Broadway an American version of the Follies Bergère, Paris's famous cabaret of showgirls and novelty acts, and he constructed a theater for this purpose at great expense. But the Follies proved to be his own folly. It failed dismally, losing over $100,000.

While vacationing in Maine the next year, Lasky's brother-in-law, a glove salesman named Samuel Goldfish, hectored him to take a flyer in the new motion picture business. Lasky, believing that the movies were beneath him, demurred, but Goldfish persisted. "One day I became so incensed at his insistence," Lasky remembered, "that I said, 'Sam, I'm a *showman*. I wonder if you know what a showman is? I'll tell you. A showman is a man who creates entertainment... something the audience wants to see.... So don't ask me to make pictures—that's the last thing in the world I'd do.'" What finally broke down his resistance was his best friend, Cecil B. De Mille, but not because De Mille sided with Goldfish. Over lunch one day, back in the city, De Mille complained that he was tired and broke and had decided to go to Mexico to write an account of the revolution going on there. Seizing anything to dissuade him, Lasky suggested they enter the movie business with Goldfish instead. De Mille immediately fancied the idea, and the deal was consummated on the back of the menu.

Lasky was now in the movie business, but he had not surrendered any of his pretensions. Like Zukor and so many of the Hollywood Jews, he had simply decided to use the movies to realize them. He began with a popular stage play called *The Squaw Man,* about an Englishman in the Old West, which he bought for $15,000 and which De Mille shot on location in California. Shortly after the premiere in February 1914, Zukor, whom Lasky already regarded as an inspiration, wired his congratulations and invited the new producer to lunch at Delmonico's, where he held forth again on the wonder of feature films. The relationship was struck.

When Zukor proposed his merger to Lasky in 1916, Lasky had become an emerging force in the industry. "Too many persons engaged in this business look upon it as a temporary means of getting money instead of a permanent business, the continued profit of which is dependent on the quality and character of the productions," he wrote a congressional committee while it was debating federal restrictions on the movies. Lasky drew a sharp distinction between himself and these "get-rich-quick artists, looking for a quick 'clean-up and a get-away.'" Late in 1914 he had closed a deal with David Belasco, another of the leading Broadway producers, acquiring the rights to ten of his plays, and by the end of the year he had completed twenty-one features—all based on plays and novels.

But Zukor, who was both extraordinarily canny and wary, never seemed to fear Lasky as a rival, and he had cultivated his friendship, meeting him regularly for lunch. Probably one reason Zukor never feared him was because he knew Lasky was malleable; he would always be a subordinate. But this also made Lasky an excellent ally in Zukor's design to take over Paramount. (On the other hand, when William Fox, a far less malleable figure, suggested a partnership in 1912, Zukor coldly refused, saying he didn't need associates.) Zukor and Lasky already produced three-quarters of the films Paramount distributed. United, they would be formidable.

Negotiations dragged on for months, possibly because Lasky and Goldfish knew the kind of man with whom they were dealing; but Zukor was implacable when he wanted something, and he held his course, even rejecting a $1.5 million offer from a banking syndicate for his share of Famous Players. "It would have been a nice nest egg for the family," Zukor said. "But I didn't know what I could do with myself. I didn't have any picture of retiring to run a shoe store or something." That understated the situation. Zukor did have a picture of himself ruling Paramount, and while he talked with Lasky, he slowly began accumulating parcels of stock with the eventual aim of replacing Hodkinson as president. Zukor even had a candidate in mind—a film distributor from Maine named Hiram Abrams.

At the same time, however, Zukor suddenly found himself having to fight a rearguard action in his own ranks. The contract of America's Sweetheart and Famous Players' biggest star, Mary Pickford, was expiring, and she was being ardently wooed by every major film company—so ardently that the bidding had already reached the vicinity of $1 million per year. Though rumors floated throughout the first six months of 1916 that Pickford had decided to leave Famous Players, Zukor said simply that he and Pickford had made a handshake agreement early in the year, and that it had only to be memorialized by a contract. His competitors weren't convinced.

While they were anticipating Pickford's defection and writing Famous Players' obituary, Zukor moved coolly and swiftly. With a meeting of Paramount's stockholders approaching and amid rumors that he was dickering with Triangle, a Paramount rival, to distribute his films, Zukor retreated to French Lick, Indiana, for a brief vacation. He returned shrouded in mystery, but it was quickly dispelled at the meeting on June 13. Abrams was placed in nomination and overwhelmingly elected. Hodkinson, realizing he had been outmaneuvered by Zukor, took his hat and stalked out of the room. On June 24, using the moral suasion at which he was so expert, Zukor resigned Mary Pickford at less than she had been offered by others. Four days later he merged his interests with Lasky's, creating Famous Players-Lasky and assumed its presidency. Zukor was now firmly in command.

The only remaining annoyance was Lasky's partner and brother-in-law, Goldfish. Zukor loathed him. As Eugene Zukor described him, "He was a very crude man . . . loud and not the most pleasant character to want to have anything to do with." Zukor felt he disagreed just to be contrary and wanted him out of the company. He got his pretext in September when Goldfish criticized him in front of Mary Pickford, and Pickford reported his comments back to Zukor. Zukor quickly issued an ultimatum to Lasky. After a weekend's deliberation, Lasky sided with Zukor, and Goldfish was bought out for $900,000. Later that same month, Famous Players-Lasky acquired Paramount itself. Zukor was king.

———

Few rulers relished their role of leadership as much as Adolph Zukor relished his. He was the self-possessed, genteel master—cautious, remote, seignorial, conscious of his position. The pose was respected. Zukor became the father confessor of his associates and friends; they would call him regularly on personal matters as well as business. Even competitors sought audiences to receive Zukor's counsel. On one occasion Carl Laemmle, the head of Universal, made a courtesy call, ostensibly to discuss the state of the industry, but he soon confessed that he was having some serious financial difficulties. Zukor offered to contact his banking connections and vouch for Laemmle, and he did.

Even at home Zukor was imperious. "He was very strict," remembered his son, Eugene. "Certain time and place for everything. If something displeased him, I would hear it. . . . There could be no misconstruing as to the way he thought and what he wanted done and what he thought hadn't been done." His daughter, Mildred, nicknamed Mickey, was his pet. She was attractive and amusing, and she was one of the only people who could break through her father's reserve, though even that ended where business began. When Mickey was nineteen she married Arthur Loew, one of Marcus Loew's twin sons. Many years later, at a hearing to prevent foreclosure of Paramount's theaters, Zukor was questioned about his connection to the Loews and admitted that when he and Marcus couldn't come to terms on showing Paramount's films, Zukor went out and built his own theaters in direct competition. "Then you did not let blood ties interfere with business?" asked an attorney. "No," snapped Zukor.

When it came to business, Eugene Zukor often took the brunt of his father's wrath. "He would give me the full treatment," Eugene said. "He'd wait until we got in the car going home [from the office], and that car would be in smoke by the time we got there." Carl Laemmle handed his studio to his heir as a birthday present. When Eugene proposed that he forgo college and enter the film business instead, Zukor was considerably less liberal. "He said, 'Well, you made your decision, and I'll tell you what my terms and conditions are: I will pay your way through college. . . . But if you're embarking on your own course, and I'm not in favor of it, I will only give you room and board. If you have any extraneous expenses, you'll have to earn the money. You'll be paid according to your talents, if you have any. If you haven't, you'll be tolerated because you're my son, but if you want to get anywhere in this business, apply yourself to the maximum.'" Zukor didn't relent. Eugene began in Paramount's shipping department. He never became head of the studio.

Zukor did dote on his wife, Lottie, a Hungarian immigrant who spent her childhood in the Dakotas, where her parents had been homesteaders. She was an attractive and cheerful woman, and Zukor did his best to indulge her. No matter how dire their finances, he never failed to give her two dozen long-stemmed roses for her birthday and a letter expressing his love. He disliked jewelry, but he always wore the gold sapphire ring she had given him when they were engaged. And though he didn't always care for her friends or her causes, when her big event, the Ladies' Aid Society Ball, arrived, he personally got on the phone and solicited stars to appear. "That night came, and Clark Gable would walk in or Maurice Chevalier would sing a song. And this was her glory," Eugene recalled.

Long before his ascendance to the throne of the industry, Zukor had been refining an imperial style for himself. It was part of his re-creation into a new man. Lottie traveled in musical circles, and the Zukors were regular subscribers to the symphony and the opera, where for years they held seats fourth row center. He bought his ties at Sulka's now, the expensive haberdashery on Manhattan's Fifth Avenue. He moved to the Savoy Plaza Hotel. And he bought himself an expensive Pierce-Arrow automobile, which even he admitted was an extravagance. But he justified his conspicuous consumption, saying, "I have always believed that if a man surrounds himself with good things, he sets a standard in his own eyes as well as those of others." And Zukor was one who always set standards.

The most dramatic example of the new imperial Zukor came after World War I, when he made a pilgrimage back to his birthplace, Risce. Zukor, like so many of the Hollywood Jews, had used the war as an opportunity to prove his patriotism; visiting Frank Wilson, director of publicity for the Liberty Loan program, which raised money from bond sales, he announced that the industry was happy "to show its patriotism [and] to prove beyond all question its worth to the Government as well as to the people of the United States," as if these had been at issue. The Jews mobilized the entire industry; Lasky and De Mille, now headquartered in California, even formed a Paramount brigade that marched up and down the studio grounds with prop rifles in preparedness.

But with the war over, Zukor had another opportunity—this one to play the prodigal and to demonstrate how the old Zukor, the secret self, had evolved into the new one. Since the railway to Risce had been destroyed, he had to charter a handcar to get there. Once in the village, he summoned the town council to tell them that he was prepared to be quite generous in allocating funds for the village's reconstruction. The way he did so, however, was in striking contrast to a similar visit Carl Laemmle made to his boyhood home after the war. Laemmle bathed in gratitude; Zukor was a cynic. "One day I visited the grave of my parents," he said, "and such a crowd of mourners I never saw. From far and wide people had arrived for the purpose of adopting me as a relative." In doling out his money, he sat behind a screen while the destitute told their needs to a lawyer Zukor had hired. After he heard each petitioner, he entered an amount. In time he was sending allowances to nearly half the residents, but he still had an agent from Budapest make regular audits to see how the money was being spent.

The postwar years were extremely good to Zukor. The war had opened new markets for American films in Europe, while the industry continued to boom domestically as the movies strengthened their hold on the popular imagination. By war's end, the movies were indisputably the most favored entertainment in the country, largely because they had matured into dramatic narratives, as Zukor had always prophesied they would. Yet because the market had grown so large and turned so competitive, there was now a much greater premium on either better pictures or more financial clout. As a result the industry was rapidly shaking down to less than a dozen major producers, and production and distribution were being merged into a single powerful entity, like Paramount, which had the resources to make those pictures or to wield that clout.

For a producer and distributor like Zukor, these were splendid developments. Exhibitors were less enthusiastic, since they were now at the mercy of the film suppliers. Thomas Tally, a one-time Texas wrangler who had become an exhibitor in Los Angeles, and J. D. Williams, a colorful entrepreneur from Australia, hit upon a solution. They would pool their resources, sign the biggest stars in the industry, and then make their own movies. They called their enterprise First National, and their first target was Charlie Chaplin, the beloved screen comedian whose Tramp was captivating the entire world. After signing Chaplin at a salary of over $1 million, they fastened on their next objective, Mary Pickford, whose contract was once again up for renewal. She ultimately signed for even more than Chaplin.

Zukor was not amused, and he devised a plan of his own to retaliate. If the exhibitors could enter production, the producers could enter exhibition. He would embark on a relentless campaign of theater acquisition and construction until Paramount had a first-run house in every major market. But to do so, he needed more capital than the company could generate internally. He needed an investment banker who would do for him financially what Daniel Frohman had done artistically—give him the sanction of legitimacy. And, as when he took over Paramount, Zukor had already chosen a candidate.

Otto Kahn looked every bit the part of an investment banker. He had dark, shrewd eyes and a long, waxed mustache that seemed as if it had been cast in porcelain. His family had manufactured featherbeds in Germany, but Otto was taken with finance and decided to emigrate to New York to find a position with a banking concern. He eventually wound up at Kuhn, Loeb and Company, possibly because it had been founded by Jews like himself. In a remarkably short time, he became a partner. Zukor had met him through Kahn's brother Felix, a tall, handsome, impeccably groomed gentleman who owned one of the largest movie theaters in New York. When Paramount bought the theater as part of its acquisition campaign, Felix became a member of the board of directors and also became a very close friend of Zukor's.

Zukor had an affinity for the Kahns. They too were lapsed Jews, desperate to assimilate, though they were rather more ruthless about it than Zukor. Otto expunged his Judaism altogether and became an

Episcopalian. They too affected an imperial style meant to confirm their position as gentlemen. And they too believed in the arts as a means of social mobility. In fact, it could have been Zukor speaking when, a few years later, Otto Kahn advised a group of film writers and producers that "in art as in everything else the American people like to be led upward and onward," and then went on to cite "the vast importance and potentialities of the 'movie' as an industry, a social influence, and an art."

Using the movies' power to uplift public taste as the inducement, Zukor asked Kahn for a $10 million loan that would become part of a public stock flotation; but Zukor, with his eye always fixed on status, was also looking at capital's power to uplift the movies. "My associates held that the request for so large a sum was preposterous," Zukor wrote later. "I pointed out that if we got it, motion pictures would be regarded as an important industry. A request for only five million dollars, I argued, might be rejected by Kuhn, Loeb and Company on the ground that the firm dealt only in larger sums."

Before committing themselves, Kuhn, Loeb made an exhaustive study of Paramount and of Zukor, examining his morals as well as his capabilities. When the study was concluded, Kahn agreed to float the public issue, but he demanded that he be allowed to place representatives in key positions. It was an indication of how badly Zukor wanted Kahn's imprimatur that he didn't balk at the terms. "Paramount was formed not at all for its own selfish ends and for the aggrandizement and profit of its officers," he said in announcing the stock issue. "That is an unworthy purpose. . . . The Paramount plan meant better times for theater patrons in providing them higher-class amusement, and the Paramount plan necessitated better and more permanent business for the producers in providing an efficient market for their films."

All of this was a cunning way of saying that Zukor had finally integrated the film industry, putting production, distribution, and now exhibition in the same hands—his. In doing so, or at least in proposing to do so, he had effected a change nearly as significant as that he had effected with *Queen Elizabeth* and Famous Players, and for some of the same reasons. He had helped establish the industry's bona fides with finance. He had helped put the industry on a sound economic footing by creating a reliable supply and constant demand, since he controlled both. And he had vastly expanded the whole scale of the movies industrially, just as he had artistically. He had, in short, won respectability and legitimacy for the *business* of motion pictures, and he had won respectability and legitimacy for himself, which had been his motive all along.

Late in 1919, now armed with Kahn's capital, Zukor began his offensive to establish his hegemony over theaters as he had over production and distribution. Where he could, he had Paramount buy property and build his theaters; if competitors converted sites nearby, Zukor was ready with threats, intimidation, and rumor to dissuade them. In the South, his agents became known as the "dynamite crew," and he was excoriated in one trade paper for his "rape of the industry." Of course, it worked both ways. When Paramount was building a theater in Seattle, a rumor began circulating that the mixture of sand in the concrete was improper and the balcony was unsafe. Zukor had all the concrete trucks drive up a ramp and across the balcony to refute it. Still, Zukor was the master at orchestrating this kind of aggression, and by 1921 he had acquired or built 303 first-run theaters. He had also enraged enough people in doing so that the Federal Trade Commission launched an investigation into his business practices and filed suit against him.

What was always difficult to reconcile about Zukor in his lifelong quest for greatness was his intractable moral authority, which he evidently identified with the genteel, and his lust for power, which was anything but genteel. One wondered how Zukor himself reconciled these. Yet Zukor's personal division in many ways paralleled a cultural division in America in the 1920s, and the convergence of the personal with the cultural may have even been one of the major sources for Zukor's astonishing sensitivity to the national zeitgeist.

On one side of the cultural divide were the nativists, white Anglo-Saxon Protestants clinging to a moralistic, traditional way of life and terrified that the the influx of immigrants would somehow destroy their values since nonnative Americans couldn't possibly share them. On the other side were the immigrants and a host of other forces that challenged any unified set of values: urbanization, mass communication, unionization, the professionalization of the middle class, education. All these had joined ranks, so to speak, to offer a fast, invigorating, tantalizing alternative to the genteel tradition in American life, where the hierarchy was rigid and values were unchanging.

One could even say that the social history of America in the 1920s was the story of the combat between these two Americas—one new and ascendant, the other old and declining; one smart and sophisticated, the other conservative and respectable.

Zukor, by temperament and situation, was positioned at the fulcrum between these Americas. He understood both because he was part of both—aspiring to remake himself as a genteel American (his moralism); using the opportunities of the immigrant, urban culture, not least of which were the movies, to get there (his power). This made Zukor, the Hungarian Jew transformed into the American gentleman, the ideal facilitator for the movies' similar transformation or, more accurately, the movies' synthesis between the new and the old, between the working class and the middle class. Zukor could—and did—bind the schism, possibly because he had spent a lifetime binding his own. Other Jews, fighting other battles, may have won over an industry. By 1921 Zukor had won over an entire nation.

Cecil B. De Mille remembered meeting Adolph Zukor for the first time in 1915, when he and his friend Jesse Lasky raced to a fire and discovered that Famous Players' studio and offices were ablaze, including the only negatives of five recently completed features. Zukor stared fixedly at the storage vault. "Jesse took me over and introduced me," De Mille wrote. "I said the futile things that are all one can say. . . . He looked away from the ruin long enough to say, 'Thank you. We'll build a better one.'" While firemen waited for the vault to cool before seeing if the negatives had been lost, Zukor called his staff to a meeting at the Astor Hotel. "I told them, 'We go ahead tomorrow, just the same as if nothing had happened.'" It was a typical Zukor performance.

But however stoical Zukor might have appeared—and he always seemed to appear that way unless his dander was up—there was evidence of banked fires inside. He smoked from eight to ten cigars every day, until much later in life he rationed himself down to five. And he had developed a psychosomatic rash, scratching his head and neck furiously whenever he was under stress. His doctor recommended a rest, someplace where he could retreat periodically from the pressure.

Having lived in the city, either Chicago or New York, nearly all his life, Zukor wasn't keen on the suggestion, but his family convinced him to look at a wooded estate north of Manhattan in Rockland County, and as his son described it, he immediately "fell in love with the place."

It had belonged to a wealthy department store executive named Larry Abrams, who had used it as a summer getaway. Abrams had designed the two houses on the property to look rustic and utilitarian, and Zukor maintained the style—the architectural equivalent of his moral austerity. The buildings were made of fieldstone and timber. The furniture was steel. There was no ornamentation, save some game trophies contributed by Felix Kahn. But Zukor was also by nature an agglomerator, and he immediately set about transforming Abrams's getaway into his own small empire. He began by acquiring large parcels of land surrounding the estate, expanding it from eighty acres to one thousand. Abrams had a nine-hole golf course. Zukor brought over a golf architect from Scotland and laid out an eighteen-hole course that was good enough to attract professional golfers as guests. Abrams had two main buildings—a lodge, where guests could gather for cards and talk, and a dormitory, where they would sleep. Zukor built a third manor for his children and grandchildren. And to transport guests there, he had a speedboat equipped with aircraft engines. (It was later sold to a bootlegger in the early days of the Depression.)

Every weekend Zukor would invite anywhere from ten to forty guests to Mountainview Farm, as he called his estate. Very few were business associates, fewer still stars—only Chevalier, silent film heartthrob Tommy Meighan, and occasionally Mary Pickford. "My father had a philosophy that certain areas had to be separated," said Eugene. "Business and family were not to mingle." Eugene speculated, however, that the separation was less a function of Zukor protecting his family than of Zukor preventing himself from compromising his power by getting too close to his employees.

Mountainview was the one place he could begin to decompress, the one place where he could lower his aristocratic facade. Over the years, before he was sovereign of the film industry, he had accumulated a secret group of friends like his secret self—those who had no expectations. One was Aaron Jones, a small Chicago exhibitor who visited Zukor every summer, pounding around the golf course with him or playing cards. And there were the Blaus, members of the family to which Zukor had been apprenticed in Hungary. Saturday nights the Blaus and the Zukors would gather for a pinochle game. Mrs. Zukor would make sandwiches and English would yield to rich, salty Hungarian. Eugene Zukor said he was afraid to go in the room "there was so much noise going on . . . but this was their enjoyment, picking on each other."

This was the lost Zukor—the Zukor made over in America and then consigned to these weekends. Though Zukor had clearly attained his goals, there was some pathos in this lifelong recreation of his; it was the awful price of assimilation that the Jewish writer Abraham Cahan had described in his novel *The Rise of David Levinsky* about another immigrant who erased himself in the process of becoming an American industrialist. "Am I happy?" Levinsky asked himself.

> *There are moments when I am overwhelmed by a sense of my success and ease. I become aware that thousands of things which had formerly been forbidden fruit to me are at my command now. I distinctly recall that crushing sense of being debarred from everything; and then I feel as though the whole world were mine. . . .*
>
> *I am lonely. Amid the pandemonium of my six hundred sewing machines and the jingle of gold which they pour into my lap I feel the deadly silence of solitude. . . .*
>
> *I can never forget the days of my misery. I cannot escape from my old self.*

Zukor certainly would have understood these pangs. But there was also a particular irony for him in the conflict between his past and his present. The man who hated losing had lost himself. The man who hated lying had carefully manufactured his entire life. Zukor had triumphed over the obstacles of his childhood. He had triumphed over his competitors. He had triumphed over class prejudice against the movies. But most of all, he had triumphed over the embittered orphan from Hungary. Most of all, he had triumphed over himself.

2

"Don't Be a Salary Slave!"

It can be done!

CARL LAEMMLE

He has often told me that as he walked about [in America] sizing things up, he kept saying to himself, under his breath, "I've *got* to be successful. I *must* be successful. I *will* be successful.

"JUNIOR" LAEMMLE

OF ALL THE MEN WHO WOULD create the majesty, the mystery, and the mythology that would be Hollywood, Carl Laemmle, founding father of Universal Pictures, was easily the most improbable. He looked like an avuncular elf— five feet two inches tall, a constant gap-toothed smile, merry little eyes, a widening expanse of pate, and a slight paunch that was evidence of the beer and the food he enjoyed. One executive recalled him as a "bald-headed little man [who] walked among his subjects being very, very friendly to everybody." Employees even addressed him as "Uncle Carl"—his own son referred to him that way—or as the "old man." Laemmle didn't mind. "He seemed to see humor in everything," said a one-time associate, and it didn't matter if he were the butt of the joke.

Though he had certain affectations, occasionally carrying a walking stick or sporting a carnation in his lapel, he was by Hollywood standards remarkably unpretentious. At a Universal *bal masque*, he dressed as a gypsy hag with hoop earrings, a long skirt, and rouged cheeks and scuttled forward to claim a door prize—until he was unmasked and disqualified. On another occasion, a young writer who had been befriended by Laemmle's son Junior was invited to the Universal lot. "There was Uncle Carl," he remembered. "He was always an old man: bald, very small, gray complexion, pallid, and he carried a tin pail with him with a top on it." After the introductions, Laemmle asked his son, "'Dump this out for me, will you?' He carried this pail with him because he had a very bad prostate, and he had to pee. So he carried this bucket with him, and wherever he was, he'd pee into the bucket. . . . There was something wonderful about it because it was so human."

Even competitors testified to Laemmle's basic decency. Thomas Ince, an important producer/director in the movies' early days, lost his studio in a fire while he was shooting an epic entitled *The Battle of Gettysburg*. There seemed no alternative but to shut down production, until Laemmle generously offered his own facilities and telegraphed, "Do not charge him a cent for them." "He is the only man in the industry who would do that," Ince said in what was probably an accurate assessment of the internecine business in those early years. Another director called him "the whitest man in the industry." The head of the Motion Picture Theater Owners of America claimed, "I have never heard anyone say anything derogatory of Carl Laemmle." Laemmle's longtime partner Robert Cochrane apparently had, but he insisted, in a curious locution, that "even the men who hate him cannot despise him."

Despite this image of affability, in his dotage Laemmle usually attributed his success to his own tenacity—not without some reason. "My success is neither luck nor happenstance," he said. But in earlier days he had dubbed himself "Lucky," and it was true that nothing in his life prior to the movies would have indicated a man of destiny. He was born on January 17, 1867, in Laupheim, Württemberg, a picturesque village of roughly three thousand inhabitants in southwestern Germany. His father, forty-seven when Carl was born, was a land speculator and sometime salesman, who, according to Laemmle's official biographer, was "philosophically disposed to let events do their own shaping." (For someone like Laemmle, who later extolled his own mastery of events, this was hardly a commendation.) His boyhood home was a large, airy cottage surrounded by loganberry bushes and with a fishing pond nearby, and his youth seems to have been routine. Years later a childhood friend couldn't recall anything particularly distinctive about the young Carl. His own most vivid memories were of visiting the town of Ulm, some twenty-five kilometers away, and seeing Richard Wagner there.

There was one deep attachment in his youth—to his mother, Rebekka. When he turned thirteen and was apprenticed out to a stationer's in a village some five hours from Laupheim, he begged his mother not to leave him. And when, several years and several American dime novels later, he began thinking about emigrating to the United States, he stayed only because his mother had exacted a promise that he wouldn't leave as long as she lived. Her sudden death in October 1883 released him from his vow, and with evidently no strong filial bonds to his father, he decided to fulfill his dream and follow his older brother Joseph to America.

It is hard to say what Laemmle hoped to find here, and he was never introspective enough to discuss his motivations, save the perfunctory nods to adventure, opportunity, and Indians. Most young immigrants of his generation came to escape poverty and prejudice, but there was little of that in Laupheim, where the Jews had made it a point to assimilate. Most immigrants came to ride the country's economic wave, and many did. But Laemmle's first two decades in America didn't conform to the inspirational immigrant sagas where industriousness was rewarded with escalating success. Instead, Laemmle failed at virtually everything he did, and, if anything, his life testified not to the justice of hard work, but to the powerful engine of failure.

For years he bounced from job to job—errand boy for a drunken, abusive druggist in New York; another job as an errand boy, this time in Chicago, where he had gone after tracking down his older brother; then as an office boy for a silk agent, who fired him and hired a nephew; and then again as an office boy for a clothing firm. Finally, with nothing to lose, he and a German friend boarded a train for South Dakota, where they had heard farmhands could earn $2.75 a day. "I found that shocking wheat was harder on the hands than any of my previous jobs," he later told an interviewer, "but there were three square meals each day and two seventy-five coming each evening at six o'clock. It was great work and made me realize the value of a dollar more than any other work I tried up to that time."

Even so, after seven weeks Laemmle was back in Chicago and on the employment carousel once again. First there was a clerking job at a wholesale house at six dollars per week (six months); then another as a bookkeeper at a jeweler's (six months); followed by work at a department store (two years); then bookkeeping for livestock buyers (eighteen months); and then back to clerking for another jeweler, this time at eighteen dollars a week. Though he lasted at this job four years, a record for him, he was clearly drifting, moving horizontally rather than vertically. At twenty-seven, he still hawked newspapers on Sunday for extra money, and he still roomed at a small boardinghouse. He was still forced to restrict his indulgences to the opera or the German theater on Sunday evenings and a ten-cent glass of beer afterward.

While Laemmle was foundering, a friend had taken a position in a Wisconsin clothing store and suggested that Carl come along. He began as a bookkeeper. He left twelve years later as the manager of Continental Clothing's Oshkosh branch. During that time, he acquired a wife—the owner's German-born niece—and fathered a daughter, Rosabelle. More, he acquired a life.

It was in Oshkosh that Laemmle, for the first time, began to find himself. The town was situated on the western lip of Lake Winnebago, halfway between Green Bay and Milwaukee, and though it wasn't exactly an outpost in 1894 when Laemmle relocated there, it did cater to the lumbermen who worked Wisconsin's forests. Why Laemmle dove into this job the way he did isn't easy to fathom, unless he himself viewed it as a last chance (of course, he never said), but he seemed to have a real aptitude for it. With the guidance of a Chicago advertising man named Robert Cochrane, from whom he bought prefabricated layouts, he began running large notices in the local papers. He printed a catalog, distributed it throughout Wisconsin, and launched a mail-order operation. And his window displays, which he tied to the season, were admired throughout the community for their inventiveness—busts of famous composers for a music festival in town or price tags in the shape of leaves for fall.

In recollection, at least, these were satisfying and emotionally rewarding years; in 1905, he was even selected one of Oshkosh's fifteen outstanding citizens. "Good you left this place," an old Oshkosh friend remarked years later. "No," said Laemmle. "I was happy here."

But at the time, approaching his fortieth birthday, something gnawed at him. After a life of fits and starts, of insecurity and disappointment, Laemmle seemed to have wanted some acknowledgment from his employer, some recognition of his contributions. For Laemmle, who was the least complex of the Hollywood moguls, this took the most obvious form: money. He decided to go to Chicago, where Continental was headquartered, and make the request personally to Sam Stern, who was, after all, his wife's uncle.

Though the details are somewhat murky, what happened in Chicago was probably the most important episode in Laemmle's life, an experience that informed everything he would do afterward. As Laemmle's official biographer related it, "On some irrelevant question, he [Stern] drove Laemmle into a quarrel." The men began to raise their voices, and Laemmle tendered his resignation. Stern promptly accepted it. Laemmle was stunned. "He took the night train, and sat awake in desperate confusion of mind until his arrival in the morning. In a few hours everybody in the town would know it—Carl Laemmle of the Continental had been sacked."

Discouraged and despondent, Laemmle now sought advice from the only source he trusted, Robert Cochrane. Cochrane was a former newspaperman who had partnered with his two brothers in a Chicago advertising agency—the one that had served Laemmle's Oshkosh store. The two men had never met—and Cochrane was actually years younger—but Laemmle had struck up a one-sided correspondence while at Continental, and Cochrane had obliged with counsel, in a sense becoming the muse of Laemmle's discontent. "Don't be a salary slave!" he exhorted in one of his letters. "If you are going to do anything in this world, you must start before you are forty, before your period of initiative has ended. Do it now!" Cochrane later admitted these pronouncements were cavalierly dispensed. For Laemmle, though, they had the effect of revelation. He read the letter over and over again and then read it to his wife. It obviously struck the nerve of failure, not least of all because Laemmle was rapidly approaching forty himself.

Two weeks later a short, toothy man with the trace of a German accent appeared before Cochrane's desk in Chicago. He told the ad man that he had managed to save roughly $2,500 and, following

Cochrane's recommendation, was now looking for a small clothing store or a five-and-dime to buy. Cochrane was so totally disarmed by Laemmle's unexpected visit and by his naive faith that he agreed to make some inquiries for him. Meanwhile, Laemmle went scouting for himself.

There are several versions of how Carl Laemmle wound up in the motion picture business, a few of them from Laemmle himself, though all indicate just how much happenstance was involved. "I went over to Chicago to close the deal [on a five-and-dime]," he told one journalist,

> and one rainy night I dropped into one of those hole-in-the-wall five-cent motion picture theaters. . . . The pictures made me laugh, though they were very short and the projection jumpy. I liked them, and so did everybody else. I knew right away that I wanted to go into the motion picture business.
>
> "Funny pictures are the thing," I said to myself. "Charge people and make them laugh." Everybody wants to laugh. . . . As I walked back to my hotel that night in Chicago, I began to build my plans, and the next day I learned everything I possibly could about the business. Three weeks after watching those funny pictures . . . I owned my own theater, which was on Milwaukee Avenue, in Chicago.

In another version, Laemmle recalled that he had regarded movies as toys until he read a long news story about the industry in the Oshkosh paper. "This induced me to go to Chicago and investigate them. What I saw there . . . convinced me that this was a business, and that it was a business I would enjoy." "I was in Chicago when Mr. Laemmle saw his first moving picture theater," an employee later recalled. "It was Dan Lingarda's house down in the Italian section on Halsted and Taylor streets, and I remember well Dan's telling me how Laemmle came and carefully counted the number of people that went in to every single show, and estimated the amount of money that the customers left in the box office."

Laemmle was impressed by the numbers, but not everyone was as optimistic about the movies prospects. Even Cochrane tried to dissuade him. His friends, he recalled, were "shocked, disappointed, and almost humiliated," and Laemmle admitted that "most everyone in the United States regarded moving pictures in about the same way that I did" before he had resolved to become a theater owner himself —which is to say, as a "toy" or "peephole sensation." This was, in fact, one of the reasons Jews like Laemmle were able to gain a foothold. Big money, gentile money, viewed the movies suspiciously— economically, as a fad; morally, as potential embarrassments.

As far as the moral issue was concerned, in February 1906, when Laemmle opened his first theater, reformers had already begun castigating the movies for their deleterious effects, particularly on children. The content of the movies supposedly undermined moral values (though the real complaint may have been that the movies existed outside the sphere of middle- and upper-class control), and makeshift movie houses themselves—dark, cramped, and seductive —supposedly bred iniquity. But while most theater operators ignored or derided the charges, they became important considerations for Laemmle. He called his theater The White Front. He meant it to conjure an image so clean and wholesome that a father wouldn't hesitate to take his family there, as he might to one of the more unsavory movie houses. And he provided amenities to make moviegoing pleasurable; in summer, the theater's awning even beckoned with the slogan "Coolest 5 cent Theatre in Chicago."

Laemmle's own family formed the work force. His future brother-in-law, Maurice Fleckles, remodeled the vacant store and transformed it into a theater. Other family members took tickets and cleaned up. The only employees outside this circle were the projectionist and a business manager Laemmle hired to show him the ropes. When it was all finished, it had cost him about $925—$400 for remodeling, $250 for seats, $250 for the projector, and $25 for a screen. The White Front could seat 214 patrons for a typical program of five short films and two illustrated songs. Each program lasted about twenty minutes, but with the movies running continuously, the nickels mounted up. On average days, Laemmle took in $180. On good days he could clear as much as $192. That came to nearly four thousand patrons. With the nickels rolling in, two months later he opened a second theater on Halsted Street in Chicago, this one charging ten cents for a better clientele. At forty, Carl Laemmle had finally made good on his pledge to succeed.

Though one always likes to trace a dramatic rise, a steady trajectory of success, for Laemmle, as for the movies themselves, success happened literally overnight, and once it happened Laemmle found himself borne along by a rush of events each one providentially bringing him more success. When a film distributor—someone who rented films to a theater owner like Laemmle—reneged on an agreement, Laemmle's projectionist suggested they raise a kitty and buy a film of their own to show. They did—an old Pathé picture called *The Pearl Fisher's Dream*—and after Laemmle ran it in his own theater, he rented it out to other exhibitors.

Again, what had begun as a casual suggestion became a cottage industry, and by October, simply by buying available movies and renting them, Laemmle had formed a full-fledged film "exchange" that grossed even more than his theaters. The next year he sold an interest in the exchange to his old mentor, Robert Cochrane, and together the two laid siege to the movie business in the Midwest, employing the same aggressive strategy they had used at Continental Clothing in Oshkosh. When a local Prohibition ordinance closed down saloons in Chicago, Laemmle and Cochrane encouraged each saloonkeeper to convert his bar to a movie theater. Two hundred did, and Laemmle's exchange gladly obliged them with film rentals. Business expanded so rapidly that the Laemmle Film Service kept outgrowing its quarters. It moved three times in the first year alone. Within two years Laemmle had branch offices in Minneapolis, Des Moines, Omaha, Memphis, Salt Lake City, Portland, Winnipeg, and Montreal. By 1909 he was, at least by his own account, the largest film distributor in America. And by 1911 his company's reach was such that he had to move his family to New York to be nearer the sources of the films he rented out.

How much of this success was propitiousness and how much design is difficult to assess, but Laemmle was certainly the beneficiary of some extraordinary timing. Harry Davis's nickelodeon, an empty storefront outfitted with one hundred to two hundred seats and dedicated exclusively to showing movies, had opened in Pittsburgh just three months before Laemmle opened The White Front. Until then, movies were shown primarily in the back of penny arcades or at vaudeville shows while audiences exited. But the nickelodeon became an instant phenomenon, triggering a national movie mania that one observer described as "nickel madness." Movie theaters now fanned out from the eastern seaboard and Chicago across the country. One contemporary journalist, calculating what a typical theater would have to take in to meet its expenses, estimated that "the average nickelodeon must have a weekly attendance of four thousand. This gives all the nickelodeons sixteen million a week, or over two million a day. Two million people a day are needed before profits can begin, and two million are forthcoming." He concluded with understatement. "It is a big thing, this new enterprise."

Why the movies had suddenly seized the imagination of America, or at least one segment of America, certainly had something to do with price and proximity. For the working poor and the immigrant masses, movies were affordable, a nickel compared with a quarter or fifty cents for vaudeville and more for the legitimate stage, and they were usually located within walking distance, saving patrons carfare, which was always a consideration. But this didn't explain the extent to which movies were capturing the imagination of the American underclass. That, as the Jews who would enter the movie industry understood, was less a matter of economics than it was a matter of culture.

By the lights of high culture, motion pictures certainly didn't qualify as art. A typical movie at the time was relatively short, seldom more than ten minutes and usually closer to five or six. There were no stars since, as Zukor would discover, professional stage actors generally eschewed the movies as beneath them, and no one was billed above the title, though audiences gradually began to pick out favorites and peg them with epithets. That's how the "girl with the curls," Mary Pickford, became a drawing card in her own right. The stage did, however, create an early movie aesthetic. The camera was set in what would have been the best seat in the house: center orchestra. The effect was static; the camera seldom moved.

The content of these early films ranged from little more than tableaux—an impersonator of then Vice President Theodore Roosevelt shooting a bear, a train roaring down the tracks, a parade—to brief vignettes. *The Life of an American Fireman* (1904) depicted a firefighter rushing to a blaze and saving a young girl. *Rescued by Rover* (1905), made in England but terrifically popular here, showed its canine hero racing the clock in another dramatic rescue. *The Great Train Robbery* (1903), the most popular film of its time and one of the most narratively sophisticated, was a Western in which bandits rob a train and then are hunted down by a posse.

Though women were the largest single component of the audience and were treated with a certain dignity on film, romances were unlikely. So were fantasies. "Subject matter was derived from American life," wrote one historian, "from the exploits of the policeman and burglar, cowboy and factory worker, farmer and country girl, clerk and politician, drunkard and servant girl, storekeeper and mechanic." These quotidian melodramas were balanced by comedies, which were as often as not simply a pretext for a chase, a prank, or a fight. Plots were scarce. At best, one got selected scenes from familiar plays or popular novels. The audience troweled in the gaps.

But what Laemmle had discovered, shaking with laughter in that Chicago theater, was that these movies, rudimentary as they were, had begun to satisfy the need of an expanding working class and a mushrooming immigrant population for some kind of cultural nucleus—something around which they could construct their recreational life. For immigrants, the movies were a powerful socializing force, acclimating them to American customs and traditions. For workers generally, they were a democratizing force, creating a sense of cultural identity and unity. The movies were an art they could call their own, constituting a fulfillment of the American bard, Walt Whitman's, summons for a native American form that comported with the "rude rank spirit of the democracies."

"The crowds not only throng to the shows," declared *The Nation* in an editorial suggestively titled "A Democratic Art," "they talk about them, on the street corners, in the cars, and over the hoods of the baby carriages. . . . The crowd discusses the technique of the moving picture theatre with as much interest as literary salons in Paris or London discuss the minutiae of the higher drama." In New York's Jewish ghetto, the movies were drawing patrons away from the Yiddish theater in droves. "There are now about a hundred movie houses in New York, many of them in the Jewish quarter," the *Jewish Daily Forward* editorialized in 1908. "They open at one in the afternoon, and customers, mostly women and children, gossip, eat fruit and nuts, and have a good time." "Everybody loves the movies," the *Forward* said a few years later, noting that even rainstorms couldn't discourage people from going. "Our Jews feel very much at home with the detectives, oceans, horses, dogs, and cars that run about on the screen."

If the movies and the new generation of working class and ethnics made an ideal marriage, it was as true for those who exhibited the films as for those who watched them. Laemmle, a simple, uneducated immigrant himself, was obviously well suited to exploit the desire for a demotic art, and he did. But in doing so, he was not only helping to create an accessible, alternative culture to the inaccessible, "official" high culture of the upper classes—there was a deep personal stake as well. He was creating a new financial empire that would validate his own aimless life. Laemmle, who had failed to scale even the lower reaches of American industry, now presided over a considerable domain—one built on outsiders and on the culturally disenfranchised like himself. And these would be his troops in the war that followed when the Jews would take over the movie industry for good.

———

Late in the spring of 1908, Thomas Alva Edison issued a call to representatives of the eight largest motion picture producers in America to discuss a proposition. With his beetle brows, long wispy hair, and beatific look, Edison might have seemed the addled inventor, but he was a shrewd businessman and a fearsome adversary who was never loath to take credit for any invention, whether he was responsible or not. For years he had claimed to have invented the motion picture camera and projector, and he had backed the claim with lengthy and expensive litigation against all pretenders. More, Edison's company, which manufactured cameras and projectors, was also one of the largest motion picture producers. Now he was asking his rival producers to consider a new scheme: monopoly.

The plan was simple. Edison owned the patents to motion picture cameras and projectors, but the American Mutoscope and Biograph Company had made patent claims of its own and had filed counter-suits against Edison. Under the proposed arrangement, the companies would drop all litigation and pool their patents in a single holding company to be known, unimaginatively, as the Motion Picture Patents Company. Any motion picture camera or projector manufacturer that used the patents would be charged a license fee. Film distributors and exhibitors who rented out or showed movies photographed with patented equipment would also be licensed and forced to pay a royalty based on footage of film. Finally, and probably most oppressively, the Patents Company signed an exclusive agreement with Eastman Kodak, the largest manufacturer of raw film stock, that prohibited any unlicensed film producer from acquiring the raw stock. The negotiations were finalized by December, and in January, while Laemmle was attending a convention of film distributors in New York, the company made its announcement that the old laissez-faire of the movie business was being abruptly terminated.

Though Laemmle was understandably livid at Edison's high-handedness, he nevertheless sought and received a license from the Patents Company, then dithered over the next three months, wondering whether, as the owner of one of the largest exchanges, he could or should take on Edison. On April 12 he gave his answer: he would continue to operate his theaters and his exchange, but without a license from the Patents Company. He would get his films from Europe, which lay outside Edison's legal jurisdiction, and from those producers willing to brave the Patents Company. Having thrown down the gauntlet, he and Cochrane then promptly launched a campaign in the trade papers encouraging others to do the same.

The response was swift. Within weeks of his initial challenge, he claimed that he had been "swamped with hundreds of wildly enthusiastic letters and telegrams, congratulating me on becoming Independent." "The Laemmle Film Service attained its success almost overnight," recounted one of its employees. "The sudden response to Laemmle's plea that exhibitors support his campaign for Independence overwhelmed us. Our business grew by leaps and bounds, and where during the previous week we had shipped one program to a city, a week later we were dispatching three, four, and five times that many." This was when Laemmle started calling himself "Lucky."

The "Trust," as Laemmle labeled Edison's cabal, didn't take this insubordination lightly. It decided that if the exchanges refused to get licenses, it would get exchanges. In February 1910 it announced that it was forming an exchange of its own, to be called the General Film Company, and began a campaign to buy out and, when necessary, force out existing film distributors by harassing them in the courts; Laemmle alone endured 289 legal actions, at a cost of $300,000 in fees. But while the desired effect had been to drive the Independents into submission, it only raised the stakes and emboldened them instead. In 1908 the Trust had a virtual monopoly on the movies. By 1912 the Independents had gobbled half the market and were closing in on a monopoly of their own.

A cluster of factors contributed to the turnabout: the Trust's inability to enforce its edicts, its arrogance toward its customers, even a lack of solidarity within its own ranks. But one major reason Edison and his cohorts had lost their hegemony was that they misinterpreted what was at stake. They never seemed to understand that they were engaged in much more than an economic battle to determine who would control the profits of the nascent film industry; their battle was also generational, cultural, philosophical, even, in some ways, religious. The Trust's members were primarily older white Anglo-Saxon Protestants who had entered the film industry in its infancy by inventing, bankrolling, or tinkering with movie hardware: cameras and projectors. For them, the movies themselves would always be novelties. The Independents, on the other hand, were largely ethnics, Jews and Catholics, who had entered the industry by opening and operating theaters.* For them, outsiders fighting the establishment, the movies would always be much more than novelties; they would be the only means available of demanding recognition and exorcising failure. When, during the wrangling between the Trust and the Independents, Laemmle claimed that he "began to fight for my life," he was expressing the gravity of the battle.

---

*Sigmund Lubin, one of only two Jews in the Trust, regularly extended his help to Jewish Independents, remembering, perhaps, when he had felt the sting of Edison's lash in the days before the Trust.

A corollary effect of the demographic division between the two opposing factions was that the aging WASPs of the Trust were increasingly losing touch with the predominantly young, urban, ethnic audience—the audience from which the Jewish exchangemen and theater owners had themselves recently risen. Even by its own admission, the Trust's movies showed it. "We sit in the Film Committee [empaneled to screen the Trust's movies before release] week after week," one of its members complained, "and pass on pictures we know will get us nothing but unfavorable comments and cancellations. We haven't the power to throw out the distinctly bad pictures, nor the courage, because as poor as they are, they represent a certain sum of money invested in negative production." Another was more succinct: "Our comedies have a bad reputation, and our dramas do not have a distinctive popularity."

When audiences began favoring longer and more heavily plotted European films, the Trust balked. As one disgruntled producer put it, "The monopoly discouraged any deviation from the status quo, which called for one- and two-reelers only. They were making easy money with little effort on short pictures and were afraid longer films would ruin the whole business. . . . " Even when individual Trust producers saw the handwriting on the wall and launched a program of feature films, they had to form an exchange outside the Trust because General Film, the Trust's own exchange, was neither willing nor ready to distribute pictures of that length or wasn't the most profitable outlet for doing so.

Though producing films wasn't something Laemmle—or most of the movie Jews, for that matter—originally had intended to do, he was finding it increasingly difficult to get a sufficient number of movies from Europe with which he could circumvent the monopoly and supply his customers, and the films he could obtain there were of variable quality. The obvious solution, Laemmle decided in the early fall of 1909, was to make his own films. This was actually less dramatic than it might have seemed. Making movies then didn't require much capital expenditure, only a camera and lab, or much technical expertise. Almost anyone could do it. One only needed to know how to load a camera, insure proper light, and turn the crank. Shooting on location across the river in New Jersey obviated the need for sets, and actors came cheap—many of them nonprofessionals off the street. As for stories, movies were so short one could practically make them up as one went along.

But there remained two rather daunting obstacles. One was harassment from the Trust, whose "bulls" pounced upon anyone suspected of using a patented camera. To thwart them, Laemmle created diversions. He'd hide his camera in an express wagon or icebox, while a "dummy" camera, one that ostensibly didn't violate Edison's patent, ground in full view. One night, when the Trust's squad made an unexpected appearance, Laemmle and Cochrane had to collect their cameras and spend the evening huddling in the studio cellar. In 1911, again to avoid Trust persecution, Laemmle sent his entire company to Cuba; but the company got homesick and the humidity proved to be as much an annoyance as Edison. Within weeks they were back in New York, practicing stealth once again.

The second obstacle was scarcity of film stock. Edison's exclusive pact with Eastman Kodak barred the Independents from purchasing the raw film necessary for production. The only alternative was stock from Europe, but demand far outstripped supply. "We used to sit around on the street waiting for the wagon to come in with stock," one of Laemmle's employees remembered. "Every independent laboratory had a crew waiting, and as soon as a wagon would arrive, everyone would make a dive to grab a couple of cans of stock and get back to the laboratory with it." Independents began cutting deals left and right with importers and with middlemen who "laundered" stock from Kodak, and Independent production continued unabated.

For his part, Laemmle entered production with a splash, obviously trying to distinguish his films from those of the Edison Trust. He promised exhibitors "the grandest American-made moving pictures you ever saw." One ad proclaimed, "My motto will be: The best films that man's ingenuity can devise, and the best films man's skill can execute." This wasn't entirely hype. Making better movies was good business, but it was also a way of legitimizing the film industry itself and the men who ran it—as powerful a motive for Laemmle as for Zukor. His first production, filmed in rural New Jersey, was a sixteen-minute dramatization of Longfellow's poem "Hiawatha." In announcing its release on October 25, 1909, his father's birthday, Laemmle boasted that "film exchanges and exhibitors by the hundred have been urging me to hurry up with this first release, but to all alike I have said: 'None of the going-off-half-cocked business for mine!' . . . [Y]ou can bet it is classy, or I wouldn't make it my first release."

Laemmle wasn't a brilliant aesthetic innovator, and *Hiawatha* was stiff and pedestrian, but he had become a brilliant exploiter, one who "knew how to use the opportunities," in the words of his nephew and one-time employee, Max Laemmle. Laemmle was now marketing movies the way he had marketed clothing in Oshkosh. Anticipating Zukor's Famous Players, he was one of the first producers to try to upgrade screen acting by luring stage performers to the movies. Virtually every major Independent followed suit. He was also among the first regularly to raid competitors for talent and then feature them as "stars"—most notably with child actress Mary Pickford. Again, virtually everyone followed, and the rush of performers and directors seeking celebrity, money, and creative power became a major drain on the Trust's pool of talent and still another reason for its collapse.

One of the first stars he spirited away from the Trust was Florence Lawrence, known by audiences simply as the "Biograph Girl" after the studio for which she worked. But shortly after signing with Laemmle and before it could be announced publicly, Lawrence was variously reported as kidnapped, murdered, or killed by a streetcar. The rumors naturally whipped up national concern, which hung on for days until Lawrence suddenly appeared, alive and well and under contract to Laemmle. Laemmle insisted that the rumors had been floated by the Trust to discredit him, but other versions attributed the story to a well-orchestrated publicity campaign by Laemmle's right-hand man, Robert Cochrane. It was the sort of stunt the stolid Trust would never have thought of doing.

Laemmle could think of it because ever since his days at Continental Clothing he had been essentially a publicist—only now he had found a product to publicize: himself. Laemmle used Cochrane's advertising apparatus not only to sell films, but to sell an image; and the image he cultivated for himself was suggestive. In his own eyes, or at least as projected in his ads, which always featured him prominently, Laemmle was straight talking, dedicated, altruistic, and incorruptible —a little man besieged by omnivorous and rapacious economic forces. He nicknamed his new production outfit "IMP" for the Independent Motion Picture Company of America. Its symbol was a mischievous little gremlin who deflated the Trust's pomposity and power. For exhibitors, Laemmle's little "imp" may have represented all the outsiders and all the put-upon in their economic and cultural warfare against a fat, entrenched establishment. For Laemmle, it represented a caricature of his life.

Yet the truth was that by 1913, Laemmle, far from being a nervy, embattled little man, was a power himself with a yearly salary estimated at $100,000 and a personal fortune at over $1 million, and a few rivals were even accusing him of the same high-handedness for which he had attacked the Trust. In May 1910 Laemmle and a number of his fellow Independents had formed an alliance, the Motion Picture Distributing and Sales Company, which consolidated their efforts by buying films made by Independent producers and selling them to Independent exchanges; those, in turn, rented the films to exhibitors. But the Independents were aptly named. Within a year the allies had divided into factions and were squabbling among themselves—warfare one observer described as without "parallel in the history of 'the show business'!"

On one side was Laemmle. On the other was Harry Aitken, who, like Laemmle, had begun his movie career as an exhibitor in the Midwest and then moved into production with his brother Roy. The alleged trigger of the dispute was a raid Aitken had made on IMP, snatching away IMP's most popular star, Mary Pickford. Laemmle quickly retaliated. He convinced the Motion Picture Distributing and Sales Company to impose sterner terms to distribute Aitken's movies. Aitken answered by withdrawing from the company and forming a new combine of his own, ultimately called the Mutual Film Corporation. Two months later Laemmle and his allies regrouped and formed still another distribution company. Pressed to name the new operation, Laemmle, according to one participant, stared thoughtfully out the window.

> *"I've got the name," he said, and paused to get their full attention. "Universal. That's what we're supplying—universal entertainment for the universe."*

> *After the meeting someone said, "C. L., how did you happen to pick the word 'Universal'?" The little giant displayed his familiar boyish grin as he answered, "I was looking down on the street as a covered truck went by. On the top was painted 'Universal Pipe Fittings.'"*

The blood of the battle between Universal and Mutual had barely dried when the partners of Universal had a falling-out of their own. This time the issue was power and who held it. Two factions claimed control—one headed by Laemmle and Cochrane and a second headed by a producer named Pat Powers, who looked like the prototype of an Irish policeman and had a brogue to match. The balance of power, however, was held by a number of small investors, and depending on which way they were leaning at any given time, either Laemmle or Powers was in command. It got so that when one faction came to examine the corporate ledgers, the other faction had them tossed out the window to an accomplice below. At one point Laemmle even dispatched a group of thugs to seize the studio of a member of the rival faction. The ensuing battle was so brutal that the police had to be summoned to stop it. But when the dust settled in 1915, Laemmle was firmly in control of Universal, was about to open the most modern and efficient studio in America, and was being lionized in the trade press as a "practically unknown man" who had risen to be "King of the Film Renters." From this point on, the Jews would control the movies.

While Laemmle was leading the charge against the Trust, the Independents' cudgels were also being wielded by a loud, indefatigable blowhard whose reputation was such that when exhibitors needed a spokesman, they recruited William Fox because Fox could "holler the loudest." Fox had been brought to New York from Hungary by his parents while he was still an infant. His father, a merchant and part-time dentist in the old country, was shiftless and irresponsible, never earning more than a thousand dollars in any given year, and the family's financial burdens ultimately fell on William. As a child he peddled stove black from tenement to tenement on the Lower East Side and sold lozenges to passengers on excursion boats and to strollers in Central Park.

When he turned eleven he quit school, and by thirteen, after lying about his age, he was a foreman at a clothing firm. Though he later claimed that "I was working for a goal and enjoyed every minute of it," he was being less than truthful. He clearly resented the role of breadwinner, and the enmity seethed in his description of his father. "My father was perfectly happy," Fox said later. "He was just as happy when he worked as when he didn't work. He never worried. . . . When I came home and told him that the butcher and the baker had refused to trust us anymore during the period he was out of work, he was sure that tomorrow would be all right, or that the butcher and baker would likely change their minds."

The younger Fox's tack was decidedly different. He was a man obsessed with success. Even as a teenager he was formulating his strategy. "Every penny was something I denied myself, with the thought in mind that if I was going forward, I had to have money. Capital was what I needed." By the time he was twenty he had saved enough to invest in a small company of his own, an inspecting and shrinking firm that prepared bolts of cloth for garment manufacturers. Within two years, riding the tide of ready-to-wear clothing that was sweeping the country, he claimed to have saved $50,000.

Tall, demonstrative, and vain, despite a stiff arm that was the result of a childhood accident, Fox had always been attracted to show business. With a friend, he had even dabbled in vaudeville himself, performing comedy routines at dances for ten dollars a night. So it wasn't entirely uncharacteristic of him to seek an investment in entertainment, though precisely how and when he did so isn't clear. Whether his interest had been piqued by a secretary at his cloth inspecting company whose father owned a small movie house or by another cloth tradesman looking for a partner to buy a theater, Fox and a friend did acquire a penny arcade in Brooklyn sometime in 1903, and after shutting it down during the summer for renovations, they installed a 150-seat movie theater on the second floor. Fox's partner sold out within six months, saying he "didn't like the business and the kind of people we had to deal with." Fox hung on and, like

Laemmle, reaped a small fortune. By giving the movie customers their change in pennies and then routing their exit past the slot machines, he cleared $40,000 on a $10,000 investment in the first year alone.

But Fox wasn't simply in the business of investment; like Zukor, he was also in the business of rehabilitation—his own—and the theaters quickly became a kind of life trope—the disreputable made reputable. A case in point was an old burlesque theater Fox acquired in the Williamsburg section of Brooklyn in 1906. It was called "The Bum" by local residents, and the city building agencies were so appalled by its condition, its roof gaping and its orchestra filled with water, that Fox had to bargain to get permits to renovate. While the repairs were proceeding, he began plotting to attract the locals by jabbing at their sensitivities—something he was skilled at doing since he had the same sensitivities himself. He circulated handbills throughout the neighborhood declaring that the theater had been called "The Bum" because some individuals, unnamed, regarded the *people* of Williamsburg as bums, and he rallied the residents to defend their besmirched honor—though it was the theater's honor that had really been besmirched, not theirs. On opening night, he recalled, "ten thousand people marched down Grand Street with ten bands playing. Yes, sir! And the people carried banners. One of 'em read, 'We are the Respectable People of Williamsburg.' That was the last ever heard of 'The Bum.' It has been a family theatre ever since." And "in a short space of time," it turned a profit of hundreds of thousands of dollars.

Like virtually all of the Jews who would be successful in the movies, Fox succeeded in part because he drew on his own life experiences and knew how to translate his own inchoate yearnings for entertainment and respectability into those of the audience. "A man who is married and earns only $12 or $15 a week can't afford to pay $2 for a seat in a theatre, can he?" Fox once asked a journalist. "Well then, what does he do? I'll tell you. He stands up at a bar until he is drunk, and then he goes home and fights with his wife. At least, that's what he used to do." But Fox had hit on an innovation. Remembering his own desire for entertainment and his own inability to afford it, he would combine movies and vaudeville at "popular prices"—fifty cents for the most expensive seats and ten cents for the cheapest. (It was the same formula Marcus Loew would follow.) If the arcades had made him wealthy, within a few years his vaudeville-movie combination had made him a millionaire with over a dozen theaters throughout New York.

Yet it was the movies, Fox realized, not the vaudeville acts, that were the real draw. "A year ago I sent out 10,000 cards requesting patrons to say what part of the performance they liked best," he told an interviewer in 1912. "Fifty-five percent of the answers were in favor of moving pictures. Interest in 'comedy scenes' and 'heart interest' photoplays seems to be about equally divided. Instructive pictures showing countries and their manufacturing industries are appreciated most in the poorer districts. But everywhere it is the pictures, more than the vaudeville acts, that hold the audiences. The only explanation I can find is that motion pictures, perhaps, realize the American idea of speed and activity."

Fox continued to promote vaudeville, and he became a serious entrepreneur in the early teens, leasing the prestigious Academy of Music on Fourteenth Street. But vaudeville was gradually being supplanted by the movies, vaudeville theaters by grand new movie palaces, and when profit for live shows declined under the competition, Fox cast his fate with the movies, until he had even the Academy of Music showing films. Fox also realized, as had Laemmle, that to cast one's fate with the movies—and to take greater advantage of the movie craze—also meant forming an exchange to buy and then rent films to the burgeoning ranks of theater owners. In 1907 he opened the Greater New York Rental Company. It was this move that eventually put him on the same collision course with the Trust that Laemmle was traveling.

Shortly after the formation of its own distribution arm, the General Film Company, the Trust had begun actively to buy out exchanges and consolidate them. Less than two years later, through a combination of intimidation and money, it had succeeded in acquiring fifty-seven of the principal exchanges. Not many exchangemen could hold out, but one of the few who could was William Fox. Fox was a fighter by nature and paranoid by experience. He had constructed an elaborate demonology in which lawyers were "reptiles" and bankers "vultures," and throughout his life he was particularly sensitive that, as a Jew, he would be exploited and destroyed by gentile powers. The Trust's threats merely confirmed his suspicions.

In the beginning Fox cooperated by securing a license, but when they approached him with an offer to buy his exchange, he set a prohibitive price of $750,000. They refused. Then, trumping up a charge that Fox had illegally exhibited licensed films in a house of prostitution, they canceled his license. Fox, in turn, set a trap. He approached the Trust and told them he had had a change of heart. He would sell, after all, and for $75,000. They readily agreed and reinstated his license. Then Fox closed the snare. He said he'd had *another* change of heart and was keeping his exchange. The Trust responded by canceling his license once again. This time they had miscalculated.

Over the years Fox had gained some powerful political connections. He had formed a partnership with two major figures in the Tammany Hall political machine to buy the City Theatre in New York; his attorney, Gustavus Rogers, had ties to prominent Washingtonians; and one of his closest associates, Winfield Sheehan, had been deputy to New York's police commissioner, Waldo Rhinelander. Fox had already filed a civil antitrust action of his own against the Motion Picture Patents Company, and within a short time he and Rogers were personally lobbying Attorney General George Wickersham in Washington to bring a federal suit as well. It is impossible to say whether Fox was instrumental in or the lucky beneficiary of a political gambit by President Taft, who was locked in an electoral battle with two outspoken trustbusters, Democratic nominee Woodrow Wilson and Bull Mooser Teddy Roosevelt. Whatever the reason, the Justice Department did file an antitrust suit on August 15, 1912. In one act, the Trust lost whatever legal legitimacy it had, and the Independent ranks swelled.

Meanwhile, amid all the legal crossfire, Fox, like Laemmle, began producing films himself in New York. One reason, he said, was that he had erected several of the largest, most opulent movie houses in the world, and the Trust producers had, in Fox's words, "grown affluent and dictatorial. They knew they had you in their grip and squeezed you accordingly." The only way to loosen the squeeze was to enter production. But Fox wasn't being entirely disingenuous either when he said he had loftier aims than profit. He was, in fact, using the movies as a form of social climbing. "When I entered, actively, the producing field of motion pictures," he stated in a 1915 press release,

> I was actuated by a double motive. The so-called features that I had been selecting with all the care possible for my theatres did not fill my ideals of the highest standard possible in motion pictures. Therefore, I was fairly driven, in the interest of my patrons, and also as a secondary consideration in the belief that there was an immense demand for really good pictures, into the manufacturing end of the business.... I decided to carry out, in my motion picture producing career, the same ideals as I had introduced at the Academy of Music. That is to say ... that the public insistently demands photoplay features by great and world-famous authors, featuring celebrated dramatic stars.

When he entered the exhibition end, he explained years later:

> I was looking for an outlet for my business acumen which hadn't found sufficient expression in the cloth examining and shrinking business.... But as I became established and expanded my business, and life was no longer merely a battle to survive, my thoughts changed. I reached the period in 1912 or 1913 where I found myself with $500,000 in cash that I wanted to invest, and I realized that there was a great deal more in life than just making money. What concerned me far more was to make a name that would stand for the finest in entertainment the world over.

He could have been speaking for nearly all of the Hollywood Jews.

Fox's own personal rehabilitation, however, was less genteel than Gothic. Out at Woodmere, Long Island, he bought a large estate among the gentry, which, with his usual flair for the dramatic, he called Fox Hall. As master of Fox Hall, he became an autocrat, assuming the role of paterfamilias to his brothers and sisters as well as to his own immediate family, trying to reshape them in the image of gentility and demanding their strict obedience. Everything came under his scrutiny and jurisdiction—from dress to language to deportment to employment. Family members were terrified lest they incur his wrath. "I watched my mother labor for a week over a 'thank you' note," recalled syndicated journalist Angela Fox Dunn, the daughter of his youngest sister, Malvina, whom Fox supported and from whom he expected gratitude. "The note should have just the right tone. It should be appropriately grateful, but it shouldn't be too groveling. One word might turn the king off. You could fall out of favor with the king, and you could be in a lot of trouble."

Trouble meant losing your stipend, a serious deprivation since none of the Foxes really worked. Women weren't supposed to; he wouldn't permit it because it wasn't genteel. (Malvina did later declare her independence with a job at Warner Brothers, but there were rumors Fox secretly paid her salary.) Fox insured that the men, husbands and brothers, had sinecures on his payroll—a kind of economic castration. The impulse was obvious. After his own father's abdication of responsibility, Fox had essentially become Man writ large to his family. He assumed all the roles—father, husband, lover, dispenser of largesse. There was no room for any man other than he. But nothing was given without strings; he would always demand an accounting. "My mother wasn't a business person; she was an actress," his niece recalled. "She used to keep shoeboxes full of receipts, and she would never find anything. It was so frustrating. The sweat would be running down her face. 'Brother Bill is coming! Go through that box!' . . . It was a horrible way to live. And yet she loved him in almost an incestuous way. They would sit and hold hands like lovers for hours, and she would stare into his eyes. . . ."

One could take Fox out of the slum, but for all his pretensions, one could never quite take the slum out of Fox. If this was one reason for his success in business, it was also a personal tragedy for someone who so badly wanted to exorcise his patrimony of failure. Fox was well aware, as a biographer put it, that New York financiers "would invite this grown-up East Side Jewish boy to luncheon at the Bankers' Club or to dinner at the Metropolitan Club for business conferences, but their wives would not appreciate him, and he would never belong to their inner circle of fashionable culture." He was extremely self-conscious about his appearance, especially his stiff left arm, which he stuck in his pocket in public, and, until even he realized it was hopeless, he went to great pains to hide his baldness, meticulously sweeping his hair across his head as camouflage. He was also sensitive to his lack of education, dreading the occasional malaprops and lapses in diction: "I seen it" or "I done it." Something of a hypochondriac, he always wore white socks for hygiene, even at board meetings, and a cashmere sweater, which he claimed his doctor had prescribed to ward off chills and subsequent illness.

His sense of disadvantage surfaced in another way, too. It made him extremely distrustful of virtually everyone and everything, a trait that often erupted in arrogance and irascibility. His only real trust resided in the fates, and superstition was a force to be observed. It wasn't a religious feeling. Judaism was identified with his father, and Fox's only recollection of religious training was a tiny *cheder* in a tenement basement where a wizened old Jewish scholar rapped his students with a stick if they gave the wrong answer. Fox's belief was closer to a naive reliance on Providence, on the one hand, and numerology, which was divination through numbers, on the other. He remembered a kindly butcher who extended his family credit and whom he later supported, as evidence of God's larger scheme. "Do you mean to tell me that God didn't give the butcher the idea to give me that meat because He knew that he was going to be taken care of?" he asked his biographer, Upton Sinclair. "During any calamity that befell me, it was always made clear to me that it wasn't any ability that I possessed that straightened me out again, but it was God Himself who came to my rescue."

As for the numerology, Fox had long contended that good things happen in threes. There were three stages to his life. Three major business decisions. Three mortal enemies. He even arranged his marriage for January 1, 1900, which also happened to be his birthday, since it would make the happy confluence of three events. His wife, Eve, claimed to possess psychic powers, and Fox himself said that he could enter another man's mind and read his thoughts.

But the most significant remnant of his childhood, as for so many of the Hollywood Jews, was fear. Jews succeeded at the sufferance of the gentile establishment. Everything gained could just as easily be lost, and it was the provisional nature of success, as much as anything else, that impelled him. Fox was a workaholic. He never carried a watch, he said, because "I never wanted to know what time it was. My day ended when my day's work was completed. Again and again, I didn't go to bed at all during the twenty-four hours." He bragged that the Fox Film Corporation was a one-man operation. Everything was given his personal attention—from the movies his company made, to the theaters it constructed, to the value of the currency of the countries it did business with. It was a desperation born of insecurity, but it would prove a powerful force in the motion picture industry, where desperation often ruled.

━━━

"I'll never forget the first time a newspaper published his picture and used the caption 'A Film Magnate,'" Robert Cochrane recalled of Carl Laemmle. "He showed it to me in high glee and with a broad grin exclaimed, 'See. I told you I'd make them recognize me.'" The idea of being a magnate was exhilarating, but the fact of the triumph, making people recognize him, seemed to be as important as its fruits. "He had absolutely no modesty about publicizing himself," recalled nephew Max, a Universal executive under Laemmle. "There was a constant flow of material that was being sent out—pictures and stories. One was always kept abreast of Carl Laemmle's doings."

Even, it turned out, his native village of Laupheim. Every year he would summer at the Carlsbad Spa in Europe, where he took the curative waters, but he always made a point of returning to Laupheim, and he had the third floor of his boyhood home renovated for his quarters. In Laupheim Laemmle played the prodigal. After World War I, he sent provisions, sugar and flour and sausages, to the destitute village, and he sponsored dozens of its residents who wanted to emigrate to America. Its citizens, especially the Jewish community to whom he was particularly generous, were grateful. On his arrival each year there would be a dinner and then a large gathering at the local pub, where he would receive old friends and their encomiums. "They loved him," his son-in-law, Stanley Bergerman, remembered.

"All of the Jewish community came to pay homage to this wonderful humanitarian." Later they named a street after him.

Yet despite the self-aggrandizement, Laemmle remained surprisingly provincial for a Hollywood mogul. After his wife, Recha, died in January 1919 during a nationwide influenza epidemic, he never remarried and never even dated. (He always kept her portrait and handkerchief in his pocket.) Disregarding etiquette, he demanded punctuality and would begin dinner promptly, even if his guests had not arrived. He would scrutinize a dinner check like a typical workingman because, he told a companion, "I don't want to be cheated." He never read books, only the newspaper, never attended the theater or symphony, never golfed, skated, or swam, and could never understand why anyone would want to.

An ebullient man even with acquaintances, Laemmle's real distractions were his children, to whom he was entirely devoted. His daughter, Rosabelle, who had been fifteen when her mother died, was headstrong and opinionated. Once affianced to the legendary young production executive Irving Thalberg, she bickered her way out of the engagement, then married a much more compliant executive named Stanley Bergerman, later moving into her father's home to care for him. Her younger brother, Julius Laemmle, or "Junior," as he was usually called to his consternation, was much more like his father—easygoing and carefree. Junior was a "colorful liver." He could usually be seen squiring pretty starlets. He loved to dance. He was an excellent tennis player. He enjoyed good food and kept a regular shipment of Nova Scotia salmon on hand. Some thought him irresponsible. Laemmle himself occasionally complained that he wasn't sure what would happen to Junior. Junior had his own idea: he wanted to become a film producer.

In the summer of 1926, Laemmle was taking his annual cruise to Europe when he fell ill. "He was sick from the first minute we left the harbor," remembered his nephew Walter, who accompanied him. "The doctor on board didn't know whether to operate or not operate. . . . He was in bed from beginning to end." At first it was thought Laemmle was suffering from appendicitis. As his condition worsened, the diagnosis changed: his appendix had burst. By the time he reached London four days later, the prognosis was grim. "The doctors gave me half an hour to live," he told a reporter a few years later. "And during that half hour, all I could think of was, 'What will become of Junior if I die now?' I didn't know. And I decided then and there that if he wanted to go into the studio, he could do it."

After a long convalescence, Laemmle decided to move from New York to California, where he had built a 230-acre studio on a stretch of mustard fields in the San Fernando Valley just over Cahuenga Pass. Though he had been one of the first of the major film producers, he was among the very last to leave New York for Hollywood, where production had gradually shifted throughout the teens. His home, located in Beverly Hills off Benedict Canyon, had belonged to producer and director Thomas Ince, who set the style for the movie moguls when he built it in 1922. Purchased for $750,000 from Ince's widow, the mansion was a two-story Mediterranean as long as a football field. The living room was thirty by seventy feet, the fireplace ten feet high, and the garage could accommodate eight cars. Surrounding it were thirty-one acres, which Laemmle had converted into a small farm with ducks, chickens, and cows. The grounds required fifteen gardeners.

Ince had named it "Días Durados," the House of Lasting Days. For Laemmle, the name would have a certain poignance. In failing health and increasingly uninterested in the daily workings of the studio, he now spent much of his time indulging an old passion: gambling. He loved to gamble—cards, horses, blackjack, roulette—it made absolutely no difference to him. At least once a week he participated in a high-stakes poker game where the players might include film executive Joseph Schenck, theater owner Sid Grauman, film attorney Edwin Loeb, or Sam Barnett, who wrote all the insurance policies for Universal and became one of Laemmle's closest friends. When the action slowed at the poker table, he might drive down to the Agua Caliente racetrack and casino across the Mexican border (where he once reportedly lost $30,000 in a weekend) or take a ferry out to a gambling boat called *The Rex*, which was anchored off Catalina.

"At that time, he used to go Saturday, and Sunday he came home," said his nephew Walter. "If he was in the studio Monday morning—let's say I wanted to ask him something—that was fine. If he was *not* in the studio Monday morning, then you knew he lost, and he tried to make it up. If he came back Tuesday, we would ask his secretary, Jack Ross, who was a good friend of ours, 'Jack, how did the old man do?' If he didn't come back Tuesday, if he came back Wednesday, we got lost. Stay out." Even on his European excursions he was seldom without a deck of cards. Ready for another game, he would yell to his entourage, "Duty calls. We're wasting time."

"He would play cards, and his daughter wanted him to be home and in bed by midnight," remembered her husband, Stanley Bergerman. "If he came home too late, he would take off his shoes downstairs and walk up because there were stone steps coming up from the main hallway to his room. . . . He would walk up in his stocking feet so his daughter wouldn't hear him coming home. . . . She'd sometimes stay up waiting for him. She loved him, and he didn't have a wife, so she was his caretaker."

Meanwhile Junior, now seventeen, went to work at Universal. His first assignment was producing a series of comic shorts about college life—ironically, since he had passed up his own opportunity to go to the University of Pennsylvania for the studio job. But everyone in the industry knew this was just a tutorial for bigger things, and the press freely speculated that he would take over the studio when he reached his twenty-first birthday in 1929, the way a prince assumed the throne. As it turned out, they were right. "Junior was always smart," his father bragged to one interviewer. "[T]hat brain of his is working every minute of the day and, I am sometimes afraid, most of the night. He is a tireless worker. I have never seen such vitality in anyone, such a determination to get a job done, not merely well, but better than anyone else could do it."

Not everyone shared this opinion. "Junior read [scripts] and very often put his finger on the heart of the story," said one executive, "and then destroyed it." Another producer, having just arrived from Europe, was counseled not to expect a job at Universal. "Junior's running this joint now, and if there's one thing the kid can't stand, it's 'great' European producers and directors." Even within the Universal family there were grumblings. Under Carl Laemmle Universal had established a policy of making "program" pictures, moderately budgeted films that would be sold to exhibitors as a package. Junior was determined to change all that. He believed in bigger, more prestigious films, but he was running into resistance from Universal's sales force.

To arbitrate the dispute, Carl Laemmle hired Sol Lesser, a major film exhibitor. After lengthy negotiations, Lesser arrived at a settlement. The "program" policy would continue, but Junior would be allowed six to eight big-budget "specials." Lesser now urged Laemmle Sr. to go to New York to give his imprimatur to the decision. Laemmle did, holing up in the posh Hotel Pierre for a week. But when he emerged, it wasn't to ratify Lesser's settlement. "Only then," Lesser said, "did I learn that he had quietly selected the successor to [General Manager] Phil Reisman."

Having passed the scepter to Junior, Laemmle now appointed Stanley Bergerman to be second in command. The idea, it seemed, was to divide authority between his children in a Lear-like gesture. Junior, bright if unmotivated, would be the strategist; Bergerman, genial and plodding, the executor. But the consequences proved to be Lear-like as well. When Universal's financial health began flagging during the Depression, Junior pinned the blame on Bergerman, opening a breach not only in the business, but in the family. Laemmle was irate. At one point he got so furious with his son over the rupture that he dismissed him, then fretted tearfully over what he had done.

Too proud to apologize himself, Laemmle recruited a young Czechoslovakian producer named Paul Kohner, whom he had sponsored from Europe, and invited him on a drive to Agua Caliente, the gambling resort that had become Laemmle's home away from home. During the drive, Laemmle appealed to Kohner to call Junior and ask him to motor to Caliente. Kohner did, and Junior consented. "I'm in your debt," Laemmle said with gratitude. "And I'll do something about it as soon as I'm back at the studio. You have never had a contract with us. I'm getting on. And as my dear mother said, 'A young man can die, an old man must die.' I will give you a long-term contract with Universal that will protect you in case something should happen to me."

Kohner was ecstatic; Laemmle had a long-standing policy of not awarding contracts. (It was one of the reasons he could never hold on to talent.) But a few months later, still without his contract, Kohner was having dinner at the Brown Derby with writer Preston Sturges when Frank Orsatti, a prominent talent agent, stopped at their table. Orsatti casually dropped some shocking news: Laemmle had sold the studio.

It was no secret around Hollywood that Universal had been in a calamitous situation for some time, and that management had yet to devise a plan to cope with it. Junior still wanted to concentrate on better productions—which meant fewer and costlier films. (He suggested cutting production by 40 precent.) Others blanched at the idea of increasing costs when the company was already strapped, and the sales force cringed at having less product to peddle. Laemmle vacillated.

By 1935 the situation had become desperate. Laemmle was in urgent need of cash, trying to stave off creditors and a possible takeover. Perhaps the cruelest twist was that at one point he even had intermediaries dun relatives for support—the same relatives who had always been subsidized by him. Finally, in November, he secured a $750,000 loan from a Wall Street syndicate headed by producer Charles Rogers and J. Cheever Cowdin, a British financier. It was a measure of his desperation that he pledged his share of Universal as collateral—that is, $5.5 million to secure a $750,000 loan. This time, however, the old Laemmle luck failed. When Universal's production of the Jerome Kern musical *Showboat* fell behind schedule and over budget, he was forced to go to the financiers a second time.

Still, outwardly at least, Laemmle remained reasonably optimistic that he would hold on to the company, and he reassured Kohner, when the young producer confronted him, that Rogers and Cowdin couldn't possibly raise the money to exercise their option even if they wanted to. But he wasn't taking chances. He had signed Junior to a long-term contract and made certain that it would be honored by new management. Within a month of the new debt obligation, the creditors called in his loan.

Now sixty-nine, Laemmle couldn't hold on. On April 2, 1936, the Universal board reorganized with Cowdin as the chairman, Laemmle's old partner Robert Cochrane as president, and Charlie Rogers as executive vice president with primary responsibility for production. All Laemmle's ties were severed; he didn't even retain a seat on the board. Junior remained for a short time, but by the fall he had left the studio as well to become an independent producer. "I'm glad to stand on my own feet," he told a reporter after returning from a sabbatical in Europe. "If I fail, then the fault is all mine. If I make good, then I should get a share of the credit. I make my own decisions. I'm using my own money—that ought to be proof that I'm in earnest over all this. Whatever the pictures, good or bad, they are my responsibility. And I want it that way, to prove that I'm not just the son of a man who happened to own a movie studio." By spring Junior had set up operations at MGM. By fall 1937 he had resigned without explanation, though there was speculation that he had lost favor.

As for Laemmle Sr., leaving the industry seemed to affect him less than the leave-taking of the other Hollywood Jews would affect them. He had long ago reached the point where he felt he had nothing left to prove. As Junior said, "I feel sure that he has realized his life's desire. I am certain that his dreams have come true." One perquisite to which his station still entitled him and one which he indulged, especially as he approached retirement, was meeting prominent people. "That is one thing which gives him an actual kick," noted Robert Cochrane. Around 1920 he even began collecting autographs, and by the early thirties, when he abdicated to Junior, this had become his favorite avocation—after gambling.

His collection was housed in two large volumes—one for personal acquaintances out of public life, which he called the Hall of Friendship, and another for celebrities, which he called the Hall of Fame. Virtually everyone of note acceded to his request—every film director and star, presidents, monarchs, artists, playwrights, captains of industry. As with everything else in his life, the symbolism was overt. Poring over these scrapbooks at Días Durados, as he did, with a childlike joy, he no doubt felt vindicated. He hadn't failed. He hadn't repeated his father's pattern of defeat. His will had seen him through. Even in retirement, Carl Laemmle was a great man. He had the signatures of the most powerful and famous men in the world to prove it.

3

Born on the Fourth of July

If someone were doing a screen biography of him, there's nothing that would convey the spirit of MGM more, the spirit of Louis B. Mayer more, than the sight of Grandpa marching out of the [Hollywood] Bowl himself to the strains of "Stars and Stripes Forever," in unison, making sure you were all in unison with him marching out.

DANNY SELZNICK

If I had to use one word to describe my father in every way, I would use "intensity."

IRENE MAYER SELZNICK

EVERY FOURTH OF JULY LOUIS B. Mayer would shut down production at his studio, Metro-Goldwyn-Mayer, and celebrate the only way he knew how: colossally. There would be picnicking and bunting and music and old-fashioned patriotic oration from Mayer himself, who could be a stirring and even eloquent speaker when the spirit moved him, as it often did. It being Independence Day, this was, of course, intended partly as a tribute to Mayer's beloved adopted country, but only partly. Claiming that he had lost his real birth records during immigration, Mayer had appropriated the Fourth of July as his own birthday, so the festivities, everyone realized, were equally a tribute to Mayer—maybe more than equally. It was an extraordinary conflation, rife with symbolism, and it condensed, as few events could, two of the chief characteristics of his life: his excess and his paternalism.

Mayer was always an extremist. There was probably no better example in Hollywood of Isaiah Berlin's "neurotic distortion of the facts"—what Berlin saw as the outsider's need to hyperbolize and glorify the prevailing culture and its values. Everything Mayer did had to be more—a relatively common affliction among Jews, particularly Jews of Mayer's generation, since Jews were often born with the racking sense of being outside and having to compensate. What made Mayer's excesses so remarkable was that they were so excessive. It wasn't enough that he became an American citizen; he had to take his country's birthdate as his own—just as it wouldn't be enough that he commanded one of the greatest of the Hollywood studios; he had to make certain that his was the largest, most famous, and the one generally regarded as the best.

Some mistook his extremism for bombast, and Eric Johnston, president of the Motion Picture Association of America, called him "a bombastic egotist. . . . Some people have a capacity for friendship. . . . Mr. Mayer's capacity was almost entirely in the field of showmanship." Others saw his extremism as a kind of voraciousness. "[L]ooking at Mayer made me think of a praying mantis," said one director. "He is carnivorous. . . . He feeds on other people, and holds them up, but never in prayer." Still others thought his emotionalism was calculating and manipulative, done sheerly for effect.

Mayer was unquestionably a brilliant performer, "the greatest actor of all of them," said his daughter Edith. "They used to call him the D. W. Griffith of actors." "If you went in to see Louis B. Mayer," one producer recalled, "it was always an experience. He was a ham. He would get down on the floor and pray and sing and illustrate the kind of pictures he would like to see you make, which were cornball pictures that nobody would dare to make, and he would go into outrageous furies. So I never went near Louis Mayer." Tears flowed easily. He was renowned for collaring balky MGM stars and pouring out honeyed words of praise and affection until Mayer himself broke down under the weight of his performance.

But this wasn't all show. Mayer was a man who pitched his own life in the highest emotional key, and he could be just as overwrought and sentimental in private moments with his own family. "He was sentimental on people's birthdays, sentimental at Christmas, sentimental about all kinds of things," remembered his grandson Danny Selznick. "By being a man who was in touch with his emotions—I think that's a good way of putting it—he was capable of being moved by a lot of situations. He certainly cried at movies. He cried at *Lassie*, cried at *The Human Comedy*. He cried at *The Great Caruso*. . . . I can think of him in a situation where he had done something for [his longtime maid] Jean, on her birthday or something, and she would come out practically weeping. 'Mr. Mayer, you realize what you've done for me?' and so forth. And he would sit there at the dinner table, and he would say, 'Isn't that wonderful? Isn't she a wonderful woman?' And then he would start to cry over his pleasure in what he'd done for her and how grateful she was to him."

The amplitude of his emotions wasn't restricted to sentiment, either. Every emotion was outsized. Though he was slow to anger, he had a terrifying temper. "He was a forceful, powerful man," said Edith Mayer Goetz. "He'd just shout. The resonance of that voice! 'God damn you!' That's it. I'd hear it and I'd run." Occasionally he would even resort to force. Once, shortly after he had signed Charlie Chaplin's estranged wife to a film contract, he, Mrs. Chaplin, and Charlie all happened to attend a dinner at the Alexandria Hotel. Chaplin accused Mayer of meddling in his wife's divorce settlement and challenged Mayer to a fight. Mayer decked him with a single punch.

If Mayer's extremism was a form of assimilation, doing more and being more to win acceptance, his excesses worked synergistically on his second characteristic—his paternalism. Mayer didn't only want to belong—he wanted to be a father to the whole world, and it colored every relationship he had. "His relationship to the studio, to the staff, to the butler, to the household maid, was that of a warm, Jewish patriarch," Danny Selznick said. "A gentile man, even a father figure, wouldn't have had that excessive caring about everything. . . . It's 'How did your son's operation go?' It's finding that so-and-so doesn't have the money to put his child through college and suddenly producing the check to put him through." To his own two daughters, Edith and Irene, Mayer was smothering—an absolute, unbrookable, strident authority. "My father was not only omnipotent, he was omniscient," Irene wrote. "In a curious way, I got him mixed up with God, because of the word 'Almighty.'" "Of course, I could not leave our home at night until I got married," Edith said. "In Boston, once, we were very little and we went to a camp. I remember I was all excited because I had hot biscuits for supper. And Dad was ferocious about food that was sautéed; he was always on a health thing with food. And the next day, it seems to me, a very large car came up and we were taken [home] in the car." But Edith understood that the biscuits were an excuse. The real reason they were taken from camp was her father's possessiveness. He took the girls out "because we were away from him. We must always be together. We would last one night [apart]—if one night. This was until I got married. I never went anywhere."

In some measure the paternalism was probably the residue of Mayer's own childhood. His father, Jacob, who emigrated from Russia to St. John, New Brunswick, in 1888 when Louis was roughly three years old, was described as "grasping and tyrannical," and there was certainly no love lost between father and son. Jacob Mayer was a peddler who later collected and sold scrap metal. The family was desperately poor. They lived near the harbor on lower Main Street in a crowded section of wooden shanties called Portland, where the residents were primarily immigrants, sailors, and unskilled workingmen. Mayer himself preferred to forget these years, and he was vague about them even to his wife and children. What he remembered was starting an operation salvaging ships from the harbor and supervising more than two hundred men, though he was barely a teenager himself. And he remembered his father signing the papers, because Louis was a minor, and calling the company J. Mayer & Sons—a usurpation that still galled Louis decades later.

Jacob Mayer was a failure in business and a failure in his family. His refuge, as it was for so many Jewish immigrants of his generation who felt emasculated by America, was religion. As late as 1880 there had been only eight Jewish families in St. John. By the time the Mayers settled there, the Jewish population had been swelled by immigrants from Eastern Europe, like Mayer, and in 1896 they organized their own congregation, largely so they could secure kosher food. Jacob Mayer was among those honored with placing the Torah, the Jewish scrolls of the Old Testament, into the ark, and he was clearly one of the pillars of the Jewish community, even though he was just as clearly not the head of one of the community's first families.

"In most people, you can perceive the child," said Danny Selznick. "You can look at them and say they were such-and-such kind of a child in relation to their parents, who were the following. With this particular person, even though I've seen pictures of my grandfather as a child, it's very hard to get a sense of what the fabric of that family was." On the scant evidence available, Louis seems to have been strong, self-sufficient, and industrious. In a press release years later, he recounted how, when a teacher asked him what he would do if he had a thousand dollars, he answered, "Invest it." He told another story about buying a little red wagon and then informing his mother that he was going "to put it to work." Education was irrelevant. He left school at twelve to assist his father, but he later claimed that "if I had my life to lead over, I'd go to work at ten."

Still, for all Mayer's retrospective bluster, it was a childhood evidently filled with dissatisfaction, which was one reason why he purged its memory. He was taunted by the local anti-Semites and forced to defend himself. He was shamelessly exploited by his father, who sent him across Canada to bid at auctions on salvage, while his mother wept, fearing for his safety. At home he was subjected to his father's abuse and humiliation and was denied the warmth and security of the family. He would gain a measure of revenge, years later, when Jacob Mayer became his dependent, living in his home—the son now the patriarch. But late in 1903, with his mother's encouragement, Mayer decided to leave his father and St. John, and on January 1, 1904, at the age of nineteen, he set out for Boston, Massachusetts, and a new life.

Boston was a relatively common destination for maritimers resettling in the United States, and Mayer was already familiar with the city since he visited it regularly as his father's agent. Mayer's daughter Irene, however, believed Boston had another, more powerful inducement than familiarity. Louis Mayer had fallen in love. Irene didn't know exactly how, but Louis had met his intended's aunt, confided his loneliness, and was shown a picture of a favorite niece who lived in Boston—Margaret Shenberg. Mayer, an extraordinary romantic, was smitten, and after traveling to Boston's Jewish South End, he rented a room nearby to begin a courtship of a girl he had never met. It wasn't easy. The Shenbergs had airs. Margaret's father was a cantor whose handsomeness, vanity, and regal mien had earned him the sobriquet Golden One, and he felt, as one confidant of Mayer's put it, that Louis "wasn't good enough. . . . They looked down on him." Still, in romance as in everything else, Mayer was relentless. Within six months he had won Margaret's hand.

For Mayer, so conscious of his own father's shortcomings, the family would always be something sacred, the source of love, morality, and security. Within this idealization, Margaret readily conformed to the role Mayer designed for her. "In the sense that my grandfather was a classic Jewish patriarch," said Danny Selznick, "I have the impression she was a classic Jewish wife—classic in the sense that she was one of L. B.'s support systems: the loving wife at home who takes care of the man and raises the family and so forth." Mayer adored her and thrived on her simple faith in him.

When Mayer came to Boston he "didn't have the price of a sandwich." He got employment with a scrap metal collector doing odd jobs, but after his marriage he heard about another scrap metal firm in Brooklyn, where he had relatives. He seized the opportunity and moved there, but it was a short stay. The 1907 depression, the one that had shaken Marcus Loew's faith in movies, ruined Mayer's business, and he was sent back to Boston, back to a room with his in-laws. Only now he had two infant daughters to support.

Back in Boston Mayer began picking up odd jobs. One of these, according to one account, was helping out at a local movie house, and it was from the proprietor, Joe Mack, who also happened to be the New England agent for a film distributor, that Mayer first got the idea of leasing a theater. According to this version, Mack noticed an advertisement announcing the availability of an old burlesque house in Haverhill, Massachusetts, some fifty miles north of Boston, and suggested that he and Mayer go up and take a look. The asking price for a six-month lease was $650, and with some assistance from Mack, who stood to gain the territory for his firm, and some from relatives, Mayer was suddenly a film exhibitor. Mayer himself told another story about how he entered the movies. In his rag-picking period, he had been given a pair of pants by the wife of a prominent banker and found some money in the pockets. He returned the bills, and as a reward the banker found him employment in a local nickelodeon, which, in turn, led to his leasing the theater in Haverhill.

Whichever story were true, when Mayer moved to Haverhill in the fall of 1907, he was a virtual novice, his only experience in exhibition being the chores he had done for Joe Mack. His sole comfort was that in Haverhill he had absolutely no competition either. Haverhill was a brute, sturdy, working-class town whose major industry was shoe manufacturing and whose motto was "The city where are made in the world's best factories shoes that tread the carpets of the globe." Cut by the green-gray Merrimack River, which snaked through the larger mill and factory towns of Lawrence and Lowell, and constructed of unrelieved brick and wood, Haverhill made a rather dreary impression, but it already had the reputation in entertainment circles of being a good stop for touring shows, and it did possess a sizable mercantile class of bankers, managers, and realtors, without also possessing a theatrical establishment to service them.

Mayer's theater, the Gem, was a six-hundred-seat burlesque house that had fallen on hard times. Located scarcely a block from the waterfront, it was an unimposing wooden structure with a long portico as an affectation and a billiard parlor above. For Mayer, who was "conservative" and "filled with moral uplift" even as a young man, the Gem was profoundly embarrassing. Before daring to open, he renovated the theater, renamed it the Orpheum, and instituted a new family-oriented policy that "won the confidence of the better element [and] held it with good, clean pictures and plays." But satisfactory would never do for an extremist like Mayer if he could devise something better. Having quickly won the trust and some of the capital of Haverhill's leading citizens, he closed the Orpheum in 1908, refurbished it once again, and reopened it as the New Orpheum.

This was just the beginning of his putative empire. Over the next two years he convinced two of Haverhill's leading businessmen to purchase and then raze a hotel in the heart of the commercial section and build a new theater—the 1,600-seat Colonial, which Mayer would manage. At its opening in December 1911, he took the stage to a loud and moving ovation, then claimed that the Colonial represented "the zenith of his ambitions." Mayer's portrait in oil hung prominently in the lobby.

In Haverhill, Mayer had won considerable respect by discovering what Zukor was discovering in New York on a larger scale—that the movies could be financially rewarding and emotionally satisfying if one tapped the middle-class audience. (He even used one of Zukor's devices, showcasing a film of the Passion Play.) "Even when I was a very little girl," Irene Selznick wrote, "my father spoke of the importance of what was being shown to the public. He deplored the way show business was being run; he thought everyone in it had an obligation to help make it respectable and then keep it so. . . . He became evangelistic about show business, most particularly movies."

Mayer loved the idea of using his business as a pulpit, but not only because it would vindicate him in the eyes of the community or because it would demonstrate his cultural legitimacy. Recognition and status meant less to Mayer than to Zukor. Mayer was driven by other personal demons. Zukor wanted to control the world. Mayer wanted to make it his family—to embrace and be embraced by it. Exhibiting movies may not have seemed like an occupation for a patriarchal moralist; to many people, it seemed quite the antithesis. But Mayer realized, as so many moral arbiters did, that the movies transmitted values, and that by controlling entertainment, he would be inculcating values, which, in turn, would make him a kind of father to the whole community—its moral and spiritual guide. So Mayer's mission in Haverhill escalated. It was not merely to bring culture to the heathens or even to bring the best entertainments from New York and Boston to the town's cultured elite. Mayer, with his paternalistic zeal, seemed bent on creating and then controlling the entire artistic life of the community, until he ran not only the New Orpheum and the Colonial, but also the smaller Bijou and the Academy of Music.

This grand design also required that he broaden his own entertainment interests to satisfy every constituency. The Bijou played movies. At the Colonial he instituted the "combination" policy of vaudeville and movies that Loew and Fox had successfully pioneered in New York. At the New Orpheum he created a repertory company to perform vignettes and plays. And at all his theaters he presented "special events," booking live acts from New York and Boston—everything from Maud Adams, the Broadway star of *Peter Pan*, to the Boston Opera Company.

Whether he had intended it or not—and he probably did—the result of this cultural siege was that Mayer became Haverhill's very own Frohman or Belasco, and he had firmly identified himself with the upper echelon of entertainment. At the same time he had made himself instrumental to the community. "Mr. Louis B. Mayer, whose inspiration and ambition it was to make grand opera in his home city a possibility, and through whose energy tonight's performance was made possible," a program eulogized on November 21, 1912, when Mayer brought the Boston Opera to the Colonial, "is undoubtedly as well known in Haverhill and its suburbs as any man in public life." "Other successes in dramatic and vaudeville endeavors," it went on, "have elevated Mr. Mayer to a plane equal with the most successful of theatrical men in New England; and Haverhill can boast, among other things, of having a citizen who is to be depended upon for those things which are necessary to enjoyment, with an assurance that everything is of the best." As the town's young impresario—he was twenty-seven—he was now also admitted to its select circle, and his wife was thrilled to be invited to their homes. "Those were happy days for him," recalled his daughter Edith. "Everything seemed to come easy."

But however important a figure he had become in Haverhill, Mayer could never have been entirely satisfied there, given his need to keep annexing more people to his "family." Encouraged by his local successes, he inevitably began to think of himself as a theatrical entrepreneur on a much larger stage—which made him the only one of the Hollywood Jews to make a frontal assault on the legitimate theater nearly all of them revered. (Lasky, who had been a theatrical impresario, forsook the stage once he entered the movie business.) On his frequent forays to New York searching for talent and material, Mayer had met Ben Stern, who for twenty years had been general manager for the late Broadway producer Henry Harris. Now, late in 1912, Mayer and Stern decided to form their own production company, which, they promised, would do "big things . . . and the theatrical world will be surprised one of these mornings to hear that certain famous stars have been contracted with by the Mayer & Stern management." Apparently dissatisfied with only one salient into that theatrical world, Mayer also formed in 1912 an alliance with another theatrical producer, Adolph Mayer, to manage the tour of an idiosyncratic tragedienne named Nance O'Neil. (She was once the companion of Lizzie Borden.)

Mayer wasn't a theatrical producer for long, despite what seems to have been a successful season. One biographer speculates that he was disillusioned after a nasty squabble with a Philadelphia theater owner over a reimbursement for some renovations Mayer had done. What seems equally likely is that Mayer discovered what the movie Jews in New York already knew—the upper reaches of theater were extremely difficult to penetrate, and the theater world, unlike that of the movies, was closed off to newcomers without prestige and enormous capital. Retreating to Haverhill, Mayer did continue to produce legitimate theater at the New Orpheum, but his brief experience in New York seems to have chastened and sobered him about the possibilities of ever being a theatrical producer. He now turned his attention exclusively to the movies.

His commitment to the movies that year, however, coincided with the first of the two most devastating events in his life. Throughout his formative years, his only ballast had been his mother. He spoke of her with such dewy idealism that even his grandson would later question whether Mayer was trying to compensate for some deprivation or dereliction. His daughter Irene wrote that "[h]e felt everything good in him had come from his mother." When she suddenly took ill after an operation, he raced to St. John with his personal physician, but he had come too late. Sarah Mayer died the next day, and her son sobbed uncontrollably. His grief would continue for the rest of his life. He would constantly invoke her memory to family, friends, and employees, and, as one intimate put it, "he continued to speak about her as if she were living." So deep was his affection that when actor John Gilbert, years later, made a disparaging remark about his own mother, Mayer felt obliged to defend the honor of all motherhood by punching him. As long as he lived, her portrait hung over his bed.

Even in death Sarah Mayer was the central influence on her son's life. A friend recalled Mayer reminiscing about his last conversation with her, as she lay dying. "'Do not grieve, Louis,' his mother had said. 'We must all die sooner or later. Now it's my turn. I wish I could have stayed a little longer, so I could see you do the big things I know you are capable of doing. But I will watch over you. I will know all about you and your work. And I will wait for you.'" Mayer always believed literally that she was watching. She became his totem, his personal divinity. He became her devoted celebrant, determined to justify her love and her faith in him.

At the time of her death in October 1913, Mayer was twenty-eight and had just made his first strike into film distribution with a two-man, Boston-based exchange called the Louis B. Mayer Film Company. It was intended to serve exhibitors like himself scattered throughout New England. (One of his earliest, and best, suppliers of films was Jesse Lasky.) But this was only the first of a plethora of companies that Mayer would either form or join over the next four years in an attempt to make his mark in a bigger arena than Haverhill. Precisely what the sequence of these various endeavors was or what each was designed to accomplish, is difficult to determine, so Byzantine were the politics and alliances of the early film industry. What they attested to, mainly, were the turbulence within the industry, the intense jockeying for advantage, and Mayer's dedication to his advancement.

Sometime shortly after the formation of the Louis B. Mayer Film Company, Mayer and three prominent businessmen from Haverhill formed yet another exchange—this one superseding the first—called the American Feature Film Company, which, according to one of the partners, "really made our organization worth some money." The same year Mayer, who was rapidly becoming a very big fish in the relatively small pond of New England, was approached by Al Lichtman, a former executive of Adolph Zukor's Famous Players, to join with other distributors and exhibitors to finance production. The company, a kind of precursor of First National, which would bedevil Zukor, was called Alco, after its founder. Due to some financial improprieties, Alco was short-lived, but several of its members regrouped to form another company on the same principal: financing feature film production. This company was called Metro Pictures, later to be the first initial in MGM, and Louis B. Mayer became secretary of the parent company and president of its New England branch. Now his ambitions had finally outstripped Haverhill. As one partner put it, "Louis was a worker—he never sleeps, you know—and he was always scheming up something. And he wanted to go into the distribution end of the business on a bigger scale, so he went to Boston."

All of these various maneuvers had made Mayer a force, albeit a modest one, in the industry. They had also emboldened him. "I remember one thing when I was a little girl," said Edith Mayer Goetz. "He'd taken us to New York from Boston, and he was so—he wasn't like Little Father [her nickname for him] anymore. He sounded tougher. He was doing business, and I'd never seen him like that. . . . I guess I saw him get more sure of himself, and I guess I realized overnight that he's a very important man."

The individual who set him on the road to becoming a major force and a very wealthy man was David Wark Griffith, the legendary director Zukor had tried to sign for Famous Players. At about the time Mayer moved to Boston, Griffith had just completed his controversial epic on the Civil War and Reconstruction, *The Birth of a Nation*. Based on *The Clansman*, a racist preacher's apologia for the Ku Klux Klan, *Birth* was a dramatically crude but cinematically rousing work that immediately stirred controversy over its racial politics and just as quickly stirred audiences for its invention and skill. European directors had already made epics; *Quo Vadis?*, *Ben Hur*, and *Cabiria* had been popular costume spectacles. But no American before Griffith had made a film on this scale, and none, European or American, had the facility with the medium that Griffith had.

When Griffith gave a private showing in New York on March 1, 1915, two days before the official New York opening and two weeks after the successful Los Angeles premiere, the jury was still out as to whether the film would win the same accolades from the judges in what was, at that time, America's capital of culture. Prolonged applause from a packed house of "opinion makers" convinced Griffith and his partners that it would. Afterward, as they lingered at a private reception savoring their victory, they received a phone call from a Boston distributor. Somehow Mayer had already received the news that *Birth* was going to be a smash, and he offered $50,000 and a fifty-fifty split, after covering his costs, for the New England distribution rights. Since Mayer wasn't yet in the financial league of the bigger distributors, the guarantee had to be hastily raised from Mayer's dependable group of investors—nearly all of them mercantile Jews in Boston who seemed less concerned about being tainted by the movies than they were about making a profit.

Mayer didn't close the deal until August, and when he did, Boston was excluded for a first-run showing—those rights being retained by the producers. Nevertheless, his judgment proved entirely sound. *Birth* was a phenomenon, the very first movie blockbuster, and Mayer in this single stroke may have made as much as $500,000 from his contract. Harry Aitken, the film's distributor, always maintained that Mayer made such an extraordinary profit because he cheated the film's producers and fudged his books, and one of Mayer's biographers, having examined the remittances, later supported the charge.

It certainly wasn't the first or the last time Mayer would take advantage of the system. A few years later he was distributing a film produced by the fledgling Warner Brothers Company, but he had failed to pay over $70,000 in fees, and Jack Warner was dispatched to recover twelve prints Mayer held. "We sparred around for a few minutes," Warner wrote, "but his footwork was too involved for me. He had no intention of handing me seventy grand, and so I left. I came back an hour later with a deputy marshal and the writ [to recover the prints], seized the twelve prints, and returned to my hotel." Within the hour Mayer anted up. "He handed me a check with his eyes smoldering behind the glasses, and he said: 'Now get out of here, whatever the hell your name is, and if I never see you again it'll be too soon.'"

With his sudden and large personal fortune from *The Birth of a Nation*, Mayer, a man of emotional extravagance but economic frugality, finally began to live a bit more lavishly. He moved from Boston to suburban Brookline, where he joined Temple Ohabai Sholem, a solidly middle-class Conservative congregation that mediated between Mayer's highly assimilative impulses and the far less assimilative impulses of his wife. He hired a complement of Irish maids. He dressed, as almost all the movie Jews would, in the height of fashion with a derby, a velvet-collared coat, and a watch fob strung stylishly across his vest. But in a career predicated on the desire for family, these things, wonderful as they were, were not especially material, or, rather, they were only material. Mayer, who understood himself surprisingly well, wanted an outlet for his emotions and his paternalism. And that is how he now deployed his wealth.

It certainly wasn't any wonder, given his inclination to overdramatize and to reign, that Mayer was drawn to producing movies as well as distributing them. He was born to produce, and he had apparently been awaiting an opportunity to do so ever since his days in Haverhill. His first essay, following rapidly upon his *Birth* windfall, was the Serial Production Company, which made a potboiler called *The Great Secret*. Its stars were Francis X. Bushman, a former male model with statuesque looks, and Beverly Bayne, Bushman's beautiful mistress, who had met him while taking a studio tour in Chicago. Bushman and Bayne were already middle-rank stars. They had a distribution deal with Metro, one of Mayer's many alliances, and they were less than enthusiastic about working for an untested producer. Mayer had to unleash all his powers of persuasion, as well as raise their salaries, to cajole them into appearing. After he had persuaded them, made the serial, and opened it in Boston, he brought the couple to his home, parading them like trophies.

Though *The Great Secret* was only moderately successful, Mayer clearly enjoyed his role as producer, and he promptly embarked on a second conquest. This time the object was one of the Vitagraph Company's beautiful stars, Anita Stewart, who, one story goes, was introduced to Mayer by a lovestruck newsboy they both knew. When Mayer returned to Boston from the meeting in Atlantic City, he was floating. "I met her, I met her!" he exulted to his secretary. "And I danced with her, too!... Everybody was talking about me!" To which his secretary sourly replied, "They were saying, 'Who's the funny little kike with Anita Stewart?'" Knowing Stewart was dissatisfied at Vitagraph, Mayer began a campaign to win her, but there was one obstacle: Stewart still had a valid contract through January 1918. Mayer had begun his courtship in May 1917.

Mayer regarded this as more of a nuisance than an intractable legal impediment, and he apparently convinced Stewart to declare her contract void on the grounds that her various grievances against Vitagraph had broken her health. Of course Vitagraph wasn't buying any of this, especially since she quickly signed a new contract with Mayer. These shenanigans resulted in a lawsuit that Mayer ultimately lost (Stewart's contract term with Vitagraph was extended until she fulfilled her obligations), but they also indicated one of Mayer's strengths in the hurly-burly of the early film industry: the man was incorrigible.

This soon became evident in his stormy relationship with Metro. When Metro's president, Richard Rowland, groused about Mayer signing a private deal with Stewart and not enlisting her for the company as a good team player would have done, Mayer resigned and took a position with the Select Picture Corporation located across the street from Metro. A month later Metro was in court seeking an injunction against Mayer, who, it claimed, had "entered upon a campaign to wreck the business of the Metro organization by intimidating its employees into leaving and joining the Select Corporation and attempting by fraudulent misrepresentations to secure its customers for the Select service." Given Mayer's previous activities with the remittances of *Birth* and the blowup with the Warners, the charges were entirely plausible.

But in joining Select Mayer had joined a figure almost as incorrigible as he was. Lewis J. Selznick was a Ukrainian Jew who had emigrated to Pittsburgh and entered the jewelry business. In 1912, many years and many enterprises later, Selznick was in New York when he ran into an old Pittsburgh acquaintance, Mark Dintenfass, then a partner in the newly formed Universal Pictures. Dintenfass told Selznick that the company had split into three factions, and none of these was speaking to the others. So Selznick, as his son David described it, simply "moved into an office, and he sent a note to each of the three factions that Lewis J. Selznick had been appointed general manager. Each one assumed that one of the other factions had done it. Of course, he had appointed himself. He ran it as general manager for some time, till he decided to form his own company."

Selznick always maintained that the movie industry "took less brains than anything else in the world," an attitude that hardly endeared him to his film confreres. Adolph Zukor was so nettled by Selznick's nose thumbing that he offered him $5,000 per week on condition that he leave for China. When Selznick refused, Zukor offered to buy half his interests for Paramount, provided that Selznick not compete with Paramount's other films and that the company name be changed from Selznick. No sooner had Selznick agreed than Zukor quietly began raiding the new company's talent and orchestrating Selznick's departure—a task made easier since Selznick's name no longer adorned the letterhead.

When Mayer joined him at Select late in 1917, Selznick was still an industry power, which was an obvious attraction for the social-climbing Mayer, but his stay was brief. By February 1918 he had moved back to Metro and assumed control of its New England branch once again. Whatever particular disagreement he had had with Selznick, he had general disdain for Selznick's life-style, which was profligate where his own was prudent, and Selznick's manner, which was openly contemptuous where his own was conservative and respectful. Mayer loathed him for years afterward, warning that his company would eventually collapse—no doubt what Mayer saw as the wages of sin. "Watch what I say, watch and see what happens to him," he told his daughter Irene. "There is no firm foundation. Things must be built stone by stone." Mayer was right. Selznick did eventually fall on hard times, pushed out by larger, better-financed companies.

By the time Mayer left Selznick, he was already preparing his first feature film, starring Anita Stewart. *Virtuous Wives*, as it was called, was based on a short story in *Cosmopolitan* magazine, and Mayer had purchased the rights for $10,000. Filmed in a studio in Brooklyn, *Virtuous Wives* was a slight melodrama about a young wife who spoils her marriage by getting swept up in the social swirl, but who eventually comes to her senses. What probably appealed to Mayer was the society setting and the ultimate moralistic resolution, again a variation on his extravagance and strict paternalism. The movie did well —well enough for Mayer to begin planning his second feature with Stewart. This time, however, Mayer had decided he wouldn't be shooting in Brooklyn. This time he had promised his star something else. Louis B. Mayer was moving to California.

———

By the late teens it may have seemed that all the Hollywood Jews had moved from exhibition to distribution to production, as Laemmle, Zukor, and Mayer had. Certainly there was an impulse to get closer to the creative side of the business where the emotional satisfactions were greater. But another group of Jews remained behind in exhibition, plying their skills and their dreams on creating a new kind of moviegoing experience—one that paralleled the transformation of the movies themselves. The most famous of these was the son of a German immigrant, Samuel Rothapfel, later known throughout the country as "Roxy," a nickname he had picked up playing semiprofessional baseball. Rothafel (he dropped the "p") had grown up in Stillwater, Minnesota, a predominantly Scandinavian milltown on the St. Croix River, where he spent "the most pleasant days of my life." But when he was twelve his father suddenly decided to uproot the family and move to New York. "A year later," Roxy recalled, "because I had already given evidence of being the black sheep of the family in not being able to see as the others saw, I was literally thrown out. . . . I was always moping about, dreaming, dreaming."

After ten years spinning his wheels at various odd jobs, Roxy joined the U.S. Marines. This seemed to have an extremely salutary effect, and after serving in the Boxer Rebellion in China, he became only the third Jew to be commissioned as an officer. When he was discharged in 1905, at the age of twenty-four, he became a traveling book salesman until he met Rose Freedman while working Forest City, Pennsylvania. Rose was the daughter of one of Forest City's leading citizens—its postmaster, justice of the peace, storekeeper, and saloonkeeper. Freedman complained that Roxy wasn't solvent enough to marry his daughter, so Roxy agreed to prove himself by tending bar for eighteen months.

Even for a former leatherneck, this wasn't easy. Forest City was a tough mining town of six thousand whose main recreation was the biweekly dance at the saloon. Almost every dance degenerated into a melee, and according to Roxy, "Each fracas was more terrible than the last." Partly in self-defense, he convinced his father-in-law to let him turn the dance hall into a motion picture theater. He bought a secondhand projector, borrowed 250 seats from the local undertaker, and trudged seven miles to Carbondale to pick up the prints. "I did everything to get every one of those six thousand inhabitants interested," he once told an interviewer.

> I painted signs myself, developed the projectors, worked out ideas of presentation. . . . I even stopped running the picture machine sometimes to explain various things to them which

*would pop into my head as I went along. In my mind's eye,
I can today see two hundred or more grizzly miners, their
wives, children, and sweethearts, turning about in their
seats looking up curiously through the dark, listening to
pearls of wisdom drop from my lips.*

What Roxy soon began to realize in Forest City was that the real
secret to film exhibition was to make the audience forget that what
they were watching cost them only a nickel or dime. The secret was
to transport them—to create an imaginative empire. And for Roxy, as
for so many of the movie Jews, the means of transportation was refinement. "It matters not how humble your theater is, or where it is
situated," he advised other exhibitors in a series of articles in *The
Moving Picture World*, "try and have an air of refinement prevail
throughout."

Refinement meant a well-drilled staff. It meant the careful arrangement of the order of films shown. ("If the programs are arranged with
care and worked up to the psychological point, the audiences will go
away contented and carry with them a definite recollection of the
entertainment.") It meant musical accompaniment that augmented
the movies. It meant clean, hospitable theaters. It meant attention to
every detail, from the uniforms the ushers wore to the lights that
bathed the screen when the movies ended. "The theatre is the thing,"
he said, "that is, the psychology of the theatre, its effect on the
audience. . . . The best pictures ever produced will never succeed in
an unattractive environment."

For the self-described ne'er-do-well, refined theaters had something
of the same magic and promise that refined movies had for Zukor,
and Roxy became every bit as apostolic. Both men even had the same
inspiration—Sarah Bernhardt. Shortly after his success in Forest City,
Roxy moved to Philadelphia, where the Keith theater circuit hired
him to supervise its lighting installations, and then to Milwaukee,
where he was engaged to light an appearance of Bernhardt. Watching
him rehearse a stage effect, the great actress put her hands on his
shoulders. "You are a great artist," she told him, "and someday you
will be heard from." This was heady praise for an ex-marine who only
a few years before had been peddling books door to door. Later that

evening, over dinner, he "poured my heart out to her. She sent me away full of inspiration."

From his theater experience, Roxy had become intoxicated with the idea of culture. Moving to Minneapolis against the advice of his friends, he converted one of the city's largest theaters into a movie house, hired a full orchestra for accompaniment, and was, according to a contemporary, "uncompromising in demanding that the same rules that prevail for grand opera [in seating the audience and in forbidding an exodus while the curtain is up] must be observed." Audiences responded enthusiastically, and in 1913 the owners of the large new Regent Theater in New York hired Roxy as their manager.

As he prepared for his New York debut, he was a difficult person on whom to get a fix. Described as a "man's man, straightforward and direct in manner," he was nevertheless powerfully drawn to the artistic and ethereal. Uneducated, untrained, and uncultured, he had nevertheless become a national figure in exhibition circles by hectoring other exhibitors not to "give the people what they want," but to "give them something better than they expect." Though he projected an image of geniality—his salutation, "Hello, everybody," would later become part of the national vocabulary when he started his own radio show—he was a man of strong convictions who bullied everyone around him, and he could be blunt well beyond the point of rudeness. When a Shriners group feted him with a poem during a visit to Minneapolis, he denounced it as "lousy," and his favorite expression was "applesauce," which he used liberally to denigrate everyone and everything.

Roxy never said what it was that converted him from a know-nothing to a culture monger in three short years, though he did suggest that his transformation was a reaction against his family's philistinism. "My ancestors were peasants," he told an interviewer in 1918. "Not one of them played the violin or eloped with a beautiful Russian opera singer. They just never did anything." Roxy's reaction, if it was one, took the most obvious form. He would not only fasten on culture, he would confirm his commitment by adducing as much culture as he could. Roxy became a monumentalist with the depth of his own enlightenment measured by the scale of his presentations. It was one reason he became an example to other monumentalists in pre-

Hitler Germany and why one of his associates was later recruited to manage one of the largest movie theaters in Berlin.

While in Minneapolis, Roxy studied audiences to see what appealed to them and came to the conclusion that the musical accompaniment was one of the prime factors in a movie's success. Now, at the Regent in New York's Harlem, he employed what he had learned. He installed an even larger orchestra than he had had in Minneapolis, and he insisted, as most exhibitors did not, that there be a strict correspondence between the movie and the music, so that each major character came to have a musical motif.

Roxy's techniques were so successful that within a year he was asked to manage the new four-thousand-seat Strand Theater on Broadway, the largest movie house in America when it was built in 1914. Here he put the orchestra on stage surrounded by a garden scene with an active fountain and introduced a musical prelude of songs and orchestral selections before the film. Within two years Felix Kahn, Otto's brother and Zukor's friend, hired him to manage the new Rialto. And when the Rivoli, named after the rue de Rivoli in Paris, which connected the Louvre (pictures) to the Opéra (music), was constructed uptown by Kahn in 1917, he ran that, too.

The Rivoli was one of New York's toniest movie theaters, and Roxy fashioned a personal style to match it, including a Japanese houseboy who cooked Roxy's beloved hot dogs in his newly furnished office. But when Kahn complained that Roxy ought to pay for his own calls to the Havre d'Grace racetrack, he resigned, claiming he was about to "take up the preliminaries of a project of significance and with a greater claim" upon his energies. By this time he was already regarded as the nation's foremost exhibitor, a man who, in the words of one trade paper, had "done much to make some of the beautiful Broadway playhouses practically temples of art" and whose "suggestions are being carried out all over the country."

For the next few months he dabbled in production, filming some of his live prologues and distributing them to theaters that couldn't afford a lavish stage show of their own before their movies, and then actually directing a few pictures on the adventures of the marines. But Roxy was an impresario rather than an artist, and by 1919 he was back at the helm of a theater, the new Capitol on Broadway. This time his monumentalism seemed boundless. Even before the Strand, Roxy had pioneered what he called "presentations" or "prologues." Prologues were elaborately staged vignettes that preceded the feature film and were intended, so Roxy said, "solely for the purpose of establishing the mood of a photoplay," though in reality the live program was often longer than the film itself and usually as magnificent. The prologues were invariably musical, most often classical. A typical program might include several arias from grand opera; symphonic selections by Roxy's orchestra, which he proudly called one of the three best in America; several ballets, choreographed by Roxy's own ballet master, a Russian immigrant with the impressive name Alexander Oumansky; a series of slides accompanied by music; and a selection from Gilbert and Sullivan or Franz Lehár. He would later say, "I now believe music makes an appeal equal to that of the screen."

In fact, Roxy loved music more than he loved film, and if Zukor used the movies as a kind of surrogate for the stage and its cachet of culture, Roxy seemed to use them as surrogate for the symphony and opera. He often talked of bringing music to the masses the way Zukor talked of bringing them great theater. But Roxy also suffered from the classic syndrome of one who revered art and genuinely appreciated it without having cultivated the taste to go along with the reverence and appreciation. Roxy, with his lengthy and massively mounted stage prologues, was essentially a king of kitsch—the leatherneck putting on culture. But since his kitsch passed for culture among many in the lower and middle classes and in the popular press, and since he was widely regarded as having brought refinement to the movies, he may have been as instrumental in making the movies palatable to the middle class as Zukor was. As one writer put it, he "gave the 'movie' a college education."

Certainly the Capitol set a standard for movie exhibition. In less than a year it had become "an institution for New York and with the splendid presentation feature offered by Samuel Rothafel, bids fair to become known throughout the nation as a picture palace that literally *must* be visited by everyone [sic] of the millions of American people who take occasion to visit the nation's mecca." Millions did. On the Capitol's fifth anniversary in 1924, one trade paper estimated that twenty-six million patrons had visited it since its opening, one-fifth the total population of the country, and it had finished in the red in only three weeks out of those five years. Its weekly average gross in 1924 and 1925 was $46,000. No other Broadway movie theater came close.

But one didn't have to examine grosses to see that Roxy had tapped into something—that he had, in fact, popularized classical music and given Americans confidence in their own taste. One only had to look at his own popularity. By the early twenties he had parlayed his image as cultural mediator to the masses into a weekly radio program in which he introduced musical acts from the Capitol, a syndicated newspaper column, and a profitable run of personal appearances. He and his "gang," as he named his troupe, played command performances for three presidents. His trademarks—"Hello, everybody," which opened his radio program, and "Good night. God bless you. Pleasant dreams," which closed it—were familiar throughout the country, and when the American Telephone and Telegraph Company, which owned his radio outlet, demanded that Roxy be less casual on the air, there was a national storm of protest. Congress even contemplated an investigation of the affair.

Regardless of his popularity, Roxy's ambitions were still driven by his passion for scale. At a dinner of New York's Rotary Club on June 2, 1925, he announced that he was leaving the Capitol to build the largest movie theater in the world. It was to cost $6 million and would seat over six thousand patrons. And it was to be called the Roxy. "I promise you this new theater will be the biggest and the best thing Roxy ever does," he told a reporter.

The Roxy *was* spectacular—a cavernous, gilded cathedral to kitsch and dreams and the movies themselves. When it opened in the fall of 1926, first-nighters included Charlie Chaplin, Harold Lloyd, Otto Kahn, and Senator Robert Wagner, and President Coolidge sent greetings on film. One hundred and twenty-five policemen were needed to keep the crowds at bay. Inside, chimes signaled the beginning of the show, then a man garbed as a monk took the stage, pointed to the balcony, and declaimed, "Let there be light!" A flood of lights suddenly bathed the orchestra. It was vintage Roxy.

Rothafel wasn't the only movie Jew to rehabilitate himself through his theaters rather than through the movies themselves. In Chicago,

Barney and A. J. Balaban, sons of a Russian immigrant grocer, owned a string of large, ornate movie palaces with grandiose names like the Valencia, the Oriental, the Tivoli, the Riviera, and the Granada. The Balabans' policy was similar to Roxy's—opulence, scale, a corps of well-drilled ushers, and long musical programs preceding the feature film. Barney's daughter, Judith, would later attribute it to the European Jew's adoration of the arts.

In California the mantle of chief exhibitor was worn by a short, mischievous man whose own flamboyance reflected the flamboyance of his theaters. (He was one of the few homosexuals admitted to the moguls' inner circle.) Sid Grauman's father had run tent shows in San Francisco before the Graumans opened an eight-hundred-seat movie house there called the Unique, later destroyed by the 1906 earthquake. After managing a theater in New York and another in Scranton, Pennsylvania, he returned to San Francisco and ran the Empress and Imperial theaters, two of the city's most impressive movie houses.

But it was in Los Angeles that Sid Grauman made his mark—first with the Million Dollar Theater, then with the 3,600-seat Metropolitan, then with the Egyptian, and finally with the Chinese, which became an American landmark. Like Roxy, Grauman loved size; his theaters were always capacious. But he was less a culture monger than a showman; where Roxy wore conservative suits to maintain an image of dignity, Grauman wore large hats rakishly tilted and parted his long curly hair down the middle, sweeping it back at the sides so that he looked as if he had stuck his finger in an electric socket. Throughout Hollywood he was famous for his elaborate pranks: convincing Paramount cowboy star William S. Hart to "ambush" a train Adolph Zukor was riding; inducing Jesse Lasky to give a speech to a group of exhibitors who turned out to be wax dummies; arriving at the cornerstone-laying ceremony of a rival theater in a hearse; dressing as a female escort to visiting star David Warfield and then crying, "Rape!" When he heard that director Ernst Lubitsch, who hated to fly, was forced to take a plane from Los Angeles to a preview in San Francisco, he hired two stuntmen to dress as pilots, run down the aisle, and then parachute during the flight. Lubitsch was so shaken that he suffered a minor heart attack.

A friend said Grauman would "spend hours plotting some outland-ish hoax that would give us no more than a moment of hysterical joy." He used the same ingenuity in managing his theaters. He was said to have originated *tableaux vivants* depicting scenes from the film to be shown, a popular feature in the movie palaces of the twen-ties; a forecourt entrance; trousered usherettes; the rising orchestra pit; and the gala Hollywood premiere where stars would exit their limou-sines and glide down the forecourt runway while searchlights roamed the skies. But his most enduring innovation was persuading stars to press their feet and hands into wet concrete blocks in the Chinese Theater court. There is some dispute over how Grauman arrived at the idea. Buddy Rogers claimed that his wife, Mary Pickford, actually came up with it when her pet dog walked over some wet cement. One of Grauman's old publicists also took credit. Another associate, Ar-thur Wenzel, remembered "walking with Sid when the Chinese was still incomplete. Sid accidentally slipped off a builder's plank into wet cement. Eyeing his own imprint, he shouted, 'Arthur, I am going to have all the stars recorded here.'" Whoever thought of the idea, the footprints helped complete the metaphor. If the theaters were cathe-drals to the movies' new status, and the movies themselves were the objects of devotion, the footprints became sacraments in the beatifi-cation of the stars. Hollywood had become America's new civic reli-gion.

During the great theater expansion of the late teens and twenties, when the movies became the preeminent form of entertainment in America and film companies bought or constructed thousands of movie houses in a heated competition to see which could erect the largest and most extravagant theaters, Roxy, the Balabans, and Grau-man occupied a unique niche in the culture—masters of grandeur. And then, suddenly, like tragic heroes, they were undone by their own too-muchness. Their escalating dreams and the escalating costs that went with them made profit impossible. Even before the stock market crash in 1929, one prophet warned that the end was near for Roxy's kind of garish theatricality. "At the Capitol Theater," he wrote, "at least two-thirds of the program is given over to music. It is stated that the picture is the least expensive part of the entertainment," and exhibitors were beginning to feel the pinch in trying to outdo one another. "The end of it will be that the exhibitors will leave off trying to educate the house and give them what they want, which is pictures at twenty-five cents, without musical culture or uplift."

Of course, that idea was anathema to Roxy, Depression or not. In 1932 he announced that he would be leaving the Roxy to take control of a new theater under construction—the Radio City Music Hall. (He had wanted to call this one the Roxy, too, but his previous employers got a court injunction preventing him from doing so.) "Not only is the International Music Hall the largest theater in the world," he said with his usual penchant for superlatives, "but it has the most lights, the biggest stage, and the most gadgets for scene shifting, lighting, and amplification to be found anywhere." A reporter, watching Roxy rehearse the 375 performers for Radio City's opening, noted "a hint of tragedy in his discovery that he had used all the superlatives and super-superlatives on lesser things." This time the theater covered six acres and seated well over six thousand, and this time Roxy's ambitions weren't limited to movies and prologues. He had been huddling with New York's Metropolitan Opera Company, trying to coax them into Radio City. "We want the Metropolitan Opera Company, and we want it very badly," he told one paper, and he spoke wistfully of the day when he would "have charge of the opera" himself.

That day never came. Opening night of Radio City was a disaster. Several weeks before the scheduled premiere in December 1932, Roxy underwent major abdominal surgery, and though he tried to conduct rehearsals from his stretcher, the show overwhelmed him. The premiere ran over four logy hours, which immediately triggered speculation that Roxy had lost his touch and would soon be replaced. Roxy fumed. "What did they think I was—a miracle man, a demigod?" he asked a reporter. "That's silly. We all make mistakes. I'm human. I make mistakes, too," and he announced that he was taking a long vacation in Corpus Christi to convalesce. "They're all wolves, this Broadway crowd," he added in a parting shot. "They're glad when somebody who has always stood for something constructive in the theater stubs his toe.... These sophisticated worldly-wise, narrow-faced, sharp-eyed low-lifes that hang around Broadway!"

By the time he returned to Radio City four months later, RKO, the parent company managing the theater, had gone into receivership. Its president ominously warned that no one man was bigger than the organization, and if Roxy wanted to leave, he was free to do so. Instead, Roxy began making plans for more extravaganzas. "We're going to put on things with vision, with a touch. . . . [W]e are going to put on a 'Bolero' that's different. And Wagner! Debussy! This isn't going bust." RKO had different plans. In January 1934, Roxy resigned, though he declared that someday he would be called back to head Radio City. By the end of the year he was running the Warner Brothers' Mastbaum Theater in Philadelphia, but after ten weeks it had reportedly lost close to $250,000, and the Warners decided to close it down until the fall.

By this time Roxy was broken—"a man attacked by immense fatigue, sorrow, and a bodily illness that defied his physician." Two years later, at the age of fifty-three, he was dead of angina pectoris. Carl Laemmle sent Roxy's widow a telegram praising him as the man who "made the motion picture theatre the community art center and compelled public appreciation of films for their true artistic values." *The New York Times* eulogized him, perhaps more accurately, as a man who "could never get enough even if he got too much."

That was both the triumph and the tragedy of his life.

In 1918, when Louis B. Mayer left Boston for California to make his second feature film with Anita Stewart, he was not simply traversing a continent. He was, whether he fully realized it or not, abandoning one way of life for another. Mayer had come from one of the first and most class-conscious metropolises in America. By comparison Los Angeles was a primitive outpost whose paved roads ended abruptly downtown and whose main architecture was small shacks engulfed by orange and pepper trees. Hollywood, the suburb where Mayer installed himself, was even less settled. Twelve miles from the Pacific Ocean and isolated on a gentle swell, it received cool ocean breezes, but a narrow horseshoe of foothills on the east repulsed both the hot summer winds from the desert and the cold blasts of winter. Intrepid midwesterners, attracted by its climate, had settled there in the late nineteenth century, and one of them, a woman from Illinois, had christened it in remembrance of her native state's holly bushes. Custard apples, avocados, pineapples, orange and lemon trees, calla lilies, and geraniums all grew wild. Skunks and rabbits roamed freely, and coyotes howled at night.

Mayer was something of a late arrival. The movie companies had started heading for California as early as 1907, when William Selig shot a film in Santa Monica and then established a studio in Los Angeles two years later. D. W. Griffith, acting for the Biograph Company, set up another near downtown Los Angeles, and Majestic, IMP, Vitagraph, Lubin, Kalem, Balboa, and many others followed. Hollywood itself wasn't invaded until 1910 when David Horsley, president of the Staten Island–based Nestor Film Company, went west for a visit. A companion on the train suggested he look up a photographer who lived in Hollywood. Horsley did and decided to rent a lot there to make pictures. It was the first Hollywood studio.

When Mayer moved west in 1918, there were well over seventy production companies in Los Angeles, and over 80 percent of the world's movies were made there. The main lure that had drawn the producers from the East was the weather. In southern California one could shoot outdoors in the dead of winter, which was a tremendous advantage, particularly since coal shortages during the war made it difficult to generate power for the huge klieg lights needed back east. Some had also come to escape the long arm of the Edison Trust, since it was far more difficult to enforce patents in the relative wilds of California than in the dense precincts of New York. Others came because land was cheap and plentiful.

But one other blandishment that must have drawn the Jews to California was that, unlike in the East, the social structure was primitive and permeable. One could even have said that California was the social equivalent of the movies themselves, new and unformed, which really made the producers' emigration there a matter of an industry discovering its appropriate spot. There was no real aristocracy in place and few social impediments obstructing Jews. There was, in fact, very little of anything. "There were practically no shops and no restaurants," recalled one early Hollywood inhabitant. "If I worked late at the studio and wanted to get a sandwich and a cup of coffee on my way home, it could hardly be done after eight o'clock. There were two small drugstores about a mile apart on Hollywood Boulevard; these provided a simple luncheon service, but that was all over and done with at half-past ten. . . . It was quite unusual to see lights in any windows after ten or ten-thirty."

In a raw, yawning environment like this, it was relatively simple to aestheticize oneself, to make oneself over, and most of the Hollywood Jews did. (*Everyone* in Hollywood did; California practically invited it.) But to a flagrant self-dramatist like Mayer, the aestheticizing was much grander and more complete. His would be a world almost totally defined by appearance, because in Mayer's eyes appearances both reflected an inner reality and helped create it; there was no sense in being virtuous if the virtue didn't show. The important question in the Mayer household, Irene Mayer Selznick would write, was "How does it look?"—which meant that the girls became Galatea to Mayer's Pygmalion. "Nails had to be short and polished only with a buffer. The clear liquid polish was frowned on, while red, so new and glamorous, was used by women of easy virtue; it advertised one's morals like smoking a cigarette. Even the tone of one's lipstick and the height of one's heels were revealing," and Mayer consequently legislated these.

The idea was to make one's virtue manifest to everyone. "I remember one of the things he taught me that became very valuable to me," said his daughter Edith.

> I must have been *fifteen or sixteen*, and we'd gone to a horse show—this stands out in my mind because it became an obsession of mine—and some people evidently came up to the box we were sitting in. And the next day when Dad came home from the studio, he asked me to come to the library. And when I heard my name being called, "Edith!" I knew I was going to get it. . . . And he said, "I don't like to have my daughter be a snob." And I said, "Why am I a snob?" And he said, "When the people came over to the box last night to meet us and I introduced you, you didn't smile." And I said, "I guess I'm shy." He said, "They didn't know that. They didn't come to meet you. They came to meet me. But you were my daughter, and it's up to you to

smile. Remember, whenever you walk into a room, smile.
You'll draw people to you."

Later, when Edith had taken dancing and acting lessons and had
been invited to audition for a role, Mayer roared his disapproval.
"Why are you giving me all these lessons, then?" she asked him. He
answered, "You're the best goddamn actress I've ever known. And you
need it for living. Remember that."

The role Mayer demanded his daughters play was part of his larger
conception of what he wanted his family to be. The family he had in
mind was nineteenth-century aristocratic, where the father was the
absolute monarch, the mother his deferential helpmate, and the
daughters demure, chaste, and obedient. (He frequently told his
daughters that he was happy to be so blessed because "if I had a son
and he disappointed me, I couldn't live through it. I couldn't live
with the shame.") Femininity and domesticity were his overriding
concerns. He took his daughters into the kitchen, demanded a meal,
and then drilled them on the cut of meat and the preparation. Every
morning he took them horseback riding and later insisted on golf
lessons, since it was a sport they could play with their husbands someday. In dress, the order was chiffon for its femininity, and years after
Edith had been married, her father criticized her clothing if it was
"too sophisticated." Higher education was ruled out completely as
unnecessary and potentially subversive. His injunction was "Be smart,
but never show it."

Ostensibly Mayer was raising his daughters to be models of the
nineteenth-century wife—the professional hostess and homemaker.
But, ironically, so firm was his dominion that Irene and Edith often
despaired of ever being allowed to fulfill that role. Nuns were scarcely
more cloistered. Sex was introduced when he gave them all five volumes of Havelock-Ellis's *Studies in the Psychology of Sex*, instructed
them to write down any questions they had, and then invited the
family doctor every Monday night to answer them. As for boyfriends,
nice girls didn't have them, and even into their twenties the Mayer
daughters were never allowed out without a chaperone—occasionally
an actress named Carmel Myers, who was considered trustworthy because her father was a rabbi. Curfew was strictly enforced on punish-

ment of losing the Chrysler limousine Mayer permitted his daughters to use. And when they finally were courted—Irene by Lewis Selznick's son David and Edith by a young producer named William Goetz—he regarded it as a breach of faith.

In as self-conscious and family-centered an existence as Mayer's, social life had a precise function and set of guidelines. One didn't associate with film people because one naturally disapproved of their morals and manners. Rather, one cultivated the powerful and the important, and by the mid-twenties Mayer did manage to ingratiate himself with a surprising number of industrial, political, and religious leaders—most notably, during those early years in Hollywood, the newspaper magnate William Randolph Hearst, whose mistress, Marion Davies, would be headquartered at Mayer's studio. "That Hearst admired and respected him meant a great deal," Irene Mayer Selznick would write. "He seemed to consult my father on all kinds of matters —politics, finance, and even the Hearst Corporation. The two men would walk and talk and sit and talk... and the affection between them was clear. Towering above him, Hearst would place his hand on my father's head for emphasis and pat it as he spoke, calling him 'Son.'" It was the affinity between two men both given to drama, to excess, and to magnificence.

If Mayer's life and his family were his first and possibly finest aesthetic products, his desire to impress obviously also found expression in the studio, which was after all a mechanism for creating impressions. At first, though he settled the family in a modest home in Hollywood, he situated his little production company out on Mission Road in southeastern Los Angeles in what was known as the Selig Zoo—because producer William Selig housed a menagerie of animals there for jungle pictures he made. It was here Mayer made *In Old Kentucky* with Anita Stewart and several pictures with his new star, Mildred Harris Chaplin, Charlie's estranged wife. These were mostly romantic, sentimental melodramas—about a country girl who saves the prize steed of a rich young horseman and then rides the horse to victory in a race (*In Old Kentucky*); about a gay young wife who narrowly escapes a brush with infidelity (*The Inferior Sex*); about a pretty young squatter who is harassed and then finally romanced by a landowner (*Polly of the Storm Country*). As one biographer put it, Mayer abided by the formula "of the poor but decent girl conducting herself with honest purpose, always against temptations and harsh assaults, with a full reward for her virtue bestowed in the happy end."

There was, of course, more than a little wish fulfillment in all of this. In the early twenties Mayer was still not one of the industry's major players, like Zukor or Laemmle, but he was well connected through a number of lucky business associations, and he did have a deserved reputation for making films of morality and quality at a time when many producers were simply "fast buck" artists. This was obviously something that cut deeply with him, as it had with Zukor. "My unchanging policy," he wrote to a director shortly after moving to California, "will be great star, great director, great play, great cast. You are authorized to get these without stint or limit. Spare nothing, neither expense, time, nor effort. Results only are what I am after. Simply send me the bills and I will O.K."

Mayer may have been well regarded, but this wasn't what suddenly vaulted him into the first rank of producers. What did was another serendipitous association, like the one with D. W. Griffith. This time Mayer's angel was Marcus Loew. By the late teens, Loew, still head-quartered in New York, was realizing that he needed more and better films for his vast theater chain if he was to compete with Paramount, First National, Fox, and the other major companies. In 1919 he purchased Metro pictures, Mayer's old alliance, but he was tremendously dissatisfied with both the studio's films and its management, and he had even briefly contemplated selling off the whole thing. While vacationing in Palm Beach, Loew discussed the idea with Lee Shubert, a stage producer who also owned a piece of Goldwyn Pictures.* Shubert advised instead that Loew buy Goldwyn and merge it with Metro, since Goldwyn, though currently in debt, had an extraordinary physical plant out in Culver City. Loew agreed and asked Metro's attorney, J. Robert Rubin, to begin negotiations.

Among the rapscallions, buccaneers, and braggarts, Rubin was an unusual man in the early movie industry. Extremely cultured, well educated, and well bred, he had given up a promising political career

---

*Goldwyn had been founded jointly by Jesse Lasky's brother-in-law, Samuel Goldfish, after Goldfish had been booted from Paramount, and a vaudeville producer named Edgar Selwyn. But Goldfish, who had legally changed his name to Goldwyn, had severed his connection with the company to become an independent producer.

in upstate New York, where he was a district attorney, for what would be a very lucrative career in the film industry, thanks largely to Mayer. When Alco, one of Mayer's first associations, went bankrupt, Rubin was appointed receiver, and when several of Alco's partners, including Mayer, regrouped as Metro, Rubin became the company's counsel, which brought him into even closer contact with Mayer. The tall, urbane Rubin and the short, relatively unpolished Mayer may have seemed an incongruous pair, and Rubin did attempt to buff Mayer's rough edges; whenever he used an obscenity, which was often in those first Hollywood years, Rubin would scowl his disapproval. But they also complemented one another—Rubin's legal shrewdness and business acumen with Mayer's gushy showmanship—and the two became partners in Mayer's production company. Not one to limit himself, Rubin also handled legal affairs for several other movie moguls, including Marcus Loew.

Whether Rubin brokered on his own or whether Mayer asked him to intervene, Rubin took Loew to visit Mayer's studio during a trip to California in 1923. Loew was apparently impressed. It was hard not to be, Mayer was such an intense and enthusiastic speaker. Loew already had a production apparatus in Metro, and he was about to acquire a lavish facility at Goldwyn. What he needed if he was to challenge his friend and rival Adolph Zukor, and what Mayer had warned Rubin he needed, was someone to manage the operation, since Loew had already acknowledged that neither the executives at Metro nor those at Goldwyn were suitable.

Mayer went to New York to press his case with Loew, and talks continued for several days with Rubin serving as the go-between. In the end Loew concluded that Mayer was the best candidate, and he offered a generous contract to buy Mayer's studio at Mission Road, to pay him a weekly salary of $1,500 plus 20 percent of the net profits of all the films the company made and to permit the credit "Louis B. Mayer Presents" before or after each film. For his part, Mayer committed himself to produce fifteen features each year. Rubin was to be made secretary and eastern representative. The contract was signed on April 10, 1924, and Mayer headed back to California to prepare for the opening ceremonies of the new studio.

The first vice presidency of Metro-Goldwyn (the Mayer wasn't officially added until 1926) was an extraordinary benison for Mayer. Allied with Loew, owner of one of the largest theater chains in the country, he was immediately thrust into a position of real importance in the industry, and even he was a bit dazed by his sudden good fortune, though he and Rubin had actively campaigned for it. Some time before, he had taken his daughter Irene on a tour of the major studios. Stopping before Famous Players-Lasky, he said, "I'll bet you'd be surprised if I became head of a studio like this someday." Now that he was, he took his captaincy more as a mandate than an opportunity. Metro-Goldwyn-Mayer wasn't simply an employer; it was a life.

The studio's opening on April 26 at the old Goldwyn tract was one of Mayer's gala celebrations. He had a wooden dais erected on a grassy space in front of the studio bungalows where its offices were housed, and he had draped it with bunting. In the center was a massive photograph of Marcus Loew. Employees from Metro, Goldwyn, and Mayer's own late company all gathered to show their fealty to the new conglomerate, and though Will Rogers made his customary cynical remarks, comparing the inauguration to the recent opening of a racetrack where they had all lost their shirts, Mayer's own rhetoric was solemn and deeply sincere. "From a production standpoint, you can count on it that Metro-Goldwyn-Mayer will reach a point of perfection never approached by any other company," he said. "[I]f there is one thing that I insist upon, it is quality." *Ars Gratia Artis*—"Art for Art's Sake"—became the studio's motto.

For a man like Mayer, who spent his entire life searching for everlarger families to command, MGM served marvelously as a big new clan, and that's exactly how he ran it. "He used to get up and make speeches at Christmas and Thanksgiving to almost the entire personnel in the commissary," remembered one MGM executive, "and would literally say, 'You don't need a contract here,' which was true. 'You are part of a family, as long as I am here. We are an MGM family.'" Mayer abhorred the usual Hollywood socializing, but every Sunday, at his home on the beach in Santa Monica, he would have a gathering for the studio. "It was almost a command appearance to go there," said the son of a studio executive. "If you didn't go there, he would be hurt. My father told me this, and I knew it. It was perfectly obvious that's why you went." "You were always aware he was the boss," said another executive, explaining why he felt compelled to attend Mayer's weekly get-togethers. "Mayer was quite demanding in his desire to have his friends in the studio with him that he felt very close to." It was really a matter of hundreds of "children" granting their father's wish, and Mayer loved it. What he didn't know was that very soon someone would be trying to take it all away from him.

Everyone knew that Marcus Loew was frail and sickly and that he suffered from a chronic heart condition, so when he spent the summer of 1927 resting at the Saratoga vacation home of his lieutenant, Nicholas Schenck, no one seemed especially alarmed. But when he complained on September 3 of suddenly feeling overwhelmed with fatigue, he was driven to the nearest harbor, where he boarded his yacht, the *Caroline* (named for his wife), and cruised down the Hudson to Glen Cove near his estate, Pembroke. There, after picking up one specialist, the yacht crossed Long Island Sound to pick up another doctor. Meanwhile, Loew rested at Pembroke and even received visitors, among them Adolph Zukor. No one regarded his condition as critical. They were simply taking precautions. By Sunday, he was dead.

Loew, only fifty-seven, was the first of the great Jewish moguls to pass away, and his funeral, at Pembroke, became a conclave of the industry's great figures. Pallbearers included William Randolph Hearst, Lee Shubert, David Warfield, and Adolph Zukor, the man whom Loew had spent a lifetime trying to exceed. Among the honorary pallbearers were Carl Laemmle, William Fox, D. W. Griffith, J. Robert Rubin, and Mayer. "All I can say," Zukor mourned, "is that I feel his loss more than that of any man in the world."

So, in many ways, would Mayer. Loew's widow was an uncomplicated, unsophisticated woman who left the business in the hands of Nick Schenck, while her twin sons, Arthur and David, remained in executive positions with the company. Nick and his older brother Joe had, like Mayer, emigrated from Russia as children. By 1901 they had managed to buy a New York pharmacy, but they made their real fortune a decade later by building and managing an amusement park at Fort George, New York. Through the park they attracted the attention of Loew, who joined them to build the Palisades Amusement Park on the Hudson River. Later, as Loew's own theater operation expanded, he hired Joe to book his theaters and Nick to run the office. Joe eventually left to produce movies. Nick remained steadfast and was rewarded with the presidency of Loew's Incorporated, Metro-Goldwyn-Mayer's parent company.

Of the two brothers, Joe was almost universally preferred. Though he had a grave poker face with what seemed a perpetual frown, he was regarded as a generous and kindly man who couldn't refuse a friend's supplication and whose old girlfriends all wound up on the payroll. His wife, film star Norma Talmadge, described him as "a sturdy oak" and always called him "Daddy," but he was also an ostentatious dresser, an inveterate gambler, and an incorrigible womanizer—all of which belied his image as an oak but also made him a legitimate character, moving freely from film company to film company and from scrape to scrape throughout his career. Through it all he maintained a wry sense of perspective. As one acquaintance put it, "Joe was a philosopher who had a comic sense. He was not opinionated, and he gave good advice, such as, 'If four or five guys tell you that you're drunk, even though you know you haven't had a thing to drink, the least you can do is to lie down a little while.'"

Nick Schenck was the much grayer of the two and far the less sophisticated. He once listed his three main interests as his infant daughter, physical fitness, and horse racing. And though the brothers had arrived in this country at the same time and Joe was the elder, Nick spoke with a thick accent while Joe had no accent whatsoever. Joe was charming. Nick did nothing to make himself more ingratiating. Like Adolph Zukor, he cultivated his power and enjoyed exercising it. Sam Marx, an MGM production executive, remembered visiting Schenck's Long Island estate for a weekend. "We were the first ones down on Sunday morning," Marx recalled, "and he said, 'Come walk with me.' And we came to a chicken coop and there were a flock of white chickens and a couple of roosters all in a caged area there, and one had been practically picked to pieces. All its feathers had been picked off, and it was bleeding. The others had ganged up on it. And he pointed out that one to me, and he said, 'Marx, you look at that and you realize that this is the way you must behave in the world. . . . You must not let others pick you to pieces.'"

For Schenck, as for many of the Hollywood Jews, this Darwinistic parable had a very practical application. When Loew died, rivals began circling his company. scheming to pick it off. Schenck, determined not to be the expiring chicken, was now turning their interest to his advantage by offering to broker a takeover himself. He had already held discussions with Zukor and the Warner brothers, but the most ardent suitor was one of the greatest of the Jewish agglomerators, William Fox. Though Fox at the time occupied a place well below the industry's summit, his biographer, Upton Sinclair, admitted that he "planned to get all the moving picture theaters in the United States under his control sooner or later. . . . I think also that he planned to have the making of moving pictures entirely in his own hands."

Like Loew, Fox had vastly expanded his theater holdings, buying up theaters by the dozen. One partner in a West Coast theater chain remembered being asked casually by a friend over a poker game whether or not he would sell out for one million dollars if he had the chance. Pondering the question briefly, the exhibitor answered that he probably would. The next day Fox was at his hotel to close the deal. Fox had also enlarged his production company, buying producer Thomas Dixon's old five-acre studio in Hollywood and then adding eight acres across the street. By 1923 he was producing so many films that he purchased an additional 250 acres in Beverly Hills, which he called the Fox Hills studio.

But Fox, like Zukor, was insatiable. Meeting with Schenck, he proposed to buy out MGM and merge it with his own holdings, financing the fifty-million-dollar deal with a combination of loans from major investment houses headed by Halsey, Stuart and Company and with the proceeds gained by selling off shares of the Fox Film Corporation and Fox Theaters. For engineering the buyout and delivering Loew's interest, Schenck would receive a healthy commission that Fox estimated at ten million dollars. It was an offer Schenck couldn't refuse. After six months of negotiations, working out the details of the financial arrangement, the sale was consummated on February 24, 1929. In one move Fox now controlled the largest and richest film studio ever assembled.

At least he did on paper. Fox and Schenck, however, had concluded their pact during the interregnum between the Coolidge and Hoover administrations. Combining two such major entities as the Fox Film Corporation and Loew's Incorporated would naturally rouse the interest of the antitrust division of the Justice Department. Fox had sought to head them off by visiting Assistant Attorney General William Donovan and soliciting his approval, and Donovan promised to have his staff examine the proposal. A few weeks later Fox's attorney phoned to tell him that one of Donovan's associates had just given them verbal sanction. Since Donovan was the odds-on favorite to become attorney general during the Hoover administration, Fox's merger seemed assured.

What Fox hadn't reckoned on was Louis B. Mayer, now MGM's head. During the negotiations, Mayer had pointedly not been consulted by Schenck, but shortly before the final sale in February he met with Fox to voice his objection and, according to Fox, to remonstrate that he, the man responsible for MGM's standing as a quality studio, hadn't been included in the spoils. Fox stoutly defended Schenck, who was, after all, his ally, and told Mayer that he hoped he stayed aboard, even though he couldn't really understand Mayer's umbrage. Not assuaged, Mayer took that umbrage elsewhere—to his friends in the Hoover administration.

It was inevitable that someone as concerned with the aesthetic contours of his life as Mayer was would sooner or later be attracted to Republican politics, where substantial, conservative businessmen all found their natural roost. Even if he hadn't been an aesthete, his rabid patriotism would have led him there, and few individuals were as rabidly patriotic as Mayer. He had probably been introduced to the political life by William Randolph Hearst sometime in the early twenties, but his real entrée was a middle-aged bulldog of a woman named Ida Koverman, who had once been secretary to Herbert Hoover. Mayer had apparently met Koverman during Coolidge's presidential campaign in 1924 when she was a staff member and he was a volunteer; after the campaign he hired her as his own personal secretary. His grandson Danny Selznick suspected it was because she reminded Mayer of his mother.

With Koverman's assistance, Mayer took as quickly to politics as he had to the movies, probably because both demanded the same skills of dramatizing and hyperbolizing. For its part, the Republican party welcomed so staunch a defender, so generous a contributor, and so hard a worker, and Mayer rapidly became a power in California state politics, rising to the chairmanship of the party's California State Committee. There was even some speculation that he would have given Hoover's nominating speech at the 1928 convention had he not been a Jew. The president-elect did reward Mayer's efforts by offering him the ambassadorship to Turkey. Mayer, after lengthy deliberation, declined.

Fox had his own contact with Hoover, having contributed heavily to his campaign, and when John Lord O'Brian, the new assistant attorney general in charge of the antitrust division, told Fox in June that there was no record of the department's having approved the merger, Fox was astounded and decided to take his case to the president personally. Hoover listened politely, promised to have his attorneys examine the record, and wished him well. Weeks passed. There was no progress. Nervous over the delay, Fox sought the advice of the treasurer of the Republican National Committee, Colonel Huston, who suggested that he speak with Louis Mayer since Mayer was the movie executive closest to Hoover. This time, according to Fox, Mayer admitted that he had lobbied the Justice Department to deny the merger, and he once again denounced Schenck for his treachery. Fox, claiming that he now saw some justice in Mayer's complaint and obviously wanting him to use his Washington influence, offered Mayer two million dollars and a new contract. Mayer accepted and now told the assistant attorney general that he was not opposed to the merger. In fact, he favored it.

During all this haggling, Schenck evidently was growing impatient, too, particularly since, Fox believed, he had gotten a better offer from Warner Brothers. To soothe him, Fox scheduled a golf match at the Lakeview Country Club on Long Island, but misfortune struck again. Fox's chauffeur lost his way, smashed into another car coming over a small ridge, and spun out of control. The chauffeur was killed. Fox and a fellow passenger were seriously injured. He lost one-third of his blood and took over three months to convalesce.

If the financial wrangling and the antitrust snafu hadn't derailed the Fox-Loew merger, Fox's accident had. With Fox laid up indefinitely, the momentum was lost and so ultimately was the financing. While he recuperated, the stock market crashed. Loew's shares lost half their value, and Fox was forced by his brokers to cover the margins on which he had bought the stock or sell it and forfeit his goal of hegemony. He chose to cover, spending four million dollars of his own personal fortune in a single day; but the dream was lost. With Fox hounded by creditors and lawsuits, Loew's Incorporated remained in the hands of Nick Schenck. Fox was ruined.

Yet if Fox's bald grab seemed a perfect demonstration of the agglomerating impulse of the Hollywood Jews, Fox himself saw it differently. For him it was a demonstration of how the gentile establishment punished Jews for hubris. Laemmle had had the good sense to be financed by S. W. Straus, Zukor by Kuhn, Loeb, the Warner brothers by Goldman, Sachs—all Jewish investment houses. Only Fox had dared deal with gentiles, and now, in his view, AT&T, Halsey, Stuart and Company, and other financiers had conspired to deny him the power to control talking pictures—an area in which Fox was pioneering and one in which they all had a financial stake.

As Sinclair imagined it, what his opponents were really saying was, "See here, this Jew who talks about himself too much wants to own patents and control the talking picture industry, which belongs to us," or "See here, I have decided to go into the moving picture business, and you know that a public utilities financier is a safer person to deal with than a little Jew upstart who won't take orders and wants to merge everything in sight." Whether or not this was an accurate reflection of the establishment's attitude toward an aggressive Jew like Fox—and there probably was some truth in it—Fox certainly believed it was. "This was the day they were waiting for," he said. The other Jews had now been forewarned.

Mayer's reaction to the whole affair was less alarm than outrage, disappointment, and finally an overwhelming sense of betrayal. Loew had been a confident and supportive employer, one who recognized Mayer's contributions and never felt challenged by them. Schenck, on the other hand, had tried to sell the company out from under him, and Mayer would never forgive him or trust him again. "Loyalty was a theme to him," Danny Selznick recalled of his grandfather. "He was very, very desirous of having people loyal to him . . . and he took an enormous amount of pride in other people's loyalty. But I have to say, what it meant was 'loyal to *me*.' He assumed his loyalty to them was taken for granted." By Mayer's governing metaphor, Schenck had been disloyal to the family. Schenck, however, had another metaphor; lest anyone mistake Mayer's paternalism for the highest authority, Schenck had everyone, including Mayer, call him "the General."

If Schenck had unnerved him, Mayer hid his insecurities behind the bold front of his life performance. "It didn't matter whether two were present or two hundred," said one employee, "he always had the floor." To his grandson, he often seemed like the comic strip character the Little King. "He blossomed at being able, in a sense, to show himself and whoever the audience was [his importance]. There was always that sense of a man who was performing a little bit to his audience and enjoying it. . . . There were always these things that were displays of his power or authority—his influence."

But inside things roiled. "He was very quiet," Edith remembered. "He used to take me often in the car . . . and drive me, it seems, way beyond, if there was a thing like Malibu, and talk to me about business. . . . And I didn't answer. And he said it comforted him to do this with me because I could listen, and he felt I was a safety valve." He was an insomniac and, like Zukor, was plagued by a nasty nervous rash. Meeting important figures, he would often be petrified, his eyes welling with tears until his secretary calmed him. He insisted on living a comparatively Spartan existence, telling his family that his economizing was a hedge against an always uncertain future. He didn't build a home of his own until 1925, fully seven years after he had arrived in California, and when he did, he chose the relatively far-flung reaches of Santa Monica rather than Beverly Hills, partly because that way he wouldn't have to move each summer to be near the ocean—saving himself the cost of a vacation home.

One of Mayer's fears, one of the fears that haunted the Hollywood Jews generally, was that it would all be taken away. Schenck's conspiracy with Fox obviously provided justification for that fear. But Schenck's perfidy had touched another, deeper fear of Mayer's as well: the fear of loneliness. Ever since his childhood, Mayer had been desperate to be connected—to a family, a community, a studio, a country. It was one of the motives behind his almost pathological possessiveness and his unbridled paternalism. He had always been desperate to belong.

Perhaps it was this need for security that also made Mayer cling so fiercely to his old provincial values. In a world of treachery and flux, he regarded them as his only touchstones. Most of the Hollywood Jews—and the gentiles, for that matter—would abandon themselves in varying degrees to Hollywood's allures. Mayer remained puritanical, using his life and his films to purvey what he regarded as virtue. "I worship good women, honorable men, and saintly mothers," he told Frances Marion, an MGM writer. These were the foundation of his studio.

Mayer's real accomplishment was translating his own way of holding on into America's. By the early thirties, MGM had clearly displaced Zukor's Paramount as the supreme studio, and Mayer certainly was due a large share of the credit—credit he wasn't always given. What Zukor had done in the twenties—what he was situated to do as an assimilating Jew—was mediate between a traditional America and a new America of immigrants and cities, between the upper and middle classes on one side and the working class on the other. What Mayer did in the thirties—what he was situated to do as a Jew yearning to belong—was provide reassurance against the anxieties and disruptions of the time. He did this by fashioning a vast, compelling national fantasy out of his dreams and out of the basic tenets of his own dogmatic faith—a belief in virtue, in the bulwark of family, in the merits of loyalty, in the soundness of tradition, in America itself.

Native born, white, Anglo-Saxon, Protestant Americans could share this fantasy with Mayer and even call it their own. But it is unlikely that any of them could have or would have invented it. To do so, one would have needed the same desperate longing for security that Mayer and so many of the other Hollywood Jews felt. One would have had to suffer the same compulsion to merge oneself with the world. One would have had to be so fearful of being outside and alone that one would go to any lengths to fabricate America as a sanctuary, safe and secure, and then promulgate this idealization to other Americans. Finally, one would have had to identify so closely with this fabricated America that one would have had to have been reborn on the Fourth of July . . . just as Louis B. Mayer had.

4

Between the Old Life and the New

Combining good picture-making with good citizenship.

MOTTO OF
THE WARNER BROTHERS STUDIO

He [Harry Warner] has two major interests, business and morals.

FORTUNE MAGAZINE,
DECEMBER 1937

JACK AND HARRY WARNER, THE two pillars of the Warner Brothers studio, loathed one another. Harry once chased Jack around the lot with a lead pipe, shouting that he was going to kill him, and had to be forcibly restrained and disarmed to keep from making good on his threat. On another occasion Harry and Jack were engaged in a typical shouting match when Harry suddenly grabbed an object on his desk and threatened his brother. This time Jack's young son was the one who intervened to save his father. At one point the hostility was so intense that neither of the brothers would enter the studio commissary if the other were there. By the end of their lives they never spoke to one another. When Harry died his widow accused Jack of having driven her husband to the grave.

It may have seemed from these incidents that Harry had a very low boiling point, and he did, but Jack was also a veteran provocateur who incited everyone. One writer described him as a "fast-talking Broadway type, who's got a flippant manner, thinks of himself as a witty man, and has pretty bad taste in the stories he tells." Almost everyone regarded him as a frustrated comedian who "liked nothing better than telling very bad jokes in a loud voice." When Albert Einstein visited the studio, Jack boasted of having told him, "You know, I have a theory about relatives, too—don't hire them." Scanning a table of Oriental guests at a banquet for Madame Chiang Kai-shek, he said, "Holy cow. I forgot to pick up my laundry." He dressed in loud jackets, yachting blazers, and patent leather shoes, and "he always sported a big smile; he had a remarkable set of flashing white teeth." He also had an annoying habit of shuffling his feet in a vaudeville soft shoe upon greeting someone.

But Jack was not only crude, vulgar, shallow, flashy, contrary, and galling; unlike the vast majority of Hollywood Jews who coveted respectability, he actively cultivated these qualities. He regarded himself as irreverent, which he was, and incorrigible, which he might have been. Others who were less charitable thought he either was a fool or acted like one, and he seemed to enjoy creating embarrassment—especially embarrassment for his older brother, Harry. Once, Harry had escorted a visiting rabbi to the dining room when Jack arrived. "Harry introduced the rabbi to Jack," remembered one witness, "and Jack said, 'How're ya, rab? I caught your act at the Palace. You were great!' Harry as always would look around and say, 'My brother, you know—sometimes he makes jokes that are not so good. . . . ' When Jack would tell a raw story, Harry would look at me and say, 'You know, my brother—he was raised in Ohio, and he didn't have the advantages of such a good education. . . .' He was always apologizing."

Harry was antithetical to Jack in almost every way—sober where Jack was silly; conservative where Jack was loud; self-conscious where Jack was thoughtless; severe where Jack was cocky—though this was probably less coincidence than design. Jack wanted to be everything Harry despised. The writer Leo Rosten described Harry, in contradistinction to Jack, as "not an impressive man to meet. He was a folksy, homey guy, who made no pretensions about himself. . . . He was a devoted family man, lived a quiet life—you never heard about him going to a night club, being mixed up in a scandal." "What would my children think?" he asked incredulously when questioned if he ever thought of succumbing to the temptations of the flesh. "That's terrible!"

According to Jack, the constant smiler, Harry seldom smiled. Like Adolph Zukor and Louis B. Mayer, he was a stern moralist who would eventually assume the role of moral adjudicator to his entire family, and he was particularly hard on Jack's transgressions. He liked to give advice, even when it wasn't solicited, and in the forties, when he decided to own and race horses, he lost one trainer after another because he insisted on telling them what to do. But if Harry was a man of plebeian tastes and manner, he was also, as Jack would discover, an implacable foe. When he thought that Lewis Selznick, who at one point distributed Warner Brothers' films, was cheating him, he went to Selznick's office and, according to his son-in-law, Milton Sperling, "beat the shit out of him. Without any questions. . . . He was a giant. He had balls."

In all of these things, Harry was very much his father's son, which probably had a great deal to do with the tension between the brothers. Benjamin Warner was a strapping Polish peasant, a *bulvon* who emigrated to Baltimore in 1883, lured by the sunny lies of a townsman who had preceded him. A cobbler by trade, he set up a shoe repair shop and within a year had earned enough to send passage for his wife, his daughter, Anna, and his son, Harry. With a hint of condescension, Jack said, "He cared more for people than for money," and that certainly characterized his career. Hearing about the money to be made by supplying railroad crews with goods, Warner invested in an inventory and moved to Lynchburg, Virginia; he sent for his two brothers-in-law from Poland to help, but one of them stole his supplies. He then moved to Canada, where Jack was born, to peddle goods to fur trappers in exchange for pelts, but when he stopped in Montreal to collect his share from a partner, he discovered he had been swindled again. "This was the experience he remembered long years later when we talked of his youth," wrote Jack. "The humiliation." Discouraged, Warner retreated to Baltimore and another shoe repair shop.

According to Jack, Harry, who was fourteen at the time, had taken a train to Ohio to catch a glimpse of presidential candidate William McKinley when a fellow traveler told him about Youngstown. Youngstown had become a magnet for Polish immigrants who came to work in the steel mills there, and the traveler suggested it might be a good place for a Pole like Harry to establish a shoe repair shop. Harry followed the advice and, given his age, apparently became something of a local phenomenon. His family arrived soon after, eventually giving up the shoe repair store for a grocery. Benjamin Warner worked sixteen to eighteen hours each day, but, Jack remembered, "there never seemed to be quite enough. We could not afford to buy shoes, so my father made them. When we boys needed clothes, my father laid us facedown on a bolt of cloth, marked it with white chalk, and made up the suits himself."

Benjamin Warner's solace was his belief. He was a devout Jew who recalled having to take his Jewish instruction surreptitiously in a Polish stable while a lookout kept watch for the police. Even in America he frequently spoke Yiddish, kept kosher, and always lived within walking distance of the synagogue in respect of the Talmudic injunction that one not ride on the Sabbath. Harry was just as serious in his commitment to Judaism, and it was one of the forces that bound him to his father. It was almost certainly the source for his passionate promotion of racial and religious tolerance. He remembered his father telling him, "Son, you're going to have to fight with the weapon you have at your command so that the children and their children may have a right to live and have a Faith, no matter what their Faith may be, in our great country, America." No studio would honor this ideal as much as Warner Brothers.

But the religion and the messianism that went with it had another effect on the Warner family: it created a moral fault line across which the Warners divided. On one side were Benjamin and the older Warner children, Anna, Rose, Harry, and Albert (anglicized from Abe). These were the more religious and moralistic, the less assimilated. On the other side were the younger Warners—there were nine surviving children in all—especially Jack and Sam. These were the more gregarious, assimilated, and rebellious. Harry could read, write, and speak Hebrew by the time he was seven. Jack took no interest whatsoever in religious instruction, and when his father hired a Boston rabbi to tutor the children, Jack said, "I didn't dig it at all." He remembered the rabbi pulling out a long hat pin and jabbing him every time he made a mistake. "So I said to myself: Rabbi, the next time you stab me with the pin I'm going to jerk your beard." When he erred and the rabbi reached for his hat pin, "I clutched the whiskers as if they were a bell clapper and gave them a mighty yank. His chin came down to his collar, and he screamed and ran to my father. 'I will not teach this boy again!' he cried." And that was the end of Jack's religious training.

Jack's defiance didn't begin with religion, nor did it end there, though the story did serve as a kind of paradigm for his life. "He was a little rebellious," said his son, Jack Warner, Jr. "He was the youngest of the brothers, and he was like a street Arab part of the time. He didn't go for the regimentation or the rules." In Youngstown he quit school after fourth grade and hung out with a street gang. When his father managed to buy his sister, Rose, a piano, Jack got attention by singing along and later performed before local groups. By his own admission he was an exhibitionist, and his mother "once became so exasperated with my behavior that she offered me two bits if I could keep quiet for five minutes." He couldn't.

With his desperate need for attention, Jack seemed destined for show business, and he soon graduated from his engagements before local groups to the Youngstown Opera House and finally to a vaudeville tour as boy soprano. Harry and Albert (who was three years younger than Harry) were far less likely recruits to the entertainment world. As young men they owned a bicycle shop in Youngstown during the bicycle craze that swept America in the late nineties, and they competed in local races, but both eventually left home for more mundane professions—Harry to work for the Armour Meat Company, using the knowledge he had gained in his father's butcher shop; and Albert to Swift and Company selling soap. Sam, who was seven years younger than Harry and much closer in temperament to Jack, became a railroad fireman. Jack, eleven years younger than Harry, stayed behind.

It was Sam, a vagabond like Jack, who introduced the family to the crazy possibility of exhibiting movies. Through an old friend who owned a machine shop in Youngstown, Sam had seen an Edison Kinetoscope, a primitive projector, and spent hours learning how to run it. He quit his railroad job and went to work at a Hale's Tours in Chicago, then returned to Youngstown when the local amusement park installed movies. Jack recalled that his brother "saw the vast possibilities in this new form of entertainment, and he was ready to do anything short of robbing a bank to get his hands on a projector of his own." A woman who ran a boardinghouse out near the amusement park where Sam worked had a son who had gone out on the road with a projector with little success. The woman confided to Sam that her son wanted to unload the machine if he could find a dupe. Concealing his enthusiasm, Sam offered to see if he could come up with someone and then raced home to convince the family to make the one-thousand-dollar investment. Ultimately, after pooling their savings and hocking their father's delivery horse, the Warners were in the movie business.

If of all the Hollywood Jews, the Warners seemed least interested in raising their status and becoming genteel, it may have been a function of growing up in a midwestern steel center like Youngstown, where culture and class distinctions were less readily apparent than in Chicago, New York, or Boston. For Sam, who had once run a portable crap game, been a carnival barker, and peddled ice-cream cones, the attractions of the movies were obvious. They were new and exciting—which made their appeal almost precisely the opposite of what it would be to the more class-conscious Jews of the East. For Jack, though he was too young to be part of the deliberations to buy the projector, the movies would ultimately be a means of satisfying his exhibitionism and of flaunting traditional values.

But for Harry and Albert, both rather staid and conventional men, the attractions were far murkier. It wasn't until many years later that Harry realized he could use the movies to promote tolerance and justice, as his father had recommended, and though he was good with figures and enjoyed the business challenge, there was nothing that militated specifically for the movies and several things that militated against them, primarily the risk and the brothers' own lack of experience.* What is likely is that Harry and Albert were attracted not to the movies generally, as were other movie Jews, but to this particular family enterprise, simply because it was a way to maintain some degree of control over their younger and wilder siblings. As head of the new company's exchequer, Harry would remain the leader of the brothers. It was a motive that would certainly be consistent with Harry's behavior over the course of his life.

The Warners launched their new venture in 1903, setting up a tent in their yard and charging admission to see their movie—*The Great Train Robbery*, a copy of which had come with the projector. A few

---

*At this time Harry was, in fact, seriously considering entering the iron business.

weeks later they took their projector to Niles, Ohio, where a carnival was bivouacked, and rented an empty store. They made $300 in one week. Afterward Sam and Albert, armed with their print of *The Great Train Robbery*, traveled a circuit of small towns until, weary of the road, they decided to find a permanent location.

The place they chose was called New Castle, a good-sized steel town some fifteen miles south of Youngstown across the Pennsylvania state line. They had chosen it because, during their circuit, they had made a greater profit there than at any other stop. Like the citizens of Louis B. Mayer's Haverhill, the people of New Castle were largely factory workers and immigrants who had very little in the way of entertainment. "They went to picnics in Cascade Park, an occasional concert by traveling musicians or to the Genkingin Opera House for vaudeville in the evenings, but there wasn't much else," said Jack.

The Warners filled that gap by renting a room above a storehouse and borrowing chairs from the neighborhood undertaker—a common practice in the early days of the nickelodeons. Harry rented the films from an exchange in Pittsburgh and ran the operation. Albert helped keep the books. Sam ran the projector. Jack and Rose would commute each weekend from Youngstown—he to sing, she to play the piano. The Cascade, as they called it, did well, but Harry, like virtually every other Hollywood Jew, realized that the profits would be far greater if one bought and then rented films than if one simply exhibited them. So in 1907, after a year in New Castle, the brothers moved to Pittsburgh to set up the Duquesne Film Exchange.

For fifteen-year-old Jack, this was traumatic. His major support within the family had always been his beloved brother and kindred spirit, Sam. While Sam had been in New Castle, he was just a long trolley ride away, but Pittsburgh seemed as if it were at the ends of the earth. Jack and Sam immediately began conspiring on how to get together and, significantly, to ease themselves out from under their older brothers' restraints. Sam suggested they move to South Africa, and Jack was smitten by the idea until his father scotched it. Jack determined he would just have to join his brother in Pittsburgh, and after a relentless campaign his father reluctantly agreed. Jack and Benjamin Warner had never been especially close—certainly not as close as Harry and his father were. It was his mother whom Jack adored. In his father he seemed to see the same antiquated values, the same inability to adjust to America, the same failure that William Fox had seen in his father. To Jack, Benjamin Warner was living proof that the values of Europe and Judaism couldn't really function in the New World. In time the father would be just as scornful of his son. But during the trip to Pittsburgh, these two antagonists shared an intimacy that would never be repeated. "We got off the train, and went down the street to a little restaurant he knew," recalled Jack.

> He handed me a menu, but I knew what I wanted. I wanted ham and eggs—a dish that was never served in our home—but I was afraid he would scold me.
> "Come now, boy," he said. "What are you going to eat?"
> "If it's all right with you, Pop," I blurted, "I'd like ham and eggs."
> "Fine, boy," he said. "I'll have the same. Country style."
> Our eyes met, and we smiled, fellow schemers sharing a secret sin. I would never again be as close to him.

———

Like that of all the successful movie Jews, the Warners' progress after Pittsburgh could be measured by leaps and bounds, surging with the boom of the movies themselves. Buying whatever movies it could get its hands on, Duquesne expanded to Norfolk, Virginia, where the Warners had relatives, and Sam and Jack were granted their wish to run it together. As Jack described it, "The Duquesne Amusement Company was in the black almost from the beginning. . . . The Warner brothers bathed in the shining river, and were getting rich." But the Warners' river to supremacy had its eddies. The first was a consequence of the Edison Trust war. As a relatively small exchange, Duquesne was susceptible to the threats and extortion of Edison's General Film Company, and when General Film launched its campaign to buy up or force out other distributors, the Warners were among the casualties. Duquesne was sold off.

Retreating to Youngstown in 1910, the brothers took their capital and regrouped. Harry and Albert, following the usual path of the movie Jews, suggested that they try to produce several inexpensive films and recommended St. Louis as a location, since there was an empty foundry that could easily serve as a studio. (Harry may have also regarded St. Louis as a reasonably safe haven from the Edison Trust.) Sam and Jack didn't need much encouragement. The Warners' very first production was a western called *Peril of the Plains*, co-written and co-produced by Sam and Jack and directed by Sam. But their inexperience showed: *Peril of the Plains* and another film they shot at the same time failed. By the time they returned to Youngstown, Harry had decided to join forces with Laemmle's Independents and reenter distribution, which was a branch they at least understood. This time, however, Harry chose California as their base of operations. Sam took Los Angeles; Jack, San Francisco. Harry himself moved to New York. Spread out on both coasts, the brothers were covering the two major centers of production.

The exchange they reestablished in 1916 was a relatively small operation, almost totally bounded by family, and initially, at least, it struggled. But even a small exchange could suddenly reap enormous rewards. The key was acquiring what was called the states' rights to a popular film—states' rights being the exclusive right to rent that film in a particular state. The Warners might pay as much as $50,000 for the California-Arizona-Nevada rights, and, according to Jack, "invariably we made a lot of money." On the other hand, they could also lose as much as $100,000 on a single film, as they did when they bought the rights to a Civil War epic called *The Crisis* and America entered World War I the same week, temporarily drying up the market for war films.

For all the money to be made in distribution, and despite his first brief and ill-fated foray into production, Harry was soon talking about making movies again. With the Edison Trust having been smashed and the movies booming, profit must have been a consideration for the money-minded Harry. He would later claim that he was chiefly motivated by a need to educate, and for Harry this was also probably true; the first films he produced, like the first films Louis B. Mayer produced, reliably promoted old-fashioned virtues. A third motive was more interesting. One longtime Warners employee speculated that the most powerful attraction for Harry was the vicarious charge he got from the chaos of moviemaking. For a man whose personal life was dull and pristine—Jack used to joke that Harry's house was maintained like a museum—making movies offered the same release that watching them provided an audience.

Whatever the attraction, Harry was now back in production with *Passions Inherited*, a sentimental poem he had acquired for $15,000. To direct, he hired a philandering Englishman named Gilbert Hamilton, but Hamilton, while carrying on an affair with one of his actresses, had gone over budget and over schedule, and communications from him had ceased. Harry dispatched Jack to the California location to discover the problem. When Jack saw that the film was still unfinished, he took the footage that had been completed and edited it into a film himself. In its truncated state, *Passions Inherited* was a commercial failure, but that didn't deter Harry. With America's entry into World War I, the Warners decided to do their patriotic part by producing a film on venereal disease for the Army Signal Corps. They also retained the rights for domestic distribution—the value of which turned out to be practically nil. What all of this proved, however, was that the Warners' success was less a product of genius than of perseverance.

Without the taste or the aspirations of most of the other Hollywood Jews, it is entirely possible that the Warners would have continued lurching along this way, throwing good distribution money after bad productions, had they not discovered *My Four Years in Germany*, which had roughly the same watershed effect on their careers as *Queen Elizabeth* had on Zukor's and *Birth of a Nation* had on Mayer's. *My Four Years in Germany* was a firsthand account by James W. Gerard, America's ambassador to Germany, of the years leading up to this country's entrance into the European conflict and of Gerard's efforts to reach some kind of settlement with Kaiser Wilhelm. The book had already become a national best-seller by the time the bidding started for the movie rights, so the Warners weren't exactly taking a major risk. In his autobiography Jack claims that he and Sam hatched the idea to secure the rights when they saw a large display in the window of the *Los Angeles Examiner* promoting the book's serialization. They immediately wired Gerard expressing their interest. Another story had Harry ringing Gerard's doorbell and offering him a share of the profits. Whatever the case, Gerard sold the rights to the Warners for $50,000, though he had received a higher bid, he said, from Lewis Selznick. "I liked you fellows because I felt you were on the level," Jack quoted Gerard as saying, "and I wanted you to make the film. And as you know, your brother Harry is a sharp one." He then proceeded to tell how he and Harry had flipped a coin to see who would pay for the fifty-cent fee to have the contract notarized.

In securing the rights, however, the Warners had a problem: their ability to pay for them. To get the funds Harry began romancing one of the industry's pioneers, Mark Dintenfass, a colorful little man with a long waxed mustache and affectations to match. Dintenfass had sold herring in his native Philadelphia before deciding to enter the film industry, and his career read like a war record. First he had run afoul of the Edison Trust when he insisted on photographing films with a patented camera. It was Sigmund Lubin, affectionately known as "Pop" and one of the Trust's two Jews, who bailed him out by letting him use one of Lubin's old facilities right under the noses of Edison's patrol. When the dust of the Trust war had finally settled, Dintenfass joined forces with Universal and once again found himself caught in the crossfire between the new company's warring factions. In the end he had an old acquaintance, Lewis Selznick, broker a sale of his shares to Laemmle, and Dintenfass went on his merry way, continuing to produce films under a variety of banners.

How and why Harry happened to latch on to Dintenfass as a potential angel is uncertain, but he took the older man to a stand-up lunch at a saloon and convinced him to put up the production costs in exchange for a significant percentage of the profits. The budget wasn't exorbitant since production itself was economized. (Harry always prided himself on his frugality.) The exteriors were to be shot on a replica of a German village street that had already been constructed as a conversation piece on the New Jersey farm of a Hearst publishing executive named Arthur Brisbane. The interiors were to be shot at the old Biograph studio in the Bronx. And because the film was done as a kind of docudrama, there were no major stars to pay.

Artistically, *My Four Years in Germany* certainly wasn't a landmark. It appealed primarily to American postwar jingoism and blood lust. In mercilessly reviling the Huns, albeit in the form of Ambassador Gerard's eyewitness account, it included scenes of a young girl being pummeled until she was permanently maimed and a Prussian officer taking another young girl from her family for obviously lascivious purposes. In another scene a girl in occupied Belgium pleads with Gerard, who is on an observation tour. "We are slaves!" And in another he challenges the use of German shepherds at a POW camp.

No one would have called the film subtle, but it was effective, and it returned to the Warners a profit of $130,000 on $1.5 million gross receipts. With both the capital and the encouragement of a success, they now left distribution altogether. While Harry and Albert remained in New York to conduct the company's business, Jack joined Sam in Los Angeles, where they set up a studio downtown and embarked on a small but steady production schedule, starting with two inexpensive serials, *The Lost City* and *The Tiger's Claw*, both of which starred a marginal actress named Helen Holmes. The Warners were obviously operating at a level far below even that of Mayer when he snared Francis X. Bushman for his first serial, and within the Hollywood constellation they were a rather dim speck with a rundown studio at Eighteenth and Main and an unimpressive roster of performers headed by a child star named Wesley Barry, an Italian comedian named Monte Blue, and a German shepherd named Rin Tin Tin.

Ironically, though, it was their lack of status that might have proved the Warners' greatest asset in those early years in Hollywood. Their studio was named eponymously for a reason: they regarded themselves as outsiders and underdogs, and they trusted no one beyond their family circle. As Harry once said, "Warner brothers personally have always construed themselves as one." That gave them a certain edge. Where other Hollywood Jews wanted desperately to appease the establishment, the Warners set themselves against it and challenged its legitimacy. It would be years before they finally became members of the club.

In this they took their style from Jack, their wariness from Harry. While no one would ever have accused Warner Brothers of being the classiest studio in Hollywood, most would have conceded that it was the most aggressive, cantankerous, and iconoclastic. "Every worthwhile contribution to the advancement of motion pictures has been made over a howl of protest from the standpatters," Jack once told an interviewer, "whose favorite refrain has been, 'You can't do that.' And when we hear that chorus now, we know we must be on the right track."

Of course, the brothers paid a price for their paranoia and insularity, particularly when it came to financing the scale of production and, later, the scale of theater acquisition that a studio needed to survive in Hollywood. Getting financing from the important investment houses was never easy, as William Fox's experience so amply demonstrated. These institutions weren't accustomed to dealing with immigrant Jews engaged in a vaguely disreputable enterprise like the movies. But it was doubly difficult when the supplicants had suspicions of their own. "Speaking from personal experience," said Milton Sperling, Harry's one-time son-in-law, "the Warners . . . distrusted the New York banks, they distrusted the eastern bankers, they distrusted Wall Street. They felt they were discriminated against just because they were Jewish."

Once the movies had clearly established their supremacy as popular entertainment, Wall Street had few compunctions about loaning money and placing its officers on the boards of movie companies. By the early twenties Wall Street was well represented in the boardroom of almost every film company.* In the mid-teens and in the smaller companies, however, the compunctions were much greater, and Jews who didn't have the clout of a Zukor were forced to fend for themselves in the banking community. "I think it was [Joseph] Schenck," remembered Sperling, "who told me the story about walking into a bank with his then partner, who was not Jewish—someone like Thomas Ince—and the bank talked to him and so forth, and he heard one banker say to Ince, 'What are you doing with a kike?' So years later, Schenck went back to this bank and to this same bank officer, and he said, 'The kike wants to borrow $100 million.' He couldn't resist it. He said, 'Now, security is Twentieth Century-Fox.' So the guy said, 'I'll be very happy to do business with you,' and he said, 'Fuck you.'"

---

*Some saw this as a tragedy. "When we operated on picture money," Cecil B. De Mille once said, "there was joy in the industry; when we operated on Wall Street money, there was grief in the industry." (De Mille, *Autobiography*, pp. 288–9)

Financing made for some strange bedfellows. One of the earliest and staunchest supporters of the fledgling film industry was an Italian immigrant's son whose own life story in many ways resembled those of the Jews he championed. Born in 1870 in San Jose, California, Amadeo Peter Giannini had a tumultuous childhood; when he was only seven he watched his father's murder at the hands of a neighbor. His mother remarried, to a produce broker, and Amadeo joined his stepfather's company when he was barely in his teens. He was so successful at brokering between the farmers and the wholesalers that he was able to retire at the age of thirty-one in 1901. What lured him out of this early retirement was a bank directorship left vacant when his father-in-law, a banker, died. Amadeo soon found himself running the bank, but he had a falling-out with the other directors over his generous loan policies. Still interested in banking, he received capital from one of the few available sources *he* had—a prominent Jewish San Francisco banker named I. W. Hellman. In 1904, with Hellman's backing, Giannini opened the Bank of Italy.

Dealing with essentially the same clientele as did the early film moguls, working-class immigrants who distrusted banks, Giannini employed many of the same commercial methods as the moguls. He solicited depositors from the Italian community in San Francisco and advertised extensively in the foreign-language newspapers. The 1906 San Francisco earthquake gave him an opportunity to provide loans to rebuild the city and, not incidentally, to build the bank. But Giannini's brainstorm—to sprinkle both coasts with branches of his Bank of Italy—was what really catapulted him into his position as one of the country's leading bankers. The conservative financial establishment was appalled and lobbied for legislation to outlaw the practice of branch banking. Giannini saw this for what it was: the genteel establishment's terror at being challenged from someone outside the cultural mainstream.

This was also one of the elements that helped forge an alliance between the Bank of Italy and the movie Jews of Hollywood and New York. Giannini and the Jews were equally marginal to the cultural establishment, and both were equally suspicious of the country's powerful economic forces. Giannini violated conservative banking practices and tweaked the establishment by playing hunches when he made loans, which meant that he would often give credit to individuals other banks disdained. "Character was his collateral," said his admirers. When Sol Lesser, a seventeen-year-old San Franciscan who had followed his father into film exhibition, came to Giannini to request a one-hundred-dollar loan for a movie that had arrived C.O.D., Giannini was skeptical. He had never loaned money to anyone in film; it wasn't regarded as a sound practice. But when Lesser insisted that he would pay because his word was his bond, Giannini not only relented, he personally guaranteed the loan.

Lesser claimed this was the beginning of the relationship between the Bank of Italy and the film community. The real engine behind the alliance, however, was not Giannini but Giannini's younger brother, Attilio, nicknamed "Doc" because he had earned a medical degree before joining the bank. When the Bank of Italy devoured the assets of the Bowery and East River Bank in New York, Doc was sent to manage it, and Sol Lesser, now one of the largest exhibitors in the country, introduced him to many of the major film executives. As a result Doc became one of the first sources of capital for Marcus Loew, Lewis Selznick, Florenz Ziegfeld, and dozens of other Jewish showmen—a collaboration of outsiders.

The Warners also kept their studio accounts with Giannini, but their major financial benefactor was another young maverick California banker—this one with the improbable name of Motley Flint. Flint was head of the Security First National Bank (no relation to the First National film company), and he was eager to form some kind of partnership with the rapidly growing film industry. For whatever reason—it was probably because the Warners, as a small but growing studio, represented a good fit for his small but growing bank—he implicitly trusted the Warners, and he became one of Jack's few close friends. "I never worry about your debts," Jack quoted him as saying. "You and Sam are going in the right direction, and I know you'll make it." Flint backed his confidence with more than $2 million in credit over the years. He also introduced the Warners to his banking connections on Wall Street.

The most significant of these, it turned out, was a financier named Waddill Catchings who had recently left J. P. Morgan for the Jewish investment house of Goldman, Sachs. With two books to his credit, Catchings was something of an economic theorist, and the theory he propounded was the power of the fearless entrepreneur and the importance of the bold initiative. Catchings met Harry Warner in December 1924, when Harry was particularly despondent over his relationship with First National, the company through which Warners distributed the films it made. Even with Flint's support, Harry complained that in order to continue production, "most of our time was spent in obtaining money from loan sharks" at interest rates as high as 40 percent. Catchings, impressed with Harry's personal and fiscal integrity, decided to make him the protagonist in an entrepreneurial drama that would play out Catchings's own theories of individual bravery and risk. The only proviso was that Harry strictly follow a master plan Catchings had devised—a condition to which Harry readily agreed. Little Warner Brothers was about to take on Hollywood.

Following phase one of the master plan, Harry appointed Catchings to the Warners board as chairman of the finance committee. Catchings then prevailed on six major banks, including the National Bank of Commerce, which had never lent money to a film company, to provide Warners with a multimillion-dollar credit fund. In phase two, Warners took $800,000 of their new credit and purchased the old, faltering Vitagraph studio. Vitagraph might have withered since its proud days as part of the Edison Trust, but it still had a valuable nationwide distribution apparatus and two studios. Now, the Warners suddenly had a large production facility and a network of exchanges. All they needed were theaters of their own to provide their studio with a reliable market, and Catchings soon supplied those by engineering the purchase of ten theaters in major markets.

Not even Catchings, however, could have fully anticipated the success of phase three. In the winter of 1925 Sam and Jack bought a Los Angeles radio station, and in the course of setting it up they met a sound engineer with Western Electric named Nathan Levinson. A few months later, after a trip to New York, Levinson visited the Warners bubbling with news over something he had seen at the Bell Labs. Bell engineers had, he claimed, accomplished something that, in film circles, had become as desirable and yet as seemingly unachievable as alchemy: they had synchronized sound with film. For decades various inventors, including Edison himself, had attempted to make sound movies, and William Fox was already acquiring patents for a sound-on-film process, but none of the processes had quite worked or proven practical, and the larger companies seemed perfectly satisfied to maintain the status quo rather than make the capital expenditures and other untold adjustments that conversion to sound would require.

The Warners and Fox, the Hollywood Jews who were most sensitive to their status as outsiders, had fewer qualms about sound, seeing it more as an opportunity to break into the front ranks than as a destabilizing upheaval (though even if it were destabilizing, neither the Warners nor Fox was likely to care). Sam left for New York to observe the process firsthand and returned to Los Angeles a fervent believer. Harry was no less desirous of beating the big studios, but he was unmoved by the idea of sound, regarding it chiefly as a way of bringing music to the movies rather than as a potential revolution.

Determined to get his brother to budge, Sam invited him to what Harry thought was a meeting of Wall Street bankers. It actually turned out to be a demonstration of sound movies. Harry admitted later that "I am positive if [he] said talking picture, I would not [have] gone." But, watching a short of a jazz band and realizing that sound shorts could be used as appetizers before the main feature, Harry conceded to experiment with sound. Catchings agreed. On June 25, 1925, Harry signed a letter of agreement with Bell, which had merged with Western Electric, to make a series of sound films. Western Electric would provide the technical competence; Warners, the artistic. The partnership was working out so well that in December both sides agreed to a more permanent arrangement—or, at least, the Warners thought they had agreed. John Otterson, however, thought differently.

Otterson was a former naval officer, former president of the Winchester Repeating Arms Company, and the new head of Electrical Research Projects, Inc. (ERPI), the division of Western Electric that was responsible for talking films. Though his predecessors had tentatively reached an accord with Warner Brothers, the only studio besides Fox that had shown any real interest in the sound process, Otterson wanted to abrogate the agreement and try to enlist one of the larger companies. How much of this was arrogance at not wanting to deal with a small-potatoes operation like Warners Brothers and how much was even anti-Semitism at having to deal with Jews at all one couldn't possibly know, but Harry was deeply embittered by the whole affair. Years later, when he and Western Electric were locked in another dispute over sound, the president of the Bell System invited him to air their grievances together. "As he [Harry] walked into the office," recalled producer Milton Sperling,

> he said, "Mr. Gray, this can be a very short meeting. I will give you all rights to our patents. I will withdraw all our suits. . . . I'll do it immediately and at no cost to you, if you'll do one thing. If you'll give me the name of one Jew who works for your company."
>
> And the man looked horrified. "What do you think—it's the policy of our company to be anti-Semitic?"
>
> He said, "No. Just give me the name of a Jew working for your company."
>
> Gray said, "Realistically, I don't think I can produce one."
>
> Harry said, "It's a policy of your company not to employ Jews. It's a policy of my company not to do business with you." And he walked out of the room.

Apparently Gray was so embarrassed that he ordered his lawyers to work out a settlement the very next week.

In the case of Otterson, Catchings went directly to the president of Bell to countermand Otterson's break-off and have the agreement reinstated. Under its terms, Western Electric granted Warners exclusive license for the sound process. For its part, Warners committed itself to sell 2,400 of the systems over the next four years, for which it would receive an 8 percent royalty. The sound process itself was to be called Vitaphone. Sam Warner, the family's greatest enthusiast for sound, was put in charge of the project and immediately began preparing short films at the old Vitagraph studios in Brooklyn, while Jack, out in Hollywood, was preparing a feature with a musical track, *Don Juan*, starring John Barrymore. The idea was that Vitaphone would be used exclusively for music, not for the spoken word; this, of course, was consistent with Harry's larger aspiration that the movies could bring culture to the masses.

Vitaphone was first exhibited on August 6, 1926, before a full house at the Warner Theater on Broadway. The program began with a "Vitaphone Prelude"—an introduction by Will Hays, president of the Motion Picture Producers and Distributors of America (the only spoken piece), and the eight musical shorts Sam Warner had produced in New York. After a ten-minute intermission came *Don Juan*. It had the intended effect, stunning the audience with its music and sounds. Sam reported back to Jack in Los Angeles that first-nighters included Adolph Zukor, Nick Schenck, William Fox, and Lewis Selznick—a roster that must have made the triumph particularly sweet for the Warners. The winds of change had blown. The next morning *Variety*, the most important entertainment trade paper, issued a special edition in acknowledgment of the impending revolution. Warner Brothers stock soared from $8 to $65 per share, and since the Warners themselves were major stockholders, they became very wealthy men virtually overnight.

What might have been even greater than the financial benefits were the psychological rewards. Having been second-class citizens within the Hollywood community, the Warners were suddenly setting the agenda for the entire industry, and even in their own eyes it must have seemed that the lowly had risen. Still, the celebrating was somewhat premature. If the investment markets were convinced about the future of sound movies, the industry itself was less sanguine. Vitaphone equipment, which consisted essentially of a large record player synchronized to a projector, was cumbersome and unreliable. Unless someone monitored the system closely, the audience was likely to hear "squawks and howls . . . [that] wrecked any of the wonder that the process might have had." Many theaters refused to install it, sending Warners' stock plummeting again, and the company wound up losing close to a million dollars in 1926—which was, however, less than they had lost the previous year. By April 1927 they were forced to renegotiate their agreement with Western Electric once again. This time they yielded their exclusive rights to Vitaphone in return for an end to the purchase agreement and a 37.5 percent royalty on all sales they made to other licensees. Meanwhile, the other major film companies signed a one-year moratorium against any sound movies, waiting to see which of the competing sound systems, if any, would finally prevail.

If the Warners were especially distressed by these developments, they didn't show it, except in Harry's fury at John Otterson for continuing to try to wrest Vitaphone from their control. Having bucked the conventional wisdom and staked their future on sound, they continued to produce sound shorts, featuring some of the biggest names in vaudeville. But as the momentum from *Don Juan* began to dissipate early in 1927, they also realized that what they really needed were more full-length Vitaphone films to showcase the system and reinvigorate the sound movement. Judging from the quality of the movies, this was less strategic than one might have thought. The second Vitaphone feature was an inconsequential comedy starring Charlie Chaplin's brother, Sydney. The third, an adaptation of the swashbuckling romance *Manon Lescaut*, starring John Barrymore again, seemed a better prospect. But the fourth, the one that would become a milestone in the history of motion pictures and would make the Warners one of the major forces in Hollywood, was a very unusual choice—one that, at first or even second or third blush, seemed a highly unlikely prospect for immortality. It was a Jewish drama.

The material on which the film was based had originated as a short story in *Everybody's Magazine* by a young Jewish writer named Samson Raphaelson and had come to the attention of the man called the greatest entertainer of his time: singer Al Jolson. Jolson felt that the story's conflict between an aged cantor and his young assimilated son who wanted to enter show business reflected the tensions in his own life. According to one account, he tried to interest D. W. Griffith in the material, and when Griffith refused on the grounds that the story was too "racial," he brought it to the attention of several studios—all of which rejected the story on the same grounds. Raphaelson apparently knew about none of this. When he and Jolson met at a nightclub about this time, Jolson told him he had read the story and now wanted it adapted as a musical revue. Raphaelson, who would later make a career writing witty, cynical comedies for director Ernst Lubitsch, objected and on his own initiative adapted it into a straight drama instead.

The Jazz Singer, as the play was titled, opened on Broadway on September 14, 1925, to generally tepid reviews. *The New York Times* called it a "shrewd and well-planned excursion into the theatre, concerned with a theme of obvious appeal, and assuredly so written that even the slowest of wits can understand it." But despite the unenthu-siastic critical response, the play picked up steam during the Jewish High Holidays and then glided along for a thirty-eight-week run that ended only because the play's star, George Jessel, had signed a con-tract with Warner Brothers. The day before the play closed, the Warners also secured the film rights for $50,000, presumably as a vehicle for Jessel.

Both signings—those of Jessel and *The Jazz Singer*—indicated something about Harry Warner's objectives. Jack claimed his brother "desperately" wanted the rights to *The Jazz Singer*. Jessel said he wasn't sure how desperate Harry was, only that Harry had told him "it would be a good picture to make for the sake of racial tolerance, if nothing else." But Jessel apparently didn't know that racial tolerance was one of the few causes that could really animate Harry. Other Jewish moguls shied away from their Judaism and hid it. Harry pa-raded it. One of the Warners' first features, *Your Best Friend*, was a soppy story of a Jewish mother who is spurned by her haughty gentile daughter-in-law until the girl discovers that her mother-in-law is the one who has been funding her own high living. Jessel, who was un-mistakably and proudly Jewish, was assigned a string of Jewish films; when he came out to California after *The Jazz Singer*, he was imme-diately cast in *Private Izzy Murphy*, about a young Jewish delicatessen owner in an Irish neighborhood who takes the name Murphy, falls in love with an Irish girl, goes off to war and becomes a hero, and then returns to confess that he is really Izzy Goldberg. His girl doesn't care and marries him anyway. Jessel followed this up with *Sailor Izzy Murphy* and *Ginsberg the Great*, which showed that the Warners certainly weren't doing anything to disguise the fact that Jessel was a Jew.

The irony that ate at Jessel for the rest of his life was that he never got to play the lead in the film version of *The Jazz Singer*, for which he had originally been signed. Jack Warner said that Jessel was as-signed the role—and the trade papers all announced that he would be starring—but when he learned that it was going to be a Vitaphone production, the star demanded $10,000 more. Jack said he quickly agreed, but Jessel demanded that Harry also approve the money. Here he badly miscalculated. The last thing Jack Warner wanted was to be held accountable to his brother. Jessel was dismissed. Years later Jessel would claim that his was less a squabble over money than over the script, which had totally revised and reversed the ending of the play. In the play, the Jewish entertainer forsakes show business and takes his father's place in the synagogue. In the film, he does not. Jessel saw this as a betrayal of the material and demanded that it be changed—a demand, he said, Jack Warner refused.

Probably neither story got at the real truth of Jessel's dismissal and his real problem—which may have been that he was too Jewish for the kind of assimilationist fable Jack Warner had in mind. Even though Harry had bought the material and had wanted to make the film, it was Jack and Sam who actually supervised the production out in California, and for them *The Jazz Singer* was less a plea for racial tolerance than a highly personal dramatization of the conflicts in their own lives and within their own family. Jack and Sam could never have identified with a strident professional Jew like Jessel, and it was almost inevitable, after searching vainly for a replacement, that they would ultimately cast a Jew as totally assimilated as they were.

Al Jolson, the phenomenally popular Broadway star who finally got the role, was not only an assimilated Jew; his own experiences so closely paralleled those of the play's protagonist, Jakie Rabinowitz, that he was practically playing himself. (In a sense he was. Raphael-son had been inspired to write the original story after seeing Jolson perform at the University of Illinois while Raphaelson was a student there.) Jolson's father was a Russian immigrant, an intransigent rabbi/cantor in Baltimore who abhorred his son's attraction to the secular world. "The chief difficulty in our home life," wrote Jolson's brother, Harry, "was that Al and I had been absorbed by American customs, American freedom of thought, and the American way of life. My father still dwelt in the consciousness of the strict, orthodox teachings and customs of the old world." It could have been Jack Warner speaking. Jack left home to join his brothers in the movies. Al Jolson left home to join a traveling show and later became a "jazz" singer—"jazz" being a loose term for any kind of up-tempo music.

The Jazz Singer opened on October 6, 1927, a date that would forever be engraved in motion picture history as the real beginning of the sound era. Even at the time, everyone seemed to recognize the stakes. Since *Don Juan*, the industry had been waiting for a confirmation, a sign that sound was part of the natural evolution of the movies and not just a short-lived novelty. Now here was one of the most popular entertainers in America giving his imprimatur to sound films, in what the Warner brothers themselves were confidently predicting would be "without a doubt the biggest stride since the birth of the industry."

The evening was brisk and clear, and the theater was filled with notables as it had been for *Don Juan* a little more than a year before. If they were waiting for an answer to the question of sound, they soon got it. Walter Wanger, a young Paramount executive by way of Oxford, raced into the lobby during intermission and called Jesse Lasky in California. "Jesse, this is a revolution!" The audience applauded wildly; according to *The New York Times*, it received the "biggest ovation in a theater since the introduction of Vitaphone." When Jolson strode to the stage afterward to be showered by the audience's plaudits, tears rolled down his cheeks. The next morning Zukor called about fifty Paramount executives to his Savoy-Plaza suite and demanded to know why *they* hadn't made a sound film. The same scene was being reenacted throughout the industry.

None of the Warners, however, was present for their greatest triumph. Sam Warner, who had guided *The Jazz Singer* through its production, had been ill since *Don Juan*, but the family had been reassured that it was just a stubborn sinus infection; after an operation to drain an abscess, he returned to work at the studio, becoming, in his brother Jack's words, "a slave driver for perfection." By the time *The Jazz Singer* was completed in August, Sam had clearly lost weight and spirit. Still, there was said to be no cause for concern. His young wife, actress/dancer Lina Basquette, continued to work, and arrangements proceeded for the premiere of *The Jazz Singer*.

Then one day Sam staggered on the set. When Jack urged that he go to the hospital, he went without protest. Doctors discovered that the old abscess had reappeared, and they operated once again. Within days the condition worsened. Albert left New York with two specialists. Harry left a few days later, but he missed his connection in Winslow, Arizona, and had to arrange with the Santa Fe Railroad to reroute him through Albuquerque. Racing the clock, he arrived in

Los Angeles at seven o'clock the next morning. Sam had died at three twenty-two; he was only thirty-nine years old.

The timing was eerie. The man most responsible for *The Jazz Singer* died one day before its premiere. He was buried on the eve of Yom Kippur; *The Jazz Singer* ends on Yom Kippur with Cantor Rabinowitz passing away and his son taking his place. But none of the brothers could quite take Sam's place. Sam was Jack's comrade in arms, his dearest friend and nearly inseparable companion. Jack had followed him to Pittsburgh, then to Norfolk, and later to Los Angeles. Sam was the one who held the balance of power in the fractious Warner family by managing to be Jack's ally without being Harry's enemy. His death would destabilize the tender truce between the family's factions and help unleash the bitter combat that would follow. The Warners would never be a family again.

———

As a historic milestone, *The Jazz Singer*'s significance was incontrovertible. It more than revivified the sound movement; by ad-libbing a few lines, Jolson had made it the first feature film with speech and introduced a whole new set of possibilities.* As a movie, however, it was decidedly less than monumental. "I had a simple, corny, well-felt little melodrama," said Raphaelson years later, "and they made an ill-felt, silly, maudlin, badly timed thing of it." Raphaelson was being kind. But even if it failed as drama, *The Jazz Singer* did something that was extremely rare in Hollywood: it provided an extraordinarily revealing window on the dilemmas of the Hollywood Jews generally and of the Warners specifically.

The plot of *The Jazz Singer* is simplicity itself. Cantor Rabinowitz, the seventh Rabinowitz to become a cantor and the patriarch of his Lower East Side congregation, assumes that his only son, Jakie, will follow the tradition. But Jakie would rather sneak off to the local saloon to entertain, and when his father catches him there and forbids him from ever setting foot there again, the boy runs away.

Don Juan, which might have rightfully claimed title as the first full-length sound movie, had only music and sound effects, no spoken words.

Years pass. Jakie Rabinowitz has become Jack Robin, a nightclub singer. But Jack is barely scraping by until a pretty chorus girl named Mary catches his act and later convinces a producer to sign him up for a new musical revue. Though Jack now returns home and is welcomed back by his mother, his father is unforgiving. The dilemma is set when Cantor Rabinowitz, apparently sagging under the weight of his broken heart, cannot sing the "Kol Nidre," the Jewish plea for forgiveness, on Yom Kippur, the Jewish day of atonement and the holiest of Jewish holidays. The congregation pressures Jack to stand in, but Jack's Broadway revue, its producers obviously insensitive to the Jewish audience, happens to be opening the same night. As the screenplay puts it, "Jack is besieged by the old life and the new, filial duty against his life's ambition, the past against the future."

What *The Jazz Singer* really examines is the relationship between these two lives and the difficulty of ever reconciling them—of becoming "at one." As the film characterizes them—Judaism identified with the desiccation and doom of the past; show business identified with the energy and excitement of the future—one wouldn't really *want* to reconcile them. Jack Warner never did. But *The Jazz Singer* acknowledges something that many of the Hollywood Jews themselves would acknowledge (though only privately, for fear it might seem to compromise their loyalty to America): Judaism somehow fructifies show business. It was one of the sources of their success in the movie industry and one of their advantages over the gentiles.

The movie defines this advantage as something like soul. "You sing jazz," says Jack Robin's girlfriend, Mary, "but it's different. There's a tear in it." "You must sing it with a sigh," he is advised by his father. Raphaelson himself likened it to the passion of prayer and wrote that jazz America "is praying with a fervor as intense as that of the America which goes sedately to church and synagogue," and "Jews are determining the nature and scope of jazz more than any other race." The inheritance of the Jews and their gift, the film seems to say, is that they inform what they do with their hearts and their pain. After centuries of persecution, Jews feel more. It is one of the things that distinguishes and exalts them, though even within the context of the movie Jack seems reluctant to broadcast this. He appears on stage, as Jolson himself did, in blackface—one minority disguised within another. It is his way of making his "soul" palatable to the gentiles.

Jack's quandary is that he can bring Judaism to show business, but he cannot bring show business to Judaism—which is to say that Judaism cannot be reinvigorated or revitalized in America or by America. It is alien to it. As Jack's mother says, "He has it [Jewish prayers] all in his head, but it is not in his heart," adding by way of explanation, "He is of America." In the end, Jakie/Jack can affect no resolution. His father won't let him be an American; America won't let him be a Jew. Caught between the old life and the new, he is like the Hollywood Jews, of both and of neither. In the play, Jack yields to Jakie and replaces his father on Yom Kippur. Of course, this surrender would never do for Jack Warner. In the film, Jack satisfies both masters. (This is what Jessel said disturbed him.) He begs off opening night, and his Broadway premiere is postponed while he sings the "Kol Nidre" in the synagogue.* Then, in an epilogue, he brings down a packed house singing "Mammy," one of Jolson's trademarks, while out in the audience his own mama beams approval.

How does Jack's (and the Jews') intractable problem suddenly get resolved? It is certainly not because Jack has found some way to navigate between these competing claims or because one has capitulated to the other, as Zukor and Mayer had surrendered their Judaism. The answer is that the movie, swiftly and painlessly, dissolves the problem altogether. Within the bounds of theatrical realism this could never happen, but the movies, after all, are a world of possibility where anything can happen, and of all the themes in *The Jazz Singer*, this might have been the most important and the most telling for the Hollywood Jews. The movies can redefine us. The movies can make us new. The movies can make us whole.

And that is precisely how the Hollywood Jews would use them.

Before *The Jazz Singer*, Hollywood waited. After *The Jazz Singer*, the rush to sound began. "Producers now realized it was a case of sink or swim," said one Western Electric sound engineer. The chief beneficiary

---

*Pointedly, the "Kol Nidre" is a song of renunciation. Its first lines are "All the vows that we made that were false to our faith and all the promises and oaths which once we swore shall be void now and forever more." In short, Jack sings his renunciation of the secular world.

was Western Electric itself, which provided the sound equipment and wired the theaters, but Warner Brothers, much to Otterson's consternation, still held a royalty agreement that paid off handsomely, and they still had a head start on every other studio. Less than a year after *The Jazz Singer*, Warners' stock, which had dipped back to $9 per share when the bloom was off *Don Juan*, climbed to $132. With Waddill Catchings's encouragement, Harry Warner now acted boldly. By 1930 he had increased the company's assets to $230 million, bankrolling part of the new investment with a $5 million personal loan.

Some of this went toward converting the Warners studios into a complete sound facility. More went toward securing theaters to show the movies and compete with the industry's giants. First, Harry bought the Stanley Company, which not only had 250 theaters but also held a one-third interest in First National, one of Hollywood's so-called Big Five. With this share he went after First National itself, buying another third outright and getting the final third from William Fox, who was conducting his own fire sale to cover his debts in the ill-fated takeover of MGM. By the time the dust had cleared, Harry had acquired over five hundred theaters and in the first six months of 1930 was averaging one new theater a day. He was also collecting record companies, radio stations, and foreign sound patents, and he was financing shows on Broadway. At the depth of the Depression, only MGM was as well diversified as Warners, and only MGM would weather the hard times as well.

But the success of the Warner Brothers company coincided with personal tragedy and dissension. Harry's twenty-two-year-old son, Lewis, was visiting Cuba in February 1932 when he contracted blood poisoning from infected gums. (This was not uncommon in the days before wholesale use of antibiotics.) Albert and Harry rushed from New York, as they had for Sam, and chartered a plane for Miami. From there they took the boy back to New York, but by this point the blood poisoning was beyond control and pneumonia had set in. For weeks he languished; on April 5 he died.

Harry's world was shattered. He had groomed Lewis, his only son, to take over the studio, as Laemmle had groomed Junior. For months he behaved erratically, calling upon Adolph Zukor at Zukor's office and then weeping for hours or awakening his daughter in the middle of the night and demanding that she accompany him to the Warners corporate headquarters. Once there he announced that she was going to take her brother's place and began inundating her with information about the industry.

Harry eventually regained his equilibrium, but neither he nor the Warners would ever be the same. Harry was now a patriarch without an heir. The studio was now a monarchy without a prince to assume power. Harry bore the loss; he never mentioned his son in public again. But in many respects it was Jack who took the heat. It was almost as if Harry regarded Jack, so many years younger than himself, as a mocking reminder of Lewis, and after Lewis's death the hostility intensified.

The Warners were to survive one more shock that year. With the Depression at high tide, David Selznick, Lewis Selznick's son and the son-in-law of Louis B. Mayer, had tried to withdraw funds from the Security First National Bank and claimed the bank had refused. Selznick promptly brought suit. The Warners' financial patron, Motley Flint, who ran the bank, was called to testify, and after he stepped down from the stand, he stopped to speak with David's mother. An irate realtor who had suffered losses in an investment scheme for which he blamed Flint, sprung up behind Mrs. Selznick, aimed a pistol directly at Flint's face, and fired. Flint died instantly. The assailant was later apprehended and convicted, but the Warners had lost their first and staunchest advocate, and Jack had lost another of his closest friends.

What finally split the Warner family, though, and brought Jack and Harry's mutual enmity into open warfare wasn't death; it was sex. In 1915, when he was twenty-three and running the Warners' exchange in San Francisco, Jack had met, romanced, and married a young woman named Irma Solomon. As had virtually all the Hollywood Jews, Jack married up. Irma was a cloistered *hochdeustche* Jew from an old San Francisco family, a variety that regarded itself as far removed from Eastern European Jews like the Warners as the WASPs were. The culture gap was evident as soon as Jack brought his teenage blond bride back to Youngstown to introduce her to the family. What she remembered was that Mrs. Warner spoke English so poorly that she was unintelligible and that the kosher food they prepared was inedible. The Warners were no more impressed by her. They called her the *shiksa*, Yiddish for "gentile."

Marriage certainly didn't trim Jack's sails for long, even after he and

Irma had a child. (Jack named him Jack M. Warner, which was consistent with German Jewish tradition but a contravention of Eastern European custom, where a child was never named for someone still living. It could only have been regarded as another of Jack's little digs at his father and brother.) Jack was a self-confessed womanizer, and with the power of his position he never lacked opportunities. As long as his father was in Youngstown and Harry in New York, Jack was accountable to no one. But in the late twenties Benjamin and Pearl Warner decided to retire to California. Their sons built them a small bungalow directly across the street from the studio, and Benjamin would visit the lot often, glowing with his newfound importance. He brought the same status to the religious community. He became a leading figure at Congregation Beth-El, a small synagogue that would claim to be Hollywood's first, and he even arranged with A. H. Giannini to retire the temple's $30,000 mortgage for $15,000. Warner gladly donated half and got other leaders in the congregation to pledge the second half. But a few days later he stormed into Jack's office, his face "distorted with fury." The other donors, he discovered, had billed the temple for interest on their loans. Jack recommended he resign. He did.

On Friday evenings Benjamin and Pearl Warner often invited their children to come observe the Sabbath with them. Even Jack frequently consented, though not without an ulterior motive. "I was his beard," remembered Milton Sperling, a young Warners executive at the time. "He was diddling on the side, and my purpose in being there [at the Sabbath dinner] was to confirm, not only from his mother and father but from an outside source, that that is where he was. But we would finish dinner and then Jack would excuse himself, and I would stay and play pinochle with his father. When he'd take off, he'd say, 'Remember, we were together tonight,'" in case his wife, Irma, should ask.

Not long afterward Jack dropped the pretense of faithfulness. This time he had fallen in love with the wife of a Valentino imitator named Don Alvarado, who had appeared in several Warner Brothers films. Ann Page Alvarado, a bit actress herself, was a remarkably beautiful woman: dark and slender with glistening black hair, large almond-shaped eyes, and the regal bearing of an Afghan hound. A Catholic from New Orleans, she was also as remote from a Jewess as one could possibly be. Jack, approaching forty, was infatuated. Even before her divorce from Alvarado was finalized in August 1932, he had already moved out of his house, and he and Ann were living together openly. Benjamin and Harry were indignant. No Warner had ever contemplated divorce.

Jack may have enjoyed provoking his father and brother, but there is little doubt that over the next two years he was subjected to unceasing pressure and abuse that must have taken its toll, even on so blithe a figure as he. Harry regularly excoriated him and called Ann a whore. His father tried reasserting his role as moral authority, lecturing him on his behavior. Nor was this a private war; everyone at the studio knew about it. Jack seemed unregenerate. Though his divorce hadn't yet been finalized, as early as 1933 he began plans to have his large Beverly Hills home entirely redecorated by William Haines, the toniest of Hollywood interior decorators, in anticipation of his marriage to Ann. But despite Jack's seeming indifference to the pressures, the wedding itself was delayed over a year and a half—largely, one must assume, in deference to the family. Then, in April 1935, Pearl Warner died after a brief illness, forcing another postponement. Several months later Benjamin returned to Youngstown to visit one of his daughters. While playing poker with a few of his old cronies, he suffered a stroke and passed away instantly.

If Harry had regarded himself as the family's leader even before his father's death, with Benjamin Warner's passing he assumed full command. "You are the oldest of my sons," he quoted his father as saying, "and it's your responsibility to keep your brothers together. As long as you stand together, you will be strong." Ironically, Harry took this injunction as further cause to goad and harass Jack. Jack responded to the death differently. Barely two months later he and Ann were finally married in New York. His one concession to his father's memory was that a rabbi officiated at the ceremony. By this time, however, the family breach was irreparable. Harry and the Warner sisters ostracized Ann, barely acknowledging her. Albert invited Jack and his new wife to visit him in Westchester and later in Miami Beach, but he pointedly refused to let Ann's maid stay in the servant's quarters—a refusal she regarded as a slight.

Jack's remarriage may have given the family quarrel new impetus and definition, but it was essentially the same old battle being fought once again: the young assimilated American Jew defying the authority of the past to establish the supremacy of the future. This, of course, wasn't just their battle. The Warners, split as they were between Harry and Jack, between obligations and aspirations, between the old and the new, between Judaism and America, were actually a kind of paradigm of the tensions of assimilation generally, just as *The Jazz Singer* was its clearest, most paradigmatic artistic expression.

But where almost every other one of the Hollywood Jews was engaged in an endless search for gentility and ultimately found himself defined by that search, the Warners, like their alter ego Jack Robin, really weren't attracted to that life. Even within Hollywood, where the genteel was often vulgarized, the Warners were regarded as antiintellectuals, and despite Harry's avowed desire to spread culture, none of them was cultured and none of them read. In fact, they seldom if ever even read film properties. When director Mervyn LeRoy, on his honeymoon after marrying Harry's daughter, saw everyone reading *Anthony Adverse*, he wired Jack to read it. "Read it?" Jack cabled back. "I can't even lift it." Or when Jack Jr. would return home from college and discuss with his father something he had learned, Jack would admonish, "Now, don't you go giving me that college talk," though Jack Jr. ascribed this less to antiintellectualism than to his father's sensitivity over his own lack of formal education.

Whether out of a grudging sense of inferiority or out of disdain, the Warners, then, were obviously energized by something other than the desire to appease and enter the establishment. They were energized by the very thing that tore them apart: the conflict between the old and new, between Judaism and America. For them, it was, as Isaiah Berlin once described it in a similar context, a tension that "sharpens the perceptions, and, like the grit which rubs against an oyster, causes suffering from which pearls of genius sometimes spring." There was no middle way—no possible rapprochement between Harry's suffocating authority and Jack's brazen defiance or between the provincial Judaic world and a new world without the old moral coordinates. For them, the only course was to continue the fight.

5

"I Don't Get Ulcers. I Give 'Em!"

He enjoyed playing Harry Cohn; he liked to be the biggest bug in the manure pile.

ELIA KAZAN

In the general run of humanity, people either give you a lift, or depress you; or bore you, or, as with most, leave you indifferent. But not Harry Cohn. Just his presence would make your hackles rise and your adrenals pump furiously. He annoyed and belittled—until he made you hate.

FRANK CAPRA

AT SOME POINT IN HIS LIFE, AP-parently very early, Harry Cohn declared war on the world, and he lived his entire life thereafter seeking vengeance for slights real or imagined. A case in point came shortly after World War II, when Cohn's personal assistant, William Graf, was reviewing applications for a receptionist's position. Graf told Cohn, "'I've got a man I'm just about to hire, but I thought I'd like to talk to you about it. . . . He's a nice fellow. He's young and he's a veteran from the war and he went to West Point.' He said, 'Hire him. Right away. Don't tell me any more.' I said, 'Why is that?' He said, 'I always wanted to go to West Point. Now, I'd like to say I *hired* a West Pointer.' And I've always remembered that, because what he was implying, to me at least, was, 'Look, I may not have gone to college, but I have gotten myself to the point where a West Pointer is coming to me for a job. Finally a retribution.'"

Among the indomitable forces of Hollywood, Cohn, bullying and contemptuous, was probably the most fearsome. "He put more people in the cemetery than all the rest of them combined," said one awe-struck observer. Like Adolph Zukor, Cohn luxuriated in power, and he exuded it. When he walked into a room, trailing the pungent scent of Carnival de Venise cologne, the effect was galvanic. "The eyes were dark and penetrating, the shoulders in the grey suit enor-mous, the smile was foreboding, ready to deliver an accolade or a crushing ultimatum," wrote one witness. "Nobody could fail to be unnerved by such concentration of personal power. The cigar pro-truded from behind the colored pocket handkerchief like a deadly weapon. If he reaches for it—duck! I thought." Cohn was fully con-scious of the effect; he was the grand eminence of Columbia Pictures, and he arrogated its power to himself the way a monarch arrogated divine right. When he suggested that director Rouben Mamoulian revise a scene in the film *Golden Boy,* Mamoulian protested. "Why? Give me one reason." Cohn said, "The reason is—I am the president of Columbia Pictures."

What he believed most devoutly was that power governed human affairs. In the early thirties, before it became impolitic to say so, Cohn had been an admirer of Italian dictator Benito Mussolini, re-leasing a documentary on his life and accepting an invitation to visit him in Rome. (It was said that what impressed him most was the story that Mussolini refused novocaine when he went to the dentist.) He was so taken by his host's imperial style that when he returned to Hollywood he had his own office redecorated to look like Mussolini's, right down to the blond, semicircular desk that surrounded him like some massive appendage; for years, even after the war, he openly displayed a photo of Mussolini there.

Yet this wasn't simply a tribute from one dictator to another; Cohn was adopting Mussolini's strategy. It was about a thirty-foot walk from the office door to Cohn's desk—a trek visitors called the Last Mile. "Why do you have the desk here—all that distance?" a friend, Co-lumbia executive Jonie Taps, once asked him. "He says, 'By the time they walk to my desk, they're beaten.' Do you hear the psychology? He knew the effect. They'd shit in their pants by the time they'd get there."

Adolph Zukor, the man who would be chiefly responsible for the rise of Paramount Pictures, in 1896 at age twenty-three, when he was still a furrier.

Friends, partners, and ultimately rivals: Adolph Zukor and Marcus Loew at Loew's Long Island estate.

Zukor and production associate Jesse L. Lasky survey the site of the new Paramount Studios in 1926. Zukor was the killer, Lasky the dreamer.
THE MUSEUM OF MODERN ART/FILM STILLS ARCHIVE

The founder of Universal Pictures, "Uncle" Carl Laemmle—the most uncharacteristic of the Hollywood moguls.
THE MUSEUM OF MODERN ART/
FILM STILLS ARCHIVE

Laemmle and his beloved son, Julius, renamed Carl, Jr., who inherited the studio on his twenty-first birthday.
THE MUSEUM OF MODERN ART/ FILM STILLS ARCHIVE

William Fox, the founder of Fox Pictures, with his daughters, Mona and Belle, in the garden of his estate at Woodmere, Long Island.
THE MUSEUM OF MODERN ART/FILM STILLS ARCHIVE

On location in 1919 at Big Bear, California, for his first major Hollywood feature, *In Old Kentucky*: Louis B. Mayer, Mrs. Mayer, director Marshall Neilan (whose flagrant womanizing infuriated Mayer), and star Anita Stewart.

The royal style: Mr. and Mrs. Louis B. Mayer outside his first studio on Mission Road in 1923, when B. P. Schulberg was subletting space. Mayer had designed it after the château of Chenonceaux.

Samuel "Roxy" Rothafel in 1925, when he was the leading movie theater impresario in America.
THE MUSEUM OF MODERN ART/FILM STILLS ARCHIVE

The Roxy, the Cathedral of Motion Pictures, shortly after its debut in 1926.

Nicholas Schenck, the power behind the throne at M-G-M.

Joseph Schenck, Nicholas's older brother, the most incorrigible of the Hollywood moguls and one of the best liked. The pose of intrigue suited him.

The Jazz Singer: Al Jolson caught between the old life, a temple *macher* (on the left), and the new, his girl Mary (on the right).

Jack Warner (on the left) with his first wife and brother Harry, Jack's nemesis, with Mrs. Harry Warner. Their attire reflected more fundamental differences.

THE MUSEUM OF MODERN ART/FILM STILLS ARCHIVE

Jack Warner with the second Mrs. Warner, Ann Alvarado, at Trocadero's in 1937. Their marriage widened the family breach.

THE MUSEUM OF MODERN ART/FILM STILLS ARCHIVE

One employee said an audience with Cohn made one feel "all of a sudden alone... wondering who's going to draw first." Usually it was Cohn, who delighted in disarming almost everyone with his shocking bluntness. Upon meeting the actress Kim Stanley for the first time, he immediately dressed down director Fred Zinnemann, who had made the introduction. "Why are you bringing me this girlie?" he said, ignoring Stanley. "She's not even pretty." Jack Lemmon remembered meeting Cohn and sticking out his hand for a handshake. Instead, Cohn smacked a riding crop on his desk. His very first words were, "The name's got to go." Cohn was worried that critics would call the young actor's films "lemons."

An invitation to Cohn's inner sanctum was regarded with dread, and one employee remembered that the first thing that came into his mind whenever Cohn demanded an appearance was, "I wonder what he wants me for? Did I do something that irritated him?" "They used to come up here trembling, absolutely trembling," said William Graf. "Even his own secretary, Duncan Cassell.... People like Eve Ettinger, who was the head of our story department, used to come down. 'What does he want me for?' I said, 'Just sit down and relax,' because I could see how emotional they were. If you were fearful of [losing] your job, he'd terrify you."

Cohn epitomized the profane, vulgar, cruel, rapacious, philandering mogul, and Red Skelton spoke for many when he said, after thousands attended Cohn's funeral, "Well, it only proves what they always say—give the public something they want to see, and they'll come out for it." But since Cohn was also shrewd and manipulative, there was usually a method behind his meanness. As Max Youngstein, a film executive who had many dealings with Cohn, explained, "To describe him with only those aspects of his character is to be so oversimplistic as to give you a picture that would carry maybe fifty percent of the truth but not a hell of a lot more."

To those who knew him well, Cohn was a master strategist, a Machiavellian who carefully gauged the effects of his behavior and seldom acted without anticipating the consequences. Being well liked was never very high on his list of priorities; in Cohn's view being popular was sissified. Being in full control and displaying it was, however. Cohn was consumed with establishing the pose of the tough guy, and though this may have seemed a very long way from the pose of gentility that most of the other Hollywood Jews tried to strike, its sources, at least, were similar. In Cohn, as in the other Hollywood Jews, class, lack of education, religion had all conspired to make a great hurt—the hurt of the outsider. But unlike the others, he was not by temperament an appeaser, playing by the rules of the establishment. His flagrant contempt and his cynicism were armaments of anger. By stripping down the dynamics of class into a kind of vicious Darwinism, Cohn obviously felt he was revealing the real rules in the game of power. While as an urban Jew he could never hope to win a contest of gentility, he could win this battle of naked aggression. He was better because he was tougher—better because he operated under no illusions.

"He rated writers and directors by their guts," wrote Frank Capra, Columbia's gutsiest and best director in the thirties, "on the raw theory that creators with mettle knew more about what they were doing than the gentle, sensitive kind. *He* might be unsure, but he wouldn't stand for uncertainty in his creative people." It was said that Cohn would berate a writer even before reading his script. If the writer admitted there were problems, Cohn went right for the jugular. If the writer protested, Cohn generally gave him his way. "[H]e was a man who believed in other people's convictions," said Academy Award–winning screenwriter Daniel Taradash,

> *but he made you prove you believed them. He would test you with innumerable negatives, innumerable questions, often apparently irrelevant, often maddeningly repetitive. He would lean back behind the desk, watching, absorbing the measure of your belief. If you hesitated even momentarily, he would also waver. But if you survived the ordeal, if you maintained a ratatatat equal to his, a moment would generally come when he'd hold up a hand. He would sigh as if in pity at your hardheadedness. Then he would say, "Go ahead."*

Cohn seemed to love a good tussle like this; tension was the catalyst in his distinctive artistic process. As writer Garson Kanin said, "He believed instinctively that it was only out of hostility, conflict, and abrasiveness that superior work could be created."

To maintain this truculent pose, Cohn had felt it necessary to banish his past, much the way Louis B. Mayer had, apparently seeing it as a possible chink in his facade of invincibility. Whatever demons lurked in his childhood, whatever abuses he suffered, he never said, even to his most intimate friends. His father was a German Jew who ran a tailor shop on New York's Upper East Side, specializing in police uniforms. What the family remembered is that when Police Commissioner Teddy Roosevelt would storm through the city during rain showers, rousting slacking policemen from their sanctuaries, Joseph Cohn's tailor shop was one of his regular stops. Harry's mother, Bella, was a Russian Jewess from the Pale of Settlement near the Polish border, and she was generally regarded as the family's moving spirit, drumming up business and collecting money for her less aggressive, more diffident husband. Harry adored her. A fiercely independent woman, she always lived according to her own lights, even after Harry had become successful. Despite his appeals, she never moved to California and never changed her life-style. She was happy in a modest apartment overlooking the George Washington Bridge, where she could watch the bustle.

Joseph and Bella had four sons: Max, Jack, Harry (born in 1891), and Nathan. Max, the eldest, was the only one who attended college and the only one who tried to maintain a distance from the film industry, but in the family he was also accounted the least successful. When his textile business failed, Harry gave him a minor job in the studio, and when Max's wife died, Harry brought his brother's two young daughters, Leonore and Judith, into his home to raise as his own—which was, no doubt, one part charity and one part revenge. Nathan, the youngest brother, was driven by few ambitions and was satisfied as Columbia's New York sales branch manager, but he was also the most intellectual of the Cohns, which meant that he kept his distance from his bullying older brother. Nathan's passion was art, and over the years he built an extraordinary collection of early Impressionist paintings. It was Jack, dough-faced, stoop-shouldered, bespectacled, and with a thin mustache that made him look like a Milquetoast, who became his brother's partner and most frequent target. For Harry, they were all guilty of the unpardonable cardinal sin—they were weak—though only Jack seemed unaware of this terminal condition and would have to pay for brooking Harry's authority.

Jack, however, had been the one who had introduced Harry to the movies. Quitting school at fourteen, as Harry would, Jack went to work for a New York advertising agency, where for six years he steadily advanced through the ranks. But he was taken by movies, and when Carl Laemmle formed his IMP production company, Jack left advertising and went to work in the lab collecting film stock and developing exposed film. At the time, 1909, IMP was a little ragtag company. Many of its films were shot in the back of a beer garden in Brooklyn and then rushed to the office on Fourteenth Street for processing in a cramped lab. "We only had a very limited number of racks to hang the films on to dry," remembered Jack. "After we used up the racks we would sit around for hours waiting for the film to dry before we could go ahead with more developing. We also sat around for days at a time waiting for raw stock." Still, Cohn turned out three thousand feet of film each day or roughly forty-five minutes' worth.

Within a few years Laemmle would beat the Edison Trust and, reincorporated as Universal, become one of the largest film producers in the country. Jack would become a relatively important part in the creative machine, inaugurating a Universal newsreel and then heading up the editing department. He was also learning lessons in economy with which he would later harass his brother at Columbia. As chief cutter it was Jack's job to broker between the tightfisted Laemmle and his employees, encouraging Universal directors to shoot more film, while at the same time assuring them that they were making only one-reelers. He would then, at Laemmle's instruction, cut the footage into two-reelers, though the directors and actors would only get paid for a one-reeler.

In 1913 one of these directors, George Loane Tucker, hatched the idea of making a film to exploit what had become a nationwide obsession with white slave traffic. Cohn, who as a child had joined the police at his father's shop when they launched their vice raids, loved the idea, but the $5,000 budget was prohibitively high for the economy-minded Universal, and Laemmle said no. So Cohn took the initiative. He conspired to make the film anyway, using company facilities, and rounded up three more Universal employees who, along with Tucker and Cohn, each agreed to kick in $1,000 to stand the costs if Laemmle, after seeing the completed picture, still refused to pay for it.

Tucker shot *Traffic in Souls*, as the picture was called, in between other assignments at the studio, while the administration was preoccupied with its own internecine quarrels between Laemmle and Pat Powers, the other major stockholder in Universal and Laemmle's nemesis. By the time the film was finished, Tucker had shot over ten reels of uncut footage, which none of the Universal executives knew about, but he had so rankled Mark Dintenfass, the temporary manager of the studio, on the pictures they *did* know about that Dintenfass fired him. That left Jack Cohn cutting the film covertly in his office at night. When he was finished a month later, he arranged a showing for Laemmle; but Laemmle, busy devising new attacks against Powers, talked throughout the screening and seemed unimpressed. Meanwhile Laemmle's rivals held him responsible for letting the picture get made at all.

At the next board meeting Laemmle, possibly to disarm his opponents, retaliated by offering to buy the picture for $10,000. Now the board, thinking that Laemmle might be trying to sew up a potential blockbuster for himself, countered with an offer of $25,000. *Traffic in Souls*, a seventy-five-minute melodrama about a rigid civic crusader who is actually running a den of white slavery behind the front of his International Purity and Reform League office, opened on November 24, 1913, and played to thirty thousand viewers in its first week. By the end of its run it had grossed $450,000, making it one of the most popular films of its time and providing a windfall for Universal—all because Jack Cohn had a fondness for the vice squad.

While Jack was learning how to squeeze nickels at Universal, Harry had embarked on a more picaresque career. A poor student, he quit school at fourteen and landed a spot as a boy singer in a Broadway play. When the play closed he took a job as a shipping clerk, but the world was full of tantalizing inducements for someone with Cohn's nerve and swagger, and he could never be slave to a time clock. Cohn, who was enigmatic about most of his youth, later bragged about fencing stolen furs and hustling pool at Bergman's Poolroom on 116th Street and Lenox Avenue. That wasn't all he hustled. In the early thirties, writers Philip Dunne and Preston Sturges formed a Thursday-night Hollywood bowling club, and Cohn, uncharacteristically, joined. "We caught on to the fact right away that Harry Cohn was a superb bowler, a *really* good bowler," remembered Dunne.

> So he told us the story himself that he and a partner used to work upstate New York and the Midwest. And their method was this: Harry would go into a town and bowl rather badly and then win a few games and make a few bets and then push the bets and bowl better and better and finally clean out the town.... Then he'd come to the alley one night and say, "Look here, fellows. I've got a confession to make. I'm a professional bowler, and I've conned you ... but I've kept a record and here's yours, Joe, and here's yours, Tom."
> He handed all the money back. He said, "I like this town and I'm thinking of opening some business here, and I'll settle down and be one of you." So then he'd stay for about a week and bowl with them and give them hints.... And then his partner would come to town. Well, his partner would go on the alley boasting and saying, "I can beat any son of a bitch in the world."
> So all the townspeople would say, "We've got the guy who can take it." Then the real bets would be made. Harry would lose, and he and his partner would move to the next town.

For roughly seven years, until he was twenty-one, Cohn sailed along this way, hustling and flimflamming; it was his real education. But however lucrative and gratifying these larcenous escapades might have been, he was still drawn to show business—possibly for the glamour, even more likely for the sex that usually came with being a performer. An exhibitionist by nature, he formed an act in 1912 singing with a popular neighborhood pianist named Harry Rubinstein. After five months playing in a local nickelodeon before the movies rolled, Cohn convinced Rubinstein to join him in Baltimore, where it would be easier to break in. As it turned out, it wasn't. After weeks of joblessness they dissolved the act and returned to New York. Rubinstein took a job playing for singing waiters at an inn out in the Bronx. Harry took a job as a trolley conductor on the line Rubinstein happened to ride. Whenever his old partner offered him the nickel fare, Harry routinely refused, saying he just wouldn't ring it up and making a gesture of derision at Rubinstein's softness for even trying to pay.

Cohn didn't stay a trolley conductor for long. According to his biographer, "The tolerant company expected conductors normally to pocket 15 percent of the fares. Young Cohn reversed the formula, allowing the company 15 percent." Instead, he got a job as a song plugger. A song plugger was hired by music publishers to sell, in the fullest sense of the word, songs to performers, who would then sing the songs in their acts, and to stores, which would then sell the sheet music. The sheet music was the publishers' profit center. The job required singing and selling in equal measure, and Harry had both the temperament and the looks, with his mesmerizing china-blue eyes and his curly hair. One of his biggest boasts was that, during this passage of his life, he had single-handedly made a hit out of "Ragtime Cowboy Joe." Years later Cohn would sing the song at every opportunity "with all the desperate energy of his younger self." "He [Ragtime Joe] taught me," Cohn would say, "that if you believe in something and you stick with it and with what you believe in, no son of a bitch around is doing to get ahead of you." As a kind of remembrance of this period, he had an oversized piano installed in his office, and he would tap out melodies with one finger as he beamed with satisfaction.

Yet song plugging didn't hold him long, either—he claimed because he couldn't stand working for someone else—and he complained that he was fired when an act of singing sisters he thought he had charmed failed to appear at the office the next day to hear some new songs. Nevertheless, Harry was a go-getter, and no doubt influenced by his older brother Jack, he sprang a new idea. Music publishers had generally plugged songs at movie theaters using song slides before the feature and conducting a singalong. Cohn thought that one could do a more effective job using movies instead of slides, and he set up an office to test his theory, cutting a short film of soldiers to fit the lyrics of a military song. Several music publishers placed orders for films of their own songs, and with Jack as his entrée, he sold the idea to Universal. Within a short time he was working for Universal himself, sent to the California studio as an administrative assistant.

By this time Jack, though only thirty, had worked for Laemmle for over a decade and was growing restless. Possibly because Laemmle was notoriously cheap, Jack began pondering the idea of starting a small film company of his own to produce shorts. Eventually he lured Joe Brandt to join him. Brandt, an attorney and Laemmle's executive secretary at Universal, had been Jack's friend since they'd worked at the advertising agency together. It isn't clear exactly how Harry became a partner, since he and Jack were less than cordial to one another even then, unless Jack realized that he needed someone with Hollywood connections. However it happened, in 1920 the three formed the C.B.C. Film Sales Company and set up New York offices in the same building as Universal. Their first efforts were a series of shorts called the Hall Room Boys, based on a comic strip about two bums who puncture the pretensions of high society; it was a subject obviously consonant with Harry's own iconoclasm. Their first capital was a $100,000 loan from A. H. Giannini, who would as a result become a revered figure, even to Harry.

Out in California, Cohn set up his offices in a little one-block enclave off Sunset Boulevard that had become known as Poverty Row because it housed dozens of fly-by-nighters trying to crash Hollywood. (Cohn actually shared his offices with another minor producer, Morris Schlank.) Poverty Row was the demimonde of production— ramshackle and chaotic. Frank Capra compared its jerry-built evolution to that of cigar boxes piled willy-nilly by playful children.

> [T]*wo sides were now three stories high; the third, two stories; the fourth, one and a half.*
>
> *Narrow halls, rising and falling with the uneven levels, tunneled through the maze; partitions honeycombed it into tiny "offices"; afterthoughts of exposed pipes for water, gas,*

and heat pierced the flimsy walls; crisscrossing electric wires
—inside and out—tied the jerry-built structure together to
keep it from blowing away. The last "crazy house" touches
were the comical stairways, interior and exterior. Some got
you places—others just got you.

For Mayer or Zukor, with their pretensions to respectability, this would have been intolerable. For Cohn, with his pretension to machismo, it was actually an invigorating environment in which to prove, once again, his jungle daring. Poverty Row was the Hollywood equivalent of the New York streets where one fended for oneself. It suited him. It suited his brusque, contentious style. On Poverty Row Cohn learned to work quickly and cheaply, pressuring his employees to get as much out of them as he could. It was an entirely different kind of satisfaction from that of a Mayer or Zukor—the rush of out-hustling and squeezing as opposed to the exhilaration of ascending.

At C.B.C—and later at Columbia—speed was of the essence. Director Howard Hawks remembered visiting his friend, Frank Capra, some years later at the studio. "Harry Cohn knew everybody who came into the studio.... So he asked me up to his office, and he said, 'I'm stuck for a story.' 'Who for?' 'Cary Grant and Jean Arthur.' 'Well,' I said, 'here's about ten pages of yellow paper that I scribbled down this morning.' And ... he looked it over and he came down to Capra's office. He said, 'When can you start?' 'Well, what do you mean?' 'We've got to have it going in a couple of weeks.'" And that's how Hawks's *Only Angels Have Wings* was born.

If Poverty Row was a fast-buck factory where artists weren't pampered and scripts weren't nurtured, it both attracted and required a certain kind of individual—the kind writer Dore Schary, in describing Cohn, called "bootleggers and icemen and butchers ... an easygoing, rough guy." In the early days at C.B.C., Cohn surrounded himself with precisely these sorts of men—other New York Jews who knew how to dish it out. Most likely no other sort of man could have stood working for him. "Needless to say, he was Jewish," wrote Frank Capra of Sam Briskin, the most important of Cohn's early lieutenants. "To stand the gaff on Poverty Row, you had to be Jewish—even if you were Italian." Briskin was fairly typical of Cohn's first henchmen. He had attended night school at the City College of New York, majoring in accounting. When he graduated, his older brother, Barney, who was also an accountant, clued him in to a position at a fledgling film company, C.B.C. In those early years Briskin helped take care of the payroll and arrange financing, but, as a kind of go-between for Jack and Harry, his duties expanded. Extremely ambitious himself, in 1924 he left to form a company of his own, called Banner Films. But he was back two years later, this time as general manager of the studio out in California.

While the major studios made certain to have a "creative" man in charge of production—Jesse Lasky and B. P. Schulberg at Paramount; former writer Darryl Zanuck at Warner Brothers; Irving Thalberg at MGM—it was apt for Harry Cohn to have an accountant, though not just because Cohn was more cost-conscious than most of the other Hollywood chieftans. Briskin, with his shock of wild hair and his thick glasses, may have looked soft and bookish like the New York accountant he was, but he was blunt and aggressive and not one to coddle his actors, writers, and directors the way the creative executives did. One writer, asking for a raise to two hundred dollars, remembered Briskin telling him in the best Cohn manner, "You're fired at the end of this term. When you come crawling back looking for work, you'll be glad to get a hundred."

Briskin had another important function at C.B.C. besides meting out Harry's punishments and absorbing his abuses. He was a one-man recruiting office. His brother Irving came to work as an executive, as did his brother-in-law, Abe Schneider, who had once delivered newspapers to the C.B.C. office and would later become president of Columbia Pictures. Schneider then brought in *his* brother-in-law, Leo Jaffe, another New York Jew. It was a formidable array of chutzpah, and it gave literal force to Capra's characterization of Poverty Row as a refuge for nervy and tenacious Jews who couldn't be bothered with the niceties of the creative process observed at many of the larger studios.

But for Cohn, at least, the role of hustler didn't end at the studio gate. It was a sign of how deeply ingrained it was in him that even his courtship became more a contest than a romance. The object of his desire was an incongruous choice for someone with Cohn's well-deserved reputation for womanizing. Rose Barker was hardly prepossessing. She was short, rather stocky, and unassuming—"very unlike Harry Cohn," recalled Sam Briskin's son Gerald. "Nothing rubbed off from him to her." Rose's sister Tillie was married to Max Winslow, a prominent New York music publisher, and Harry had met her back in the late teens when he was plugging songs. The relationship was casual. Harry moved to California to head up C.B.C. Rose married a wealthy attorney in New York. That was that.

Or so it seemed. Oddly, or perhaps not so oddly given Cohn's strange psyche, it was only after Rose had married that his ardor suddenly seemed to intensify—almost as if he had lost a contest in which he hadn't even been engaged. Part of this was almost certainly the fact that she had married an attorney; Cohn would always envy attorneys, and he made the law into one of his avocations, poring over casebooks and memorizing rulings. Part was probably that she had married "above" him. Both motives gave impetus to Cohn's Darwinistic tendencies, in which he would assert his superiority over his social betters, and when Cohn was set on something he was an extremely difficult man to resist. In 1923 he began to woo her, asking her to come out to California for a visit. With a friend as companion and beard, Rose eventually agreed. Handsome, brash, and charming when he wanted to be, he apparently dazzled her, though she returned home to her husband two weeks later as planned. According to Cohn's biographer, it was the traveling companion who finally confessed to Rose's husband that Rose had been seeing Cohn. The attorney, gracious in defeat, granted her a divorce and bestowed a healthy settlement on her—a good deal of which, everyone knew, was then pumped into Cohn's company after they married in 1923. A short time later—it was said because C.B.C. was often disparaged as "corned beef and cabbage"—Cohn reincorporated the company under a new name.

Henceforth, he would be the head of Columbia Pictures.

Like so many of the Jewish moguls themselves, Frank Capra was an immigrant. He had come to America from Sicily in 1903 when he was six years old. His family settled in Los Angeles, where he worked at a number of odd jobs to add to the family treasury. But Capra also had lofty ambitions. He graduated high school and then received an engineering degree from the Throop Institute (later renamed the California Institute of Technology). After serving briefly in the army during World War I, Capra couldn't find a job in engineering, so he knocked around the Southwest, conning and panhandling as Harry Cohn had done in the East and Midwest—"hopping freights, selling photos house to house, hustling poker, playing guitars." During one stretch, he sold a set of inspirational books door to door, tugging customers' heartstrings with a story of how he had been orphaned and was breaking his back picking rocks from a field when a solicitous bookbinder took pity on him and taught him the trade. Now he only wanted to place these books in the customer's home, so he could return to the bookbinder and make more.

Though he had no filmmaking experience whatsoever, he answered a San Francisco newspaper ad of a putative film company and convinced the head that he was actually a prominent director currently vacationing there. He got the assignment and made a short film adaptation of Rudyard Kipling's ballad "Fultah Fisher's Boarding House." Even though the film turned out reasonably well, he wasn't to direct another for four years. He resolved instead to learn everything he could about the business from the ground up. He worked in a small film lab, then prepared props, then edited, then wrote gags for silent comedies, and finally directed three films for Harry Langdon, a baby-faced comedian whom Capra described as a "man-child whose only ally was God" and whose fame in the mid-twenties nearly rivaled that of Chaplin, Buster Keaton, and Harold Lloyd. But Langdon jealously prized the credit for his success, and when Capra started getting recognition, the star abruptly fired him. In 1928, after directing a flop and beating the pavement, he went back to work for producer Mack Sennett writing gags.

Though this was obviously a demotion, Capra later confessed that it didn't seem like a reprieve when his agent called saying that Columbia Pictures wanted to see him. He had never heard of Columbia, and Sam Briskin admitted that it had never heard of him, either. Cohn had instructed him to call Capra because Capra's name was the first on an alphabetical listing of unemployed directors. Capra, who would always be audacious and independent, announced his terms: he wanted to write, direct, and produce his films for a flat fee of $1,000 per picture. Briskin practically choked and couldn't wait for Capra to make his demands directly to Cohn. Capra remembered his introduction to the man he would later call the Crude One.

"The room was so long I could barely see the other end," he wrote. "In the distant gloom I made out a balding, pugnacious man standing behind a large desk covered with phones and dictographs. Around the edge of a large chair with its back to us I caught a glimpse of two shapely crossed legs." When Briskin tried to make the introductions, Cohn snapped, "For crissake, Sam, will you get your ass outta here. I'm busy. Put 'em to work." Thus began one of the most extraordinary collaborations in the history of American film.

It is safe to say that no other studio was as dependent on a single artist as Columbia would be on Capra, and no other studio was built through a single talent the way Columbia was built through Capra's. It is equally safe to say that no other studio would have acceded to Capra's demands in 1928 to have total responsibility for his own films. Cohn and Capra had a strange, symbiotic relationship, and in it were the lineaments of almost every relationship Cohn would have. It began with hunch and impulse. Cohn was almost totally a hunch player; he prided himself on his instinct, even if everyone else at the studio disagreed and sometimes especially if they disagreed. In his own mind this was one of his gifts, and though it certainly wasn't unerring, it was surprisingly sharp. His hiring of Capra, a director of little experience and less renown, was purely instinct.

Next came the test—the psychological vise Cohn repeatedly applied to his employees to see if they were made of sterner stuff. Capra endured any number of these tests—short-changed in manpower and then dared to complain, thrown into a big picture already under production while the first director pleaded with Cohn not to replace him, pressured to complete pictures on tiny budgets. (If one needed evidence of Cohn as taskmaster, Capra made seven films in 1928, his first year.) Laemmle, Zukor, and Mayer wanted men of art. Cohn wanted men of steel, and though Capra might not have wanted to admit it, there was a lot of Harry Cohn in him, which is one of the reasons they managed to coexist as well as they did for as long as they did. Both had been street hustlers. Both were iron-willed and uncompromising. And if they were often like two immovable objects, it was this very obduracy that created a grudging mutual respect. Capra wasn't effete. Cohn called him "Dago" as a kind of compliment that he was one of the boys.

There was one other similarity, and it probably had as much to do with the direction of Columbia in the thirties as anything else. Both men desperately wanted the acknowledgment of Hollywood, the way Laemmle, Zukor, and Mayer wanted the acknowledgment of the eastern establishment. For all his protestations to the contrary and for all his disdain for the hoity-toity, Cohn was genuinely awed by the Hollywood elite and genuinely envied them, especially Louis B. Mayer. Mayer, as head of the largest and best studio, was a symbol of what power really meant in Hollywood, and Cohn regarded him as a kind of exemplar. There was nothing Cohn wanted more than to wrest some kind of concession from Mayer, to get Mayer in his debt, preferably by having a talent that MGM wanted. It became a fixation throughout the thirties—Cohn's proof of his own power.

For Capra, though the motive was the same, the object was different. He prized his independence too highly ever to want to work for Mayer or any of the other moguls for whom realpolitik counted for far less than it did with Cohn. What Capra wanted was an Oscar, the award given for achievement by the industry itself. The Oscar became Capra's grail. By his own admission, in the early thirties he began making films in the hope and expectation that he would be nominated—"a secret ambition that would soon aggravate into a manic obsession." It would be his reproof for the ups and downs, the retreats and the rebuffs in his career. It would also be a validation of having to work on Poverty Row.

Cohn's desire for power, which he rightly conflated with status, and Capra's desire for recognition dovetailed perfectly. "Cohn was determined to crash the feast of the majors," said Capra. "He used me as his battering ram. I used his ambition to get control of my films." It was another of those Hollywood alliances between outsiders. Nevertheless, Capra still had to demonstrate the talent to fulfill their ambitions. His first films for Columbia were a potpourri of melodramas, romances, comedies, and adventures, skillfully made and commercially successful, though one would have been hard put to find anything distinctively Capraesque about them. By 1929 he had graduated to "A" pictures, which at Columbia meant movies with budgets of roughly $150,000 (the average "B" picture was budgeted at roughly $50,000). This was as opposed to the budget of an "A" picture at a studio like Cohn's coveted MGM, where the bottom line sometimes exceeded $1 million.

Cohn obviously had other directors besides Capra, but none had Capra's brass or, ultimately, his talent, and after his string of successes Capra was routinely assigned the prestige projects, including Columbia's first talking picture. Curiously, like *The Jazz Singer*, which had propelled the sound era, it was a Jewish melodrama adapted from a Fannie Hurst story about an aggressive Jewish businessman who repudiates his roots, moves himself and his parents to Park Avenue, and then denies his father when the old man arrives one day, like a delivery boy, loaded down with packages. How and why Cohn chose this material is impossible to say. He was seldom forthcoming about his motives, and it may have simply been a matter of imitation—Cohn making *his Jazz Singer*.

But Cohn's *Jazz Singer*, called *The Younger Generation*, is different. This time, instead of working for a rapprochement, the mother sides with her son, scolding her peddler husband for his laziness and telling him that their son Morris "will be a businessman like you ain't." (Very likely this echoed the sentiments of Cohn's own mother.) This time show business isn't counterpoised against Judaism, since Morris's sister Birdie (played, incidentally, by Sam Warner's widow, Lina Basquette) is affianced to a songwriter and she is the one who upholds traditional old-world values. And this time the film ends not with some sudden, magical reversal reconciling the poles, but with Morris alone in what his sister calls his "cold Italian tomb," the striped shadows from the blinds falling over him like bars. Forsaking his family and his traditions for money and power, he is condemned —a prisoner of assimilation.

It is hard to believe that Harry Cohn endorsed any of this or that he ever felt the slightest stress over assimilation himself. If he did, he concealed it brilliantly. Though his mother was devoutly religious and though all the Cohn boys were bar mitzvahed, Harry promptly jetti-soned Judaism as he jettisoned anything he found disadvantageous. Years later, when he was approached for a contribution toward a Jew-ish relief fund, Cohn yelled, "Relief *for* the Jews! How about relief *from* the Jews? All the trouble in this world is caused by Jews and Irishmen." "Harry Cohn would have liked to escape being Jewish," said one longtime associate, Judge Lester Roth. "I worked for him for a period of time, and I think that if he could have come to California to produce pictures as a gentile—because he didn't look particularly Jewish—[he would have]. . . . I doubt if Harry ever went to a temple or a synagogue. I'm sure that Rose [who practiced Catholicism] didn't." Even on the holiest of Jewish holidays, Yom Kippur, Cohn would be at the studio—not out of ignorance, but from a kind of defiance.

Other Hollywood Jews effaced their Judaism as a means of being accepted. Cohn more than effaced it; he exhibited active contempt toward it, as if it were something repellent. Not that this was totally unheard of. There were a great many Jews who resented being branded as outsiders or being regarded as "soft," and they reacted against their Judaism aggressively the way Cohn did. For them it wasn't enough to deny the faith; they had to demonstrate their superi-ority over it, and this often took the form of a kind of Jewish anti-Se-mitism. Writer Garson Kanin remembered Cohn telling a joke about "two little Jews." Kanin's wife, actress Ruth Gordon, stormed out of the room. "She just doesn't like that kind of comedy," Kanin ex-plained to a puzzled Cohn. "What kind of comedy? Jew comedy?" asked Cohn. "I don't get it. She's not even Jewish." On another occa-sion, interviewing the screenwriter Lewis Meltzer, Cohn asked Meltzer what his ethnic origins were. "I'm an American and a Jew," answered Meltzer. "I like that," said Cohn. "American first."

Nominal attachment to Judaism seemed endemic to the entire Cohn clan. Jack's son Robert recalled a family scandal when Leonore and Judith, the two young nieces Harry had taken into his home and then raised as his own, decided to undergo plastic surgery to expunge what they saw as genetic vestiges of their Judaism. "I remember now as a kid what a stir it was. They both had their noses done by a fellow named Maltz, who was a very famous plastic surgeon. They had them done together at the same time. Then my middle brother changed his name, which was quite a dramatic moment at home. . . . He changed his name because he was going into the advertising business. And he had *his* nose done." It was all very much like *The Younger Generation*, only without the tragic denouement.

Still, assimilation itself had no particular allure for Cohn. His real pursuit was power—"to break into the elite inner circle of major studio Rajahs who had the production and distribution—and, in some cases also the exhibition—of films sewed up tight," as Capra put it. What made this especially difficult was that Cohn, unlike the other moguls who had broken into the movies in the teens, had entered an industry that was already reasonably stable and increasingly impenetrable. A small-timer by the standards of a Zukor or a Mayer, he had too little capital to acquire theaters as all the major film companies had, and in any case his brother and Joe Brandt back in New York were opposed to that policy. Cohn's only option—ironically, very much like the option that the earlier moguls originally exercised—was to demand recognition by dint of the films his studio made.

Needless to say, this was an extremely problematic course. To crack the inner circle, as Cohn so desperately wanted to do, meant making commercially successful pictures that were also good enough to earn him a certain envy from the so-called majors. For this he was almost entirely at the mercy of Capra. "He was frightened of Capra," claimed producer Pandro Berman, "because Capra was good and Cohn knew and he didn't dare interfere." Of course Capra was in the grip of his own status-mongering demons. His pace had slackened considerably after he made *The Younger Generation*; he was down to three pictures a year. But as the quality of the pictures and his own skill steadily improved, the studio's status did begin to rise—slowly. At least insiders knew who Capra was. In April 1931, with an adventure film by Capra called *Dirigible*, Cohn had his first opening at Grauman's Chinese Theater, where the majors premiered their big pictures. Less than two years later Capra's melodrama about miscegenation, *The Bitter Tea of General Yen*, was chosen to open Roxy's Radio City Music Hall, another significant milestone for the Poverty Row studio.

Capra, however, was distressed. He had made *Bitter Tea* to appeal to the arty tastes of the Academy of Motion Picture Arts and Sciences, which awarded the Oscars, but the film had failed to fetch a single nomination. Now he realized he was trapped in a paradox. Working at a Poverty Row studio proscribed him from being considered for an Oscar, yet getting an Oscar was the fastest, perhaps the only, way of elevating the studio's status—and his own. In an industry where evaluating quality was always a slippery thing, the Oscars were avidly pursued because they were about the only certification of value one had, and they had escalated from a casual dinner dance where winners were announced at the end of the evening to a fierce competition, where studios bullied their employees to vote in blocs for the company's nominees. The spoils were prestige, which, among the Hollywood Jews, was nearly everything. "[T]hey all talk about business, and they all talk about making a profit," recalled writer (and later executive) Dore Schary of his days at Columbia, "and they give you the usual cliché things about 'Look, I'm not interested in winning any Academy Awards. I don't want the New York critics, I don't care what they say as long as the people come.' They all give you that. But they are all beautifully comforted by good notices... and if they don't get the Academy Awards, they then say: 'What's happening around here?'"

Though Cohn might have pooh-poohed the Academy himself, hissing to Capra that "they only vote for that arty junk," the Oscar was a kind of totem for him, too—and more. If the strategy was to make quality films that compelled recognition, the surest recognition was the Oscar. But neither he nor Capra wanted to leave the Oscar to fate. Capra had actually mapped out a deliberate campaign to win acknowledgment—beginning with an attack on the Academy for neglecting the smaller studios like Columbia and browbeating the Academy leaders into issuing him an invitation to join their ranks; followed by another complaint, once inside, that the Academy was "unfair" to independent producers outside the major studios; and climaxed by Cohn's own howl of protest that the smaller studios were inadequately represented on the Academy's board of governors.

The plan worked even more felicitously than Capra had expected. *He* was appointed to the board, but this only set in motion another tactical assault to breach the enclave of important directors who made the initial nominations for the Oscars. "Two status-building maneuvers were open to me," Capra wrote. "One, to become an officer in the Academy—perhaps President—and preside over the world's most glamorous event, an Academy Award Banquet. The other—and more practical scheme—was to make a 'loan-out' picture at a major studio where I could meet and hobnob with the Brahmins. . . . " Conveniently, at about this time Louis B. Mayer began making overtures to Cohn to borrow Capra. Cohn naturally regarded this as a major coup and happily complied. Columbia finally had something that MGM wanted.

The arrangement turned out to be short-lived—Capra had a run-in with one of the MGM producers—but his politicking, not to mention his filmmaking, was having its effect. In 1933 *Lady for a Day*, a wistful comedy starring May Robson as an aged derelict who is rehabilitated for one day so she can impress the visiting daughter she sent to boarding school years before, was nominated for four Oscars—including one for Capra as best director. It made him the first directorial nominee from outside the club of major studios. Though Capra didn't win—neither did any of the other contenders from *Lady for a Day*—the nominations did confer legitimacy on Columbia. The next year, with *It Happened One Night*, the Oscars would confer power.

Like *The Jazz Singer*, *It Happened One Night* might have seemed an incongruous candidate to make a studio. Based on a short story Capra had read in the *Saturday Evening Post* about an heiress who goes on a bus ride with a bohemian painter, the script had been rejected by nearly half a dozen stars, and the studio brass, notwithstanding Capra's reputation, were urging him to scrap it. Only Cohn, the hunch player, sided with Capra, though Capra and screenwriter Robert Riskin were beginning to have their own doubts. Three events saved the project. First, Capra's friend, the screenwriter Myles Connolly, suggested they change the hero into a newspaper reporter and the heroine from a spoiled brat to a bored one. Both changes made the leads more sympathetic. Second, Mayer loaned out a young contract player at MGM, Clark Gable, as punishment for insubordination of one sort or another. (To be sent from MGM to Columbia was more than punishment; it was disgrace.) And third, Cohn acceded to Claudette Colbert's outrageous salary and schedule demands—demands to which she was sure no one could possibly agree.

It wouldn't have been accurate to say that Columbia was built solely on *It Happened One Night*; the studio produced a number of successful, inexpensive films that kept it afloat. But *It Happened One Night* was the film that brought Columbia and Capra the cachet that would hoist them out of Poverty Row. A brilliant comedy that set the standard for the comedies of the thirties, it became, in the words of one contemporary critic, "an absolutely gilt-edged source of reference for lowbrow and highbrow alike."

As reconstituted by Capra and Riskin, the plot involved a willful, snobbish rich girl (Colbert) who is affianced to a simpering aviator named King Wesley. When her father objects to the impending marriage and keeps her captive on his yacht, she jumps off, swims to shore, and buys a bus ticket for a trip from Miami to New York, where she'll rendezvous with her lover. But on the bus she meets a bibulous newspaper reporter (Gable) who is everything she is not: practical where she is careless, worldly wise where she is sheltered, down-to-earth where she is ethereal. He soon catches on that she is the missing heiress, and as a reporter he realizes he has a great story, so he agrees to accompany her. Of course, along the way she slowly begins to surrender her pretensions (in one of the most famous scenes in movie history, she hikes her skirt and sticks out her leg to stop a car for a ride), and the two grudgingly fall in love. But when he briefly abandons her to write the story and collect enough money so they can marry, she believes she has been deceived and proceeds with her marriage to Wesley. Only at the ceremony, in the nick of time, does she change her mind and run from the altar to her true love.

When it opened in February 1934, *It Happened One Night* became a national phenomenon. "Capra had already made a few pictures, his *Lady for a Day* and *The Bitter Tea of General Yen* being clearly recalled by a small but intense following," wrote critic Otis Ferguson in *The New Republic*. "What made him on this comedy was the public, which went back to *It Happened One Night*, and went back again. They talked it up, and it kept replaying dates all year and became an outstanding example of what the trade calls word-of-mouth build-up. It made history while the historians were asleep. The pay-off was that, while it was just a picture at the beginning of the year and was in only third place in the fall when five hundred national movie reviewers were rounded up in a *Film Daily* poll, it swept the field of awards by Christmas."

In large measure, the film's reception was attributable to Capra's brilliant execution; from his apprenticeship with Sennett and Langdon, he understood the rhythms of comedy better than any of his contemporaries. In some measure, however, it was also attributable to the film's theme—which bridged class divisions during the Depression and suggested that the rich had a good deal to learn from those in the trenches. It was a theme that Capra would sound again and again throughout the Depression in a string of successes: *Mr. Deeds Goes to Town, You Can't Take It with You, Mr. Smith Goes to Washington, Meet John Doe.* In all of these, Capra, a lapsed Catholic, propounded what one could have called a theology of comedy—a secularized displacement of Christ's tale in which a common-man hero, blessed with goodness and sense, overcomes obstacles, temptations, and even betrayals to redeem his own life and triumph. (In his most extraordinary film, *It's a Wonderful Life*, made in 1946, the hero actually attempts suicide and is "resurrected" by divine intervention.) If he was occasionally sentimental and overidealized the virtues of small-town Americans, Capra also created a powerful myth for the nation—one that would help sustain and define Americans for decades. "The ecumenical church of humanism," he called it. Others called it simply "being an American."

For all the balm this myth provided to a country divided by class and riddled with anxiety, it also had a very particular resonance at Columbia. Harry Cohn may not have recognized that Capra was Americanizing and democratizing the life of Christ in his films, but he certainly understood that Capra's "little men" fighting against and often converting entrenched powers had direct application to him. It was, after all, a description of his life in Hollywood, and significantly, only the Warner brothers, the other outsiders to come crashing into the Hollywood elite, demonstrated anywhere near the same sensitivity to the ordinary fellow. What Capra's heroes were doing, Cohn himself had been doing, and what others generally regarded as boorishness and discourtesy in Cohn, he saw as the pretension-piercing honesty of a Capra hero. He hated airs, in life and in the movies. He may have envied the power and status of Mayer, but he trusted and cultivated his own boorish unpretentiousness.

By the time *It Happened One Night* won its Oscars—an unprecedented sweep of Best Picture, Best Actor, Best Actress, Best Screenplay, and Best Director—the awards were almost anticlimactic. Opening the envelopes with the winners' names, humorist Irvin S. Cobb, the master of ceremonies, would shout, "You guessed it. It is something that—" "Happened one night!" the audience would answer in refrain. Cohn cleared a spot behind his desk for his statuette, which would stare down visitors like a sentinel. (All his Oscars would ultimately be stationed there.) He tore up Capra's contract and tendered him a new one, giving him $100,000 per picture and 25 percent of the profits. Like Capra's heroes, he had won. Harry Cohn now had to be reckoned with, and ironically, the vulgarian had done it the way the Hollywood Jews usually did it—with quality.

But the Capra saga didn't end there. Something galled Cohn. Despite Columbia's extraordinary success, very few credited him. He got the power, but not the glory. That went to Capra. Even a decade later the slight would enrage him. When he mentioned Capra's name to actress Shelley Winters, then a novice doing a screen test, she suddenly started. "Frank Capra? He's the one who made *It Happened One Night*, isn't he? I saw it ten times." Cohn fumed. "*I* made it. He just directed it, Shelley, don't you ever forget that the executive producer is the most important person on a picture. Never mind the director." But everyone *did* mind the director, even Cohn himself, and that is what exacerbated the hurt. For a lone operator who never wanted to be indebted to anyone—who even welshed on a boxing bet once because he claimed a fight-ending blow the referee had ruled a foul was actually a clean punch—the debt he owed Capra was intolerable. It meant that Capra had something on him, yet Capra had something on him because he was Cohn's bread and butter. Columbia practically sold its entire program of pictures on the basis that buying them all was the only way exhibitors would get Capra's movies.

Cohn was a superb psychologist who knew how to attack his adversaries' vulnerabilities. With his resentment building, he decided to strike Capra where it would hurt most—at his reputation. Capra had only gotten wind of the scheme while on vacation in England in 1937. Acquaintances were snickering over a new Jean Arthur film, behaving as if Capra had directed it, though Capra hadn't the slightest idea what they were talking about. What stung him is that when he disavowed any knowledge of the picture, the acquaintances said they didn't blame him; it was a clunker compared with *It Happened One Night* or *Mr. Deeds Goes to Town*. Determined to find out what was going on, Capra visited the Columbia offices in London and asked to see the press book used to publicize the film. There in bold letters he saw *If You Could Only Cook* directed by Frank Capra. Capra was incensed.

He continued his European tour, then went directly to Hollywood to confront Cohn, who tossed the whole thing aside, saying that someone in the New York office had come up with the idea as a way of charging exhibitors more for the picture, and if Capra were angry, they would cut him in for a piece. Capra fired back that he would never put his name on someone else's picture, regardless of the price. "Oh, price my ass," Capra quoted Cohn as saying. "What are you, the Pope or something? What about the price you've made Columbia pay? Full control of your pictures. Producer-director. Critics even write up that *Capra* is Columbia, instead of Cohn. So what the hell is wrong with playing ball with *me* a little? Is it a deal, or isn't it a deal?" Both understood the stakes. It was a showdown; whoever blinked first lost. Cohn was threatening Capra's authority. Capra, as expert at brinksmanship as Cohn, stood his ground. He threatened to sue unless Cohn tore up his contract. Cohn refused, invoking the sanctity of the contract, and Capra stormed out.

The legal proceedings dragged on for months. First there was a change in venue because Columbia was headquartered in New York, though suit had originally been brought in Los Angeles. Additional months passed as the charges were refiled in New York. Then there was a second dismissal on the grounds that the New York courts had no standing because the offense had actually occurred in England. Meanwhile Capra, an Academy Award–winning director, remained unemployed. No other studio would touch him.

This wasn't so unusual in Hollywood. Studio heads could be bitter rivals, scheming to gain advantage of one another, but there was a certain honor among them, even if it was bred out of self-interest. Balking stars and insolent directors would find themselves on a blacklist. Actress Loretta Young remembered being blackballed for nine months when she left Twentieth Century-Fox. "See, the studio heads would get together over a game of poker and say, 'Well, you're not interested in Loretta Young, are you?' and the other producer would say, 'I guess not if you say not.' When you were with a studio, you would get maybe four or five scripts coming in at a time. When you leave, *nothing*."

Cohn had obviously put out the word on Capra, and when the suit was dismissed in New York, he told everyone that his star director would now come crawling back, penitent, which is what Cohn had wanted all along. Hearing these vaunts through his collaborator, writer Robert Riskin, Capra raced out of his house, yelling at his children to keep their distance. Then he went to the nearby cliffs and hurled stones and driftwood into the ocean until he was exhausted. It was a scene Capra, consciously or not, would borrow for *It's a Wonderful Life*, when the villain, a sour, dictatorial magnate, tells the hero that *he'll* come crawling back. Weaving home, distraught and panicked, the hero turns on his family and destroys a model bridge he had been building. In *It's a Wonderful Life*, the hero then goes off and contemplates suicide by jumping off a bridge. In Capra's life, the episode had a different ending. He returned home, resolving never to surrender to Cohn. Instead, he promptly arranged to bring suit against him in England as he had in Los Angeles and New York.

Roughly six weeks later—on Armistice Day, appropriately enough—Cohn unexpectedly arrived at Capra's house in Malibu. Now, for the first time, he was contrite. He explained that Capra was almost certain to win the suit in England. As a result it was likely that exhibitors would demand refunds and refuse to book other Columbia pictures; that Columbia's executives in England would be fined and possibly imprisoned; and that Cohn himself would be ousted by irate stockholders. For all their sakes, would he drop the suit? Capra remained impassive. Then, according to Capra, Cohn exploded with what would be one of the most unusual tirades in his career. "You think this is easy for me, you goddam dago?" he shouted.

> *"Yes! I'm crying! I started Columbia with spit and wire and these fists, made one-reel comedies with no money to pay bills. I stole, cheated, beat people's brains out to build Co-*

lumbia; got known as a crude, loudmouth son-of-a-bitch.
But I built Columbia. Into a major studio. Yes, you helped.
But I picked you out of the gutter and backed you. Now you
wanna leave Columbia. It's dreck to you. Poverty Row. But
to me, goddam you, Columbia is—is—not just my love.
It's my baby, my life. I'd die without Columbia!"

It was a bravura performance, intended to soften Capra with the very sort of appeal a Capra hero might have used—his devotion and integrity. Whether Cohn was dissembling or not, not even Capra could tell, but the sentiment certainly seemed legitimate.

Capra relented, dropped the suit, and returned to Columbia. Two years and another Oscar later, to add to the ones he had won for *It Happened One Night* and *Mr. Deeds Goes to Town*, he fulfilled his contract and left Columbia to form his own independent production company. Harry Cohn sent a telegram. "You'll be back," it said. He wouldn't.

━━━━━━

By the mid-thirties, when Columbia joined the ranks of major studios, Harry Cohn knew he had an image to protect: that of the toughest, least cultivated man in Hollywood. "He enjoyed it," said his friend Jonie Taps. "He wanted to be known as a son of a bitch," and he admitted to Taps that "nobody likes me, but I want them to like you." "You could sense he liked to be considered the tough guy, the guy who was a ball breaker," said William Graf. Graf remembered an exchange between Cohn and a Columbia producer named Jules Schermer. Schermer had previewed a new film, and though Cohn had been unable to attend, several of the Columbia executives did, including a quiet vice president named Ben Kahane. Afterward Kahane recommended some cuts and changes. Schermer, feeling that his creative prerogatives had been usurped, tendered his resignation to Cohn. "Harry looked at him," recalled Graf. "He said, 'Jules, I heard you're quitting the studio because you couldn't get along with Ben Kahane.' And Jules said, 'That's right, Harry.' Cohn said, 'Let me give you a tip. If you go out there and try to get a job at another studio and say you had a fight with Ben Kahane, you won't get anywhere in town. Go out and tell them you had a fight with me, and they'll hire you in a minute.'"

Nevertheless, underneath the bravado there was a charitable spot in Cohn. In one case he arranged to have some rare medicine flown from New York to aid a dying writer who had once testified against him in a legal matter. When the writer lavished thanks, Cohn warned, "Don't tell anybody. I don't want to lose my reputation." When a group of influential California women approached him during World War II requesting that he contribute a portion of his pictures' receipts to a fund-raising effort of theirs, he declined, saying that the profits belonged to Columbia stockholders. Then he turned around and wrote them a $10,000 check from his personal funds.

At Christmas Cohn would sign bonus checks and then ritually grumble to his secretary that the holiday had become too commercialized. "So one time I took the checks in to him," remembered Dona Holloway, "and I said, 'Come on, Scrooge. Sign these checks.' . . . The next morning he came into the office and glared at me. So I went into his office and closed the door. He said, 'Don't you ever call me Scrooge again. I saw him last night on television, and he's a mean, ugly old man.' . . . He was dead serious. Apparently he was aware of the story but had never seen it. And when he saw Lionel Barrymore [as Scrooge], he really reacted."

Then there was Cohn's relationship to his black chauffeur, Henry Martin. When Henry retired, Cohn, out of loyalty, gave him permission to open a coffee stand on the studio lot. Later Sam Briskin, Cohn's head of production, admitted a family of refugees to open a stand of their own and the two proprietors, Henry and the refugees, soon found themselves fighting off the other's threats. Henry strode up to Cohn's office, where Harry assured him that "as long as I'm around here, nobody's going to take that stand away from you." A few years later Henry contracted Buerger's disease, a vascular condition in which clots obstruct the arteries and the veins, often necessitating amputation of the limbs. Cohn immediately assigned the studio physicians to the case. Before leaving for the hospital, Henry handed Graf a cigar box. It held all his savings, he said—$7,500—and he wanted all of it willed to Harry Cohn.

Sometimes, it seems, even Cohn himself had trouble distinguishing his kindness from his pose. One evening Gerald Briskin, Sam's son and a recent employee at Columbia, was dining with his parents at the Brown Derby restaurant in Hollywood—a hangout for movie people. Cohn happened to be in a nearby booth and shouted to Gerald, "I heard you're doing well and all. . . . Maybe you should have a raise." Briskin groped for words of appreciation. "The next day or the day after that," Briskin recalled, "I was out at the Columbia ranch and there was a phone call for me. . . . It was him. And I got on the phone and his first words were, 'What is this I heard that you're supposed to get a raise?'" I said, 'I don't recall saying anything. *You* said [something] at dinner the other night across the aisle.' . . . He said, 'I don't remember saying anything.' . . . And I don't know whether it was a put-on, really. It could be he was that kind of guy. Yet when I went to get married, he called me up to his office and gave me a [large] check as a wedding gift."

Part of Cohn's pose required an open hostility to culture; he once responded to an invitation to the ballet with an incredulous, "Watch those fags chase each other for three hours and not catch each other?" He just as certainly wanted others to believe, as Lester Roth said, that "he lived for bread alone." "He insisted he made pictures for one goal: money," wrote screenwriter Daniel Taradash. "He maintained defiance to Art. ('I wouldn't make *Peter Ibbetson* if they gave it to me for a quarter. Let Rembrandt make character studies, not Columbia.')"

But what belied his cultural philistinism, as his good deeds belied his apparent cruelty, was that Cohn legitimately admired men of intellect and refinement and, at some level, deeply regretted not being one of them. He was always forced to take his culture vicariously, increasingly hiring men of gentility. Some even believed that his truculence was really a defense mechanism against his lack of education and breeding. "I always felt that," admitted Dona Holloway, "because he reacted to people who were better educated than he. . . . He was sensitive to that. If, for instance, a writer or director would come in and use words with which he was not familiar, he would comment on it. 'Speak my language.' He'd say something like that." "That [his lack of education] was his biggest frustration," said Jonie Taps, who remembered Cohn reading the script of a swashbuckler and then tossing it down in disgust. "'How can you put this kind of language in a script?'" he asked the producer, Sam Bischoff. "'You use words like yesiree and nosiree.' Bischoff looks at him and says, 'Harry, that's "No, *sire*," "Yes, *sire*."' I'll never forget that. I fell right off the couch. But he just kept on—next page."

Writers, most of whom detested Cohn, worked on this sensitivity mercilessly. On one occasion Cohn got into an argument with writer Norman Krasna in the Columbia executive dining room. Krasna said, "'You're an illiterate bastard. You're so illiterate, I bet you can't even spell the name of your own company.' Cohn says, 'You mean I can't spell Columbia? What are you talking about?' Krasna says, 'I'll bet you a thousand dollars.'" Cohn took the bet and began spelling. "'C-O-L-O-M-B-I-A.' Somebody said, 'It's U.' He said, 'It is?' Krasna knew because Cohn had written him a letter once—a handwritten letter—saying, 'You're working for Colombia. Remember that.'"

The pathos, if one could admit any pathos in Cohn, was that he was, finally, a man divided—not between the man he was and the one he aspired to be, as Zukor had been, but between two disparate personae he felt he had to maintain. On the one hand he wanted to be the toughest, most brutal executive in Hollywood—the one they all feared. On the other hand he wanted to be regarded as a man of good taste and judgment—the one they all envied. Negotiating between these—the vulgarian and the patron—required an excruciating balancing act, and it was one apparently important enough for Cohn to perform, yet it took its toll. For a man of such expansive temperament, he seldom socialized and usually continued work at home in his bedroom until the early hours of the morning. "He called me one night about a quarter to three," recalled William Graf, "and obviously I was asleep. I said, 'Yes.' And the operator said, 'Mr. Cohn.' I said, 'Yes, Mr. Cohn.' He said, 'Now what did I call you about?' I said, 'I'm listening.' He said, 'I don't know what it is. I'll call you tomorrow morning.' That was very unusual, but it did happen."

He had few friends. He was wary of intimacy—wary of lowering his defenses to anyone. Once, during a labor strike, a minor producer at Columbia was griping about Cohn. A studio publicist named Whitney Bolton shot back, using Cohn's favorite phrase, "Who eats my bread, sings my song." Somehow Bolton's defense got back to Cohn, who summarily fired *him*, not the offending producer. "His last words to me were these exactly," remembered Bolton. "'If you stay here, every time I see you on a sound stage or in a studio street or at lunch in the executive dining room, I shall be acutely aware of my obligation to [you], and I don't want that obligation or discomfort. I'll help you night and day and with anyone in the film business to get another job—but you can't stay here. Thank you for defending me —and so long.'"

Professionally, at least, Cohn had good reason to be cautious. With his badgering management style, which infuriated practically every-one, he was an ideal target for a palace coup, and the rumblings of an impending revolution were constant. Keenly aware of all this, Cohn never knew whom he could trust, so he wound up trusting no one. His nephew, Robert, actually felt Cohn's bellicosity was a result of these threats, not a source. "I think, after a time, he became what he was because he had experiences that others have had where [you] put your faith in certain persons and then they would turn. I do know that his circle [of friends] was smaller and smaller. He would find a friend . . . and they would really lock in."

The threats against him originated in New York among the money men who resented Cohn's power and arrogance. For his part, Harry referred to the New York office as "they," as if it constituted a rival firm. In every film company there were bitter divisions between the coasts—between the men in the West who made the movies and those in the East who tallied the profits and losses, held the purse strings and ultimately the real power.* Neither side understood the other, and each chafed at its dependency on the other. But at Colum-bia the rivalry was particularly intense, hostile, and petty. Every pro-duction failure jeopardized Cohn—gave the New York office a possible reason to dismiss him. Every success was occasion for Cohn to vaunt, and it got so that many of the New Yorkers began secretly wishing for failures just so they could rid themselves of Harry.

What added fury to the conflict was that it wasn't just a matter of artistic temperaments clashing with financial ones, as it was at most

---

*Cohn was a major stockholder of Columbia, as Zukor was of Paramount, Laemmle of Universal, Mayer of MGM, and the Warners of Warner Brothers, but all were ultimately accountable to a board of directors in the East. Each of them served at the sufferance of the board, though in artistic matters it almost always deferred to its creative people.

studios when the coasts warred; like Warner Brothers, it was a matter of one sibling clashing with another. Jack Cohn, who had stayed behind in New York when Harry went out to Hollywood, was always regarded as the "nice" brother. He had a mild, softspoken manner and a ready laugh. Personally he could never have contended with Harry, and he knew it. He didn't have the fortitude. But Jack had the apparatus of the New York office behind him, and Harry knew that. So, through New York, Jack kept the pressure on his brother, constantly cajoling him at arm's length about expenses and grosses. Harry's revenge was to humiliate his brother.

"I saw Mr. Cohn do some things or say some things to his brother that I don't think he should have," said William Graf. Each day executives from each coast would gather around the telex machines to pass information. "Sometimes, when I would be doing the telex, he'd say, 'Get that son of a bitch away from the thing,' and I would type, 'Mr. Cohn wants Jack Cohn to leave the machine.' And he'd come in and read the telex and he'd say, 'Bill, I thought I told you to get that son of a bitch away from there.' I'd say, 'Mr. Cohn, you don't want to have them read that back there.' He'd say, 'You put down what I say.'"

Occasionally Jack would visit the studio, and then the fur would really fly. Harry would scream at him, while Jack shuddered silently. Sometimes it got so bad that afterward Jack's wife would call Harry, begging him to desist. "My mother was so concerned about it," said Jack's son Robert, "because she was concerned with my father's health, and she knew that after those sessions, he really felt it. And I know that a lot of times she pleaded with him to get out of it. He never could."

Jack learned instead to keep his distance, and after one particularly savage blowout he never visited Harry's office again. Still, Harry was rightfully suspicious of his brother's machinations. It wasn't just that no one from New York was to be trusted. No one who even socialized with Jack was to be trusted. "When I came to New York I used to play gin . . . and Jack Cohn always wanted to tag along," remembered Jonie Taps. "So he'd go and meet me at the hotel. I couldn't get rid of him. He said, 'I'm going to play gin with you.' . . . So, as we get into the lobby, [I hear] 'Paging Mr. Taps.' Long-distance call. It was Harry Cohn from California." After a brief argument over a business matter,

Taps snapped, "'I'll see you in two days, Harry.' 'Where are you going?' 'I'm going to play gin, and your brother is going with me.' That blew Harry up sky high. . . . He didn't want me to be so close to everybody in New York." On the other hand, if anyone else disparaged Jack, Harry would fly to his defense, reserving the right to make the assaults himself.

These internecine quarrels not only made him eternally vigilant, they also conveniently fit Harry's dark cynicism in which it was every man for himself. Years later, in the forties, Cohn was courting Daniel Fuchs, a novelist and screenwriter. Fuchs kept resisting Cohn's advances, turning down project after project. "He couldn't believe a writer would turn down an assignment just because the material was unsuitable," wrote Fuchs.

> *He thought there had to be a deeper, intricate motivation. He thought I was maneuvering. "Everybody that walks into this office is a prostitute," he said. "They don't come in here unless they're out for something. Everybody cares only for their self-interest. Here, I'll show you—I got it right here in my desk. . . ." He pulled the paper out. It was a garish act of betrayal by some close relative, a son or a brother. They had manipulated stock against him, had labored in an effort to push him out of his company. The betrayal had occurred many years ago, but he always kept the letter of dismissal with him—it was a comfort, he needed to believe that people were base and abject."*

For Cohn this was the gospel—the only verity. In a world based on self-interest and power, one had to be the most powerful. In a world where one lacked the advantages of class and education, one had to compensate with muscle and nerve. In a world of dissembling, one either had to dissemble better or be brutally honest. In a world of prostitutes, one had always to be the procurer.

Anything less would have been conceding defeat in his private war.

PART TWO

The Empire

6

In Their Image

Studios had faces then. They had their own style. They could bring you blindfolded into a movie house and you opened it and looked up and you knew. "Hey, this is an RKO picture. This is a Paramount picture. This is an MGM picture." They had a certain handwriting, like publishing houses.

BILLY WILDER

THIS IS HOW IT WORKED IN THE thirties. Each morning Jack Warner would rise at about nine o'clock and immediately head for the phone to talk to the production manager about the day's agenda. That done, he would then call his administrative assistant to review the mail and the Hollywood trade papers, which were culled and digested for him as they were for every major film executive. Over breakfast—usually half a grapefruit, two slices of toast, and a watered-down cup of coffee—he would scan synopses of scripts and books that the studio might be considering. Then he would repair to the shower. He would usually arrive at the lot, out in Burbank, at about noon, checking once again with the production manager and occasionally with the legal department if a deal for a star or property were pending.

At about one-thirty he would head for lunch in the Warner Brothers executive dining room, where he had installed a Swiss chef and a German maître d'. The general lunchtime conversation ran to small talk—usually gossip and horse racing tips. After lunch Jack would go to one of the studio's projection rooms to watch the unedited footage that had been shot the day before—"dailies," as they are called in the business. He watched all of it (practically all the moguls did), and it took the better part of the afternoon—two to three hours.

When he returned to his office, he would generally see visitors and petitioners and exchange information with the head of production, whose office was adjacent to his, though these weren't the only precincts where business was conducted. "I had some papers to deliver to [head of production] Darryl Zanuck," remembered production executive Milton Sperling, then an office boy at Warners, "and I went into his office and he was not behind the desk, but I heard voices from the next room. So I said he must be in with Warner. I walked into the alleyway between the two offices, and Warner was sitting on the toilet, taking a crap and pressing, and then I heard the plop, and Zanuck, who was talking to him, pulled the chain and continued talking."

After business Warner would customarily retire to the studio barber shop for his daily shave. Often he would fall asleep in the chair while the barber worked, and often he would follow this nap with a trip to the steam room, which was just off the executive dining area. (Warner was fastidious about health and fashion; a shirtmaker would come to the studio regularly, and Warner would buy thirty shirts at a crack. Everyone wondered what he did with them all.) He always returned from these sessions at the barber shop and steam room reinvigorated, ready for more meetings and conferences.

By the time these ended it was early evening, but the workday wasn't over yet. The studio brass, including Warner, would attend previews of their new films, usually in the outlying suburbs of Los Angeles and sometimes as far away as Santa Barbara, which was at least an hour's ride. During the screening, Jack, who had an uncanny memory for dailies he had seen three or four months earlier, would sit next to the editor making comments and suggestions. The editor would then write these down with a lighted pen on a clipboard so they could be transcribed and implemented. Jack was always the final authority. It was only after the preview, late in the evening, that Warner finally went home.

The others—Cohn, Mayer, Zukor—followed similar routines. The studio consumed. It consumed, however, not because the demands of the industry necessarily made it that way, but because the Hollywood Jews wanted it that way. They had cut their lives to the contours of their environment and discarded the rest, because only here were they in complete command. The studios were repositories of dreams and hopes, security and power. If one couldn't control the world of real power and influence, the august world of big business, finance, and politics, through the studio one could create a whole fictive universe that one *could* control. And that was exactly how the studio apparatus came to function. What gave each studio its distinctive personality was an elaborate calculus of economic circumstance, the location of its theaters, tradition, geography, and a hundred other things, but most of all it was a product of the personality of the man or men who owned and ran it. The moguls made the studios in their images to actualize their own dreams.

━━━━

"They had different kinds of ambitions and different methods of achieving them," said Viennese-born writer and director Billy Wilder, who came to Hollywood after working in the pre-Hitler German film industry. "Warner Brothers, let us say, was a little tougher on its writers. You had to clock in. Not at Paramount. Not at MGM. I came. I went. But Harry Warner would go around and kill the lights in the toilets because that's the kind of boss he was." Warners, which had suffered a series of economic tribulations before and after the introduction of sound, always played it tight. It had to. After its rapid expansion into theaters and its plunge into sound, the company found itself over $100 million in debt. Some stockholders, irate that the Warners had voted themselves 90,000 additional shares of stock at their 1928 board meeting, filed suits charging mismanagement and nepotism and demanded the company be put into receivership. Harry reacted by drastically cutting costs. "Listen, a picture, all it is is an expensive dream," he later told a reporter. "Well, it's just as easy to dream for $700,000 as for $1,500,000."

"MGM was a studio that spent," said Milton Sperling, a Warner Brothers executive at the time. "It was a studio of white telephones. Warners had black telephones," which was another way of saying that everything there was geared toward economy.* Eventually, however, the economizing itself began to contribute to a certain unmistakable

---

*This was literally true since Louis Mayer's office was decorated all in creams with white telephones on the desk.

style. Warners' pictures were blunt and tough and fast. Their mise-en-scène was flat and cold; their visual cadences were clipped. One producer remembered cutting individual frames of film from each scene to quicken the pace. (After seeing Frank Capra's *It Happened One Night*, and comparing its more leisurely rhythms to those of Warners' films, production executive Hal Wallis even fretted that "maybe we are cutting our pictures too fast and making them too snappy.")

It was also a style that was particularly appropriate for a certain kind of material—contemporary and urban—and those were the properties to which the studio gravitated both by temperament and necessity. "I remember distinctly being called in once," recalled another Warner writer, Jerry Wald, "and saying that we could not compete with Metro and their tremendous stable of stars, so we had to go after the stories, topical ones, not typical ones. The stories became the stars.... We used to say 't - t - t: timely, topical, and not typical'—that was our slogan.... We were all searching frantically, looking through papers for story ideas."

Warner Brothers did have stars of first magnitude, but they seldom conformed to the traditional Hollywood images of glamour and romance. Jimmy Cagney worked there, and Humphrey Bogart, Edward G. Robinson, Paul Muni, John Garfield, Bette Davis, and Joan Blondell. Only lithe, handsome Errol Flynn, who starred primarily in costume epics and swashbucklers like *Captain Blood*, *The Sea Hawk*, *The Charge of the Light Brigade*, and *The Adventures of Robin Hood*, could have qualified as a conventional romantic lead (his films were also the most conventional Warners made). The others were all decidedly smart and urban, small and explosive. Even the women were hard-bitten and cynical, and no one, not even Flynn, could possibly have been regarded as passive.* At Warner Brothers people acted; they weren't acted upon—which was precisely how Jack Warner thought of himself.

In part that was because Warners' actors were cut in the mold of Jack, or at least cut in the mold of how Jack idealized himself. They were his alter egos, acting out his own fantasies of power and suprem-

---

*This was even true of Warners' animation, which was famous for its fast, smart, cynical approach as epitomized by Bugs Bunny.

acy. Not for him the tall, elegant, aestheticized heroes of MGM or the continental swains of Paramount. Like Harry Cohn, Jack imagined himself in rebellion against the niceties and hypocrisies of the establishment, and that's what he projected on his actors and in his films. He was reflected, his son believed, "in some of Edward G. Robinson's characters—Rico in *Little Caesar*. 'This is the way it's going to be or—*bang*!' He didn't use a gun; he used to use other people. . . . I think he's reflected in Jimmy Cagney—the smart guy, the survivor, the tough little guy. I think that's a real thing. And Humphrey Bogart—the cynical onlooker who realizes that this happy guy here is agreeing with you now but is going to screw you."

It also worked reflexively. If stars were often chosen because they were idealizations of Jack, he assumed their dimensions as well. He even picked up their mannerisms—his soft-shoe shuffle; the habit he had of lighting a cigar and then twirling it; his constant smirk that recalled a knowing Robinson or Bogart. He ran the studio the same way, preemptively and cynically, as if he were an urban tough free of illusions. "He was the father. The power. The glory," wrote Bette Davis. "And he was in business to make money." Screenwriter Henry Ephron compared Warner's ego to that of "Louis B. Mayer of Metro, Harry Cohn of Columbia, and Darryl Zanuck of Fox," but he didn't nurture or pamper the way they, even Cohn, could and "[a]t times he was violent in his hatreds," as well as capricious in his exercise of power. Once, during his rounds on the lot, Jack heard a gateman singing and asked what he would rather be doing—singing or manning the studio gate. When the man said, "Sing," Jack snapped, "You're fired."

Employees at Warners were driven ruthlessly. James Cagney said, "[I]t seemed as if the Warner boys were confusing their actors with their racehorses. The pace was incredible. I think I did about six pictures in the first forty weeks." "Frequently we worked until three or four in the morning," he later wrote. "I'd look over and there'd be the director, Archie Mayo, sitting with his head thrown back, sawing away. He was tired; we were *all* tired. This kind of pressure the studio put on us because they wanted to get the thing done as cheaply as possible. At times, we started at nine in the morning and worked straight through to the next morning."

But as much as Jack might have wanted an autocracy, Warners was far from being one. On the one hand, by driving his employees as hard as he did, he had created an atmosphere of dissatisfaction. On the other hand, by hiring tough, uncompromising personalities, he had collected a group that was almost assured of mutiny. Everyone fought back. "I had to fight for everything at Warners," recalled actress Ann Sheridan. "From the casting director up to Jack Warner. Of course, at Warners everybody seemed to have to fight. Cagney and Davis. That's the only way it was done. A knock-down, drag-out fight. You didn't always win, but it let them know you were alive."

Most stars in the studio days were under long-term contracts, but the studios held all the cards. Contracts weren't guaranteed, and performers weren't paid for "down time," the weeks they weren't actually working on a picture; if they were deemed responsible for the lost time, the time missed was added to the length of the contract, which could in most cases be canceled at the studio's option. Moreover, very few stars had any approval over the material in which they would appear. With restrictive covenants like these, when stars felt mistreated their only recourse was to walk off the set, hoping that the disruption and subsequent costs would pressure the studio executives to compromise.

At Warner Brothers walkouts were part of the normal course of business. "I did an entire series of these walkouts over the years," wrote Cagney. "I walked out because I depended on the studio heads to keep their word on this, that, or the other promise. . . . I'd go back East and stay on my farm until we had some kind of understanding." Bette Davis, refusing to do another potboiler she had been assigned after winning an Oscar, fled to Europe to make pictures, but Warner filed a suit for breach of contract, won, and got an injunction. Olivia De Havilland tried the same thing and also failed.*

Harry Warner could be as stern and impulsive as Jack, and he had even less regard for talent. When, early in the Depression, his highly regarded young production head, Darryl Zanuck, balked at enforcing a 50 percent pay cut, Harry didn't hesitate. Hal Wallis, another young

---

*Years later, in 1945, Jack unilaterally extended De Havilland's contract for twenty-five weeks to compensate the studio for her numerous walkouts. De Havilland sued and won. It was the emancipation for contract stars.

production executive, was having dinner with Zanuck at the Brown Derby. "Suddenly, Harry Warner poked his head in the front door and motioned Darryl to come outside. Several diners looked up in astonishment." Zanuck followed him outside, and the two engaged in a shouting match. When Zanuck returned, he announced that he was leaving the studio. On another occasion, after Errol Flynn had made a large contract demand, Jack was expatiating in the executive dining room on the ingratitude of actors. Harry entered and derisively told him that they could always make another Errol Flynn and pointed to an attractive young producer. "Take this fellow here and we'll make him a new star and forget about these other temperamental actors." Jack countered that if the young man actually became a star, *he* would soon be making the same demands. Harry turned on the producer and said, "In that case—the hell with you."

For Harry Warner, ferocity came naturally. Jack wanted to seem tough, yet unlike Harry Cohn, whom he superficially resembled in many ways, he really didn't have the temperament to be a tyrant, nor did he elicit that kind of fear. His was a fake, and most of his employees knew it. "Jack was a frightened man," said Milton Sperling, who worked under him. "The typical Jack Warner story is that the man who had been his assistant and associate for forty years—he suddenly decided to fire him. And he didn't have the courage to do it. So he waited until his annual trip to the south of France, and he talked to this man, Steve Trilling, and he said, 'While I'm away I want this done and that done.' He left. When he was safely on the plane and in the air, the studio vice president in charge of finance came to Trilling's office and said, 'Steve, I don't know how to tell you this, but Warner told me to fire you as soon as he was out of the country.'... He was afraid he might have been punched out—that's what he said later. Jack was Byzantine. He was a conniver. Harry was a bull."

If the Trilling story was an example of Jack's weakness and insecurity, there were numerous other examples of his pettiness and self-aggrandizement. When Zanuck left the studio, Hal Wallis was appointed to replace him, but Wallis negotiated a contract giving him not only the authority to supervise production, but the right to produce several films himself under the Warners' aegis. One of these became the romantic wartime classic *Casablanca*, starring Humphrey Bogart as a disillusioned café owner nursing his amatory wounds in neutral Morocco and Ingrid Bergman as the woman he felt had once jilted him but who now reenters his life as the wife of a resistance leader. After *Casablanca* was announced as the Academy Award winner for Best Picture in 1943, Wallis naturally rose to accept, "when Jack ran to the stage ahead of me and took the award with a broad, flashing smile and a look of great satisfaction. I couldn't believe it was happening. . . . As the audience gasped, I tried to get out of the row of seats and into the aisle, but the entire Warner family sat blocking me. I had no alternative but to sit down again, humiliated and furious." Wallis was contractually obligated to continue at Warner Brothers, but he couldn't easily forget Jack's usurpation. When his contract expired he left the studio and later became a successful independent producer at Paramount.

Even this behavior, however, was probably less a reflection of Jack's egocentrism than of his fear. Like virtually all the Hollywood Jews, he was petrified lest someone take advantage of him, lest someone betray him. He once glued together the pages of a script, sent it to Harry Rapf, a production associate, and then called to find out how he liked it, though he was really calling to see if Rapf would lie about having read it. Another time he peremptorily cut off one of his oldest friends because he had heard a rumor that the man had bad-mouthed him. Though the man pleaded with Jack to let him present his side of the story, the remonstrations went for naught. The two never spoke again.

At Warner Brothers the siege mentality ran deep, and it didn't end with Jack. All their lives the Warners had been acutely aware of their status as outsiders, even within the relatively déclassé encampment of Hollywood and even after they had achieved success there. All their lives they felt they had had to fight—everyone from AT&T to Bette Davis to their own stockholders. "The fight has left its mark on the brothers," wrote one reporter as late as 1937. "They have not yet lowered their guard. They are neither in Hollywood nor of it." But unlike Harry Cohn, who sought to appease the Hollywood establishment artistically while maintaining his personal vituperation, the Warners could never quite make that separation; and since virtually everything in the studio was filtered through the scrim of Jack or

Harry's sensibility, a great deal of their suspicion and hostility ultimately surfaced in the Warner Brothers movies. It was one of the
things that made their films so distinctive.

In practice this meant that Warners' films, like the Warners themselves, were permeated with a vague underdog liberalism, and if their
films lacked refinement and glamour, they did have a conscience—
deliberately so. Even the Errol Flynn swashbucklers were cast in
terms of class conflict with Captain Blood or Robin Hood befriending
the weak and poor against the entrenched powers of privilege—a
displacement of what the Warners saw as their own situation within
Hollywood. In any case, Warner Brothers films seemed to have a
mission. "More and more is the realization growing that pictures can
and do play an all-important part in the cultural and educational
development of the world," Jack told a reporter. "I do not mean we
should strive for so-called intellectual films, but we should strive for
pictures that provide something more than a mere idle hour or two of
entertainment."

In this Jack was merely mouthing the sentiments of his brother
Harry, who served as the self-appointed conscience of the Warner
family. Largely because of his profound sensitivity to his own Judaism, Harry could be tirelessly and often tiresomely messianic about
racial and religious prejudice. (At one point, after attending the bar
mitzvah of Edward G. Robinson's son, Harry was so moved he convinced Robinson to let the studio film a reenactment and release it
along with films of Protestant and Catholic ceremonies as a special
Brotherhood Week presentation. But after a preview the elder Robinson began to worry that "stardom" would go to his son's head, and he
dissuaded Harry from releasing the picture.) One could see the messianism most palpably in the Warners' attacks on prejudice in the
brave antilynching film *They Won't Forget*, where a southern schoolteacher is falsely accused of rape, and in their biographical pictures,
many of which showed the contributions and victimization of Jews:
Disraeli, The Life of Emile Zola, Dr. Ehrlich's Magic Bullet.

But one could also see the conscience at work, if less palpably, in
dozens of films that embraced the losers and the loners, the prize-
fighters, meat packers, truck drivers, coal miners, cardsharps, gum-
shoes, racketeers, con artists, and the rest of what might have seemed

like the detritus of Depression America. These were Warners' heroes, and Warners' films demonstrated an unusual—unusual for Holly-wood—sympathy for these people and their plight—so much so that they became favorite targets for outraged moralists who attacked them not only for depicting antisocial behavior, but for seeming to condone it. Harry answered, "The motion picture presents right and wrong, as the Bible does. By showing both right and wrong, we teach the right."

This time it was Harry's turn to be disingenuous. Warners' films certainly weren't antisocial in the sense that religious tub-thumpers thought, but they were far more ambivalent toward traditional Ameri-can values than the films of any other studio, just as the Warners themselves were more ambivalent than the heads of any other studio. The energy with which their films throb is almost always accompa-nied by a dark shade of despair—in *I Am a Fugitive from a Chain Gang*, a Kafkaesque descent into a hell of southern prisons where a man unjustly accused of robbery discovers there will never be excul-pation or release; in *Four Daughters*, a family saga that introduced John Garfield as an embittered drifter who casts a pall of hopelessness over the lives he enters; in *The Roaring Twenties*, a gangster epic with Cagney as a war veteran who becomes a bootlegger because nothing else is available and then finds himself in the inexorable slide to death; in *The Charge of the Light Brigade* with its denouement of doom; in *Forty-Second Street*, a cheerless musical about a fallen im-presario who desperately rouses his talents for one last show; in the score of Bette Davis melodramas where romance is inevitably be-clouded by the gray billows of fate; and later in the Joan Crawford tearjerkers where fate lay waiting like a trap. All of this was personi-fied by the studio's leading director, Michael Curtiz, a moody, feral Hungarian whose slithering camera and dark frames were the visual equivalents of despair.

Out of this mix of energy, suspicion, gloom, iconoclasm, and liber-alism came not only a distinctive kind of film, but also a distinctive vision of America—particularly urban America. It was an environ-ment cruel and indifferent, one almost cosmologically adversarial, where a host of forces prevented one from easily attaining virtue. It was a world that daunted and dared—a world where one's only hope and only meaning lay not in higher morals, not in love, not in family, not in sacrifice, but in action leavened by a vague sense of honor. Warners' stars, more than those of any other studio, were defined by kinesis. They *move*, and through movement they invent themselves. In fact, one could almost say that in Warners' pictures—and in Cagney, Robinson, Bogart, Raft, Garfield, Flynn, Muni, Davis, and the others who populated them—heroism is action, at least when the action is informed by an understanding that it is all we have. Hence the speed.

This was, of course, a particularly apt vision for the under- and working classes of urban Depression America, who felt their own sense of betrayal, suspicion, and anxiety, and for many of them these films came to frame their experience. More, they came to form a powerful, enduring mythology of urban America with which dispossessed Americans, like dispossessed film executives, could identify and through which they could gain a kind of sustenance. Warner Brothers' films certainly didn't provide the security that Columbia's or MGM's did, that pervasive sense of American decency that served as a shield in times of distress. Warners' heroes are faintly disreputable and uprooted; they draw less on American traditions than on themselves. (Again, one thinks immediately of Cagney or Bogart.) But because they ennoble energy and because they are low born, cocky, and self-sufficient, they demonstrate what one can accomplish against all the odds and outside the traditions. They exalt the small rather than the outsized, the people at the margins rather than those at the center.

The Hollywood Jews would create other versions of America, bent to their own fantasies and needs, but it is fair to say that the Warners' version was the least assimilative. Reflecting the divisions within the family itself, what Warner Brothers' films acknowledged was that there were deep divisions—divisions of class, of roots, of style, of religion, of values. There was a difference between us and them, between the outsiders and the insiders. One might not have been able to move from the first to the second, as the Warners learned from their own experience, but one could, by mythologizing the qualities of the poor and the marginal, forge a community of energy and mount an artistic challenge to the insiders. Cagney, Bogart, Robinson, Davis, and the others were Harry and Jack's answer to being thrown out of Louis Mayer's party years ago when the Warners were upstarts and Mayer was Hollywood aristocracy. They were also the answer to millions of Americans who felt they had been thrown out of genteel America. For the thirties, at least, this group could live imaginatively in Warnerland among the smart, the tough, and the cynical.

In the studio pecking order, working at Columbia was even less desirable than working at Warners. Harry Cohn "ran Columbia like a private police state," according to one writer who toiled there. "He was tough, feared, ruthless and courageous, unbearably crude, profane, quirky, a hammer-headed power machine who held total financial and physical control over his self-made empire. . . . It was said that he would fire and blacklist a man for mentioning *verboten* subjects like death or disease in his private studio dining room. It was said he had listening devices on all sound stages and could tune in any conversation on the set, then boom over a loudspeaker if he heard anything that displeased him. It was said that every evening he personally toured his big studio, trying to catch anyone who might have left on a light." Writer Ring Lardner, Jr., recalled that at Warner Brothers Jack demanded a full measure of work even on Saturdays and had the gatekeeper monitor when employees arrived and departed. But "Columbia was the most extreme. Harry Cohn used to look out his window because it was a building with a kind of quadrangle with a court in the middle, and he could see in writers' offices. He'd call up a writer and say, 'I see you're not working.'"

When it came to talent, Cohn did enjoy courtship. He enjoyed wooing a star, a director, or a writer, and to certain creative people, particularly those who demonstrated intellect, he would be genuinely respectful. Once the relationship was consummated, he seemed to lose interest. "No sooner would he win you," said producer Pandro Berman, who experienced the process firsthand, "than he would lose respect for you—because, basically, I don't think he thought too highly of himself, and he thought that anybody who would come to work for him must not be very good. Louis B. Mayer was the exact opposite. He would do the same thing: get you over there. And when he got you, he prized you, because he thought you were very smart to come to work for him." Mayer adored his stars. Cohn, on the other hand, would say of a recalcitrant actress, "I can get a broad off the street. Fuck her."

In part Cohn's contempt was a clever assertion of power. If everyone was replaceable, even the stars, it meant that everyone was subservient to him. Yet, psychological components aside, Cohn's dictatorial style was more than a way of dramatizing who ran the ship. It was also, and primarily, a way of shaping his world. A studio was nothing if not a controlled environment in which one could mold the materials—scripts, sets, actors, and the like—to conform to one's own vision. It was an instrument to satisfy certain needs. Though filmmakers might have cringed to think of him that way, this meant that Cohn was, after his own fashion, an artist, too, forcing his will, his personality, and his sensibility on the studio and ultimately on its films the way any other artist willed himself on his materials. What made it seem more unruly and more mercenary than art was both the fact that the instrumentality, namely the studio, was an artistic product itself, an extension of the man who ran it, and that the man who ran it seemed to have a temperament far too coarse and unrefined to be called artistic. To some degree, however, this was an idea first promulgated and then perpetuated by the people who had to work under him—the writers, directors, and stars who felt Cohn was interfering with their vision rather than using them to establish one of his own.

Like Jack Warner, Cohn supervised virtually every aspect of his studio. "In the midst of a vital casting discussion," recalled screenwriter Daniel Taradash, "he would stop, flip an intercom key, demand to know whether the lights had been turned out by a certain director when he left his office. But his probing didn't stop at minutiae. He wanted to know everything, everything that was happening in his studio and in the others. If you spent an afternoon with him, with the Dictograph buzzing and the phones ringing and the teletypes ticking, the secretaries popping in and out, you were in attendance at the business of the entire town."

As the final authority, the maw through which everything passed, Cohn unmistakably set Columbia's agenda, though the tolerances for talent were somewhat greater and consequently the movies somewhat more diverse than at Warner Brothers. Overall one might have thought, given Cohn's experiences as a hustler and knockabout and given his revulsion at pretense, that Columbia's America might have closely resembled Warners'—combative, iconoclastic, vigorous. To some extent, it did. Through most of the thirties, Columbia's America was really Frank Capra's America. It was sturdy, resilient, decent, blessed with a kind of ingenuous wisdom best represented by Gary Cooper's Mr. Deeds or Jimmy Stewart's Mr. Smith. But for all that, it was an America that also countenanced corruption, mendacity, and manipulation at the very highest peaks of power.

Capra's villains were customarily ruthless industrialists exploiting the symbols of democracy for their own ends, and his films were always confrontations of values and sensibilities: rural against urban, the common against the rich and mighty, the innocent against the shrewd, the individual against the corporation, the traditional against the new. Capra's emotions may have often seemed primitive and his approach naively affirmative. His films, however, demonstrated how one had to wrest optimism from forces that everywhere endangered it. As one critic said, comparing Capra with the ostensibly more acidulous director Billy Wilder, Wilder was bilious on the outside, sugary on the inside; Capra was sugar on the outside, bilious on the inside.

How much of this was Capra and how much Cohn isn't open to dispute. Capra made the films. Still, the sensibilities jived, and through Cohn these values came to inform the studio's films the way the Warners' insecurity and rancor informed theirs. What one remembers most fondly of the Columbia of the thirties and early forties are the smart, usually astringent, and finally moral comedies: *The Awful Truth*, with Cary Grant splitting from wife Irene Dunne only to have them both realize that they belong together; *The More the Merrier*, with Jean Arthur sharing rooms with Joel McCrea and Charles Coburn in apartment-scarce wartime Washington; *The Talk of the Town*, starring Cary Grant again, this time as a small-town provocateur accused of arson who hides out at the country retreat of a distinguished jurist, played by Ronald Colman, and winds up humanizing Colman's view of the law; *Here Comes Mr. Jordan*, about a cloddish prizefighter who is mistakenly snatched away by an angel before his time has come and is temporarily placed in the vacated body of an overweening industrialist; and *His Girl Friday*, a brilliant reconstruction of Ben Hecht and Charles MacArthur's *The Front Page*, with Cary Grant as a fast-talking newspaper editor who bamboozles his ex-wife and former top reporter, Rosalind Russell, into covering an electrocution for old times' sake.

Taken together, these formed a moderately coherent populist America of sinister forces at the top pitched against decency at the bottom, though it was a less class-conscious configuration than that of Warner Brothers and a less embittered one as well. Even the bumpkins, the Stewarts and Coopers in the Capra films, were middle class, not working class, and no one was vaguely ethnic. Cohn's stars were cooler—Ronald Colman, Jean Arthur, Barbara Stanwyck, and Cary Grant, who, as one of the few free agents in Hollywood, shuttled regularly between RKO and Columbia. They inhabited a more homogenized stratum where houses were spacious, money plentiful, style abundant, values reasonably clear, and Jews absent. They weren't enacting an existential drama in which the world was metaphysically ominous, as it was at Warner Brothers. Columbia's world had its villains, namely those industrialists and demagogic politicians, but somehow they seemed more easily identifiable and conquerable, sometimes even convertible.

Columbia purveyed life partly as it was for Harry Cohn and partly as he wished it to be. On the one hand, Cohn the individualist, Cohn the populist, Cohn the keen-sighted debunker of pretension and duplicity. All of these Cohn thought he was. On the other hand, Cohn the verbal duelist, Cohn the rhetorician and philosopher, Cohn the moralist. All of these Cohn aspired to be to compensate for what he believed were deficiencies. (For a man who had difficulty expressing himself without expletives, his stars were among the most verbally dexterous in the movies.) In reimagining Depression America as a place of wit, resource, security, and basic values, then, he had also reimagined himself. At Columbia Harry Cohn could live vicariously through the screen—a new man. What was remarkable was that millions of Americans evidently shared the same thrill of revision.

At Paramount, at least for the better part of the twenties and into the early thirties when disaster struck, the pictures purred with the smooth hum of sophistication. It began with Paramount's president, Adolph Zukor. Ever since he had sponsored *Queen Elizabeth* with Sarah Bernhardt, Zukor had envisioned movies as a source of intellectual elevation, and he was so dedicated to this proposition that, according to one reporter, he was "surprised when anybody criticizes his gestures for improving the social tone of the cinema as publicity schemes." He established a school on the Paramount lot to teach young would-be performers decorum—an education that included classes in literature, sociology, and sobriety. He created a fund to reward those writers who best advanced the status of the motion picture. He enjoyed the company of novelists and playwrights and cultivated their friendship, becoming particularly close to James Barrie, the highly regarded dramatist and author of *Peter Pan*.

Every studio scoured Europe for new talent, but Zukor was especially zealous, bringing over, among others, Emil Jannings, the great German tragedian of *The Last Laugh* and *Variety*; Maurice Chevalier; Josef von Sternberg, a Viennese-born, New York–educated filmmaker who knocked about Europe and Hollywood before catching on with Paramount in 1926; and Marlene Dietrich, von Sternberg's German protégé and a middle-rank European star whose sultry daring made her a first-rank American star. He also managed to lure the brilliant German satirist and farceur, Ernst Lubitsch, from Warner Brothers, which never quite knew how to use him. Paramount even enticed Sergei Eisenstein, the Soviet D. W. Griffith, to Hollywood to adapt and direct Theodore Dreiser's *An American Tragedy*, but the changing political climate within Hollywood and the disarray within the company aborted the project, and Eisenstein left, gravely disappointed and hopelessly disillusioned.

Initiated by Zukor, the policy of sophistication was encouraged by his associates, chiefly Jesse Lasky, who headed the California studio while Zukor remained in New York. (To Zukor, with his acute sensitivity to caste, California would always be somewhat abject, a "factory," and Paramount continued to maintain a studio in New York's

Astoria long after the other companies had permanently decamped to the West.) Lasky may have lacked Zukor's arrogance, but he shared his artistic aspirations. "Lasky was a dreamer," said Adolph's son, Eugene. "He was as far removed from Wall Street and what was going on there as one could be. The world was a beautiful place in which to paint pictures. . . . He loved to be with writers and creators. And the money? So what! Even the budgeting—he said, 'Well, it's true it's too much, but it isn't too much if you get what you want for it.' His attitude was, it wasn't going into anyone's pocket. It was going toward a good purpose—a good objective."

"The greatest aspect of Jesse Lasky was his tremendous enthusiasm," remembered director Rouben Mamoulian, "the ease with which he liked stories and new people, and the enthusiasm he brought to it. He had an enormous quality of appreciating whatever he saw. I don't believe I ever put on a play that he had seen, or made a film, without getting a long wire from Jesse. You could always count on it. . . . I think that was his most valid contribution [at Paramount]—he was afire with enthusiasm for a great many projects and with appreciation for a lot of talented people. . . . That is quite a virtue. He had this more than some of the other pioneers because he was an idealist, and when he saw something beautiful, he gave you a tremendous reaction to it."

Heading up production under Lasky was a former newspaperman, screenwriter, and publicist from New York named Benjamin P. Schulberg. Schulberg didn't have the physical delicacy of Lasky; with his broad nose and wide mouth, he looked like a roughneck. But he had the same pretensions. His wife, a woman of considerable refinement, actually conducted a kind of salon for the children of several film executives, including those of Louis B. Mayer. Schulberg himself had an extensive library, and he would spend Sundays reading aloud from selected classics. "The trouble with your old man," the curmudgeonly writer Herman Mankiewicz once remarked to Schulberg's son, Budd, "is that he's read too goddamn many books. That can get you in a lot of trouble out here."

But not at Paramount—at least not in the late twenties and early thirties—when the studio basked in its own daring, discrimination, taste, and élan. "We were always trying to lift public taste a little bit," admitted Walter Wanger, a Paramount executive by way of Dartmouth and Oxford. "Zukor and Lasky were dedicated men who would produce pictures that they thought should be done, even though they weren't going to be profitable." As probably best typified by Lubitsch, whose sly, stylish comedies contrasted so vividly with Capra's open, homespun films, Paramount pictures were decidedly nonegalitarian. They didn't ennoble the audience; they whisked them away to a world of sheen and sex where people spoke in innuendo, acted with abandon, and doubted the rewards of virtue. Paramount's was a universe of Marlene Dietrich's smoky come-ons, of Chevalier's eyebrows arched in the boulevardier's worldliness, of Mae West's double entendres sliding out the corner of her mouth, of Gary Cooper's aestheticized handsomeness, and of the Marx Brothers' leveling chaos. Though Cary Grant later left for independence, he began there—his stylishness and savoir faire the quintessence of the studio Zukor built.

On artistic matters Zukor was never as intrusive an executive as Jack Warner or Harry Cohn, but as the man who approved contracts, read scripts, gave go-aheads, and vetted budgets, Zukor permeated his studio every bit as much as they permeated theirs. The modernity, the class, the dedication to quality—all of which had been part of Zukor's personal rehabilitation—surfaced in his movies as well. In the worldliness of Chevalier, there was the self-created Zukor, cagey and continental. In the boldness of Cooper there was Zukor, intrepid and unbeatable. In the one-upmanship of the Marx Brothers, there was Zukor, faster and smarter than his rivals. And in the heroes of Lubitsch, there was Zukor again, tonier and more sophisticated than the rest of the Hollywood Jews.

But as Zukor's life was rent by contradictions, so too were many of Paramount's films individually and the product of the studio as a whole. The studio of glossy sophistication was also the studio of grand patriotic spectacles like *Old Ironsides* and *The Covered Wagon*, which treated American history with the textbook reverence that Zukor felt toward his adopted country. The studio with visualist sensualists like Von Sternberg and Cecil B. De Mille, their cameras languid and caressing, also made the most popular of the biblical spectacles—many of them by De Mille himself, who wrapped moralism in sensualism, thereby mediating between the genteel and the Jazz Age much the way Zukor did. And the studio of Lubitsch's canny, glancing wit was also home to the Bob Hope-Bing Crosby "road" comedies, which, however funny they might have been, were neither canny nor glancing.

But deepest within Zukor was the old contradiction between his aspirations to respectability and the means it took to attain them, and this he turned into a strength of Paramount's, if only by being attracted to talent who embodied a resolution. What Lubitsch, Von Sternberg, De Mille, Dietrich, Grant, Mae West, and many of the others on the studio's roster all shared was the ability to combine sophistication with a certain hard-edged realism—the gentleman with the con artist, the civil with the steely, the genteel with the tough—just as Zukor himself had. "I love you as a crook. I worship you as a crook," declared the heroine of Lubitsch's *Trouble in Paradise* to her con artist boyfriend. "Steal, swindle, rob—but don't become one of those useless, good-for-nothing gigolos!" At Paramount, at least, one didn't have to choose between soft, idle respectability and realpolitik. At Paramount, the house that Zukor built, one could always have both.

Carl Laemmle, the oldest of the Hollywood Jews, hadn't fared especially well during the twenties. His studio, Universal, had slid from one of the most important, early in the decade, to an also-ran by the end, and Laemmle had to shoulder a good deal of the responsibility for the decline. Conservative, frugal, and distracted, he had, after pioneering the industry's struggle against Edison's Trust, trailed the other studios in virtually every advance and new economic configuration. While they invested heavily in theaters to provide a reliable market for their films, Universal made no acquisitions. While they cultivated stars as drawing cards, Laemmle lambasted rising salaries and inveighed against the star system as "a ruinous practice that has been responsible for high-priced but low-grade features that have weakened many exhibitors." (Bette Davis, who had worked there, said, "From the evidence they wanted us to fail. They did nothing to help us.") While other studios embraced the Jazz Age and enlarged their audience among the young, the urban, and the sophisticated, Universal, which had once given free rein to Erich von Stroheim, an Austrian Jew who posed as an aristocrat and specialized in sensual Ruritanian romances, now retreated from the risqué and suggestive. Its audience was largely rural, and its films were tailored to appeal to them. And while other studios rapidly converted to sound, Universal found itself a latecomer, in part because the rural theaters that showed its films were the last to be rewired.

By the late twenties and early thirties, Universal's pictures had neither the economy and speed of Warners', the screwball inventiveness of Columbia's, nor the continental sheen of Paramount's. If anything, the studio was best recognized for its Westerns, which constituted nearly a third of its output, and for its horror films, which actually constituted a very small percentage but remain Universal's most enduring legacy. In varying degrees, both of these took their inspiration from Laemmle. The Westerns harkened back to the dime novels he had devoured as a boy in Germany when he had imagined America as a vigorous landscape of cowboys and Indians, but they were also distinguished by the repetition of a rather unusual narrative archetype. In film after film—with titles like *Set Free*, *The Western Whirlwind*, *Clean Up Man*, and *Greased Lightning*—a seemingly shiftless cowpoke arrives in town and falls in love with a local girl. The girl, however, is already coveted by the town sharpie, often a banker or other magnate, who abducts her in an attempt to frame the cowpoke, forcing the cowpoke to rescue her. In the end, of course, the hero clears his name and wins the girl. Occasionally he also reveals himself to be something more than he appears to be—a detective or the scion of wealth. In short, the seeming failure turns out to be a success—a parable with direct application to Laemmle's own years of seeming failure.

Universal's horror films, the most famous of which were *Frankenstein*, *Dracula*, and *The Mummy*, also harkened back to Germany, and they bore the stylistic marks of the school of German Expressionism: the encroaching shadows, the skewed and rather overelaborated Gothic sets, the fixation on man's delicate relationship to Nature and Fate, and the general sense of the grotesque. Laemmle obviously cultivated this look in his films. Like Zukor, he regularly scouted and signed European talent on his yearly sojourns there, and the studio built a sizable stable of emigrés: directors Von Stroheim, Paul Leni, Paul Fejos, E. A. Dupont, and Edgar Ulmer; cinematographer and later director Karl Freund, who had been responsible for the distinctively gloomy style of many of the German Expressionist classics; actors Conrad Veidt and Rudolph and Joseph Schildkraut. In this Laemmle was clearly motivated by more than a personal preference for things German. Universal made almost half its profits in foreign markets, and in any case European talent contributed a certain luster to the images of the Hollywood Jews—gave them a certain cultural legitimacy.

Still, the films reflected the man. When stripped down to its basics, *Frankenstein*, adapted freely from Mary Shelley's novella, is a tale of the assertion of will—the quality Laemmle most celebrated in himself and the one to which he attributed his success. "Have you never wanted to do anything that was dangerous?" Dr. Frankenstein asks his mentor in defense of his ambition. "What should we be if nobody tried to find out what was beyond—have you never wanted to look beyond the clouds and the stars or to know what causes the trees to bend? And what changes darkness to light? But if you talk like that, people call you crazy." Then he adds significantly, "Well, if I could discover just one of those things, what eternity is, for example, I wouldn't care if they did think I was crazy." It could have been Laemmle speaking about his early tribulations, and when the monster that Dr. Frankenstein has created runs amok, and the doctor is punished for the hubris of arrogating God's work to himself, one got the sort of homiletic lesson in humility that Laemmle might have delivered against the Edison Trust.

Arrogance certainly wasn't the trouble at Universal in the thirties. Informality bordering on haphazardness was, and it contributed to a lack of clarity in the studio's image as well as to a breakdown in the studio system, which would ultimately wreck the studio itself. One writer described working at Universal in the thirties as "a mess. . . . They didn't have any management there to speak of." Another screenwriter, George Oppenheimer, remembered Laemmle calling his agent to arrange an appointment. "Papa [Laemmle] greeted me warmly and, since he looked in miniature and sounded in caricature like my maternal grandfather, I immediately felt at ease. My tranquillity increased as he launched into a panegyric of my qualities and qualifications. According to his honeyed words, he and Junior had combed Hollywood and found no one better suited to fill this position. On and on he went, extolling me and reiterating my suitability to the job." But when Oppenheimer interrupted to ask what the job was, Laemmle admitted he didn't yet know, but that Junior would call him. That was the last he heard from Senior or Junior.

Increasingly, Laemmle was surrounded by sycophants. "I think he was a very amiable sort of man who was very intuitive in his business attitudes," said Max Laemmle, his nephew and one-time Universal sales executive. "He was always surrounded by a lot of people whose opinions he looked to, and he was easily influenced by various people. Many felt that the last one always won out in influencing him. . . . He did look for opinions constantly. After a screening, he wanted to hear what you thought." But one learned generally to give him the response he expected, and when Max once criticized a film, Laemmle thundered, "How can you sell it if you don't like it?"

By far the most important factor in the management miasma at Universal was nepotism, especially after Junior Laemmle ascended to power. Not that nepotism wasn't everywhere in Hollywood; in some measure it was a defense mechanism for the Hollywood Jews to surround themselves with their own kin, and during the Depression, when the studio heads might have felt personally obligated to support their extended families, the studio payroll allowed them a way to fulfill their obligations without personal liability. Even so, nowhere was nepotism as rampant as at Universal, where by one count over seventy relatives, friends, and pensioners were on the payroll even during the depths of the Depression. "The place was so jammed with relatives," wrote one reporter, "that a producer would always say 'sir' to a janitor because the latter would probably turn out to be a second cousin of the big boss's wife's brother-in-law." "Most of them [relatives] were unable to do anything—you took them whether you liked them or not," recalled director and actor Erich von Stroheim. "Some were nice, others were arrogant bastards."

Industry insiders joked about Laemmle's blatant nepotism—"making the world safe for nephews," Jack Warner once quipped—but at Universal nepotism held powerful compensations for Laemmle, and after a time it, more than making movies, became his reason for running the studio. Movies had never really been the point anyway. Since his own string of setbacks in the days before he opened his first theater in Chicago, the point had been establishing proof of his own value and providing an inheritance for his family. While the other Hollywood Jews imposed themselves on their studios and their movies, using them as instruments of social aggression and mobility, Laemmle, having achieved both his goals, seemed to have lost interest. Universal's *lack* of direction by the early thirties reflected Laemmle's own indecision, indifference, and eclecticism.

So Universal foundered between its inexpensive horror pictures and expensive epics like *All Quiet on the Western Front* and *Showboat*, with which Junior, who did burn compulsively for status, tried to challenge Paramount and MGM. But Universal would never be as central to the creation of a national mythology as the other studios were. Unable to find itself, it never found America, either. For Laemmle, it was enough to pass the baton.

"From the time you were signed at MGM you just felt you were in God's hands," related actress Ann Rutherford. "Somebody was looking after you. . . . They cared about you." "Louis B. Mayer knew that the coin he dealt in was talent," director George Cukor told an interviewer. "He would husband it and be very patient and put up with a lot of nonsense if he really believed in it. . . . I think people don't understand how a place like MGM had to be fed, sustained, and organized every day. The organization was really wonderful. It was so convenient to work there, a marvelous research department that could tell you about the rights on a European property within forty-eight hours." Writer Leo Rosten said of MGM, "They had all the attributes of immense wealth and immense success, and their theory was different. The theory is that you cannot channel creative talent to order— that you have to create an atmosphere in which it will flourish."

In the thirties there was no question that Metro-Goldwyn-Mayer was the "Tiffany" of studios—the one to which most talent in Hollywood aspired and the one that paid the highest salaries and gave the most creative latitude. To a very large degree, Louis B. Mayer was responsible. Though he could be overbearing and reptilian, he was also obsessed with making *his* studio the best, and he had a very high regard for talent. "If anybody was good," said production executive Pandro Berman, "he wanted them." After producing a string of Fred Astaire-Ginger Rogers musicals, Berman had just signed a new five-year contract to head RKO when he received a call from Mayer. "'I want you to work for me.' And I said, 'Mr. Mayer, there's nobody in this business I'd rather work for. But unfortunately I just made a five-year deal and I'm tied up.' He said, 'Did I ask you *when?*' I said, 'No.' He said, 'When your deal is up, I want you to come work for me.' Now there wasn't any other man in Hollywood who would have been interested five minutes. . . . And when I left RKO five years later, that was the man I called and that was the man I went to work for."

Everything about MGM bespoke quality. Though it wasn't the largest studio in physical size—Universal City, over the Cahuenga Pass, occupied several hundred acres—it was easily the grandest, from its colonnaded facade on Washington Boulevard to its white sound stages and, later, its sleek, art deco administration building. One reporter observed, "In operation, the plant presents the appearance less of a factory than of a demented university with a campus made out of beaverboard and canvas." In the early thirties, during the worst of the Depression, its pictures' budgets averaged at least $150,000 more per film than any other studio. Even its commissary was regarded as the finest. (An executive named Al Lichtman once incurred the wrath of Loew's boss, Nick Schenck, when he told an interviewer, "MGM is the only place in the world where you can make $5,000 a week and free meals.") The whole atmosphere was one of composed confidence, and while at other studios the lunchtime conversation generally rang with pictures and profits, the executive dining room conversation at MGM never did. It was almost as if the producers there were above business.

They weren't, of course. Writer Ben Hecht complained that studio executives would support their creative decisions by taking writers to production manager Joe Cohn's office and "showing you their last picture had made a million dollars, therefore they knew what should go into a picture." This wasn't a common grievance, but there were others who found the milieu oppressively rarefied and resented being subsumed by the company. Actress Mary Astor said she always found it "a cold place. . . . I felt the producers to be remote in their heavily carpeted soundproof offices." "Here the slogan was not 'one man, one film,'" wrote director Frank Capra after Harry Cohn had loaned him out to MGM. "It was 'many films, many assembly lines.' A sign on [Vice President] Eddie Mannix's desk warned: 'The only star at MGM is Leo the Lion.'" Another director, William Wellman, recalled being ushered into Mayer's capacious office—"big enough to house a comfortable little cafe, to put wings on and fly first-class, to play badminton in." Mayer "didn't look up because he was concentrating on papers with rows of figures on them, profits and losses, but no scripts —the whole room was money. He said, 'sit down,' not in a particularly commanding tone, not a 'please-sit-down' or a 'be-with-you-in-a-minute' sit down, just an unusual 'sit down'; it had an uncomfortable ring to it." When Mayer complimented him for the speed with which he made pictures and offered to make him a "soldier" in MGM's army, Wellman said no thanks, got up, and walked out.

Hecht, Capra, and Wellman were all rather independent and cantankerous souls, and MGM wasn't the studio for free spirits like them. That's because Mayer never felt he was simply running an organization with hired hands; he felt he was raising a family in which he, of course, was the patriarch and his employees were the children, expected to obey and to work for the family's greater good rather than their own narrow interests. This may have made Mayer seem patronizing to some and high-handed to others, but those who accepted their roles loved him. "I don't think you can be a public figure and have everything kind said about you," MGM star Joan Crawford once recollected. "To me, L. B. Mayer was my father, my father confessor; the *best* friend I ever had. And I think most of us growing up at Metro can say the same things. I know Judy [Garland] would always go to him; Lana Turner would always to go him; every time we had a problem. And he never turned any of us down. Even if he was in a conference." Mayer, in turn, took them under his wing, directed their destinies. "They would chide you if you went out with someone that they deemed not good for your image," said Ann Rutherford. "Not good for your image meant dating a gentleman who was too old for you or someone who was living in an unsavory way or someone who was a lousy or unimportant actor. They were right."

It wasn't just stars Mayer groomed. He was just as solicitous of his lieutenants, even on the smallest of matters. Watching one eat an oversized corned-beef sandwich, he launched into a lecture on a proper diet. "You're ruining your stomach," he tut-tutted like a Jewish mother. "Have some boiled chicken instead." (Diet was a subject about which Mayer, with his delicate digestive system, was fanatical; on a trip to Italy with his family, he was so appalled by the Italian cuisine of pasta, veal, cheese, and wine that he dispatched his wife, Margaret, to find a kosher butcher for some "wholesome food.") On another occasion he took his daughters to a preview with the rest of the studio high command, including Irving Thalberg, the vice president in charge of production. "Dad came in the car," remembered Edith Mayer Goetz, "and Irving Thalberg was there and said, 'How did you children like it?' We said, 'We don't like it very much.'" Mayer was furious that they had been so impolite as to offend Thalberg, even though Mayer's own relationship with him was often acrimonious. In a family, one tried to spare another's feelings. "Don't ever say that to him," he scolded. "You have to be more tactful. After all, he created this thing." It was not counsel likely to be voiced by Jack Warner or Harry Cohn.

This concern was very much a component not only of *how* Mayer ran his studio, but of *why* he ran it. Where Warner and Cohn got their satisfaction from the surge of peremptory power, Mayer got his out of playing father to hundreds of employees—from top executives to studio technicians. "He was the kind of man whose door was always open at the studio," remarked producer/director Mervyn LeRoy, "and the little people on the lot often walked right in and began chatting away about his current projects."

Masterminding lives was obviously a powerful compensation for his own unsatisfying childhood, but the concern he demonstrated, though wholly genuine, also had a strategic benefit. It turned out to be a brilliant way to run a studio, engendering a strong sense of loyalty and care and community, if not to one another, then to the company. One never wanted to let down one's father, particularly when the father was as caring as Mayer and as generous. "My boy, I don't know why you want to make this picture," he once told Pandro Berman when Berman proposed *The Seventh Cross*. "I don't like it. I hate it." Berman argued, "Well, Mr. Mayer, I like it and I think there's a great picture in it. I can take Spencer Tracy. I can make it for a price. . . . I can make something fine—something you can be proud of." "I'll tell you, I think you're wrong. I hate it. But you're my man. You want it. You make it." And Berman, like a son, was then certain to try to justify Mayer's faith.

Like everything else at MGM, it was a management style that was predicated on having the resources to support it. Loew's Incorporated, MGM's parent company, had ridden out the Depression better than any of its rivals largely because it had been better situated going in. Most of its theater expansion had occurred prior to 1928, before increased competition sent prices skyrocketing, and in any case it held far fewer theaters than its rivals, preferring to concentrate on lavish, first-run houses in major metropolitan areas. (Paramount held nearly 1,600 theaters at its height; Loew's less than 200). Moreover, most of these were held separately, through locally financed corporations, so that Loew's had access to the theaters for its films and received a major portion of their profits but was not legally liable for possible defaults. Under this complex arrangement, the company turned a profit even in the worst years of the Depression and never failed to grant a dividend on its stock. It also managed to keep Wall Street from its boardroom. "As I understand it," Loew's president Nick Schenck told a Senate hearing in 1941, "a few years ago the bankers came there [to Hollywood] and went through the business and said we were all crazy—that they would do this and that. But that went on because they did not understand it. After all, it is just a business where you deal with brains and imagination and creative ability, and you cannot buy that from us."

What Schenck was acknowledging, though he often did so grudgingly and didn't fully understand it himself, was that Mayer and his top executives were accomplishing something mysterious and very nearly miraculous out in Culver City—at least by the cut-and-dried practices of most businesses. In an industry where the real capital was as intangible and unpredictable as talent, MGM had an astonishing run of success, almost from the moment Mayer took command in 1924. From here came dreams. From here came a world sometimes awesomely resplendent, sometimes movingly simple and naive— sprung from the fabrications and riven with the contradictions of Mayer's own life.

What most distinguished MGM's films was their general air of unreality. One writer who worked there said that Mayer "would have liked MGM to remain a Graustark or a Ruritania, a mythical kingdom that ignored realities," and this was certainly manifest in the studio's pictures. Mayer loved beauty as an aesthete did. He particularly believed, in accordance with his somewhat antiquated nineteenth-century view of women, in idealizing his female stars, and that became one of the benchmarks of the MGM look. Cameramen "had to photograph the movie queens and make them look damn good," said director George Cukor, whose specialty was women. "Louis B. Mayer was a great believer in his movie queens 'looking right.'" "Jules Dassin—then beginning as a director, treading carefully—once made a photographic study of his leading lady, shading her face with the flickering play of leaves," wrote screenwriter Daniel Fuchs, "and Mr. Mayer swiftly had him on the carpet for the shot, upbraiding him for the shadows, wanting nothing that would mar the clear, crystalline beauty of his company's stars. He lectured Jules severely on the point, so that Jules told me of the incident, startled by the older man's vehemence, by his notions, by his odd possessive insistence. It was a deep personal involvement with Mr. Mayer, a seemingly life and death concern."

Personal because what Mayer was playing out through his stars and their opulent romantic melodramas were his own fantasies of attractiveness and social mobility. He took these fantasies seriously, which is one reason why he took the movies seriously; watching the films, he was transported the way audiences were. At MGM the women were beautiful, elegant, smart, and yet coolly unapproachable. Greta Garbo, whom Mayer had discovered in Sweden as a plump young film actress and brought to Hollywood, was the quintessence of the Mayer woman: unspeakably divine with her large, languid eyes, her ascending cheekbones and brows, and her long, almost severe mouth, but for all her sensuality, she also seemed remote and rather pristine. (This may, in fact, have been one of the sources of her sensuality.) Other MGM women were more accessible than Garbo—Joan Crawford, Norma Shearer, Jean Harlow, Myrna Loy—but they were all similarly stylized, and one wasn't likely to find in them the nerve, sass, and fire one got at Warners or even Columbia. Here cool prevailed. It was equally true of the male stars. Clark Gable, Robert Taylor, William Powell, Walter Pidgeon, Melvyn Douglas—all were tall, stylish, and rather aestheticized. With the glaring exception of Spencer Tracy, these were men who didn't muss their suits.

But Mayer seemed to draw a sharp distinction between this cosmopolitan world of glamour and wealth, with its icy inhabitants and their amorphous morality, and the more domestic, though no less stylized, place he called America. If the first played out his fantasies of beauty, the second played out his fantasies of family and security, and if the first was best exemplified by Garbo and Gable, the second was probably best exemplified by Mickey Rooney starring in a series of films as Andy Hardy, an all-American teenager living in an all-American town with his sage father and his tolerant, loving mother.

"When you look at the Andy Hardy pictures," said Mayer's grandson Danny Selznick, "you think of a man who had a very strong morality—a kind of straitlaced morality. . . . These were pictures in which children learned from their parents. And that was a very strong reflection of Louis B. Mayer. Obviously the writers and producers on the lot, in order to get a picture made, must have known these kinds of things appealed to him and therefore kept bringing them forward." Mothers in particular were beatified at MGM, as Mayer beatified his own mother. Mary Astor complained that "Metro's mothers never did anything but mothering. They never had a thought in their heads except their children. They sacrificed everything; they were domineering or else the 'Eat up your spinach' type. Clucking like hens"—which was precisely how Mayer thought mothers ought to behave.

Some—most, perhaps—may have thought that Mayer was hopelessly naive in this vision of small-town America with its simple pieties and Norman Rockwell preciousness, but Mayer knew that he was confecting, not reflecting. According to his grandson, who attended many of the screenings with him, he saw these films "as artifacts of Americana and really saw them as shaping the taste of the country—consciously *hoped* that they would shape the taste of the country. The one part of life in Communist Russia he would have admired if he had stayed behind was the way in which art is forced to shape society. . . . He wanted values to be instilled in the country and knew how influential films could be and very much wanted to capitalize on it."

Like the glamorizing of his stars, Mayer took this mission seriously—sometimes to comical effect. "We were writing a script for Lubitsch called *Ninotchka*," Billy Wilder recalled, "and the windows gave onto a little bridge which connects this old building with the new Thalberg Building. We looked out the window because there was screaming going on, and Louis B. Mayer held Mickey Rooney by the lapel. He says, 'You're Andy Hardy! You're the United States! You're the Stars and Stripes. Behave yourself! You're a symbol!'"

Probably because he took them so personally, because they were so very much a product of his own needs and desires, Mayer would watch MGM's movies with the most profound joy. "I would sit next to him at sneak preview after sneak preview," recalled Danny Selznick.

> He had that quality of somebody who knows what's going to happen: "Now, watch this—yes!" He was watching the audience for confirmation of his own taste. "I thought they'd like a [musical] number about so-forth-and-so-on. Let's watch and see if they do because I have this hunch. . . ." His total success was, of course, not just shaping American tastes, but being able to anticipate them. He adored movies with a relish that, I suspect, may have been unique. I mean, I wonder whether Jack Warner or Harry Cohn loved movies the way Mayer loved movies. You talk about people who love restaurants or love eating—the incredible relish with which they anticipate each dish on the menu, the rel-

ish taken in each bite. [That was] the incredible pleasure he took in the movies he'd made.

What may have seemed incongruous for someone so passionately devoted to popular culture was that Mayer was just as passionate about high culture, and he had never abandoned the role he had assumed back in Haverhill as a purveyor of the fine arts. While he loved leading the MGM contingent out of the Hollywood Bowl to a Sousa march, his face glowing with a wide grin and his arms pumping, he also attended the annual recitals by Heifetz and Rubinstein. He regularly attended the ballet and opera, as Zukor had in New York, and gained a considerable knowledge of both. In his house a large Capehart phonograph wafted classical music (the Russian Romantics were, as one might have suspected, his favorites), and he would play certain records again and again and again, answering his family's complaints with "If you love it, you love it." When his grandchildren were barely school age, he bought them records of *La Bohème*, *Aida*, and *Carmen*, bragging to studio executives that the boys could already differentiate one from another. And it was he who brought opera stars Grace Moore, Lauritz Melchior, and, later, Mario Lanza to the screen.

Mayer's penchant for cultured people was so pronounced that the waggish writer Charles MacArthur devised an elaborate practical joke to exploit it. MacArthur and his wife, actress Helen Hayes, were playing tennis one afternoon when MGM publicist Howard Dietz dragooned a young English accountant for doubles. MacArthur promptly dubbed him "I. C. Nelson" and the next day began spreading his name around the lot as "the English theater genius." As MacArthur anticipated, Ida Koverman, Mayer's assistant, called to request that Nelson join Mayer for lunch. MacArthur coached the accountant to say only, "I came over to escape the fog and rain." Impressed by this studied detachment, Mayer offered the Englishman a $1,000-per-week contract to produce films. He accepted with alacrity, this time following MacArthur's advice to return every script, saying, "It's not up my street" or "It's not up my alley."

The joke revealed something important about Mayer. Of all the disparagements he would suffer, he most bitterly resented being regarded as venal and uncultured, and over the years he boiled at the injustice of being denied credit for MGM's loftiness, as he usually was; in Hollywood, after all, it was difficult to reconcile an Eastern European Jew, uneducated and unsophisticated, with the high-blown ambitions and pretensions of MGM. He was looked upon as the administrator and the money man. The credit for the studio's sublimity would always go elsewhere. It was the pretender, as Mayer saw him, who would become the legend. Mayer would be the fool.

———

He was the prince of Hollywood. "He darted in and out of the role of 'one of the boys' with dexterity," said Cecilia Brady of his alter ego in F. Scott Fitzgerald's *The Last Tycoon*, "but on the whole I should say he wasn't one of them. But he knew how to shut up, how to draw into the background, how to listen. From where he stood (and though he was not a tall man, it always seemed high up) he watched the multitudinous practicalities of his world like a proud young shepherd to whom night and day have never mattered. He was born sleepless, without a talent for rest or the desire for it." He "was a genius," said Ben Hecht. "He was like a man who hadn't learned to write, who hadn't even learned to think, because he hadn't the faintest idea of what was going on anywhere in the world except his office. But he had a flair for telling stories like comedians have for telling jokes. He could make them up. It was a fantasy-ridden head he had, and it was good. . . . He lived two-thirds of the time in the projection room. He saw only movies, he never saw life . . . but he knew what shadows could do." George Cukor said "[h]e had a kind of instinct for refinement." His wife called him "a cold, calm, logical, impersonal judge. He is never wrong."

The prince, Irving Thalberg, had been born in a middle-class section of Brooklyn in 1899. His father, a lace importer, had emigrated from a small town near Coblenz, Germany, and his mother, whose family owned a large New York department store, was also a German Jew—which, in the pecking order of Jewish society, gave him a leg up on the Eastern European Jews of Hollywood. Irving, with his aquiline nose, his sculpted cranium, his fine features, seemed almost dainty, and the impression was an unfortunately accurate one. A congenital heart deformity confined him to bed, where, shut off from the world of action and immersed in a vicarious world of books, it is likely he developed what became a very active fantasy life.

Irving's mother, Henrietta, a protective, indomitable woman, regarded her son's disability as a peculiar sign of grace. She was determined that he would lead as normal a life as possible to fulfill his special destiny, and despite the doctors' bleak prognosis, she ministered unceasingly to him and practically willed him to go to school. By the sixth grade he had contracted bronchitis. By high school he was felled by diphtheria, but he nevertheless managed to graduate. Realizing his life would probably be abbreviated by his illnesses, he decided to forgo college and enter business instead.

For a time he worked in his grandfather's store, writing ads, but he also took secretarial classes and learned Spanish, and at the age of seventeen he placed an ad of his own: "Situation Wanted: Secretary, stenographer, Spanish, English, high school education, inexperienced; $15." From the responses, he chose a job at a small trading firm in Manhattan, then later became a stenographer at another export firm. Within a year he had risen to assistant manager.

There is some dispute over precisely what happened next. By most accounts he was vacationing at his maternal grandmother's home out in Edgemere on Long Island when he encountered Carl Laemmle, who happened to have a home nearby. Laemmle was impressed and offered Thalberg a job. In another account Laemmle's wife, Recha, was a girlhood friend of Henrietta Thalberg, and the two got together for weekly kaffeeklatsches. Henrietta was reluctant to have her son go into the movies, but Recha convinced her it was a lucrative industry. Whatever the truth, Thalberg got a job as a secretary at Universal's New York office through family connections—though according to his official studio biography, he rejected Laemmle's initial offer, only to apply at the Universal office without Laemmle's knowledge or assistance.

As Sam Marx, who also worked in the New York Universal office, remembered it, Thalberg was indefatigable despite his health—or even possibly because of it. Thalberg knew he had limited time to accomplish his ends, and everything in his life seemed to move with a rush. He was always the first in and the last to leave, lingering to talk to Marx about what he would do if he were in charge of a studio. His industriousness eventually caught the attention of Laemmle, for whom industriousness was second only to will on the list of cardinal virtues, and he was elevated to the post of Laemmle's personal secretary. Again according to the lore, Laemmle was making a hastily arranged trip to the California studio and mentioned that he could use Thalberg's assistance answering correspondence on the train. Henrietta rushed from Brooklyn with an extra suit, and Thalberg was off. By the time the visit to California was over, he had so amazed Laemmle with his acuity and maturity that Laemmle asked him to stay there as a kind of watchdog. He always remembered the date of departure—July 6, 1920—because from that day on, California would be his home.

Thalberg's ascendancy at Universal was as swift as it was unlikely. With the studio high command hopelessly fragmented and Laemmle's brother-in-law, Isadore Bernstein, nominally in control, Thalberg recommended the appointment of an overseer, not necessarily to run the studio, but to coordinate production there. Laemmle agreed and appointed Thalberg. Whether by design or default, within six months Thalberg had steered his way through the bureaucratic maze and emerged as general manager—the head of the California operation. He was barely twenty years old.

Gossip columnist Louella Parsons remembered getting a call at the time from Universal's vice president, Robert Cochrane, asking if she would be interested in interviewing the new general manager before he returned to California. When she arrived at the designated spot, a tea room on Forty-eighth Street, Thalberg approached her. "'Mr. Cochrane said you wanted to see me.' I replied briefly and I fear none too gently, 'Well, what's the joke? Where is the new general manager?' 'I am,' replied the boy modestly. To save my embarrassment, Irving started ordering luncheon. Five minutes' talk with him and I knew he might be a boy in looks and age, but it was no child's mind that was being sent to cope with the intricate politics of Universal City."

Partly what was so arresting about Thalberg, and what created an immediate mystique about him, was his age. Anyone so young was bound to attract attention in a community as insular as Hollywood was in the 1920s. And partly what was so arresting about him was that tragic sense of mortality he radiated. He was a strange and unique combination of someone who had not grown up at all, as distanced from or uninterested in ordinary experience as he was, and of someone who lived with a ferocious intensity, as if all his forestalled growing up had to be compressed *now,* in the time left him. This idea of the doomed prince was a powerful one in Hollywood, and it acquired even greater power as Thalberg himself did. For women, it was a kind of aphrodisiac. Few men were more ardently pursued than Thalberg, and one studio chief even exacted a promise from him that he would not romance either of the chief's daughters for fear he might leave one a young widow.

Carl Laemmle felt differently. Long before he rose to general manager—in fact, when he was still a secretary back in New York—Thalberg had apparently been smitten by Laemmle's attractive daughter, Rosabelle. Sam Marx remembered that his conversations with Thalberg in those days almost always got around to the subject of Rosabelle. By the time he was ensconced as the studio head in California, she was returning the interest, but Thalberg was the object of so much attention now that his ardor for her had cooled, and in any case Rosabelle was an extremely willful, headstrong young woman who continually tried his patience. Their arguments, like their romance, had become a kind of continuing saga, followed regularly by the Hollywood gossip mongers. For the family-conscious Laemmle, who wouldn't have been at all unhappy to see his wunderkind enter the dynasty, the situation was especially vexing. For Thalberg himself, it was compromising.

A restless man even when things were calm, Thalberg, sometime in 1922, apparently put out feelers through his close friend Edwin Loeb, a diminutive attorney who, with his brother, Joseph, represented most of the Hollywood Jews in the twenties. ("The boy is a genius. I can see it. I know it," Cecil De Mille told Jesse Lasky when he learned Thalberg was available. "Geniuses we have all we need," said Lasky.) By most accounts, Thalberg met Louis B. Mayer for the first time at Loeb's home late in 1922. All the parties knew this was a kind of audition, and there was nervous expectation as Mayer posed a problem. A director of his had made a film called *Pleasure Mad* that Mayer found embarrassingly risqué, but the film was already presold to exhibitors. Should he write it off? he asked, fixing his gaze on Thalberg. Thalberg said *he* would, believing the ultimate authority at a studio had to be the producer, not the director. Pleased, Mayer rose and was escorted out, telling Loeb that if Thalberg wanted to work for him, he would treat him like a son.

The partnership wasn't consummated immediately, but with the demise of Thalberg's relationship with Rosabelle and his growing dissatisfaction over his salary, it was just a matter of time. Thalberg's own motto, which guided the headlong rush of his career, was "Never remain in a job when you have everything from it you can get." On February 15, 1923, he joined Louis Mayer as vice president and production assistant, forming what would be regarded as the most formidable production team in the history of movies. It was certainly one of the most perfectly complementary pairings. Mayer was close to forty but seemed much older. Thalberg was twenty-three but seemed much younger. Despite his hypochondria, Mayer was robust and powerfully built, with a barrel chest so well muscled that he gave a mistaken impression of fat when he was anything but. Thalberg was painfully frail to look at. Mayer was melodramatic, loud, and overbearing. Thalberg was, in one observer's words, "very quiet, soft-spoken, absolutely the opposite of Mayer." Mayer was self-aggrandizing. Thalberg was disarmingly modest.

This was, wrote Ben Hecht of Thalberg, a "quality so incredible in Hollywood as feathers on an eel." Thalberg never even took a credit on the movies he supervised because, he often said, the credit you give yourself isn't worth having. Charles MacArthur, Hecht's friend and writing partner, said, "Entertainment is his God. He's satisfied to serve him without billing, like a priest at an altar, or a rabbi under the scrolls." With talent, he could be surprisingly demure for the head of production—quite different from Mayer. Though he was largely responsible for shepherding Garbo's career, George Cukor remembered "he was always quite shy with her. He came on the set of *Camille* one day and she was preoccupied, so he said, 'Well, I've been turned off better sets than this,' and left with the greatest grace. He looked and behaved like a prince." Another at MGM said he had "a wonderful candid humility which reminds you of Abe Lincoln. The most simple, unaffected person you can imagine." It was hardly what one would have said about Mayer.

Perhaps the most striking dissimilarity between Thalberg and Mayer, however, was that while Mayer was playing father to the world with a kind of desperation to possess it, Thalberg, perhaps with that dread sense of his mortality, was remaining aloof and unapproachable. (This remoteness, in fact, may very well have been mistaken for modesty.) Thalberg moved through the world; he didn't live in it. He customarily arrived at his two-story bungalow on the MGM lot around ten o'clock and remained until two in the morning. Nothing mattered to him but the movies. "He was thoughtful when he thought of you," wrote publicist Howard Dietz, "but he rarely thought of you unless you were useful to a picture project. . . . I never had a conversation with him about anything except movies."

Waiting to see Thalberg was an endurance test to which all MGM employees were regularly subjected. Writer George Oppenheimer was once summoned to Thalberg's office for an appointment at 9:30 one morning, then wound up waiting two or three more days before finally being ushered in to the inner sanctum, where he admitted "it took only thirty seconds or so for the Thalberg charm and the Thalberg praise (he liked what I had done) to heal all wounds. . . . After a while I became inured. If you waited through dinner, you were served an excellent meal in his private dining room, and enough drinks to take the edge off annoyance. There was also plenty of company in that outer office." Humorist S. J. Perelman had landed an assignment at MGM but had such difficulty getting to see the production head that he "seriously began to question whether Thalberg existed, whether he might not be a solar myth or a deity concocted by the front office to garner prestige." When he was finally summoned to the office, he found "cooling their heels in the anteroom . . . a dozen literary artisans of note like Sidney Howard and Robert Sherwood, George S. Kaufman, Marc Connelly, S. N. Behrman and Donald Ogden Stewart. . . . I discovered that everybody there had been seeking Thalberg's ear without success and was seething."

It isn't likely Thalberg's discourtesy was a conscious slight, though Perelman was right: it fueled the myth. Still, it is more likely he was simply distracted and preoccupied. No one in Hollywood was more dedicated to his fictive world than Thalberg, and he demanded of his employees the same dedication—calling them at odd hours, requesting their appearance for conferences, drilling them for ideas. The system he helped devise—a system as fantastic and self-indulgent as the films themselves—was directed toward one end: perfection. It may have been his way of retaliating against fate for his precarious health. "It was the most amazing set-up," said screenwriter Anita Loos.

> I don't think Thalberg ever produced a picture that five years of work hadn't gone into. . . . It was Thalberg's theory to have an enormous staff, so he would hire writers by the dozens. . . . Conferences, rewrites, conferences again. At least twelve scripts were written on every story that was ever done. Sometimes, you'd go back to the first one. But anyway, every resource was uncovered, of every story, and they looked so smooth when they reached the screen that the hard work that went into them was not apparent. They seemed easy, but they were really worked over.

Even then, with the film edited and shown, "Irving was never satisfied with a picture," said one actor. Like most of the moguls, Thalberg attended previews religiously, studying the audience's reactions and mumbling comments to his editor. But where most executives would then relay instructions to recut the film, Thalberg relayed instructions to reshoot it, frequently adding whole new scenes. It was said that at MGM movies weren't made, they were remade, and Culver City became widely known as "Retake Valley." "We always made a picture with the idea we were going to retake at least twenty-five percent of it," said director Clarence Brown. "They didn't figure when a picture was complete that it was finished. That was the first cut—the first draft."

One reason even highly talented individuals suffered Thalberg's interference—and often suffered it gladly—was that in the legend his instincts were regarded as close to infallible. "There was a certainty in Thalberg to which Charlie responded," Ben Hecht wrote of the relationship between Charles MacArthur and MGM's vice president. Another MGM writer remembered Thalberg leaning over the desk and declaring imperiously, "I, more than any single person in Hollywood, have my finger on the pulse of America. I *know* what people will do

and what they won't do." The writer took this audacious pronounce-
ment at face value, but it is more likely that the boy wonder was
giving a demonstration in what sustained authority. Fitzgerald remembered a little parable Thalberg had once told him about sur-
veyors determining over which route to build a mountain road. "You
say, 'Well, I think we will put the road there'... and you know in
your secret heart that you have no reason for putting the road there
rather than in several other different courses, but you're the only
person that knows you don't know why you're doing it and you've got
to stick to that and you've got to pretend that you know and that you
did it for specific reasons, even though you're utterly assailed by
doubts." That was the Thalberg style.

He worked impulsively, intuitively, restlessly. He paced the room,
twirled his watch chain, or jangled the change in his pocket, his mind
racing with ideas. Director Clarence Brown said, "You would be
working with your writer, and you would come to this scene in the
script. It didn't click. It just didn't jell. The scene was no goddam
good. You would make a date with Irving, talk to him for thirty minutes, and you'd come away with the best scene in the picture."
Watching *Tugboat Annie*, a comedy about two crusty old dockside
salts (played by Marie Dressler and Wallace Beery), Thalberg told
director Mervyn LeRoy that a scene would play better if Beery's shoes
squeaked, and when LeRoy said he agreed but that the set had already
been struck, Thalberg parried, "Mervyn, I didn't ask you how much it
would cost. I asked you whether it would help the picture." Another
time, at a story conference for *Camille*, he suggested the lovers plan
their marriage as if they were plotting a murder, and suddenly the
scene worked. Thalberg himself explained his uncanny success with
three rules.

Never take any one man's opinion as final.

Never take your own opinion as final.

Never expect anyone to help you but yourself.

Of course, Thalberg could only operate in his imaginative aerie,
imposing his will to perfect his world, because Mayer, as head of the
studio, permitted him to do so. ("That was one thing about Stahr,"
Fitzgerald wrote, "the literal sky was the limit. He had worked with
Jews too long to believe legends that they were small with money.") In

this, as in all things, Mayer was the indulgent father, and he viewed Thalberg very much as a surrogate son. "Between them they created MGM," said David Selznick, a great producer in his own right and Mayer's son-in-law. "I don't think either of them could have created it without the other. They were a great team. Thalberg was freed from the responsibilities of administration and finance and dealing with New York, by Mayer; and Thalberg's every wish was Mayer's command. Thalberg had only to say what he wanted and Mayer would deliver it." Another compared them to the War Office providing the men and matériel (Mayer) and the commander in the field actually fighting the war (Thalberg), though this also meant that while Thalberg relentlessly drove his troops, Mayer provided the morale and soothed them—"the one that you went to whenever you were in trouble and needed help."

Mayer had never been one to enjoy sharing his power, but the reason he ceded so much authority to Thalberg was that the boy genius clearly came to function not simply as a surrogate son, but as a vessel of dreams, the way movie stars did—a direct link between the Eastern European Jews' own rough roots and the high culture to which they had always aspired. "The original guys were all fur merchants and bouncers out at Palisades Park and things like that," said producer Pandro Berman. "The next generation, the Thalberg-Selznick generation, were educated, calm, cultured men." Thalberg was young, ethereally handsome, boyishly charming, confident, intelligent, and, above all, possessed of a natural refinement. He wasn't formally educated beyond high school, but he was extremely well read, and he lacked any self-consciousness about himself, his background, or his Judaism. He was, in short, everything Mayer—or any of the Hollywood Jews—thought he might have been and certainly would have liked to be if he had been born a generation later, and that was the primary reason he became a living legend to them. Thalberg was their Jewish American Prince.

By most standards he couldn't really have been considered an intellectual; his tastes ran more to the middle brow than to the high brow, and one writer who worked for him admitted he couldn't "call him a man of intellectual content." But Thalberg liked to rub shoulders with intellectuals, which gave him a kind of legitimacy by association among the older Hollywood Jews, and he conspicuously displayed what learning he did have. At the studio he hired a bookish young critic from New York named Albert Lewin, who had earned a masters degree in English at Harvard and had completed everything but his dissertation while working for his doctorate at Columbia. "Thalberg always had him present at conferences where there was a need to compare [books]," said writer Maurice Rapf. "After all, they were all doing subjects that had literary antecedents. Even if they couldn't read the damn books themselves—which they didn't very often— he'd have Albert read the book." At the very least, it made Thalberg *seem* conversant with literature.

He was also one of the few executives who actually socialized with literary people—which is, no doubt, one of the reasons they treated him so kindly in their reminiscences. One writer remembered attending a party at Thalberg's beach house where Fitzgerald got drunk and sang an embarrassing song about dogs. "I could see the little figure of Thalberg standing in a doorway at the far end of the room, with his hands plunged deep in his pockets, his shoulders hunched slightly in that characteristic posture of his which seemed to be both a withdrawal and a rejection at the same time. There was a slight, not unkind smile on his lips as he looked down toward the group at the piano. But he did not move." Fitzgerald returned the favor of not getting tossed out—and others—with his unfinished hagiographic novel inspired by Thalberg, called, with redolent nostalgia, *The Last Tycoon*.

Thalberg may have been Hollywood's Jewish intellectual, but his pretensions occasionally exposed his cultural limits, too, as when he met the Olympian composer Arnold Schönberg. Schönberg had fled the Nazis in the early thirties and joined a growing colony of emigrés in Hollywood, where many of them served the film industry in various capacities from research to writing. Thalberg hadn't known that Schönberg had abandoned symphonic conventions for the dissonance of twelve-tone music, so after listening to a radio concert of some of Schönberg's earlier pieces, he decided that the modernist was just the man to compose the score for the film version of Pearl Buck's Chinese saga *The Good Earth* and arranged a meeting. "Last Sunday when I heard the lovely music you have written..." Thalberg began. "I don't write 'lovely' music," Schönberg curtly corrected. A bit startled, Thalberg recomposed himself and explained the assignment, but again Schönberg interrupted even before the translation was finished. He hated the way movies used music and sound. He wouldn't consider undertaking the assignment unless he was granted complete control over the sound. "What do you mean by complete control?" Thalberg questioned incredulously. "I mean that I would have to work with the actors," Schönberg said. "They would have to speak in the same pitch and key as I compose it in. It would be similar to *Pierrot Lunaire*, but, of course, less difficult."

The meeting broke inconclusively, but Thalberg believed it would only be a matter of time before Schönberg understood the difference between composing an opera and composing for film. He was wrong. After pondering the offer, Schönberg now demanded twice as much money, since he realized he would have to assume responsibility for the entire production. According to Salka Viertel, the writer who relayed Schönberg's answer, Thalberg shrugged and said he had found some Chinese folk songs that had inspired the head of the sound department to compose some "lovely" music. Schönberg was never asked to compose for MGM again.

This was the myth. Thalberg the intellectual, Thalberg the practical executive, Thalberg the genius, Thalberg the fated, and, finally, Thalberg the romantic—the most eligible bachelor in Hollywood. Falling into the company of several first-class carousers—directors Howard Hawks and Jack Conway, scenarist Jack Colton, romantic actor John Gilbert, who lived with Greta Garbo, and producer Paul Bern, who would later marry Jean Harlow—Thalberg came to know his way around the Hollywood night scene, and he squired an assortment of beautiful women: Bessie Love, a blonde, oval-faced starlet; Peggy Hopkins Joyce, a leggy showgirl who made a career of marrying and divorcing wealthy industrialists; Constance Talmadge, a brassy and scintillating actress whom Thalberg met on the yacht of her brother-in-law, Joseph Schenck. Thalberg fell hardest for Talmadge; he could scarcely take his eyes off her in public. But she was a self-confessed free spirit, and while she roamed, he took up again with Rosabelle Laemmle, who had settled in Hollywood with the stated intention of recapturing Thalberg's affections.

As this romantic whirligig spun, Thalberg also occasionally dated a young Canadian-born actress whom he had first met when she was called on the carpet by her director for ineptitude. Thalberg bucked up her spirits, then asked her for a date, though she admitted, while commiserating with Henrietta, that she was only Irving's "spare tire." Meanwhile, when Talmadge hastily entered into marriage, his affair with Rosabelle Laemmle suddenly intensified—at least until Thalberg, running late for an engagement they were to attend together, called to tell her he would send his car and meet her there. Rosabelle answered brusquely that she did not arrive at affairs unaccompanied. Thalberg, who seldom lost his composure, burned with rage but raced home to dress and then to Laemmle's home to pick up Rosabelle.

The relationship never recovered from what he considered an act of unprovoked wilfullness, and after another brief dalliance with Talmadge, who had divorced just as quickly as she had married, his interest was rekindled in Norma Shearer—particularly when she arrived at the Mayfair Club ball in a shocking scarlet dress while the other women all wore the suggested white. It was the kind of spine Thalberg liked, and sometime late in the summer of 1927 he invited her to his office, produced a row of engagement rings, and casually asked her which one she wanted.

They were married at four-thirty in the afternoon on September 29 in the garden of the Beverly Hills home Thalberg had rented from silent screen star Pauline Frederick. Norma had wanted an intimate affair—at least by Hollywood standards—and Thalberg, who wasn't exactly convivial in any case, complied. The studio's art director, Cedric Gibbons, designed a flower-studded trellis as a backdrop, and Norma wore a gown of soft ivory velvet with a yoke of handmade rose lace punctuated by a diamond pin Irving had given her. Rabbi Edgar Magnin officiated. Norma, largely out of courtesy to Henrietta, had studied Judaism with Magnin and spent the morning nervously practicing her Hebrew responses for the Jewish ceremony. When the time came she "muffed" her lines, but she insisted on repeating each one until she got it right. It was the only glitch in the production. Irving's sister, Sylvia, was the maid of honor. Mayer's daughters, Irene and Edith, were the bridesmaids. The best man was Louis B. Mayer.

This was the honor due Mayer, and it was the honor he expected, but it belied some severe strains ahead between father and surrogate son. Part of it was the inevitable course of Hollywood bloodletting. Thalberg was the legend—something that was initially a source of pride to Mayer, but which became increasingly bothersome, not simply because the boy genius was getting all the credit, but because there were those who believed Mayer was actually an impediment to the studio's progress. For Mayer, who took his studio's success personally, the idea that he was irrelevant was devastating. Moreover, as much as Thalberg represented the new Hollywood Jew for Mayer, Mayer began to realize that over time this new order would clearly endanger the old one. Who needed the suit cutters, junkmen, and bouncers when they could have bright, assimilated Jews like Thalberg and Selznick? For Thalberg's part, he was beginning to live the legend and demanded to get paid for it. "Why the hell am I killing myself so Mayer and Schenck can get rich and fat?" he supposedly told one associate.

Mayer, the great reconciler, usually pacified his production head by whittling off a piece of his own percentage of the company's profits, since Schenck insisted there were no profits *but* Mayer's left to carve up without making the stockholders howl. This had worked in 1927 and again in 1929, but by 1932, with his contract expiring, Thalberg was beginning to play hardball with Loew's. Rumors circulated that he was ready to leave MGM, and he was forced to issue the perfunctory denials: "Reports that I am leaving Metro-Goldwyn-Mayer have absolutely no foundation. My association with Nicholas Schenck, Louis B. Mayer, J. Robert Rubin [MGM's East coast vice president], and other members of the organization has been, and I am confident will continue to be, a most happy and inspiring one." It wasn't the strongest endorsement, but then, Thalberg wasn't the happiest employee. With Thalberg besieged by offers from rival studios, Nick Schenck raced to California to negotiate. Thalberg was obdurate. He stated frankly that he, not Mayer, was responsible for MGM's success, and he expected to be compensated accordingly. The discussion became so vehement that Mayer excused himself. When it ended, Schenck had conceded to let Thalberg purchase 100,000 shares of Loew's, Incorporated, at a price lower than market value. This placated him—Mayer was placated with a similar offer—but it also widened the breach between Mayer and his surrogate son.

To Mayer it was all arrogance. To some degree he was probably right, despite the testimonials to Thalberg's modesty. Studio manager Eddie Mannix felt that money changed Thalberg. "He wanted as much as L. B. was getting and that touched off the rivalry between them." But Thalberg was also painfully aware of his own precariousness (his health could have been a metaphor for the precariousness of the Hollywood Jews generally), and with a new infant son, he was determined to leave a legacy for his family. The justification for his concern came swiftly. In October he was weakened by a bout with influenza. He recovered, negotiated his new deal with Schenck, and was in seemingly high spirits at the annual Christmas party, which, on this last dry holiday before Prohibition was repealed, was particularly boisterous. Even Thalberg drank and lowered his customary reserve, leaving the party occasionally to embrace his employees on the lot.

That evening he suffered a heart attack. Thalberg now looked especially delicate—like a wounded bird, his head oversized, his limbs limp and etiolated. He could scarcely rise from bed, and Norma halted her work to nurse him round the clock. By the end of February he was able to take a short Sunday ride in his car and began planning a cruise through the Panama Canal to New York and then to Europe for a tonsillectomy, since his doctors suspected that inflamed tonsils might have contributed to his attack. In the meantime, partly to fill the vacuum created by Thalberg's absence, Mayer begged his son-in-law David Selznick to join MGM. Selznick, who then headed up RKO, resisted, as he had resisted all his father-in-law's pleadings. But when Selznick's beloved father died, a distraught David was softened by Mayer's appeals to family. In what he later regretted as a moment of weakness, he accepted. "The son-in-law also rises," was the studio joke.

Technically, Selznick wasn't replacing Thalberg; he was operating an independent production unit within the studio rather than supervising the studio's entire output as Thalberg had done. He and Thalberg were actually friends after a fashion, and Selznick had praised him lavishly as "the greatest producer the industry has yet developed." But Thalberg was nevertheless dismayed that Mayer should make any attempt to usurp his authority during his convalescence by making production decisions, and the two had a very heated exchange. Unsettled by the contretemps himself, Mayer wrote:

> I felt an air of suspicion on your part towards me, and want you to know if I was correct in my interpretation of your feeling, that it was entirely undeserved. . . . Instead of appreciating the fact that I have cheerfully taken on your work, as well as my own, and have carried on to the best of my ability, you chose to bitingly and sarcastically accuse me of many things, by innuendo, which I am supposed to have done to you and your friends. Being a man of temperament, I could not restrain myself any longer and lost my temper. Even when I did so I regretted it, because I thought it might hurt you physically. . . .
>
> And now let me philosophize for a moment. Anyone who has said that I have a feeling of wrong towards you will eventually have cause to regret their [sic] treachery, because that is exactly what it would be, and what it would be on my part if I had any feeling other than what I have expressed in this letter towards you. I assure you I will go on loving you to the end.

Thalberg responded that their disagreement had less to do with sowers of discord than with Mayer's own violation of the principle of shared authority and accountability. But he added, "Please come to see me as soon as it is convenient for you to do so, as nothing would make me happier than to feel we had parted at least as good personal friends, if not better, than ever before." A few days later, the Thalbergs, accompanied by a large retinue of servants and by their close friends Helen Hayes and Charles MacArthur, set sail.

As soon as Thalberg left, the studio was rent by factions, and Selznick was caught in the middle. He was far too independent to be his father-in-law's man, but the Thalberg loyalists regarded him as a threat. "He found increasing resistance to working with him, even from people recently well disposed," wrote his wife. "This was the worst penalty." Inevitably, new rumors circulated that Thalberg was about to be overthrown while in Europe—though Schenck denied these publicly as Thalberg had earlier denied leaving MGM. Nevertheless, Thalberg's supporters feared the worst. Everyone knew that Mayer was pressing executives to take sides—his or Thalberg's—and in the absence of his vice president of production, he had moved forcefully into the breach, obviously hoping not only to reassert his own authority, but also to gain the cachet that attached to production. None of the Hollywood Jews, least of all Mayer, wanted to be considered a businessman.

Some of these maneuvers, however much they may have offended Thalberg, were a matter of necessity. As Thalberg's sabbatical dragged on for months, the studio needed clear lines of authority to produce its fifty-two pictures. Even a maverick like Selznick believed that "a single centralized production head, operating under a company head such as L. B., and having a dictatorship over all the production and editorial activities of the studio, is the soundest plan of operation. No compromise oligarchy or system of dual or triple control can, in my opinion, be very effective. . . ." To Mayer and Schenck, it seemed increasingly likely that Thalberg would no longer be able to fill that role, though he evidently felt the position should be held for him until his return. It wasn't. In part out of retribution for his hubris, in part out of respect for the hard facts of producing a schedule of films, that summer Thalberg, still in Europe, was relieved of his responsibilities as vice president in charge of production.

When he returned to MGM in August, after a nine-month absence, it was as an independent producer dedicated to making the best films. "Idealism is profitable," he told a reporter. "That is the reason I retain my conviction that it is the thing. Quality pictures pay. We're in this business to make money, naturally, but the quality production, which is more often than not the expensive production, is the one that pays the big returns." Thalberg plunged into his own schedule of films, and he would still be regarded as one of Hollywood's best, most idealistic producers, but the halcyon days of power, where all of MGM was at his disposal, were gone now. He was the son once again.

In a similar situation in *The Last Tycoon*, Fitzgerald's Stahr perishes in a plane crash on his way to New York to retake the studio from the business infidels. Thalberg chose not to exhaust himself fighting back—a futile gesture in any case—but to devote himself to movies, among them *Mutiny on the Bounty*, which won an Oscar for Best Picture; *The Barretts of Wimpole Street*, adapted from the drama about Victorian poets Elizabeth Barrett and Robert Browning; *A Night at the Opera*, starring the Marx Brothers; *Romeo and Juliet*, long a pet project of his, starring his wife, Norma, and Leslie Howard; and *The Good Earth*.

With Thalberg now relegated to the role of producer, Mayer had regained the power at the studio. Perhaps, in time, he might have even gained the prestige he really wanted as a creative force equal to Thalberg had fate not taken what must have seemed like revenge and memorialized the prince forever. Over the Labor Day weekend 1936, Thalberg and Norma took a brief vacation at Del Monte in northern California, where they had honeymooned nearly a decade earlier. When they returned Irving had apparently caught a cold and was having some labored breathing. His physician, suspecting pneumonia, ordered tests. By Tuesday, however, he was at the Hollywood Bowl supervising the dress rehearsal of a pageant organized to promote brotherhood, and on a cold, damp Thursday evening he attended the premiere, receiving an ovation from the crowd of twenty thousand. The next day his condition worsened, and he was confined to bed.

That Sunday, for the first time in memory, Thalberg missed the MGM picnic, where he and Mayer traditionally headed opposing teams in a game of tug-of-war. Cabling his regrets, he said, "Only illness keeps me from being with you today." Later that day several of the MGM brain trust came to visit him at his home on the ocean out in Santa Monica. He was clearly very ill. "I'm not getting the right treatment," he told his longtime assistant, Bernie Hyman, after a coughing spell. "They don't know what they're doing. They're killing me." Hyman tried to reassure him, but Thalberg interrupted. "No, Bernie. This time I'm not going to make it." He rallied briefly early the next morning, then fell into a coma. Mayer waited in his office with other MGM executives. Shortly after ten-thirty that morning, the phone rang. It was Norma. Mayer put down the receiver and turned to the group. "Irving is dead." As the news spread around the lot, employees wept openly.

The funeral was held two days later at the Wilshire Boulevard Temple. Nearly ten thousand onlookers clogged the streets around the synagogue to gawk at the stars in attendance. "He was simple as a child, despite his greatness," eulogized Rabbi Edgar Magnin to the 1,500 mourners. "He was sweet and kind and charming." Opera star Grace Moore, in the choir loft high above the congregation, then sang the Psalm of David but broke down in tears. Magnin read condolences from President Roosevelt, who praised Thalberg's "high ideals, insight and imagination," and Norma swooned when Magnin extolled the love between Irving and her. When the service ended Mayer and Joe Schenck accompanied Norma to Forest Lawn, where the burial took place. As the casket was carried into the sanctuary, Wallace Beery, piloting his own plane, dropped flowers from the sky.

Thalberg's death may not have ended an era in Hollywood; his career may have actually begun one, since every studio wanted a Thalberg of its own. But, as Fitzgerald recognized, he was an era's most remarkable symbol and, in many ways, its soul, and his premature death at thirty-seven would always keep him that way—wrapped in nostalgia and romance. MGM continued, now with Mayer firmly in control. "I came to California to pay my respects to his memory and to give my sympathy," said Mayer's new supporter, Nick Schenck. "This has been done and I am leaving for New York. As for the rest, MGM is an organization managed by and composed of those who honored and respected Irving Thalberg, and his unfinished work will be left for completion in those capable and willing hands."

Two weeks later Schenck and Mayer began dismantling Thalberg's production unit. The prince may have been dead, but they weren't going to be haunted by his memory any more than they had to. But Thalberg couldn't really be expunged. He would always remain the paragon—the young Jew who embodied Hollywood's hopes and dreams and who stood in such contrast to the first generation of Hollywood Jews. For most of the film community, it was as Fitzgerald wrote of another fictional film executive he had modeled after Thalberg: "What a hell of a hole he leaves in this damn wilderness." For them, Hollywood had gained its first martyr.

7

How They Lived

The rich and vulgar and pretentious Jews of our big American cities are perhaps the greatest misfortune that has ever befallen the Jewish people. They are the fountain of anti-Semitism. When they rush about in superautomobiles, bejeweled and furred and painted and overbarbered, when they build themselves French chateaux and Italian palazzi, they stir up the latent hatred against crude wealth in the hands of shallow people; and that hatred diffuses itself.

WALTER LIPPMANN

SOMETIME LATE IN 1931, WHEN Paramount was reeling from the effects of the Depression, the studio's eastern brass met for their weekly luncheon at the Astor Hotel across the street from the imposing new Paramount office tower on Times Square. "We were sitting at a long table, and Lasky and all the others were present," recalled Eugene Zukor, by then a Paramount executive,

> *and Katz* banged on the table. We thought, Well, he's going to put on an act. Every once in a while somebody would play the big guy for the hell of it and you would*

---

*Sam Katz, one-time nickelodeon piano player, was a successful exhibitor from Chicago who had sold his chain to Paramount and then moved to New York to head up the company's vast theater holdings.

> *laugh. . . . This particular day he said, "Lasky, we are on*
> *the verge of destruction. This company is collapsing. This*
> *company is going to ruin. This company is going to hell and*
> *gone, and you know the reason why. You are the direct*
> *cause. Your ideas are not in the best interests of the com-*
> *pany, and your function as head of the studio no longer*
> *exists. You are not considered capable."*

The room was stunned. "I just couldn't believe what I was hear-
ing," said Eugene Zukor. "I thought, Where does the joke come in?"
Shaken, Lasky asked if Katz wanted him to tender his resignation.
Katz answered that he did—on behalf of the company's shareholders.
Lasky rose. "I am withdrawing. I can't work under these circum-
stances. I'm leaving." And he calmly strode out of the room.

Over the course of the next five years Paramount would become
the spoils in a savage war between Wall Street, which had apparently
thrown its weight behind Katz, and Adolph Zukor, who boiled at the
interference of his board of directors, composed, by one board
member's own admission, "mostly of railroad presidents, bank presidents and similar tycoons selected, so it seemed, for their complete
ignorance of the motion picture industry." For a time Zukor would be
banished to California, where he would become such a pariah in a
community addicted to success that, by one account, he sat alone for
hours at a nightclub, no one feeling the need any longer to pay their
respects to the man who had just a few years before been the power of
the industry. And in 1936 he would rise again when Barney Balaban,
a blunt, uncomplicated theater chain owner from Chicago, was asked
to take control of the company. "The headwaiter and captains of the
same night club" where he had been snubbed, wrote one columnist,
"scurried frantically about trying to get him a ringside table. From all
sides, producers, directors, screen stars left their own tables to rush
over and talk to him. Some of them sat down with him. They made
plenty of fuss about Adolph Zukor that night—and will continue to,
you can bet."

The one who would never recover was Jesse Lasky. Lasky, a gently
dispositioned innocent, had lived Hollywood to the hilt. He could
afford to. As one of the principals of Paramount, he made a weekly

salary of $2,500 plus 7.5 percent of the company's net earnings. He had three Rolls-Royces (among other automobiles), two butlers, a lady's maid, a valet, a French governess, two cooks, and two chauffeurs. Every morning he sparred two rounds with middleweight boxing champion Kid McCoy. When he traveled he took a private train car. The premiums on his life insurance alone came to $40,000 each year.

All that was over now. The Depression had wiped out his fortune, and his ouster had wiped out his power. For weeks the normally ebullient Lasky was sullen and despondent. At his oceanfront house in Santa Monica he would pace the beach for hours as his family watched, fearing he would try to take his life. Harry Warner, seething over what he saw as Lasky's destruction by the hated eastern establishment, offered him a $250,000 loan to pay off stock Lasky had bought on margin, but he had had to put up his beloved beach house as collateral. "Of course he lost it," remembered Lasky's daughter, Betty. "As a child I wouldn't have known that the house wasn't ours anymore, and I must have been at the beach club with a school friend, and being very young, we would have walked over to the house. . . . We went into the swimming pool, and I remember two of the Warner brothers were there. One of them must have been living in the house temporarily. And they were maybe a little bit embarrassed, but they were very nice. They could see right away I didn't know what was going on. But I remember being struck with them. They were very animalistic types. I wasn't used to types like that—the ghetto types. It was their appearance. They were so ugly-looking but so ghetto ugly. . . . It was like a child going to a circus and looking at a freak."

Gradually Lasky emerged from his depression and got a contract producing films independently at Fox Pictures, but his life and lifestyle never fully recovered. "It changed everything," recalled Betty Lasky. "He had never licked a stamp and put one on an envelope in his life. He probably had never made a phone call; he always had a secretary. He had never been to the market. And all of these things were great discoveries. They thrilled him. He would go mad in the cheese section. . . . And also he was able to drive again. The chauffeur was gone. In the early days he had raced his Stutz Bearcat across the country and driven his Rolls roadster at breakneck speed with the top down. He'd terrify us if we happened to be in the backseat. He'd go whirling around Malibu Canyon—we had a ranch up in Malibu—and if you asked him to go slower, he'd go faster. He was absolutely fearless and a speed demon." These might have been small compensations, but they were the only ones Jesse Lasky had left.

If Lasky had waxed suicidal, it was because he realized that in losing the trappings of his success he had lost something much more than material comforts. For Lasky, as for nearly all the Hollywood Jews, making movies was a metaphor for one's entire life—for the imaginative transformation to which those lives would be subjected. The Hollywood Jews lived their movie. Their wealth was another way of acting out the genteel, of buying their way out of Eastern European Judaism and into America, which is to say that, while they all lived well and displayed their wealth conspicuously, their extravagance had a very particular design and function beyond display. Its function was to emulate rich gentiles in the hope of becoming them.

"They represented what we wanted to be," admitted Eugene Zukor. "They represented the intellectual, the well groomed, the cultured people. My father's group—they were still first-generation Americans. They hadn't grown up to this." One could see the imitation in the Hollywood Jews' palatial homes, which usually resembled European manors; in their smart clothes, which were custom tailored by the finest haberdashers; and in their luxurious automobiles. Though occasional vulgarizations crept in—Louis Mayer's Chrysler limousine had an illuminated plastic lion on the hood—the Hollywood Jews were, by and large, aggressively tasteful rather than boorish. Tastefulness, after all, was the object, even if it became inflated in a contest of being *more* tasteful than anyone else.

"I knew we were in for trouble," recalled Paul Wurtzel, son of sour-tempered Fox production executive Sol Wurtzel, "when he built a home in Bel Air. I had this instinct—this feeling of doom. It was like a movie. They got the best architect, and they started building this goddamn Italian villa. It had nothing to do with the farm in Krakow, you know. Or Second Avenue in New York. . . . They built this goddamn mansion, and we all moved in there. There were butlers and maids. . . . That was the beginning of the whole baloney. People get to you, and they say you have to live up to your image."

Later Wurtzel, a gruff, uneducated little man from the Lower East Side of New York, went to Europe to acquire furnishings for his villa, but he couldn't shake the Lower East Side entirely. Still budget conscious, he demanded his son report back to him on what Mrs. Wurtzel was planning to spend. "He'd say, 'I want to know what the hell's going on. Tell me!.'"

Acquiring class never came cheap. When Joe Schenck, brother of Loew's president Nick Schenck and himself the head of Twentieth Century-Fox, was brought to trial on charges of income tax fraud in 1941, one got what amounted to the only public accounting of what it cost a mogul to maintain his life-style. Schenck's secretary testified that he always kept $50,000 in pin money in a steel box in his office. Schenck's accountant testified that his client spent over $16,000 on hotels in one year, $1,500 on laundry, $5,000 on meat, $3,000 on gas and oil for his car, $500 for his barber (Schenck was nearly bald), $32,000 on charity, and $63,000 for an item called "exchange"— which turned out to be a euphemism for his gambling debts. That didn't include his French lessons or the yacht he sailed to Cuba or the parties he threw or the generous gifts he bestowed. "Believe it or not," Schenck joked to reporters after numerous payments to various female friends had been revealed, "I don't keep any women."

However steep the monetary costs, though, the Hollywood Jews' imitation of eastern aristocracy exacted a much greater hidden cost: the sacrifice of a reasonably normal family life. That was because the family itself became less a refuge from the world than another way of proving one's gentility to it, so that, ironically, while the studio became a kind of surrogate family, the family itself became a kind of studio. The children in this domestic drama were cast to give the lie to the anti-Semitic stereotype of the Eastern European Jew. "You could even see the physical change in the family in the second generation—not resembling the first generation at all," observed writer and director Philip Dunne. "Of course, this is true all across the country, but it is particularly noticeable in people who come out of very poor families. . . . One dear friend and colleague of mine was a product of a Lower East Side slum. He was desperately poor. And he grew up a rickety, tiny man who obviously had suffered as a child. At school, he told me, the goyim would scream at him. Growing up in California, his two sons were tall, tanned, and blond. Both excelled academically and in athletics. One became a military officer, the other a physicist. They were California kids. Not only American but Californian."

But healthy and handsome was only the beginning. The children were also meant to be embodiments of the breeding and deportment their fathers lacked—a role that made most of them miserable. Eugene Zukor recalled how his father always demanded perfection, yelling at him for the slightest infraction. Mayer's daughters complained about a childhood dedicated to making the proper impression. "My childhood was so terrible that I blanked out on a lot of it," said Betty Lasky, whose molding was left to others. "I wasn't a princess. I was very lonely. . . . The best time would be in the summer. We'd go up to the mountains for about two weeks for a camping trip. Other than that I never saw my father." Most of her time was spent with her French governess. She and Betty, who spoke French fluently, would sit on the beach reading French novels. It was an image as removed from the ghetto as one was likely to find.

Education, which the Hollywood Jews embraced desperately, was to be the badge of their children's inner enlightenment. The Mayer daughters attended a private facility called the Hollywood School for Girls, where the daughters of Cecil B. De Mille and William de Mille, the "old" Hollywood aristocracy of the time, matriculated. (As vessels of domesticity, they were forbidden higher education.) For the sons, who were not only reflections of their fathers' glory but their legatees, the most popular institution was a military academy in Beverly Hills called Black Fox, where Jack Warner sent Jack Jr. and Harry Cohn sent his two sons. Others removed their children from Hollywood entirely. When Jesse Jr. started hanging around sets and consorting with actors, Lasky shuffled him off to an eastern prep school and then to the University of Dijon in France, where he was to train to be a diplomat. (He wound up being a screenwriter instead.) Michael Korda, nephew of producer Alexander Korda, went farther still —to a Swiss boarding school, where he rubbed shoulders with the shah of Iran's nephews, the Aga Khan's grandchildren, the brother of the king of Belgium, the son of the deposed king of Italy, and the duke of Kent. Another classmate was Warner LeRoy, son of producer/director Mervyn LeRoy and grandson of Harry Warner. Here, where aristocracies merged, Warner won friends by passing out autographed photos of movie stars his father sent over.

Like Thalberg within the industry, one of the sons' functions was to provide certain vicarious satisfactions for their fathers, the most important of which was to crash the gates of real American society, to translate wealth and power into genuine status. Show business power, however great, was always déclassé, and it was a sign of the Hollywood Jews' attitude toward their own industry that all of them but Laemmle carefully steered their children away from the movies toward something more respectable. But it wasn't just respectability that moved them. Most felt that in making their sons genteel, they had also softened them. The boys hadn't the ghetto steel one needed to survive in movies. Sol Wurtzel, the chain-smoking head of production at Fox Pictures, put it most forcefully. Wurtzel, whose face was twisted into a nervous grimace that some mistook for a perpetual smile and who drank gallons of a cathartic called pluto water because he was so tense, forbade his son to enter the movie industry. "You're not emotionally equipped for this business," he told him. "I'll buy you a farm. Become a farmer. You'll be happier."

But the sons seldom complied. Born into their fathers' artistocracy where they had all the perquisites, few cared to challenge the aristocracy outside. Paul Wurtzel, who had seen the industry turn his father into a walking coil, nevertheless went to work on the back lot. Jack Warner, Jr., did too. Budd Schulberg, son of Paramount production executive B. P. Schulberg, and Maurice Rapf, son of MGM production executive Harry Rapf, were both shipped off to Dartmouth, but both returned to Hollywood to write screenplays. Eugene Zukor, defying his father's exhortations that he continue his education, joined Paramount. Junior Laemmle begged off college and began producing films at his father's studio.

For the daughters, the role was somewhat different and almost medieval. Mayer could scarcely bear to part with his girls, Edith and Irene, but when he did he was determined that they would marry up. Edie, lively, cheerful, extroverted, had a passel of suitors—those her father couldn't scare off—but her attentions fell on a fast-talking, small-time production executive named William Goetz, whom she had met one winter when illness forced the family to leave their oceanside house and stay at the Ambassador Hotel. "When we got back to the beach house in the summer," Edie remembered, her father asked, "'What's Goetz calling all the time for? Bring him to dinner.' And Bill, being Bill, said some awfully funny things at the table. And my father just looked at him. He said later, 'What's with this kid and the jokes?' 'If you want to know the truth,' I said, 'he's a very, very funny, witty man.'" Mayer wasn't appreciative. No one would have been good enough for his daughters, and Goetz, bawdy and down-to-earth, certainly wasn't the kind of man he had had in mind. But Edith could be as obstinate as her father, and eventually Goetz went to the studio to ask for her hand. When Mayer asked how he intended to support her, Goetz answered, "If necessary, Mr. Mayer, with my own two hands." It was the sort of thing Mayer loved to hear.

Meanwhile, Mayer's younger daughter, Irene, was being courted by David Selznick, a rising executive at Paramount whose bull-headedness was gradually cracking the protective wall Mayer had erected around her. Though he had grown up in Hollywood, Selznick didn't look like a Hollywood prince. Large and ungainly, with short curly hair and thick glasses, he was a wonky moose of a man, but he had a manner, a kind of innocent hedonism, that was at once charming and infectious. He was also intelligent, blunt, stubborn, and impulsive—and not the sort of son-in-law Mayer had in mind either. As the child of Lewis J. Selznick, with whom Mayer had once had a short-lived partnership, Selznick had bad bloodlines. Like his father, he lived high. He wasn't old-fashioned and deferential. When Mayer advised Selznick to postpone the marriage, the young producer shocked his future father-in-law by telling him that he could barely control his sexual urges as it was, and that he wanted to go ahead.

Reluctantly Selznick did agree to wait until after Edith had married Goetz. The nuptials occurred on March 19, 1930. "I just wanted to be married quietly," Edith said, but her father insisted. "The wedding is for *me*," he told her. "You want to marry this kid? Then keep your eyes on him." There were 650 guests and 8 bridesmaids. Adrian, the top designer at MGM, dressed the bride. William Randolph Hearst played Mayer at the rehearsal. "It was such a production!" Edith recalled. Still, the effect was more funereal than festive. The Mayers

weren't gaining status; they were losing a daughter. Riding in the car
with Edith to the Biltmore Hotel for the ceremony, Mayer was stern
and silent. Margaret Mayer sobbed. "Be strong," Mayer whispered to
Edith. "Your mother's very emotional about this." Two months later
Selznick married Irene, and Mayer had lost both his daughters,
though he never relinquished the dream of shaping their lives. "My
father often talked about the degree to which he had to keep his
father-in-law at bay," said David's son, Danny, "keep him from interfering, dictating."

William Fox, who also had two daughters, married them off reasonably well to men outside the industry, but he took his control to
even further extremes than Mayer. "Possessive is just barely touching
it," said Fox's niece, Angela Fox Dunn. "He let both girls marry, and
luckily they both got pregnant shortly thereafter. According to my
mother, as soon as both girls gave birth, to boys, the two mothers and
their infant sons were brought back to Fox Hall, where cottages were
built on the estate for them, and the husbands were 'dismissed,' to use
my mother's word. One husband was named Taussig. I never heard
what happened to him. The other was an attorney in New York City
named Maurice Schwartz. The way my mother told it, what happened to Schwartz was like one of those bad mystery stories. She said
he came home from work one day, put his key in the front door, and
found a totally empty apartment. No wife. No son. No furniture. He
thought he had walked into the wrong apartment. He had a heart
attack and died right there on the bare floor. . . . Then Fox raised
those boys [his grandchildren] as his own sons." As a kind of coup de
grace, he legally adopted them and renamed one William Fox II and
the other William Fox III.

Still, the children at least were born into their roles. It was the
wives of the Hollywood Jews who paid the greatest price for their
husbands' affected gentility. Most had married them when the men
were struggling and when the marriage could have been regarded as
coups for the ambitious young Jewish grooms. Mayer married a cantor's daughter, Laemmle the niece of his boss, Fox the daughter of a
successful clothing manufacturer, Zukor the niece of his fur partner,
Marcus Loew the daughter of a prosperous furniture dealer, Jack
Warner a German Jewess, Harry Cohn the ex-wife of a wealthy attor-

ney, Jesse Lasky a beautiful girl from Boston Jewish society. None of these women could have reckoned on their husbands' success or on the demands, sacrifices, and humiliations they would have to endure as a result.

Their spouses, as Jack Warner, Jr., said of his own father, were "creatures of a drive that didn't leave them much time to be good husbands or fathers." Jesse Lasky admitted, "I was absorbed in company business and making money to the exclusion of any real personal life." But that absorption didn't exclude extracurricular sex; and while their wives were meant to be decorous and refined and sexless, essentially young society matrons, many of the Hollywood Jews found sexual release elsewhere—sometimes flagrantly. "Amour in Hollywood, as I remember it in its heyday," Ben Hecht said, "was about seventy-five percent exhibitionism. I don't know what the other twenty-five percent was, but you saw most of it, after dark, reeling around dance-floors and tables and getting photographed." Hecht was probably right that sex, like family, power, wealth, and culture, was meant to be conspicuous in Hollywood. It was a symbol of power, which may be why so many of the Hollywood Jews behaved with such little discretion. Jack Warner bragged about his conquests as if they were trophies. Bess Lasky knew that when her husband sneaked away to make a quick business call he was not talking to Adolph Zukor. B. P. Schulberg, Paramount's head of production in the early thirties, was so shameless in his affair with actress Sylvia Sidney that Zukor fired him because he refused to intercede with Sidney when she decided to walk off a picture. "Miss Sidney's health came first and must be protected," he said.

The most notorious and insatiable sexual predator was Harry Cohn. Geraldine Brooks remembered her father, a friend of Cohn's, recommending her for a part in a film. Cohn seized on the idea and began inundating her with calls until she finally conceded to come to his office for a meeting. "She was still a teenager," wrote Budd Schulberg, later Brooks's husband. "She came in with a dirndl skirt and off-the-shoulder peasant blouse." Cohn charged from behind his massive desk. "'What kind of a blouse is that—going around with your shoulders naked—your father would be ashamed of you!' And on that pious note he yanked her blouse down from her shoulders and grabbed her. She ran for the door. 'You'll never work in this town again!' were Cohn's parting words to his friend's teenage daughter." Corinne Calvet, a beautiful, amply proportioned French starlet, received a command from Cohn that she appear on his yacht to discuss a contract. That evening Cohn, in his pajamas, bulled his way into her room and attacked her. Calvet, who found him physically repulsive, managed to fend off his advance and hide until her boyfriend, actor Rory Calhoun, could arrive later that night to spirit her off the boat to safety.

"A lot of the girls he went with—quite a few of the cover girls—he used to take to his house," said Columbia executive Jonie Taps, who often accompanied Cohn on his forays. "I think he liked the intrigue." On one vacation he took his wife to Honolulu, where he ran into a girl he had known and liked back in Los Angeles. She was traveling with a banker named Al Hart, who was a friend of Cohn's, so Cohn suggested the couple join him and his wife, and he and the girl spent the rest of the vacation together. On Saturday afternoons in the fall, Mrs. Cohn would pack a picnic basket for her husband and send him off to watch football. Then he would pick up his latest girl and take her to Taps's apartment, where they would devour the lunch and presumably each other.

Some wives adjusted to the new expectations. Lottie Zukor enjoyed her role as much as her husband enjoyed his. She became a patron of the arts and a society matron, and like the dowagers in her husband's movies, she held musicales in her spacious apartment. Eve Fox also relished the role, and there were those who felt she was as tough-minded and conniving as her husband. Marcus Loew's wife surrounded herself with the rewards of wealth at their magnificent estate out on Long Island, but she remained lively and unaffected.

Those who couldn't adjust were often replaced, and in the end divorce among the top Hollywood Jews was usually less a product of sexual temptation than of inadequate social performance. For the husbands, their wives could no longer be provincial Jewish mamas any more than their cars could be jalopies or their homes shacks. They had an image to maintain. Harry Cohn, sounding like Henry VIII, told Shelley Winters he divorced his first wife because she couldn't have children, and he desperately wanted a son. To add to her inadequacies as he saw them, Rose Cohn was also self-effacing and unpretty and not at all the proper consort for a king. Cohn decided he would have to find a new one.

After a long search, the woman he finally chose to play the role of Mrs. Cohn was a bit actress and model named Joan Perry (actually Cohn had renamed her that; originally she was Betty Miller from Pensacola, Florida), whom he had first seen on the dance floor of the Central Park Casino. Cohn brought her out to California as his first marriage was unraveling, and from the outset he showed unusual interest in her career—the studio shot 1,200 feet of film for her screen test—though it soon became apparent that it wasn't just the movies he was grooming her for. She was young, stately, attractive rather than brassy, refined, and gentile—everything Cohn could have desired in a professional wife. On June 28, 1941, he obtained a divorce in Reno, Nevada. Three days later he married Joan Perry at the St. Regis Hotel in New York. Within a year she had borne him a child.

The new Mrs. Cohn was, as one of Cohn's associates described her, "a bird in a gilded cage." She entertained superbly. She raised their children—their daughter had died in infancy, but they had two sons and later adopted a daughter—to be models of decorum. She collected paintings and painted herself. Cohn's urbane colleague Nate Spingold hung one of her canvases among his Chagalls and Braques and Picassos. She studied French. She dressed exquisitely in Jean Louis gowns designed at the studio. She suffered indignities silently. And, most of all, she knew how to recede when her husband wanted her to.

For the birds in their gilded cages, however, it wasn't always a very satisfying life, and the wives, like their children, often complained bitterly. Margaret Mayer, who was basically shy and homely, preferred the company of her family to the social demands of the film industry and increasingly remained home. Bess Lasky, ethereally fragile, was the hostess for her husband's famous parties, but she also gradually retreated from the role of Hollywood wife, complaining about having to associate with the other Hollywood Jews, whom she found contemptible. "The more things I gave my wife and the more successful I was," Lasky wrote years later, "the more she withdrew." She sought

The young Harry Cohn, founder of Columbia Pictures. Even the photo's inscription, which warns the recipients to fix their elevator, is typically Cohn.

Harry Cohn, in his studio
photo, as he liked to
be seen.
THE MUSEUM OF MODERN ART/
FILM STILLS ARCHIVE,
COURTESY OF
COLUMBIA PICTURES

Cohn and Frank Capra, the men who made Columbia, with one of Capra's three Oscars.
THE MUSEUM OF MODERN ART/FILM STILLS ARCHIVE

Quintessential images: Frank McHugh, James Cagney, and Humphrey Bogart in *The Roaring Twenties* from Warner Brothers, where the films were permeated with toughness and a vague underdog liberalism.

The gothic expressionism of Universal's *Frankenstein.*

Rosalind Russell and Cary Grant in *His Girl Friday* from Columbia Pictures, where the movies were generally fast and sassy.

The continental sheen of Paramount: Cary Grant and Marlene Dietrich in *Blonde Venus.*

The two sides of M-G-M: Greta Garbo and John Barrymore in *Grand Hotel*, Judy Garland and Mickey Rooney in *Love Finds Andy Hardy*.

THE MUSEUM OF MODERN ART/FILM STILLS ARCHIVE, COURTESY OF M-G-M

The prince of Hollywood: Irving Thalberg.

The prince and his consort, Norma Shearer.
THE MUSEUM OF MODERN ART/ FILM STILLS ARCHIVE

A congregation of power at Irving Thalberg's wedding: (left to right) director Edmund Goulding, William Thalberg, producer Lawrence Weingarten, producer Bernie Hyman, director Robert Z. Leonard, Thalberg, director Fred Niblo, executive Eddie Mannix, William Randolph Hearst, Louis B. Mayer, Howard Hawks, Rabbi Edgar Magnin.
PRIVATE COLLECTION

Wilshire Boulevard Temple on September 16, 1936: Irving Thalberg's funeral.

solace in her painting but also in a string of romances—the most serious with Edward G. Robinson, whose own wife couldn't withstand the rigors of a Hollywood life, either. Ann Warner, Jack's beautiful second wife, also rebelled. "After she was married for about fifteen years," recalled William Schaefer, Warner's administrative assistant, "she suddenly said on one trip, 'You know, I'm awfully tired of the Hollywood society routine. I'm not interested in being part of it anymore.'... When she stopped being the hostess, there was a change in their relationship as well. ... He never discussed his wife except [to say], 'I don't know why the hell she doesn't do this or why she stays up all night and sleeps until noon.'" She spent the better part of her time poring over books on antiques and then browsing stores for objets d'art. Sol Wurtzel and his wife, a Polish immigrant he had married in New York long before he became a film executive, separated, though they never divorced. She took up painting and decided to learn languages, becoming fluent in four or five.

But none of this dissatisfaction really surfaced where it counted most—publicly. Publicly, the families of the Hollywood Jews were as beautiful, loving, secure, serene, and American as the families in the movies the Jews made. Publicly, the children were successes, the wives brilliantly domestic. Publicly, everything was as genteel as could be. For here, life not only imitated art. Here, among the Hollywood Jews, life became art itself.

———

Among the many ways the Hollywood Jews rejected the eastern establishment, which they felt had rejected them, was to pretend that it didn't really matter. "Hollywood was a company town, with me not in the company," wrote Ella Winter, wife of screenwriter Donald Ogden Stewart. "Everyone talked movies, inhaled movies and inevitably went to movie parties. After dinner, if there was a projection room at a producer's house, movies were shown." "Even my doctor had as his clientele mostly movie people," said screenwriter George Oppenheimer. "In his waiting room you were more apt to hear about previews than about symptoms. A call at your druggist, especially if it was Schwab's on the [Sunset] Strip, resulted in more prescriptions for the health of a sick picture than for your health. You were shaved and had your hair trimmed to a choir singing selections from the *Hollywood Reporter* and *Daily Variety*. And in the markets there was more talk of grosses than groceries. . . . "

The irony was that for all the community's insularity and self-absorption, its social life was still modeled after that of eastern high society, and anyone searching for the wild parties of lore was likely to be disappointed. One visiting potentate from Europe asked quietly if he could attend one of these bacchanals with starlets and spirits and sex. Mayer quickly got wind that the visitor wanted a Hollywood party and set to work arranging a bash. But when the poor dignitary showed up, ready for adventure, he found instead precisely the sort of sedate, classy affair he had hoped to avoid.

By the late twenties and throughout the thirties, the big affairs were conducted by a loose confederation of film executives, stars, and directors called the Mayfair Club, which some also labeled the Hollywood Four Hundred. The Mayfair Club met nine times a year at the Biltmore Hotel ballroom in downtown Los Angeles for a candlelit dinner and dance. Since the idea was to keep the outside world at bay, admission was by invitation only, and only the elite were invited. Valentino, Gloria Swanson, Chaplin, Mary Pickford, Mayer, Zukor, Joe Schenck all regularly attended, and when a newcomer entered the community—say, Maurice Chevalier or heavyweight champion Jack Dempsey—the Mayfair was usually where he had his coming-out.

As Hollywood's answer to the East, the Mayfair nights were intended to be dazzling, and they were. The colonnaded ballroom, hung with long, elaborately brocaded draperies, would be decorated with palm fronds, and the guests would be dressed in coordinated finery; one month all the women would be asked to wear red, another month white. That the effect of this orchestrated glamour was more important than the socializing wasn't lost on all the Hollywood Jews. "I marveled at this new world of iridescent splendor representing many millions, many romances, many miracles," remarked another transplanted New York Jew, comedian Eddie Cantor, "and it had all come into being through the imagination and the business brains of a former furrier, a former druggist, and former coronet player—Adolph Zukor, Joe Schenck, and Jesse Lasky."

For Cantor, the Mayfair was an achievement—a source of pride.

For others, the aping of genteel society was comically incongruous. "The food was good, the music was the best," wrote actress Mary Astor. "But as for people being themselves, it was absurd. The men wore top hats, white tie and tails. Everybody got a good look at everybody else, and who was with who, and who got drunk and who looked terrible, and the columns duly reported the long lists of important names the following day; and if your name wasn't there you called the paper and raised hell."

Even the private social functions were intended primarily as conspicuous displays of status, and the social competition was fierce. "Everyone was giving parties," wrote Jesse Lasky, Jr., whose father was one of the most extravagant party givers. "We attended swimming parties, beach parties, tennis parties, country club parties, buffet parties, cocktail parties, masquerade parties, game parties, lawn parties, come-as-you-are, come-as-you-aren't." On any given Saturday night there were at least twenty-five parties throughout Hollywood bidding to capture the biggest stars, the most powerful executives, the hottest writers and directors. The ubiquitous symbol of the Hollywood party in those days, the thirties, was the capacious peppermint-striped tent in the backyard. At the better affairs, dinner was usually buffet prepared by one of a small, select list of caterers. Generally a wooden dance floor was laid, a string of lanterns hung, and a long ribbon of striped canvas unfurled along the yard's borders.

If it looked like the set for a swanky soiree in a movie, in a sense it was. These people, whose lives were absorbed by artifice and performance, really didn't know how to socialize except by entertaining— literally. "When we really threw a party," wrote Jesse Lasky, "the roster of entertainment would have done credit to a charity benefit." The Ballet Russe de Santa Monica, an impromptu troupe that included Eddie Cantor, Harpo Marx, and Douglas Fairbanks, Jr., might perform. Maurice Chevalier or Jeanette MacDonald might sing. Chaplin might do a pantomime. George Gershwin or Jerome Kern might play some of their compositions at the piano.

When executives entertained, they would usually show a film in their private projection rooms. "I remember there was only one immovable house rule," said Jack Warner, Jr. "If the man who made the picture was the host, you didn't criticize it. But if it was a picture you ran from another studio, you could talk back to the screen and say anything you wanted to, and there was a lot of that happening." MGM executives went one better. They actually *made* movies to be shown at their parties. "They were usually very dirty," recalled Maurice Rapf, the son of MGM vice president Harry Rapf.

> They were funny in a very "in" way, but nobody would ever make fun of Mayer. They were silent movies... very short. I was in one. I look about eleven. And Mervyn LeRoy [producer and director] is in it. [MGM vice president] Thalberg and my father are in it. The presumption of this is a look into the future, and I'm running the studio and Thalberg and my father are in the waiting room waiting to see me. And I'm riding in Thalberg's car with his chauffeur, now a very old man, all whited up. That's the kind of thing they used to do for parties. A twenty-minute film on 35 mm.

The master of this sort of elaborate entertainment was Mayer himself. "I went to Mayer's house one night when he threw a party for a Jewish general named Julius Klein, who was head of the National Guard division in Illinois," said producer Milton Sperling.

> At the end of dinner, about forty people, we went into Mayer's projection room, which was a small theater with banked seats, a pitched floor, and a stage. And we all sat in armchairs, and Mayer sat down at the front in a wooden chair facing the audience.
> "Tonight," he says, "you're going to see something you'll remember the rest of your lives. All right," and he snapped his fingers. The band played, and out came Judy Garland, Gene Kelly, etc., etc. He never looked at them. He had his back turned and [was] watching the audience. He said, "How about that, hah? Isn't that something?" He never turned to look at them. They were performing to his back. He was the master of ceremonies. It was absolutely unbelievable.

Even where there weren't formal performances like these, the parties became individual performances of power by the guests. The men and women customarily divided—the men talking business, the women discussing the servant situation. "Every male was automatically drawn to the most influential and useful person present," wrote scenarist George Oppenheimer. "The drones would gather about this king bee and pay him court, while the women were left to fend for themselves usually until dinner was announced, at which time the sexes could chastely mingle." Reginald Fernald, a friend of Edmund Wilson, recounted attending one of these parties and hearing the kind of vaunting over money that went on among the men—a macho rite. "[H]e had gone into the next room and found a friend who had disappeared pacing the floor there," wrote Wilson. "'What's the matter?' 'All that kind of talk's damn embarrassing, you know, when you're trying to decide whether you've got enough money to get new linoleum for the kitchen floor!'"

Aside from creating an atmosphere of competition, all of this constant preening made real friendship extremely difficult, and people seldom formed the sort of deep, abiding associations that are typical elsewhere. Relationships tended to be utilitarian—whomever one happened to be working with, whomever one happened to need—which meant that friendship took on an entirely different meaning in Hollywood. One Christmas, MGM executive Sam Marx remembered, the husband-and-wife writing team of Dorothy Parker and Alan Campbell was working with Garson Kanin. Parker said, "You know, I always hate the holidays in this town. As long as we're working, why don't we just go up to Arrowhead or somewhere and get out of town for this period." Kanin replied without a hint of irony, "No. I'm going to stick around because Sam and Marie Marx are my best friends and they always have a party, and I haven't seen them since last Christmas." Then, realizing what he'd said, he fell to the floor laughing.

This lack of genuine friendship was especially true of the community's upper crust, where, unlike eastern society, one's current success counted for practically everything. No one, certainly not the Hollywood Jews, many of whom had narrowly escaped failure themselves, wanted to be associated with failures, and Hollywood could be particularly cruel to those on the way down. Producer Milton Sperling, after reading that a consortium had made a sizable offer to buy Columbia, asked Harry Cohn if he was going to sell. Cohn said, "'Are you crazy? If I sell the company, who's going to call me on the telephone?' And that was absolutely true. Everyone knew this. Once they didn't have the job, that was the end." Budd Schulberg, son of one-time Paramount production head B. P. Schulberg, remembered a studio truck pulling up to their home on Christmas Eve and unloading gifts while a parade of sycophants stopped by to leave expensive presents. Then suddenly—no truck, no well-wishers, no phone calls. B. P. Schulberg had been deposed.

"Society consisted of the top executives, the most successful producers, the brightest stars, the visiting firemen, social, intellectual, or financial, and the various hangers-on," observed one screenwriter. "Since statuses were constantly changing with the success or failure of films, the guest list at parties was apt to be kaleidoscopic. The cynical brother of a producer once pointed out to me that on the occasion of the latter's annual birthday party, you seldom saw more than three or four faces from the year before." "They came and went," said Jack Warner, Jr., of his father's carousel of friends. "There weren't any long-term friends. . . . He sort of pushed people away."

The moguls seldom fraternized with one another, except at charitable functions, and even then they were likely to confine themselves to their own studio's table. In part this was a matter of self-defense, since these were men with oversized egos and tempers. "I remember my uncle and father saying that they had been physically thrown out of Louis B. Mayer's house one night," recalled Jack Warner, Jr. "They were angry as hell about it because it had never happened before, and it never did again." Occasionally Louis Mayer would socialize with Harry Cohn, largely because Cohn so aggressively pursued the relationship that Mayer was flattered. And at the level beneath the top, executives might gather for a weekly high-stakes poker game (they were the only ones who could afford it). But generally there was an almost collegiate rivalry among the studio heads, with each wanting to prove his empire paramount, each trying to prove himself the greatest.

At its most playful, this took the form of athletic competition.

"They would hire all the guys from the college teams to work for the studio," remembered the son of one executive. "They'd make them grips and electricians, and they'd have teams and leagues. . . . I remember working with a guy who was an assistant who was a United States handball champion." Warners' executives actually formed a polo team in the mid-thirties with Jack as one of the players. ("From Poland to Polo in one generation" became a studio joke). Warner production head Darryl Zanuck would walk around the lot swinging a polo mallet, and Jack, in a rush of enthusiasm, went out and stabled eight horses, twice as many as a player customarily needed. The team played weekly matches until injuries forced it to disband.

Of course, competition only began on the playing fields. The real contests were in the executive suites and boardrooms. Periodically, at least until the labor wars of the thirties forced them to maintain a united front, studios would launch raids on the talent of rivals and then brace for the inevitable retaliation. (One particularly savage skirmish, between Paramount and Warner Brothers, saw nearly a dozen stars change uniforms.) Harry Cohn, at Columbia, struck closer. He repeatedly tried to hire members of Warner's own family, including Jack Jr. "'Why do you keep working for that no-good son of a bitch?'" Cohn asked Jack Jr. "'Why don't you come over here and work for me?' He was saying that to hurt my father, because if I did leave Warner Brothers to work for Harry Cohn, he knew that would upset my father." Cohn tried the same tactic on Harry Warner's son-in-law, Milton Sperling—again to no avail.

A few, like Jack Warner, took the rivalry seriously. Most of the others seemed to realize there was a certain gamesmanship to all of it. Eugene Zukor remembered his father and Harry Warner screaming at one another during a phone conversation because the Warners had decided to build a new theater near one Paramount had recently built.

> They called each other names: colorful, brilliant, dirty names. I was sitting in the office, and there was another party, the treasurer of the company or someone. . . . Then my father gets a call from the coast that we have a problem getting Gary Cooper to appear in a picture because he's

*being held up in a production of Warner Brothers. So he
calls Harry Warner, the same guy he'd talked to five minutes before.*

*"Harry, what is the situation with Gary Cooper?" Just as
if nothing had happened.*

"I'll tell you. We're behind and the weather is bad."

"Well, do you think we could work something out?"

*"Sure we will. No problem. We'll be through with him in
two weeks. If we need retakes, we'll call you up and I'm sure
we can get a day."*

*The fellow sitting there said, "How can he talk to this
man after this guy called him every name under the sun?
They were archenemies five minutes ago."*

*My father said, "We're in so many lines of business, you
can't be the same person in each one without affecting the
others. It's an unwritten law in our business: our paths
cross unexpectedly, and if we're developing enmities, it's
going to affect all of our businesses adversely. We have to
play the game according to the immediate situation."*

But there was something more than pragmatism at work. Despite
their lack of social contact and their heated rivalry, the Hollywood
Jews always sensed that their real adversaries were outside the industry, on Wall Street and in the boardrooms of the East, where they
believed, not wholly without reason, that gentiles were plotting to
take their studios away. Particularly after the Depression hit, the Jews
had an unspoken convenant. That explained why Harry Warner put
aside his differences and rushed to Lasky's defense when he was
ousted from Paramount and needed money. And it helped explain a
more curious act of solidarity a few years later when Zukor himself
was being besieged by the eastern financiers.

Eugene Zukor received a call from Louis Mayer inviting him to
visit MGM. Mayer, whom Eugene had met only once before, asked
him for an assessment of the state of Paramount. Eugene replied
frankly that "our house is invaded by vermin or worse," but that his
father, despite the humiliation of being demoted from company president to head of production, intended to stick it out, believing that in
the long run the eastern financiers would come to see that they

needed his expertise. Mayer shot back, "I don't agree with that at all. They are bent on destruction, and they're going to seek it out. They're going to do everything to scuttle it [the company]." Then, always the master dramatist, he dropped his bombshell. "I want you to come over here."

Eugene was amazed at the offer. Mayer continued, "Beginning now, I want you and your father, and I'll give you anything you want. You've *got* to come over here. Not only that—but I have taken a position to this effect." And with that, Mayer opened the door from his office that led to the boardroom. Assembled there was the entire production staff of the studio—ironically including Sam Katz, who had deserted Paramount after helping to engineer its takeover. "I have just told young Zukor what I have already told you: I want him and his father to join our staff over here as an independent unit and to tell Paramount to shove it." Mayer strode over to a telephone on the board's table and announced that he was calling Nicholas Schenck, president of MGM's parent company, Loew's Incorporated, to demonstrate to Eugene that the offer was extended with Schenck's support. "I want these people here," Mayer told Schenck in front of the gathering, "and I want you to subscribe to it [his offer]." Hanging up the phone, he turned to Eugene for an answer.

Eugene groped, saying he was "grateful and honored and also exhilarated, stupefied, and whatever else a person can be under these circumstances," but that he could only convey the offer to his father, which he did. When told, the elder Zukor was adamant. He would not leave Paramount. It had become a point of honor to pull himself and his company through, and nothing would change his mind. To leave now would be admitting defeat. To leave would be surrendering the company to financiers who cared nothing for the movies, and this he would not do. Eugene disagreed but consented to call Mayer and thank him for his gesture. "Gesture! Goddammit!" Mayer raged. "They deserve to sink. Let's sink them!" It was the voice of Jewish Hollywood.

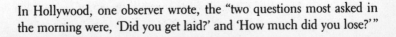

In Hollywood, one observer wrote, the "two questions most asked in the morning were, 'Did you get laid?' and 'How much did you lose?'"

As vices went, Jews seldom drank or indulged in drugs, which even in the thirties were readily available. They did, of course, womanize, but women were really a distraction that became a metaphor for power. The Hollywood Jews had another vice—a metaphor that became an obsession. They loved to gamble. Virtually everyone—even Mayer played penny-ante canasta or bridge—gambled. They would wager on anything: football, cards, horses, movies, elections. Al Lichtman, a longtime film executive, once proposed his usual wager on the golf course; when his partner balked, Lichtman offered to lower the bet, and when that failed he gave the fellow the stake just so he could bet it. That was the gambling madness.

The real showdowns were the all-night, high-stakes poker and bridge games—sometimes poker and bridge simultaneously at adjacent tables. Thalberg was a regular and Joe Schenck and B. P. Schulberg and David Selznick, and others would drop by—Irving Berlin, Sid Grauman, bandleader Ben Bernie, and half a dozen more. The amounts wagered were staggering, and that was part of the metaphor. In Michael Korda's words, "The mark of a man's position in the hierarchy of movies was the amount of money he could afford to lose." More, "[t]he ability to play for high stakes was one of the few ways to win the respect of men like Mayer, Cohn and Zanuck, all of whom were capable of betting fortunes in card games, and would have killed their own children for an advantage." Sam Marx remembered a typical game where Thalberg stood up and said, "Fellows, I've got to get to work. This is as far as I go. Cash me in." He was $16,000 ahead. Marx seized the opportunity to cash in his $200 worth of chips, but he didn't get the check for another two and a half months. It turned out that after Marx had left, Schulberg had dropped $48,000, and it had taken him that long to pay off.

Jack Warner hosted another game to inaugurate the poker room of his brand-new Beverly Hills mansion. (Actually, it wasn't quite "brand" new; Warner's second wife, Ann, demanded that he knock down his old house where he had lived with his first wife and build another on its foundation.) "Whatever the house cost," said Warner's son, Jack, "my father lost it that night. He always complained the house cost him twice what it should have." Warner was luckier than some. David Selznick, a bearish hedonist with the appetites and discipline of a child, was an inveterate gambler and an inveterate loser, but no matter how much he lost (and he lost small fortunes), how much he borrowed, begged, forestalled, he couldn't let go. Gambling was the inexorable demon. His brother-in-law, Bill Goetz, bragged that he maintained his standard of living off Selznick's debts. His wife wrote, "[I]t took the fine edge of happiness off our marriage" and "undermined both his self-esteem and his independence."

What bit so deeply in Selznick and the other Hollywood Jews was not just the pagan demonstration of wealth, as Korda said. The wealth was what made it easy to gamble. Gambling was a kind of therapy that cut through all the affectations and reduced everything to basic naked aggression. It tested the skills of bluff and nerve and judgment, which were the measure of a film executive, and it provided a small arena for tremendously competitive and insecure men to intimidate one another and prove themselves. At the same time it provided anxiety, which, writer Leo Rosten observed, "is provoked, nursed, and kept alive in a manner which suggests self-punishment for obscure and disturbing guilts"—possibly, though Rosten made no conjecture, the Jews' guilt for having rejected themselves or possibly guilt over their sense of unworthiness in the face of success. And, finally, it provided a way to cheat destiny by mastering it. For the Jews, most of whom felt they had been matched against destiny, the last may have been the most important. Thalberg seldom lost. Lasky always did. In Hollywood, that meant something.

The most profligate of the gamblers and the towering figure of the gambling community was Joe Schenck. At fifty-nine Schenck was so outwardly saturnine with his icy-blue eyes and thin-lipped inscrutability that he had been nicknamed "Buddha," but that was far from the essential man. In reality he embodied just about every cliché of Hollywood decadence and debauchery, and he had even gone to jail for it when he was convicted of taking excessive deductions on his income tax. (He had claimed 83 percent of his salary as a business expense.) Still, the jury foreman admitted to reporters that Schenck would have been acquitted if he had been guilty only of taking those excessive deductions. What clinched the case was chicanery involving some stock in a racetrack—Schenck sold the stock to friends for a pittance and claimed heavy capital losses—and a $15,000 bet on Roosevelt's election, which Schenck won but didn't declare. That, the jury decided, was the last straw.

One who testified as a character witness at Schenck's trial was Al Wertheimer. Al and his brother Lew may have been Schenck's main contributions to the Hollywood gambling scene in the 1930s. The Wertheimers had a somewhat beclouded and unsavory past in Detroit —there were vague references to the Purple Gang—until Schenck invited them out to Hollywood. By his own admission, Lew had absolutely no experience in show business, but Schenck nevertheless offered him $500 a week as an executive for Fox, and Mayer, possibly at the instruction of Nick Schenck, even matched the offer. What the Wertheimers lacked in experience, however, they seemed to make up in charm, attractiveness, toughness, and a certain insouciance. One summer when Schenck was away, the Wertheimers rented his Hollywood home, knocked down a wall without telling him, and set up a gambling den in the newly expanded room. Another time Al was seriously injured in a car accident in Palm Springs; every bone in his body was broken, save his wrist. When he arrived at the hospital, he broke the wrist himself.

Whatever the Wertheimers were doing in the movie business, they soon gravitated back to the illicit by opening the Clover Club in Hollywood, where gambling was prohibited. Compared with the tony casinos of Monte Carlo and even Palm Beach, the Clover was small potatoes, but it had a kind of cathouse showiness—one patron described it as "sleaze"—that attracted the big rollers in the film industry, and in any case Joe Schenck steered business there. The Clover had an air of intrigue. Guests approached down a quiet street off the Sunset Strip, then had to be checked off at the driveway to insure they weren't in cahoots with the police. A boy took your car, and you were checked again at the door. Inside, the dominant color was blood red. At the end of the room was an oversized mirror that opened up, in a touch of Hollywood drama, as a secret passageway to the really high-stakes poker games. To complete the effect, the bouncers wore forty-fives under their jackets.

For many of the Hollywood Jews, the Clover became an informal meetinghouse. Things happened there. It was lively and loud and electric. Harry Cohn went. And Jack Warner. And Frank Orsatti,

Mayer's boon companion, took him there. Benny Thau, an MGM executive, lost so much money there that Nick Schenck garnisheed a portion of his salary each week just so he wouldn't have anything to gamble with. And, of course, there was Joe Schenck. "Everyone that knew Joe Schenck," testified his friend Harpo Marx at Schenck's trial, "knew that Mr. Schenck played poker and chemin de fer," and that he gambled "extensively."

Eventually the Clover, like most things in Hollywood, passed out of fashion. Gambling moved to the Trocadero, which wasn't a gambling club per se, but which hosted a nightly poker game, often with writer Herman Mankiewicz presiding. (Schulberg had to put Mankiewicz under contract, it was said, because it was the only way he could get what was owed him.) The Wertheimers moved on to Palm Springs and opened a new gambling club there called the Dunes. Al bought himself a ranch in Montana.

Meanwhile, the big Hollywood money moved south to a Mexican resort called Agua Caliente in the desert just outside Tijuana. Schenck had leased the land from Mexico's president, Rodriguez, and with his partners he erected an impressive monument of pink adobe to the things he liked best: gambling and fun. Its brochure claimed that Agua Caliente "is synonymous with thoughts of carefree days, of laughter, joy, and life to its fullest, in a balmy sun-kissed land of glamorous romance." Agua Caliente had tennis courts, a golf course, hot baths, and available women. It also had a racetrack, a dog track, and a casino, so the Jewish executives who went there had a variety of things on which to wager.

To get to Agua Caliente by car from Hollywood took about six hours, and the wait at the border on the way back could be as long as two, but that didn't seem to deter anyone. On weekends it resembled a bivouac of film executives, writers, and stars all drinking, gambling, and whoring amid the mariachis. On Saturday nights, wrote director William Wellman, "the huge barroom was loaded and so was everyone in it. The bar six deep with actors, actresses, jockeys, doctors, lawyers, and an Indian chief from Oklahoma. . . . It was so noisy that everyone wanting to be heard had to yell and everybody had the floor." Schenck scarcely spent a weekend away from it.

But that party ended, too. General Rodriguez was ousted from power, and the new government outlawed gambling, making the resort, in the words of Schenck's attorney, "as dead as a cock in a cockpit." It reopened two years later, in 1937, but by this time Schenck had already unloaded his stock and claimed his loss in the complicated tax dodge that would send him to prison. It closed again in September after just two months, and five days before its scheduled grand re-reopening in December, the Mexican government expropriated the complex and turned it over to the labor unions. Thus ended Hollywood's favorite den of iniquity.

But the gambling would continue—in the back rooms of other clubs, at restaurants and mansions and apartments and weekend retreats in the mountains. "There used to be a kind of floating Jewish population," remembered producer Pandro Berman, who belonged to a group of cardplayers that included Ben Schulberg, Harry Warner, and Sam Briskin, production head at Columbia. "We'd go to Palm Springs. We'd go to Coronado. We'd go to Pebble Beach and Arrowhead Springs and Arrowhead Lake. . . . They'd go down on a Saturday afternoon and come home on a Sunday night, and they'd stay overnight and play cards. . . . They never discussed anything. They just played cards." Jack Warner eventually bought a home in France near the Monte Carlo casinos, where he would sit for hours at the gaming tables. Schenck gambled in Cuba. In the late forties Harry Cohn practically commuted to Las Vegas. The venues changed. The gambling continued. It would continue as long as the Hollywood Jews needed to exercise their primal instincts and as long as they needed to test fate. As it turned out, it would continue for a very long time.

───

If their social and family lives were stamped in the image of eastern gentility and their recreational lives stamped in combat, the Hollywood Jews ultimately discovered something that solidified their claims to status while at the same time providing the therapeutic benefits of gambling. They discovered horses. In Fitzgerald's *The Last Tycoon*, Monroe Stahr speculates that "the Jews had taken over the worship of horses as a symbol—for years it had been the Cossacks mounted and the Jews on foot. Now the Jews had horses and it gave them a sense of extraordinary well-being and power." Fitzgerald was right that the horses came before the racing. The Hellmans, one of the first families of Los Angeles' Jewish community, organized a Bridle Path Association in Beverly Hills even before the Hollywood Jews arrived, and by the late twenties more than half the members of the Hollywood Polo and Riding Club were Jews. Given their fixation on aestheticizing themselves, it wasn't surprising that when the movie Jews moved out to Hollywood from the clotted cities of the East, they assumed the same affectation; and so there was Louis Mayer, like a country squire, joining the Griffith Park Riding Academy and bobbing in the saddle on his morning horseback ride.

This image may have seemed ridiculous to anyone outside Hollywood, but the Jews there took it very seriously. Still, to be gentlemen riders wasn't enough. The deepest satisfactions, not to mention the surest signs, of the horsey set were owning and racing thoroughbreds. The problem was that the premier track in Los Angeles, Santa Anita, had an unspoken policy excluding Jews, which forced them back to the solution they had always employed in similar situations: they would create a track of their own. The prime mover, if not the instigator, of the new track was Harry Warner. Warner loved horses and racing, in that order, and he had purchased a large spread in the San Fernando Valley, when land was cheap and plentiful, to accommodate, among other things, a horse ranch. Warner's son-in-law, director and producer Mervyn LeRoy, was also a horse fancier and had already become part of the Jewish cabal trying to build a track. It was he who approached Warner, though it apparently didn't take too much convincing to get him to put up the final capital. The Jews' track was named Hollywood Park. One observer called it "Hillcrest with furlong markers," after the Jewish Hillcrest Country Club.

As it turned out, most of the Hollywood Jews were only adequate breeders. Warner himself had little success. Harry Cohn owned some horses and bet heavily (he even hired an old tout named Doc Salter to phone him reports from the track) until, characteristically, he realized it was *their* game, not his, and quit. Even Joe Schenck had more luck with women and cards than with ponies. The one who fared best was Louis Mayer. Mayer had actually come to horse racing relatively late, when, according to one account, his doctor suggested he find a form of recreation to provide a release from the pressures of the studio. Why he decided to take up horse racing isn't entirely clear—his daughter Edith attributed his interest to a friend and avid horseman named Neil McCarthy—but its rewards must have soon become obvious to him, and they exerted a powerful hold. He plunged into horses the way he had plunged into nothing else save the movies nearly twenty years before. There were even faint rumblings that the horses had displaced the studio as his first passion.

For Mayer, in fact, the two had a great deal in common, and his success as a breeder was attributable to the same urges and techniques that had made him a success as a movie magnate. As one of the most status conscious of the Hollywood Jews, what Mayer obviously recognized was the status that attached to racing and breeding. "It was a kind of classy thing for him to be doing," admitted his grandson Danny Selznick. As at MGM, everything had to be the best. He spent extravagantly, offering $1 million for the legendary Man o' War. (The horse's owner declined, saying, "They would not know how to treat this old fellow.") He offered the same for the great English horse Hyperion and was again refused, but he did acquire one of Hyperion's offspring named Alibhai and a fabled thirteen-year-old stallion from Australia named Beau Pere. These became the nuclei of his stable. Now he had the studs but not the stud farm. So next he bought five hundred acres of land in Perris, California, just off the Mojave Desert with the mountains as a backdrop, and proceeded to build the most modern, sophisticated, and certainly one of the most beautiful horse farms in the country. From MGM came dreams. From here came champions.

But what was touching—what was always touching about Mayer —was the way in which the horses also satisfied his sense of dynasty —a longing that had recently been undermined both by his separation from his wife and by renewed grumblings from Nick Schenck over Mayer's command of the studio. His stable brought him closer to his cherished dream of patriarchy; at Perris he had become the patriarch of horseflesh. "As he had his own specially developed relationship with each secretary on the [MGM] lot or a certain chef on the lot or a chauffeur," remembered Danny Selznick, "so he had a relationship with certain horse trainers, certain jockeys, and the individual horses. He had a sort of playful dialogue that he entered into with each of his horses that I believe he improvised just for us. It was as if different members of his family were being introduced to one another. He would say to Busher, 'You know my grandson Daniel Selznick' or 'You know my grandson Jeffrey Selznick.'"

Mayer rapidly became one of the most successful racehorse owners in the country and one of the most important breeders. By 1945, scarcely seven years after he bought his first horse, he was the second leading money winner in America. That same year the New York Turf Writers named him their leading breeder. The irony was that in conquering a world of the gentile gentry as he did, he won as much envy as respect. Even bettors weren't satisfied, since Mayer's horses won so consistently that the odds on them were short and the payoffs meager. And that worried the Hollywood Jews.

So one day a delegation of Jewish community leaders, headed by a prominent entertainment attorney named Mendel Silberberg, arrived at Mayer's office and suggested that he get out of racing. His name was being booed at the track, they said, and this was making it difficult on all the Jews in Los Angeles. Mayer was furious. "What do you think I'm going to do—live in a closet because I'm Louis B. Mayer?" he yelled. "Is that what you're asking me to do?" And before waiting for their reply, Mayer, who was known for his proclivity to violence, threw them all bodily out of his office.

Rabbi to the Stars

8

Consider this. A Jew becomes Americanized only in direct proportion to his becoming de-Judaized. But that's a tightrope performance. Yearning to be Americanized, that is, to be accepted at par by the *goyim*, he begins by renouncing everything Jewish about him. He sheds his accent, shaves his beard, changes his clothes, curtails his names, plays golf and tennis, subdues his fire, and makes his whole religion conform to an elite Protestantism. Then, suddenly, he becomes aware that he has nothing left which is intrinsically himself. He has a crazy quilt make-up of foreign patches which serves as a good temporary covering.

FROM *RABBI BURNS,* A NOVEL

HE LOOKED AS IF HE HAD BEEN hewn out of a sequoia. He was tall, heavy, and shapeless, and he carried himself with the kind of studied gravity that befitted an institution—which is what he was. He had officiated at the weddings of many of them, including Thalberg, and in time he would officiate at their funerals. When he conducted Sabbath services on Friday evenings at the magnificent tabernacle he erected for himself on Wilshire Boulevard, the Hollywood Bowl canceled its concerts. Some in Hollywood joked that they would eventually have to reschedule the Friday-night fights rather than compete with him. He had his own newspaper column and network radio program, and his listeners included the misanthropic comedian W. C. Fields, who once arranged a dinner just because he wanted to meet him. "He was the most important Jew in Los Angeles," one writer said. The subject of this encomium was no less immodest. "I really was *the* rabbi. . . . I was the only one the public recognized." To the Hollywood Jews, he was the closest thing they had to a spiritual adviser.

Edgar Magnin had been born on July 1, 1890, in San Francisco, where the Jewish community was comprised largely of prosperous old German families who prided themselves on their ability to assimilate. Magnin's own family were actually Dutch Jews. His paternal grandfather had started a successful department store, eponymously named I. Magnin, but his parents divorced when he was an infant, and his mother forbade him to have anything to do with the Magnins. He never heard from his father again. Edgar was told that, years later, his father would sneak into the temple to hear him speak and then silently slink out.

For a religious leader, Magnin had less than a pietistic upbringing. Taken into the home of his grandfather Fogel, who owned a clothing store on the waterfront, Edgar would sit with the old sea captains who docked there and listen to their tales. The prizefighter Jim Corbett lived in the neighborhood, and nearby was the Tivoli Theater. An uncle of his was related to one of the chorus girls there, and that gave Edgar the privilege to go backstage—a privilege of which he frequently availed himself. A close childhood friend was Sol Lesser, whose father operated one of the first nickelodeons in San Francisco and who would himself eventually become one of the leading film exhibitors on the West Coast and later a producer.

Lesser's uncle, M. S. Levy, also happened to be the rabbi at the local shul the boys attended each day. For a man of God, Levy was something of a showman, and this wasn't lost on Magnin. He remembered him as a "character out of Dickens." He always wore a silk hat, a white tie, and a Prince Albert coat, and when he spoke he had a rich, stentorian delivery that spellbound the children. He was also a man of tremendous warmth—buying the boys chewing gum or purchasing a stack of papers from a newsboy. Magnin could never say what steered him into religion, since his family wasn't particularly religious, and he never felt he had been inculcated with any special religious feeling. His real love was literature, and years later he remarked, "I don't know why I didn't start to be a writer, a novelist. I should have done it, I think." But Levy became a role model, and when Magnin was sixteen he left for the Hebrew Union College in Cincinnati—in large part, he said, to release himself from his mother's apron strings and enter a new world.

Hebrew Union College was where the sons of wealthy German Jews trained for the rabbinate under the tutelage of old German Jews. "A Russian Jew or a descendant was like a barbarian to them," said Magnin. Each day he would walk from the small boardinghouse where he roomed for $25 a month to the school, which was squeezed in between the brothels and stockyards of downtown Cincinnati. He never felt entirely comfortable among his brethren and his teachers. To him they were all desiccated and dull—deadened by faith rather than enlivened by it. Writing a sermon for a class, he composed a parable about geese who live isolated in their own hermetic world until one of them finally peeks outside and returns to report what he has seen. The other geese dismiss him, calling him insane. Magnin's professor didn't have the vaguest idea what Magnin was saying and advised that he stick to the Bible.

But Magnin was unbowed. "I used to go to temple on Saturday morning," he recalled. "And one of the rabbis, you knew what he said before he spoke, and the other one you didn't know what he said when he was all through. And all they had in the congregation were a few old ladies with bladder trouble and men with prostates. . . . And I used to study these men to find out what not to do. I figured if there's anything that I do that's the very opposite, then I can't go too wrong." One day Emil G. Hirsch came to the college to lecture. Hirsch was a brilliant firebrand of a rabbi from Chicago—Carl Laemmle used to attend his lectures there—who had made it his mission to break through the piety and pomposity of religion and make it live. "Nine turns of the crank and every sausage comes out alike," Hirsch told the nine members of Magnin's graduating class. Magnin said to himself. "That's my man."

With Hirsch's admonitions ringing in his ears, Magnin returned to California in September 1914 to head a congregation in Stockton, where a relative of his exercised some clout in the Jewish community. Here, in this small sullen outpost that consisted of not much more than a main street and a cluster of stores, Magnin was determined to put his style into practice. Where his predecessor seldom mingled with the congregants, Magnin went to their homes for dinner and after the Friday-evening services went out and ate tamales with them. He wrote a weekly column for the local newspaper and gave talks at the library and before the women's club. He lectured on the Jewish Chautauqua circuit, which served as a kind of floating adult education course. In his own words, he "got down to the people's level." No one had ever seen a rabbi quite like him.

Sometime late in 1914, Magnin was on the Chautauqua in San Francisco delivering a lecture entitled "The Renaissance of Hebrew Literature," when a small elderly man approached and introduced himself. Max Newmark was a member of one of the most elite German-Jewish families in Los Angeles. Back in 1862 Max's father, Joseph Newmark, had founded the first Jewish congregation in that city, B'nai B'rith. Now Max had been delegated to make a proposal to Stockton's young rabbi. Rabbi Sigmund Hecht, whose daughter was married to one of the Newmarks, had been the spiritual leader of B'nai B'rith since 1899, but he was aged and, at least in the minds of the synagogue's board, no longer capable of handling his work load alone. At the time, there were less than a dozen Reform rabbis on the whole West Coast, and Magnin's reputation as a maverick had already reached Los Angeles. "Why are you picking me out?" Magnin questioned when Newmark made his offer. "Anybody who can make that subject interesting," replied Newmark, "is the kind of man we're looking for." Several months later, with a group of his congregants to see him off, Magnin boarded the Angel, as the train to Los Angeles was called, for his new job as associate rabbi of B'nai B'rith.

What Magnin didn't know when he arrived in Los Angeles was that Rabbi Hecht had never conceded the need for an assistant and took Magnin's hiring as a personal affront. The wound deepened when, on what Magnin called "opening night," there was a large turnout to see the controversial young rabbi whose pulpit style was reputed to be entertainingly informal. (His sermon was titled "The Stuff Dreams Are Made Of.") Hecht talked bitterly of a new broom sweeping clean, but Magnin publicly declared what a privilege it would be to work beside a scholar like Hecht ("He wasn't that scholarly," Magnin admitted years later), and that seemed to salve the old man's feelings. Seven years later, when the prestigious Isaac M. Wise Temple of Cincinnati asked Magnin to assume a position there, the young rabbi interrupted Hecht's weekly domino game to tell him. Hecht broke down in tears, pleading with Magnin not to leave him. He didn't.

"I always had my eye on New York," Magnin remembered. "I didn't know that Los Angeles would be the second-largest Jewish city in the world. I had no concept like that. So this was only going to be a transition for me." In fact, Los Angeles in 1915, when Magnin arrived there, was a rustic patch of rose-covered bungalows, sighing palms, dirt roads that got impossibly rutted when it rained, an ostrich farm, and roughly 400,000 residents flung over its wide expanse. The Jewish community Magnin entered there had increased nearly tenfold since the turn of the century, but it still numbered less than 20,000, and the great influx of Eastern European Jews that packed the ghettos of New York and Chicago hadn't yet reached the West.

In Los Angeles the German Jews were predominant and preeminent, and they were by and large a moneyed bunch who regarded themselves as genteel and felt they had much more in common with other American elites than with their co-religionists. "Just the other day we noticed several Russian Jewish immigrants walking the streets, wearing their beaver head coverings," noted an observer in a typically disdainful report in the *B'nai B'rith Messenger*. "It was quite a novelty here in this city and their friends should remind these fellows that they are in Los Angeles and not in Siberia." It was an injunction the German Jews themselves scrupulously abided—most demonstrably in a peculiar institution they called the Concordia Club. The Concordia was a convocation of German Jewry's one hundred preeminent families, where the best Jewish girls, like their gentile counterparts, could hold their debutante balls as they came out into society. It was a sign of the German Jews' own religious identification that one of the Concordia's major social events was Christmas and that a large decorated tree stood watch over the group's seasonal festivities.

These German Jews controlled the money, power, and status in the Jewish community, but by the late teens, when Magnin and the Hollywood Jews had arrived, they were only one enclave. "Where do the Jews live?" a New York Jew visiting Los Angeles asks a policeman in a novel about the Los Angeles Jews. "Young feller—do you mean the kikes or the clean Jews?" "I mean the kikes." "Over in Boyle Heights." "Boyle Heights. Named after a good Irishman." When the Eastern European Jews, the "kikes," belatedly made their appearance in Los Angeles in the late teens and early twenties and clustered in an area known as Boyle Heights, there were bound to be frictions with the "clean" Jews. The German-Jewish establishment high-hatted them, excluding them from its organizations and charitable boards and treating them as if they were some kind of contagion spreading the infection of overt Judaism. Even the sick didn't mingle because the Jewish medical community was divided between Kaspare Cohn Hospital, which had been established by the German Jews, and Mt. Sinai, which was supported by the Eastern Europeans. Rabbi Magnin said the breach would be healed only when "the bright, upcoming young Jewish lawyers and doctors descended from [Eastern Europeans] marry the ugly girls of the Germans."

The Hollywood Jews, Eastern European in origin, German in attitude, stood apart from both enclaves. The Boyle Heights Jews ignored them. The German Jews were rankled by them, since their visibility gave them an importance out of all proportion to their numbers. To the German Jews, these newcomers from the East were no better, and in some respects worse, than the Eastern Europeans they reviled. They were the vulgar nouveau riche. "Those [Hollywood Jews] that you met at the time were aggressive," admitted one member of the establishment, a well-connected jurist named Lester Roth, "some of them abrasively so, not too literate and always with a feeling that they ought to impress you with the fact that they were important." The Jews who were really important, at least in the Los Angeles Jewish community, hotly resented this arrogance and even more hotly resented that the attention was being deflected from them. As Roth said, "None of them received the receptions from royalty when they went to Europe that were accorded to any big motion picture director, not just the head of the studio."

Such was the Jewish community over which Magnin would preside: wary, divided, status conscious. But to the gentiles in Los Angeles, all Jews, regardless of rank, were suspect, and their hands were to be kept from the levers of power. In 1909 there were only five Jewish attorneys in the city, in part because most firms proscribed hiring Jews altogether, and those that did hire proscribed making them partners, so that Jewish attorneys could really only serve the small Jewish community.

In this, at least, the gentiles' loss was the Hollywood Jews' gain. Dissatisfied with their lack of progress in the firms they were with, Edwin and Joseph Loeb, two diminutive brothers who were well connected among the Jewish first families, formed a firm of their own. Since many of the Hollywood Jews, new to Los Angeles, preferred to deal with other Jews, Loeb & Loeb ultimately came to represent many of the film companies. "I was working in the library one lunch hour," remembered an attorney who apprenticed at the firm in the twenties, "and I get a call from the switchboard, and he said, 'Mr. Loeb would like to see you in his office at once.' . . . And I went in there, and he casually introduced me to Carl Laemmle and Joe Schenck and Louie Mayer—all in one room. . . . That indicates what a monopoly they had on the motion picture industry."

Jews were also excluded from the best schools, which was especially agonizing to the Hollywood Jews, who held a naive faith that education would enable their children to enter the precincts of the gentile elite from which they themselves had been banned. "It was a terrible thing for me in my childhood," recalled Betty Lasky, daughter of Jesse Lasky. "I couldn't go to Westlake School for Girls. I had to go to public school. . . . They were very polite. We toured the campus and what have you. Then they had some way of notifying us that I couldn't go. What it said, I don't know, because my grades were acceptable. They must have made up some kind of an excuse. But I know at the time I was very upset about it." Louis B. Mayer's daughters met the same resistance when he "begged" gossip columnist Hedda Hopper to use her influence to get them admitted to a private school whose principal was a friend of hers. "Mr. Mayer, they don't accept them," insisted Hopper. To which Mayer remonstrated, "But they'll take my daughters. Can't you tell the headmistress how important I am?" "It won't do any good. . . . They will not take Jews." When Michael Korda, nephew of producer Alexander Korda, was asked by his father how he liked the Beverly Hills military academy he was attending, Michael innocently replied, "Well, the commandant says it's the best school in Los Angeles because there aren't any kikes there." Enraged, Korda took the boy's uniform, burned it in the incinerator, and then went to the school to withdraw his son and excoriate the commandant.

Schools at least made excuses. The least veiled anti-Semitism was reserved for the social clubs. As a policy, none of the country clubs accepted Jews—not the Lakeside Country Club, which was adjacent to the Warner Brothers studio in Burbank; not the Los Angeles Country Club, which was a stone's throw from the Fox studios; not even the Santa Monica Beach Club, which was just down the road from Jesse Lasky's and Louis Mayer's homes. "The only [Jewish] family that I ever saw there would have been Eddie Robinson's," said Betty Lasky. "Eddie Robinson didn't go [himself]. His wife, Gladys, and Gladys's daughter. I would see them there sitting alone under an umbrella, and nobody would ever speak to them. It didn't matter that he was a famous actor. They still wouldn't have spoken to him." The Jewish wife of a famous screenwriter, seeing a chart with the names of a few prominent Jewish members on the club's wall, went to apply for membership herself. "The old man handed me a paper for me to fill out, and it said 'Religious affiliation,' and I said, 'What does that mean?' I really didn't know what it meant. So he said, 'It means are you Jewish or not?' I said, 'I'm Jewish.' He reached for the paper to take it back. I said, 'Oh, no, I want the pleasure of tearing this up myself.' As I was tearing it, I said to the old man, 'How come you have a lot of Jewish people there on your chart as members?' He said, 'Well, they got in before we made this rule.'"

Even the prestigious gentlemen's clubs that had once accepted the wealthy German Jews—the University Club and the California Club —had a change of heart lest they now be invaded by the rich, illiterate immigrant Jews of Eastern Europe. It happened when Joseph Loeb left the University Club to protest an increase in fees and later applied for reinstatement. He was refused. So, it turned out, was every other Jew. When the California Club rejected the application of the son-in-law of one of its founders, a well-heeled Jewish banking magnate named Kaspare Cohn, Cohn and the other Jews resigned. It would be fifty years before another Jew was accepted.

For some, exclusion from these social clubs was more than just another minor indignity. Those who fancied themselves Jewish society and those who modeled themselves after the gentiles required a social center where they could play tennis and golf, where they could transact business, and where, perhaps most of all, they could reestablish their own pecking order. What it came down to is that, with the Concordia Club having faded into oblivion, the Jews needed a new social arbiter. Once again Magnin served as a facilitator. In June 1920 Magnin and a group of German Jews, most of them from his B'nai B'rith, formed the Hillcrest Country Club and authorized its board to purchase a 142-acre plot out in western Los Angeles just south of Beverly Hills. Within a year, in this essentially barren territory, they had erected something splendid enough to rival the bastions of the gentiles they envied and emulated.

Hillcrest, controlled as it was by the Newmarks, the Hellmans, the Cohns, the Loebs, and the Schiffs, was the klavern from which all power emanated. It was the Jewish court of nobility for, in Magnin's words, "the aristocrats and Jewish big shots at the time." By definition this meant that the Hollywood Jews, fresh from the East and with disreputability clinging to them like tar, weren't welcome, though it also meant that the Hollywood Jews wanted in—seeking the blessing of their social betters. For a decade, by and large, they were denied. But the Depression decimated Hillcrest, especially since so many of its members were in the hard-pressed banking industry. Its rolls declined from 350 to 200. The high command couldn't pay the interest on the "gold notes" that had been sold to members to provide the club's initial capital or on its mortgage. To stave off a default, a special three-man committee, which included Joseph Loeb, advised the board to file for bankruptcy. The court accepted the petition, most of the creditors settled for 25 percent of the value of their notes, and the club secured a new mortgage. But there was still the problem of the depleted membership.

Writer-producer Milton Sperling, who was then working across the street from Hillcrest on the Fox lot, remembered a man knocking on his office door. "'I saw your name on the door. Are you Jewish?' And I said, 'Yes. Why?' He said, 'Where are you from?' 'New York.' He said, 'How long have you been here?' I said, 'Two and a half years.' And he said, 'When was the last time you had a bowl of chicken soup and a little chopped chicken liver and some marinated herring? When you left New York, hah?' I said, 'That's right.'" So the man invited Sperling across the street to have a Jewish lunch in the Hillcrest dining room, and after the lunch he said, "'Do you see this place? This is the only place in Los Angeles where a Jew can play golf.' I said, 'I don't play golf.' He said, 'But you're *going* to play golf. You're a nice Jewish boy. You have to support this club. We'll have to close down if people like you don't give money.'" When Sperling protested that he was only earning $300 per week, the man offered to give him a $100 membership on credit and threw in a month's worth of free lunches. And that's how Sperling became a member of Hillcrest.

Of course these inducements weren't necessary for most of the Hollywood Jews. Mayer joined, and the Warners and Harry Cohn and Adolph Zukor and dozens of others who now linked themselves to the Jewish power structure and arrogated its status to themselves. But if the German Jews had founded their club as the genteel seat of the Jewish community, the Hollywood Jews used Hillcrest differently. Regardless of why they applied and regardless of the formality of the setting, Hillcrest became a sanctuary for their Jewishness. At Hillcrest Louis Mayer was "in his shirt-sleeves," said his grandson Danny Selznick, "and he really *was* in his shirt-sleeves, quite literally. He was more relaxed, funnier, freer to be funny, freer to tell jokes . . . because so many of the men at Hillcrest had come from origins similar to his. . . . The clearest sense I have of it was of a lunch that was constantly interrupted—people coming to the table. No story that he was in the process of telling would ever go totally uninterrupted. We might as well all have been standing at a cocktail party because there was a continuous flow of people in and out. That doesn't happen at the Waldorf Astoria. . . . You didn't wander by somebody's table at the Pavilion."

The Hollywood Jews never came close to commandeering Hillcrest; they were there to enjoy the conviviality and the prestige. But whether by design or by nature, they did pierce the curtain of gentility. On Sunday nights there were loud and lively dinners, and afterward the movie Jews would show their recent films. Once each year they would arrange their own golf tournament—the Pow Wow, it was called—with the players dressing in costumes and trying to avert obstacles like gunshots, animals crossing the fairways, and Harpo Marx charging around the course in a gorilla suit. (It was Groucho who had said of Hillcrest, "I wouldn't want to be a member of any club that would have me.") In time they came to conduct business there, too. Abe Lastfogel, the cherubic little boss of the William Morris Agency, held forth at one table. So did Phil Berg and Bert Allenberg, two other top agents. "It was known as a very elite place for the transaction of business," said one executive. "Usually if you went there, you were dealing with someone important, someone who was wealthy and prominent and influential. If you went there to deal with somebody, you were up on important levels."

Meanwhile, the Hollywood Jews at Hillcrest were also rearranging the power configurations within the Jewish community. Hillcrest not only signified the grudging acceptance of the Hollywood Jews by the German Jews, whose power was, in any case, declining by the time the Depression hit; Hillcrest forged an alliance between these groups that would strengthen the entire Jewish community, especially when it was confronted by the virulent anti-Semitism of the thirties or when it needed to raise funds for Jewish causes. At Hillcrest the movie Jews and the German Jews who had originally ostracized them found they had more in common than wealth. They had their Judaism. They had their enemies. And they had their fear.

"Jewish people have to change a lot to get friends," Rabbi Magnin said, expressing the social gospel that was to legitimize the Hollywood Jews' self-denial, "and I don't know if it's possible. . . . I don't think the average Jew has the capacity of cultivating the average gentile in a way to make him like him." Of course that shouldn't stop them from trying. Magnin took enormous pride in being the Los Angeles gentiles' favorite Jew. As the young rabbi in the community, he solicited dinner invitations from the old moneyed gentile clans to prove that Jews didn't have horns, and he accomplished this largely because he was almost totally unself-conscious about his own Judaism. "What was so beautiful about that damned shtetl?" he once said. "They lived like pigs, and they treated their wives like dogs, and their children were beaten by the *melamed* in the Hebrew school." This wasn't Europe. This was America.

For the Hollywood Jews whom Magnin served, his philosophy had the added force of self-defense. It hadn't taken long for anti-Semites to seize the issue of Jewish control of the film industry. The movies, fulminated Henry Ford's *Dearborn Independent* early in 1921, are

> *Jew-controlled, not in spots only, not 50 per cent merely, but entirely; with the natural consequence that now the world is in arms against the trivializing and demoralizing influences of that form of entertainment as presently managed.... As soon as the Jews gained control of the "movies," we had a movie problem, the consequences of which are not yet visible. It is the genius of that race to create problems of a moral character in whatever business they achieve a majority.*

A month later, the *Independent* conceded, "It is not that producers of Semitic origin have deliberately set out to be bad according to their own standards, but they know that their whole taste and temper are different from the prevailing standards of the American people.... Many of these producers don't know how filthy their stuff is—it is so natural to them."

Others couched their attacks against the European-born Hollywood Jews in a cloak of nativism—the notion that immigrants were corrupting this country. "No foreign bunch can come over here and tell us how we ought to observe the Lord's Day," preached evangelist Billy Sunday while thumping for laws that would prohibit the showing of movies on the Sabbath. "The United States at heart is a God-fearing and a God-loving nation and most of our laxity on this point I lay at the door of those elements which are a part of our population, but are not yet assimilated." Another religious zealot blasted the movies' alleged "seduction of hundreds of thoughtless girls every day," which he saw as part of America's general "Europeanization," and he pressed for federal censorship laws.

The Hollywood Jews said little in their own defense—what could they say?—but William Brady, Zukor's old partner who had become president of a trade group called the National Association of the Motion Picture Industry, promised, "If these slanderers, Jew-baiters and Catholic haters are not silenced, we must fight to the finish with no quarter." Ten years later, in 1931, *The Christian Century*, a popular conservative Protestant journal, was still flogging the movie Jews—this time in the form of an open letter from one embarrassed Jew to his Hollywood confreres. "I am a Jew," he wrote, "but I am ashamed of my kinship with you Jews of Hollywood. I am ashamed of kinship with a people who have wholly forgotten their spiritual mission and are now engaged only in the feverish acquisition of wealth by pandering to the worst instincts of humanity."

Even within Hollywood itself there was mumbling about Jewish control. For some it was the handiest rationale for thwarted dreams. Theodore Dreiser had been lured out to Hollywood in the thirties to oversee the film production of his monumental novel *An American Tragedy*, but he had battled hammer and tongs with Paramount over what he felt was the "traducing" of his masterpiece, and now he had departed, trying to raise money for a new project on tobacco monopolist James Buchanan Duke. When that failed, Dreiser blamed the Jews. He wrote a Swiftian satire suggesting that Jews be rounded up and packed off to Kansas where they could do no more harm. To a friend he wrote, "The movies are solidly Jewish. They've dug in, employ only Jews with American names. . . . The dollar sign is the guide—mentally & physically. That America should be led—the mass—by their direction is beyond all believing. In addition, they are arrogant, insolent and contemptuous." Director Howard Hawks complained that Jews were loud. "Do you notice how noisy it is in here suddenly?" he asked actress Lauren Bacall over lunch. "That's because Leo Forbstein [head of the Warner Brothers music department] just walked in—Jews always make more noise." Bacall, née Betty Perske from New York, said nothing—afraid that Hawks might find out she was Jewish and fire her.

Sadly, the Hollywood Jews' self-contempt over their Judaism ran so deep that they often talked about themselves in the same terms. "Through the years I had heard many of the top-drawer Jewish studio executives lose their tempers at meetings or in card games," wrote Dore Schary, recollecting Louis B. Mayer dressing down one of his vassals, "and I was always dismayed when one of the first pejorative terms they used was 'kike'—usually 'dirty kike.'" Schary thought it was an attempt by the Jews to assert their superiority over their antagonists by appropriating their language and thus neutralizing it, and to some degree he was probably right. But Jewish anti-Semitism was also a way for Hollywood Jews to assert superiority over themselves.

A case in point was Herbert Somborn, a smooth Jewish New York film executive. Somborn had talked his way into marrying movie star Gloria Swanson and immediately started grumbling about getting her "out of the hands of these Eastern European Jews," by which he meant Adolph Zukor and Jesse Lasky. Deciding to consult an attorney to see if he could have her contract with Paramount voided on the grounds of inequitability, he snarled, "That's the only way to deal with these Eastern European Jews."

Of course, it was one thing for Jews to disparage themselves and another for gentiles to do it. The Hollywood Jews were never thick-skinned as far as anti-Semitism was concerned. For them it lurked everywhere, constantly menacing. Watching a bearded Greek Orthodox prelate walk down the aisle of an airplane, Jack Warner complained bitterly to a companion, "If he was a rabbi, everyone would make a nasty comment. 'Look at the Jew!'" Calling someone an anti-Semite was one of the surest ways of blackening him among the Hollywood executives. When RKO production head George Schaefer refused Louis Mayer's offer to buy the negative of Orson Welles's masterpiece *Citizen Kane* (Mayer made the offer to destroy the movie, which was loosely and unflatteringly based on the life of his friend William Randolph Hearst), Schaefer suddenly found himself the victim of a whispering campaign accusing him of anti-Semitism.

Determined to find the source, Schaefer later traced the rumors to a close associate of Mayer's. Naturally, none of this prevented the Hollywood Jews from practicing a reverse discrimination—"Those goyim!" Harry Warner would yell in derision, or "He's a nice fellow for a goy," a Jew might say—but only in their inner sanctums, when they were safe among fellow Jews, and only verbally. Otherwise gentiles were to be courted and given deference.

In calling for an Americanized Judaism, then, Magnin wasn't only speaking as a fully assimilated San Francisco Jew. He was also accommodating and sanctioning the views of his congregation. What the German Jews wanted, what the Hollywood Jews wanted, was a way of maintaining their Judaism (they couldn't avoid it) without being too pushy about it and rousing the gentiles. That was Magnin's function, and he served it brilliantly. He "was the right rabbi in the right temple in the right city at the right moment in time," wrote Budd Schulberg, who attended B'nai B'rith as a child. "If he had not presided over our B'nai B'rith, God and Louis B. Mayer—whose overpowering presences tended to overlap—would have had to create him. Or maybe they did."

Magnin certainly seemed like the product of a very vivid Hollywood imagination. He was young, loud, earthy, gregarious, dynamic, frank, and disarming—one of the boys. Except when he got carried away in the pulpit, he avoided piety as if it were a sin, attacking the pretensions of other rabbis with their sonorous voices and holier-than-thou demeanor. Mayer claimed that "Edgar would fit into any group." Magnin called himself "a democratic person." He lived out in Beverly Hills among the movie moguls in a Spanish hacienda he designed himself because he believed the Spanish period was the golden age of Judaism. He knew how to function in the secular world and ran the temple like a business, dispensing bar mitzvahs to the children of the wealthy in exchange for the parents' becoming dues-paying members of the congregation. "How do you know so much about business?" a banker once asked him after witnessing Magnin's financial acumen, then added, "Oh, you're with I. Magnin." "No, that's my grandfather," answered Magnin. "I'm not in business. I know two and two make four. It's just plain common sense."

All of this made Magnin extremely attractive to the Hollywood

Jews, who had forsworn the dogmatic Orthodox Judaism of their fathers. (The fathers, in fact, formed a small congregation of their own,
renting a bungalow and converting it into a "real *shul* like the ones
they had left behind in their cozy Eastern ghettos.") Carl Laemmle,
Harry and Jack Warner, Louis B. Mayer, Irving Thalberg, William
Fox, and dozens of other film executives, directors, and actors became members of the B'nai B'rith, but Magnin admitted the attraction wasn't the opportunity for religious observance; if anything, it
was the opportunity to secularize religion. Here was a rabbi, in one
reporter's words, "with human interests throbbing freely in his heart
and soul, who wasn't afraid or ashamed to reveal his being one of the
mortals." Magnin was shrewd enough to realize that his style was his
power, among both the Hollywood Jews and the gentiles. "I don't care
about religion," Mayer once told him, "but you could do anything
you want with the community." Mayer respected that.

Magnin not only ministered to the Hollywood Jews; he liked to
mingle with them. If a production unit were going overseas to shoot a
film, Magnin would often come to the studio to give it his benediction. "The tables and desks would be piled with liquor bottles," recalled onetime MGM story editor Sam Marx, "and the rabbi would
stand in back of them and talk just as if they weren't there." Though
he regarded himself as a friend to all of them, he was especially close
to Louis Mayer. On Sunday mornings he was one of the regulars at
Mayer's royal brunches out in Santa Monica. He and Mayer lunched
together two or three times a week, and they and their wives often
attended previews of MGM films together. When Mayer's wife, Margaret, was away, Magnin would go out to the beach house to keep
him company. "He loved me," Magnin said with his customary im-
modesty, and it was probably true.

"Louis, I want to have lunch with you, but not here," Magnin said
one day in Mayer's office. When Mayer scowled, Magnin snapped,
"Get off your cross. One Jesus is enough." Now Mayer cracked a
slight smile. They walked to the end of the studio lot and sat down on
a bench among the carpenters constructing sets. "I want to change
your life," Magnin began. "I want to run your life." Mayer was perplexed. "I said, 'Not the picture business. I think you're fairly successful at that. Your *life*! I want six months for you to do what I say, and

people will love you and bless the day your mother brought you into this world. You're a good man, and people don't know this about you. They don't know the lovely things that you've done." What Magnin was offering, essentially, was to ply his own strategies of public relations for his good friend as a kind of gift. But Mayer was far too authoritarian to ever place himself under another's control, and he demurred. "'Edgar, your chemistry is different from mine.' I said, 'If you're going to talk chemisty, just go back to Mussolini's office. To hell with that.'" And the proposal died.

But sometime later, in the early thirties, Mayer invited Magnin out to Hillcrest for lunch. This time it was his turn to make a proposal. "Do you want to go to MGM?" Mayer asked. "Doing what?" "What do you want to do? You want to act? You want to direct? You want to write? You can do anything. I'll give you more money than you could ever make in the ministry." "How much will you give me?" queried Magnin, innocently or not. Mayer pulled out a pencil to write a figure, but Magnin grabbed his hand. "I love you," he said. "I'll never, 'til my dying day, forget you. But I'm going to be a rabbi for life. I'm not going to work for you for two weeks."

The fact was Magnin didn't need the movies. He had his pulpit, where, in Budd Schulberg's words, "[l]ike a peacock he seemed to expand in his rabbinical robes, delivering his sermon with a kind of professional piety that always made me feel he was auditioning for L. B. Mayer and Harry Warner." To him, sermons were performances. Early in his career, when his wife told him she didn't like the way he was reading the prayers, he learned where actors were going for voice lessons and went there himself. "I had the voice, I had the timing, I had the feeling, but I didn't know how to use it," he said later, sounding like an actor groping his way into a new role. "And in those few lessons I learned how to read so that when you say 'Break, break, break, On thy cold gray stones, O sea!' there's tragedy in it. . . . When you go to a theater," he continued, "if you don't come out laughing or crying, there is something wrong with the show." Services were the same way.

So Magnin became the Roxy of religion. He freely interpreted and changed prayers because he considered them "third-rate poetry, typical of the early twentieth century," and he wouldn't "stoop to read such unaesthetic material." He would call for silence, then read a poem with dramatic emphasis, or, in another vein, he would be as folksy as a politician on the stump. Most of his sermons were free association; in his mind, that kept them honest and colloquial and seemingly artless, though that was clearly by design. "The pulpit is a work of art," he believed, "just like making a painting, or sculpture, or dancing, or anything in music. It's an art. And you have to be born to it. And every generation has its great men," of whom Magnin surely considered himself one.

As the rabbinical Roxy, Magnin also realized by the late twenties that he needed a larger stage than the nondescript building in downtown Los Angeles where B'nai B'rith was housed. He needed a physical edifice to symbolize the spiritual edifice he had created—a kind of high church that was, in one Jew's words, the Jewish equivalent of the Episcopalians. The new Wilshire Boulevard Temple—Magnin had changed the name, he said, to avoid confusion with the B'nai B'rith lodges, though it also had the effect of further secularizing the synagogue—occupied a full block in an area that was then dotted with mansions. It was designed after the Pantheon in Rome, buff-colored and squat with a diadem of a dome as massive and resolute as the rabbi who presided beneath it. The interior was capacious—it seated over 1,500—and opulent with dark walnut benches, and its contours were broad rather than narrow. "I wanted the proportions like a theater," said Magnin, "so I can talk with people, not at them." The walls were covered with biblical murals donated by the Warner brothers and painted by Hugo Ballin, head of that studio's art department. It was a grace note. In a synagogue designed to house a rather attenuated form of Judaism, it was somehow appropriate that it be decorated by a Hollywood art director.

Religious observance among the Hollywood Jews was rather attenuated, too. In the early days Louis B. Mayer and Ben Schulberg would meet for delicatessen on Sunday nights, and Mayer's wife actually kept a kosher house (until Louis demanded, as a gesture of assimilation, that she throw away the extra set of dishes required for keeping kosher), but that was about the extent of their Jewishness. When it came to services, they were all what was known as "holiday Jews," which meant that on the Jewish High Holidays, Rosh Hashanah and Yom Kippur, they attended Wilshire out of what must have been a sense of tribal obligation. The rest of the year they stayed home. Of the major moguls, only Laemmle and Harry Warner conducted a Passover seder in their own homes. The others, when they observed Passover at all, did so at their parents' homes and after their parents died not at all. Mayer's granddaughter, Barbara Goetz, was surprised when her mother objected to a Christian wedding ceremony. "It was the first time I'd heard of any reference to my being Jewish," she said. In her home there were grand Christmas parties and Easter egg hunts, not seders. It was no different in the home of Mayer's younger daughter, Irene. Danny Selznick said his father, producer David Selznick, regarded Judaism like cousins from Lithuania: "You let one of them in and soon you'll have all of them. You let a little Judaism in the house and where does it stop?"

One congregant at another temple remembered Harry Cohn attending a funeral service and sitting in the middle of the synagogue puffing on a large cigar, until an usher requested that he put it out. Another member of the same temple recalled a wedding there for a prominent Jewish film director named Lewis Seiler. "They were going down the aisle to the altar, and an agent got out of his seat and asked the director to see a client. . . . He says, 'Lew, can I see you after the ceremony? I got a guy—' an actor or something. It was unbelievable."

All this really demonstrated, however, was that making movies was a deeper obligation than religion. Until 1956, when the unions won a concession, the studios were open on Saturday, the Jewish sabbath. They were also open on the High Holidays. Harry Cohn always made a point of coming to the studio on Yom Kippur, and though he made a concession by refusing to take calls, he was flabbergasted that anyone would take religious observance seriously. Michael Blankfort, a Jewish writer, remembered closing an important deal with Cohn and the boss then suggesting they go out and celebrate. "And I said, 'Harry, today is Erav Yom Kippur [Yom Kippur eve]. I've got to pick up my father and go to the synagogue.' He said, 'What! You mean, a day like this, a grown man like you is going to go to shul on Yom Kippur? What are you talking about?' He couldn't get over it. . . . 'You still do that? . . . Jesus Christ! I never believe that.'" When Blankfort's agent called him a few days later to tell him the deal had been consummated, he said that Cohn kept raving about what a "crazy son of a bitch" Blankfort was to take his father to temple.

It was different for many of the movie Jews who were still stationed at corporate headquarters in New York. In New York, with its large Jewish community, Judaism wasn't something exotic and reproachful as it might have seemed in the West. Marcus Loew wasn't himself religious, but his wife was a major contributor to Temple Rodeph Shalom on Manhatttan's Upper West Side. Barney Balaban, president of Paramount, frequently attended a local synagogue in Westchester, where he lived. Adolph Zukor enrolled his children in Rabbi Stephen Wise's Free Synagogue, which was known for its liberalism and social consciousness. When a scandal erupted over a religious schoolteacher who was caught romancing a student, Zukor, ever the moralist, withdrew Eugene and Mildred, but he continued to attend temple irregularly throughout his life.

But for some of the Jews in Hollywood itself, including several who made obligatory holiday appearances at Wilshire, even Magnin's attenuated Judaism was too much. As his daughter Edith put it, Louis Mayer was "very Catholic prone. He loved the Catholics." He was a close friend and a great admirer of New York's Cardinal Spellman, with whom he dined every time he visited New York, and a large portrait of Spellman in his red vestments was the first sight that greeted visitors to Mayer's library. Edith remembered being awakened abruptly one morning by an urgent call from her father. Spellman had come to visit him, and he wanted his daughter to come immediately to witness the occasion.

Some speculated, especially later in his life when he was hospitalized after falling from a horse and a priest stood vigil, that Mayer had contemplated converting. He never converted, but there is little doubt that he felt a spiritual affinity for Catholicism. To some degree he was probably attracted to the drama, the pomp, and the color of Catholicism, not to mention the dogma. Magnin believed, however, that the attraction was less spiritual than temporal. "Louis admired power, clout, importance," and Spellman had them. "He was *the* cardinal in America, probably *the* cardinal in the world," said Judge Lester Roth, a friend of Mayer's. "As a consequence Mayer could use Spellman and did. . . . When the Catholic church or its censors were about to ban some picture or insist upon having something cut out of a picture, Mayer went to the court of last resort. And he could do it by telephone. He'd pick up the phone and call the cardinal." In return Mayer provided "very effective service to help build the kind of image of their church that they wanted to build." As one writer recalled, when it came to religious matters, the Hollywood Jews were always "very tender with the Catholics."

Beyond the spiritual and political motives, for Louis B. Mayer there was always the cultural: culture as virtue. Mayer's grandson Danny Selznick felt it was the respectability of the Church that made the deepest claim on Mayer's allegiance, and he compared it to his grandfather's absorption with classical music and ballet. While Catholics themselves might have seemed as marginal as Jews and subject to many of the same prejudices, the Catholic church was as far from Judaism and as close to the kingdom of God as one was likely to get. Catholicism had that aura of the august and the holy. Or so Mayer thought. Besides, Danny Selznick said, the head of MGM probably identified with the pope.

Harry Cohn was another who felt the tug of Catholicism, though he was far too much the cynic to subscribe to any faith. Like Mayer, he regarded Cardinal Spellman as a friend and visited him every time he was in New York. Yet Catholicism struck much closer. Cohn's first wife had been a Catholic, and his second wife, Joan, was a converted Catholic who took her religion very seriously—so seriously that Cohn unhesitatingly let her raise their children in the Church. As with Mayer, his attraction to Catholicism led to rumors that he would convert, but it is likely Cohn would have considered this a capitulation of some kind, and he was a man who never capitulated. One close associate felt he wore his Judaism as a threat. "Why isn't it Jewish?" he asked his companion at producer Mark Hellinger's funeral service, the suggestion being that, even in death, Hellinger was trying to hide something.

Ironically, the very appeal of Catholicism to the Hollywood Jews— its seeming distance from anything Jewish—may have also been the very thing that made them hesitant to convert. For many Jews, however, there was a convenient way station from the faith of their fathers to complete acculturation in America: Christian Science. Quasi-religion, quasi-mysticism, the beauty of Christian Science was that it made one less Jewish without demanding total surrender in return.

Jack Warner's first wife, a San Francisco German Jew, was a Christian Science practitioner with virtually no knowledge of Judaism. As such, she had to withstand the pressures that Jack's Jewish Orthodox father placed on him. "My father used to argue with my mother about her wanting me to go to Christian Science," said Jack Warner, Jr. "I went to both. I went to the temple [Wilshire Boulevard], and I went to the Ninth Church of Christ Scientists, but I quit after a while because I guess my tribal memories, my Jewishness, my grandparents' influence were pervasive." Jack Cohn's wife was another practitioner who raised her children in the faith. So was Barney Balaban's brother and former partner, A. J.

When Jesse Lasky hit bottom after a purge at Paramount during the Depression, he began to investigate religion as a means of relief and sustenance. He became especially interested in spiritualism, which led him to Christian Science, too. His son, Jesse Jr., used to watch him lying in the grass, practicing deep breathing with books on the Science of Mind, Religious Science, Unity, and Christian Science strewn about him. "If it weren't for his religious reading," said his wife, who always feared that he would succumb to the pressures, "I don't know what he'd do!"

Bess Lasky was the beautiful daughter of Orthodox Russian Jews who fled the pogroms and settled in Boston. Perhaps as a way of armoring her against possible anti-Semitic assaults in their new home, her parents sent her to the Sacred Heart Convent in Boston, and though she never formally converted, she retained a deep attachment to Catholicism; in her bedroom there were tables covered with rare crucifixes she had collected. Too rarefied for her robust and affable husband, Bess withdrew into spiritualism herself. She discovered she was a natural medium who could readily go into a trance. She took up what she called "cosmic painting," placing her brush on the canvas and letting otherwordly forces guide her, and she practiced "automatic writing," which was the literary equivalent. Lasky, with a look of perfect satisfaction, would sit and watch her paint for hours. It uplifted him, he said. Lost in spiritualism—it was also at this time he began consulting the son of spiritualist Edgar Cayce—he was lost to Judaism. His religion, like his movies, was a product of imagination and a means of escape.

Neither Jesse nor Bess Lasky felt even nominally Jewish, but however tenuous the religious identification of the Hollywood Jews and
their offspring, "the worst illiterate Jew was still a Jew," as writer
Michael Blankfort put it. "And he functioned at the root level as a
Jew. . . . If you said to them [Hollywood Jews], 'It is the ethical goal
of Jews to help other Jews,' they would have said, 'Fuck off! Don't
give me that shit! Is there a Jew starving? Here's some money.
Don't talk about ethics or morality and the Talmud and the
psalms. Don't talk to me about Jews having an ethical duty.' He
might even say, 'I'll help *anyone* who's starving.' What he really
meant was, 'Yes, I'll help a Jew.'"

Ben Hecht thought the Hollywood Jews' philanthropy originated in
the guilt they felt over abandoning their faith; it was a relatively pain-
less way to pay penance. If so, the larger Jewish community certainly
knew how to exploit it. The German Jews had what they called the
Federation of Jewish Welfare Organizations, with its fund-raising
arm, the United Jewish Welfare Fund, which had been organized by
Magnin and David Tannenbaum, a prominent entertainment attorney. The Eastern European Jews had the Jewish Community Council, which opened its lines to the film industry and the industry's
coffers by reserving one of its vice presidencies for a Hollywood Jew.
In addition, by the late thirties there were Los Angeles branches of
the B'nai B'rith Anti-Defamation League, the American Jewish
Committee, the American Jewish Congress, the Hillel Foundation,
and the Brandeis Institute—all of which solicited funds. Louis
Mayer's sister, Ida Mae Cummings, ran the Jewish Women's Auxil-
iary, which raised money for a Jewish nursing home. And there were
the Jewish hospitals. And the synagogues. And the Jewish Blind. And
a dozen other ad hoc groups with their hands outstretched. The
Hollywood Jews gave and gave and gave.

Hecht may have been right in attributing this largesse to guilt, but
guilt was seldom an operative principle among the Hollywood Jews,
and even if it had been, it wasn't the whole story. In the gentile
aristocracy and among the rich German Jews of the East, philan-

thropy was a mark, as well as an expectation, of status. For the Hollywood Jews, for whom status was far more critical than assuaging guilt, charity was a way of buying respectability by doing what the respectable did. Like so many other things in Hollywood, however, philanthropy became a contest, vulgarized by the notion that the more you gave, the more respectable you were.

Jack Warner demanded that his Jewish employees donate a percentage of their salary to the United Jewish Welfare Fund. During a fund-raising drive, he would call them into the studio commissary. "When we were all assembled," remembered screenwriter Alvah Bessie, "[Warner] marched in and—to our astonishment—brandished a rubber truncheon, which had probably been a prop for one of the anti-Nazi pictures we were making. He stood behind his table and smashed the length of rubber hose on the wood, and then he smiled and said, 'I've been looking at the results of the Jewish Appeal drive, and believe you me, it ain't good.' Here he paused for effect and said, 'Everybody's gonna double his contribution here and now—or else!' The rubber truncheon crashed on the table again as everyone present . . . reached for our checkbooks." "All he had to say," admitted his son, Jack Jr., "was, 'You won't ever work here again if you don't give to the United Jewish Appeal.'"

The big Jewish fund-raisers were held at Hillcrest, where they became festivals of philanthropic virility. "If they wanted big contributions," said MGM executive Sam Marx, "they would call for these meetings at Hillcrest, and then they would call out your name so that you're standing up among your peers and being asked what you will contribute. Now we had a comedy writer on the lot named Harry Ruskin, a Jewish boy, and I was sitting next to him, and he gets up and he said he was going to give $25,000 to whatever it was at the moment. When he sat down, I said, 'Come on, Harry. You know you're not going to give $25,000.' He said, 'Yeah. But *they* don't know that. So what the hell. I make the promise. Let them try and collect.'" At one fund-raiser Hal Wallis, head of production at Warner Brothers, rose to make a magnanimous pledge, as he was expected to do. The next day he called one of the functionaries and asked to reduce the amount. When Jack Warner heard, he was furious, and according to this account, at least, it had as much to do with the frosty relations between the men as the contretemps over credit for *Casablanca*.

Not all the Hollywood Jews were givers. Some resented contributing *because* of the kind of vaunting that occurred. (The United Jewish Welfare Fund actually circulated a magazine listing the amount each contributor donated.) Others were afraid of rousing sleeping lions by calling attention to their Judaism. Ben Hecht, the cantankerous ex-newsman from Chicago who had come to Hollywood in the late twenties when it beckoned anyone who could write dialogue for the new talkies, had become radicalized by the rise of nazism, and his outspokenness had attracted the attention of a Jewish Palestinian named Peter Bergson. Bergson, the nephew of the former chief rabbi of Palestine, was the head of a Jewish Palestinian terrorist group called Irgun Zvai Leumi, which was preparing to hound the British, then in custody of Palestine, and drive them out. What Bergson needed was a propagandist to stir passions and, more important, raise money in America. He found his man in Hecht.

But Hecht didn't find *his* men in Hollywood—at least not at first. The Irgun, with its commitment to violence, had drawn the opprobrium of most of the respectable Jews outside Hollywood, and now it was drawing the opprobrium of those within. Harry Warner, an ardent Zionist, rejected Hecht's solicitation and threw him out of the office. Louis Mayer and producer Samuel Goldwyn also refused. William Morris, head of the largest and most important talent agency in Hollywood, offered to contribute, but only if the word "Jew" were dropped from the fund-raising literature. "A Jew, each explained in his own way, could do anything he wanted to as an American, but as a Jew he must be very careful of angering people and very careful not to assert himself in any unpopular way."

David Selznick was more blunt. "I don't want to have anything to do with your cause," Selznick fumed when Hecht asked him to co-sponsor a fund-raising dinner, "for the simple reason that it's a Jewish political cause. And I am not interested in Jewish political problems. I am an American and not a Jew. . . . It would be silly of me to pretend suddenly that I'm a Jew, with some sort of full-blown Jewish psychology."

Hecht, who knew his quarry was a habitual gambler, then made

Selznick a proposition. Selznick could name any three individuals he liked. If one of them, when the question was put, agreed that Selznick was an American and not a Jew, Hecht would concede defeat. If not, Selznick would co-sponsor the dinner. Selznick, his sporting instinct triggered, agreed. "I'd say David Selznick was a Jew," answered Martin Quigley, publisher of the *Motion Picture Exhibitors' Herald*. One down. Nunnally Johnson, a screenwriter, "hemmed a few moments, but finally offered the same reply." Two down. Leland Hayward, a powerful talent agent, snapped, "For God's sake, what's the matter with David? He's a Jew and he knows it."

Selznick paid up, and eventually other top Hollywood Jews, browbeaten by the Nazi atrocities then going on in Europe, agreed to attend a meeting in the commissary at Twentieth Century-Fox. But when one of the speakers, a British colonel who had commanded a group of Jewish soldiers during World War I, excoriated the British for their behavior in Palestine, the Hollywood Jews, most of whom were Anglophiles, were unsettled. The subsequent solicitation for funds met with stony silence until gossip columnist Hedda Hopper pledged $300. Then the philanthropic contest took hold, and by the end of the evening Hecht had raised $130,000 for the cause—only $9,000 of which was actually paid. For many of the Hollywood Jews, the contest was, after all, more important than the cause.

By the mid-thirties, when his power was unchallenged, Rabbi Magnin had come to serve many functions among the Hollywood Jews: legitimizer of assimilation, safe bond to the past, fund-raiser, advocate with the larger Jewish community, friend. But one function he consciously forswore was moral guide. If any of the Hollywood Jews came to Magnin with a personal problem, he claimed he told them, "I'm your rabbi, not Dear Abby. Don't bother me." Still, the moral life of Hollywood, such as it was, never quite escaped the grip of Judaism, and among many of the old-guard Hollywood Jews, at least, a certain anachronistic code still obtained. Hollywood "was basically a provincial city," said playwright and screenwriter Samuel Spewack. "Its whole mental and spiritual climate was definitely small-town." Writer Philip Dunne concurred. "In achieving a state of sin, I would rate Hollywood about on a par with the New York Social Register." And Dunne added, "This probity may have been a quotient of the high percentage of Jews in the upper echelon which set the moral tone for the rest of the community."

Basically, the first rank of Hollywood Jews were the products of a deeply conservative Jewish upbringing that none of them had ever entirely shaken. As incongruous as it seemed, even a vulgarian like Harry Cohn could be courtly when it came to profanity, and though he had an extensive vocabulary of expletives that he didn't hesitate to use among his colleagues, he would reprimand anyone who used vulgarity in front of a woman. "Don't you know there's a lady here?" he would say. "Don't let me hear that language in my office." Harry Warner might tell a slightly off-color story in the executive dining room, but he would also beg his listener's pardon. The worst oath Mayer's daughter Edith ever heard him utter was "goddamn."

No matter that he had helped create it, Mayer was extremely suspicious of Hollywood and viewed it, as did many in the gentile establishment, as if it were a modern Sodom. His great fear was that its values, apparently the values of the talent, might taint his daughters. "If you have the right values, the *dignity*," he counseled them, "none of this will touch you." "He was a very unsophisticated man threatened by a sea of iniquity," said his daughter Irene.

Once, at a wedding party Mayer was throwing in his home for a close friend, a guest asked what the newlyweds were going to do on their honeymoon. Before either could answer, Mayer's son-in-law William Goetz interjected, "Fuck." This drew howls of appreciative laughter, but Mayer hadn't heard it, and he asked Edith what her husband had said. Discretion being the better part of valor for any daughter of Mayer's, she tried brushing him off. He persisted. "And finally he pestered me so long, I told him what he said." The next day he called asking her to come to lunch. The joke—actually the fact that Edith would repeat it—disturbed him. "A married woman with children," he scolded. "Anything as fine as you to use a word like that."

The same moral rigidity extended to other peccadilloes. Harry

Cohn once fired a carpenter who had been with Columbia for over twenty-five years because the man was caught smuggling home a hammer belonging to the studio. William Graf, Cohn's assistant, remonstrated in the man's behalf, but to no avail. "Fire him. He's a crook. He's a thief," answered Cohn. Some time later Cohn and Graf were transacting business at the Bank of America on Sunset and Gower. The carpenter was now selling papers at a newsstand nearby. Cohn passed, staring straight ahead as if he hadn't noticed. But when he and Graf got to the corner, Cohn said, "Did you see the crook there?" "Mr. Cohn, the man is not a crook for a dollar eighty." Cohn snapped, "I told you never to mention that again," and Graf never did.

Nevertheless, the Hollywood Jews operated in a tough, licentious business, and if they practiced the stern morality of their fathers on minor transgressions, they could also just as easily chuck their morality when it was expedient to do so. In fact, as Harry Cohn so often demonstrated, one's lack of honor frequently became a *point* of honor in the movie jungle—a sign of one's superiority. "If a thing worked, it was moral," Jack Warner, Jr., said of his father. "That's a terribly cynical thing to say, but I think that's how he felt. If somebody broke a contract with him, he was outraged. But if he could work it out to break a contract with someone and it was to his benefit . . . He had made an agreement with somebody. They shook hands on it. He was not to release a certain story because it couldn't be done until a certain date had passed. It could really hurt this other man if it got known that he was negotiating with Warners before a certain date." But no sooner had Warner and an associate returned to the studio than he called gossip columnist Louella Parsons and announced that he had acquired the property. Warner's associate was aghast. "How could you do that? You had a gentlemen's agreement." Said Warner, "I'm no gentleman."

———

"A group in the motion picture industry is seriously considering setting up some form of organization through which it could be far more articulate in both the general effort for democracy and the correlated effort against anti-Semitism," Mendel Silberberg wrote Maurice Wertheim of the American Jewish Committee in May 1942. Silberberg said that a "group of the outstanding younger men in the motion picture industry" had already met several times to outline the reasons for a new organization to mobilize Hollywood Jews, and they had cited the "[c]ontinued prevalence and growth of anti-Semitism and activity of anti-Semitic groups in California and the United States; [t]he fact that the motion picture industry has been made a primary target for anti-Semitic activity; [t]he necessity that the truth regarding the Jew and the motion picture industry be presented to the people of the United States." Among the activities of this new group, Silberberg recommended that it "militantly meet attacks on Jews or upon the motion picture industry by using for these purposes the talents and abilities of those engaged in the motion picture industry," and he concluded, "I feel that if the opportunity Hollywood presents were properly harnessed to some of your activities, it could not fail to be of advantage."

Advantage to whom, Silberberg didn't say, though it turned out to be extremely advantageous to him. Silberberg was the Rabbi Magnin of the secular Jewish community. He came from an old-line Los Angeles Jewish family that was so deeply assimilated it practiced Christian Science and raised him that way. After working briefly at the *Los Angeles Times*, he became an attorney, but when the head of his firm brought in his son as an associate, Silberberg and a close friend named Shepard Mitchell quit and formed a firm of their own. Years later, when it had become one of the most powerful law firms in Los Angeles, they liked to reminisce about its infancy. Their income was so paltry that they served their own papers and ate at a local bar where the lunch came gratis with the beer. Nevertheless, Silberberg upbraided their principal client for recommending they do something illicit. "If you weren't my partner and didn't have to bear half the cost," he told Mitchell when the partner poked his head in to see what the commotion was, "I'd throw this son of a bitch through this partition." Mitchell told him to go right ahead, and Silberberg did.

Silberberg was a man of stern values and acknowledged probity, but his real talent was as a fixer, and his real arena wasn't law but politics. As a young attorney he had gotten himself deeply involved in what turned out to be a successful campaign to remove a crooked Los Angeles mayor named Shaw. That and his relationship with the Chandler family, which owned the *Los Angeles Times* on which he had worked, led him to a privileged place in the inner councils of the Republican party. Silberberg had clout. "There were more judges sitting on the bench by the grace of Mendel Silberberg than anybody else," said one associate. "He was one of what were then called the 'five kingmakers' in the Republican party." He was also the first Jew to be offered a federal judgeship in Los Angeles. For Silberberg, however, that would have been a demotion, and he gratefully declined, hand-picking another candidate instead.

It was probably through his GOP connections that he met Louis B. Mayer sometime in the twenties, and through Mayer that he was introduced to the elite Jews in Hollywood. (Silberberg already had some association with the film industry through his close friend Sol Lesser, Rabbi Magnin's old childhood companion and the owner of a significant theater chain and through his wife, Dorothy Howell, a screenwriter.) Hollywood and Silberberg made a perfect match. It had visibility and money. He had prestige and power. More problematic was his match with Jews. Silberberg had always been something of a nominal Jew. He couldn't even pronounce "Chanukah" until someone told him how, and he found lox and cream cheese a revelation. Like Magnin and the German Jews, he had little understanding of or tolerance for Jews of Eastern European origin who paraded their Judaism. He believed in discretion. In fact, said Joseph Roos, an organizer for Jewish groups in Los Angeles and a longtime associate of Silberberg's, "Mendel Silberberg wasn't aware that he was Jewish until Louis B. Mayer made a Jew out of him for Mayer's Republican purposes."

What Roos meant is that Mayer had involved Silberberg in the convoluted politics of the Jewish community as a way of giving himself and the other Hollywood Jews power within the convoluted politics of the Republican party. First, though, he had to demonstrate to Silberberg that he had a community of interest with the Hollywood Jews. It happened in 1933. A small crackpot group of Bundists who supported the new German chancellor Hitler had found two sym-pathizers working in the printing plant of the *Los Angeles Times* and managed to sneak an anti-Semitic pamphlet into editions of the paper. When the Jews saw the insert they were distressed and fright-ened, and they called a meeting to determine a course of action. Among those attending were representatives from the major studios, including Mayer. The group resolved to approach Otis Chandler, owner of the *Los Angeles Times*, and enlist his help. This is where Silberberg, with his relationship to Chandler, became instrumental. He became the emissary.

The result was that the *Times* promised renewed vigilance at its plants. But the Bund of Nazi sympathizers was particularly active in Los Angeles, and when another episode of anti-Semitism erupted the following year, these Jews decided to create an apparatus of their own that could serve as part watchdog, part educator. It was called the Community Committee. Its professional secretary was a wealthy semi-invalid named Leon L. Lewis, who had been gassed in World War I and had retired to California after serving as secretary of the Chicago B'nai B'rith, a Jewish fraternal organization. Its chairman was Mendel Silberberg.

The Community Committee, later renamed the Community Rela-tions Council, was the official liaison between the Jews and the rest of Los Angeles, and that made Silberberg a kind of Jewish ambassador not only from the Los Angeles Jews generally, but from the Holly-wood Jews who dominated the CRC. He loved the role, and it was fair to say that it loved him. As a rather tenuous Jew himself, he was extremely sensitive to the image of the Jew among gentiles, which was exactly the way the Hollywood Jews wanted it. He was also articulate, cultured, magnetic, intelligent, rich, and powerful, which was ex-actly how the Hollywood Jews wanted to be represented to the gen-tiles.

But the benefits weren't all one-sided. If the Hollywood Jews got themselves a perfect front man, what Silberberg got in the CRC was an extraordinary power base among the Jews. "He was *the* accepted Jew by the establishment," said Joseph Roos. The Los Angeles Jews, who seemed to meet each problem by forming a committee, had created a morass of anagrams, and from the CRC Silberberg's tentacles extended into practically all of them. He sat on the executive committee of the American Jewish Committee, a deeply conservative, primarily German-Jewish agency, which in turn had created a Community Council under whose jurisdiction fell all other Jewish community activities, including Silberberg's CRC. He also sat on the Uptown Committee, which was the motion picture branch of the CRC; its function was to present Jewish concerns about prospective movies to the movie executives—mostly the same executives who constituted the committee. (Why these Jews needed a separate group when they monopolized the CRC itself is one of those little bureaucratic riddles that can be answered only by the Hollywood Jews' fondness for new clubs to join.) Finally, Silberberg was a board member of the Free World Association of Hollywood, which, while not technically a Jewish organization, still was dedicated to many of the same programs—"to promote ideals of sound Americanism, to oppose fascism, to advance democratic thinking in respect to the international scene." With all these bureaucracies at his disposal, Silberberg probably was, as one film executive called him, "the most valuable piece of manpower in Hollywood."

By this time, just before the war, Silberberg was not only the most important Jew in Los Angeles after Magnin; he was also the most important entertainment attorney in the country. He did work for MGM, and his firm was the general counsel for both Columbia and RKO. Such was his power that when millionaire eccentric Howard Hughes, who had just purchased RKO, kept him waiting for an hour and fifteen minutes, Silberberg rose, told Hughes's secretary that if he wanted a meeting he could come to the law office, and walked out. "Now that was our most important client," remembered Arthur Groman, who was then an associate at the firm. "And, by God, Hughes called up the next day and came to our offices."

At Columbia Harry Cohn respected very few people, but Silberberg was one of them and one of the few Cohn knew he couldn't make cower. They made an odd pair—the refined, engaging attorney and the boorish, detested movie mogul—though Cohn, who loved law, probably saw a lot of himself in the confident Silberberg, and Silberberg, who loved the art of brokering, probably enjoyed the constant negotiation that constituted Cohn's relationship with the world and with his own company. They met daily, and for a brief time Cohn even enticed him to take a vice presidency at the studio. "Silberberg was the peacemaker," said Cohn's nephew Robert. "He was the guy in between Harry and Jack. . . . Harry used to berate him. I would hear him knock him. . . . I never saw him do it to his face, but he would refer to him out of annoyance, because Mendel would say, 'This is the way it has to be done,' and Harry would do it, but reluctantly." Cohn listened, said Groman, because he knew that "Mendel was not a 'yes-man.' "

When Silberberg wrote Wertheim in 1942 about creating still another Jewish agency, this one designated specifically to utilize the movie industry for a variety of Jewish campaigns, he was reacting as much to concerns over his own jealously guarded turf as to his concerns over anti-Semitism. For several years the major Jewish organizations of the East had looked yearningly at Hollywood for its ability to influence public opinion. Through Silberberg, these groups had contacts with the movie Jews, but they desired some more formal mechanism for involving the movie Jews in their activities and consequently gaining their cooperation.

Silberberg's proposal was a way of satisfying the eastern Jewish establishment while maintaining his own prerogatives. Wertheim responded favorably to the idea of having "close contact with the right sort of men in the industry," but the Hollywood Jews themselves, possibly sensing that they might be creating a new pressure group on their own industry, demurred. After discussing the project "with a number of the men in the community whose viewpoint and leadership would be necessary if such a project were inaugurated"—presumably Mayer, Cohn, and the Warners—Silberberg concluded that "they are all so deeply engrossed in various kinds of war and industry related activities that they do not have necessary interest."

Still, the idea would not die. After a trip to the West Coast in 1944, Nate Spingold, an East Coast vice president of Columbia Pictures and one of Harry Cohn's closest associates, suggested that the American Jewish Committee send a representative to check into the feasibility of reviving the proposal. Silberberg introduced the AJC representative, Dick Rothschild, to the leading producers, directors, and writers, and Rothschild returned to New York supporting the notion of a new organization of Hollywood Jews and believing that the "most satisfactory results could be achieved only through some individual who could serve as liaison between our office and our friends on the West Coast." Whether he had Silberberg in mind, he didn't say.

Neither Rothschild, Spingold, nor Silberberg did anything more to pursue the idea, but shortly after the war it was suddenly revived once again—this time in a very different context. On another trip to California, in February 1947, Rothschild had learned that RKO was making a film of *The Brick Foxhole*, a contemporary novel that used the murder of a homosexual as the pretext for a sermon on tolerance. There was nothing wrong with that, except that in adapting the book, RKO had decided to make the victim a Jew instead. "Dick understood perfectly that the producers of the picture were animated by the best of motives," stated an AJC memo, "but he felt that the basic idea of killing Jews just because they are Jews, was an extremely dangerous idea to project on the screen before 50 million or more people of all shades of emotional maturity or immaturity."

Rothschild swung into action. The new production head at RKO, Dore Schary, was a former screenwriter with the face of a blade. He was also a committed Jew who served on the CRC. Rothschild immediately contacted Schary to dissuade him from making the film about Jews; with astounding insensitivity, he suggested making the victim a black instead. But Schary, who had lectured on anti-Semitism to soldiers during the war, wouldn't budge. A few days later Rothschild received the film's script, now called *Crossfire*, from Silberberg and arranged to meet RKO's president, Peter Rathvon, who apparently expressed his own doubts about the movie. (How much of this was concern over Jews and how much over box office is hard to say; *Crossfire* had tested poorly in an audience survey asking moviegoers whether they wanted to see a film about its subject.) Silberberg and Schary were incensed that a fellow Jew had gone over their heads to lodge a complaint, and when an AJC member who had seen a preview of the film criticized it at an AJC meeting, Silberberg, more Hollywood than Jew, rose to its defense.

Crossfire, starring Robert Young, Robert Mitchum, and Robert Ryan, became a modest commercial success, but it had a profound effect on the leaders of the Jewish community, especially in the East, by sensitizing them to a new issue: since Hollywood promulgated the image of the Jew to most Americans and since Jews controlled Hollywood, why couldn't they be coaxed into presenting a more positive image of their own people? Prior to World War II, the question of Jewish identity on the screen was never very significant because Jews were very seldom seen there. "Jews are for killing," one Jewish studio executive of the thirties was reported to have said, "not for making movies about." Years later, when writer Garson Kanin suggested Judy Holliday, a Jewess, for the lead in *Born Yesterday*, the producer, also a Jew, told him, "This show is *by* Jews and *for* Jews, but it can't be *with* Jews." (She was hired anyway.)

Usually the Jewish executives invoked the box office; regardless of how they felt personally, they said, no one else wanted to see a movie about a Jew. (Harry Cohn once employed a research company to wire the audience during a preview of *The Jolson Story* and plot which scenes they liked and which they didn't. When Jolson sang a Yiddish song, the graph plummeted. "I don't believe this," Cohn said. "We got a bunch of anti-Semites or something in this audience." But at each preview the result was the same, and Cohn ordered the scene cut.) Some Hollywood Jews admitted that they deliberately avoided Jewish subjects because they didn't want to "ruffle the goyim." Louis B. Mayer's argument was more ingenious. When Magnin asked him why MGM didn't make any films about Jews, Mayer answered that "rabbis don't look dramatic. A priest has all these trimmings and all this stuff." Mayer was more honest when Ring Lardner, Jr., and Michael Kanin submitted their script of *Woman of the Year* and Mayer immediately vetoed a scene where the heroine, a diplomat's daughter and cosmopolite, spoke Yiddish. "Our impression," said Lardner, "was simply that from Mayer's point of view, this kind of thing would be interpreted as the Jewish-dominated motion picture industry trying to promote Jewishness or the acceptability of the Yiddish language. . . . It didn't make sense, but he was afraid. . . . "

Beneath the lame excuses, this was the deeper truth: Hollywood was itself a means of avoiding Judaism, not celebrating it. Most of the moguls had no stake in and no attachment to so-called Jewish projects, and those projects that were attempted often got lost in ambivalence and unresolved feelings about Judaism. Ring Lardner, Jr., was hired by producer Sam Goldwyn to write one such project—an adaptation of a novel about a Catholic woman and a Jewish man who decide to marry. Goldwyn had himself divorced his Jewish wife—Jesse Lasky's sister—and married a gentile, and "when he first called me into conference, it was all that he wanted to do this really relevant, important story, and I was to know how strongly *he* felt about the issue." Then Lardner turned in his first draft, and Goldwyn began leafing through the script, citing passage after passage that touched on anti-Semitism. Lardner had betrayed him, he said. "What do you mean, I betrayed you?" Lardner asked, nonplussed by Goldwyn's outburst. "Well, one of the reasons I hired you to work on this script was the fact you were a gentile," Goldwyn answered. "You betrayed me by writing like a Jew!" Goldwyn's wife, Frances, prevailed on Lardner to do a rewrite, but Goldwyn still wasn't satisfied. Over the next two years he hired a succession of writers—none of whom ever produced a script he liked, which led Lardner to conclude that "he was just too mixed up, too torn about this thing, to be able to produce it."

The ones who were hardest hit by the shunning of Jewish films were the Jewish actors. "With acting there was very definitely the feeling that a Jewish personality would not work," said screenwriter Maurice Rapf, who grew up in Hollywood. "There were some hidden Jews. Not that in their private life they made any secret of it. But they were not known to the general public, and the studios perhaps didn't want it known, either." The names went. Jacob Krantz became Ricardo Cortez. Stella Adler became Stella Ardler. Sophia Kosow became Sylvia Sidney. Emmanuel Goldenberg became Edward G. Robinson (the "G" adopted as a continuing reminder of who he really was). "What kind of a name is Garfield, anyway?" Jack Warner asked a young actor from New York's Group Theater. "It doesn't sound American." Jules Garfield, formerly Julius Garfinkle, protested that it was the name of an American president, so Warner countered that it was the Jules that had to go. How about James—James Garfield? "But that's the president's name," Garfield objected. "You wouldn't name a goddamn actor Abraham Lincoln, would you?" "No, kid, we wouldn't," answered a Warner executive, "because Abe is a name that most people would say is Jewish and we wouldn't want people to get the wrong idea." So Julius Garfinkle became John Garfield.

And Muni Weisenfreund became Paul Muni. Muni had been born

in Lemberg, Austria (now Lvov), the son of itinerant performers. His family emigrated when he was seven and settled in New York, where Muni became a star on the Yiddish stage and later on Broadway. He came to Hollywood in 1929 and quickly won an Oscar nomination, but after a second film he returned to the stage. When he came back to Hollywood, starring in *Scarface* as a knockoff of Al Capone and in *I Am a Fugitive from a Chain Gang*, and later as a Frenchman in *The Story of Louis Pasteur*, a Chinese in *The Good Earth*, and a Mexican in *Juarez*, he assumed stature as one of Hollywood's most distinguished actors. At the same time his career became a paradigm for the tortured identity of the actor Jew in Hollywood—always dressed in someone else's ethnicity. A man of almost desperate intensity and equally desperate loneliness, he was, according to his friend Hy Kraft, "one of the unhappiest men I ever met. And the thing that depressed Muni was that he was always playing character parts. He was never playing himself, and he never did find an opportunity to play a lover. . . . Even as a child, he was playing an old man." He had so effaced himself that he would answer the door in makeup.

If anyone changed the Jews' self-effacement in Hollywood, it was Hitler. By the end of the war Jewish leaders were lobbying Hollywood executives to accept Jews as a valid and dramatic subject for movies. "For a while there, the screen was Judenrein," said entertainment attorney Martin Gang, who was one of the lobbyists. "And we said, 'For God sakes, don't wipe them out completely to avoid problems.'" But what Rothschild was recommending in 1947 after the tempest over *Crossfire* was something more than a lobby. What he was proposing was a kind of Jewish clearance board that would look at scripts involving Jews and give its approval. The attitude of the big New York Jewish organizations, the American Jewish Committee, the American Jewish Congress, and the Anti-Defamation League, was, "We left it to Mendel Silberberg and his guys to watch over this and look—they fell down." So now each organization began scouting Hollywood with an eye toward establishing its own clearinghouse and, not incidentally, establishing its own connections with Hollywood money and influence. Drilling to a deeper motive, writer Leo Rosten put it bluntly. "Hollywood was a huge, untapped source of money, and it had been reluctant to contribute to eastern causes."

For the eastern Jews, patrolling the portrayal of their co-religionists on screen was a perfectly legitimate and plausible way to get to that money and influence. "Jewish organizations have a clear and rightful interest in making sure that Hollywood films do not present Jews in such a way as to arouse prejudice," declared a memo from an umbrella group of Jewish organizations called the National Community Relations Advisory Council (NCRAC), early in 1947. "In some cases, such pictures should be taken out of production entirely. In other cases, scripts should be edited carefully to eliminate questionable passages. Everything should be done to eliminate unfortunate stereotypes of the Jews. . . ." What NCRAC recognized, however, was that the highly suspicious movie industry was apt to resent anyone interfering in its business—even, or especially, other Jews.

They were right. Silberberg exploded over this incursion into his territory, and he reacted early in 1948 by calling a conclave of representatives from all the major Jewish agencies in NCRAC to hammer out a solution over who would tell the Hollywood Jews how they should be portraying Jews on screen. Essentially, it amounted to a showdown between the Hollywood Jews and the Jews of the eastern establishment who wanted to use them. For two days the sides traded charges, with the New York Jews accusing Silberberg of dereliction and Silberberg accusing them of ignorance. When the smoke finally cleared, a truce had been arranged, and yet another new organization had been born: the Motion Picture Project.

Ostensibly, the function of the Motion Picture Project was to maintain a full-time liaison with the Hollywood Jews. Less ostensibly, it functioned to give each of the major Jewish organizations a piece of Hollywood, a touch of its glamour and power, and all of them contributed to it through NCRAC. The project's chairman was a former English teacher from New York who had come to Hollywood as a writer in 1919 and later moved into production. John Stone, formerly John Strumwasser, was to be a watchdog on the industry—reviewing scripts, cajoling producers, keeping the big Jewish organizations informed of any movie that might help or hurt the Jews. One member of the Motion Picture Committee described the project's operation this way: "They'd give us the scripts. We'd tell them what was right or wrong. They would do it."

In effect, though, Stone's work mainly came down to picking nits: influencing the producer of *The Sands of Iwo Jima* to incorporate a fictitious Jewish soldier; advising the producer of *I Can Get It for You Wholesale*, a film about the garment industry, that he must proceed cautiously since the general public associated Jews with the garment trades; trying to beef up the role of Justice Brandeis in a film biography of Oliver Wendell Holmes; leaning on the writer of *Murder, Inc.*, about the Jewish gangster Louis Lepke, to include a crusading Jewish prosecutor as well; and, most ludicrously, suggesting that Sammy Glick, the conniving Jewish protagonist of Budd Schulberg's novel *What Makes Sammy Run?*, be changed to someone of indeterminate ancestry.

Silberberg and the Motion Picture Committee of the CRC, which survived even though it was essentially deprived of any function now except to pressure the Motion Picture Project, suggested that none of Stone's activities be publicized, fearing that it could draw "the charge that [a] Jewish group is trying to censor the industry," which, in fact, was exactly what it was trying to do. The Jewish organizations of the East that supported Stone felt differently. Those that had once scorned Hollywood now clearly enjoyed their Hollywood presence and regarded the Motion Picture Project as a kind of plum, if only because, as such a dramatic and obvious example of Jewish activism, it helped attract funds for other activities. The problem was that in financing the project each organization was subsumed under the aegis of NCRAC, so none got full credit for supervising Hollywood or reaped the rewards for doing so.

This was particularly vexing to the American Jewish Committee and the Anti-Defamation League, which together provided roughly 50 percent of the project's budget. By the early fifties both organizations were making rumblings about pulling out of NCRAC, which they apparently hoped would kill the project, and then forming a new project of their own to oversee Hollywood. When the American Jewish Congress offered to fill the breach and assume full financial responsibility for the project, a leader of the American Jewish Committee nervously wrote an associate, "We must keep our hands on Hollywood, because in the future it may be necessary to have the right influence in the industry," adding that the "Hollywood activity is a talking point with welfare funds."

In the end this minicrisis was mediated by the man most of the eastern Jews had been trying to usurp: Mendel Silberberg. The last thing Silberberg wanted was another group of Jews running around Hollywood telling the Jewish movie executives what to do; that was the reason he had consented to the Motion Picture Project in the first place. What Silberberg proposed was that NCRAC, the American Jewish Committee, and the Anti-Defamation League contribute *separately* to a new—always a new—national committee to work with the Los Angeles Motion Picture Committee, the subsidiary of the CRC that Silberberg had headed. This Byzantine rapprochement meant that the AJC and the ADL would exercise greater control over and have higher visibility in the Motion Picture Project than they had when they were folded within NCRAC, while Silberberg and his ally Dore Schary would wield the real power as they had before the eastern Jews discovered Hollywood.

The Motion Picture Project continued under this new arrangement, with Stone still needling Hollywood and applying pressure under the watchful eyes of Silberberg and Schary and the AJC and ADL pointing proudly to their efforts. Whether any of this had a real impact on movies or not is difficult to say; for the Hollywood Jews themselves, the effort probably was at worst an annoyance. But for anyone with a sense of irony it did constitute a turnabout that a few of the Hollywood Jews must have enjoyed. After having spent the better part of their lives trying not to antagonize gentiles, they now found they had to be careful not to antagonize Jews as well. So it went in Hollywood.

———

"When he was young in Berlin, he was like a meteor coming on under Hitler," said the woman who would marry him. "Everybody heard about Max Nussbaum in Berlin because he was such a novelty. Berlin had a very sedate and sober old Jewish community. I did not go to a liberal temple. I went to an old Orthodox synagogue with my father. My mother never went to a temple. She was a completely assimilated Jewess. . . . But when Nussbaum appeared, my mother started to go to temples where he was speaking because everyone was so fascinated by this young, beautiful man who came and told Hassidic stories and was so different from all the old rabbis they had had. When I met him, I didn't particularly like him because he was much too glamorous for my taste. I made fun of him. I said, 'You belong in Hollywood.' That was in 1937." Five years later that is exactly where he was.

Nussbaum had been invited to Los Angeles to lead the congregation at Temple Israel, which was not only located in Hollywood, but was of Hollywood. The temple had been founded in 1926 by seven men, five of whom were prominent in the film community: Sol Wurtzel, head of production at Fox Films; Isadore Bernstein, then head of production at Universal; I. E. Chadwick, the president of Chadwick Studios, a small, independently owned production company; Jesse Goldberg, an independent producer; and John Stone, the same man who would later head the Motion Picture Project. Of the other two founders, Jack Weiner was an important talent agent and Herman Appel was a physician who was regarded as "the doctor of the movie colony at the time, and thus a part of the social set of the industry."

Their stated aim was to create a religious institution with which, in Nussbaum's words, "Jewish members of the industry could affiliate and where they could have a spiritual home." What they were really doing, however, was creating a religious and cultural alternative to Hollywood's house rabbi, Edgar Magnin. Magnin may have been extremely well liked among gentiles and many of the major Jewish film executives like Mayer and the Warners, but his Rotarian style and cautious philosophy also made him an object of some derision as well. One Jew called him "a car dealer sort." Another called him "the most reactionary man you've ever met." A third attributed the Hollywood Jews' self-hatred to his counsel and called him "Cardinal Magnin" for the way he curried favor with the Catholics.

One writer used him as the basis for a novel entitled *Rabbi Burns*, in which the protagonist is an ambitious young Hollywood rabbi who "ignored the gloomy spirit and concentrated upon entertainment and stimulating externals, just as they did in the successful churches." Burns, once Moishke Bernstein, has a dream: "To preside over a house of worship as elaborate and magnificent and costly as Sid Grauman's Chinese Theater." But he has also fallen in love with the daughter of a rich congregant and accepts a job at one of the studios to prove he can support her. "Talk moving pictures, big money, and pretty girls," she laughs when he tells her. "Say—that's pretty funny for a rabbi."

Temple Israel was also assimilationist—the masthead of the temple bulletin paired Moses with the Statue of Liberty—but it didn't seem to exact as high a price for it as Magnin's Wilshire Boulevard Temple, and it was infused with a much greater sense of the Hollywood Jews' obligations to other Jews. That, in fact, was one of the reasons for its existence—a kind of noblesse oblige from Hollywood. "We had a desire to do good in the community," said John Stone, "but not really to become too involved in the religious angle. We wanted to provide for a community need." Its first rabbi, Isadore Isaacson, was a compact, stocky man from Iowa who understood, as Magnin did, how to ingratiate himself with his congregants; he was the best pinochle player in the temple. Unlike Magnin, however, he viewed Judaism as an active, practical moral force with relevance to the issues of the day, and he delivered sermons on the Kellogg Peace Pact, the Scopes monkey trial, the challenge of Einstein's theories to faith, and the role of religion in easing unemployment—subjects Magnin would never have touched.

By the end of the thirties Isaacson had died, another young rabbi had come and gone, and Hitler had made Nussbaum, one of the most charismatic rabbis in Europe, available—but just barely. One evening in 1938, while Nussbaum was still in Berlin, he received a call from an Associated Press correspondent telling him that his temple was in flames. He rushed to the synagogue, and, as he told it twenty-five years later, he saw a "very small Torah scroll lying almost untouched, though the flames started already to kindle up on the mantle of it, which, with the help of the custodian, I was able to wrap and hide it under a raincoat and walk away with it in the middle of the night." Within two years of that evening—Kristallnacht, so named after the smashed windows of Jewish businesses—Nussbaum had escaped Germany. He sneaked across the border to Switzerland, then traveled through Vichy France, Spain, and Portugal until he crossed the ocean to the United States and ultimately Hollywood. The small Torah scroll he retrieved traveled with him, placed finally in the ark of Temple Israel, where, he said, it would always bear witness to the events in Germany.

Experiences like these had obviously made Nussbaum a very different kind of religious leader from Magnin, which is no doubt one reason why Temple Israel originally courted him. Magnin, as Joseph Roos described him, was a "cold" Jew. Nussbaum "was completely the opposite. He was an intense Jew. He was a Jew before he was anything else—before he was an American, almost before he was a human being, he identified so strongly." "When Nussbaum came here he was very young," remembered an admirer, "and he was a firebrand. He was a man that really—it's very hard to explain—he was like an actor. He was like a star. When he started to talk, you just were sitting there in absolute awe. You would listen to every word. He had a fantastic magnetism."

Inevitably, as the two most important religious figures among the Hollywood Jews, Nussbaum and Magnin became rivals—nothing public or nasty, just the mutual antagonism of two very self-confident men with two radically different ideologies. ("I wouldn't blame you for being jealous," Magnin said he told his fellow rabbis, "but have the good taste not to show it publicly.") Even physically they seemed embodiments of their differences: Magnin tall, raw-boned, hardy, and American; Nussbaum smallish, delicately handsome, intense, and unmistakably European. Magnin's speech was broad and calculatingly demotic; Nussbaum's was deliberate, each line solemnly and dramatically inflected, each word pulled, each syllable enunciated as if he were examining the language through a crystal. Magnin in the pulpit had bonhomie; Nussbaum had charisma. Magnin had the authority of one who had passed with the gentiles; Nussbaum had the moral authority of one who challenged them.

That helped account for why Hollywood Jews who attended synagogue during and after the war increasingly attended Temple Israel rather than the more majestic Wilshire Boulevard Temple. Nussbaum cut a better figure and authored a better drama. But just as Magnin was a man of his moment, when the Hollywood Jews needed an acceptably sanitized Judaism, Nussbaum was a man of *his* moment, when a second generation of Hollywood Jews, their consciousness raised by the war and the Holocaust, were shamed into a rededication to Judaism and a recommitment to social activism. And that is what Nussbaum provided them. On religious matters, he was a conservative in the sense that he believed in conserving tradition and ritual. On social matters, he was an outspoken crusader, raising his voice in support of civil rights, unionization, peace, and the state of Israel.

For all his overt religiosity and moral fervor, though, Nussbaum was no less a Hollywood rabbi than Magnin, only a more thoughtful, refined, and progressive one, and, like Magnin, he rather enjoyed the Hollywood connection and the attention that came with it. Certainly there wasn't another temple in the country that raised funds through gala benefits as Temple Israel did—headlining Jews like Sophie Tucker and Jack Benny and non-Jews like Martha Raye and Bill "Bojangles" Robinson. (After one benefit a group of congregants repaired to the Brown Derby for an after-theater repast with Robinson, but when Robinson, a black, was refused service, Nussbaum calmly shepherded the group out.) There wasn't another temple, save Wilshire, where the interior had been decorated by a movie studio, as Fox Pictures, under Sol Wurtzel, had decorated Temple Israel. And there wasn't another rabbi whose list of converts was as glamorous: Sammy Davis, Jr.; his actress wife, May Britt; and, shortly after she married the Jewish crooner Eddie Fisher, Elizabeth Taylor. Their pictures adorned his office walls. And surely only in the peculiar universe of Hollywood could a rabbi go to a television studio to appear on a program about the meaning of the High Holidays, as Nussbaum did in September 1958, and instead have Ralph Edwards sneak up and suddenly declare, "Rabbi Max Nussbaum—this is *your* life!"

The song of Hollywood, like the song of the sirens, was irresistible. Not even those strapped to the mast of religion could deny it. But the song of Judaism also insinuated itself—a stubborn, haunting melody of tradition and trial. Not even those strapped to the mast of the movies could deny it, however much they tried. And so, what had happened in Hollywood was a symbiosis between Hollywood Judaism and the Hollywood Jews. Judaism got the rush of celebrity—the exhilaration of moving among the gilded. The Hollywood Jews got their dispensations—the older Jews to assimilate without guilt; the younger ones to *be* Jews again without guilt. This may not have seemed like a function of religion, but in a community that had been shaped out of fear and atonement, it was precisely what the Hollywood Jews required of their God.

Refugees and British Actors

I sort of went back to the twenties.... It was a period in which I think most young men who were interested in ideas accepted the premise that the system of government or this government that we had all grown up under had failed —there was—there weren't any more horizons; there weren't any more promises. ... I felt that I was looking— for new horizons, for a new kind of society, something I could believe in and become part of, something in—well, in a sense, I felt I wanted to attach myself to history....

ROBERT ROSSEN, DIRECTOR

Utopia is the opiate of the Jewish people.

LUDWIG LEWISOHN

UPTON SINCLAIR DID NOT SEEM to be the sort of man who would shake the foundations of American civilization the way he might have shaken oranges out of a tree at his Pasadena bungalow, but from the vehemence with which Hollywood executives reacted to him in 1934, one would have thought that he was Lenin reincarnated and come to California to launch the revolution. Sinclair, a genial and modest muckraking novelist who had most successfully raked the muck of the meat-packing industry in *The Jungle*, was a Socialist. During interregnums between books, he had run for Congress and for the Senate on the Socialist ticket, losing handily both times, but in the summer of 1933 he suddenly discovered an affinity for Franklin Roosevelt ("He has barely got started on his journey, but he is headed in the right direction . . . and I am shoving"), registered as a Democrat, and declared for governor of California.

None of Sinclair's economic nostrums, which he called End Poverty in California (EPIC), seemed to have the faintest chance of being actualized, except that to his and everyone else's surprise, he won the Democratic primary that August, collecting 500,000 votes, and suddenly found himself head to head with California's incumbent, a pallid political reactionary named Robert Merriam. Good-humored and homespun, Sinclair made an appealing candidate, and two months before the election he was even thought to be running ahead. "A quiet, slight figure, with a pleasant smile constantly on his lips, suggesting inner certainty rather than humor or a political winsomeness," wrote a *New York Times* reporter, "Mr. Sinclair avoids emotional appeals and the stage tricks of fighting virility. In an even, bland voice, almost a monotone, with all the intimacy of an informal lecture on the better society in some one's front parlor, he talks at once plainly and brilliantly. With uncanny definiteness and concreteness he creates out of things which have not happened yet but are about to happen, a California as real as—if manifestly more agreeable than—the daily tangle of Los Angeles traffic."

The Hollywood Jews viewed him differently. Before Sinclair's candidacy, Hollywood had dabbled with him and he with it. MGM, of all studios, had bought the rights to one of his novels, *The Wet Parade*, though Irving Thalberg warned his story editor, Sam Marx, "to keep that Bolshevik away from me." (At the movie's premiere on March 17, 1932, held at Grauman's Chinese Theater, Sinclair lamented, "I was present, but was not called upon by the theater owner [Grauman] because I had failed to honor the occasion by wearing a dress suit.") Still, the radical actively solicited movie work, and Edgar Selwyn, a favorably disposed producer, invited him to dinners where he could defuse his incendiary image with the major executives and demonstrate, his wife said, that "he's had his fill of politics." No one was buying the transformation—not even Sinclair. "I don't think I am egotistical in saying that I have offered to the motion picture studios some good opportunities," he said later. "There is only one thing wrong with them, they indict the profit system."

There was, however, one mogul who felt he himself had been victimized by the profit system. Early in 1932, shortly after Sinclair had struck out with the movie studios, William Fox wrote asking to see him. The recently deposed head of Fox Pictures arrived with his lawyer, whom Sinclair described as "humble and obedient" and behaving "just like an errand boy." Dispatched by Fox to fetch the documents, the rotund little man returned with a bulging suitcase, and Fox launched into his threnody on how he had been undone by Nicholas Schenck, Louis B. Mayer, and large gentile banking interests determined to thwart his master plan to take over MGM. Now he was imploring Sinclair to chronicle his demise and condemn his tormentors, for which the writer would be paid $25,000 upon receipt of the manuscript. Sinclair, in the middle of another project, tried begging off, but his wife, "who knew the smell of money when it came near," accepted in his behalf.

And so Upton Sinclair embarked upon a lengthy attack on the movie and banking interests who had ganged up on William Fox. Three times a week Fox would arrive at Sinclair's home in Pasadena with his lawyer and his suitcase, sit down before a pitcher of lemonade Mrs. Sinclair had prepared, and dictate to a stenographer while Sinclair asked questions and clarified points. Sometime in late May Sinclair sent the first draft of the manuscript to Fox, who had returned with his family to New York. "And what happened then?" Sinclair wrote in his autobiography. "Well, to be precise—nothing. I waited patiently for two or three weeks, and I heard not a word. Then I received a letter from my friend Floyd Dell, who happened to be in New York. How Floyd got the information I have forgotten, but the substance of it was that Fox was using the threat of publishing my manuscript in an effort to get back some of the properties of which he had been deprived."

When Sinclair verified the information, he sent his carbon copy of the manuscript to his publisher in Indiana and instructed them to put the book into print. Fox wired, demanding Sinclair desist, but it was too late. "When those beautiful yellow-covered books hit Hollywood," Sinclair said, "it was with a bang that might have been heard at the moon if there was anybody there to listen." Fox Pictures posted a warning that any employee caught with the book would be immediately fired.

Now that Sinclair, the polemicist and adversary of the movie industry, appeared to have a legitimate chance at becoming California's next governor, Hollywood panicked. Suddenly, false stories were circulating that Mrs. Sinclair had admitted the race was a big publicity stunt to sell more of her husband's books or that Sinclair was raking profits from EPIC. Joe Schenck told reporters that Sinclair's election would destroy the film industry. "I'll move the studios to Florida, sure as fate, if Sinclair is elected." When asked if the studios were banding together to defeat him, Schenck answered, "Not as yet. But I'm going to tell the moving picture people who don't come along with us that they will cut their own throats."

Schenck wasn't being entirely truthful about Hollywood's collusion. Within a few weeks the studios were turning out "newsreels" in which an inquiring reporter would ask ordinary citizens whom they were voting for. "I am voting for Governor Merriam," said a little old lady, her voice quavering. "Why, Mother?" "Because I want to have my little home. It is all I have left in the world." "Vy, I am foting for Seenclair," boasted a bedraggled, bewhiskered, wild-eyed immigrant in another newsreel. "Vell, his system vorked vell in Russia, vy can't it vork here?" In another, an army of hoboes descended upon California in anticipation of Sinclair's election. In still another, a popular black Los Angeles minister said he was voting for Merriam because he liked to preach and play the piano, and he wanted to keep a church to preach in and a piano to play. In all, the industry raised nearly half a million dollars for the cause—most of it by exacting two days' wages from each employee. "This campaign against Upton Sinclair has been and is dynamite," exulted *The Hollywood Reporter* eleven days before the election. "When the picture business gets aroused, it becomes AROUSED, and boy, how they can go to it. It is the most effective piece of political humdingery that has ever been effected." In November Sinclair was soundly thrashed.

One night shortly after the election, there was a party at Fredric March's house in Hollywood. The partygoers, who included Irving Thalberg, got into a heated argument over what Hollywood had done to defeat Sinclair, especially the bogus newsreels. "I made those shorts," Thalberg said quietly. "'But it was a dirty trick!' shouted Freddy March, leaning forward angrily. 'It was the damnedest unfairest thing I've ever heard of!' 'Nothing is unfair in politics,' said Thalberg, evenly. 'We could sit down here and figure dirty things out all night, and every one of them would be all right in a political campaign.'" Thalberg recalled his childhood when he gave speeches for the Socialist party in New York and Tammany waded into the crowds to disperse them. "Fairness in an election is a contradiction in terms. It just doesn't exist."

The Sinclair campaign demonstrated probably better than anything else the political proclivities and activities of the Jewish executives. At its topmost levels, Hollywood was a reactionary enclave of Jews wearing the fashions of American gentility and giving no quarter to anyone who threatened their pretensions to prestige. Politically, genteel fashion dictated fealty to the Republican party, though until the late twenties *most* of the Eastern European immigrant Jews had affiliated with the Republicans, largely because most of them had emigrated during Republican administrations early in the century and wanted to express their gratitude to the party in power, but also because most of the German Jews, who served as models for the Eastern Europeans, were Republicans. Adolph Zukor said he became a Republican "because all the people I knew were Republicans."

The realignment began with the presidential campaign of New York Governor Al Smith, the Democratic candidate in 1928. Impeded or prohibited from gaining access to the real avenues of power in America—education, professions, business—Jews began to see a deeper community of interest with the downtrodden and dispossessed, the minorities, the workers, the city dwellers who would later form the core of Franklin Roosevelt's coalition. The Hollywood Jews never realigned, and most felt little real affinity with the forgotten men of the Depression—at least most of them never wanted to exhibit any affinity. (Jews who feel subordinate, one analyst of Jewish political behavior found, "are least likely to be tolerant of political nonconformists and altruistic toward other deprived groups.") The Hollywood Jews were after acceptance from those they regarded as their betters, and they saw their community of interest lying with the rich and the powerful of Los Angeles—a conservative lot in a deeply conservative place. It didn't hurt, either, that their mentor in things political was newspaper magnate William Randolph Hearst, a man of decidedly conservative temperament.

Of course, there was an economic as well as a psychological basis for their Republicanism. By the mid-thirties nineteen of the twenty-five highest salaries in America and forty of the highest sixty-three went to film executives. Louis Mayer earned more money than any other individual in the country—well over $1 million, even in the depths of the Depression. No one else in any industry approached Mayer, but other top Loew's executives received very substantial remuneration just the same. J. Robert Rubin and Nick Schenck, Mayer's boss, had the second and fourth highest salaries in the country, respectively, and Adolph Zukor, as a standard of comparison, earned close to $2 million and ten thousand shares of Paramount stock from 1927 to 1931. It was one of the reasons Sinclair's candidacy, with its threat of higher taxes, mobilized the film executives the way it did.

The most activist of the Hollywood Jews was the one most deeply possessed by the power of gentility: Louis B. Mayer. "When anyone important—senator, congressman, governor, or any important public official—came to town," explained Judge Lester Roth, a friend of Mayer's, "he entertained them at the studio. He would call together some of his important directors and acting personnel, whether it be Garbo or Gable or whoever, and entertain them at a luncheon. And he'd invite them to speak to this luncheon." These would be relatively small gatherings—no more than twenty or thirty guests—and Mayer, who was a gifted and impassioned speaker, would make the introductions himself, often turning them into orations. It was the Hollywood equivalent of the political salons of the east, where power brokers rubbed shoulders. "So they began to know him. . . . And that's how Louis Mayer built himself up."

When Californian Herbert Hoover was elected president in 1928, Mayer's rank in the party rose dramatically. He and his family were the new president's very first dinner guests—his daughter Edith remembered him complaining that the gravy was too thick—and then spent the evening in the White House. "He was so at home there," Edith said. Four years later, working for Hoover's renomination at the

Republican convention in Chicago, Mayer "seemed often at the head of the Golden Gate [sic] delegation and was so reported in the news services' accounts of the proceedings. . . . [T]hrough the President, Mayer becomes in his way pretty much of a leader in the Republican Party. . . ." Four years after that, with Hoover having been repudiated by the electorate, Mayer and his close friend William Randolph Hearst were back at the convention, again trying to play the role of kingmakers. There was even talk that Mayer himself would be a candidate for office someday.

Among the top echelon of Hollywood Jews, the only avowed Democrats were Mayer's lifelong adversaries the Warners, though how much of this was political conviction and how much a tactic to seize the political initiative in Hollywood is hard to say. According to Jack, sometime in 1932 his brother Harry summoned him to New York to attend what Harry said would be a clandestine meeting. When Jack arrived at the New York Warners' offices, he found Al Smith; industrialist Joseph Kennedy; John Raskob, former General Motors chairman and the new chairman of the Democratic National Committee; and several of New York Governor Franklin Roosevelt's advisers. Though the Warners had been Republicans of long standing, these Democratic chieftains, no doubt realizing that the Warners were the black sheep of the Hollywood establishment, were now asking their support to help nominate and elect Roosevelt president. Jack was puzzled by his brother's turnabout. Harry's answer was, "The country is in chaos. There is a revolution in the air, and we need a change." So Jack became chairman of the motion picture division of "Roosevelt for President," organizing a spectacular rally of stars at the Los Angeles Coliseum with every searchlight in the studio commandeered to strafe the sky. When Roosevelt carried the state by 500,000 votes, Jack was invited to head a delegation of film stars at the inauguration. Soon afterward he became the Los Angeles chairman of Roosevelt's National Recovery Act.

"I think he enjoyed having me around," Jack later said of his relationship to Roosevelt, "and there was to be a period when I virtually commuted to the White House, because I was an amusing fellow who wanted nothing in exchange. Court jester, I was, and proud of it." That was Warner's interpretation. Yet Roosevelt got a good deal in exchange—namely, access to Hollywood and the support of Warner Brothers on screen—and according to Jack, the president once tried to reward him with an ambassadorship.*

Still, the Warners' dalliance with liberalism was short-lived, and by 1936 they had returned to the Republican fold, embittered and disillusioned by what Harry saw as Roosevelt's ingratitude. The split centered on a dispute Harry had with a contentious banker. In 1926, when the studio bought the rival First National studio, it had also acquired a controlling interest in a chain of St. Louis theaters that First National owned. In 1931 the value of the theaters had plummeted, and a minority stockholder in the chain maneuvered it into receivership. Harry Warner tried manfully to maintain control, but the court instead appointed a financier named Harry Arthur.

Arthur was to learn that Harry Warner was not a man to cross. Fighting back, Harry secured short-term leases on several large first-run theaters and immediately struck deals with RKO and Paramount to exhibit their films exclusively. Arthur, believing that Warner was trying to freeze him out by sealing up first-run movies, brought a court action claiming that Warner had gotten Paramount's films only after threatening to challenge Paramount's theaters in Detroit in the same kind of cutthroat battle Zukor had patented in the early twenties. The trial took place in St. Louis, and even Harry was sure he was going to be convicted after the judge charged the jury in a way that (to Harry, at least) seemed extremely prejudicial. When, to his astonishment, he was acquitted, he thought the issue had finally been put to rest. Now, however, the *government* brought suit against him. Jack tried to intercede with Roosevelt but was rebuffed. "For what I did, they could have given a little help," he complained acidly. Harry was infuriated. One magazine, apparently expressing Harry's own pique, reported, "The New Deal, as Harry sees it, pays off its friends with the Sherman Act and causes him to lose his theaters." It was the last time any of the first generation of Hollywood Jews would support a Democrat.

---

*One thinks immediately of the "Forgotten Man" number in *The Gold Diggers of 1933*, or *Footlight Parade*, where the chorus forms ranks in a pictogram of Roosevelt and then the NRA eagle.

In the summer of 1934, just before Sinclair's campaign, Maurice Rapf, the teenage son of MGM executive Harry Rapf, convinced his father to let him tour the Soviet Union. In Russia Maurice was struck by the ubiquitous anti-Nazi propaganda—"Keep the Nazi slop out of the Soviet garden," read the caption of one poster with a red fist poised against a Nazi storm trooper over a brown wall—and by what he saw as the Soviet tolerance toward Jews. "Speak Yiddish! This is the Soviet Union. You don't have to hide it," said one Russian Jew when the American tourists tried conversing with him in German.

By the time he returned to Hollywood, Maurice had seen the future and been radicalized. "My father was very sad," he recalled, "but he couldn't counter what I had to say. After all, I had been there, and he was very respectful. But he sent me to see a series of his associates and friends and let them talk to me . . . and I had some really hair-raising experiences." Harry Warner, who had once been Harry Rapf's partner, was barely civil. "I don't want to talk to no goddamn Communist. Don't forget you're a Jew. Jewish Communists are going to bring down the wrath of the world on the rest of the Jews." Albert Warner, called the "Major," lacerated him. "Don't come into my office and start spouting any of that." Mayer argued that Maurice owed it to the Jewish people to forswear radicalism. "Everybody thinks that Jews are Communists," he said. Maurice thought, Everybody thinks that Jews are capitalists. I'll give up being a Communist if you give up being a capitalist.

Thalberg was calm. He brought in his resident intellectual, Albert Lewin, a former university professor, and let them debate Marxism. Then he said, "I understand why you're for the poor and why you want change. I did too when I was a young man." But Thalberg, the boyhood Socialist orator, said he had outgrown those feelings and advised that if Maurice were smart, he would get over them, too. David Selznick sympathized. He said he read *The Nation* and *The New Republic*. He was aware of injustice and he knew the left-wing prescriptions to ameliorate it. "Be a radical," he said. "Think anything you goddamn please. But don't wear it on your sleeve. Don't go around talking about it all the time because it's going to get in the way of your career. If you want to be a moviemaker, that's all you can do."

What was interesting was how much the Hollywood Jews' hatred of communism seemed really to be a fear that Jewish radicals would make all Jews suspect, rather than any ideological opposition. The Hollywood Jews would have done almost anything to disassociate themselves from the old canard that linked Jews to political radicalism; ironically and rather sadly, their efforts often made them bedfellows with the same reactionary groups that had attacked *them* for controlling Hollywood in the first place. A case in point was the brief American career of the famous Russian director Sergei Eisenstein, whom Paramount had, astonishingly, brought to Hollywood in 1930. No sooner had Eisenstein—a Communist, a homosexual, *and* a Jew —arrived than he fell victim to an unrelenting campaign of anti-Semitism and anticommunism orchestrated by a right-wing functionary named Frank Pease. The campaign began with slanders in letters and pamphlets, but when it escalated to threats against the studio and against Eisenstein personally, his contract was terminated. *

Appeasement and fear were reasons enough for the Hollywood Jews to be reactionaries, but their dread of being lumped with agitators and subversives acted upon another, equally disturbing fear. This was the fear that if the American Cossacks outside the industry didn't club them to death, the radicals within the industry would ultimately bleed them to death. To the Hollywood Jews, who acted like military dictators in a banana republic, these forces had to be eradicated before they took root.

It began with unions. By the time of Sinclair's campaign for governor, there was already a growing cadre of disaffected workers within the industry talking about organizing into guilds that could bargain with the producers. In the Neanderthal political environment of Hollywood—not to mention the environment of southern California generally—this kind of union activity was tantamount to treason. Union busting was a way of life there, and the film industry had, amazingly, managed to avoid any real labor strife into the thirties by

---

*It was Upton Sinclair who later raised funds so that Eisenstein could go to Mexico to make an epic about primitive Indians there. After shooting thousands of feet of film, Eisenstein abandoned the project and returned to Russia, where he languished under Stalin. (Sinclair, *Autobiography*, pp. 276–8.)

coopting union sentiments through the Academy of Motion Picture Arts and Sciences. Formed early in 1927 by thirty-six luminaries of the film industry who met at the behest of Louis B. Mayer, the academy was essentially a sweetheart union where producers invoked the sanctity of their common artistic mission with their creative employees and thereby deflected dissatisfaction that might have translated into genuine political action. Even the Oscar, which the academy awarded to recognize artistic merit, was just another way of striking filmmakers where they were most vulnerable—at their vanity.

But early in March 1933, the week of Roosevelt's inauguration and of the bank holiday that immediately followed, the labor peace was suddenly shattered. The studios declared they weren't going to be able to meet their payrolls. Even that might not have fomented an insurrection among the stars, writers, and directors, a notoriously soft and obsequious bunch, had the studio heads not then collaborated on March 9 and decided to inflict a Draconian pay cut of 50 percent for any employee earning over fifty dollars a week—the cut to last eight weeks.

Weary and moist-eyed, Louis Mayer collected his MGM family into the Thalberg Projection Room to lay out the grave facts about the industry's financial debility. He could barely speak. "Don't worry, L. B. We're with you," shouted Lionel Barrymore when Mayer broke down, but a Hungarian-born writer named Ernest Vadja was unmoved, protesting that of all the studios MGM was clearly in the best fiscal health. Let the other studios mete out pay cuts—not the roaring lion. "Mr. Vadja is like a man on his way to the guillotine, wanting to stop for a manicure," Barrymore said in his famous grandfatherly purr. That rallied the family. May Robson, an elderly actress, stood up and offered to take the cut as the oldest person in the room. One of the child actors immediately followed, taking the cut as the youngest person in the room. Mayer called a vote, and the assemblage agreed to accept the cuts. According to Sam Marx, as Mayer strode back to his office, he turned to his crony Ben Thau and asked, "How did I do?"

Regardless of the initial support, the measures ultimately and irrevocably destroyed solidarity in Hollywood by demonstrating to the workers that they really had no choice in the matter, and most of the studio heads were so bent on seizing the opportunity to cut costs that they didn't seem to care about the long-term ramifications. The wiser ones, however, understood. Darryl Zanuck, who had opposed the wage cuts in the first place, insisted that Warner Brothers restore the cuts as promised after eight weeks. When Harry reneged, Zanuck had the scene at the Brown Derby that resulted in his ouster. Thalberg had been in Europe at the time Schenck and Mayer imposed the cuts, but when he returned he lambasted Schenck for destroying morale and threatened to quit—a threat he never made good on. But Thalberg was right about the effects. A few weeks after the imposition of the cuts, a group of dissatisfied writers formed the Screen Writers Guild to represent them against management, and left-wing political sentiment intensified. Screenwriter Albert Hackett quipped that Louis B. Mayer had "created more Communists than Karl Marx."

In some inchoate way, Upton Sinclair's campaign a year later became a flashpoint for the divisions between capital and labor, assuming symbolic proportions far greater than Sinclair's own election. For the Jewish executives, Sinclair came to symbolize all the portentous radical forces within their community. For the discontented stars, directors, and especially the discontented writers of Hollywood, the campaign represented a way to fight back. Once these lines were drawn, they remained. By serving as a vicarious battleground, Sinclair's campaign also set one group of Jews against another: the Jewish executives against the Jewish writers.

The writers had, by and large, come from the East when Hollywood issued its call with the advent of the talkies. They were playwrights and novelists and newspapermen and magazine journalists and college boys with fresh English degrees, many of them of indifferent talent, most of them attracted by the money and the promise of paradise. "Millions are to be grabbed out here, Herman Mankiewicz cynically wired his friend Ben Hecht, "and your only competition is idiots." But they also came, many of them, with a conscience. Poor, young, educated Jews growing up in New York in the twenties and thirties, which described so many of the writers in Hollywood, could scarcely escape it. "My father read the *Forward* [the Jewish Socialist newspaper]," recalled Milton Sperling, who came to Hollywood as a young writer in the thirties. "He was a member of a union. And my grandfather was a member of a union. The Jews in New York were socialists. They were old-country Socialists . . . and unions and left-wing thinking of that simple sort that was so Jewish in those days was translated to their children."

The heritage of political conscience obviously gained impetus from the Depression and the ferment that followed. Politics and aesthetics merged. Young Jews with a gift for writing wanted to use it to right wrongs, expose injustices, redress grievances, and create new worlds, and that is precisely what they tried to do on the New York stage. They brought the same passionate commitment to Hollywood when it beckoned. "There were a number of people who came out about that time, young writers, who felt very deeply about motion pictures, and began to take a point of view about them," said Dore Schary. "There were some of us who would not take assignments unless we liked them. We would begin to argue with the producers. We would search for material we felt had some sort of integrity." Alvah Bessie, screenwriter and one-time drama critic for the left-wing *New Masses*, admitted surprise when Warner Brothers' executive Jerry Wald told him they deliberately hired progressives "because these boys knew what society in general and fascism and the war in particular were all about and could create characters and situations that bore some re-semblance to reality."

Yet Hollywood had a strange effect on the writers' own sense of reality—something at once narcotizing and unsettling. These young Jews who back in New York had been the shock troops of a new political order suddenly found themselves softened and spoiled by California and their messianism momentarily coopted. "I loved the hills back of Hollywood," rhapsodized transplanted New York playwright Jerome Chodorov. "I loved the air, I loved the sunshine, and going to the beach was so easy and then I had a car for the first time in my life. . . . You don't know what it is to live in a city where the jackhammer wasn't going and the pile driver. . . . " New York the-atrical director Harold Clurman remembered visiting playwright Clifford Odets in Hollywood and being struck immediately by "its overpowering pleasantness. On my first walk I thought I had suddenly moved into a new never-never land. When I met Eddie Robinson outside his imposing property, he nodded toward it and said: 'This is

the millennium,' and grinned like a pumpkin." One hot Sunday afternoon, Clurman lay floating contentedly in actor Franchot Tone's
pool when Tone "observed me with friendly malice and remarked:
'The life of a prostitute is pretty comfortable, isn't it?'"

For the writers, the answer was deeply ambivalent. For all the
wonderful blandishments of California and its promise of sunny comfort, writers, traditionally solitary and self-respecting, paid the price
with their independence and status. It was a cruel adjustment—men
of art treated like laborers. "You had to punch the clock," Milton
Sperling recalled. "They would walk around and see if everybody was
typing. There'd be a lookout in the writers' building. When Warner
or Cohn would be seen coming toward the building, somebody would
say, 'He's coming!' And all the typewriters would start.... He [Jack
Warner] couldn't understand why people weren't always typing. He
didn't realize they have to think." "We had a six-day week," remembered writer and director Billy Wilder. "On Saturday, you only had to
work until lunchtime.... You just delivered about eleven pages every
Thursday to the head of the writers' department. You knocked out like
two or three scripts a year."

Almost all complained about the awful sense of helplessness as
other writers were assigned to do rewrites of one's original draft until
one's relationship to the script became tenuous—the paternity questionable. F. Scott Fitzgerald, confessing to his daughter that he was
too cocky the first time he came to Hollywood and too humble the
second time, now wrote, "I want to profit by these two experiences—I
must be very tactful but keep my hand on the wheel from the start—
find out the key men among the bosses and the most malleable
among the collaborators—then fight the rest tooth and nail until, in
fact or in effect, I'm alone on the picture. That's the only way I can
do my best work."

What Fitzgerald would never comprehend—what most of the
writers would never comprehend—is that, in the minds of the executives, film wasn't essentially a writer's medium the way the novel was.
In Hollywood writers were hired hands on a project that was not and
would never be the product of any single sensibility, much less theirs.
Though Fitzgerald did recognize that "these people are more impressed with what comes out with the imprimatur of an important

magazine in the East than in almost anything done here" and that "[h]ardly a man here is in the big money who has not had a best seller or some striking stories or a successful play to his credit," he could never draw the appropriate conclusion. Distinguished writers weren't hired for their literary talent—which, in any case, usually proved negligible in the peculiar craft of screenwriting. Distinguished writers were hired for the distinction they brought to the men who hired them. As Jack Warner once boasted at a party after signing William Faulkner, "I've got America's best writer for $300 a week."

The writer was a trinket for men of dubious breeding and culture. He was another affectation along with the racehorses, the mansions, the limousines, the tailored suits. He was a reproof of the accusation of vulgarity. "The higher the class of talent he could tell what to do and how to do it," Ben Hecht noted, "the more giddily cultured he could feel himself." (Philip Dunne once noted that in Hollywood it was always "my" writer but "our" director.) But this also made the writer an ideal target for the Hollywood Jews' contempt: a scapegoat for the indignities they felt they had had to suffer for their lack of education and refinement. "They were afraid," writer Michael Blankfort said of the moguls. "If you're an illiterate and you're talking to someone who's literate and can do something you have no conception of. . . . So it isn't that I envy them. I fear them."*

Despite the fact that they conferred status, writers in Hollywood had very little status of their own. Socially, they kept to themselves, hanging out at Musso & Frank's Grill, a spacious, noisy watering hole of dark banquettes on Hollywood Boulevard where the favored writers—Faulkner, Nathanael West, Donald Ogden Stewart, Dorothy Parker—had a back room to themselves. Often they would repair next door to the Stanley Rose Bookshop, where men of letters—Irwin Shaw and John O'Hara were frequent visitors—congregated to discuss literature. "At a Hollywood party, there would be forty or fifty celebrities," said Ben Hecht, one of the highest-paid screenwriters, "but I don't think you'd find any writers, possibly one, at the most

---

*For their degradation, however, the writers did exact a small measure of revenge, since it is almost exclusively through writers that we know what we know of the Hollywood moguls. Our whole history of Hollywood is framed by the writers' prejudices. It is history by retribution.

two. They were never invited out in mixed company. They were treated much like butlers, socially." Hecht added, "If you could alter your status from that of writer to that of card-player or drinking companion, it was a tremendous step up." Said another screenwriter, "Jews are the writers of the business and writers are the Jews of the business."

The contempt was, of course, reciprocated. It was really the only weapon writers had against the executives who commanded them; they could buy their words but not their respect. "Don't you think it's a shame that you and I, intelligent men with some talent, should be the pot-boys of the common ruffians that run this joint?" one writer asks another in a novel that captured the writers' umbrage. "Somebody should go to the chair for a serious crime in order to make the world realize the position of the intellectual in Hollywood." "The main topic of conversation [at the studio commissaries]," remembered Michael Blankfort, "was how stupid the producers and directors were. . . . The resentment was the resentment of the coal miner who resents the boss because he's digging coal, he's getting all dirty. The boss is nice and clean and sitting in an air-conditioned office."

The writers' contempt for the moguls was matched only by their self-contempt for having surrendered. "Nobody would live in Hollywood except to get what money he could get out of it," Faulkner once said. Ben Hecht told an interviewer, "There was no art to the film. There never was, any more than there is to making toilet seats or socks or sausages. It's a commodity for mass consumption. . . . They're platitudes strung together, repetition of plots." Most of the writers regularly attended foreign films at cramped art houses and pined afterward over what they believed they could accomplish if only they had the license. Self-contempt, conspicuously displayed, actually became a badge of honor among the writers—the only way of asserting one's superiority over the process. Skewering Hollywood as he regularly did, Fitzgerald wrote a friend, "The heroes are the great corruptionists or the supremely indifferent—by whom I mean the spoiled writers, Hecht, Nunnally Johnson, Dotty [Parker], Dash Hammett, etc." It may have seemed the only heroism left a writer.

Those writers who couldn't feign indifference often found themselves swinging between extravagance and guilt. ("You didn't live through the Depression," one screenwriter's brother told him. "You lived in Hollywood.") "I began to realize why people believe the legend that Hollywood corrupts writers," wrote Dalton Trumbo, himself a screenwriter. "But they're quite wrong. All Hollywood does is give them enough money so they can get married and have kids like normal people. But it's getting married and having kids that really corrupts them." For the New York Jewish writers, infused with the faith of street corner socialism, this made for some particularly ridiculous contradictions. After a Sunday buffet hosted by playwright Clifford Odets and his new wife, actress Luise Rainer, Rainer tearfully phoned her friend Ella Winter, wife of screenwriter Donald Ogden Stewart. "Cliff is furious at me," she said of her breast-beating left-wing husband, "because we did not have servants to bring the food and wait on table. 'Even if it was their Sunday off, you should have hired others,' he said. I told him all theatrical people did it like this on Sunday nights in Vienna, but he said this wasn't Vienna, it was Hollywood, and in Hollywood one had servants; otherwise why come here?" Sometime later Harold Clurman was spending an evening with actress Stella Adler and Odets, all three Jewish veterans of New York's leftish Group Theatre, when Adler blurted at Clurman, "I feel that I need to sin, and you make me feel I have no right to." To which Odets rejoined, nearly shouting, "She's right."

For the New York Jews particularly, to contempt, guilt, and sin there was one last, cleansing alternative, and that was politics. "It started with much fewer people in the Upton Sinclair campaign," recalled Philip Dunne, "and then in 1936, when the Spanish Civil War started, that was the catalyst.... All of a sudden people like Ernest Hemingway and Andre Malraux, who were gods, came to Hollywood and sat in your living room and talked to screenwriters who were still partially despised" by the eastern literary establishment. This was a heady appeal for self-reproachful writers, but there were others. Political activity assuaged guilt. It gave higher purpose to men and women who desperately needed it and who realized they were regarded as a "self-contained community of self-centered people who were so corrupt on every level that they could scarcely be bothered with something so small as a world war." And it provided a sense of camaraderie to the diffuse, downtrodden cadre of Hollywood writers. In politics, they lived.

For writer Tess Slesinger, the question was, "Are we history or are we mice?" but she left no doubt as to the answer. The drumbeat of history seemed to be everywhere around them—in Roosevelt and the New Deal, in the Spanish Civil War, in the rise of nazism, in their own efforts to unionize. All of these were conflated into a political crescendo that, for a time, swept Hollywood. "We're up to our necks in politics and morality now," one screenwriter lamented. "Nobody goes to anybody's house any more to sit and talk and have fun. There's a master of ceremonies and a collection basket, because there are no gatherings now except for a Good Cause. We have almost no time to be actors and writers these days. We're committee members and collectors and organizers and audiences for orators." Writing in *The New Republic*, Ella Winter concurred: "There is hardly a tea party today, or a cocktail gathering, a studio lunch table or dinner even at a producer's house at which you do not hear agitated discussion, talk of 'freedom' and 'suppression,' talk of tyranny and the Constitution, of war, of world economy and political theory."

The "Good Causes" were, of course, primarily liberal ones, and Philip Dunne estimated that "probably 70 percent of the writers, directors, actors, and so on were liberally inclined," if only because it was the only way to salve their guilt and demonstrate their compassion. Hollywood Jews had a narrower interest. Actor Melvyn Douglas, a Jew, remembered returning from Europe early in 1936 and hearing several midwestern businessmen lavishly praise Hitler and viciously attack Roosevelt. By trip's end Douglas felt "congealed with a kind of horror" that so few seemed to be aware of the Nazi threat. A short time later, back in Hollywood, he joined several other political activists who had formed the Hollywood League Against Nazism, soon renamed the Hollywood Anti-Nazi League.

The Anti-Nazi League cast its net much wider than its title would have suggested. From 1936 through 1939 it was really the primary vehicle for most of the community's left-wing activism. The league proselytized, pressured, and picketed for everything from condemnation of the Germans and, after their invasion of China, the Japanese to support for Roosevelt's beleaguered Federal Theater Project, but even though its embrace was wide and unwieldy, in many ways it resembled less the large, lumbering political tumbril so characteristic of Hollywood organizations than a well-oiled, thundering steam engine. It sponsored two weekly radio programs, published its own bi-weekly tabloid, *Hollywood Now*, and generated a number of subcommittees to address and educate specific constituencies—women, youth, labor, race, religion, professions—all of which led the right wing to accuse it of being a Communist front.

There was certainly a basis for suspicion. At roughly the same time the league was formed, the Communist party of the United States of America dispatched V. J. Jerome and Stanley Lawrence to Hollywood to channel the inchoate political sentiment there. Lawrence, a tall shaggy dog with glasses the thickness of pop bottle bottoms, had been a Los Angeles cabdriver who had gone overseas to help organize workers there and returned with the fire of a true believer. Jerome's bloodlines were nobler. He was born Jerome Isaac Romain in Poland in 1896, but by the time he had been naturalized in this country in 1928, he was known as Victor Jeremy Jerome. Educated in England and at New York University, Jerome was one of those leftist intellectuals who was attracted to the CPUSA, and by the time he arrived in California he had become chairman of the Party's Cultural Commission, its cultural commissar.

Jerome was doctrinaire and, in one Party member's words, "diffident," but he was also articulate and indefatigable. He spoke often and easily on any issue of the left: on the Spanish Civil War, on Hitler, on Mussolini, on unionization, and, perhaps most important for Hollywood, on the role of the writer. Jerome could and did argue that "agitprop drama was actually better drama because Marxists better understood the forces that shaped human beings, and could therefore write better characters." To a writer who already felt unappreciated, this was like evangelism to a redeemable sinner. To be told, as one observer cited, that "the status they achieved in making featherweight movies, however worthless in itself, contributed mightily to the Cause in the long run" was almost enough to justify their lives. It was the political equivalent of salvation.

Communism, of course, held other appeals for the writers: there was really no organized liberal opposition in Hollywood, so that liberals and Communists tended to meld; writers naturally tended to the dramatic, and the aesthetics of communism were not, as it turned out, very different from the aesthetics of Hollywood, so that, colum-

nist Murray Kempton commented, the "slogans, the sweeping formulae, the superficial clangor of Communist culture had a certain
fashion in Hollywood precisely because they were two-dimensional
appeals to a two-dimensional community"; the Party served as a social
club where the rigid distinctions between high-priced screenwriters
and their younger brethren fell; and finally, the writers, alienated
from their own labor and bowing to capital, viewed Hollywood as a
perfect if rudimentary model of a capitalist economy. "It is not accidental that Hollywood workers speak always of the industry, never of
the medium," Dalton Trumbo wrote the editor of the radical *Masses
and Mainstream* magazine. "For motion picture writers are purely
industrial workers, subject to a great many of the economic ills of
industrial workers in other industries." It wasn't surprising, then, that
by the time Jerome departed for the East after nine months of agitating in Hollywood, the Party had a firm hold in the film community;
estimates ranged as high as three hundred members during the decade
from 1936 to 1946—nearly half of them writers.

But as much as the Hollywood Communist party was a writers'
party, it was also, to the everlasting regret of American Jews generally,
a Jewish party. (Indeed, to be the former really meant being the latter
as well.) Jews had first forged ties to the parties of the Left, and to the
Communist party specifically, back in Europe, where they had been
susceptible to the Party's call to internationalism (they had few nationalist ties) and to its incantation of working-class utopianism (they were
all skilled and semiskilled laborers). Though the CPUSA, right up
through the mid-thirties, did little to encourage Jewish participation
here, Jews still constituted a sizable minority of the Party, partly as a
vestige of their European roots and partly as a response to their own
sensitivity to injustice in this country. Elsewhere in the world, the
Party was a group of committed workers roused by a cadre of intellectuals. In America, the Party was a group of committed intellectuals
roused by the romance of workers, and the intellectuals were dispro-
portionately Jewish.

None of this was lost on the Party organizers. However large a
Communist cohort the Jews formed before 1935, they formed an
even larger one afterward, when the Party joined forces with other
left-wing groups that year in the Popular Front and began actively

soliciting Jews. Zionism and anti-Semitism suddenly moved to the top of the Party's agenda. As a result, one leading Communist estimated that 50 percent of the Party's members were Jews during its heyday in the thirties and forties, and a large minority—sometimes a majority—of the Party leadership was Jewish.

What was true of the national Party was even truer in Hollywood, where Jews already formed a large part of the left-leaning artistic community. "There were a lot of liberals like me in Hollywood then who weren't communist," said screenwriter Samson Raphaelson. "But most Jews, because of their fear of anti-Semitism, contributed to all of the antifascist causes. I felt that if the world were going to go communist or fascist, I'd rather see it go communist." One member complained that nearly 90 percent of the Party in Los Angeles was Jewish, and while that probably exaggerated the situation, Ring Lardner, Jr., himself a Party member, had the "impression that it was well over 50 percent, somewhere like, maybe, two-thirds." The role of Jews "was discussed to a certain extent within the Party," Lardner remembered. "There were certainly education discussions on anti-Semitism and on the forces at work within the United States that were producing a largely middle-class Communist party. This was regarded as a danger and a weakness in the CP—that it didn't have the strong working-class base. And this was a result of the number of Jewish people in it at a time when this generation of Jews in America was becoming less working class."

In Hollywood it couldn't be avoided. After V. J. Jerome returned East in 1937, the reins of the Hollywood Party had even passed to a Jewish screenwriter whose personal history read like a résumé of all the Jewish screenwriters who had ventured West. Bushy-haired and affable—he was described as a boon drinking companion—John Howard Lawson had grown up in New York, attended Williams College, and then gone off during World War I with Hemingway, Cummings, and Dos Passos to drive ambulances in France and Italy. When he returned from Europe he gravitated, like so many middle-class Jews in his generation, to the left-wing theater. He had an early success with a didactic, fire-breathing play titled *Processional* (1928) about a coal miners' strike, but left-wing politics had so deeply infected him that he found himself constantly and unsuccessfully negotiating between his art and his mission. When MGM asked him to move to Hollywood and write for the movies, he grabbed the opportunity as a possible palliative for his discontent.

But if Lawson thought a sojourn in Hollywood would provide a breathing spell from his internal combat, he quickly realized he had come to the wrong place. Assigned to write a feature for Cecil B. De Mille, he was appalled at how little control he had over the final product and at how generously writing credits were tendered to others, even though he did the vast bulk of the work. (Control over one's material would remain one of Lawson's most fervent causes, dovetailing with his communism; he always insisted that the real issue during the dark days of the blacklist was freedom of expression.) Disillusioned, he returned to New York in 1930 to continue work in the theater, where, he averred, he could speak in his "true voice." Two years later, working with the Group Theatre that would later send Clifford Odets and other putative left-wing radicals to Hollywood, he turned out what would be his last dramatic triumph, *Success Story*.

Though radical critics—and Lawson himself—tended to dismiss *Success Story* as politically irrelevant, it probably went as far as anything he wrote in suggesting what personal demons he was struggling to tame. Like *The Jazz Singer*, *Success Story* was about a young American Jew who wants desperately to arrive and assimilate but who realizes, as he fulfills his ambitions, that success comes at the expense of his deeper self and his roots. (Lawson's own father, Simon Levy, had changed the family name and assimilated, only to be wrecked by the Depression.) It was, of course, the classic American-Jewish dilemma—the same one that haunted the Hollywood Jews whom Lawson would later battle and despise. For Lawson it became the central configuration of his life.

Whether it was Jew versus American, artist versus politico, intellectual versus activist or middle class versus working class, Lawson was very much a man in between searching to be whole. He continued to write for the theater, but he admitted he was still distracted and unhappy, unable to reconcile his contradictions. The Party took note. Critic Michael Gold, seizing on Lawson's ideological confusion, condemned him in *New Masses* as a "Bourgeois Hamlet of Our Time," who kept "repeating the same monotonous question: 'Where do I belong in the warring world of the two classes?'" For Gold the answer may have been self-evident. For Lawson it was much more vexing.

When he finally did take sides, sometime in 1934, it was predictably as a left-wing zealot. Dorothy Healy, the chairperson of the Los Angeles Communist party, later described him as "a tragic figure." "He was a man of talent and ability, but he was struggling so hard to prove he was not a petty-bourgeois intellectual." To establish his political credentials, he largely suspended his dramatic writing throughout 1934, traveling to Scottsboro, Alabama, to show support for the Scottsboro Boys. On two occasions he was ordered to leave Birmingham—once for demonstrating in behalf of striking black steelworkers and again for writing a corrosive series of articles on civil rights. He later wrote that his foray down South "deepened my conviction that *commitment* is essential to the artist's creative growth." In November Lawson openly declared in *New Theater* that he was now a member of the Communist party. "As for myself, I do not hesitate to say that it is my aim to present the Communist position and to do so in the most specific manner."

Taking sides, becoming orthodox, seemed finally to bring Lawson the peace he had sought for so long. The irony was that the Communist party served his needs and those of the other Jewish writers in very much the same way that the Republican party met the needs of the Jewish executives. One could lose oneself in communism. One could become attached to something larger and distinctively non-Jewish—in the case of Republicans, a genteel America; in the case of Communists, a classless state. One could fashion a utopia where Jews would be fully accepted. This, beyond the traditions of radicalism and self-contempt, may have been the most powerful appeal of the Party for the Jewish writers in Hollywood. Ring Lardner, Jr., had married a Jewess and brought her into the Party. "She was very much of an assimilationist in all of her attitudes," he said, "and I think one of the things that really appealed to her about the Party was the fact that it was kind of a channel for her assimilationist viewpoint. I think that was certainly true of a lot of people I knew. There was certainly, among the people I knew in Hollywood, much less identification with Judaism generally than there was during and after the war or than there is today." One social historian went further. "From the start,

Jewish self-hate and the striving for total assimilation was characteristic of those Jews attracted to Bolshevism," he noted. The Bolsheviks'
"conceptions of class war and the supremacy of the workers appealed
primarily to those Jews who wanted to destroy both the bourgeois
Christian society that rejected them and the petty-bourgeois Jewish
society they blamed for that rejection."

When Lawson returned to Hollywood in 1937, to write and to
command the Hollywood Party, he was no longer a vacillator. Always
articulate and brilliant, he was now also dogmatic, and he quickly
became, in one Communist's words, the Party's "high lama." "He
settled all questions," testified one-time Party member director Edward Dmytryk. "If there was a switch in the Party line, he explained
it. If there were any decisions to be made, they went to John Howard
Lawson. If there was any conflict within the Communist party, he
was the one who settled it." One writer called him "ruthless." Few
dared tangle with him. "The important thing is this," F. Scott Fitzgerald wrote about Hollywood Communists generally but in what
seemed a perfect description of the new Lawson.

> They had best be treated not as people holding a certain set
> of liberal or conservative opinions but rather as you might
> treat a set of extremely fanatical Roman Catholics among
> whom you might find yourself. It's not that you should not
> disagree with them—the important thing is that you should
> not argue with them . . . whatever you say they have ways of
> twisting it into shapes which put you in some lower category
> of mankind ("Fascist," "Liberal," "Trotskyist") and dispar-
> age you both intellectually and personally in the process.

At the time, though Lawson's bullying orthodoxy terrorized many
Party members, there were just as many who idolized him for it.
(Among the transplanted New York Jews in craven Hollywood, intel-
lectualism went a long way.) He had the certitude and fervor of the
converted, and his rhetorical skills—among people, after all, who
made their living with words—were extraordinary. When he addressed a meeting, he had a way of laying out policy with the cool,
imperturbable logic of a general explaining a stratagem. One writer

compared him to Lenin. It was the sort of comparison for which Lawson lived.

But the rumpled Jewish intellectual was also, as events would prove, the Hollywood Party's Stalin. Budd Schulberg, the son of former Paramount production head B. P. Schulberg, had joined the Party in 1937 after several years of youthful left-wing idealism (he had accompanied Maurice Rapf to Russia in 1934) and had generally bowed to its discipline. In 1939, however, when Schulberg announced his intention to turn one of his short stories into a novel, the Party was not pleased. First published in *Liberty Magazine* in 1937, "What Makes Sammy Run?" was an account of an ambitious first-generation American Jew named Sammy Glick who claws his way to the top of the Hollywood heap by forsaking everything decent. Whether the Party felt the story insufficiently "progressive" and too "individualistic," as Schulberg reported he was told, or whether Lawson and his functionaries feared the book might offend the Jewish membership and raise anti-Semitism, Schulberg was alerted not to proceed without a review of the situation. Schulberg said he was advised to submit an outline and then "discuss the matter further"—one of Lawson's signature phrases. Instead, Schulberg decided "I would have to get away from this if I was ever to be a writer." He jumped in the car with his wife and daughter and headed for Vermont.

He returned in March 1940 with his completed manuscript and the wrath of the Party ringing down around him. Lawson reprimanded him for breaking discipline and offered a detailed criticism of the book itself. V. J. Jerome, the cultural commissar, denounced him. "I was wrong about writing; wrong about this book; wrong about the Party; wrong about the so-called peace movement at that particular time. . . . I felt I had talked to someone rigid and dictatorial who was trying to tell me how to live my life, and as far as I remember, I didn't want to have anything more to do with them." But that was far from the end of it.

Charles Glenn, the young book reviewer for the *People's World* and *Daily Worker*, bumped into Schulberg at Larry Edmund's bookstore in Hollywood and, being a fan, asked if he could read the galleys of the new novel. On April 2, 1941, a few weeks after *Sammy* was published, Glenn praised it effusively in *People's World*. "For slightly fewer years than they have awaited the great American novel, whatever that may be," Glenn wrote, "American bibliophiles and critics have been awaiting the Hollywood novel. While they may argue its merits and demerits, I've a feeling that all critics, no matter their carping standards, will have to admit they've found *the* Hollywood novel in Budd Schulberg's *What Makes Sammy Run?*"

The Party was appalled. Glenn had failed to clear his review with Lawson or Jerome, and if Schulberg had committed the sin of individualism, of not sufficiently appreciating and explaining the workers' struggle in Hollywood, Glenn had compounded it. Glenn was now asked to attend a public meeting to recant his views (Schulberg declined Lawson's invitation), and on April 23, bowing to the pressure, he wrote a revised review in the *Daily Worker*. "On the basis of quite lengthy discussion on the book, I've done a little reevaluating," Glenn hedged. "To say I felt more than a trifle silly when these weaknesses [in the novel] were called to my attention is putting it a bit mildly. It is precisely the superficial subjective attitude shown in this review which reflects the dangers of an 'anti-Hollywood' approach, conscious or unconscious." Lawson had spoken.

If the Communists had been speaking aesthetically, they might have had a point. As novels go, *What Makes Sammy Run?* was coarsely written and quaintly primitive in its application of psychology to the drives of the Hollywood mogul, but Schulberg was certainly on to something in making an effort to locate those drives rather than assume a kind of spontaneous aggression. Glick, ferret-faced and nervous, is an irrepressible schemer and user, a bolt of ambition who climbs his way from errand boy at a newspaper to columnist to screenwriter to producer without missing a beat. "I wonder if the thing that makes Sammy so fascinating for us," says a character in the book, "is that he is the *id* of our whole society." Schulberg's titular question, which could have been asked of any of the Jewish moguls, was *what* drove them to their obsession with power.

It wasn't genetics, concluded Schulberg's narrator, Al Manheim. There were too many "Jews without money, without push, without plots, without any of the characteristics which such experts on genetics as Adolf Hitler, Henry Ford and Father Coughlin try to tell us are racial traits." Sammy himself shuddered at the notion. "What the hell did the Jews ever do for me?—except maybe get my head cracked open for me when I was a kid. . . . 'Jews,' he said bitterly and absently. 'Jews,' he said like a storm-trooper." Sammy's response, however, shocks the narrator into a new line of investigation. Traveling to Sammy's boyhood neighborhood on the Lower East Side of New York, he discovers a "tenement laced with corroded fire escapes and sagging washlines" squeezed in between a synagogue and a fish store. And he discovers that Sammy's late father, like the fathers of virtually all the Hollywood Jews, was an extremely religious Jew who barely eked out a living with a pushcart. Meanwhile, Sammy was matriculating on the streets—fighting, conning, whoring. "While you was being such a goddam good Jew," he curses his father, "who was hustlin' up the dough to pay the rent?"

And so, Manheim concludes, what really made Sammy run was his war against his father, his Judaism, his environment, his poverty, his world. "I thought of Sammy Glick rocking in his cradle of hate, malnutrition, prejudice, suspicions, amorality, the anarchy of the poor," Manheim muses. "I thought of him as a mangy little puppy in a dog-eat-dog world. . . . I saw Sammy Glick on a battlefield where every soldier was his own cause, his own army and his own flag, and I realized that I had singled him out not because he had been born into the world any more selfish, ruthless and cruel than anybody else, even though he had become all three, but because in the midst of a war that was selfish, ruthless and cruel Sammy was proving himself the fittest, the fiercest and the fastest."

Obviously Sammy Glick struck a nerve with the Hollywood Jews, and the clamor over *What Makes Sammy Run?* within the Party was matched only by the clamor it raised among the Jewish executives. Schulberg's own father advised that he put the book in a drawer and publish another novel first to establish some literary clout before he took on the industry's Jewish powers. Mayer, who probably cared more about his image as a man of culture than any of his fellow executives, was incensed and lit out after B. P. Schulberg. "I blame you for this. God damn it, B. P., why didn't you stop him?" Budd Schulberg remembered the assault. When Mayer suggested that Budd be deported for his infraction, B. P. laughed. "'Deported? Where? He was one of the few kids who came out of this place. Where are we going to deport him to? Catalina? Lake Helena? Louis, where do we send him?' And Mayer didn't think it was funny and he said, 'I don't care where you send him, but deport him.'"

The Jewish executives were obviously concerned that Sammy Glick would reinforce stereotypes about the industry and create a backlash against the Jews—against *them*. The Communists were more circumspect. Lawson and Jerome had initially upbraided Schulberg for not keeping faith with the cause, for being self-indulgent and not consulting the Party for guidance, for failing to limn the real class basis of the Screen Writers Guild battles that the book chronicles. That was how the Party theoreticians framed the issues. But among the rank and file, the focus of the debate was quite different. Ring Lardner, Jr., remembered meeting to discuss *Sammy* with half a dozen left-wing writers, including Schulberg, at the home of director Herbert Biberman. Obviously nothing was finally resolved, but it was clear that what roused the Jewish radicals was the same thing that roused the Jewish executives: whether the book implicitly promoted anti-Semitism. Judaism made strange bedfellows.

Whatever he was doing to their co-religionists in Germany, Adolf Hitler placed the Jewish executives in a curious position. The radicals could condemn him roundly from political, if not religious, conviction. But the executives, who had spent the better part of their lives transforming themselves *from* Jews, had the comfort neither of religion nor dogma. Some simply ignored the Nazis. Mayer asked his friend William Randolph Hearst to have a chat with Hitler and was relieved when Hearst assured him that Hitler's motives were pure. Irving Thalberg returned from Germany in 1934 sanguinely pronouncing that "a lot of Jews will lose their lives" but that "Hitler and Hitlerism will pass; the Jews will still be there." When his astonished listeners pressed him, he insisted that German Jews should not fight back and that Jews throughout the world shouldn't interfere. Again, "Hitler would eventually disappear; the Jews would remain."

Who *is* Hitler? Carl Laemmle asked Joseph Roos at a cocktail party.

Roos, a German-born public relations specialist and Jewish activist, had recently conducted an investigation on the Nazis for Colonel, later General, George Marshall, and he was eager to share what he had learned. Laemmle, in turn, was so eager to hear that he gave Roos a job at the studio. What prompted Laemmle's inquiry were reports that in his birthplace of Laupheim, Germany, public streets and buildings that had once borne his name now bore the name "Hitler." Laemmle couldn't understand it. "Here I did everything for my little town and now it's no longer Laemmle Strasse," he complained, and he hired Roos to give an explanation "over and over again." "He would call me either there at Universal or in the evening and say, 'Can I pick you up?'" Roos recalled. "So he would come in this fancy big car and pick me up and go out to Venice on the Boardwalk, and we would enjoy walking up and down and talk for an hour or two or three.... It must have been a dozen times, maybe even more. Sometimes he would ask me to come to dinner, talk even during dinner."

"I don't know when they took the street name down," said Laemmle's nephew Walter, "but I know that since Hitler came to power every letter he wrote to my father, he said, 'Get out! Get out! Sell your business. If you can't sell it, bring the things along.' And my father had the philosophy: 'I've never done anything wrong in Germany. Why should I leave?'" Louis Laemmle probably would have stayed had his wife not suffered a stroke and given an ultimatum that she would leave Germany without him. Reluctantly, he went to the American consulate to get visas for him and his wife. When some petitioners in the office protested that the woman was half-paralyzed yet was still granted a visa, Louis Laemmle told them, "Yes, if you have Carl Laemmle as a brother-in-law, you can get it, too."

They left for America on September 30, 1938, the day of the Munich Conference. Walter stayed behind and was eventually sent to Dachau, though he was later permitted to emigrate. Meanwhile, Laemmle offered to provide affidavits vouching financial solvency for virtually anyone who wanted to come to America. "Tell me how many inhabitants Laupheim has," joked the American consul because so many of the villagers had come to the United States with Laemmle's support. In all, he assisted over 250 German Jews who were threatened by Hitler, and when the State Department started questioning his affidavits, he began hectoring friends and relatives to provide affidavits in *their* names, giving a written guarantee that if they were asked to make any financial contribution to the people they sponsored, he would reimburse them.

Adolph Zukor was also touched directly by the rise of Hitler. His brother Arthur had become a prominent rabbi in Berlin, and long before Hitler became chancellor, he was discussing the potential dangers the Nazis posed to the Jewish community. In 1932 he finally decided it was unwise to remain, but rather than come to America he resettled his family in Palestine, where he remained until his death. Notwithstanding his own family's escape from the Nazis, just three weeks before Hitler invaded Poland, Adolph Zukor told an interviewer, "I don't think that Hollywood should deal with anything but entertainment. The newsreels take care of current events. To make films of political significance is a mistake. When they go to a theatre they want to forget. If it's entertainment, it's all right—but not propaganda."

What finally mobilized the Jewish executives was not what Hitler was doing to the Jews in Europe, but what his minions threatened to do to the Jews in Hollywood. The Los Angeles Bund was especially active—picketing, pamphleteering, badgering—and its central targets were the Hollywood Jews. *Liberation* and *Silver Ranger*, two Bund periodicals, regularly attacked the movie industry, and G. Allison Phelps, a radio commentator with close ties to the Bund, continued the attacks on the air. On March 13, 1934, Mendel Silberberg, Hollywood's Jewish fixer, invited the most prominent Jewish executives to a meeting at Hillcrest to discuss whether they wanted to retaliate. MGM story editor Sam Marx remembered that terror gripped the room. "Being kind of unterrifiable, I offered to go outside to Pico Boulevard, stop the first ten motorists, and ask, 'What do you think about the Jews?' and they wouldn't know what I was talking about. But they wouldn't take my bet." Mayer took the floor, steaming. He said he for one wasn't going to take these attacks lying down, and that two things were required: money and intelligent direction. He then enjoined the participants to provide both. Goaded into action, they immediately appointed a committee to raise funds. Thalberg represented MGM; Cohn, Columbia; Joe Schenck, Twentieth Century; Jack Warner, Warner Brothers; Manny Cohen, Paramount; Sol Wurtzel, Fox; and Pandro Berman, RKO. It was this group that eventually evolved into the Community Relations Committee, the political instrument of wealthy Los Angeles Jews.

How active the committee became in combatting Nazis is difficult to say, though its main function seemed to be to monitor the activities of the Nazi sympathizers and issue broadsides of its own. Mayer joined with Rabbi Edgar Magnin and two other old-line German Jews, Marco Newmark and Louis Nordlinger, to publish a newspaper on anti-Semitism, and Leon Lewis of the B'nai B'rith ran a News Research Service, which exposed pro-Nazi and anti-Semitic activities in Los Angeles. At the same time its members were also applying subtle pressure on the community's media barons not to publicize the Bundists.

But these were essentially defensive strategies to deal with domestic threats; the Jewish executives resented the more open and aggressive activities of the Jewish writers. Screenwriter Hy Kraft, who was active in the Anti-Nazi League, said his group met as much opposition from the "rich Jewish community" as from the Bund itself. "We met with them several times, but we could never get them committed to our program." Instead, the CRC's main objective seemed to be to convince the group to change its name from the Hollywood Anti-Nazi League to the Hollywood Anti-Nazi, Anti-Communist League.

The Jewish radicals had their own answers for why the Jewish executives remained supine. Some speculated that the Jews didn't want to call attention to themselves, lest they come under attack as foreigners and subversives. Some saw it as the Jews' way of proving they were less Jews than they were Americans. Still others suspected the real reasons were economic. "There was a feeling," explained Maurice Rapf, "that because it was known as a Jewish industry, it should not take a leading role in doing any activities—such as organizing anti-Nazi organizations or making films [against the Nazis]. . . . I always thought it was a cover-up for lack of real zeal about the Nazis. You have to face the fact that they began to have a lot more zeal about the Nazis when the Nazis closed down distribution offices in Germany, which they did by about 1934." "It was a matter of business," Hy

Kraft agreed. "The motion picture companies had large interests in Europe for distribution of their pictures." They tried to hold on as long as possible, and Warner Brothers only closed its German office when a band of Nazi thugs chased and murdered its representative there, a Jew named Joe Kauffman.

But among the Hollywood Jews, nazism was a subject that could scarcely be avoided, and early in 1936 Jewish writers and executives agreed to meet once again at Hillcrest, this time to formulate some position toward Hitler. "It was a pretty representative group of the important people in the motion picture industry who were Jewish," recalled attorney Martin Gang. "What stands out in my mind was David Selznick, who wanted to do it in the usual Jewish way of being on the fringes and not letting yourself appear as involved in it. . . . Don't get too public. Do it quietly. Behind the scenes. And Walter Wanger, who was a pretty powerful man in those days, was more forthright. Walter Wanger spoke out. . . . That to me was the first time that picture people joined in a group meeting to recognize the fact that the shots were aimed at them, too."

Others remembered it differently. In these recollections, Mayer and several of the older executives implored the Jews not to display militance. "Their attitude," according to one, "was Jews should not stick their necks out"—an argument that enraged the anti-Nazi Jews among the writers. With the issue joined, the verbal sallies began and didn't end until three in the morning, when the meeting finally degenerated into a violent argument among left, right, and center. When an MGM executive warned that by calling attention to themselves the Jews would only be inviting trouble, one of the leftists shouted, "You mean like L. B. Mayer, who's chairman of the Republican party in California . . . and is flaunting his wealth everywhere?" Jerome Chodorov claimed he knew at least a dozen Jews who became Communists the very next week because their eyes had been opened to the "reactionary indifference of people like L. B. Mayer."

Indifference overstated the case. Privately, most of the Jewish executives did express concern over the plight of the Jews in Europe. Their dilemma, as they saw it, was that they had to balance their roles as businessmen with their roles as prominent Jews. Even someone as sensitive to Jewish issues as Harry Warner searched his soul before

committing the studio to anti-Nazi movies. "Are we making it because we're Jews or because it can make a good movie?" his nephew,
Jack Warner, Jr., remembered him asking. "We've got to be aware
that we are Jews," Harry said frequently, "and that we will be looked
upon by the community, not just Hollywood, of saying certain things
because of being Jewish, but that we're really making films." By fall
1936 the more conservative Hollywood Jews began issuing tentative
attacks on the Hitler regime. Visiting his boyhood home in St. John,
New Brunswick, to receive an honorary degree, Mayer warned that
war in Europe was imminent and urged the United States to merge
forces with Britain. Two weeks later four hundred motion picture
luminaries gathered at the Hotel Roosevelt "to openly fight any cause
that threatens our country," and though the group still defined these
threats as "communisms and all other dangerous isms," fascism was
nevertheless included among the ills. The group dedicated its work to
Irving Thalberg—the man who, two years before, had scoffed at the
menace of Hitler.

This was the nature of the executives' opposition to Hitler over the
next three years—tentative and even-handed, making sure to condemn Stalin as well as Hitler. But when war broke out in Europe, and
the United States moved closer to open hostility toward Hitler in the
late thirties, the Hollywood Jews suddenly found themselves spinning
in the dance of neutrality. On the one hand, President Roosevelt
seemed to encourage them to take sides, having said, "This nation
will remain a neutral nation, but I cannot ask that every American
remain neutral in thought as well. Even a neutral has a right to take
account of facts. Even a neutral cannot be asked to close his mind or
his conscience." The Warners knew an offer, even a veiled offer,
when they saw one and wired the president that "personally we would
like to do all in our power within the motion picture industry and by
use of the talking screen to show the American people the worthiness
of the cause for which the free peoples of Europe are making such
tremendous sacrifices." A few months later Nick Schenck offered to
place his entire studio at the president's disposal "in connection with
the movie of national defense and foreign policy in which you
[Roosevelt] were interested."

On the other hand, there were elements both within the administration and outside it—Nazi sympathizers, anti-Semites, and sincere isolationists—who kept watch on the executives and sent them into a panic. "There is a great deal of hysteria at the moment in the film industry and no little defeatism," Douglas Fairbanks, Jr., wrote Roosevelt's assistant, Steve Early, just a few weeks after the Warners made their offer. "Most companies are wary of *any* subject likely to offend the Germans. They go so far as to suggest that the U.S. Government has expressed a wish to the Producers that they refrain from all controversial subjects." Early answered by quoting the president's statement on neutrality and personal conscience and added that "the spirit which prompted your inquiry is deeply appreciated."

The Jews' paranoia wasn't entirely unjustified. Late in 1940 the United States ambassador to England, Joseph P. Kennedy, suspected as a nazi sympathizer, paid a visit to Hollywood and requested an audience with the major Jewish executives. "He spoke to the gathering for about three hours," Fairbanks wrote the president after talking to a number of individuals who attended. "He stated that although he did not think that Britain would lose the war, still, she had not won it yet. He repeated very forcefully that there was no reason for our ever becoming involved in *any way*." But Kennedy didn't stop there. "He apparently threw the fear of God into many of our producers and executives by telling them that the Jews were on the spot, and that they should stop making anti-Nazi pictures or using the film medium to promote or show sympathy to the cause of the 'democracies' versus the 'dictators.' He said that anti-Semitism was growing in Britain and that the Jews were being blamed for the war. . . . He continued to underline the fact that the film business was using its power to influence the public dangerously and that we all, and the Jews in particular, would be in jeopardy, if they continued to abuse that power." The executives were shocked. "As a result of Kennedy's cry for silence," Ben Hecht later wrote, "all of Hollywood's top Jews went around with their grief hidden like a Jewish fox under their gentile vests."

Kennedy wasn't alone, though having owned a studio himself, he must have known the Hollywood Jews' particular sensitivities. Isolationists across the country had seized on the movies as one of the prime engines for American intervention in the war in Europe, and wartime public opinion surveys disclosed that Americans distrusted

The empire's splendor: Marcus Loew's estate, Pembroke, off Long Island Sound.
THE MUSEUM OF MODERN ART/FILM STILLS ARCHIVE

Mendel Silberberg, the ambassador from the Hollywood Jews to the Los Angeles Jewish community, receiving an award in 1950.
DORIA STEEDMAN

Rabbi Edgar F. Magnin, the religious leader of the Hollywood Jewish community, presents Eleanor Roosevelt with a token of appreciation at the Jewish Home for the Aged in Boyle Heights.

Rabbi Max Nussbaum with his most famous convert, Elizabeth Taylor, and her husband, Eddie Fisher.

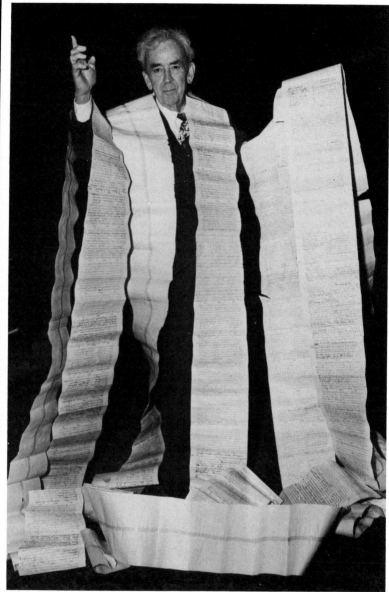

Representative John Rankin of Mississippi, whose anti-Semitism and anti-communism launched a congressional investigation of subversion within Hollywood, here wrapped in a toga of petitions supporting his forays against the motion picture industry, January 1947.
WIDE WORLD PHOTOS

The House Committee Room in Washington on the morning of October 20, 1947, the day HUAC began its hearings into Communist subversion of Hollywood.
WIDE WORLD PHOTOS

Screenwriter John Howard Lawson, the leader of the Hollywood Communists, leaving the witness table after his shouting match with Chairman John Parnell Thomas.
WIDE WORLD PHOTOS

HUAC Chairman J. Parnell Thomas on November 24, 1947, having just left the floor of Congress with a stack of contempt citations after the House had voted the Hollywood Ten in contempt.
WIDE WORLD PHOTOS

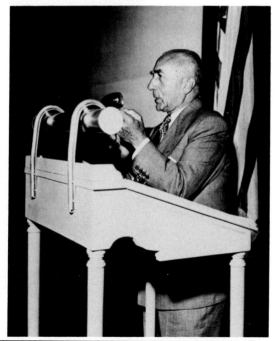

Harry Warner, the most strident of the Hollywood anti-Communists, at a meeting in September 1950, haranguing 2,000 studio employees to reject any "un-American organization." "You're good honest Americans —why not stand up and fight? There can be no divided allegiance here."
THE MUSEUM OF MODERN ART/
FILM STILLS ARCHIVE

The King and the Dauphin, Louis B. Mayer and Dore Schary, meeting the press in July 1948 after Schary's anointment.

Forced to sell his race horses to satisfy his divorce settlement, Louis Mayer (second from left) watches the auction with the future Mrs. Mayer, Lorena Danker, and Mr. and Mrs. Henry Ford II, February 27, 1947.
WIDE WORLD PHOTOS

At seventy-two, Adolph Zukor, executive emeritus, in his Paramount office, where he spun tales of power.
THE MUSEUM OF MODERN ART/ FILM STILLS ARCHIVE

The one-hundredth birthday celebration on January 7, 1973: Zukor encircled by (left to right) Paramount production executive Frank Yablans, Bob Hope, Charles Bluhdorn, chairman of Paramount's parent company, Gulf & Western, and Paramount production head Robert Evans.

THE MUSEUM OF MODERN ART/FILM STILLS ARCHIVE

Jews more than any European group with the sole exception of Italians. Pressed by isolationist senator Burton Wheeler for an explanation of why Hollywood insisted on propagandizing for America's entry into the war, Will Hays, president of the Motion Picture Producers and Distributors of America, felt compelled to reassure him that "there will be no cycle of 'hate' pictures. The primary purpose of the essential service of motion pictures is entertainment."

The senator wasn't impressed. Late that summer Wheeler, who headed the Senate's Interstate Commerce Commission, appointed a subcommittee to investigate whether the movie industry had encouraged America to end its neutrality. Though Wheeler and the other Senate isolationists insisted they had no animus against Jews, the new subcommittee was strongly supported and assisted by a rabid isolationist group called America First, which obviously did. (America First's most prominent spokesman was Colonel Charles Lindbergh, who had warned an audience in Des Moines that the Jews' "greatest danger to this country lies in their large ownership and influence in our motion pictures, our press, our radio, and our government," and one of the leaders of the group, a myopic reactionary named John T. Flynn, had actually drafted the resolution that called for an investigation.) On the day it was submitted, August 1, Senator Gerald Nye of North Dakota, one of its co-sponsors, was delivering a speech before a rally of America Firsters in St. Louis. Proclaiming that it was the movies that were agitating for war, Nye asked the crowd, "Who are the men who are doing this? Why are they trying to make America punch drunk with propaganda to push her into war?" The senator then named the executives of the major film companies and drew the inevitable conclusion: "In each of these companies there are a number of production directors, many of whom have come from Russia, Hungary, Germany, and the Balkan countries"—people who were "naturally susceptible" to "racial emotions."

When the subcommittee convened on September 9, Nye, the first witness, was less euphemistic. He began his testimony by defending himself against charges of Jew baiting. "I was not naming those names because they might seem to be Jewish names, for the moment," he swore. That said, he continued, "Those primarily responsible for the propaganda pictures are born abroad. They came to our land and took citizenship here, entertaining violent animosities toward certain causes abroad.... However, if I had it to do over and were I determined to name those primarily responsible for propaganda in the moving-picture field, I would, in light of what I have since learned, confine myself to four names, each that of one of the Jewish faith, each except only one foreign-born." Missouri Senator Bennett Clark, who co-sponsored with Nye the resolution creating the subcommittee, picked up the same theme the next day. There was not one word in the movies against intervention, he said, because "the moving-picture industry is a monopoly controlled by half a dozen men and because most of those men are themselves dominated by these hatreds."

This was the sort of talk that ordinarily terrified the Hollywood Jews and sent them groveling in appeasement. But this time the monopolists, knowing they had the support both of public opinion and of the Roosevelt administration, didn't permit themselves to be cowed. To represent them as counsel before the committee, Mendel Silberberg engaged Wendell Willkie, the unsuccessful Republican candidate for president and an articulate advocate of America's global responsibility. Howard Dietz, the brilliant publicist from MGM, assisted him. "The best men in the Industry are ready to go into these hearings fighting," Lowell Mellett, President Roosevelt's aide, informed him. "They say they'll proclaim they are doing everything they know how to make America conscious of the national peril; that they won't apologize— just the reverse."

The Jews did, in fact, take the stand with a confidence that bordered on arrogance. Nick Schenck, looking tanned and grizzled, repeatedly drew laughter when he attacked the premise that Hollywood was run by a dynasty. "When you live in a society, after all, with a small group of people," he said, explaining why the children of Hollywood executives occasionally married one another, "it is the natural thing for boys to be thrown with girls, and for girls to be thrown with boys, and they will get married." Schenck was less flippant on the Nazis. "I would not produce pictures that would make one race of people hate another; there is no doubt about that. But I would produce pictures of this sort when something is happening on the other side, in the balance of the world that is occupied by Nazis. I certainly feel that I would like to show as much of it as the public wants." Harry Warner was belligerent, suggesting that Senator Clark was stirring just as much prejudice as any film could when he insisted he too abhorred the Nazis' behavior. "You can correctly charge me with being anti-Nazi," he declared. "But no one can charge me with being anti-American."

It soon emerged that with the single exception of Charlie Chaplin's *The Great Dictator,* Senator Nye hadn't seen any of the purportedly prointerventionist movies he was attacking. Willkie remarked sarcastically that since the subcommittee's aim seemed to be to have movies made that present both sides of the interventionist question, it followed if "Chaplin made a laughable caricature of Hitler, the industry should be forced to employ Charles Laughton to do the same on Winston Churchill." President Roosevelt ridiculed the whole proceedings at a press conference, claiming *he* had gone to the movies and found no propaganda and held up a cartoon of Chaplin from the *Washington Evening Star* captioned, "Now what could I possibly tell those pastmasters [on the committee] about comedy?"

If it had hoped to prevent America from catching war fever, the committee's timing was execrable. It adjourned after three weeks and forty witnesses to assess the information it had received. Before it could reconvene, the Japanese had attacked Pearl Harbor, America was at war, and the Hollywood Jews were on the side of the angels.

———

For the Hollywood Jews, war was peace, a brief idyll where for once their obligations as Jews and their obligations as Americans not only merged, but received official sanction. Roosevelt, who recognized the power of the media as clearly as anyone, welcomed their assistance, and scarcely a year after Pearl Harbor four hundred executives, artists, and technicians had been commissioned as officers in the armed forces to make training and propaganda films. Once again Congress was suspicious. Early in 1943 another Senate committee was empaneled—this one to investigate whether the executives should have been commissioned and whether they were profiting off the war—but the probe ended inconclusively. "I have never found such a group of wholehearted, willing, patriotic people trying to do something for the Government," testified the chief of the Army Pictorial Division, "and they are urging us to give them more scripts so they can turn out more training films for the war effort."

He was right. Draped in the flag, the Hollywood Jews were deliriously patriotic, turning out film after film about the Nazis' cruelty, the sedition of Nazi sympathizers here, the bravery of our soldiers, the steadfastness of our people, and the rightness of our mission, and they were no less zealous against the Japanese. Even the radicals found common cause with the reactionaries once the Popular Front was revived in 1941. Everyone hated the Axis. The Jewish executives, however, were eager to demonstrate that they were motivated even more by love of this country—that it was their citizenship rather than their religion that spurred them. "I want all our films to sell America 'long' not 'short,'" Jack Warner told columnist Louella Parsons shortly after the war. "My brothers and I are examples of what this country does for its citizens. There were no silver spoons in our mouths when we were born. If anything, they were shovels. But we were free to climb as high as our energy and brains could take us." Barney Balaban, the president of Paramount, claimed, "We, the industry, recognize the need for informing people in foreign lands about the things that have made America a great country." He promised to convey this message in Paramount's films, and "We are prepared to take a loss in revenue if necessary."

The war didn't make Americans of the Hollywood Jews, but the aftermath of the war *did* make Jews out of the Hollywood Americans —at least temporarily. To involve Hollywood more deeply in disseminating the message of democracy, the State Department and the army commissioned several film executives to visit Europe shortly after the war's end and see firsthand what Hitler had done. They visited Hitler's quarters, cruised on his yacht, and toured the war zones. Then they visited the concentration camps. Harry Cohn, according to one associate, "never expressed a feeling about it one way or another." But others were badly shaken. Barney Balaban was devastated. Plagued by nightmares, he begged off describing the scene even to his family.

Rabbi Magnin, the spiritual leader of the Hollywood Jews, had a different response. He complained that the Holocaust, rather than creating sympathy for the Jews, would actually reopen the divisions between the Jews and the gentiles. "All they talk about is the Holocaust and all the sufferings. The goddamn fools don't realize that the more you tell gentiles that nobody likes us, the more they say there must be reason for it. They don't understand a simple piece of psychology. . . . They've got paranoia, these Jews."

In point of fact, the Hollywood Jews were probably less paranoid in the eighteen months after the war than they had ever been before and certainly than they would be after. They now not only felt secure enough to make several pictures condemning anti-Semitism, a subject they had always timorously avoided, but they actually competed for the privilege. At RKO, left-wing producer Adrian Scott, who was not a Jew but who had wanted to make a film about prejudice, finally received the studio go-ahead to make *Crossfire*, about a psychopath who murders a Jew, even though a survey indicated the public had little interest in the subject. Scott admitted he got severe stomach pains fretting over whether the studio would lose its nerve and rescind its approval, but it was actually the Jewish community outside Hollywood that was lobbying to stop the picture.

Meanwhile, Darryl Zanuck bought *Gentleman's Agreement*, Laura Hobson's best-seller about a gentile reporter who masquerades as a Jew to experience anti-Semitism himself. Zanuck was a Protestant from Wahoo, Nebraska, but he had been in Hollywood so long he might have been called a Jewish fellow traveler, and his closest friend was a Jewish talent agent named Charles Feldman. "You have no idea how deep the anti-Semitism in this country is," Zanuck lectured an associate who complained that the script for *Gentleman's Agreement* wasn't hard-hitting enough. To prove it, Zanuck told about a recent visit to a resort hotel with his wife. "It took me two hours to convince them that I wasn't a Jew." He said it without a trace of irony.

When Zanuck heard that RKO production head Dore Schary had already put *Crossfire* before the cameras, he took it as a personal affront. *He* was preparing *his* film on anti-Semitism and acted as if Schary were trying to co-opt him. To which Schary replied: Zanuck had not discovered anti-Semitism, and it would take more than two pictures to eradicate it. Zanuck was not amused, but *Gentleman's Agreement* with Gregory Peck as the investigative journalist went on to capture the Oscar for Best Picture, proving that anti-anti-Semitism was now not only acceptable, it was highly respectable.

So was Zionism. Taking their cues from Rabbi Magnin, the Hollywood Jews had never shown much interest in a Jewish homeland, since, as Magnin suggested, this would be yet more evidence of divided loyalties. Mayer was ardently anti-Zionist, believing that it would lead to nothing but trouble. Harry Cohn was pressured by Mendel Silberberg to attend a fund-raiser for Israel with Golda Meir as speaker, but he left incensed when Meir reprimanded them all for not contributing enough. Jack Cohn visited Israel and was appalled by the beards and *payess*. He never went again.

But the war did have an effect on many of the Hollywood Jews' feelings toward a Jewish homeland. Ben Hecht, a notorious cynic on all other issues, was agitating for the Irgun, Harry Warner was petitioning President Truman to create a Jewish homeland in Alaska, and a number of Hollywood personalities, Jew and gentile, formed a branch of the American Arts Committee for Palestine. Rabbi Max Nussbaum, Magnin's chief rival for Hollywood's affections, visited Palestine in 1948 and returned to plead its case after narrowly escaping an Arab ambush. Even Magnin, who refused to have the flag of Israel in his temple, decided to visit Israel and conceded that American Jews should work to help "those" people.

"Most of us... had a feeling that we were homeless, waiflike people who got pushed around, not really accepted," said film executive Robert Blumofe about the Hollywood Jews. "And suddenly Israel, even to the least Jewish of us, represented status of some sort. It meant that we did have a homeland. It meant that we did have an identity. It meant that we were no longer the stereotype of the Jew: the moneylender, the Jew businessman. These were fighters and they were farmers and they revived the land there.... All of this was terribly, terribly uplifting."

In January 1934 Representative Samuel Dickstein of New York, himself an Eastern European–born Jew, introduced a resolution to create a committee to investigate Nazi propaganda and activities in this country. During the rancorous debate, several congressmen objected that this was essentially a Jewish bill. One of them declared that most Germans thought Hitler was doing a fine job and that German Americans would resent the investigation. When the dust settled, however, the bill had carried overwhelmingly, 168 to 31, and the House Committee on Un-American Activities was formed.

Though Dickstein realized the committee would be more effective if headed by a non-Jew, he couldn't have realized that he was unleashing a whirlwind that would eventually turn on the Jews themselves. At one session the editor of *Healey's Irish Weekly* tarred Dickstein as part of the "radical Jewish minority influence in Washington," and several hundred German Americans picketed the committee's last session with placards reading "Down with Dickstein" and "Heil Hitler." Thus ended the first investigation by HUAC.

But Dickstein wasn't finished and neither was HUAC. In 1937 he introduced a bill to create another investigating committee to report on un-American activities. This time the House mysteriously tabled the motion. Three months later Dickstein discovered why. "Many of our Jewish citizens wanted Dickstein eliminated," Representative Martin Dies admitted, "because they felt he was furnishing ammunition to the Nazis and other anti-Semitic movements." So Dies, a Texas Democrat, submitted a resolution to create an investigating committee of his own. "They knew that as a member of the powerful Rules Committee, my resolution would be preferred over Dickstein's, and by custom I would be named chairman." Dies was right. Adding insult to injury, Dickstein wasn't even selected to sit on the new committee.

If the Jews hoped to find a defender in Dies, as he claimed, they had certainly picked an improbable candidate. The son of a conservative Texas congressman who fervently opposed immigration, Dies took up the cause and introduced legislation on his first day in the House to suspend immigration for five years. Some opponents suspected he was motivated by anti-Semitism. Dies waved off those accusations, but he spoke frequently of restoring "Christian influence" in America, and he openly consorted with anti-Semites. The committee's first investigator was a prominent speaker for the Nazi Bund. A notorious anti-Semite from Chicago named Harry Jung collaborated with the committee, and so did Joseph P. Kemp, who published the Fascist magazine *The Awakener*. Dies received verbal support from James True, the man who invented a blackjack nicknamed the "kike killer"; from the Reverend Gerald L. K. Smith, an anti-Semitic evangelist; from William Dudley Pelley, who headed the pro-Nazi Silver Shirts; and from James Colescott, the Imperial Wizard of the Ku Klux Klan. When one committee witness repeated some anti-Semitic remarks allegedly made by a second individual and said the comments "would more or less indicate to me at any rate that he wouldn't care about sleeping with any of them [Jews]," Dies quickly interposed, "That doesn't necessarily show that a man is prejudiced."

"In the beginning, our Committee obtained much valuable information from Jews and Jewish organizations, including the Anti-Defamation League," Dies later wrote. "However, over a period of time, I noted that the Anti-Defamation League, apparently influenced by the power which it had acquired, became arrogant, overbearing and uncooperative in some of its activities...." That was Dies's reading. In actuality it didn't take long for the Jews to see that nazism didn't really interest Dies. His war was against Karl Marx, whom he believed was locked in mortal combat with Jesus Christ for the future of Western civilization. For Dies, however, the line between Marxism and Judaism seemed to be indistinct. In May 1939 Dies uncovered a dastardly scheme and sicced his committee to investigate. Rich Jews, he said, were planning to seize the government that August with the aid of 150,000 Spanish mercenaries routed through Mexico. At the same time, these Jews intended to manipulate the stock market, sending it crashing and triggering a wave of strikes. How did Dies know? He had all this on the authority of no less than General George Van Horn Moseley and George E. Deatherage, two outspoken anti-Semites.

That same month Dies turned his committee's attention to some other Jews—the Jews in Hollywood. As he later explained it, he was visiting Los Angeles to address the American Legion when two of his committee's investigators showed him their files. Dies was shocked. "It was apparent that un-Americanism had made more progress in

California and on the West Coast than in any other part of the country." After the Legionnaires had filled him in on the situation, "I told the producers we had reliable information that a number of film actors and screen writers and a few producers either were members of the Communist Party, followed the Communist line, or were used as dupes, and that there was evidence that the Hollywood Anti-Nazi League was under the control of Communists." When the producers allegedly admitted they knew about these elements but that the radicals were under contract, Dies blithely suggested the industry start making some anti-Communist movies.

Dies hadn't made any connection yet between Hollywood sedition and Judaism, but at least a few of the Hollywood Jews knew he was on a witch-hunt. Art Arthur, a producer at Twentieth Century-Fox, recommended they take the offensive against HUAC. Writing to Sidney Wallach of the American Jewish Committee, Arthur said they should take the allegations linking Judaism to communism and "not only reply to them—but make each of them a springboard for a true report of what Jews mean to America, just who and what they are, etc. It is important to end the impression that Jews are an 'alien element.'..." That never happened. Possibly a certain hesitancy about openly declaring their Judaism dissuaded the Hollywood Jews from taking action, and in any case HUAC seemed to enjoy widespread public support. But it is also possible, as many left-wing writers suspected, that the producers had actually invited Dies to Hollywood to help smash the nascent Screen Writers Guild on the eve of its negotiations with the studios.

If the producers had cooperated, they soon discovered they had unleashed a monster in their midst. In February 1940 Dies announced his plan of action. Two subjects were to be investigated— the use of Mexico as a launching pad for propaganda and the subversion of Hollywood by Communists. In July the chairman produced his first evidence. John L. Leech, a former Communist from Portland, Oregon, met Dies in closed session in Beaumont, Texas, and described how the Party had infiltrated the National Guard by luring soldiers to "socials," where they were indoctrinated with Communist propaganda. Where did these Communists get their funding? Dies wanted to know. The next day, Leech answered and dropped his bombshell. He fingered Hollywood as a hotbed of subversion and produced a list of forty-two "members, sympathizers, or contributors" to the Communist party. This was all the chairman needed. Thus armed, Martin Dies, looking, with his poached eyes, his jowls, and brilliantined hair, like a sagging Edward G. Robinson, came to Hollywood.

Dies obviously knew that in communism he was touching a very sensitive subject with the Hollywood Jews, and they were eager to disarm him. He had scarcely settled in his hotel room when a delegation of producers, headed by a gentile from Georgia named Y. Frank Freeman, welcomed him. "Thirty-two thousand motion picture workers in Hollywood are not willing to yield to anyone in their true Americanism," Freeman told him. "We welcome a complete and impartial investigation. . . . It is and always has been the desire of all loyal Americans in this industry to cooperate with the government's representatives." Freeman added that if the committee discovered individuals who brought discredit on the industry, "there will be no attempt to protect these individuals or groups of individuals."

Dies held court in Hollywood throughout August. One by one, the accused came to his hotel to seek absolution: Humphrey Bogart, Fredric March, Luise Rainer, Franchot Tone, even Jimmy Cagney, who left telling reporters that the charges claiming Hollywood was permeated by communism were "so exaggerated that they are ridiculous." "Jimmy, I see by the papers you've been a bad boy," President Roosevelt joked a few days later at a special birthday celebration. Cagney smiled. "All I did, Mr. President, was believe in the things you believe." And Roosevelt said, "Attaboy, Jimmy."

The big headlines never really came, and the investigation ended almost as quickly as it began. By month's end Dies had pronounced Hollywood clean and returned to Washington—*why* was never entirely clear, though it was possible he had reaped all the publicity he was likely to get, or that he had simply exhausted his evidence. The next year Nye came. Then war came. The menace of communism momentarily diminished beside the menace of nazism. And the Hollywood Jews enjoyed their glorious bout of patriotism—until HUAC made its return visit.

"You should tell your Jewish friends that the Jews in Germany stuck their necks out too far and Hitler took care of them and that the same thing will happen here unless they watch their steps." That was how one investigator from HUAC, while in the presence of the committee's chief counsel, warned a Columbia University professor early in 1946. For Hollywood, the handwriting was already on the wall. Though Dies, in poor health, had decided not to run for reelection in 1944, his committee survived, thanks to the parliamentary machinations of a Mississippi congressman named John Rankin. Since its inception, HUAC had always been a temporary committee created for a specific purpose. With its authorization about to expire and the committee about to pass into oblivion, Rankin moved that it be made a standing committee of the House. Since it was the first day of the new Congress and the rules hadn't yet been voted on, he was able to bypass the House Rules Committee, where the motion would have almost certainly gotten tabled, and instead steered it to a narrow victory, 207 to 186. HUAC was back in business.

Despite his efforts, Rankin was not named chairman of the standing committee. A New Jersey Democrat named Edward Hart was, but Rankin was still very much HUAC's voice and conscience—the one who set its agenda and its tone. Gaunt, with hollow eyes and generous tufts of gray hair that made him look like a biblical prophet, Rankin had been a decorated war veteran and a local prosecutor before moving on to Congress in 1921, where he had mainly distinguished himself by insisting on the links between Judaism and communism. "If I am any judge, they are Communists, pure and simple," he said of a delegation of women who protested one of his bills. "They looked like foreigners to me. I never saw such a wilderness of noses in my life." Columnist Walter Winchell was called a "slime mongering kike" for attacking him. He labeled another Jewish writer "that little Communist kike . . . a scavenger who stooped to as base a level as that of the loathsome ghoul at night who invades the sacred precinct of the tomb." During debate on the House floor, he even addressed Congressman Emmanuel Celler as a "Jewish gentleman." "I have no quarrel with any man about his religion," Rankin told the House. "Any man who believes in the fundamental principles of Christianity and lives up to them, whether he is Catholic or Protestant, certainly deserves the respect and confidence of mankind."

Sometimes his anti-Semitism led him through tortuous logic to peculiar conclusions. "Stalin is a gentile and Trotsky was a Jew," he said. "Stalin was educated from the priesthood. The Bible says, teach a child the way he should go and when he is old he will not depart therefrom. It was but natural therefore that when Stalin got into power he should open the churches.... Stalin broke up the Comintern.... He restored rank and discipline in his army and introduced the incentive payment plan among the men who work in his factories."

With its commingling of Communists and Jews, Hollywood was obviously an ideal quarry for Rankin, and he was poised to finish the job Dies had begun. What he seemed to lack was an opening, and he got that quite unexpectedly when Edward Hart fell ill and resigned the committee's chairmanship at the end of June 1945. Rankin was appointed acting head. Though only fourteen days passed between Hart's abdication and the appointment of a new chairman, a conservative Democrat from Georgia named John S. Wood, Rankin made the most of them. At his very first session he offered a motion to send investigators to Hollywood. "We don't know what information he has," admitted one committee member, "but the motion was agreed to on the theory that we ought to find out whether our acting chairman is having nightmares or whether there really is something that ought to be investigated."

Rankin had no doubts at all. A day after taking charge, he announced he was about to unearth "one of the most dangerous plots ever instigated for the overthrow of the government.... The information we get is that this [Hollywood] is the greatest hotbed of subversive activities in the United States. We're on the trail of the tarantula now, and we're going to follow through. The best people in California are helping us."

The next week Rankin, still the chairman, assured his fellow congressmen that the committee members "are not trying to hound legitimate producers. We are not trying to hound legitimate writers, but we are out to expose those elements that are insidiously trying to spread subversive propaganda, poison the minds of your children, distort the history of our country, and discredit Christianity." It didn't take any particular insight to recognize what Rankin was really up to, and several Jews and liberals in Congress strenuously objected. "Are they planning to follow up a previous investigation of Hollywood which resulted in the assertion that Shirley Temple was a Communist?" asked Samuel Dickstein, referring to a witness before the old Dies committee who had accused Miss Temple of being a Communist dupe. "Do they feel that her growing up has resulted in her being a stronger Communist?... Not one member of this committee can present to me or to the House sufficient evidence justifying such action [hearings]." Several members of the California delegation even met with HUAC's new chairman, John Wood, to brief him on how little Dies's investigation of Hollywood had turned up.

Rankin tartly accused them of trying to thwart the committee and then delivered his most blistering salvo yet against the anti-Christian heathens. "Communism is the most dangerous influence in the world today," he declaimed on the floor of the House when his motives were challenged by a representative from California.

> I am talking about the communism of Leon Trotsky that is based upon hatred for Christianity. Remember that communism and Christianity can never live in the same atmosphere. Communism is older than Christianity. It is the curse of the ages. It hounded and persecuted the Savior during his earthly ministry, inspired his crucifixion, derided him in his dying agony, and then gambled for his garments at the foot of the cross; and has spent more than 1,900 years trying to destroy Christianity and everything based on Christian principles.

Now, Rankin continued, these "alien-minded communistic enemies of Christianity, and their stooges, are trying to get control of the press of this country.... They are trying to take over the radio. Listen to their lying broadcasts in broken English and you can almost smell them." But it was Hollywood that most powerfully inflamed Rankin's passions. "They are now trying to take over the motion-picture industry, and howl to high heaven when our Committee on un-American Activities propose to investigate them. They want to spread their un-American propaganda, as well as their loathsome, lying, immortal, anti-Christian filth before the eyes of your children in every community in America."

The rhetoric was pure Rankin—hyperbolic, impassioned, paranoid, euphemistic—but it was also, almost verbatim, what a group of extreme right-wingers and Nazi sympathizers had been saying about Hollywood just a few months before—before Rankin had gotten the scent of the Hollywood Communists himself. The Reverend Gerald L. K. Smith was another of the self-styled political saviors who had emerged during the Depression when it seemed that anyone with a panacea or a scapegoat could attract a following. A boyish rabble-rouser from Wisconsin with a feverish stump style that no less an authority than H. L. Mencken described as more impressive than that of William Jennings Bryan, Smith had assisted Senator Huey Long in the thirties and then, after Long's assassination, tried lassoing the remnants of Long's support into a coalition with other disaffected populists. The effort failed when he proved so overbearing, egocentric, and unpredictable (he was once jailed for using obscenity and disturbing the peace) that not even the other political crackpots wanted much to do with him.

By the late thirties, what finally erupted from under his surface of southern populism was a distinct appeal to neofascism and Jew baiting. Like other reactionaries, Smith had opposed America's entrance into the war, but unlike most of them, he was unregenerate even after Pearl Harbor, regrouping the more extreme isolationist elements into a new America First Party, which gave vent to his hatreds. Among the planks of its 1944 platform were a call for a negotiated peace with Germany, a congressional investigation to determine who conspired to bring this country into the conflict, an end to immigration, and a solution to the "Jewish problem."

Smith was clearly a kindred spirit with Rankin, but when it came to Hollywood he may have been an inspiration as well. For months Smith had excoriated Hollywood for undermining the "influence and teachings of the Church, the Christian home, and the Sunday School." At the same time Rankin was urging HUAC to investigate the Hollywood Jews, Smith's party organ, *The Cross and the Flag*, was launching a six-part series titled "The Rape of America by Hollywood." "Controlled by foreign-born, unassimilative upstarts, many of whose records smell to high heaven, Hollywood has been raping American decency, national honesty and financial well-being," spewed an anonymous writer. "Christ was crucified on Calvary; and the same despisers of Christ are still busy in this world, especially in Hollywood, crucifying all of the Savior's fine principles." This was followed by a long open letter to Rankin recommending that the committee "not waste too much time on the 'small fry' Reds with which Hollywood is overrun. I hope they will start right in on the major traitors, many of whom, hypocritically wrapping themselves in the Stars and Stripes and pretending to be in favor of our form of government, have been boring undercover and using the 'small fry,' whom they've assisted to reach our shores, to undermine the very foundation of our Constitutional Republic."

In Hollywood, the Jews could have and probably would have ignored this sort of lunatic screed, except that by October it became clear that Smith and Rankin were in league and that the lunatic fringe might actually be setting the agenda for the proposed HUAC hearings. That month Smith visited Washington with a 150-foot petition supporting Rankin in his investigation. "We Christian Nationalists must give this investigation our full support," Smith told the Mississippian, "because the anti-Christians and anti-Americans are doing all in their power to smear Mr. Rankin and the committee with which he is associated." Rankin happily posed for photographers with the petition wrapped around him like a long toga. That same month Smith paid a visit to Los Angeles to deliver a series of anti-Semitic speeches. The community was so alarmed, it formed a group called the Mobilization for Democracy, the express purpose of which was to picket Smith. The line of marchers stretched four square blocks, four abreast.

Up to this point, though, there really had been no investigation of Hollywood; there had only been Rankin's campaign for one, and Chairman Wood, possibly responding to pressure from the California congressional delegation, had not even scheduled any hearings into the matter. But Smith's bombardment had its effect. By year's end Wood and HUAC investigator Ernie Adamson—the man who had stood idly by while one of his underlings warned of the Hitlerian consequences for left-wing Jews—conducted a one-day hearing in

Los Angeles behind closed doors. They emerged with the news that there was definitely a Communist plan to take over films, and Adamson promised that a subcommittee would be revisiting Hollywood soon to smoke it out.

When the committee began its hearings in Washington in January on general issues of subversion, one of its first witnesses was none other than Gerald L. K. Smith, just back from his foray in California. Smith recounted his boyhood, rhapsodized about his family, attacked those who had persecuted him, and berated the usual assortment of liberals, unions, and Communists. Though Smith bridled at suggestions he was anti-Semitic, he readily provided the committee with statistics about how the Jews controlled the press, the radio, and the movies. "There is a general belief that Russian Jews control too much of Hollywood propaganda," he said, "and they are trying to popularize Russian Communism in America through that instrumentality. Personally I believe that is the case."

Even within the committee itself there was dissension over Smith's wild charges toward Hollywood, and Representative Gerald W. Landis of Indiana apparently scolded Rankin for the friendly reception Smith received. Other congressmen objected when they were denied the right to interrogate Smith themselves as "America's most raucous purveyor of anti-Semitism and of racial and religious bigotry." Rankin responded by sneering that this was "the usual Communist propaganda." As for the Jewish community, it was appalled and frightened that Smith had suddenly gained legitimacy. "Although Congressman Wood is the nominal chairman of the House Committee on Un-American Activities," wrote one member of the American Jewish Committee in a report on Smith's testimony, "it was apparent throughout the hearing that Congressman Rankin was the actual head of the committee and spearheaded its activities. Ernie Adamson, the committee's counsel, was obviously friendly to Smith."

Still, the actual hearings stalled throughout 1946 or until the congressional elections that November, when the Republicans won control of the House and Senate. Now, finally, the long-simmering battle against the New Deal and its alleged left-wing minions could reach full boil. Leading the charge was HUAC's new Republican chairman, a bumptious former insurance broker from New Jersey named John

Parnell Thomas, who was a veritable caricature of small-town prejudice and fear. Like many of the Hollywood Jews, Thomas had
changed his name. He was born John Parnell Feeney, Jr., but after
his father's death he assumed his mother's maiden name because, he
said in his court petition, "he can get recognition and business under
the name of Thomas that he could not get under the name of
Feeney." Just to make sure his past wouldn't compromise his future,
Thomas, an Irish Catholic, also started attending Baptist services,
though he occasionally claimed in the press that he was an Episcopalian.

Beefy and balding with sad eyes and a pug nose, Thomas looked
and acted like a small-time vaudevillian. One magazine even described him as "Pickwickian," and no doubt he enjoyed the characterization. No colorless political functionary, he liked to grandstand,
which made witch-hunting the perfect vehicle for him. As a legislator
in New Jersey back at the beginning of the Depression, he had stum-
bled upon the issue of communism when a group of indigent lobbyists descended on the Capital to support a bill for relief and Thomas
discovered that one of the mob had once run for governor of Ohio on
the Communist ticket. This was evidence enough for Thomas of a
Communist conspiracy, and it became the turning point in his life.
Henceforth he would be a professional anti-Communist, and after he
was elected to Congress and HUAC was formed, he became one of its
charter members, not to mention one of John Rankin's staunchest
allies.

Thomas's predecessor as HUAC chairman, John Wood, had certainly been no respecter of civil liberties, but neither was he the self-
publicist Thomas was. In Thomas's hands the committee shot from
the line, its Klaxons sounding. Within weeks he had launched probes
into the nefarious activities of various unions that he suspected of
Communist taint. Meanwhile, Hollywood lay on the horizon.
"Those who signed the petitions and helped circulate them," Gerald
L. K. Smith announced in the January issue of his *Cross and Flag*
long before Thomas had made his plans public, "will be happy to
know that the Congressional Committee has already started its investigation and has promised that the full committee will sit in Hollywood early this year. There is much to uncover. . . . The lovers of

Christ and the lovers of America have been ridiculed." Within months the committee's cannons were aimed at Hollywood, and in May 1947 Thomas, Wood, Representative John McDowell of Pennsylvania, and two of the committee's investigators, Robert Stripling and Louis Russell, ensconced themselves at the Biltmore Hotel in Los Angeles to "confer" with a number of individuals concerning Communist infiltration in movies.

The people Thomas consulted on May 8 and 9 could hardly have been considered a representative group. James Kevin McGuinness, a favored writer at MGM, was an arrogant, vociferous reactionary who had organized opposition to the Screen Writers Guild and who had once claimed, "In this world, some people will ride and some people will walk. I'm gonna be one who rides." Rupert Hughes, Howard Hughes's uncle, was an aging literary jack-of-all-trades who had worked with McGuinness to abort the guild, and so had screenwriter Howard Emmet Rogers, a dour alcoholic who was so deathly pale he had been nicknamed the "Grey Eminence." Actor Robert Taylor was another conservative who had whined to HUAC about Communist writers and complained about being pressured by the Roosevelt administration to star in a film favorable to the Russians. Lela Rogers, Ginger's mother, saw Communists everywhere. So did boulevardier Adolphe Menjou.

By the time Thomas had finished, fourteen witnesses had testified in closed session—all "frank and cooperative." One described Hollywood as "the hub of Red propaganda in the United States." The committee itself concluded that "up until recently there has been no concerted effort on the part of the studio heads to remove the communists from the industry, but that in fact they have been permitted to gain influence and power which has been reflected in the propaganda which they have been successful in injecting in numerous pictures which have been produced in the last eight years."

In some ways the real question was not why HUAC came to Hollywood, but what had taken it so long. One answer, possibly, was that for all its tub-thumping, the committee really had very little hard evidence of Communist infiltration—only what it had collected through the neo-Nazi hate groups—and that this made the commit-

tee itself immediately suspect. Who could believe the wild accusations of Gerald L. K. Smith? Another answer was that in the
aftermath of war, the Hollywood left and the Hollywood center, whatever their disagreements, seemed reasonably unified in their opposition to HUAC and that, in any case, the Jewish executives themselves
were defiant. "Nobody can tell me how to run my studio," Louis
Mayer, a political troglodyte if ever there was one, told a radical
screenwriter.

The two answers, of course, were not unrelated. The Jewish
executives were as anti-Communist as the most ferocious Red-
baiters, but they were acutely aware of HUAC's anti-Semitic bent
and realized that the tautology of Jew and Communist would ultimately destroy not only the Hollywood Reds, but the executives
themselves. (It was a very short step from their having permitted
propaganda in their movies to their having actually condoned it.)
That was reason enough to keep HUAC at bay, but after years of
receiving the benediction and the gratitude of the president for their
help during the war, they knew they would be doubly damned.
"The New Deal is either for the Communist Party, or is playing
into the hands of the Communist Party," Thomas had once testified
before the Dies committee. That made the Hollywood Jews part of
an inescapable syllogism that would once again connect them to
communism. They felt they really had no choice but to hold firm
and wait for the storm to pass.

Not all the denizens of Hollywood, and particularly the non-Jews,
were as complacent. One of them, a competent if undistinguished
director named Sam Wood, had been festering with anger and disappointment for years—ever since 1939 when he'd failed to win the
Academy Award he felt he deserved for *Goodbye, Mr. Chips*. Wood
was a close friend and a great admirer of William Randolph Hearst;
he had directed Hearst's mistress, Marion Davies, in two films. When
Hearst turned on Roosevelt during the war, Wood's own frustration
suddenly curdled into a hatred of the New Deal and a conflation of
liberalism and communism. He began carrying a little black book in
which he jotted the names of those radicals, often no more than
supporters of the New Deal, he hoped someday to purge from Hollywood. Possessed by his mission—his daughter said that "iron entered

his soul"—Wood decided to organize like-minded film people into a new group. The Motion Picture Alliance for the Preservation of American Ideals was announced in February 1944. "The American motion picture industry is, and will continue to be, held by Am .ri-cans for the American people, in the interests of America and dedicated to the preservation and continuance of the American scene and the American way of life," Wood declared.

Though Wood didn't use the word "Christian" the way Rankin did, and though Jewish screenwriter Morrie Ryskind was a member, the Alliance did have its anti-Semitic tinge. Among its officers were McGuinness, a snobbish anti-Semite, and Walt Disney, whose company refused to hire Jews.* The Jewish executives, who must have suspected that the alliance was as much an attempt to realign power in Hollywood as to exorcise Reds, didn't join. More, they attempted to disarm it. Shortly after the war the Alliance presented them with evidence of Communist infiltration. The Jews called a meeting at Hillcrest. "Who were the Communists in the industry? Name names, they demanded. Pressed, one of the speakers mentioned the son of one of MGM's leading producers as a ringleader in the Soviet group. It was an unfortunate reference, for all the elder statesmen around the investigating table had known this lad as a *schnook* from the day he was born. Sam Goldwyn got to his feet. 'If this snot-nosed baby is the Red boss in Hollywood, gentlemen, we've got nothing to fear. Let's go home.' The meeting broke up."

It soon became clear that they had much more to fear, in fact, from the Alliance. Since its formation it had repeatedly invited HUAC to come to Hollywood to investigate not only Communist propaganda itself, but the "flagrant manner in which the motion picture industrialists of Hollywood have been coddling Communists." Now, with Roosevelt's death, with a Republican Congress, with the beginning of the Cold War, with a series of bitter labor disputes in Hollywood, the Alliance had asked again, and this time HUAC had accepted. Vir-

---

*When David Swift, a longtime Disney employee, accepted a job at Columbia, Disney snapped in a Jewish accent, "Okay, Davy Boy. Off you go to work with those Jews. It's where you belong, with those Jews." (Leonard Mosley, *Disney's World* [New York, 1985], p. 207.)

tually all of HUAC's witnesses during Thomas's visit in May were members of the Alliance, and most of them, on the available evidence, confirmed the committee's worst suspicions.

As for the Hollywood Jews' worst suspicions, those were confirmed, too. What was now arrayed against them in the summer of 1947 was an unholy alliance of HUAC, its neo-Fascist supporters, and extreme gentile reactionary elements within Hollywood. (Lest there have been any doubt, and there couldn't have been much, Robert Stripling, HUAC's new counsel, was a southern white supremacist who had previously assisted Ernest Sullivan, a former publicist for the Bund.) Still, most of the Jewish executives remained remarkably sanguine. At a meeting a few weeks after Thomas's closed-door sessions, Eric Johnston, the recently appointed president of the Motion Picture Association of America, proposed that the studio heads commit themselves not to employ any suspected Communist. They demurred. At Johnston's suggestion, they did, however, make a perfunctory nod to the committee, asking it to hold open hearings to investigate the matter. They had nothing to hide.

Throughout the summer HUAC's investigators hounded, intimidated, and threatened the executives, trying to get them to suspend the suspected Communists to which the Alliance had alerted them. The leader of the harassment was a former FBI agent named H. A. Smith, an associate of FBI chief J. Edgar Hoover, and Smith's team was comprised largely of other agents—a circumstance that gave the hunt at least the appearance of official favor. In Hollywood that was important. Hoover was especially close to Harry Warner. Once a year they would go down to the Del Mar Race Track and spend a few weeks together watching the ponies. Whether it was Hoover's influence, their own Red-baiting resurfacing, or a reaction to the violent strike that had hit their studio not long before, the Warners were the first to break ranks with the other Jewish executives; when Thomas came in May, Jack was the only executive who met with him—partly to condemn the Communist menace, but just as likely to clear his own name.

Whatever the motive, even Jack seemed less than enthusiastic. "What sort of questions did they ask you?" director John Huston inquired when Warner told him he had appeared before Thomas.

"They wanted to know the names of people I thought might be Communists out here."

"What did you say?"

"Well . . . I told them the names of a few."

"You did?"

Now Warner was contrite. "Yeah . . . I guess I shouldn't have, should I?" When Huston told him he believed Warner had made a mistake in cooperating, Jack became distraught. "I guess I'm a squealer, huh?"

At roughly the same time, Harry Warner called his son-in-law, writer-producer Milton Sperling, to his office. As Sperling entered he saw two FBI agents standing there with a dossier on him. Hoover had instructed that they show it to Warner. As Sperling recalled it, Harry said, "'They got it on you.' I said, 'What do they got on me?'" Harry threw a sheet of paper across the desk. On it was a list of the various liberal organizations Sperling had joined. Beneath these was his service record: he had volunteered for the U.S Marine Corps and had been discharged as a captain. And beneath that was a single sentence: "Sperling is a premature anti-Fascist." Harry demanded an explanation. Sperling insisted that his crime apparently was that he had hated the Nazis before it was fashionable to do so. Harry seemed temporarily pacified, but the FBI men suggested he keep the file. Evidently Hoover didn't want it getting in the wrong hands.

While the FBI and H. A. Smith were sniffing out Communists in Los Angeles, Thomas announced in September that he would finally be holding his long-promised hearings on Hollywood and pledged to expose seventy-nine prominent members of the industry who were Communists or fellow travelers. Forty-three subpoenas were issued. Of those summoned, twenty-four were regarded as "friendly" witnesses, many of them the same individuals who had testified in Thomas's closed session. Nineteen were regarded as potentially uncooperative—left-wingers who had been fingered by the Alliance. Of the nineteen, ten were Jewish. "There was considerable feeling," said Ring Lardner, Jr., one of the nineteen, "that this was a force in which anti-Semitism played a strong part."

With the subpoenas issued, the old fear now began rippling through the executive ranks. "Every executive in the business knew that it was just a question of time before a drive would be made to take it away from them," recalled Judge Lester Roth, at the time a vice president at Columbia. "There's always the complexion that, 'Hell, we're the Jews and we built this thing up. They wouldn't let us get into the banks. They wouldn't let us get into the insurance companies. They wouldn't let us get into any of the nationally wealthy hard industries. Now we've built up this one, and they want to take it away.'" By October, when the hearings began in Washington, the Jews had to decide whether they would resist the committee or capitulate to it—whether they would tell the anti-Semitic right where to go or let it tell them how to run their studios.

For most of the Hollywood Jews, the choice between abetting HUAC and unleashing anti-Semitic forces that they believed might soon be aimed at them or opposing HUAC and risking charges of anti-Americanism posed a terrible dilemma, far more excruciating than the left-wing writers thought—for it placed the means of their life's work against the end. Their control of Hollywood, which would be endangered if they did support HUAC, had been the avenue for gaining American respectability, which would be doomed if they didn't. How they resolved this crisis when HUAC summoned them in September turned out to be contortion rather than contrition. They would cooperate with the committee, defer to it, and concede the presence of Communists in Hollywood, while refusing to acknowledge subversive content in their own films.

Jack Warner, who had so eagerly given names of suspected radicals to the committee in May, was the first to testify in October. He delivered an oration so reactionary that even conservatives must have blanched, but when he finished, what they really wanted to know was why he hadn't fired the writers he had named as radicals in the closed session last May. Warner now told the committee that he had gotten carried away in naming names. "I was rather emotional," he said, retracting some of the wild charges he had made during his anti-Communist rhapsody, "being in a very emotional business." Nevertheless, Warner suggested that subversive writers had tried smuggling their messages into the studio's movies and that he had, vigilantly, removed them. Who were these subversives? the committee wanted to know. Warner admitted he didn't know. "I had never seen a Communist and wouldn't know one if I saw one." In his prepared statement, Louis B. Mayer defended himself as having as much contempt for communism "as anybody living in this world," and he denounced Communist writers. But when pressed to cite examples of their propaganda, Mayer, like Warner, pleaded that he did not know of any Communists employed in his studio.

According to Lester Cole, an MGM writer who had been called by HUAC as an "unfriendly" witness, Mayer wasn't being entirely truthful. "Your kind don't grow on trees," he told Cole after the latter had been subpoenaed. "I don't want to lose you." Cole assured him that he most likely wouldn't. The law didn't permit someone to be terminated on the basis of his political beliefs. "I don't give a shit about the law," Mayer snapped. "It's them goddamn Commies that you're tied up with. Break with them. Stick with us. With me. . . . You'll do what you want. Direct your own pictures? Say so. I believe you'd do great. Dough means nothing. We'll tear up the contract, double your salary. You name it, you can have it. Just make the break."

Cole was stunned and numbly shook his head. "I know about communism," Mayer shouted. "I know what happens to men like that. Take that Communist Roosevelt! A hero, a man of the people! And what happens five minutes after they shoveled the dirt on his grave? The people pissed on it! That's what you want, Lester? Be with *us*, be smart. You got kids, think of them." Cole thanked Mayer for the offer but declined. "You're nuts!" Mayer screamed. "Goddamn crazy Commie! Get out! Goddamn it, get out!"

Still, for reasons that are complex and murky, the idea of an official Hollywood blacklist, which had already been rejected in June, hadn't taken hold that October. One reason was certainly the fear that a list would violate the dismissed writers' constitutional rights—a fear that sprang not from any deep-seated commitment to civil liberties, but from the very real danger that those blacklisted would bring suit. (This, in fact, was the reason the executives gave to the committee when asked why they hadn't acted to purge Hollywood of its Communist cancer.) Another motive may have been a resistance to any outside interference. And another, possibly, was a kind of native recoiling at deploying against others the tactics that had often been deployed against them as Jews. Instead, the executives did nothing.

Meanwhile, liberal screenwriter Philip Dunne had been roused by HUAC's cavalier attitude toward constitutional rights. He suggested to directors William Wyler and John Huston that they form a committee to go to Washington to demonstrate Hollywood's support for the beleaguered principle of free political association. The three of them wound up assembling an impressive collection of liberal writers, directors, and stars including Humphrey Bogart and Lauren Bacall, Judy Garland, Frank Sinatra, Kirk Douglas, Katharine Hepburn, Henry Fonda, Edward G. Robinson, John Garfield, Groucho Marx, and Gene Kelly, who had been begged by MGM vice president L. K. Sidney not to make the trip to Washington. Meeting in high spirits at the home of Ira Gershwin, the group was giddy with hope that it might shame HUAC and turn the tide. It elected to call itself, augustly, the Committee for the First Amendment.

As a dozen representatives of the CFA arrived in Washington two days before the first of the so-called hostile witnesses, John Howard Lawson, was to testify, the battle lines were being drawn. For its part, HUAC had decided not to let the unfriendlies make any statement that it had not already examined and would give no approval to anything that disparaged the committee. For their part, the nineteen, after exhaustive strategy sessions, decided finally that they would deny HUAC's right to question them at all on the grounds that no legislative committee had any right to inquire into a person's political beliefs—a First Amendment as opposed to a Fifth Amendment defense.

Lawson entered the hearing room the morning of October 27 prepared to lob his constitutional grenades at the committee. He told the congressmen that he had a statement he wanted to make. Thomas asked that it be brought to him, and after reading silently for a moment at the rostrum, he looked up and told Lawson he would not be permitted to make his presentation. When Lawson objected, a shouting match ensued, with Thomas noisily banging his gavel. In this cacophony, Thomas and Stripling began their interrogation—they questioning, Lawson yelling back his denial of the committee's authority. Asked if he were a member of the Communist party, Lawson tried to give a civics lesson. "It is unfortunate and tragic that I have to teach this committee the basic principles of American—" He was broken off in mid-sentence. When Thomas demanded he leave the stand, Lawson held his ground until police were called to forcibly remove him.

From an aesthetic and public relations standpoint, it was a thoroughly depressing and undignified display, and it shocked the innocents of the CFA who were observing it, not to mention the Jewish executives. Witness after witness loudly denounced the committee, all for its illegitimacy, but several also for its implicit anti-Semitism. When asked if he were a member of the Screen Writers Guild, Albert Maltz answered, "Next you are going to ask me what religious group I belong to." "Under the kind of censorship this inquisition threatens," scolded Ring Lardner, Jr., "a leading man wouldn't even be able to blurt out the words 'I love you' unless he had first secured a notarized affidavit proving she was a pure, white Protestant gentile of old Confederate stock." Samuel Ornitz, an aging screenwriter who had once written a popular Jewish novel, *Haunch, Paunch and Jowl*, had prepared a statement that read, "I wish to address this Committee as a Jew, because one of its leading members is the outstanding anti-Semite in the Congress and revels in this fact. I refer to John E. Rankin. . . . When constitutional guarantees are overridden, the Jew is the first one to suffer. . . . As soon as the Jew is crushed the others get it."

All the Hollywoodites—the unfriendlies, the members of the Committee for the First Amendment, the executives—returned to the West Coast that week in a state of agitation and uncertainty. Jack Warner felt he had been deceived. There had been a prepared list of questions, and the committee hadn't stuck to it. He really couldn't understand what it was the committee wanted from him. "I was only trying to help my country at war," he remonstrated to anyone who would listen.

"When he came back to the coast, he came in time for lunch," Milton Sperling remembered. "He came right to the dining room, and I was sitting there. I said, 'Hello, Jack.' And he didn't answer me." Sperling was puzzled. Warner sat down and got up several times, clearly distressed. "I don't think I should be eating lunch in the same room with you," he said. Sperling asked why. Now Warner exploded. He snarled about that "fucking telegram with your name on it," referring to a CFA petition that Sperling had signed to protest the committee, and said, "One of us will not be eating in this dining room." Sperling rose quietly. "I'm going to leave. It's your studio," and he started out of the room. But Warner called him back. "We gotta stick together," he implored. "They're after all of us."

When Philip Dunne returned from Washington, the first thing he did was contact his friend, attorney Mendel Silberberg, the chief operative in the Jewish community. Dunne realized that with the hostile witnesses having behaved badly, the pressure for a blacklist would now intensify; Silberberg, with his close ties to the Jewish executives and his conservative pedigree, would be both a facilitator and a conscience. No one was more rock-ribbed a Republican than Mendel Silberberg, but he opposed a blacklist on the grounds that once it started, there would be no stopping it. The Jews, he feared, would be hoisted on their own petard.

Over the next week, Dunne and Silberberg met with the studio heads one by one—all except Jack Warner, who declined. The meetings were brief and strained. Mayer wouldn't meet their eyes but kept insisting that he wanted no part of a blacklist. Harry Cohn was adamant against one. Dore Schary at RKO strongly opposed a blacklist. Joe Schenck at Twentieth Century-Fox, Dunne's own studio, said he didn't believe there should be a blacklist but added that he didn't think they should hire Communists, either. ("I couldn't parse that one myself," Dunne said.) But Dunne and Silberberg had at least received assurances that the studios didn't want to capitulate, even after the sorry display by the unfriendly witnesses in Washington.

Three weeks later, on November 24, the House voted the ten uncooperative witnesses in contempt. During the debate over the contempt citations, Rankin once again rose to the occasion. The committee was only trying to "protect the American people against those things in which these people are now engaged who want to undermine and destroy this Republic, to destroy American institutions, and to bring to the Christian people of America the murder and plunder that has taken place in the Communist-dominated countries of Europe." Rankin then cited the petition from the Committee for the First Amendment. "One of the names is June Havoc. We found out from the motion-picture almanac that her real name is June Hovick.

"Another one was Danny Kaye, and we found out that his real name was David Daniel Kaminsky.

"Another one here is John Beal, whose real name is J. Alexander Bliedung.

"Another one is Cy Bartlett, whose real name is Sacha Baraniev.

"Another one is Eddie Cantor, whose real name is Edward Iskowitz.

"There is one who calls himself Edward Robinson. His real name is Emmanuel Goldenberg.

"There is another one here who calls himself Melvyn Douglas, whose real name is Melvyn Hesselberg."

The citations passed overwhelmingly.

Two days before that vote, Eric Johnston, president of the Motion Picture Association of America, was on his way home to Spokane, Washington, for Thanksgiving when he received an urgent call at the airport in Chicago from Nick Schenck. Schenck was in a frenzy. He believed that the industry had to coordinate some strategy toward dealing with the alleged subversives, and he demanded that Johnston return to New York immediately or be fired.

That is why the same day Congress held the ten in contempt, Eric Johnston was calling the major film executives to a meeting in a public room at the Waldorf-Astoria Hotel in New York. Schenck was there, and Mayer and Barney Balaban and Jack Cohn and Jack Warner and Samuel Goldwyn and Walter Wanger and Dore Schary —about twenty executives in all and three times as many attorneys representing them. Schary, a liberal activist who had graduated to the executive suite from the writers' ranks and claimed he detested the idea of blacklisting them for their political beliefs, immediately sensed that the executives' resolve had softened considerably in the last two weeks. Johnston addressed them "as if we were members of an industry manufacturing secret deadly weapons by employing Communists." A parade of speakers followed, including Mayer, with the obligatory patriotic rhetoric. When producer Samuel Goldwyn, a naturally contrary fellow, said it sounded as if they were panicking, Johnston exploded. If ever they wanted to earn the respect of the American people, he barked at the assemblage, they would have to fire the uncooperative witnesses.

Though Johnston, a former president of the Chamber of Commerce, was undoubtedly moved less by the Hollywood Jews' yearning for respectability than by the right wing's dire threats to organize boycotts of the movies, he had struck one of the most sensitive nerves of the group. Older and wearier now, as Lillian Hellman described them, and frightened, the executives paid heed. The new special counsel of Johnston's MPAA, former Secretary of State James Byrnes, assured them that no one in government would hold them accountable if they fired the uncooperative ten. Every studio contract had a "morals clause" forbidding scandalous behavior; they had only to invoke that. But Goldwyn, Wanger, and Schary still balked—at least according to Schary's version. Johnston, who had been listening silently to the debate while nervously slapping his hotel key against the table, abruptly threw down the key and, quivering with rage, threatened to quit unless they voted to fire the ten.

No vote was necessary; it was understood. The group then selected a committee to draft a public statement: Mayer, Joe Schenck, Walter Wanger, and Dore Schary. Curiously, the chairman of the committee was none other than Mendel Silberberg, one of the prime movers in forestalling an official blacklist. Silberberg might have glossed his participation by saying that he was trying to limit the damage already done, but whatever his motives, there was something telling about the fact that the leader of the Hollywood Jews was the one who articulated the industry's position toward the unrepentant radicals. No one in Hollywood was more conscious of the image of Jews in the public mind. No one was more keenly aware of the practical consequences of the Hollywood Jews' seeming to harbor Communists. No one more accurately represented the Hollywood Jews' fears and hopes.

As Silberberg drafted it, the Waldorf Statement deplored "the action of the ten Hollywood men who have been cited for contempt. . . . [T]heir actions have been a disservice to their employers and have impaired their usefulness to the industry." Under the circumstances, the signatories agreed to discharge the ten until they purged themselves of their contempt citations or renounced communism under oath. It was their next declaration that was to cause the turmoil and tragedy. The producers also agreed that they would not knowingly employ a Communist. They admitted that "there is the danger of hurting innocent people. There is the risk of creating an atmosphere of fear. Creative work at its best cannot be carried on in an atmosphere of fear. We will guard against this danger, this risk, this fear." Fifteen producers signed the statement. Ten of them were Jews.

It was easy to revile these Jewish executives for cowardice and, worse, expedience, to accuse them of abandoning in the face of economic disaster what few principles they held. It was easy to view them as arrogant and stupid and reactionary—all of which they were. But, though it doesn't absolve them to say so, they were also in the grip of a deep and legitimate fear: the fear that somehow the delicate rapprochement they had established between themselves and this country would be destroyed, and with it their lives. "I don't think the heads of movie companies, and the men they appointed to run the studios, had ever before thought of themselves as American citizens with inherited rights and obligations," wrote Lillian Hellman, standing one of the typical right-wing anti-Semitic attacks on its head. "Many of them had been born in foreign lands and inherited foreign fears. It would not have been possible in Russia or Poland, but it was possible here to offer the Cossacks a bowl of chicken soup."

To save themselves from the wrath of the anti-Semites, that is what they did.

═══

And so the plague descended. The ten were fired. Dozens of others who were Communists or liberals or "premature anti-Fascists" were blighted. The American Legion threatened to picket films that bore credits of those they considered subversive. Lists circulated. The studios established clearance offices for those who felt unfairly accused. And of the Jewish executives, some forgot and some despaired, but all went on. "I didn't want to do anything," Mayer still insisted. Harry Cohn argued aggressively with his legal staff against dismissing suspected radicals, and he called HUAC unconstitutional, but he said New York demanded that he terminate them, and he had to comply, handing the job over to one of his associates, B. B. Kahane.

The larger Jewish community had been watching all this with profound interest and divided opinions about how to respond. In November, shortly after the contempt citations, Sidney Harmon, a member of the American Jewish Committee's board and an executive at Fox, wrote AJC's executive director John Slawson, proposing that the AJC take up its cudgels against HUAC by demonstrating "one of the prime purposes of the Un-American Activities Committee is to spread anti-Semitism." Quoting Billy Wilder, Harmon claimed that HUAC was implementing the same strategy the Nazis had used in wresting control of the German film industry from the Jews there—namely, tying Jews to communism—and cited the insistent equation of HUAC and its supporters between the Jews who ran the film industry and the subversives there plotting against the country. The anti-Semitism, Harmon believed, was patent in the fact that ten of the nineteen unfriendly witnesses subpoenaed were Jews. "What position is the American Jewish Committee to take in relation to the ten unfriendly Jewish witnesses?" Harmon wanted to know.

In January 1948 Slawson responded that the AJC would not get involved with the so-called Hollywood Ten because it was a legal matter that affected all citizens regardless of their religious or ethnic affiliation, rather than a matter that was pertinent only to minorities. Slawson was, of course, being extremely disingenuous. The larger Jewish community didn't want to touch the Jewish Communists any more than the Jewish executives did for fear they would get tainted, too, but they did have a vested interest in calming the troubled waters, if only to prove that not all Jews were Communists.

Jewish agencies funneled affidavits from suspect Jewish actors, writers, and directors who wanted to be cleared to the individuals who could clear them—usually the FBI or self-appointed vigilantes from the American Legion and other ad hoc anti-Communist groups. Arnold Forster, the general counsel of the Anti-Defamation League, lent his matchmaking services to suspected Jews and put them in touch with such right-wing contacts as columnist Victor Riesel. Similarly, Leon Lewis, the disabled World War I veteran who had been dispatched to Los Angeles by the ADL years before, maintained close ties to the FBI, and when the Los Angeles Jewish community had a sensitive matter that needed taking care of, Lewis could always go to the local office for assistance.

In effect, the need for the Los Angeles Jews to involve themselves somehow in the process of accusation, information, and clearance also converted Mendel Silberberg's Community Relations Council, the umbrella group of Jewish organizations, into a strange social club that informally brokered among the accusing, the accused, and the Jewish executives who had tried to stand above the battle. "The CRC was a natural place for the process to take place," Jewish activist Paul Jacobs told one investigator, "because you had the studios represented through Silberberg; you had the Jewish war veterans there, who were able to go to the Legionnarie types, and you had other people who were close to union people who could go to [Roy] Brewer [anti-Communist president of the International Alliance of Theatrical Stage Employees]; and you had in the case of Roos himself a very knowledgeable, sophisticated political guy. Roos came out of the German Social Democratic movement, he was a refugee, and he knew a hell of a lot about the CP and all about CP activities."

Joseph Roos, a tiny man with a delightfully thick German accent, had become the executive director of the CRC after years in public relations, but through watchdogging groups for the council, he had also gained a certain investigative expertise, which he now turned to the accused Jews. The process often began with Silberberg himself. He would ask Roos to assist some beleaguered Jew—someone who felt he had been unfairly accused or someone who wanted to repent for youthful indiscretions so he could work again. Roos would then spend hours interviewing the victim. He would comb through the man's financial records, searching for evidence that he had been misled or misguided. (For Edward G. Robinson, who had been gray-listed, Roos examined check stubs to determine which allegedly subversive organizations he had contributed to, then presented a list of other, unassailably anti-Communist contributors to those same organizations. It was innocence by association.) Once he had compiled a dossier, he would pass it along to one of his own contacts in the American Legion or to Martin Gang.

Gang was a high-powered show business attorney whose clients included Bob Hope, Burt Lancaster, Paulette Goddard, and Art Linkletter. He had gotten where he was because he had a reputation for being a tough negotiator when it came to bargaining with the executives. Dalton Trumbo, one of the Hollywood Ten who had retained Gang in a suit against MGM for back pay, called him "the industry expert in frying producers." But in 1950 one of Gang's clients, Sterling Hayden, had a different sort of problem. During the war, Hayden had joined Tito's partisans in Yugoslavia and subsequently became a Party member. Now, in the hysteria that gripped Hollywood after HUAC, he came to Gang asking what he should do. Gang also happened to be an active member of the Los Angeles Jewish community —one of those who hobnobbed at the CRC with Silberberg and Roos. It was through the CRC that Gang learned about the unofficial contacts between the FBI and the establishment Jews. Not knowing what else to do, he decided to use them in Hayden's behalf.

So Gang sat down and wrote J. Edgar Hoover a letter explaining that Hayden was repentant. Hoover wrote back, "We really don't know what to tell you, except take Mr. Hayden down to the local office—we'll write him a letter so they'll see him—and you tell him to tell them his story." "Get it on the record, and if anything comes up, they'll help you," Gang advised Hayden, and Hayden did just that. "The sad thing was that Mr. Hoover was not a gentleman," Gang later recalled. Rather than clear Hayden, Hoover fed the information to HUAC, and a year later Hayden was subpoenaed to appear before the committee. Gang thought it was a "dirty trick." He immediately flew to Washington and warned HUAC's counsel, Frank Tavenner, that Hayden would not answer the question, "Are you now or have you ever been a member of the Communist Party?" Gang wanted instead to lay the groundwork for why Hayden entered the Party, or his client would not cooperate.

Hayden did eventually testify and did name names—an act for which he was eternally remorseful. Meanwhile, Gang became a one-man clearinghouse. "Other lawyers referred people to me," Gang recalled. "Some came to me directly. When they had a problem, I felt I would solve them." The executives, who had so often fought with Gang over perks and money in his clients' contracts, welcomed him in his role as self-appointed purifier. "They had somebody here whom they could call and talk. Ben Kahane [in charge of security at Columbia] would call me on the phone. Frank Freeman [production head at Paramount] would call me on the phone when he had problems. I'd get Roy Brewer. And we'd go down and talk to Steve Broidy, who was then down at Allied Artists. . . . I'd give them affidavits. What were we going to do? These guys wanted to work, and they were being kept from work by this O'Neill [of the American Legion] and the nuts with the lists. I phoned. There was nothing secret about it."

Roos, who had his own close contacts with HUAC, introduced Gang to HUAC's chief investigator, William Wheeler. That added a new wrinkle to Gang's service. Gang would now invite Wheeler to dine with blacklisted clients, apparently to show him that they didn't wear horns. "There used to be a Japanese place—I remember taking him to dinner with two clients of mine whom he wanted to talk to. And he became convinced they were in the clear, and he never bothered to subpoena them." Occasionally Wheeler would even hold an executive session in Gang's office.

Still, Gang was distressed. The problem, as he saw it, was that virtually *anyone* could make an accusation, lack of evidence notwithstanding, but there was no systematic way to defend oneself against an accusation or repent for past transgressions. The only recourse a suspected subversive had was to beg forgiveness from one of the dozen or so clearinghouses or go to Gang and have *him* do the begging. "You had James O'Neill of the American Legion running a clearance," Gang said. "You had *Red Channels* [a magazine] running a clearance. You had the union guy... Roy Brewer running around here. You had the crazy ones like James McGuinness with his Motion Picture Association for the Preservation of American Ideals. He was running around with Ward Bond.... You had all this nonsense."

In the Jewish community the problem was compounded by the fact that "a lot of them [blacklistees] were Jewish," and the reckless charges were beginning to throw suspicion once again on the Jews generally. Eager to demonstrate their cooperation and protect their own reputations, some officials of organized Jewry, including Gang, began hunting for a mechanism that would somehow rationalize the anarchic clearance system. In doing so, Gang and the others no doubt hoped that they would be demonstrating their patriotism to HUAC and its fellow travelers, while at the same time assisting Jews in need.

The idea for a new committee that would serve as a central clearinghouse apparently originated with Edwin Lukas, a staff member of the American Jewish Committee, but it was Gang who seemed to promote the idea most enthusiastically. What Gang proposed early in 1952 was a Citizens Committee for Cooperation with Congress to be composed of representatives from the entertainment world. The committee's function, he wrote in a letter to the major film executives, would be "to provide for the first time effective liaison between the entertainment industry and the House Committee on Un-American Activities." While the industry debated its response, Lukas made a counterproposal: a tribunal of prestigious citizens, non-Jews, from which blacklistees could seek and receive absolution. Funding would be provided by AJC. Gang, warming to the suggestion himself, recommended Judge Learned Hand head the tribunal.

Looking back, Gang conceded it was "a terrible idea. It's a rotten idea to have private courts," and it died through lack of enthusiasm from the only people who could make it effective: the industry and the blacklisters. But the Jews kept searching for ways to control the damage. Some tried to influence the blacklisters by infiltrating their organizations the way the subversives had been accused of infiltrating the studios. "What we did," confessed Joseph Roos, "is we built up this person, Al Chamie, who was in World War II as a naval officer. . . . We built him up in the American Legion where he finally became state commander and then finally national commander. And the objective of building him up in the American Legion was for the American Legion to say, 'The motion picture industry is not Communist,' which is nicer than for you or I to say it."

But there were other Jews in Hollywood for whom collaboration with the blacklisters wasn't sufficient. They wanted to outdo them. "Why should Jews sit back if every other citizen and every other religion and group are against communism? As though we were Communists," asked Rabbi Edgar Magnin, the spiritual leader of the Hollywood Jews. "You have to concern yourself with the other side. You are a very small minority. You can't do things that other people can do and get away with them. You may think so, but you see what happened in Germany. It can happen here. . . . What's the virtue of antagonizing?"

Magnin certainly wasn't alone in feeling this way. On March 15, 1948, two and a half months after the Hollywood Ten had been voted in contempt, a rabbi in Yonkers, New York, formed the American Jewish League Against Communism. Even by the standards of Jewish conservatism, Benjamin Schultz was unusual. An unattractive man with a spatulate nose, baggy eyes, and black beetle brows, he had come to prominence the week before HUAC convened with a series of three articles in the *New York World Telegram* titled "Communists Invade the Churches," which said, among other things, that one-third of the college students in New York were under the influence of Communist doctrine. The New York Board of Rabbis promptly condemned him for violating the commandment against bearing false witness, and Rabbi Stephen Wise, who had been personally attacked in the articles, called Schultz "a professional and probably profiteering Communist baiter, unworthy to be a member, not to say a rabbi of a Jewish congregation." Leaping to Schultz's defense, Gerald L. K. Smith praised him for trying "unsuccessfully to recruit the Jews of America in a campaign against Communism."

In June twelve Los Angeles Jews formed their own chapter of Schultz's league and named screenwriter Morrie Ryskind, a charter member of the Motion Picture Alliance, as its chairman. This was a group full of fire and brimstone, and as a measure of their fanaticism, they chose as their first guest speaker California State Senator Jack Tenney. Tenney, another jowly Pickwickian with slicked-back hair, had entered the California State Legislature as a left-wing assembly-man; when he submitted a resolution calling for the end of an arms embargo to the Spanish Republicans, a fellow legislator proclaimed, "This resolution was sent out by the emissaries of Moscow."

But all that was to change rapidly. Tenney was also a musician—he had composed "Mexicali Rose"—and had been elected president of Local 47 of the American Federation of Musicians. When he was defeated for reelection as head of the local, he immediately blamed a Communist faction, and like Parnell Thomas before him, he turned overnight into a right-wing zealot. In January 1941 he proposed and then became chairman of a joint legislative committee to investigate subversive elements in California, a kind of miniature Dies committee. He continued to chair the committee when he was elected to the state senate in 1942.

Tenney quickly realized that there were no Communists like Hollywood Communists—at least no investigation of Communists that could attract the publicity an investigation of Hollywood Communists could. Though repeated probes failed to expose any Communist conspiracy there, as Tenney promised, he persevered. When Rankin announced his own probe of Hollywood, Tenney not only offered to channel the information he had gathered to HUAC, he accused Rankin of being "guilty of understatement in his announcement that Hollywood was full of Reds."

All of this was reason enough for the Los Angeles chapter of the American Jewish League Against Communism to honor him—except for one thing. Tenney was also widely regarded as an anti-Semite. Just a few months after appearing before the league to discuss the "problem of communism in its relation to California Jewry," he launched an investigation into the Soto-Michigan Jewish Center for taking funds from the community chest and then allowing alleged Communist front groups to use the premises. Just a few years later he was Gerald L. K. Smith's running mate on the Christian Nationalist party ticket. And two years after that, in a letter to his constituents, he wrote:

> During the nearly ten years of my chairmanship of the California Committee on Un-American Activities I have experienced the pressure of organized Jewry in its attempts to influence Committee hearings, investigations, and even the Reports of the Committee. . . . Jewish leaders will go to any length to destroy any public official or person who they believe interferes with their plans or is a threat to their program.

Most of the organized Jewish community considered Schultz and his league an embarrassment. "Most Jews realize that a 'Jewish League Against Communism' makes about as much sense as a 'Jewish League Against Rent Gouging' or a 'Jewish League Against International Banking.' The very name is self-defeating," wrote one Jewish leader. Others feared that the league conferred legitimacy on anti-Semitic Red-baiters and proposed an investigation of their own to document the ties between anti-Semites and the Red-baiting vigilantes. "This is a scandalous business—an overt surrender to the Commie line that anti-Communism and anti-Semitism are somehow intertwined," Eugene Lyons, a vehemently anti-Communist journalist and league member, wrote Edwin Lukas of the AJC, "and could only have been started by a dope acting as stooge for some Partyliner." "I agree that 'investigation of anti-communists' is not a 'Jewish problem,'" Lukas replied. "That is, it is not a Jewish problem so long as the forces that seek to eliminate communist activity from the stream of American life do not turn their anti-communist activities into an anti-semitic drive.... I might also suggest to you, in all candor, that if the investigation of anti-communists is not to be undertaken by a Jewish organization as a 'Jewish problem,' it would follow—as day follows night—that the fighting of Communism is not to be undertaken by a Jewish organization (i.e., the American Jewish League Against Communism.) Or is there a distinction that has eluded me?"

━━━━━

The HUAC hearings in October 1947, while frightening the Jewish executives into submission, hadn't been a particular triumph for J. Parnell Thomas. In fact, the irony was that the Hollywood Jews' panicky reaction to the hearings went a long way toward giving them credibility and legitimacy. At the time, however, newspapers editorialized against the committee; the Committee for the First Amendment had demonstrated wide if short-lived opposition within the film industry itself, and the Gallup poll showed the public was evenly divided. It wasn't a particularly good *year* for the committee's prime movers, either. Rankin, whose bombast had set the whole thing in motion, was forced to surrender his membership on the committee when it was decided that committee chairmen—Rankin headed the House Committee on Veterans' Affairs—should be limited to one assignment.

For J. Parnell Thomas, the committee's gavel-pounding chairman, fate was much more cruel and wry. In August 1948 an unhappy secretary told columnist Drew Pearson that Thomas had padded his payroll by billing the U.S. Treasury for individuals who had not worked in his office. Two days after he had won election to the House for the seventh time, he was called before a grand jury. Thomas took the Fifth Amendment. Within a week he was indicted for conspiracy to defraud the government. He later pleaded nolo contendere and was sentenced to eighteen months in Danbury Prison.

Thomas stalled his imprisonment for nearly three years with claims of failing health. Meanwhile, the Hollywood Ten had been appealing their contempt citations, and the process slowly wound its way to the Supreme Court, where the group anticipated vindication. Instead, on April 10, 1950, the Supreme Court denied certiorari. Their citations were upheld, each was eventually sentenced, and each served a prison term. The Motion Picture Alliance celebrated with a full-page advertisement in the Hollywood trade papers warning, "Our top level executives must not make the same mistake this time that they did last. Whether they like it, or not, the American public will not let them off with the legal shrug of the shoulders. . . . America is insisting on a complete delousing."

Ring Lardner, Jr., and Lester Cole, two of the convicted ten, were sentenced to Danbury, where they found their old antagonist, Parnell Thomas. Working in the prison yard one afternoon, Cole cutting the grass with a machete, Thomas cleaning a nearby chicken coop, Thomas yelled, "Hey, Bolshie! I see you still got your sickle. Where's your hammer?" Cole riposted, "And I see just like in Congress, you're still picking up chickenshit."

All this time, or ever since the Hollywood Ten had caused their ruckus in 1947, HUAC had been dormant. Whether it was waiting for the Court's ruling on its citations or was simply waiting to catch another wave of anti-Communist hysteria was impossible to say. By 1951 it had gotten both, and the hearings suddenly and surprisingly resumed—this time with dozens of witnesses penitently taking the stand and naming names of political associates. What was new this time was the poignance—the Hollywood Ten had been obstreperous and unbowed—and the stridency, even among the previously cautious Jews of the establishment. "Without getting into a debate with a witness," Marcus Cohn, the AJC's Washington counsel, wrote Edwin Lukas shortly after the hearings began, "I feel two or three questions would probably devastate the next Commie witness who starts hiding behind his Jewishness. . . . Obviously, it is going to be a source of real annoyance in the future; the House Committee wants to be cooperative and I think we should take advantage of their cooperative attitude by suggesting the best possible technique for handling the situation."

During the first HUAC inquisition in 1947, the Jewish executives had felt betrayed by the sudden Orwellian attack on what they had regarded as their patriotic duty in the war. During the second HUAC inquisition, the Jewish leftists felt a similar sense of betrayal and disorientation at the sudden attack on what they had regarded as their moral duty in fighting fascism. These two factions, at opposite ends of the political spectrum, still shared that Jewish sense of never being able to set the terms for their relationship to this country and, more, knowing that no matter what their motives, they would always be suspect.

John Garfield was a perfect example of the way in which the Orwellian turned into the Kafkaesque for the Hollywood Jews of the fifties. Garfield had come to Hollywood in 1938 after a successful career with the left-wing Group Theatre in New York. Young, idealistic, impassioned, and liberal, he had naturally contributed time and money to various liberal causes, though he was decidedly nondoctrinaire and even claimed once that the Party had rejected him because he was "too dumb." Even so, the word had gone out, and Garfield found himself stigmatized by his liberalism.

"I went to Twentieth Century-Fox to meet with the general manager, Lew Schreiber, about the Sol Hurok story and suggested Garfield for it," remembered Garfield's agent, George Chasin. "Schreiber said, 'He's wrong for it.' 'Wrong for it? Sol Hurok was a Jew. John Garfield did *Humoresque* at Warner Brothers. It's relatively the same kind of character.' I said, 'Are you saying no because you think John Garfield is a Communist?' He said, 'No, no, no.' So I went to Garfield and I said, 'Would you make a test?' He never made a test for anything. He said, 'Yes.' So I went back to Schreiber and said, 'Garfield is willing to make a test.' He said, 'It would be a waste of money —of *our* money.' I went back to Garfield and I said, 'Will you *pay* for the test and could you get Elia Kazan to direct it?' He said, 'Yes.' So I went back to Lew Schreiber and I said, 'Garfield will pay for the test and get Kazan to direct it. But as evidence of your good faith, could you give me one page of dialogue?' And he said, 'No. It would be a waste of Garfield's money and Kazan's time.' So I was convinced that because Garfield was on the blacklist that the test was not going to be made."

Perhaps it was just that the Jewish executives who instituted the blacklist were themselves mystified and terrified by the chaos. Jack Warner stormed into the studio commissary one afternoon after hearing virtually his entire contract list mentioned as possible subversives at the hearings. "He ran wildly about," remembered one writer, "jabbing his thumbs at his lunching help. 'I can do without you!' he yelled. 'And you! And you! I can do without you!' He came to Jerry Wald, who at that time was producing a good half of all the Warner Brothers films. 'I can almost do without you!' he screamed."

"You just had to look at them," said screenwriter Jerome Chodorov of the moguls. "They were frightened to death. . . . And the so-called power was nothing, you know. . . . The American Legion was the front; they were going to picket the theaters and they were going to put you out of business if you didn't fire people, and of course it was a joke, you know. The American Legion would have sent up one picket line for an hour and that would have been the end of that. . . . But the producers were the most frightened people in the world." Harry Warner fired a writer whose name had been listed. "This is a mistake," the man pleaded, opening a briefcase full of documents that substantiated his opposition to communism. "The plain fact is that I am an *anti*-Communist." Harry fired back, "I don't give a shit what kind of Communist you are, get out of here."

Harry Cohn, the world hater, remained ambivalent. On the one hand, he had rushed to join the Jewish American League Against Communism; he was the first studio head to do so. On the other hand, when one of his best film editors, Robert Parrish, asked Cohn if he should sign a loyalty oath as his agent requested and banish any suspicions, Cohn growled characteristically, "I'm suspicious of everybody. What have you done?" Parish said his agent wanted to know if he was a Communist. "Tell him to go fuck himself," Cohn said. "It's none of his goddamn business. Ask him if he's a Jew." Cohn got up to go to the bathroom. When he returned he said casually, "By the way, are you a Communist?" Parrish snapped, "No. Are you a Jew?" "It's none of your goddamn business. Now let's get to work."

Back at the time of the Waldorf Statement, the Hollywood Jews had blamed the New York executives for forcing their hand. This had always been Cohn's own defense, and it wasn't without justification. The Jews actually *in* Hollywood were nobles who resented incursions on their empire, but everyone knew the American Legion had been applying enormous pressure on the New York executives, and those corporate Jews were much more susceptible to anything that adversely affected the bottom line—which is one reason the American Legion usually applied its pressure in New York rather than in Hollywood. When Darryl Zanuck fired Ring Lardner, Jr., as he was obligated to do under the terms of the statement, and Philip Dunne went to Zanuck to tender his resignation in protest, Zanuck remonstrated that the coercion from New York was beyond Dunne's comprehension. The Hollywood Jews had no choice: fire or be fired.

But even the idea of New York bogeymen was too pat an explanation. Barney Balaban, president of Paramount and an organization man right down to his fingertips, was as baffled and tense as the Jews of Hollywood. "I don't think it's okay," he told his daughter when she questioned why he wasn't doing anything to stop the Red-baiting madness. "There's something about it that's okay, but there's something about it that's terrible, and I don't quite understand it all yet." At the premiere of a preposterously overwrought anti-Communist film Paramount had released, *My Son John,* an executive from a rival studio approached Balaban and praised the picture effusively. "I'm glad you feel that way," Balaban said. "I wish you had made it."

Of course, their ambivalence didn't prevent the industry Jews from participating in the process. But if, in doing so, they had hoped to secure their empire against the vandals, the cooperation had quite a different effect. Hollywood was a community of utopians—genteel utopians on the right who envisioned a brave new world of decent, upright, upper-middle-class Americans; and starry-eyed utopians on the left who envisioned a world of compassionate, morally lathered comrades smiting injustice. In the balmy unreality of southern California, one could actually believe in the realization of these images, in the perfection of the world, just as one perfected the world in the movies. HUAC and all the things that came in its wake destroyed that innocence and shattered that faith. The Jews who tried appeasing Hollywood's tormentors only demonstrated their tormentors' strength and the Jews' own weakness. Paradise was lost. It would never be regained.

10

The End

Now, these aren't men who know pictures. They've got ticker tapes in their brains.

FROM *WHAT MAKES SAMMY RUN?*

They're mechanical bastards. All they care about is what sold last year.

HARRY COHN

OF ALL THE FILMS HE HAD SU-
pervised at MGM, Louis B. Mayer loved *The Human Comedy* best.
He had only to see the first scene—of a small boy staring curiously at
a gopher hole—to weep unashamedly, and he proudly told the writer
that "tears poured out of my eyes" simply having the outline read to
him. The author, William Saroyan, was a burly, somber-faced young
American-Armenian from Fresno, California, who had flabbergasted
Broadway not only with his talent (he won the Pulitzer Prize for
drama in 1940 for *The Time of Your Life*), but even more with his
bohemian disregard for all the little civilities of high-brow culture.
Saroyan was a plebeian, rough and irreverent. He was garrulous, sentimental, histrionic, hardy, and unbowable—which is, no doubt,
why Mayer was immediately attracted to him. In Saroyan he found a
kindred spirit—a chip off his own youth and his secret self.

Saroyan was less impressed. He later wrote of Mayer that he "could
make or break movie people, in all departments, and he did so whenever desirable or necessary. . . . Anybody who got sarcastic with old
L. B., even only in the eyes, giving him only a sarcastic *look*, would
soon enough learn that L. B. would take it slow and easy, and then at
an unexpected moment take his revenge. Like death itself." But for
the time at least, in 1942, Saroyan was Mayer's protégé. Mayer even
touted him as the new designated heir to Thalberg and set him up in
the studio to write whatever he desired on whatever timetable he

desired. "No Jew can ever cheat an Armenian," Saroyan gloated when it was suggested that Mayer would ultimately try to sucker him. "The Armenians have been cheating the Jews for centuries."

Saroyan didn't last long at MGM, but he did produce a story about a family in a small California town during the war that was written precisely to Mayer's specifications. *The Human Comedy*, as he called it, freely blended patriotic bromides with domestic ones, images of American unity with images of Rockwellian bliss. Saroyan's Ithaca was the hometown in American middle-class dreams: composed of capacious white clapboard houses with broad verandas, gleaming white streets, and shops with friendly picture windows, a quaint town square where one could pitch horseshoes on a lazy summer's evening, a library the size of a small cathedral, an archetypal high school with matronly teachers whose lives were dedicated to inculcating virtue. Its citizens were industrious, religious, wholesome, and decent, and though they were of different classes and ethnic origins, they were knitted together by a larger, almost spiritual sense of family—the weave of Mayer's own sensibility.

Even Saroyan must have understood that this was less his America than Mayer's and as close to an ultimate expression of the Mayer philosophy as one was likely to get. The film, starring Mickey Rooney as Homer Macauley, a high school student who must sustain his own family after his father has died and his older brother has gone off to war, and directed by Mayer's close friend, Clarence Brown, was life as Mayer idealized it—fresh and genteel. Yet for all its preachments on the flag and motherhood, *The Human Comedy* was also a dark and rather sober film—as much about the imminence of death as the immanence of God's spirit. The film is narrated by Homer's dead father. Homer's boon companion at the telegraph office where he works is an aging drunkard terrified of being pensioned out. His older brother dies in battle. "Almost everything you find out is sad, isn't it?" Homer confides to his mother, who agrees that ours is a world laced with pain and endured through faith.

For Mayer himself, the difficulty of synchronizing his life to its idealization, the difficulty of maintaining his own genteel domestic autocracy, must have led him to the same conclusion. In weeping for the Macauleys, he was weeping for his own lost dreams, which had begun to slip away nearly a decade before with the failing of his wife's health. Late in 1933 Margaret Mayer entered the hospital for a "female complication," which, the doctors determined, would require a hysterectomy. Though the operation was itself uneventful, it would become, in Irene Selznick's words, "the worst calamity that ever hit our family." Mrs. Mayer, her hormones discombobulated by the surgery, fell into a deep, unshakable depression. She complained of unremitting pain. She "moaned and wept." She became a hypochondriac, hunting for new maladies. For her husband, who showed the same implacably rosy sensibility manifest in MGM's movies, this was incomprehensible. (And frightening. A hypochondriac himself, whose desk was cluttered with medicine bottles, Mayer was terrified by illness.) While he searched for scapegoats—her doctors had bungled—she retreated to a small home near her two daughters, where she permitted fifteen-minute audiences. Later she was packed off to the Austen Riggs Center in Stockbridge, Massachusetts, for psychotherapy.

Alone for the first time since their marriage, Mayer was shaken and inconsolable—the very foundations of his life knocked out from under him. His wife returned, but she ignored her daughter Irene's counsel of moderation, thrust herself into her old routine, and was soon back at Riggs, where she would spend nearly a third of her time over the next ten years. Gradually Mayer reemerged from his own melancholia and began complaining to friends that he'd be damned if he was going to "stay home and sit in front of the fire in a smoking jacket and carpet slippers, the way my wife wants me to do!" There was one more thing: his wife's doctors, as was customary at the time after a woman had a hysterectomy, discouraged her from having sexual intercourse.

Mayer once insisted that "the Talmud says a man is not responsible for a sin committed by any part of his body below the waist." But this was all bluff. He was exactly what he appeared to be—a prude. His daughter Irene called him "probably the most unsophisticated, straitlaced man in town." He believed in the homilies he preached about family, which made his wife's condition or, more accurately, the condition of their marriage, especially distressing to him. "I believe that he was such a moral man," said his grandson Danny Selznick, "that he felt he could not have affairs, go chase women, pursue. It's fascinating because . . . you see Louis B. Mayer pictured as a lecher asking secretaries for their home numbers, as if he was bedding down everything in sight. I think precisely the opposite was true. I think he was so moral and so ethical that he felt he could not pursue any of these potential partners until he was separated from his wife."

Still, there were those who encouraged Mayer to blossom. One was Joe Schenck, Nick's prodigiously high-living brother. Schenck was both an inveterate party giver and womanizer, and he coaxed Mayer to join him on his romps. Another was Frank Orsatti, an unpretentious bootlegger whom Mayer had met at a party, befriended, and then convinced to open a talent agency. With Mayer's wife either gone to Stockbridge or moping at home, Orsatti became a confidant, companion, crony, and loyalist. Eventually he was able to persuade Mayer to start stepping out with him, though the only gratification to which Mayer could admit was dancing. "He has a theory that dancing is an excellent cure for insomnia," a *New Yorker* profile reported, "and three or four nights a week he goes to the Trocadero, on Sunset Boulevard, or another night club, and whirls gracefully around the floor until he is weary." Orsatti offered to set up his friend with women, but Mayer refused. He felt uncomfortable. When Orsatti did succeed in arranging tête-à-têtes, Mayer, as unschooled in romance as adolescent Andy Hardy, inquired after the girl's family. One said, "It would have been like doing it with my father!"

But as love came to Andy Hardy, so it came to fifty-year-old Louis B. Mayer—in the form of a twenty-four-year-old starlet named Jean Howard. Howard was a Texas-born Ziegfeld showgirl whose beauty—long almond eyes, ovalescent face, lovely white complexion, and sensual mouth—had already gained her access to men of prominence. One of these, Bert Taylor, president of the New York Stock Exchange, had introduced her to J. Robert Rubin, MGM's East Coast vice president, and Rubin sent her west with instructions that she be given a screen test. By one account, Mayer saw her test and became infatuated, though he demonstrated his ardor rather peculiarly. "Do you have a dentist if you get a toothache?" he asked. "Do you know any doctors if you need one?" If not, Mayer offered his services. It was his way of making an overture. By another account,

Mayer met her at one of Joe Schenck's parties. By both accounts, Mayer was so diffident with her that he hired her friend, a former showgirl named Ethel Borden, to write scripts and, more importantly, to intercede on his behalf. For the deeply conflicted but lovestruck Mayer, Miss Borden also functioned as chaperone.

The romance, such as it was, remained chaste throughout the spring of 1934 ("I'm sure I would have gone to bed with him if he had asked me," she told Sam Marx years later), but Mayer had promised to take his ailing wife to Europe that summer and now arranged to have Miss Borden and Miss Howard follow soon after on another ship. Mayer met them at the pier in Le Havre, and on the train to Paris he was flushed with enthusiasm. He said it had all been settled. His wife had agreed to divorce him so that he could marry Miss Howard. The prospective bride was astonished. What she hadn't told Mayer—what she saw no need to tell Mayer—was that she had been having a torrid affair with a young talent agent named Charlie Feldman, and that she had promised Feldman she would marry him in New York as soon as she returned from her trip.

Miss Howard kept silent on the train about her plans, but as she was unpacking in the Georges V Hotel where the party was staying in Paris, Mayer's publicity chief, Howard Strickling, knocked on her door and gravely demanded she visit Mayer. When she arrived she found Mayer storming about the room in a rage. He had received a report from a private detective in Hollywood detailing Howard's affair with Feldman. At one point in his tirade, Miss Howard, Miss Borden, and Strickling had to restrain him from jumping out the window. Mayer spent most of the rest of the evening numbly wandering the streets. Very shortly after, Miss Howard left for New York and married Feldman. One account reported that Mayer actually saw her off at Le Havre.

Meanwhile, Margaret Mayer contracted pneumonia in Paris. When she suddenly took a turn for the worse, her husband, who was in London at the time, coerced both the Prince of Wales's personal physician, Lord Horder, and the personal physician to the king, Lord Dawson of Penn, to fly to her bedside. She made a dramatic recovery, but Mayer, the fatalist who always believed his mother was watching over him, must have seen her illness as divine retribution for his moral infraction. Penitent and chastened, he remained in Europe during her convalescence, even though he chafed at being away from his studio, where he knew he could bury his shame in work. His companion, Howard Strickling, compared him to a "caged lion. He had two or three telephone conversations all going at once, and he'd jump back and forth between one phone and the next, champing at the bit because everything had to be done long distance." Back in Hollywood, Irene Selznick wrote, her father was "neither married nor unmarried, had neither his freedom nor his home. Though he had his business to distract him, he had a painful time of it."

And so it continued for nearly a decade—a long impasse of tension and recrimination. Margaret blamed him for her condition. "This came on because I dieted," she insisted. "Louis likes slim girls, and it's left me like this." Mayer blamed her for a provincialism that he thought compromised his status. "He felt she didn't grow with him," was how his daughter Edith explained it. (Once, Mayer enlisted gossip columnist and fashion plate Hedda Hopper to accompany his wife on a shopping expedition and introduce her to haute couture, but Maggie kept finding fault with the stylish clothes Hopper showed her. She returned with only a girdle.) "On an emotional level, he never lost his ties to Maggie, as he called her," said Danny Selznick. "But he had to have other kinds of things going on. It wouldn't have surprised me if he never remarried, but he seemed to want a younger partner and a more contemporary style of living."

In 1944, the year after *The Human Comedy*, Louis and Maggie Mayer finally separated. She stayed at the beach house they had built in Santa Monica, listening to the ocean. He rented a massive, high-ceilinged mansion in Benedict Canyon from his friend William Randolph Hearst, where, like Hearst's fictional counterpart, Charles Foster Kane, he lived in what he himself felt was aching solitude.

"There was something funny—either funny or poignant or both—about this small man rambling around in this big house with enormous ceilings," recalled Danny Selznick, who visited his grandfather often during this time. "I was just very aware of his loneliness and his need for companionship in that particular period.... He needed someone to enjoy the pleasure and pain of life with. He needed an audience." At one point Mayer suggested he move in with his daughter Irene, who had divorced David Selznick not long after her parents had separated. She gently refused. His cronies visited frequently, Joe Schenck and Frank Orsatti and Clarence Brown, and he had even tried convincing Mervyn LeRoy, an MGM producer and director who had been recently divorced himself, to move in. LeRoy declined, but he would come out to the mansion for long, discursive, soul-baring discussions, often tinged with bitterness. "Look out for yourself," Mayer told LeRoy in one of these sessions, "or they'll pee on your grave."

Whether Mayer had anyone in mind at the time, by 1948 his loneliness, anguish, and unhappiness had clearly fastened on two targets whom he had come to believe were jeopardizing the only family he had left—his studio. One was his old nemesis, Nick Schenck. The other was Dore Schary. Ever since Thalberg's death in 1936, Schenck had let Mayer run MGM without interference, and Mayer had insured his autonomy by keeping Thalberg's position, essentially vice president in charge of production, vacant. In its place he had set up a committee of executives that was dubbed "the College of Cardinals." No one doubted who the pope was. Each executive ran a unit that was assigned movies to produce, and each reported to Mayer, who, loath to trod on the artistic prerogatives of his employees, functioned more as a guiding spirit, setting the studio's tone, than as an engaged creative force. Mayer suggested, nudged, extolled, and lamented. The executives executed.

This may not have been the most efficient system—Mayer had designed it less for efficiency than to reassert those prerogatives he felt Thalberg had usurped—but for nearly a decade it had worked splendidly, and MGM remained the envy of Hollywood. It was only when Mayer hit his blue period that its weaknesses began to surface. The main problem was that with Mayer distracted by his personal crisis and without a hands-on production executive like Thalberg at the top to coordinate all the various films and supervise the development of scripts, stagnation set in. "You could never get a decision," complained one staff member, "because half the people would be for it and half the people would be against it." It was frustrating, cumbersome, and, in the end, debilitating.

For his part, Schenck, a cool and rather taciturn individual, prided himself on being a hard-nosed businessman. However much he might have begrudged Mayer his power, independence, and compensation, so long as MGM remained prosperous, he had little warrant to criticize Mayer's performance or trim his sails. More, the stockholders wouldn't have let him. Mayer, after all, remained a symbol of considerable magnitude. But when the studio's profits declined precipitously in 1947 (in fairness, the entire industry suffered a severe slump), he inevitably fixed blame on Mayer and the system of authority he had devised, even to the point of suggesting that he had spent too much time on his horses and not enough attending to the studio. As many saw it, MGM had in a few short years become the dowager of Hollywood, imposing but tatty and clearly past her prime. She needed to be reinvigorated. And that was where Dore Schary came in.

Schenck had met Schary on the train back to New York after the HUAC hearing in Washington in November 1947, and the two, as Schary recalled it, hit it off immediately—so much so that, Schary later surmised, Schenck recommended Mayer contact him. Mayer and Schary, who at the time headed production at RKO, had worked together briefly at MGM a decade before, and they had a nodding acquaintance from various Jewish fund-raisers, but they didn't travel in the same circles and were hardly the kind of men who seemed compatible. Schary was a first-generation American Jew from Newark, New Jersey, where his father, a mustachioed behemoth of a man, ran a catering hall called Schary Manor. Hugo Schary dreamed the dreams of a Hollywood Jew. He often talked about buying a large tract of wooded land where he would build a home for each of his children. In the center would be a baronial mansion for him and his wife.

His son dreamed of show business, and after quitting school at thirteen and working a number of odd jobs, including assistant recreation director at a Catskills resort, he became an actor and amateur playwright. One of his efforts came to the attention of Columbia's story editor at the very moment Harry Cohn had issued an edict for new blood, so Dore Schary came to Hollywood in 1932 as a young contract writer. ("She writes tough like a man," producer Walter Wanger had advised Cohn before meeting Schary.) He rapidly worked his way up from B movies to A movies, winning an Academy Award in 1938 for his original story of *Boys Town*. When he asked to direct an inexpensive film he had written for MGM, Mayer called him into his office and questioned why he would possibly want to direct rather than produce and why he would want to make an inexpensive film rather than a big one. Schary answered that a B movie didn't necessarily have to be an inferior movie. The next day Mayer, obviously acting on impulse, asked Schary to head up MGM's entire B unit. A year later he was working for producer David Selznick, Mayer's son-in-law. Three years after that he was heading up RKO.

As production executives went, Schary was an anomaly. Ben Hecht called him "the most imbecilic of the producers, the weakest, the saddest. The reason he was an imbecile as a producer is that he had some talent. He had to put it in his back pocket all the time." In Hecht's view he was miscast in the role of executive. "A producer is a man who can take over the owner's attitude, which is a very simple one: make money." Schary took a higher, more principled line. He always insisted that he wanted to make movies that mattered, and when he quit MGM's B unit it was because he had been thwarted in making a parable about Hitler and Mussolini in the form of a Western.

Schary made other executives uneasy. He avoided the Hollywood social scene and preferred quiet gatherings at his home with friends. He was an outspoken liberal Democrat while most of the executives were fervent Republicans. He was an active and religious Jew while most of the Jewish executives concealed their faith. And he abhorred combat while most of the executives found combat one of their primary talents; it was said he never wanted to make an enemy. Tall, with a long, horsey face and glasses, Schary even looked the part of an intellectual. Mayer, who often characterized people as animals, once described him as an elephant—"strong, big, surefooted, firm." It fit.

Why all of this didn't immediately make Mayer as uneasy as it made most of the other old-line executives is difficult to divine, unless Mayer felt that Schary was weak and manipulable. Even Schary expressed surprise when, late in the spring of 1948, he received a call inviting him to Mayer's home, and Mayer, without preliminaries, offered him the job as vice president in charge of production—the first since Thalberg's death over twelve years before. Some speculated that Mayer was impressed by Schary's devotion to his mother and by his deep religious faith, though they were hardly the same kind of Jew—Mayer, remote and assimilative; Schary, aggressive and proud. Danny Selznick had a different theory. He postulated that Schary, who had trained under David Selznick, was the closest thing to Selznick that his grandfather could acquire, since Selznick himself had repeatedly rejected offers to work at MGM. Schary had a slight physical resemblance to Selznick. He appropriated Selznick's dress, his manner, his executive style, his donnish high-mindedness, and like Selznick he had been an active creative producer rather than a pencil pusher. In getting Schary, then, he would be getting still another surrogate son.

But there was another, simpler theory that might have gone further toward explaining Schary's ascension: Nick Schenck wanted it. Schary was young (forty-three), intelligent, and successful, having done particularly well for RKO. With his predilection for what he called "simple, down-to-earth pictures, the ones about everyday life," he complemented Mayer, who obviously preferred a different kind of picture. (Mayer derided Schary's approach as "realism.") More, he was available. Howard Hughes had taken over RKO just a few months before, and Schary, who always insisted on his independence and feared it would be compromised under the unpredictable Hughes, had asked for his release. The deal was set that June at Mayer's house. Schary insisted on autonomy; he would not work within the College of Cardinals. Schenck and Mayer, who was now over sixty and claimed he was going to retire in a few years anyway, acceded. Dore Schary had become the new dauphin.

"When we heard it was Dore Schary, we said, 'Oh, boy! That's not going to be good,'" remembered Edith Mayer Goetz. Almost from the start, it wasn't. Schary, whether he wanted to admit it or not, resented having to work within the shadow of a legend and not a placid one at that. (Later, when asked what it was precisely that Mayer did at the studio now that Schary himself was responsible for production, he said, "He calls me and tells me what he thinks of the pictures.") Schary saw Mayer as vain, self-involved, unstable, paranoid, and untrustworthy. He had seen his temper during an earlier hitch at MGM when Mayer summarily fired Harry Rapf, one of the original partners at MGM, for interfering with the B unit Schary headed. "You stupid kike bastard," Mayer yelled at Rapf, "you ought to kiss this man's shoes—get on your knees." Witnessing the scene, Schary left the office and ran to the men's room, where he vomited.

By the same token, Mayer resented Schary's incursions into his domain. To him Schary was an upstart and interloper, and he couldn't help but treat him as a know-it-all pupil who would have to learn from his mistakes. Naturally, the relationship was colored by Mayer's experience with Thalberg, whom he still regarded as disloyal. "I had a premonition I would hear the story of Mayer and Thalberg many times," Schary wrote, recalling one of Mayer's lectures about Thalberg's greed and ingratitude. "I did."

But it turned out it wasn't really the ghost of Thalberg that Schary conjured. It was the power of Schenck. The chill began shortly after Schary returned from New York, where Schenck announced his appointment. Schary noticed that Mayer was uncommunicative and discovered why from Eddie Mannix, a former bouncer who had become one of Mayer's lieutenants: Mayer felt slighted by having the announcement made in New York. Schary, always the diplomat (or the weakling, depending on how one looked at it), decided to approach Mayer and express his belief that they were working together in common cause, sharing the accolades. Mayer responded by launching an attack on Thalberg, but his ire soon turned to Schenck. "He'll bring you caviar when you leave New York and flowers in your room when you get back there—but he's only smiles and caviar and roses—and the rest of him is all shit." Schary took this to be more evidence of Mayer's intemperance. He didn't seem to realize that Mayer saw *him* as Schenck's man and that Schenck was a lifelong enemy—the pall over all his dreams.

When faced with crisis, Mayer, like the Macauleys, customarily sought solace in his family. Now, with his extended family at MGM endangered by Schary and Schenck, the two "grave peers," and with his own family shattered by his separation, he had no family on which to rely—so he went out and created one. Mayer had been introduced to Lorena Danker on the Hollywood party circuit. She was the young, resourceful widow of an advertising executive and had herself worked at the J. Walter Thompson Agency. She wasn't a striking beauty as Hollywood women went, but she was a woman of considerable charm and decorum, and she fit perfectly Mayer's idea of a genteel/gentile spouse—young but not too young, attractive, steady, and compliant. She was also the mother of an eleven-year-old daughter, Suzanne, which, if anything, made her more appealing in Mayer's eyes. It enlarged the family.

Avoiding the prying eyes of Hollywood, Mayer and Lorena Danker decided to elope to Yuma, Arizona. Overcast skies made flying impossible, so they took the overnight train, disembarked at four o'clock in the morning, checked in at a motor hotel, and then went to a drive-in for a quick breakfast. By this time the press had been alerted that Mayer was about to marry, and they hounded the party from the diner back to the motel and then to the courthouse, where a justice of the peace officiated and the Yuma jailyard served as backdrop. It was December 1948—six months after Dore Schary had taken over production at MGM.

Like his first family, his studio, and his stable of horses, Mayer viewed his second family as an aesthetic object—something to be shaped and then displayed as a reflection of its creator. For a time, this, even more than the studio, engaged his attention and seemed to rejuvenate him. He liked the idea of starting over from scratch. The first order of business was a home, since the Hearst mansion in which he had lived only reminded him of his period of melancholy. The new home he was building in Bel Air was not only a large, fashionably modern domicile that befitted his station and symbolized his achievement, it was also a rather moving monument to the cultural aspirations of an Eastern European Jew.

"Everything was white," his daughter Edith remembered. "White draperies, white sofa, white rugs.... It looked like a hospital room." The decorator, a studio designer from MGM named Ed Willis, called her in a panic. That was the scheme Mayer had demanded, as if the slightest hint of color would be too showy and déclassé, but Willis hated it and so did Edith. "This looks like a display window in W. and J. Sloane or something. It's terrible." Willis wanted to know what he should do. Edith recommended he paint the living room walls a very pale green and send to New York for expensive European and Chinese wallpapers for the dining room. She would take care of her father, who at the time was still living in Benedict Canyon while the construction proceeded.

"What's with the wallpaper?" Mayer demanded as soon as he heard. "In Boston, Massachusetts, you take wallpaper to clean dirty walls. That's what you use wallpaper for. And *you* use wallpaper in the dining room?" Edith, whose temper was as hair-trigger as her father's, hung up on him, but that evening when she and her husband arrived for dinner, he greeted her effusively and told her she could do whatever she liked to the house. "Yudele, Yudele," he said, using his nickname for her. "You know what you can do? You can use wallpaper over the entire house." Edith agreed to oversee the decorating, but on one condition: that he not set foot in the house until she finished.

Mayer had trained his daughters well, and Edith, essentially a professional wife and hostess, had impeccable taste. She redid everything, putting up her wallpaper, repainting the walls, coordinating the furniture. Then, at dusk one winter's day, Edith invited her father to the house for its unveiling. "I sat in the living room. And the candles were lit in the dining room. The whole effect. It was a performance. He came in the living room and he was crying like a child." For Mayer, it was the fulfillment of a life aestheticized, though not everyone saw it that way. For his grandson Danny Selznick, it was aestheticized but also depersonalized—not so much an extension of his grandfather as a camouflage of him.

Yet some of the essential Mayer, the Jewish junkman from Russia, still peeked through the decoration. In his library, prominently displayed in silver-and-leather frames, were photographs of his friends Cardinal Spellman, Herbert Hoover, and K. T. Keller, the chairman of the board of the Chrysler Corporation—the parvenu's symbols of having arrived. And on the walls, in virtually every room, were other signs of the parvenu: paintings by Mayer's favorite artist, Grandma Moses. "Her paintings are life," he said.

Settled in his new house with his new family, Mayer was once again what he most liked to be, a patriarch, which in practice meant that Lorena and Suzanne had to surrender to his authority just as Maggie, Edith, and Irene had had to do. For Lorena, who was even-tempered and submissive, this was sufferable. The real stress fell on

Mayer's poor, baffled adopted daughter, Suzanne. The problem was that Mayer, at sixty, remained a Victorian. "The degree of strictness!" Danny Selznick recalled. "I mean, I could go out on a date with her. I was acceptable companionship for her. . . . Suzanne and I had something called the Wednesday Afternoon Swimming Club, which was kind of a joke between us. I would bring over a friend of mine, male or female—sometimes two—for swimming and lunch on the patio every Wednesday afternoon. But if I wanted to go out at night, let's say I thought it would be fun to have a double date, Grandpa would say, 'Well, who is this boy? Who's his father?' There was a fairly intense screening process of anybody. If somebody wanted to take Suzanne out, he would say, 'Well, I'll place the limousine at their disposal.' This is fine when you're thirteen or fourteen, but when you're fifteen or sixteen, you can drive in California, and I'd say, 'Grandpa, they want to pick her up in his car.' He'd say, 'I'm not trusting this boy to go out with Suzanne. Frank [his chauffeur] will take them in the Chrysler.'"

Suzanne tried to conform to her stepfather's image of her, just as Edith and Irene had, but it was an exacting performance for a teenage girl in the fifties. "Suzie found her situation confusing," wrote Irene Selznick. "Her mother, inclined to flatter, kept telling her to do as she herself did—say yes to my father, always smile and be affectionate. My father told her to pattern herself after me. I told her to be herself and never say what she didn't mean." Suzie finally took a different course of action entirely. She decided to become the one thing her stepfather had really trained her for: a nun.

Meanwhile Maggie Mayer, Louis's ex-wife, was suffering her own form of coventry at the beach house they had built together. Quiet to the point of self-effacement, she stayed at the house, occasionally entertaining close friends, but mainly keeping to herself, her solitude made somehow more poignant by her proximity to the sea. And she dreamed. She dreamed that Mayer might someday realize his mistake and return to her. She never voiced it that way. In fact, *she* never talked about him at all—she didn't even have a picture of him in her home—but she would ask her grandchildren how he was, what he did, how his new home was decorated, what kind of reception he gave them at the studio, whether they liked his new wife—a stream of questions the purpose of which was unmistakable.

Pathetic as these interrogations were, there was something even more pathetic. She decided to reconstruct her face through plastic surgery. "She was a beautiful woman," Danny Selznick recalled. "She didn't need to have anything done to her nose or her chins or anything else. . . . I didn't understand it. The only way I could justify it was that on some subconscious level, she was hoping to get him back, I think, or hoping to have him realize that he still loved her." What was worse, the operation had gone badly. Nothing seemed to be quite right, and with her nose covered in ointments, her chin botched, and her eyes eerily magnified by her bifocals, she retreated even more deeply into herself. The last vestige of her husband's past, the remnant of the days before he had become a great man, she had aestheticized herself out of existence.

It almost seemed a rite of passage for the Hollywood Jew. Like Mayer, Harry Cohn had married his young gentile wife, fathered a family, moved into a mansion—his in Beverly Hills, across the street from the Beverly Hills Hotel—and fended off threats to his empire from those who believed he was aging and vulnerable. But Cohn could never settle comfortably into his dotage. His family was a prerogative of his power rather than a solace—perhaps he felt being too intimate with one's family exposed a weakness—and he was restless and lonely.

"He was looking for a fellow like me to be his confidant," admitted Jonie Taps, a successful music publisher from the rougher precincts of New York. Taps, a squattish man who talked with a Runyonesque twang, was unpolished and unaffected. Cohn obviously felt comfortable with him and brought him out to Columbia's music department, where he became, in effect, Cohn's Sancho Panza. "We had a switchboard that went twenty-four hours a day. No matter where I went I had to notify the switchboard where I was at because he changed my contract to twenty-four hours a day. And I was glad. I didn't care."

Joan Perry Cohn suspected Taps of being her husband's procurer. In reality he was more like Cohn's beard, lending Cohn his apartment for trysts and then covering for him, though Taps was also likely to accompany Cohn on his womanizing jaunts. Cohn loved Las Vegas.

In its gaudy vulgarity, its naked greed, its noise, its lights, its action, and its women, Vegas was his kind of city, and he would visit frequently, sometimes every weekend, with Taps as his companion. "Harry Cohn was a player with women. There was no doubt about it," Taps recalled. On one typical foray Taps had been introduced to "the most beautiful girl in the line at the El Rancho," which was owned by Beldon Katleman, the husband of Cohn's niece. "After the two o'clock show we went out. . . . This girl had on a gray mink stole that you couldn't miss. We got back to the bungalows, she took off her mink stole and threw it over the dining room table, and we ended up in the bedroom. The telephone rings. It's Harry Cohn." Cohn, on his way back to his room, had spotted the mink through the window and reprimanded Taps for being indiscreet. Taps snapped that he wasn't married, saw no reason to be discreet, and hung up.

The next morning Cohn asked Taps if he could take the girl out himself that night. Taps said he didn't mind. "So that day he did something extraordinary. He gave her chips to play with. He bought her stockings. He bought her a dress. This was not his usual way, but she was so beautiful." Then that night, again after the last show, Cohn propositioned her, but engaging in a kind of sexual one-up-manship with Taps, he decided he wouldn't take her back to the bungalow. He'd heard she had a house a few miles out in the desert, and he suggested they go there. Katleman's deputy drove them, and when they arrived Cohn dismissed the car. What the woman hadn't divulged was that she lived with her mother and young son. Cohn politely excused himself and asked her to call him a cab, but the woman didn't have a phone. "How did you get home?" Taps asked him the next morning when Cohn recounted his adventure. "Did you see It Happened One Night—with the thumb, hitching the ride?" Cohn answered. That was how he'd done it.

These were dalliances—little conquests to demonstrate his prowess and indulge his appetites. But there was in this period one serious affair of the heart. He first saw her at Lindy's in New York escorted by a dress manufacturer named Sam Chapman and immediately pronounced her the most beautiful woman he had ever seen. Cohn had come to New York for a board of directors meeting and to attend the premiere of Desiree, a costume epic starring Marlon Brando as Napoleon. Rita Hayworth was supposed to accompany him to the premiere, but she and Cohn had another of their stormy rows, and now the mysterious girl with Sam Chapman started entering his conversations.

Taps, taking the hint, phoned Chapman and discovered she was a high-fashion model from England who was staying at the Plaza Hotel during a shoot. Taps also got Chapman to ask her if she would attend the premiere with Cohn, and she agreed. "The next few days he saw this girl day and night," Taps recalled. "In front of me that's all I saw." Two weeks later Taps and Cohn were deplaning in Las Vegas for another of their revels. The fashion model greeted them at the airport. "You son of a bitch!" Taps gasped.

Back in Hollywood, Cohn installed the model at the Beverly Hills Hotel a few minutes' from his home. Each night he would tell his wife he was going for a walk to get the newspapers, when in actuality he was visiting the model's bungalow. One evening he called Taps into his office, and there were tears in his eyes. The model had issued an ultimatum: either he married her or she would return to England. As Taps told it, Cohn begged him to intercede and convince her to stay.

Later that night Taps took her to dinner. He handed her an airplane ticket to London and one thousand dollars cash and told her that Cohn wanted her to return to England. Taps took her to the airport that same night. Meanwhile, Cohn was waiting at the Polo Lounge to hear whether Taps had succeeded in persuading her to continue the arrangement. "She's on her way back to England," Taps said. Cohn was stunned. "What do you mean?" Taps explained that he had, on his own initiative, sent her back, believing it was the only way to save Cohn's marriage and family. Furious, Cohn stormed out of the restaurant. It was three months before he spoke to Taps again.

There was to be one more doomed affair of the heart in this period, but this was love of a much different order. Cohn adored Sidney Buchman. Movie star handsome, Buchman was an erudite screenwriter from Minnesota who had attended Columbia University and then Oxford, staying on in England to work as assistant stage manager at the Old Vic. Back in New York he began playwrighting in earnest and, like so many moderately successful dramatists, wound up in Hollywood in 1930 as a contract writer for Paramount. In 1934, when Cohn was conducting one of his periodic talent searches, Buchman, then thirty-two, moved to Columbia. He would stay until that fateful day in 1951 when everything collapsed.

At first blush Buchman may have seemed an unlikely compatriot for Cohn. Well spoken, well educated, fiercely intelligent, highly political, he seemed the sort of man Cohn usually excoriated. But Buchman wasn't only an extremely capable writer; he was also confident and combative, and he understood, as perhaps only Frank Capra did, how to win Cohn's respect. Buchman's secret was that he never capitulated, while at the same time he never got himself drawn in to Cohn's style of combat. He was unswerving but also temperate and reasonable—the only one who wasn't either cowed or belligerent. Cohn would enter the dining room and immediately badger his writers, demanding to know what each had done to earn his bread. Most fumbled. Buchman said wearily, "I'm too tired to play games, Harry. Drop it." No one, save Capra, talked to Cohn that way.

Buchman's name adorned some of the smartest comedies of the thirties and forties—*Theodora Goes Wild, Holiday, Mr. Smith Goes to Washington, Here Comes Mr. Jordan, Talk of the Town*—and Cohn frequently used him as a troubleshooter on pictures Buchman didn't write. In time he became a producer and then a production executive, eventually second in command to Cohn himself on creative matters. But while he was rising through the ranks of Columbia, he was also ascending through the political sphere of Hollywood. He was a charter member of the Screen Writers Guild at a time when executives were threatening its members with dismissal, and during the war, he was its president. He was a founding member of the Motion Picture Guild, Inc., a loose confederation of left-wing filmmakers that pledged to make socially conscious documentaries. He was active in the Hollywood Democratic Committee, which endorsed and worked for progressive candidates. Later, he was a vocal opponent of the conservative Motion Picture Alliance for the Preservation of American Ideals, and he publicly denounced HUAC.

Among all his other activities, Buchman also happened to be a member of the Communist party. On September 21, 1951, he appeared before HUAC in Los Angeles. Cohn was shattered. "Harry would have protected Sidney Buchman with his life," Jonie Taps averred, and certainly Buchman's situation was one reason why Cohn, who otherwise hadn't shown himself to be a civil libertarian, privately groused about HUAC and questioned its constitutionality. For nearly three hours Buchman testified, freely admitting to his own membership in the Party but refusing to implicate others or to invoke the Fifth Amendment. Ordinarily Buchman would have been found in contempt, but before he could be cited one of the interrogating congressmen, Ronald Jackson of California, suddenly left the hearing room. With his departure the quorum had vanished, and Buchman was spared. Many believed it had all been engineered by Cohn, though Buchman had explicitly asked him not to interfere.

If Cohn had, it was only a temporary expedient. Four months later Buchman was subpoenaed once again. This time he chose to fight the subpoena in court, claiming he was being harassed. Twice the courts refused to quash it, so Buchman simply refused to appear. This time the House did vote him in contempt, 314–0. He was convicted on March 12, 1953, fined $150, and given a suspended one-year sentence. His days at Columbia, however, were finished. Blacklisted, unable to find work in Hollywood, he ran a car park for a time, then left for Europe, where a decade later he was finally able to return to films. Cohn never blamed Buchman for being a Communist. He blamed Columbia's New York executives for not letting him work.

For Cohn, Buchman's leave-taking was a painful loss. He had lost more than his most valued friend and heir apparent; he was beginning to lose the sense that his world could be bent to his will—the sense that had driven so many of the Hollywood Jews, but especially Cohn. Things weren't the way they once were. The empires were getting soft and shapeless. Cohn's response was to tighten his circle once again. Now his intimates were Taps, Nate Spingold of Columbia's New York office, and Lillian Burns and George Sidney, a husband-and-wife team—he a producer/director and, ironically, the son of the man who headed Mayer's blacklisting unit, she a former drama coach and now Cohn's executive assistant. Stationed almost nightly in Cohn's cavernous bedroom, where he liked to work, they kept watch with him as it all began to slip away—not, as he had always feared, because it was being pulled from him, but because he was now too old, too tired, and the world too complex for him to defend it.

Families for solace. Families for display. Families as a demonstration of gentility and status. Smiling Jack Warner had always regarded his family as something else—a threat, an intrusion, a burden, perhaps most of all an entanglement. Warner hated emotional involvement. "I've had self-searching sessions, thinking back to him and remembering my trying to open up areas of warmth and closeness," said his son, Jack Jr., "and finding that it was very, very difficult. Maybe I saw too many Andy Hardy movies. You couldn't handle him like the old judge. . . . He didn't throw many compliments to me. It's funny. I think he was proud [of Jack Jr.'s education]. I did very well. I graduated with honors. . . . But he wouldn't express it to me. To others. Then it got back to me. That was part of his nature. You know, you compliment an actor and right away he'll want a raise. You compliment your son and you don't know what he's going to want, so you don't compliment him."

Part of the estrangement from Jack Jr. was that the son was a living indictment from Jack's first marriage, which had ended in a swirl of anger and accusation. Humiliated that her husband was living openly with another woman, the first Mrs. Warner relinquished her bitterness very slowly, and, whether she passed it on to her son or not, Jack always regarded him slightly askance. When Jack Jr. returned from service after World War II as a major in the Army Signal Corps, it was actually the new Mrs. Warner who invited him to stay in their home, hoping to reach some accommodation, but all three were uncomfortable, and he returned to his mother's home the next day.

Out at the studio in Burbank, Jack Jr. became an assistant director on the back lot, far from the center of power. He was diligent and knowledgeable about cameras and anything but arrogant, but in his father's eyes that was a sign of weakness that disqualified him for consideration as a possible successor. "The trouble with Jackie is that he doesn't have any balls," Jack told associates. When he married a woman of whom his father disapproved—ironically, given Warner's experience with his brother Harry's denunciation of Jack's own marriage—Jackie was furloughed to the Warners' office in London. Unhappy there, he was shifted back again—this time to the documentary unit, where he seemed to fritter his time away in nepotistic exile.

Warner's daughter, Barbara, progeny of his second marriage, was more a chip off the old block, though that made her no less the subject of his disapprobation. Rebellious, spirited, and irresponsible, she had been packed off to a Swiss boarding school to little apparent effect. Eventually she graduated from the Spence School in New York and then attended Sarah Lawrence. After college she spent most of her time in Europe, living gaily in the company of socialites and scamps. One of the latter was an Englishman named Michael Caborn-Waterfield. Friends called him "Dandy Kim." During a party at her father's Riviera home, Kim blackmailed Barbara into helping him find the keys to the safe on threat of telling Warner "everything about what happened last year." (Kim fled prosecution but was arrested seven years later by Scotland Yard.) Meanwhile, Barbara married Claude Terrail, owner of the famous Tour D'Argent restaurant in Paris.

With Barbara in Paris and Jack Jr. exiled at the studio, Jack was comfortably unencumbered of responsibility. Jack's brother Harry took a different attitude entirely. By the mid-forties he had decided to move to California from New York, partly to be closer to the studio, but primarily to be closer to his daughters. Even being in the same city didn't prove close enough for him. He purchased a large tract of land out in the San Fernando Valley, where he tried to actualize the patriarchal dreams Dore Schary's father had harbored. Around his own home, he built homes for his children. They, however, refused to move, and Harry lived there as a kind of Hollywood King Lear.

Of course everyone in Hollywood knew that Harry Warner took the same patriarchal attitude toward his younger brother, Jack, and everyone knew how deeply Jack resented it. Though it may have been true of Jack that, to paraphrase Gertrude Stein, there was no underneath underneath, there seemed to be one hidden agenda to his life: to avenge himself on his brother and assert his independence. Harry seemed oblivious to the depth of Jack's hostility, preferring to believe in the strength of family to heal breaches or in his own power to influence Jack. As a sign of their mutual trust, the brothers—Abe, Harry, and Jack—had even made a gentleman's agreement. None of them would sell their shares in Warner Brothers unless all decided to sell.

Selling out had become an option because Warner Brothers, assaulted as every studio was in the late forties and fifties, by the divestiture of its theaters under the consent decrees, by the competition of television, and by the rise of independent production, was seeing its profits decline dramatically.* For someone like Louis Mayer, whose life was virtually inextricable from the company he built, voluntary retirement was impossible. But Major Abe Warner had already retreated from an active role in the company and settled in Florida, and in 1953, when the discussions to sell became serious, Harry was in his seventies and disengaging himself from the studio's affairs. One deal to sell the company had apparently even been concluded, then was abruptly canceled when Harry learned Jack intended to breach their agreement and renege on the sale of his own shares.

Jack did finally get his revenge. Three years later the brothers sold their interest in Warner Brothers to a syndicate organized by the First National Bank of Boston. Jack, however, had made a prior arrangement to buy back his shares and keep his title—at least, that is what Harry believed. "I've got the old bastard by the balls at last," Jack reportedly told another executive after the coup. "He can't do a goddamn thing." The brothers never spoke to one another again after the buyout. "The treachery really killed Harry," said his son-in-law, Milton Sperling. Shortly after the sale, as in a bad melodrama, he suffered a severe stroke. He died two years later on July 27, 1958. Rabbi Magnin officiated at his funeral, and one thousand mourners attended.

Jack Warner wasn't one of them. "Jack had just gone over to the south of France—just like two days before [Harry's death]," recalled

---

*Roosevelt's Attorney General, Thurman Arnold, invoking the Anti-Trust Act, had pressured the studios to peel off their theater holdings back in the late thirties, but the studios refused. Now, nearly a decade later, having already been ruled a monopoly by the Supreme Court in May 1948, and realizing it was fighting a losing battle, the industry finally agreed to a series of consent decrees, the effect of which was to divorce production and distribution from exhibition. The grand scheme Zukor had engineered back in the twenties had been wrecked on the shoals of its own ambition: to control the industry.

William Schaefer, Jack Warner's executive assistant. "Now he knew his brother was quite ill, but there was this thing. And so he never made any bones about coming back." A week later, returning at 2:00 A.M. from a long gambling session in Cannes, Warner smashed into a truck. The car bounced off the truck and flew off the road, where it burst into flame. Warner was thrown forty feet. His condition was critical.

"I think I'm going to go over to see my father. I think I should," Jack Jr. told William Schaefer, evidently looking for encouragement before flying to France. But at the hospital in Cannes, Jack Jr. committed one gaffe by not paying his respects to Ann Warner before visiting his father and committed another when he gave reporters the impression that his father would not survive. Jack Warner did recover, and he was enraged by the reports of his imminent death—perhaps because he imputed an element of wish fulfillment or perhaps because he wanted a pretext for ending the intimacy. (It was extraordinary how much of his relationship with Harry, his own father figure, he would reenact with his son.) When Jack returned to Hollywood three months later, he had his attorney dismiss Jack Jr. from the studio. Over the next twenty years they barely spoke to or saw one another, and Warner saw one of his grandchildren only when he and his son happened to cross paths at a doctor's office.

As for his injury, Jack recuperated for a year and then reassumed his role as studio boss, but he was no longer presiding over a studio in his image. Production was down, the contract players were gone, the efficient studio system of the thirties and forties was now obsolete—a casualty of fewer films, higher costs, and greater independence among the creative people. The studio monarch was obsolete, too, and Jack kept looking for scapegoats. He blasted the independent producer, "who goes from studio to studio, or works in his home" and whose "stake is only in a single motion picture" rather than the studio, but he was whistling in the wind. At a Screen Producers Guild dinner, he lashed out at movie critics, calling them "downbeat bums," and issued a call to arms against the press generally. "It is high time that we in the film industry struck back. No one strikes back except me." When he finished, the master of ceremonies, George Jessel, asked, "How the hell did you become the head of a great studio?" The audience applauded, shouted, and rapped its silverware against its goblets.

Like Mayer and Cohn and the other old Hollywood Jews, Warner had become an anachronism from a time when the studio *was* an instrument to translate the Jews' yearnings into film and to create a kind of psychological *lebensraum* for themselves. But postwar Hollywood was like the South after the Civil War—the plantations wasted, the slaves emancipated, a way of life gone forever. In 1966 Warner sold his own interest to a holding company called Seven Arts, Limited, for $32 million. No longer head of the studio, he nevertheless remained on the lot, meeting friends and planning productions of his own. He produced two films—*Dirty Little Billy* about Billy the Kid and *1776*, adapted from the Broadway musical about the drafting of the Declaration of Independence—but neither was a success. "From the old Warners people there was certainly a lot of deference," remembered William Schaefer, who remained as his assistant. "But the Seven Arts people—they just practically ignored you. I think it [galled him], but he didn't show it. It was amazing how he could hide his personal feelings." Two years later he left the Warners lot for good and set up in a suite in Century City.

From there, one last battle was to be launched. Jack had gotten it into his head that he was going to be a Broadway producer and he had selected as his vehicle a lavish musical based on the life of flashy New York mayor Jimmy Walker. From the outset it was a folly. Budgeted at well over $1 million, it too failed—its director pleaded with Warner to close it out of town and spare them all the embarrassment—and Warner, bankrolling it for several weeks for appearance's sake, finally retired—not so much chastened, for it was impossible to chasten him, as unconcerned. For him it had never been a matter of proving himself, as it was for so many of the Hollywood Jews; it had always been a matter of demonstrating how little he cared what anyone thought.

His dotage consisted mainly of gambling and playing tennis, which even at eighty was a passion. One afternoon in 1974, during a game, he tripped, fell, and struck the court, cracking his sternum. This time, he never did fully recover. Disoriented and bedridden, he died on September 9, 1978, like his brother Harry, of a stroke. His son, who wasn't permitted to visit him during the final illness, was invited to the funeral.

———

"How could he pick Dore Schary over me?" Louis B. Mayer would ask, less with incredulity than with anger at Nick Schenck. But Schenck, at least in Mayer's view, had. In 1951, while Schary was vacationing with his family in Boca Raton, Florida, Schenck, who had a vacation home in Miami, suggested they get together. Schenck was obviously pleased. In the three years since Schary's ascendancy, MGM had improved its performance markedly, and now he was about to be rewarded. Over lunch Schenck offered to extend his contract another six years. More, he offered him stock options in the company. Schenck told him that Mayer had concurred in all of this but that Schenck had reserved the right to tell Schary the news.

"What would you do if you were me and you wanted or had to retire? Be honest," Mayer asked Schary back in Hollywood, the implications of the new contract clear. Schary waved off answering, but Mayer persisted. Reluctantly Schary suggested he would travel, write, set up a foundation, possibly establish a fund for needy individuals in the film industry. Mayer scoffed, calling Schary a *kabtzen*—Yiddish for peasant—for suggesting he be humble. "Nobody gave me anything. Screw the company and screw the stockholders." Schary chalked it up to Mayer's wounded pride at no longer being the sole authority at the studio.

A few months later, in the spring of 1951, Schary was again in Mayer's office for some routine matters when the phone rang and Mayer answered. Listening, Mayer fixed his eyes sternly on Schary, who from the salutation assumed the caller was Robert Rubin, MGM's counsel and an associate of Mayer's since the Alco days. "I have no intention of talking to Nick Schenck," Mayer said. There was a pause while Mayer listened. "Never, Bob, never. You can tell Mr. Nicholas Schenck that he and Dore Schary can take the studio and choke on it." Schary stood there dumbfounded. "Sit down and I'll tell you everything, you little kike," Mayer commanded. But Schary was already out of the office and on his way to call his attorney and Schenck.

Schenck tried to mollify him, asking him to return to Mayer's office and see if he could reach some kind of accommodation with him. Schary, always conciliatory, agreed, but Mayer again lacerated him, and Schary said, "L.B., I've been through this before, and you're too old a man for me to fight with. I'm leaving." Still uncertain what was transpiring between Schenck and Mayer, Schary decided to go home. The next morning Mayer announced his resignation from MGM. He promised that his career would resume "at a studio and under conditions where I shall have the right to make the right kind of pictures—decent, wholesome pictures for Americans and for people throughout the world who want and need this type of entertainment."

For Schenck it had always been a matter of power. For Mayer it was something much deeper—a matter of morality, really. What he was fighting for was not just whether he or Schary made the movies, not just whether Schenck placed the balance of power on his or Schary's side. Mayer was fighting for his vision of the world, fully realizing it was rapidly fading. Schary was simply the symbol of the forces that threatened it. "Schary had become the message maker," recalled producer Pandro Berman. "He was more than most of us determined to make messages on the screen. We were all doing it, but he lived for it. And Mayer was not the message man. That's where the tensions really were." "I know what the audience wants," Mayer told a reporter shortly before his resignation, sneering at Schary's liberal realism. "Andy Hardy. Sentimentality! What's wrong with it? Love! Good old-fashioned romance. Is it bad? It entertains. It brings the audience to the box office."

Two days after the resignation, the MGM brass met in Chicago, midway between the East and West, to chart the company's course without Mayer. Afterward, Schenck asked them to leave the room so he could have a word with Schary. "He showed me a letter Mayer had written him in which Mayer had laid it on the line that he was tired of Dore Schary usurping authority and getting credit for his work, and that Schenck had to make up his mind: it was either Mayer or Schary. Then he showed me his response, which was that he had gone over the records, and if Mayer was forcing a flat choice, he just had to opt for Schary." Schary protested that if he had known, he might have been able to pacify the old man. "No," Schenck said, "that was impossible because he doesn't like you." So Mayer had left the studio he had created and loved.

Louis B. Mayer in exile was like Napoleon on Elba. At first he had planned to become an independent producer. He purchased the film rights to the musical *Paint Your Wagon* and had commissioned a script for a movie of Joseph and his brethren, but he hadn't really produced films since his days with Anita Stewart, and he didn't really have the temperament to supervise logistics. He was a weaver of dreams, an orchestrator, a facilitator, an agenda setter. None of these plans bore fruit. There was also a rumor that he would take over Warner Brothers when Abe, Harry, and Jack were negotiating a sale, but this was aborted, too. A year later he was offered a position in a company promoting a new widescreen process called Cinerama. He accepted, but the process never moved beyond novelty, and he wound up settling his contract for a substantial sum.

For a time horses piqued his interest again. In 1947 he had auctioned all his thoroughbreds to satisfy his divorce settlement with Maggie and had sold his beloved ranch to the Mormon church.* A few months after leaving MGM, he purchased $300,000 worth of yearlings, which he boarded in Kentucky, and in September he bought a piece of Joe Schenck's share in the Del Mar Turf Club. But even here there wasn't quite the same zeal as before. Without his studio he was a lost, forlorn man—"like Knute Rockne without a football team to coach," observed David Selznick, his former son-in-law. "Maybe he felt he could not associate with the big men of other industries without a big position of his own."

"Once he left MGM," remembered Danny Selznick, "loneliness became a theme in his life again because he didn't have the same degree of friends, the same degree of social activity, and so, again, you were aware of the loneliness. It immediately manifested itself in his restlessness. He would pace. Watch television. Get up from the television set. Sit back down in front of the television. Since his

---

*Of the auction, Ned Cronin of the *Los Angeles Times* wrote, "Mayer sat there quietly, with his head down, listening intently to the singsong bedlam of the auctioneer's voice. He lifted his head once in a while to gaze down upon the platinum glow of spotlights where his horses were going under the hammer. . . . His eyes were mirrored with mist." (Quoted in Humphrey S. Finney with Raleigh Burroughs, *Fair Exchange: Recollections of a Life with Horses* [New York, 1974], p. 54.)

emotions... were on the surface, you'd see it in an instant. Other people would be able to disguise their loneliness cleverly. With him, whatever he was feeling was always evident." Writer Daniel Fuchs remembered seeing him at a party, "idling by himself on the fringes now, no one any longer obligated to listen to him." Lillian Burns brought Fuchs over to introduce him to Mayer and mentioned that he had written a film of the realistic, unsentimentalized sort Mayer despised. He "instantly took his hand back, turned on his heel, and stalked off, still haughty, still fierce, indomitable."

His wife, Lorena, bore the brunt of his frustration, suffering such verbal abuse that his daughters and grandsons tried to intercede in her behalf. "I stayed with him for three weeks," recalled Danny Selznick. "I'm glad I had the experience of really seeing, in a sense, the real man, because obviously I had put him on a pedestal. I suppose I learned painfully the price of being a Louis B. Mayer without the support system." The relationship with his daughters also took a strange turn, as if they had to compensate him for the loss of his beloved studio family. Mayer tested them—tested their loyalty. Irene, who had divorced David Selznick shortly after her parents' separation and had since become a successful Broadway producer, passed. Without another man in her life, her father could always claim primacy. Edith didn't.

She claimed it began back in the thirties after she had married William Goetz. Goetz was a voluble young producer with a reputation for bawdy wit that hardly endeared him to his prudish father-in-law—later, Edith claimed, Goetz had only to speak to set her father laughing—but even if he had been genteel, Mayer would have regarded him, as he was to regard his other son-in-law, David Selznick, as a rival trying to displace him in his daughter's affections. Like a jealous suitor, Mayer apparently thought he could reestablish himself as the primum mobile of his daughters' lives by subjugating their husbands, and he tried. With Thalberg gone he asked Goetz to come work for him, but Goetz refused, and Mayer took it as an affront. "Snoogie, did you turn down an offer from Dad?" Edith asked her husband after a dinner at which her father pressured her to get him to change his mind. Goetz said he had. "The first thing I would do is fire your father. You wouldn't like that, would you?" So Goetz followed his own course, eventually becoming head of production at

Universal-International and then a successful independent producer.

They had a second run-in over horses. Mayer had bred a three-year-old named Your Host, which was an early favorite for the 1950 Kentucky Derby. Since he had liquidated his own stable, however, he ran the horse under Goetz's colors. As Irene told it, Goetz ignored Mayer's advice on how to train the horse, and though it went into the Derby at eight to five, Mayer wasn't optimistic about its prospects. When it faded badly and finished ninth, as he had predicted, he phoned Goetz and blamed him for dashing the dreams for a Derby victory. Seizing the phone, Edith came to her husband's defense—she admitted that, like her father, she would "fight like a tigress for her family"—then slammed down the receiver.

The final breach came two years later, after Mayer had left MGM. Goetz was a liberal Democrat and a champion of the Democratic presidential candidate, Adlai Stevenson. (Mayer, of course, found all Democrats anathema.) Dore Schary was another Stevenson activist, and he called Goetz asking if they could stage a reception at his house. According to his wife, Goetz tried begging off. "I no way want to hurt the old man." Nevertheless, when the party proceeded with Goetz and Schary as co-hosts, Mayer felt hurt and betrayed that his son-in-law would collaborate with the enemy.

"I got word: Dad was upset with me, upset with me, upset with me, and I have to call," remembered Edith. "So I called . . . and boy, did I yell. He said, 'I don't want you to turn your face away from me.' And I said, 'You're committing a cardinal sin. You'd like me to divorce him, wouldn't you? I have something to tell you. I've lived longer with him than I have with you, and there's no way that I'll ever divorce this man. Remember that.' So finally he says, 'All right, then. When we're out, you turn your face away.' I said, 'If that's the way you want it, good-bye.' And I hear, 'Yudele! Yudele!'" Edith hung up. Lorena would call pleading with her to apologize. He couldn't sleep, she said. His hands were outstretched for her. But Edith, who was incensed that her father, in an intemperate moment, had called Goetz a Communist, felt Mayer should be the one to apologize. He never did. He couldn't.

Both realized that the jobs, the horses, the politics, important as these all were to Mayer, were really a pretext for the deeper issue: love. He needed it—not only because he had been abandoned, but because love validated his domestic vision of America. Mayer often shared confidences with a Russian-born endocrinologist named Jessie Marmorston, whom he had met back in the forties and who was widely reputed to be Mayer's unofficial psychoanalyst. (He would have never gone to a real psychiatrist.) "He couldn't really love anybody," Marmorston told Edith after his death, "but you belonged to him. He created you, and you were an obsession with him." And when she chose Goetz over him, as she had to do, he had much the same reaction as when Schenck chose Schary over him. Her name was never again to be mentioned in his presence.

Mayer could never contain his feelings; he needed something to magnify them, which was one reason he created the studio. Without the studio Mayer's personal disappointments now found an extraordinarily apt political channel—one that seemed to project his own frustrations on a national screen. Wisconsin Senator Joseph McCarthy was Mayer's kind of man. Young, dramatic, Catholic, and conservative, he subscribed to the same pieties as Mayer, and when McCarthy launched a campaign to purge the government of Communists in 1950, Mayer became a fervent supporter. In April 1954, with McCarthy making headlines, Mayer returned to Haverhill, Massachusetts, where his film career had begun, for a Chamber of Commerce dinner honoring him. "The more McCarthy yells, the better I like him," he told the group. "He's doing a job to get rid of the 'termites' eating away at our democracy. . . . I hope he drives all the bums back to Moscow. That's the place for them." McCarthy's opponents were all "leftists," and he expressed the wish that "there was some way we could give every American a trial of Communism. I wish it would be like running water, and we could turn the faucet on for about thirty days and then turn it off and go back to our American way."

God was the answer. "If children get a love of God in their hearts they'll keep that love through their lives. Why is it that there are so few Catholic converts to Communism?" he asked his audience. "It is because they learned the love of God when they were children. Why don't Jews and Protestants do the same thing?"

He gave the same harangues to his family and friends. "I remember L. B. Mayer coming up to me early on, while the witch-hunts were at their peak, and telling me that he thought Joe McCarthy was one of the greatest men of our time," wrote director John Huston. "Then he looked at me speculatively. 'John,' he said, 'you've done documentaries. . . . How about doing one that is a tribute to McCarthy.'" Huston, an ardent liberal, laughed. "L. B., you're out of your God-damned mind!"

"I'm sorry to have to say he saw it [McCarthyism] in incredibly oversimplified terms," said Danny Selznick, who was about to attend Harvard University, which his grandfather regarded as a hotbed of subversion. "He was very angry at anyone who deviated from the party line—the Republican party line and finally the McCarthy party line. . . . I was really quite horrified to learn that he had personally supported Joe McCarthy, had sent money to Joe McCarthy. . . . But he really felt that if you didn't understand *his* point of view about this, you were not loyal to your country."

But however much he invoked it—and he invoked it frequently— patriotism wasn't really the point, either. As in his blowout with Schary, the point was loyalty to a certain kind of world—the world of Andy Hardy and Homer Macauley, the world of homespun truths, strong families, beloved mothers, and virtuous children, the world of religion and high morals. In the end, it was this world, *his* world, that he was trying to protect from the leftists, freethinkers, cynics, and realists who were already destroying it. McCarthy was just another stalwart trying to hold the line against these modern demons. In the end, they would both lose.

Though it was a purveyor of sentiment, Hollywood itself was, as Mayer learned, a notoriously unsentimental place. When one had fallen from power, he inevitably fell from grace as well, banished and forgotten. It happened to virtually all the Hollywood Jews. Luckier than most, Carl Laemmle, who had fought the Edison Trust and founded Universal, had taken what he called a "permanent vacation" after selling out in 1936. With a fortune estimated at $4 million, he spent his time dandling his grandchildren, playing cards, and betting at the races. On September 23, 1939, he went for a drive to escape the suffocating heat. When he returned he said he felt wobbly and retired to bed. The next morning he suffered the first of three heart attacks. The last, that evening, proved fatal.

As for Junior Laemmle, Carl's son, he never worked in Hollywood again. A hypochondriac of legendary proportions, he seldom left the city, believing that he would die if he didn't sleep in his own bed. "He had a shelf this big with pills," recalled a friend, "and he always had a bodyguard. It destroyed him." Another remembered that he had a dread of physical contact, instructing his barber never to touch his ears. Despite a reputation as a lady-killer, he never married. ("No woman in her right mind would be likely to marry him," admitted Sam Marx, a friend.) He lived alone in his father's mansion, where, even after he was severely disabled by a degenerative muscle disease and confined to a wheelchair, he clung to one ritual: every New Year's Day he hosted a big Rose Bowl party for a hundred or so of his cronies.

Very few of the old Hollywood Jews went into the night as gently. William Fox, who had been undone by the stock market collapse when he was on the verge of snatching MGM, vowed to regain his empire. "They formed a conspiracy to drive me out of my business," he complained to the Senate Banking and Currency Subcommittee investigating Wall Street. To which one of his alleged tormentors replied that Fox was suffering from "conspiracy hallucinations." Fox fought back. In October 1934 he won a suit against six motion picture companies, including MGM, for infringing on patents he claimed he owned for the standard optical sound process that all the studios were using for their talking pictures. "Mr. Fox is now not only in a position to fix royalties to suit himself," said one newspaper report, "but can virtually dictate to motion picture companies to admit him in active participation in their affairs." That was precisely what he had in mind. He soon announced that he would be returning to production, using movies "as an influence for good."

His victory, however, was short-lived. Six months later the Supreme Court held his patents invalid. Without them he was no longer a threat. He tried valiantly to stave off the merger of his old company Fox Pictures and Twentieth Century—a merger being engineered by the Chase National Bank, which had wrested Fox's company from him—but the attempt failed. All told, he had spent over $1 million in legal fees from 1930 to 1934. In September 1935 he received another blow: the government demanded $3.5 million in back taxes. His only recourse was to declare bankruptcy.

But Fox was, as H. L. Mencken characterized him, a "very slippery fellow." Rather than leave his bankruptcy proceedings to chance, he and his attorney decided to confer with the bankruptcy judge, J. Warren Davis. Davis listened sympathetically, but he had a problem of his own. His daughter was getting married, and he needed $15,000. Fox sent the money through his attorney. A few months later the judge had another request. Could Fox possibly loan him $12,500 more? This time Fox came personally to Philadelphia with twelve one-thousand-dollar bills folded into a newspaper. In the hallway of a building, he handed Davis the money. The government later traced five of the bills from the Philadelphia Federal Reserve to an Atlantic City bank and then to the account of Davis's daughter in Florida. Fox was charged with conspiracy to obstruct justice and defraud the government. He pleaded guilty and was sentenced to one year in prison.

On May 3, 1943, after serving five months and seventeen days of his sentence, William Fox was paroled from the Northeastern Penitentiary in Lewisburg, Pennsylvania. Though sixty-five years old and kept alive by insulin, he was far from broken. "I started with nothing and I'm not afraid to try again," he told a reporter. He had, in fact, taken an option on 1,500 acres in California and was planning to build a new studio. "He never said a word about it [jail]," said his niece Angela Fox Dunn. "I got the feeling that this man was a giant and that it was a temporary setback he was suffering. . . . Fox kept the imperial attitude to the end."

Of course the studio was never built, and Fox never did regain the stature he so desperately wanted. Weakened by a stroke, he died at Doctors Hospital in New York on May 8, 1952. One day, not long before he died, his niece was sitting at his feet as she was expected to do, and Fox, quite out of the blue, said, "Don't ever marry a gentile." Only a child, she was perplexed, but the explanation was forthcoming. "Someday he will turn on you and call you a 'dirty Jew.'" It was his own explanation for everything that had happened to him.

For Jesse Lasky, Zukor's old partner at Paramount, it wasn't a conspiracy of jealous gentiles; it was Hollywood's own cold disregard that did him in. After his ouster from Paramount in the early thirties, he tried to revive his career by becoming an independent producer, but even his single success, a film biography of World War I hero Sergeant Alvin York starring Gary Cooper, had disastrous consequences. He had claimed the profits as a capital gain, and the Internal Revenue Service disallowed it. Desperately in need of money to pay his assessment, he optioned Mrs. Caruso's biography of her husband, opera legend Enrico Caruso, and peddled it from studio to studio without success. Finally Louis Mayer, almost as a favor from one anachronism to another, agreed to assume Lasky's installments to Mrs. Caruso.

Meanwhile Howard Hughes had taken control at RKO and offered Lasky a three-picture deal including *The Great Caruso*. Ebullient at this turn of events, Lasky rushed over to Mayer with a check for $30,000 to buy back the option. Mayer, ingenuously or not, said he had to call Dore Schary for approval. ("Have to get approval from him to go to the toilet," he said.) By the time he hung up, he was in tears. Schary had made a deal with opera singer Mario Lanza and wanted to keep the property. The best Mayer could do was offer Lasky a job as co-producer at $500 a week. Lasky accepted, but it was a humiliating turn for the man who had once headed production at Hollywood's foremost studio.

"There was a big rift between the old Hollywood and the new Hollywood—Dore Schary's crowd and the moguls who were dying off," said Lasky's daughter, Betty. "I think that all the moguls, the founders and the originals, all the pioneers who were still alive, were like castoffs and treated like nobodies. . . . If you went to an important affair where you felt you should go and be seen, it would be embarrassing, almost humiliating. . . . Dore Schary would just cut Dad. He just didn't see you. He didn't speak to you. He wasn't polite. He wasn't even courteous." Lasky became a memento mori of Hollywood's fortunes. Hounded by the IRS, jobless, aging, he decided to write his memoirs. He had just finished signing copies at a hotel reception when he collapsed and was rushed to the emergency room. "Religion?" he was reportedly asked by a hospital attendant. "American," he said. Then he died.

By November 1956 Dore Schary was out. He wasn't exactly sure why, but reports had been circulating in the press for weeks that his departure was imminent, and when he confronted Joseph Vogel, who had recently been appointed Loew's president, Vogel told him it was true. He was being fired. Schary demanded some kind of explanation. Vogel produced a letter complaining about Schary's political activities in behalf of Stevenson, about alleged sexual indiscretions, about gambling with stars. "You've got enemies on the board of directors, among the stockholders, and in the studio," Vogel told him. "They don't say good things about you."

Two days later, with Schary and his attorney sitting in Vogel's office to negotiate the contract settlement, Vogel was more specific. Schary was a casualty—probably the last casualty—of the war between the first generation of Hollywood Jews and the second generation, just as he had been a beneficiary in that battle a few years before. "You see, Dore, you're strange," explained Vogel expansively in the voice of the fading old guard. "You're—an egghead. People don't understand that. Those guys on the coast, they cut you up, Dore—cut you up terribly. And then there are people here in New York—stockholders —some of the board of directors—who are your enemies." He went on, citing Schary's community work and his political activism as evidence of his peculiarity. "Joe, there's something else you might add, which makes their case even better," Schary said. "I'm also taking lessons in conversational Hebrew." According to Schary, Vogel waved his hand and said, "That's what I mean."

Vogel had never liked Schary; he told a reporter he had vowed to fire Schary some years before when he refused to show Vogel, then head of Loew's theater operations, the rough cut of a film. But the real mastermind behind the plot wasn't Vogel or even Nick Schenck, who now occupied the titular role of chairman emeritus. The real mastermind might have been Louis Mayer himself. Since Mayer's resignation—and to his profound satisfaction—MGM had not fared well. After three successful years under Schary, profits had once again declined and so had dividends, setting angry stockholders on an uneasy board of directors.

Schenck, now seventy-four, took the immediate heat. The board demanded a new president, and Schenck complied. In November 1955 he became chairman of the board, and Arthur Loew, son of the company's founder, Marcus Loew, and for years the head of the company's foreign operations, ascended to the presidency. Loew was an extremely urbane and charming individual whose career was checkered by numerous romantic imbroglios, but he had no desire to command Loew's, had accepted the position only because the board had asked him to, and within a year had tendered his resignation. Schenck, attempting to regain control, submitted the name of Charles Moskowitz, the company's longtime treasurer and a servile Schenck man. Instead the board compromised on Vogel, a former usher. Loew became chairman. Schenck was named honorary chairman—an empty title.

Watching these battles from his exile in Bel Air was Mayer. He was hardly a disinterested party. Whether he had approached them or they had approached him, Mayer had gotten himself entangled with a faction of stockholders, headed by a Canadian industrialist named Joseph Tomlinson, which was maneuvering to take control of the company. Mayer, whose reputation had been burnished since his departure, was their link with past glory and a persuasive argument for board members who had little experience with film. He became the ghostly force lurking behind the various boardroom machinations.

Schary suspected that his own dismissal was the result of Schenck trying to strike a deal with Mayer to avert a proxy fight, and Schenck nearly confirmed as much when he asked Schary to lunch shortly after the firing. Schenck told Schary he had been fired because he wouldn't listen to anyone. "I got into trouble because of you, and I'm responsible for getting you out of this studio. It was my decision," he said casually, startling Schary, who had once told a reporter that "you always know where you stand with him." But if Schenck had hoped to pacify Mayer by sacrificing Schary, he was badly mistaken. A month later Schenck himself was bounced after fifty years in the Loew's organization.

Nick Schenck had been, as John Huston put it, "the ruler of rulers. . . . Schenck never gets his picture in the papers, and he doesn't go to parties, and he avoids going out in public, but he's the *real* king of the pack." Schenck himself had been more blunt. When asked by a Senate committee whether he was "it" at Loew's, he replied in third person, "Mr. Schenck and the board of directors are responsible for it all; there is no doubt about that." With his power gone, he retired to his estate in Sands Point. In his final years he was obsessed by the idea that he was destitute, and he refused to enter the posher venues because he was certain he couldn't afford them. When he died in 1969, he was eighty-eight years old.

Back at Loew's, wrangling between the Vogel and Tomlinson factions continued, while Mayer, like de Gaulle, waited to be called. In July 1957 the invitation actually seemed imminent. While Vogel and Tomlinson were fighting to a standoff, each controlling half the board, a management consultant and the board's one swing vote, New York publisher Ogden Reid, who had been appointed by two investment houses with interests in Loew's, sounded Mayer out. Would he be interested in assuming the presidency of Loew's, Schenck's old job? Mayer, obviously flattered, agreed to take it under advisement, though by this point he had already received vindication. The next day, according to one account, Mayer told Reid he would not become president.

Theories differed as to why Mayer finally refused to take control— that he was tired of the squabbling and didn't want to have to defend his own flanks from counterattacks by Vogel; that it was never the presidency of Loew's that had really interested him, only the command of the studio in Hollywood, which was now no longer the wonderful extended family it had once been; that he realized he was too old to run the company; that it would have all been fruitless anyway. "He couldn't be happy without MGM," observed Danny Selznick about his grandfather's efforts to win control. But in the end he couldn't be happy with it either. MGM had changed irrevocably. So had Mayer.

That summer he became ill, checking into the Stanford University Hospital for an extensive battery of tests. He returned to Los Angeles, apparently without a diagnosis, but within days he was back in the hospital, this time at the UCLA Medical Center. Mayer had always been fanatical about his health—he would often get a complete physical in one city only to have the procedure repeated in another—and he told his daughter Irene that he was only there for a routine checkup. As the stay stretched into weeks, however, Mayer asked Irene to engage an eminent specialist from Harvard named Sidney

Farber, which she did. While Farber examined the case, Irene, cooking up a pretense so as not to alarm her father, came to Los Angeles herself. Consulting with his doctors the next morning, she found out he had leukemia, and that it was terminal.

Perhaps nothing so exemplified Mayer's life as the leaving of it. No one told him he was critically ill, and if he suspected anything, as surely he must have, he never mentioned it to anyone. Instead he seemed to conspire in the fiction that this episode, like so many of his MGM movies, would have a happy ending. "In unstated collaboration," Irene later wrote, "we stayed away from anything provocative. He closed his mind to all else but getting well, and conserved his energies to better endure the necessary therapies. . . . High-strung though he was, he demonstrated a self-control that I found extraordinary." Friends visited. Howard Strickling, MGM's publicity chief, kept him apprised of the latest developments in the battle for the corpse of Loew's. Lorena endured as best she could.

The only crack in the fiction was that Edith never made an appearance. Ten years before, when Mayer had suffered a serious spill from one of his horses and was listed in critical condition, Edith had sat by his bed in his darkened room. "He opened his eyes and he grabbed me and he kissed my hands," she remembered, "and he said, 'Yudele, supposing I had died. You wouldn't have me anymore.' It was the most emotional scene. I was a wreck." Now, on his deathbed, he had asked Dr. Marmorston for her, but the doctor didn't make the call, telling her years later that she didn't believe Edith could have borne it. "You'd never forget the scene," Marmorston said. "He was going to die any minute, and you would never forget that scene."

To maintain the fiction that nothing was seriously wrong with him, Irene had left for New York, but she was summoned soon after her return. Her father had taken a serious turn. By the time she arrived, he had dropped into unconsciousness. He died at half-past midnight on October 29, 1957. The funeral the next day befitted him. It was produced by David Selznick, who had offered to make all the arrangements, directed by Clarence Brown, written by Carey Wilson and John Lee Mahin, two of Mayer's favorite screenwriters, and performed by Spencer Tracy. In the organ loft where Grace Moore had sung at Thalberg's funeral, Jeanette MacDonald sang "Oh, Sweet

Mystery of Life." And Rabbi Magnin, who began by eulogizing him as the vigilant enemy of "pseudo-liberals, Reds and pinks," concluded by calling Mayer's passing "the end of an era. It is the end of a volume, not a chapter."

Harry Cohn had a premonition that he would die when he reached the age of sixty-seven. All the Cohns died at that age, he said, and when his brother Jack, then sixty-seven, died suddenly after a routine operation, Cohn's fatalism deepened. One Saturday afternoon he returned from the studio with his secretary Dona Holloway for his children's birthday party. (The boys celebrated jointly since their birthdays fell just a week apart.) "It was a beautiful day, and we had ponies and clowns and everything," Holloway recalled. "We went up in his rooms that overlooked the garden, and I was sitting at his desk waiting for him. He was standing at the window watching the kids get on and off the pony. And suddenly I realized he was crying. So I ran over to him and said, 'What's wrong?' And he said, 'It makes me sad to know that I will not live long enough to see my sons fully grown.'"

Cohn hadn't suddenly turned melodramatic. Several years before, in March 1954, he had been treated for throat cancer. Almost everyone knew why he had been hospitalized, but Cohn, like Mayer, never discussed his illness, and even his closest friends respected this. "I think he always wanted to be seen at his best," said Holloway, "and he had this image as a very strong, powerful, healthy man." In any case, after several operations he appeared to have beaten it and returned to the studio, but he was distracted, enervated, and even conciliatory— not the same man who had once struck terror in the hearts of his employees.

One example was a minor incident with Irving Briskin, a Columbia executive with whom he had less than cordial relations. Briskin despised Cohn's longtime secretary, Dona Holloway. It had reached the point where Briskin refused to enter Cohn's office because she occupied the anteroom. Finally Cohn decided to dismiss her rather than continue to fight about it. He told his friend Jonie Taps in confidence, but Taps told Briskin anyway, and Briskin informed Holloway, who naturally asked Cohn for a confirmation or denial. Cohn called Taps "every dirty name in the book" for breaking his confidence, and Taps offered his resignation. In his prime Cohn would have almost certainly accepted it, but now his eyes welled with tears. "Do me a favor," he told Taps. "Forget about it and go back to the office." Taps saw it as evidence of Cohn's decline. "I knew how sick he was, and that was the end of it."

"I certainly saw a change in those last years," said his nephew Robert, who worked at the studio, but he attributed it as much to the pressure of running Columbia in an era of uncertainty as to his health. New York kept demanding more pictures, but the studio was no longer a fiefdom where Cohn could commission his employees to make them. Like all studio heads, he now had to contend with independent producers and pricey talent. "He quieted. He slowed," said Robert Cohn. "The business was getting so tough. He couldn't turn out those pictures. It was very hard. You could see it. It was just frustration."

"Harry and I went to a board meeting in New York," related Jonie Taps, "and they aggravated him so, that in the airport he fell over. Then on the plane, he had a heart attack. They got him some oxygen because he wouldn't let them land. He was afraid the stock would go down. We radioed ahead. An ambulance was waiting for us." Again Cohn recovered, though he was, in Taps's words, "popping nitroglycerin pills like candy." Two months later he and Joan flew to Phoenix for their annual vacation at the Arizona Biltmore Hotel. He was dressing for a reception he was to host later that evening when he admitted he felt queasy. At dinner he took six nitroglycerin tablets— his prescription called for one—and Joan arranged for a wheelchair to be brought to the table. Cohn waved it off and left the dining room on his own, but his wife did cancel their reception, countermanding his wishes.

The next morning, February 27, 1958, he was carried to an ambulance and rushed to St. Joseph's Hospital. "Too tough," he told his wife, who sat beside him. "It's too tough." He died of a coronary occlusion before reaching the hospital. A memorial service was held three days later, not in a synagogue or church (Cohn was posthumously baptized at Mrs. Cohn's request because she said he had invoked the name of Christ), but on a Columbia sound stage where

1,400 camp chairs had been set up. Danny Kaye delivered the eulogy, which he had written with Clifford Odets's assistance. "Men cannot be all things to all men," he said. "They cannot, unfortunately, be all things even to themselves—but in this constant battle of man with himself, Harry emerged with a true sense of what you are and let the chips fall where they may. Harry was always himself—always."

In the early fifties, when he was the company's "grey eminence," Adolph Zukor would sit in his office in the Paramount Building and like Scheherazade unfold tales from his past. "He intrigued me because of the schizoid reputation he had," said Max Youngstein, who was a young Paramount employee at the time. "This little delicate man who looked sometimes like a tailor and sometimes like a guy whose head would explode with ideas. . . . I found out very early that, come postlunchtime, he would be sitting in his big leather chair, a kind of greenish-brown mixture—a big, old-fashioned overstuffed chair. It almost hid him because he was a rather small man. And I would very frequently—as often as I could, as a matter of fact—come back to the office, just check in, then immediately take to the intercom, saying, 'Mr. Zukor, are you in there? I'd like to see you.'"

Youngstein would ask him questions, prompting him to recall the past when he was fighting to establish Paramount and the movies. Occasionally, during the telling, Zukor would doze off for a few minutes, but he would reawaken with startlingly acute perceptions about what was currently going on in the company. "What I did see was this enormous grasp for power," Youngstein observed. "He figured that unless you controlled the whole ball of wax to the furthest extent the law permitted [you were weak]. . . I know that he was very much of the idea that softness in this business, compromising, being the nice guy, would not get you very far." He believed in conquest. "There was no dream with respect to power that was too big for him."

But by this time these were dreams from the past. Zukor was now into his eighties. In 1948 he had sold his eight-hundred-acre estate in Rockland County to a syndicate that intended to convert it into a country club, and he had relocated with his wife to the Savoy Hotel in Manhattan. "What am I doing?" he told an interviewer. "Well, I come down [to Paramount] every day. I'm here at 9:30. I attend meetings where we discuss plays, or any other policy of the company. . . . I have a great deal of pleasure in being able to study the public reaction to certain types of pictures. Then, based on that, I realize what would be a good story for the future, and I tell them and I talk about it. I don't say that they can't get along without me—maybe they could—but in the meantime, it keeps me busy three or four hours a day, and the week goes by."

Paramount's president, Barney Balaban, a conservative and rather prosaic man, treated Zukor respectfully as a reminder of the company's origins (Zukor called Balaban "the boy,"), but he was equally a testament to how much things had changed. Zukor was the last of the old Jewish buccaneers. In 1927, when Paramount was riding high and Zukor was in control, twelve of the nineteen directors on the company's board were Jewish. In 1953 two of ten were, and virtually none of the board members were movie men. The financiers and industrialists—the genteel to which the movie Jews had always aspired—had moved in. Zukor's own dreams for the movies had been realized, but in the process most of the Hollywood Jews who had shared those dreams had been displaced.

Zukor rolled on, even after his wife, Lottie, died in 1956. "She had a little closet in the hotel with an electric outlet in it, which the hotel didn't know about," remembered Zukor's son, Eugene. "And she bought herself a two-burner unit to put in there to cook on—a couple of pots and pans and things. And that's where she prepared what was to be their last supper together." She had gone out that afternoon and bought all the preparations for an old-fashioned Hungarian dinner. "And when he came home that night, she had closed the closet door. There was no aroma or anything. He said, 'Well, we ought to go out tonight.' She said, 'We've been going out so much. I'm going to surprise you.' So she set the table in the dining room with all the best dishes and everything and she marches in with the [dinner]. He said they never had such a time." The next day she suffered a stroke that ultimately proved fatal, but Eugene said his father took her death "very philosophically, because he remembered their last night together."

During his salad days, Zukor had once promised that he would outlive all his enemies, and he had. "There was barely anyone around to remember how rough and ruthless he could be," said Irene Mayer Selznick. Now, wizened and benign, the man who had been known for his implacability had become a living monument of the old Hollywood—a nostalgic artifact. Zukor enjoyed the status, but he made as few concessions to his age as he could. At ninety-three he still smoked three cigars a day, though he had been forced to surrender his daily steambath. At ninety-six he was living alone in an apartment at the Beverly Hills Hotel. At ninety-seven he was still spending two hours at the studio each day, scanning the Paramount grosses every Monday morning just as he always had. At one hundred he had moved to a high rise in Century City and hired a young housekeeper, but he shuffled out for daily lunches at the Hillcrest Country Club and then watched the afternoon bridge games. He spurned using a wheelchair. It took him ten minutes to walk the fifty yards from his apartment to the elevator, another ten minutes to walk from the Hillcrest parking lot to the dining room. He no longer attended movies, but Eugene did and would report back.

On January 7, 1973, Paramount held a gala party to celebrate Zukor's one hundredth birthday. While Zukor sat in his suite upstairs, welcoming well-wishers and dining, over twelve hundred celebrants were being entertained in the Beverly Hilton ballroom, which had been decorated as the Crystal Hall, Zukor's original theater. President Nixon awarded him the Certificate of Distinguished Achievement. Charles Bluhdorn, chairman of the board of the Gulf & Western Corporation, which had acquired Paramount, said, "Mr. Zukor exemplified the American dream." What he really exemplified, however, was the tenacity of the Hollywood Jews' dreams for respectability and their belief in the power of gentility.

At eleven-fifty, three and a half hours after the gala began, a fourteen-foot-high frosted plywood cake with one hundred candles was wheeled out, and Zukor made his appearance. "I'm very grateful for this wonderful party," he said, visibly moved. "This is the best possible medicine I could have. It will last the rest of my life." Rabbi Magnin delivered the benediction. All he said was, "Well, Moses lived to a hundred and twenty. Who knows?" Then he turned to Zukor, placed both hands on his head, and blessed him.

"He was still going strong at one hundred and one," said Eugene.

"He started to fade about one hundred and two, when things began to bother him physically. His jaw began to bother him, his teeth became loose.... This was catastrophic when he couldn't bite into a piece of steak. He had to eat mushy foods. It really made life unpleasant for him. He wouldn't complain. He just wouldn't eat, so he lost a lot of weight.... When you cease to enjoy biting into whatever your favorite morsel is, that's pretty near the end of the line. You can't live for anything else."

People still visited, and he still insisted on being presentably genteel when they did. "He was always conscious of how he looked," remembered Eugene. "He always insisted on being dressed with a tie and waistcoat. He never was seen in pajamas or a bathrobe by anybody. I never remember a day that he wasn't shaved. He went to the Hillcrest Barber Shop, and it used to kill me to think of him going there, getting into a wheelchair, getting into a car, out of the car, into a wheelchair, helped by two people into the barbershop. But he insisted on going.

"When he was right at the tail end, I'd say, 'We'll be over to see you.' He'd say, 'Well, come over at about four o'clock.' He figured everything would be taken care of. He'd be dressed. He'd be rested. And that's the way he passed on. He died in his chair, all dressed with his tie and his shirt and everything immaculate. That's the way he wanted to go."

Epilogue

All lives are metaphors. All lives resolve themselves into themes. The old Hollywood Jews created the American film industry at a certain time, in a certain place, and for certain reasons. The time passed, the place changed, the reasons no longer obtained, and the men themselves resigned and died, unable to maintain their hold on what they had devised and ultimately rendered irrelevant by it. New men, many of them Jews, came—lawyers and businessmen and talent agents with connections to the new source of power in Hollywood, the stars.

The studios have survived, though fragmented and empty: places in which others create visions rather than monarchies promulgating the visions of their rulers. Conglomerates and industrialists have assumed financial control in what amounts to a kind of vicarious assimilation for the old Hollywood Jews. MGM, after Mayer and Schary, foundered badly and was bought by Kirk Kerkorian, a hotel magnate, who auctioned its props and costumes and eventually even sold the studio grounds. Warner Brothers was gobbled first by Seven Arts and then by the Kinney Company, a parking lot conglomerate that later changed its name to Warner Communications. Paramount was acquired by the Gulf & Western Company, another multinational conglomerate. Universal was assumed by MCA, the largest and most powerful of the talent agencies—which was only fitting since its head, Lew Wasserman, was the brilliant agent who perfected the percentage deal, giving stars new clout and contributing to the demise of the old studio feudalism. Harry Cohn's Columbia held out longest against the corporate invaders. But it finally surrendered, too, acquired by the Coca-Cola company.

And so the empires have crumbled. The moguls' names have faded. The estates are gone and the power and the panache and the fear. But what the Hollywood Jews left behind is something powerful and mysterious. What remains is a spell, a landscape of the mind, a constellation of values, attitudes, and images, a history and a mythology that is part of our culture and our consciousness. What remains is the America of our imaginations and theirs. Out of their desperation and their dreams, they gave us this America. Out of their desperation and dreams, they lost themselves.

REFERENCE NOTES

INTRODUCTION

PAGE

1   *"Russian-Jewish immigrants came..."* Quoted in Studs Terkel, *American Dreams: Lost and Found* (New York, 1980), p. 58.

1   *"They not only believed..."* Interview in William E. Wiener Oral History Library at the American Jewish Committee, p. 27.

1   *"The quintessence..."* Will Hays, *See and Hear* (New York, 1929), p. 4.

2   *"Of 85 names..."* *Jews in America*, editors of *Fortune* (New York, 1936), p. 61.

2   *"A Jewish holiday..."* Notes for *The Last Tycoon*, Princeton University Library, quoted in Matthew J. Bruccoli, *Some Sort of Epic Grandeur* (New York, 1981), p. 423.

2   *"500 un-Christian Jews..."* Press release from the International Reform Bureau, cited in Terry Ramsaye, *A Million and One Nights* (New York, 1926), p. 483.

2   *"Outside the moral sphere..."* Anonymous, "An Analysis of Jewish Culture," in *Jews in a Gentile World*, eds. Isacque Graeber, and Steuart Henderson Britt (New York, 1942), p. 256.

2   *"Neurotic distortion..."* Isaiah Berlin, *Against the Current: Essays in the History of Ideas*, ed. by Henry Hardy (New York, 1979), p. 258.

3   Spit on coffin. Angela Fox Dunn interviewed by author.

5   *"That's the important thing..."* Milton Sperling, interviewed by author.

5   Impediments. Carey McWilliams, *A Mask of Privilege: Anti-Semitism in America* (Boston, 1948), pp. 146–48. McWilliams puts the issue very well: "Jews have been excluded from participation in the basic industries of the country, the industries that exercise a decisive control over the entire economy.... Generally speaking, the businesses in which Jews are concentrated are those in which a large risk-factor is involved; businesses peripheral to the economy; businesses originally regarded as unimportant; new industries and businesses; and businesses which have traditionally carried a certain element of social stigma, such, for example, as the amusement industry and the liquor industry."

5   Less than four hundred dollars. Adolph Zukor quoted in *The Story of the Films*, ed. Joseph P. Kennedy (Chicago, 1927), pp. 57–58.

5   *"They were the audience."* MS.

6   *"I'm living in America..."* "Rabbi Edgar F. Magnin, Leader and Personality," interview by Malca Chall, unpublished manuscript in the Regional Oval History Office, the Bancroft Library, University of California (Berkeley, CA, 1975), p. 132.

6   *"A sustained attempt..."* Berlin, p. 275.

1: THE KILLER

11   *"With the power..."* Max Youngstein, interviewed by author.

11   *"Loew came out..."* Niven Busch, Jr., "Profile" in *The New Yorker*, September 7, 1929, p. 32.

11   *The victory was all.* Jesse Lasky with Don Weldon, *I Blow My Own Horn* (Garden City, NY, 1957), pp. 120–21.

12   *"My father took the deck..."* Eugene Zukor, interviewed by author; Eugene Zukor interview in the William E. Wiener Oral History Library at the American Jewish Committee, pp. 59–60.

12   *"Mr. Zukor always remained..."* William de Mille, *Hollywood Saga* (New York, 1939), p. 180.

12   "Creepy" and "long eyes"... *New York Times*, January 4, 1966; Mary Pickford, quoted in Adolph Zukor with Dale Kramer, *The Public Is Never Wrong* (New York, 1953), p. 97.

12   Lasky terrified of Zukor's moral rigidity. Jesse Lasky, Jr., *Whatever Happened to Hollywood?* (New York, 1975), pp. 65–66.

13   *"Judaism was a question..."* Adolph Zukor interview in the William E. Wiener Oral History Library at the American Jewish Committee, p. 3.

13   *"What I was interested in..."* Ibid., p. 14.

13   *"I am sure that he looked upon this man..."* Eugene Zukor interview, Wiener Oral History Library, pp. 37 and 39.

13   *Eugene also speculated...* EZ

14   *"I didn't believe..."* Adolph Zukor interview, Wiener Oral History Library, p. 13.

14   *"A new pair of shoes..."* Will Irwin, *The House That Shadows Built* (Garden City, NY, 1928), p. 15.

14   *"Dipped me into a sewer."* Ibid., p. 16.

14   *"'What's next?'"* Adolph Zukor interview, Columbia University Oral History Collection, p. 1.

14   *"I had no father..."* Adolph Zukor interview, Wiener Oral History Library, pp. 17–18.

15   *"No sooner did I put my foot..."* Zukor with Kramer, p. 32.

15   Assimilation. Irwin, p. 36 and pp. 46–47.

15   Eating lobster. Eugene Zukor, interviewed by author.

15   *Like most young immigrants...* Irwin, pp. 28–35; Adolph Zukor interview, Columbia Oral History Collection, pp. 4–5; Adolph Zukor interview, Wiener Oral History Library, pp. 28–29.

15   *"Fairly successful."* Adolph Zukor interview, Columbia Oral History Collection, p. 5.

16   Each cleared $8,000. Irwin, pp. 48–49.

16   *He averted bankruptcy...* Ibid., pp. 71–76; Adolph Zukor interview, Columbia Oral History Collection, pp. 6–7.

16   Profits soared. Zukor with Kramer, pp. 33–36; Irwin, p. 85.

17   *"It's not like making shoes..."* Adolph Zukor interview, Columbia University Oral History Collection, p. 37.

17   *Whatever the motive...* Zukor with Kramer, pp. 37–39.

18   *"I looked around..."* As told to Richard Schickel.

18   *"Filled with automatic fortune tellers..."* Lasky, p. 100.

18   *"Our fur offices were nearby..."* Zukor with Kramer, p. 39.

18   *It took in between...* Ibid., p. 39.

19   *"I wear 'em to impress 'em."* Irwin, pp. 83–84.

19   *"Undersized and slightly pathetic..."* William Brady, *Showman* (New York, 1937), p. 269.

19   *"I'm another Napoleon."* Cleveland Leader, June 9, 1918.

19   *"I was poor."* Kansas City Star, October 23, 1927.

19   *Small and sickly as a child...* New York Times, September 6, 1927, p. 23. For secondary source account of Loew's life, see Bosley Crowther, *The Lion's Share* (New York, 1957), pp. 19–22.

20   *"It is pretty sentiment..."* Kansas City Star, October 23, 1927.

20   Warfield and Loew. Marcus Loew III, interviewed by author.

20   *"Ambition!"* Arthur Prill, "The 'Small Time' King," *Theatre*, March 1914.

20   *When Zukor opened the Automatic Vaudeville...* ML III; Irwin, p. 111.

21   *"We were surprised..."* Cleveland Leader, June 9, 1918.

21   *Loew wasn't being entirely truthful...* Crowther, p. 26.

21   *Within six months...* New York Times, September 6, 1927, p. 23.

21   *"The next night..."* Irwin, p. 81.

22   *"It ran maybe a minute..."* Adolph Zukor interview, Columbia University Oral History Collection, p. 8.

22   *"We had this empty floor..."* Quoted in undated, untitled clipping in Zukor file in the New York Public Library of the Performing Arts at Lincoln Center.

22   *With the success of Crystal Hall...* Adolph Zukor interview, Columbia University Oral History Collection, p. 8.

23   *One thing Brady knew...* Brady, p. 266.

23   *"This is a big thing..."* Adolph Zukor interview, Columbia University Oral History Collection, p. 10.

23   *Zukor agreed with him...* Brady, p. 266; Irwin, p. 104. Irwin puts the debt at $180,000.

23   *"I can hardly remember..."* "Hollywood, From A to Z," by Aljean Harmetz, *New York Times*, February 4, 1973.

23   *"Well, so we move again..."* Eugene Zukor interview, Wiener Oral History Library, pp. 47–48.

23   *"With each crash..."* Eugene Zukor interview, Wiener Oral History Library, p. 49.

24   *"It was as though I'd touched him..."* Irwin, p. 105.

24   *At the end of two years...* Brady, p. 266.

24   *"These short films..."* Adolph Zukor interview, Columbia University Oral History Collection, p. 11.

24   *"You couldn't head him."* Brady, pp. 267–68.

25   *Since his Comedy Theater...* The Moving Picture World, Vol. 6 (1910), p. 885.

25   *"Every Hungarian is either..."* Irwin, p. 91.

25   Became a Republican. *Ibid.*, p. 53.

26   *"Everybody thought I was crazy..."* Adolph Zukor interview, Wiener Oral History Library, p. 46.

26   *"Nobody believed..."* Quoted in *The Story of the Films*, ed. Joseph P. Kennedy (Chicago, 1927), p. 64.

26   *Zukor obviously disagreed...* Kennedy, pp. 58–60.

26   *"I made a condition..."* Ibid., p. 61.

27   *Zukor attributed his partner's skepticism...* Zukor with Kramer, p. 49.

27   The story of opening night. *Cleveland Leader*, June 9, 1918.

27   *"I don't offer widely advertised..."* Theater, March 1914.

28   *When his company reorganized...* Crowther, p. 32.

28   "*I traveled all through Europe...*" Kennedy, p. 61.
28   Acquiring *Queen Elizabeth*. Irwin, pp. 155–56; Zukor with Kramer, p. 61. Here the figure is $40,000, and the money was given to help complete the production.
28   "*Famous Players in Famous Plays.*" Zukor with Kramer, p. 59.
29   "*Breaking down the prejudice...*" Zukor with Kramer, p. 71.
29   "*Possibility of a higher class...*" *Ibid.*, p. 72.
29   "*In order to give himself validity...*" Eugene Zukor, interviewed by author.
29   "*You're out of your head.*" Brady, p. 268.
29   *Frohman agreed to meet...* Zukor with Kramer, pp. 64–65.
30   "*He talks the English...*" Busch, Jr., p. 32.
30   *Famous Players would improve...* Daniel Frohman, *Daniel Frohman Presents* (New York, 1935), p. 278.
30   "*The time is not ripe...*" Zukor with Kramer, pp. 73–74.
30   "*What they were making...*" Adolph Zukor interview, Columbia Oral History Collection, p. 14.
31   *Loew was dismayed.* Zukor with Kramer, p. 63. Irwin places the liquidation sometime later, in 1913, and claims it was the result of a financial crisis at Famous Players that Frohman ultimately bailed him out of. See Irwin, pp. 184–87.
31   "*If I talked to an actor...*" Adolph Zukor interview, Wiener Oral History Library, p. 45.
31   "*All Daniel Frohman had to say...*" Eugene Zukor interview, Wiener Oral History Library, p. 78.
31   "*My father had a great way....*" *Ibid.*, p. 77.
31   "*Realized that this was an art...*" Kennedy, p. 64.
32   *He had even hired...* Terry Ramsaye, *A Million and One Nights* (New York, 1926), p. 628.
32   "*The most notable figure...*" "Adolph Zukor, The Elevator of Moving Pictures," *New York Journal*, December 24, 1912.
32   "*Seven wonders of the motion picture business.*" *New York Clipper*, February 14, 1914.
32   "*Perhaps the greatest single phase...*" "Adolph Zukor Quit Furs for Films," *The Moving Picture World*, July 15, 1916, p. 415.
32   "*I dropped into my seat...*" Frohman, pp. 281–82.
32   *Zukor had more success...* *Ibid.*, pp. 248–49.
33   "*I must say I am getting on...*" Letter to wife, Adolph Zukor Correspondence, Margaret Herrick Library at the Academy of Motion Picture Arts and Sciences.
33   "*Mr. Zukor enjoys power.*" Cecil B. De Mille, *Autobiography* (New Jersey, 1959), pp. 153 and 156.
33   "*When he meets a new acquaintance...*" Irwin, p. 283.
34   *65 percent of the holes.* Lasky, p. 124.
34   "*Jesse Lasky in no way...*" Philip Dunne, *Take Two* (New York, 1980), p. 26.
34   "*He did not crawl...*" Betty Lasky, interviewed by author.
35   *After a series of ill-fated...* Lasky, pp. 66–67.
35   "*I yearned to trespass...*" *Ibid.*, p. 74.
35   "*One day I became so incensed...*" *Ibid.*, p. 90.
35   *Over lunch one day...* *Ibid.*, p. 91; Cecil B. De Mille, pp. 69–70. De Mille, however, claims that Lasky had already decided to enter the movie industry.

36   *Shortly after the premiere...* Zukor with Kramer, p. 123; Lasky, p. 101. Lasky believes he was the one who set up the lunch with Zukor.

36   *"Too many persons engaged..."* Letter from attorneys for Jesse L. Lasky Feature Play Co., to Rep. D. M. Hughes, January 25, 1916, in *Twentieth Century Quarterly*, June 1916, p. 8.

36   *When William Fox suggested a partnership...* Zukor with Kramer, p. 92.

36   *"It would have been a nice nest egg..."* Ramsaye, pp. 745–46.

37   *"He was a very crude man..."* EZ.

37   *Zukor felt he disagreed...* Zukor with Kramer, pp. 176–79; Lasky, p. 123; Ramsaye, pp. 741–52.

38   *On one occasion, Laemmle...* EZ.

38   *"He was very strict."* Eugene Zukor interview, Wiener Oral History Library, p. 57.

38   *"If something displeased him..."* EZ.

38   *At a hearing to prevent foreclosure...* New York Times, November 2, 1933.

38   *"He would give me the full treatment."* EZ.

39   *"He said, 'Well, you made your decision...'"* EZ.

39   *Zukor did dote on his wife...* EZ.

39   *"I have always believed that if a man surrounds..."* Zukor with Kramer, p. 133.

40   *"To show its patriotism..."* Moving Picture World, August 3, 1918.

40   *Once in the village...* Zukor with Kramer, p. 240.

40   *In doling out his money...* Irwin, p. 267.

40   *In time, he was sending...* Busch, Jr., p. 32.

41   Otto Kahn. See Mary Jane Matz, *The Many Lives of Otto Kahn* (New York, 1963), for a biography of Kahn.

41   *Otto expunged his Judaism...* Ibid., p. 9. A letter from Kahn to a friend in 1918 claims that he had been reared without any religious instruction. "It has had the natural and irreparable effect of preventing me from feeling that personal concern and taking that serious interest in Jewish affairs which I might as a matter of course be assumed to possess."

42   *"In art as in everything else..."* Speech to Author's League Committee in charge of the International Congress on Motion Picture Arts, June 8, 1923, quoted in Otto H. Kahn, *Of Many Things* (New York, 1926), pp. 35–36.

42   *"My associates held that the request..."* Zukor with Kramer, p. 181.

42   *Before committing themselves...* EZ.

42   *"Paramount was not formed..."* Quoted in Gertrude Jobes, *Motion Picture Empire* (Hamden, CT, 1966), p. 132.

43   *"Rape of the industry."* Exhibitors' Herald quoted in "Paramount," *Fortune* magazine, March 1937, p. 92.

43   *When Paramount was building a theater...* EZ.

44   *"Jesse took me over..."* Cecil B. De Mille, p. 152.

44   *"I told them, 'We go ahead...'"* Adolph Zukor interview, Columbia University Oral History Collection, p. 16.

44   *His doctor recommended...* EZ; Irwin, pp. 263–64.

45   *"Fell in love with the place."* Eugene Zukor interview, Wiener Oral History Collection, p. 42.

45   *It had belonged...* EZ.

45   *Zukor's business philosophy...* Eugene Zukor interview, Wiener Oral History Library, pp. 62–63.

46   *"Saturday nights . . ." Ibid.*, pp. 15–16.
46   *"There are moments when . . ."* Abraham Cahan, *The Rise of David Le-vinsky* (New York, 1917), pp. 525, 526, 530.

2: "DON'T BE A SALARY SLAVE!"

47   *"It Can Be Done!"* Legend underneath portrait in Laemmle living room, *Motion Picture*, September 1932, n.p., in Laemmle file at New York Public Library of the Performing Arts at Lincoln Center.
47   *"He has often told me . . ."* Gladys Hall, "Uncle Carl and Junior Laemmle Have Made Movie History," *Motion Picture*, September 1932.
47   *"Bald-headed little man . . ."* Sam Marx, interviewed by author.
47   *"He seemed to see humor . . ."* Garson Kanin, *Hollywood: Stars and Starlets, Tycoons and Flesh-Peddlers, Moviemakers and Moneymakers, Frauds and Geniuses, Hopefuls and Has-Beens, Great Lovers and Sex Symbols* (New York, 1974), p. 72.
47   *Bal masque. The Moving Picture World*, March 16, 1916, p. 66.
47   *"Dump this out . . ."* Milton Sperling, interviewed by author.
48   *"Do not charge him . . ."* Quoted in *Film Daily* by Isidore Bernstein, February 28, 1926, p. 41.
48   *"The whitest man . . ."* Rupert Hughes quoted in John Drinkwater, *The Life and Adventures of Carl Laemmle* (New York, 1931), p. 241.
48   *"I have never heard . . ."* Peter Woodhull, quoted in Drinkwater, p. 267.
48   *"Even the men who hate him . . ."* Robert Cochrane, quoted in *The Moving Picture World*, March 16, 1918, p. 1526.
48   *"My success . . ."* Quoted in Drinkwater, p. 263.
48   *"Philosophically disposed . . ."* Drinkwater, p. 26.
48   A childhood friend. *Ibid.*, p. 17.
49   *"I found that shocking wheat . . ."* "Filmdom's Famous Fighter," by Stanhope A. Selwyn, *Movie Pictorial*, August 14, 1914, n.p.
50   Employment carousel. *Ibid.*, and Drinkwater, pp. 31–47. The exact accounts differ, but the idea is the same: Laemmle had little sense of direction.
50   *"Good you left . . ."* Drinkwater, 57.
51   *"He took the night train . . ." Ibid.*, pp. 58–60.
51   *"Don't be a salary slave!"* Ramsaye, p. 447.
52   *"I went over to Chicago . . ."* Selwyn.
52   *"This induced me . . ."* Quoted in *The New York Times*, February 22, 1931.
52   *"I was in Chicago when . . ."* Charles Chasteen, quoted in "How the Laemmle Exchanges Started," *Film Daily*, February 28, 1926, p. 75.
53   *"Shocked, disappointed and almost humiliated . . ."* New York Times, February 22, 1931.
53   When it was all finished . . . I. G. Edwards, *Big U* (South Brunswick, NJ, 1977), p. 20.
53   On average days . . . Paul Gulick, "Carl Laemmle Made Start in Chicago 'Store Show,'" *The Moving Picture World*, July 15, 1916, pp. 420–21.
54   *Laemmle's projectionist suggested . . .* Film Daily, February 28, 1926, p. 75.
54   Saloonkeepers. *New York Times*, September 25, 1939.
54   *Within two years . . .* Selwyn, n.p.
54   Largest film distributor. Drinkwater, p. 67.

55   *"Nickel madness."* Barton W. Currie, "The Nickel Madness," *Harper's Weekly,* vol. 51 (August 24, 1907), p. 1246.

55   *"The average theater..."* Joseph Medill Patterson, "The Nickelodeons, the Poor Man's Elementary Course in the Drama," *Saturday Evening Post,* November 23, 1907, pp. 10–11.

56   *"Subject matter was derived..."* Lewis Jacobs, *The Rise of the American Film* (New York, 1939), p. 67.

56   *"Rude rank spirit..."* Walt Whitman, *Specimen Days, Democratic Vistas,* ed. Louise Pound (New York, 1935), p. 276.

56   *"The crowds not only throng..."* *The Nation,* August 28, 1913, p. 193.

57   *"There are now about a hundred..."* *Jewish Daily Forward,* May 24, 1908, and July 28, 1914, quoted in Irving Howe, *World of Our Fathers* (New York, 1976), p. 213.

58   The Patents Company. There are a number of accounts of the formation of the Patents Company. For the most detailed, if not necessarily the most reliable, see Ramsaye, pp. 465–72.

58   Laemmle's reaction. Drinkwater, p. 73.

58   *"Swamped with hundreds..."* *Ibid.,* p. 75.

58   *"The Laemmle Film Service attained..."* Abe Stern, quoted in *Film Daily,* February 28, 1926, p. 77.

59   Legal actions. Drinkwater, p. 110.

59   Monopoly of their own. Robert Sklar, *Movie-Made America* (New York, 1975), p. 37.

59   *"Began to fight..."* Selwyn, n.p.

60   *"We sit in the Film Committee..."* L. W. McChesney memo to C. H. Wilson, January 2, 1915, cited in Robert Conot, *A Streak of Luck* (New York, 1979), p. 396.

60   *"Our comedies..."* Letter in *Motion Pictures,* January 13, 1915, quoted in *Ibid.,* p. 397.

60   *"The monopoly discouraged..."* Jesse L. Lasky with Don Weldon, *I Blow My Own Horn* (Garden City, NY, 1957), p. 97.

60   Exchange outside the Trust. Ramsaye, p. 716; and Jeanne Thomas Allen, "The Decay of the Motion Picture Patents Company," in *The American Film Industry,* ed. Tino Balio (Madison, WI, 1976) pp. 119–34. Allen wholly discounts the idea that the Trust fell because of feature films, but she does suggest that Trust members, for whatever reasons, were no longer satisfied with its operation. See also Janet Staiger, "Combination and Litigation: Structures of US Film Distribution, 1891–1917," *Cinema Journal,* vol. 23, no. 2, pp. 41–72. Staiger argues, essentially, that the Trust broke up primarily because its members found more advantageous economic alliances. This may be so, but I think it leaves out the personal, psychological, and cultural components. The fact remains that virtually every member of the Trust was defunct by 1920, with Vitagraph the only one lasting until 1925. Economics alone doesn't explain it.

61   Unexpected appearance. Winthrop Sargent, a Trust employee, quoted in *Film Daily,* February 28, 1926, p. 49.

61   *"We used to sit around..."* Jack Cohn, quoted in *Film Daily,* February 28, 1926, p. 57.

61   *"The grandest American-made moving picture..."* Drinkwater, p. 81.

61   *"My motto..."* *Ibid.,* p. 82.

62   *"Film exchanges and exhibitors..."* *Ibid.,* p. 81.

62   *"Knew how to use..."* Max Laemmle, interviewed by author.

62   Upgrade screen acting. Robert Grau, *Theatre of Science* (New York, 1914), p. 206.

62   Raiding competitors. *New York Times*, February 22, 1931.

62   Florence Lawrence. See *Moving Picture World*, March 26, 1910, and Ramsaye, pp. 523–24, for varying accounts.

63   Personal fortune. Selwyn, n.p.

63   Warfare without parallel. Grau, p. 111.

63   *"I've got the name . . ."* *Film Daily*, February 28, 1926, p. 31.

64   The ensuing battle. For the best accounts, one is referred to the contemporary trade journals. For the most colorful accounts, one is referred to Ramsaye, pp. 580–81, 590–93, and Grau, pp. 38–48.

64   *"Practically unknown man . . ."* Editorial quoted in Drinkwater, p. 78. For some idea of Laemmle's wealth, see *The Moving Picture World*, August 5, 1916, p. 919, where Laemmle announces the purchase of his exchanges by Universal for over $1 million.

64   *"Holler the loudest . . ."* Ramsaye, p. 478.

65   *"I was working for . . ."*; *"My father was . . ."* Quoted in Upton Sinclair, *Upton Sinclair Presents William Fox* (Los Angeles, 1933), pp. 17, 18–19. This book, dictated to Sinclair by Fox, is the only detailed account of Fox's life. To its credit, it is refreshingly candid about Fox's feelings and motivations.

65   *"Every penny . . ."* *Ibid.*, p. 25.

65   Saved $50,000. *Ibid.*, p. 31.

65   *"Didn't like the business . . ."* Ramsaye, p. 452.

66   Cleared $40,000. Press release from Fox Film Corporation, May 1915.

66   *"Ten thousand people marched . . ."* Quoted in *New York Evening World*, November 30, 1912. For more on the arcade, see also *Theatre*, May 1920, and Sinclair, pp. 34–35.

66   Turned a profit. Sinclair, p. 38.

66   *"A man who is married . . ."* *New York Evening World*, November 30, 1912.

66   Combining movies and vaudeville. *New York Telegraph*, December 13, 1910.

67   *"A year ago I sent out 10,000 . . ."* *Ibid.*

67   Demonology. Angela Fox Dunn, Fox's niece, interviewed by author. See also Sinclair, p. 10.

68   Fox's political connections. Sinclair, pp. 40–41; Ramsaye, pp. 529–530; *Toledo Blade*, January 22, 1916.

68   *"Affluent and dictatorial."* Undated, untitled newspaper clipping in the William Fox file in the New York Public Library of the Performing Arts at Lincoln Center.

69   *"When I entered . . ."* Press release from Fox Film Corporation, May 1915.

69   *"I was looking for an outlet . . ."* Sinclair, p. 51.

70   *"I watched my mother . . ."* AFD.

70   *"My mother wasn't a business person."* AFD.

70   *New York financiers would invite . . .* Sinclair, p. 3.

71   Religious feeling. *Ibid.*, p. 17.

71   *"Do you mean to tell . . ."* *Ibid.*, p. 11.

71   Psychic powers. AFD.

72   *"I never wanted to know . . ."* Sinclair, p. 5.

72   *"I'll never forget the first time . . ."* *Film Daily*, February 26, 1928, p. 5.

72   *"He had absolutely . . ."* ML.

72   "*They loved him . . .*" Stanley Bergerman, interviewed by author.
73   "*I don't want to be cheated.*" Walter Laemmle, interviewed by author.
73   "*Colorful liver.*" Samuel Marx, interviewed by author.
73   "*He was sick . . .*" WL.
73   "*The doctors gave me . . .*" *Motion Picture*, September 1932.
74   Dias Durados. Michael Regan, *Stars, Moguls, Magnates: The Mansions of Beverly Hills* (Los Angeles, 1966), pp. 31–34; and SB. Laemmle himself spelled it "Dios," which would mean "enduring God," but Ince was apparently memorializing his wish that the house survive for five hundred years.
74   Gambling. *New York American Journal*, July 18, 1965; and SB.
74   "*At that time . . .*" WL.
75   "*Duty calls.*" ML.
75   "*He would play cards . . .*" SB.
75   Assuming the throne. Lionel White, "Mr. Laemmle's Boy Carl," *Cinema*, December 1930; and undated, untitled clip in the Carl Laemmle file at the New York Public Library of the Performing Arts at Lincoln Center: "It is said that it is very probable in about five years' time, on attaining his twenty-first birthday, that young Carl will be elected Vice-President of Universal Pictures Corporation, which will make him the youngest film magnate in the picture industry."
75   "*Junior was always smart . . .*" *Motion Picture*, September 1932.
75   "*Junior read . . .*" SM.
75   "*Junior's running this joint . . .*" Director Gregory La Cava, quoted in Joe Pasternak, *Easy the Hard Way* (New York, 1956), p. 159.
76   "*Only then did I learn . . .*" Sol Lesser interview, Columbia University Oral History Collection.
76   Laemmle recruited a young Czechoslovakian. Frederick Kohner, *The Magician of Sunset Boulevard* (Palos Verdes, CA, 1977), pp. 80–81.
78   "*I'm glad to stand . . .*" *New York Sun*, October 20, 1936.
78   Speculation he had lost favor. *New York Times*, November 12, 1937.
78   "*I feel sure . . .*" *Motion Picture*, September 1932.
78   "*That is one thing . . .*" *Film Daily*, February 28, 1926, p. 2.

3: BORN ON THE FOURTH OF JULY

79   "*If someone were doing . . .*" Danny Selznick, grandson of Louis B. Mayer, interviewed by author.
79   "*If I had to use one word . . .*" Irene Mayer Selznick, *A Private View* (New York, 1983), p. 26.
80   "*A bombastic egotist . . .*" Eric Johnston interview, Columbia University Oral History Collection, sec. III, vol. 3, part II, p. 896.
80   "*Looking at Mayer made me think . . .*" William Wellman, *A Short Time for Insanity* (New York, 1974), p. 227.
80   "*The greatest actor . . .*" Edith Mayer Goetz, interviewed by author.
80   "*If you went in to see . . .*" Pandro Berman, interviewed by author.
80   "*He was sentimental . . .*" DS.
81   "*He was a forceful . . .*" EMG.
81   Fight with Chaplin. Bosley Crowther, *Hollywood Rajah* (New York, 1960), pp. 77–78; Selznick, p. 36.
81   "*His relationship to the studio . . .*" DS.

81   *"My father was not only . . ."* Selznick, p. 20.

82   *"Of course, I could not leave our home . . ."* EMG.

82   *"Grasping and tyrannical."* Selznick, p. 4.

82   *As late as 1880 . . .* Eli Boyaner, "The Settlement and Development of the Jewish Community of Saint John," *New Brunswick Historical Society,* New Brunswick Historical Society Collections, number 15.

83   *"In most people, you can perceive . . ."* DS.

83   *"Invest it."* Metro-Goldwyn-Mayer press release in the Louis B. Mayer file at New York Public Library of the Performing Arts at Lincoln Center.

83   Taunted by anti-Semites. Crowther, p. 16.

83   Shamelessly exploited. Selznick, p. 4.

83   *Boston was a relatively common destination . . . Boston Globe,* November 23, 1930. Article states that Mayer visited Boston twice each year.

83   *Irene didn't know exactly how . . .* Selznick, pp. 5–6.

84   *Louis "wasn't good enough . . ."* Rabbi Edgar Magnin, interviewed by author.

84   *"In the sense that my grandfather . . ."* DS.

84   *"Price of a sandwich."* Mayer quoted in *Variety,* May 24, 1939.

84   *According to this version . . .* Crowther, pp. 26–29

84   *Mayer himself told another story . . .* Letter from Mrs. Lloyd Smith of Haverhill to the author.

85   *"The city where are made . . ."* *Haverhill Board of Trade Tidings,* April 1914.

85   *For Mayer, who was . . .* Selznick, pp. 7–8.

85   *Before daring to open . . .* MGM press release in Mayer file in the New York Public Library of the Performing Arts at Lincoln Center.

85   *At its opening in December 1911 . . .* Account in *Haverhill Evening Gazette,* quoted in Gary Carey, *All the Stars in Heaven* (New York, 1981), p. 18.

86   *"Even when I was a very little girl . . ."* Selznick, p. 27.

86   *The grand design also required . . .* *Haverhill Evening Gazette,* June 22, 1940.

87   *"Mr. Louis B. Mayer whose inspiration . . ."* Colonial Theatre Programme, November 21, 1912.

87   *"Those were happy days . . ."* EMG.

87   *"Theatrical world will be surprised . . ."* *Haverhill Evening Gazette,* November 18, 1912.

87   *Apparently dissatisfied . . . Ibid.*

88   *One biographer speculates . . .* Carey, p. 22. Unfortunately, no footnote is given to indicate on what Carey based this conclusion.

88   *He spoke with such dewy idealism . . .* DS.

88   *"He felt everything good in him . . ."* Selznick, p. 8.

88   *Sarah Mayer died . . .* EMG.

88   *"He continued to speak about her . . ."* Mervyn LeRoy, as told to Dick Kleiner, *LeRoy: Take One* (New York, 1974), p. 135.

88   *So deep was his affection . . .* Selznick, p. 69.

88   *"Do not grieve . . ."* LeRoy, p. 135.

89   *Sometime shortly after the formation . . .* George C. Elliott, quoted in *Haverhill Evening Gazette,* June 22, 1940.

89   *"Louis was a worker . . ." Ibid.*

90   *"I remember one thing . . ."* EMG.

90   *Birth of a Nation.* Richard Schickel, *D. W. Griffith: An American Life*

(New York, 1984), pp. 273–74.

91 Fudging the books. Crowther, p. 50.

91 *"We sparred around..."* Jack Warner with Dean Jennings, *My First Hundred Years in Hollywood* (New York, 1965), pp. 92–93.

92 *Mayer had to turn on...* Crowther, p. 52.

92 *After he had persuaded them...* Selznick, pp. 28–29.

92 *"I met her, I met her!"* Crowther, pp. 55–56.

93 *A month later Metro was in court...* The Moving Picture World, November 10, 1917, p. 864.

93 *Selznick moved into an office...* David Selznick interview, Columbia University Oral History Collection, p. 4.

93 *Movie industry took less brains...* Ibid., p. 3.

93 *Adolph Zukor was so nettled...* Terry Ramsaye, A Million and One Nights (New York, 1924), p. 765.

94 *By February 1918...* The Moving Picture World, February 23, 1918, p. 1103.

94 *"Watch what I say..."* Selznick, p. 96.

95 *"The most pleasant days..."* St. Paul Pioneer Press, June 21, 1925.

95 *"Black sheep of the family..."* Avery Strakosch, "And They Thought He Was the Black Sheep of the Family!" *National Brain Power*, May 1923.

95 *Almost every dance degenerated...* Ibid.

95 *"I did everything to get..."* Ibid.

96 *"The theatre is the thing..."* The Triangle, January 15, 1916.

96 *"You are a great artist."* Boston Herald, February 8, 1925.

97 *"Poured out my heart to her."* Ibid.

97 *"Uncompromising in demanding..."* Robert Grau, *The Theater of Science* (New York, 1914), p. 291.

97 *"Man's man."* New York Telegram-Mail, radio section, January 24, 1925.

97 *"Give the people what they want..."* William Reynolds, "Don't Give People What They Want," *Green Book Magazine*, August 1914.

97 *"Applesauce."* Variety, May 22, 1934; Louis Nizer, *Bulletin of the Motion Picture Club*, December 1, 1931.

97 *"My ancestors were peasants."* New York Tribune, February 17, 1918.

97 Popularity in Germany. See *Deutsche Amerika*, Seite 26, Heft 47, and *LBB*, #77, Seite 7, in the Samuel Rothapfel file in the New York Public Library of the Performing Arts at Lincoln Center; and *Variety*, July 15, 1925.

98 *"Take up the preliminaries..."* Untitled news clipping, January 8, 1918, in Rothapfel file in the New York Public Library of the Performing Arts at Lincoln Center.

98 *"Temples of art."* The Dramatic News, February 17, 1917.

99 *"Solely for the purpose..."* Philadelphia Inquirer, August 14, 1927.

99 *"I now believe that music..."* Broadway Brevities, circa 1921, in Samuel Rothapfel file in the New York Public Library of the Performing Arts at Lincoln Center.

99 *"College education."* New York Commercial, February 26, 1923.

99 *"An institution for New York."* National Magazine, circa October 1920, in Rothapfel file in the New York Public Library of the Performing Arts at Lincoln Center.

100 Weekly average gross. *Exhibitors Trade Review*, November 22, 1924; *Variety*, May 27, 1925.

100 National storm of protest. *New York Daily News*, February 3, 1925; *New*

York American, February 8, 1925; *New York Evening Star*, February 5, 1925. A few days later, AT&T buckled to the pressure and let Roxy be his old, informal self.

100   *"I promise you . . ."* *New York Telegram*, July 25, 1925.

101   *Barney's daughter . . ."* Judith Balaban, interviewed by author.

101   *Grauman pranks.* See Adolph Zukor with Dale Kramer, *The Public Is Never Wrong* (New York, 1953), p. 163; *New York Post*, January 8, 1938; and Jesse Lasky, Jr., *Whatever Happened to Hollywood?* (New York, 1975), pp. 103–6.

102   *Grauman would spend hours . . .* Warner, p. 96.

102   *"Walking with Sid . . ."* Letter from Arthur S. Wenzel in *Variety*, September 24, 1975.

102   *"At the Capitol Theater . . ."* *Los Angeles Times*, July 31, 1921.

103   *"Not only is the International Music Hall . . ."* *New York Herald Tribune*, December 19, 1932.

103   *"A hint of tragedy . . ."* *New York Herald Tribune*, December 19, 1932.

103   *"We want the Metropolitan Opera . . ."* Untitled press clipping, December 29, 1932, in Rothapfel file in the New York Public Library of the Performing Arts at Lincoln Center.

103   *"What did they think . . ."* *New York Herald Tribune*, February 15, 1933.

104   *"We're going to put on things . . ."* *New York World Telegram*, March 1, 1933.

104   *"A man attacked . . ."* *New York Sun*, undated clipping in the New York Public Library for the Performing Arts at Lincoln Center, MFL + n.c. 1830.

104   *Carl Laemmle sent . . .* Telegram from Carl Laemmle to Mrs. Samuel Rothafel in the New York Public Library of the Performing Arts at Lincoln Center, MFL + n.c. 1824.

104   *"Could never get enough . . ."* *New York Times*, January 14, 1936.

104   *Hollywood's name.* But see Bruce T. Torrence, *Hollywood: The First Hundred Years* (New York, 1982), for another version. Torrence claims the name came when the wife of land speculator Harvey Wilcox took a train back East and talked to a woman who described her summer home, which she called "Hollywood." (p. 25).

105   *Custard apples . . .* Edwin O. Palmer, *The History of Hollywood* (Hollywood, CA, 1937), pp. 9–13.

105   *Hollywood itself wasn't invaded . . .* Ibid., pp. 190–91.

105   *Over seventy production companies . . .* Grau, p. 289; Kevin Brownlow, *The Parade's Gone By* (New York, 1968), p. 36.

105   *"There were practically no shops . . ."* William de Mille, *Hollywood Saga* (New York, 1939), pp. 84–85.

106   *"Nails had to be . . ."* Selznick, p. 65.

106   *Making virtue manifest.* See David Riesman, *The Lonely Crowd: A Study of the Changing American Character* (New Haven, CT, 1950), for the classical articulation of the other-directed man as opposed to the inner-directed man, whose sense of self is internally generated. Playwright Sam Shepard may have put this phenomenon best when he said of Hollwood, "people here/have become/the people/they're pretending to be." *Motel Chronicles* (San Francisco, 1982), p. 42. That was certainly the aspiration of Mayer and many of the other Hollywood Jews.

106   *"I remember one of the things . . ."* EMG.

107   *"Why are you giving me . . ."* Ibid.

107   Femininity and domesticity. EMG; Selznick, pp 51–52, 67.

108   *"That Hearst admired . . . "* Ibid., p. 84.

108   *"The poor but decent girl . . . "* Crowther, p. 81.

109   *"My unchanging policy . . . "* Telegram from Mayer to director Lois Weber, quoted in *Ibid.*, p. 69.

110   *Rubin would scowl . . .* Samuel Marx, *Mayer and Thalberg: The Make-Believe Saints* (New York, 1975), p. 51.

110   *Mayer went to New York . . .* Crowther, pp. 94–95.

111   *"I'll bet you'd be surprised . . . "* Marx, p. 41. Though Irene was the probable source for Marx, in her own book she claims the studio visited was Metro (Selznick, p. 54).

111   *"If there is one thing . . . "* Motion Picture News, July 19, 1924, p. 321.

111   *"He used to get up . . . "* Sam Marx, interviewed by author.

111   *"It was almost a command . . . "* Maurice Rapf, son of Harry Rapf, interviewed by author.

111   *"You were always aware . . . "* SM.

112   *"All I can say . . . "* New York Times, September 7, 1927.

113   *"Sturdy oak."* Margaret L. Talmadge, *The Talmadge Sisters* (Philadelphia, 1924), p. 146.

113   *"Joe was a philosopher . . . "* Howard Dietz, *Dancing in the Dark* (New York, 1974), p. 110.

113   Three main interests. Henry F. Pringle, "Profile," *The New Yorker*, April 30, 1932, p. 25.

113   *"We were the first ones down . . . "* SM.

114   *"Planned to get all the moving picture theaters . . . "* Upton Sinclair, *Upton Sinclair Presents William Fox* (Los Angeles, 1933), p. 73.

114   *One partner in a West Coast theater chain . . .* Sol Lesser Oral History, Columbia University Oral History Collection, pp. 68–71. Fox offered a fabulous deal to Lesser, but Lesser's partners called him away from Fox's office as they were about to consummate the agreement and convinced him not to sell lest the wily Fox undermine the entire First National with whom they had an arrangement. Fox told Lesser, "You're too trusting, my boy. If any of them get the chance to sell and can work out a deal like I've offered you, they'll sell and nothing will keep them from it." He was right. Three months later First National's franchise holders for Illinois, Balaban and Katz, sold out to Paramount.

114   *Meeting with Schenck . . .* The best and primary source for this account is Sinclair.

115   *Mayer had apparently met Ida Koverman . . .* Crowther, pp. 127–28.

115   Reminded him of his mother. DS.

116   Speculation about nominating speech. Crowther, p. 137.

116   Ambassadorship to Turkey. Associated Press dispatch in *Haverhill Evening Gazette*, February 2, 1929.

116   Mayer and Fox. Sinclair, p. 91; Crowther, p. 148.

117   *"See here, this Jew . . . "* Sinclair, p. 129.

117   *"This was the day . . . "* Ibid., p. 120.

117   *"Loyalty was a theme . . . "* DS.

118   *"It didn't matter . . . "* Dietz, p. 117.

118   *"He blossomed . . . "* DS.

118   *"He was very quiet . . . "* EMG.

118   *"Meeting important figures . . . "* Crowther, pp. 72–73.

118   *He insisted on living . . .* For years Mayer drove a secondhand Ford. Col-

umnist Hedda Hopper once asked him why. "See those cars down there? Pretty, aren't they?" he said. "Yes, and I've seen too many of them, belonging to directors and stars, taken out of there by the finance company. I'm going to use my Ford until I can afford to buy three Cadillacs — for cash." Hedda Hopper, *From Under My Hat* (Garden City, NY, 1952), p. 133.

119   *"I worship good women . . ."* Frances Marion, *Off With Their Heads* (New York, 1972), p. 99.

4: BETWEEN THE OLD LIFE AND THE NEW

120   *"He has two major interests."* "Warner Brothers," *Fortune* magazine, December 1937, p. 208.

120   *Harry chased Jack . . .* Milton Sperling, Harry Warner's son-in-law, interviewed by author.

120   *On another occasion . . .* Jack Warner, Jr., interviewed by author.

120   *When Harry died . . .* JW, Jr.

120   *"Fast-talking Broadway type."* Leo Rosten interview, Columbia University Oral History Collection, p. 2224.

120   Frustrated comedian. Hal Wallis with Charles Higham, *Starmaker* (New York, 1980), p. 14.

120   *"You know, I have a theory . . ."* Michael Freedland, *The Warner Brothers* (New York, 1983), p. 1.

120   *"Holy cow. I forgot . . ."* Jack Warner with Dean Jennings, *My First Hundred Years in Hollywood* (New York, 1965), p. 9.

121   *"He always sported a big smile."* Wallis, p. 14.

121   *"Harry introduced the rabbi . . ."* Rosten interview, Columbia University Oral History Collection, p. 2224.

121   *"Not an impressive man to meet."* Rosten interview, p. 2227.

121   *"What would my children think?"* MS.

122   *"Beat the shit . . ."* MS.

122   *"He cared more for people . . ."* Warner, p. 294.

122   *"This was one experience . . ." Ibid.*, p. 24.

123   *"There never seemed to be . . ." Ibid.*, pp. 33–34.

123   *"Son, you're going to have to fight . . ."* Letter to Warner Twyford, February 25, 1949, Harry B. Warner Papers at the American Jewish Archives.

123   *"I didn't dig it at all."* Warner, p. 17.

124   *"He was a little rebellious."* JW, Jr.

124   *"Once became so exasperated . . ."* Warner, p. 35.

124   *It was Sam . . .* This is Jack's version. (Warner, pp. 49–52). In other versions, Albert and Sam pitched in with Harry, joining them later, only after they realized they needed someone with accounting experience.

124   *"Saw the vast possibilities . . ." Ibid.*, p. 49.

126   *"They went to picnics . . ."* Warner, p. 56.

127   *"He handed me a menu . . ." Ibid.*, p. 61.

127   *"The Duquesne Amusement Company . . ." Ibid.*, pp. 65–66.

128   *"Invariably we made . . ." Ibid.*, p. 81.

129   *Jack used to joke . . .* William Schaefer, Jack Warner's administrative assistant, interviewed by author.

129   *Jack claims that he . . .* Freedland claims Sam got the idea to bid on the rights after reading a serialization in the *Philadelphia Public Ledger* but

gives no citation (p. 20).

129   *They immediately wired...* Warner, p. 90.

129   *Another story had Harry...* "Warner Brothers," *Fortune* magazine, December 1937.

130   *"I liked you fellows..."* Warner, pp. 90–91.

130   *Artistically,* My Four Years in Germany... See Clive Hirschhorn, *The Warner Brothers Story* (New York, 1979), for a capsule of this film and every other Warner Brothers picture.

131    $130,000 profit. Warner, p. 92.

131   *"Warner brothers personally..."* *Fortune* magazine, December 1937.

131   *"Every worthwhile contribution..."* Quoted in *Brooklyn Eagle*, April 1, 1938.

132   *"Speaking from personal experience..."* MS.

132   *"I think it was Schenck..."* MS.

133   Giannini. For a fuller account of Giannini's life, see Julian Dana, *A.P. Giannini: Giant in the West* (New York, 1947). For a fuller account of the bank itself, see George W. Dowrie, "The History of the Bank of Italy in California," *Journal of Economic and Business History,* February 1930.

134   *"Character was his collateral."* Director Frank Capra used Giannini as his model for Walter Huston's honest, sympathetic banker in *American Madness* (1931). See Charles Maland, *Frank Capra* (Boston, 1980), p. 70.

134   *When Sol Lesser...* Sol Lesser interview, Columbia University Oral History Collection, pp. 28–29.

134   *"I never worry..."* Warner, p. 102.

135   *"Loan sharks..."* *Fortune* magazine, December 1937.

135   *Following phase one...* For a full account of the various machinations behind the Warners' campaign, see J. Douglas Gomery, "The Coming of the Talkies: Invention, Innovation, and Diffusion," *The American Film Industry,* ed. Tino Balio (Madison, WI, 1976), pp. 193–211.

136   *"I am positive..."* Harry Warner quoted in *General Talking Pictures Corporation et al.* v. *American Telephone and Telegraph Company et al.,* 18F. Supp 650 (1937), Record, p. 1108, in Gomery, p. 200.

137   *"As he walked into the office..."* MS.

138   *Sam reported back...* Warner, p. 177.

138   *The next morning,* Variety... Kevin Brownlow, *The Parade's Gone By* (New York, 1968), p. 658.

138   *Warner Brothers stock...* Alva Johnston, "Profile," *The New Yorker,* December 22, 1928, p. 24.

138   *"Squawks and howls."* Brownlow, p. 658.

139   *The material on which the film was based...* Robert L. Carringer, "History of a Popular Culture Classic," in *The Jazz Singer,* Robert L. Carringer, ed. (Madison, WI, 1979), p. 12. This is the most detailed account of the origins of the film.

139   *"Shrewd and well-planned."* New York Times, September 15, 1925, quoted in Carringer.

140   *"Desperately wanted the rights."* Warner, p. 174.

140   *"It would be a good picture..."* George Jessel, *So Help Me* (New York, 1943), p. 85.

140   *Jack said he quickly agreed...* Warner, pp. 174–75.

141   *Years later Jessel would claim...* Jessel, p. 88.

141   *Raphaelson had been inspired...* Samson Raphaelson, interviewed by author.

141   *"The chief difficulty..."* Harry Jolson, as told to Alban Emley, *Mistah Jolson* (Hollywood, 1951), p. 47.

142   *"Without a doubt the biggest..."* "The Jazz Singer," in *Souvenir Programs of Twelve Classic Movies, 1927–1941,* ed. Miles Kreuger (New York, 1977), p. 9.

142   *"Jesse, this is a revolution!"* Walter Wanger interview in Bernard Rosenberg and Harry Silverstein, *The Real Tinsel* (New York, 1970), p. 94.

142   *"Biggest ovation in a theater..."* *New York Times,* October 7, 1926.

142   *When Jolson strode...* George Morris, "Opening Night," *Take One,* January 1978, p. 32.

142   *"A slave-driver for perfection..."* Warner, p. 170.

143   Sam Warner's death. For accounts of Sam Warner's death, see *New York Times,* October 6, 1927, p. 25; *Variety,* October 12, 1927, p. 11; *Film Daily,* October 6, 1927, p. 1; *Motion Picture News,* October 14, 1927, p. 1171. These reports vary, and it seems uncertain whether the exact cause of death was a cerebral hemorrhage or an abscess on the brain.

143   *"I had a simple..."* Samson Raphaelson interview, Columbia Oral History Collection, quoted in Carringer, p. 20.

143   *But even if it failed as drama...* See J. Hoberman, "Is 'The Jazz Singer' Good for the Jews?" *Village Voice,* January 7–13, 1981, pp. 1, 31–33, for another analysis of the film. Hoberman calls it "the bluntest and most resonant movie Hollywood ever produced on the subject of American Jews. For *The Jazz Singer* is a metaphoric account of Jewish modernization—it deals with the secularization of the religious impulses and the ensuing crisis of Jewish identity."

144   *"Jack is besieged..."* Carringer, p. 130.

144   *"Jews are determining..."* Samson Raphaelson, "Preface to 'The Jazz Singer'" in Kreuger, p. 14.

145   *"Producers now realized..."* Stanley Watkins, quoted in Brownlow, p. 660.

146   *Less than a year after* The Jazz Singer... Johnston, p. 24.

146   *By the time the dust had cleared...* Fortune magazine, December 1937.

146   *For months he behaved erratically...* Milton Sperling, quoted in Freedland, p. 61.

147   *They called her* shiksa... JW, Jr.

148   *"Distorted with fury."* Warner, p. 212.

148   *"I was his beard."* MS.

149   *Though his divorce hadn't yet been finalized...* New York Evening Journal, December 21, 1933.

149   *"You are the oldest..."* Quoted in letter to Warner Twyford, February 25, 1949, Harry Warner Papers, American Jewish Archive.

149   Divorce. To a surprisingly large degree—or, perhaps, not so surprising, given Jack's exhibitionism—a disproportionate number of the studio's films in the late twenties and early thirties dealt with marital discord—movies with titles like *Her Marriage Vow, A Lost Lady, Compromise, Other Women's Husbands,* and *Don't Tell the Wife.* In all of these the conflicts between old and new, between obligation and freedom, between roots and dreams, find a sexual rather than a religious context, although the conflicts are essentially the same as in *The Jazz Singer.* This was obviously both a personal and a professional preoccupation of Jack's.

150   *"Read it?"* Mervyn LeRoy, as told to Dick Kleiner, *LeRoy: Take One* (New York, 1974), p. 114.

150   *"Now, don't you go giving me..."* JW, Jr.

150   *"Sharpens the perceptions..."* Isaiah Berlin, *Against the Current: Essays in the History of Ideas* (New York, 1979), p. 256.

5: "I DON'T GET ULCERS. I GIVE 'EM!"

151   *"He enjoyed playing Harry Cohn."* Quoted in Bob Thomas, *King Cohn* (New York, 1967), pp. xviii–xvix. This is the only book-length biography of Cohn.

151   *"In the general run..."* Frank Capra, *The Name Above the Title* (New York, 1971), p. 84.

151   *"I've got a man..."* William Graf, interviewed by author.

152   *"He put more people in the cemetery..."* Daniel Fuchs, "Writing for the Movies," *Commentary*, February 1962, p. 109.

152   *"The eyes were dark..."* Jesse Lasky, Jr., *Whatever Happened to Hollywood?* (New York, 1975), p. 290.

152   *"The reason is..."* Leonard Lyons, "Lyons' Den," *New York Post*, February 28, 1958.

152   Mussolini and novocaine. Jonie Taps, Columbia music executive and one of Cohn's closest friends, interviewed by author.

152   *"Why do you have the desk here?"* JT.

153   *"All of a sudden alone..."* Anonymous, quoted in *New York Herald Tribune*, February 28, 1958.

153   *"Why are you introducing this girlie?"* Kim Stanley, quoted in John Kobal, *People Will Talk* (New York, 1986), p. 693.

153   *"The name's got to go."* Jack Lemmon, quoted in Walter Wagner, *You Must Remember This* (New York, 1975), p. 301.

153   *"I wonder what he wants..."* Gerald Briskin, Columbia executive and son of Columbia production head Sam Briskin, interviewed by author.

153   *"They used to come up here trembling."* WG.

153   *"Give the public..."* Quoted in Thomas, pp. xvii–xviii.

153   *"To describe him..."* Max Youngstein, interviewed by author.

154   *"He rated writers..."* Capra, p. 92.

154   *"He was a man who believed..."* Daniel Taradash, "I Remember Him Well," in *Hello, Hollywood!*, eds. Allen Rivkin and Laura Kerr (New York, 1962), p. 123.

154   *"He believed instinctively..."* Garson Kanin, *Hollywood* (New York, 1974), p. 212.

155   Despite his appeals... Robert Cohn, son of Jack Cohn and nephew of Harry, interviewed by author.

156   *"We only had a very limited number..."* Film Daily, February 28, 1926, p. 57.

156   Traffic in Souls. Terry Ramsaye, *A Million and One Nights* (New York, 1926), p. 613.

157   Grossed $450,000. *Ibid.*, pp. 613–17.

158   Fencing furs. JT.

158   *"We caught on to the fact..."* Philip Dunne, interviewed by author.

159   Whenever his old partner... Thomas, pp. 10–13. Harry Rubinstein later became Harry Ruby, a successful Broadway and Hollywood composer.

159   *"The tolerant trolley company..."* Ibid., p. 21.

159   *"He taught me..."* Kanin, p. 211.

160   Their first capital... Robert Cohn recalled going to an Italian restaurant

with his father and uncle when Giannini appeared. "And I remember for some reason calling him 'Doc,' because he was Doctor Giannini. And Harry grabbing me...and saying, 'He's *Doctor* Giannini to you.'...But he was God to them."

160   *"Two sides were now three stories..."* Capra, p. 81.

161   *"Harry Cohn knew everybody..."* Howard Hawks, quoted in Kobal, p. 92.

161   *"Bootleggers and icemen..."* Dore Schary, quoted in *The Real Tinsel*, eds. Bernard Rosenberg and Harry Silverstein (New York, 1970), p. 128.

161   *"Needless to say, he was Jewish."* Capra, p. 78.

162   *"You're fired..."* Dore Schary, *Heyday* (Boston, 1979), p. 75.

163   *"Very unlike Harry Cohn."* GB.

163   *According to Cohn's biographer...* Thomas, p. 39.

164   *"Hopping freights..."* Capra, p. 17.

164   *During one stretch, he sold a set...* Charles Maland, *Frank Capra* (Boston, 1980), p. 24.

165   *"The room was so long..."* Capra, pp. 79–80.

166   *"A secret ambition..."* Ibid., p. 105.

166   *"Cohn was determined..."* Ibid.

167   *The Younger Generation.* For a more detailed description, see Patricia Erens, *The Jew in American Cinema* (Bloomington, IN, 1984), pp. 87–89.

168   *"Relief for the Jews!"* Thomas, p. 230.

168   *"I worked for him..."* Lester Roth, interviewed by author.

168   *There were a great many Jews...* See Kenneth B. Clark, "Jews in Contemporary America: Problems in Identification," in ed. Norman Kiell, *The Psychodynamics of American Jewish Life* (New York, 1967), pp. 111–26.

168   *"Two little Jews."* Kanin, pp. 219–20.

168   *"I'm an American..."* Thomas, p. 257.

168   *"I remember now as a kid..."* RC. There is something of an irony here, since the son of the brother who changed his name reclaimed "Cohn" when he decided to enter the film business. It seems that what was a disadvantage in advertising was a decided advantage in Hollywood.

169   *"To break into the elite..."* Capra, p. 105.

169   *"He was frightened of Capra..."* Pandro Berman, interviewed by author.

170   *"They all talk about business..."* Dore Schary interview, Columbia University Oral History Collection, pp. 17–18.

170   *"Two status-building maneuvers..."* Capra, p. 117.

172   *"An absolutely gilt-edged source..."* Otis Ferguson, *The Film Criticism of Otis Ferguson*, ed. Robert Wilson (Philadelphia, 1971), p. 18.

172   *"Capra had already made..."* Ibid., p. 19.

173   Bridging class. For an extended discussion of the "class-bridging" function of screwball comedy, see Andrew Bergman, *We're in the Money* (New York, 1971).

173   *"Ecumenical church of humanism."* Maland, p. 92.

174   *"Frank Capra? He's the one..."* Shelley Winters, *Shelley Also Known as Shirley* (New York, 1981), p. 70.

174   Welshed on a boxing bet. Schulberg, *Life* magazine, March 3, 1967.

174   *If You Could Only Cook.* Capra, pp. 217–18.

175   *"Oh, price my ass."* Ibid., p. 218.

176   *"See, the studio heads..."* Quoted in Kobal, p. 410.

176   *"You think this is easy?"* Capra, p. 233.

177   *"He enjoyed it."* JT.

177   *"You could sense..."* WG.

178   *"Don't tell anybody."* Taradash in Rivkin and Kerr, p. 124.
178   *When a group of influential California women . . .* Whitney Bolton, *New York Morning Telegraph*, March 4, 1958.
178   *"So one time I took the checks . . ."* Dona Holloway, executive secretary, interviewed by author. Barrymore never played Scrooge, and Holloway obviously meant someone else, but the meaning of the story remains.
178   Henry Martin. WG. Fortunately Henry survived, and Graf later convinced him to will the money to a black scholarship fund.
179   *"I hear you're doing well."* GB.
179   *"Watch those fags . . ."* JT.
179   *"Lived for bread alone."* LR.
179   *"He insisted he made pictures . . ."* Taradash in Rivkin and Kerr, p. 123.
179   *"I always felt that."* DH.
179   *"That was his biggest frustration."* JT.
180   *"You're an illiterate . . ."* Milton Sperling, film producer, interviewed by author.
180   *"He called me one night . . ."* WG.
180   *"His last words . . ."* Whitney Bolton, *New York Morning Telegraph*, March 7, 1967.
181   *"Because he had experiences . . ."* RC.
182   *"I saw Mr. Cohn do some things . . ."* WG.
182   *"My mother was so concerned . . ."* RC.
182   *"When I came to New York . . ."* JT.
183   *"He couldn't believe a writer . . ."* Fuchs, p. 109. Fuchs doesn't mention Cohn by name, but the implication is unmistakable. What Cohn was almost certainly referring to was an attempt by Jack in 1932 to seize control of the company and fire Harry. Harry successfully parried but apparently never forgot.

6: IN THEIR IMAGE

187   *"Studios had faces . . ."* Billy Wilder, interviewed by author.
187   Jack Warner's day. William Schaefer, Jack Warner's administrative assistant, interviewed by author.
188   *"I had some papers . . ."* Milton Sperling, interviewed by author.
189   *"They had different kinds of ambitions . . ."* BW.
189   *"An expensive dream . . ."* Quoted in "Warner Brothers," *Fortune* magazine, December 1937, p. 110.
189   *"MGM was a studio that spent . . ."* MS.
190   *One producer remembered cutting . . .* Louis Edelman in John Baxter, *Hollywood in the Thirties* (London, 1968), p. 71.
190   *"Maybe we are cutting our pictures . . ."* Memo from Hal Wallis to Jack Warner, dated March 8, 1934, in *Inside Warner Brothers (1935–1951)*, ed. Rudy Behlmer, (New York, 1985), p. 15.
190   *"Timely, topical, not typical."* Jerry Wald interview, Columbia University Oral History Collection, pp. 2031–32 and 2067.
191   *He was reflected . . .* Jack Warner, Jr., interviewed by author.
191   *"He was the father . . ."* Bette Davis, *The Lonely Life* (New York, 1962), p. 183.
191   *"Violent in his hatreds . . ."* Henry Ephron, *We Thought We Could Do Anything* (New York, 1977), p. 70.
191   *Once, during his rounds . . . Fortune* magazine, December 1937.

191   *"Confusing their actors with racehorses."* James Cagney, *Cagney by Cagney* (New York, 1976), pp. 55 and 69.

192   *"I had to fight for everything..."* Ann Sheridan, quoted in John Kobal, *People Will Talk* (New York, 1985), p. 421.

192   *"I did an entire series of these walkouts..."* Cagney, p. 64.

193   *"Suddenly, Harry Warner poked his head..."* Hal Wallis and Charles Higham, *Starmaker* (New York, 1980), p. 28.

193   *"Take this fellow here..."* Leo Rosten interview, Columbia Oral History Collection, pp. 2235–36.

193   *"Jack was a frightened man."* MS.

194   *"Jack ran to the stage ahead of me..."* Wallis and Higham, p. 95.

194   *"He once glued the pages..."* WS.

194   Peremptorily cut off friend. JW, Jr.

194   *"The fight has left its mark..."* *Fortune* magazine, December 1937, p. 111.

195   *"More and more is the realization growing..."* *New York American*, August 11, 1936.

195   Edward G. Robinson's son's bar mitzvah. Edward G. Robinson, Jr., with William Dufty. *My Father, My Son* (New York, 1958), pp. 72–76.

196   *"The motion picture presents..."* *Fortune* magazine, December 1937, p. 220.

198   *"Ran Columbia like a private police state."* Jesse Lasky, Jr., *Whatever Happened to Hollywood?* (New York, 1975), p. 289.

198   *"Columbia was the most extreme."* Ring Lardner, Jr., interviewed by author.

198   *"No sooner would he win you..."* Pandro Berman, interviewed by author.

199   *"Fuck her."* Jack Cole, Columbia choreographer, quoted in John Kobal, *People Will Talk* (New York, 1985), p. 605.

199   *"In the midst of a vital casting discussion..."* Daniel Taradash, "I Remember Him Well," in *Hello, Hollywood!*, eds. Allen Rivkin and Laura Kerr, p. 124.

200   Capra and Wilder. William Pechter, *Twenty-Four Times a Second* (New York, 1971), p. 124.

202   *"Surprised when anybody criticizes..."* Niven Busch, Jr., "Profile," *The New Yorker* magazine, September 7, 1929, p. 29.

203   *"Lasky was a dreamer."* Eugene Zukor, interviewed by author.

203   *"The greatest aspect of Jesse Lasky..."* Rouben Mamoulian interview, Columbia University Oral History Collection, series 1, vol. 6, part 2, pp. 74–75. It was Lasky who was responsible for the most incongruous of Paramount's films: De Mille's epics. Though Zukor often resisted these as garish and overpriced, they played beautifully into Lasky's sense of grandiosity and pomposity.

203   *"The trouble with your old man..."* Budd Schulberg, *Moving Pictures: Memories of a Hollywood Prince* (New York, 1981), p. 358.

203   *"We were always trying to lift public taste..."* Walter Wanger interview in *The Real Tinsel*, eds. Bernard Rosenberg and Harry Silverstein (New York, 1970), p. 84.

205   *"Ruinous practice..."* Quoted in I. G. Edmonds, *Big U* (South Brunswick, NJ, 1977), pp. 80–81.

205   *"From the evidence..."* Davis, p. 139.

206   Latecomer to sound. Richard Koszarski, *Universal Pictures: Sixty-Five Years* (New York, 1978), p. 8.

206   Western archetype. The archetype also surfaces repeatedly in films that are not Westerns.

207   *"A mess."* Allen Rivkin, interviewed by author.

207   *"Papa greeted me warmly..."* George Oppenheimer, *The View From the 60s* (New York, 1966), pp. 115–16.

208   *"A very amiable sort of man..."* Max Laemmle, interviewed by author.

208   *"The place was so jammed with relatives..."* *New York World-Telegram*, May 8, 1937. An earlier article from the same newspaper cites fourteen of Laemmle's relatives working at Universal (March 22, 1936).

208   *"Most of them were unable to do anything..."* Erich von Stroheim on tape, recorded by John Huntley for the British Film Institute, London, 1953, quoted in Kevin Brownlow, *The Parade's Gone By* (New York, 1968), p. 476.

209   *"From the time you were signed at MGM..."* Quoted in Walter Wagner, *You Must Remember This* (New York, 1975), p. 205.

209   *"Coin he dealt in was talent."* Gavin Lambert, *On Cukor* (New York, 1972), p. 105.

209   *"All the attributes of immense wealth..."* Leo Rosten interview, Columbia Oral History Collection, p. 2240.

210   *"If anybody was good..."* PB.

210   *"In operation, the plant presents..."* "MGM," *Fortune* magazine, December 1932, p. 51.

210   *"MGM is the only place..."* SM

211   *"Showing you their last picture made a million..."* Ben Hecht interview, Columbia University Oral History Collection, p. 722.

211   *"A cold place."* Mary Astor, *A Life on Film* (New York, 1971), p. 140.

211   *"Here the slogan was..."* Frank Capra, *The Name Above the Title* (New York, 1971), p. 118.

211   *"Big enough to house a comfortable little cafe..."* William Wellman, *A Short Time for Insanity* (New York, 1974), pp. 226–28.

211   *"I don't think you can be a public figure..."* Joan Crawford, quoted in Kobal, p. 279.

212   *"They would chide you..."* Quoted in Wagner, p. 206.

212   *"You're ruining your stomach."* SM.

212   Trip to Italy. Irene Mayer Selznick, *A Private View* (New York, 1983), p. 58.

212   *"Dad came in the car."* Edith Mayer Goetz, interviewed by author.

212   *"He was the kind of man whose door..."* Mervyn LeRoy, *LeRoy: Take One* (New York, 1974), p. 135. Though this is doubtful if taken literally—Ida Koverman was a fearsome palace guard—the sense is accurate: Mayer was far from an imperious ruler.

213   *"My boy, I don't know..."* PB.

213   Loew's complex theater arrangement. "MGM," *Fortune* magazine, December 1932, p. 114; and "Loew's, Inc.," *Fortune* magazine, August 1939, pp. 25–30.

213   *"A few years ago the bankers came..."* U.S. Congress, Senate. Committee on Interstate Commerce, *Hearings, Moving Picture and Radio Propaganda*, September 23, 1941, p. 248.

214   *"A Graustark or a Ruritania..."* Oppenheimer, p. 118.

214   *"Movie queens 'looking right.'"* Lambert, p. 187.

214   *"Jules Dassin..."* Daniel Fuchs, "Writing for the Movies," *Commentary*, February 1962, p. 112.

215   *"When you look at the Andy Hardy pictures..."* Danny Selznick, interviewed by author.

215   *"Metro's mothers..."* Astor, p. 171.

216   *"Artifacts of Americana..."* DS.

216   *"You're Andy Hardy!"* BW.

216   *"I would sit next to him..."* DS.

217   I. C. Nelson story. Dietz, pp. 299–300.

218   *"He darted in and out..."* F. Scott Fitzgerald, *The Last Tycoon* (New York, 1941), pp. 22–23.

218   *"He was like a man who hadn't learned to write..."* Ben Hecht interview, Columbia University Oral History Collection, p. 723.

218   *"Instinct for refinement."* Lambert, p. 106.

218   *"Cold, calm, logical, impersonal judge."* *New York Evening Journal*, September 14, 1936.

219   *"Situation wanted."* Cited in *Brooklyn Eagle*, September 15, 1926.

219   Thalberg's job. See Bob Thomas, *Thalberg* (New York, 1969), p. 39. Thomas, in an undocumented story, says that Laemmle set up a projector on his porch for the entertainment of the neighborhood. See also *New York Times*, September 15, 1936, and *New York Herald Tribune*, September 15, 1936, for similar accounts.

219   *In another account...* Samuel Marx, *Mayer and Thalberg: The Make-Believe Saints* (New York, 1975), p. 30. When in doubt, Marx is often treated as the reliable source because he was an acquaintance of Thalberg's and spent a good deal of time with him.

220   *"Mr. Cochrane said you wanted to see me."* Louella Parsons, dateline November 20, 1927.

221   *One studio chief exacted...* Marx, p. 64.

221   *Their arguments, like their romance...* Walter Laemmle, interviewed by author.

221   *"The boy is a genius."* De Mille, p. 100.

221   *Thalberg met Mayer...* Bosley Crowther, *Hollywood Rajah* (New York, 1960), pp. 86–88; Marx, pp. 17–18. The source of this story is probably Loeb himself, whom Marx interviewed.

222   *"Never remain in a job..."* Quoted in Brownlow, p. 487.

222   *"Very quiet, soft-spoken..."* Philip Dunne, interviewed by author.

222   *"Feathers on an eel."* Ben Hecht, *Charlie, The Improbable Life and Times of Charles MacArthur* (New York, 1957), pp. 171–72.

222   *"He was always quite shy with her."* Lambert, p. 106.

222   *"Wonderful candid humility..."* Quoted in S. J. Perelman, "The Great (and Invisible) Man," in *Hello, Hollywood!*, eds. Allen Rivkin and Laura Kerr (New York, 1962), p. 76.

223   *"He was thoughtful..."* Dietz, p. 157.

223   *"It took only thirty seconds..."* Oppenheimer, p. 122.

223   *"Seriously began to question..."* Perelman, pp. 78, 79, and 80.

224   *"It was the most amazing set-up."* Anita Loos interview, Columbia University Oral History Collection, pp. 131–32.

224   *"Irving was never satisfied..."* Conrad Nagel in *The Real Tinsel*, Bernard Rosenberg and Harry Silverstein (New York, 1970), p. 188.

224   *"We always made a picture with..."* Brownlow, p. 488.

224   *"There was a certainty..."* Hecht, p. 171; *"My finger on the pulse..."* Allen Rivkin in Rivkin and Kerr, p. 74.

225   *"I think we will put the road here."* Quoted in Matthew J. Bruccoli, *Some Kind of Epic Grandeur* (New York, 1981), p. 259.

225   *"You would be working with your writer..."* Quoted in Brownlow, p. 487.

225   *"Mervyn, I didn't ask..."* LeRoy, p. 121.

225   Thalberg's rules. *New York Evening Journal,* September 14, 1936.

225   *"That was one thing about Stahr."* Fitzgerald, p. 54.

226   *"Between them they created MGM."* David Selznick interview, William Wiener Oral History Library, American Jewish Committee, p. 8.

226   *Another compared them...* Loos interview, p. 141.

226   *"The original guys were all fur merchants..."* PB.

226   *"Man of intellectual content."* Samuel Spewack interview, Columbia University Oral History Collection, p. 2.

227   Albert Lewin. MR.

227   *"I could see the little figure..."* Dwight Taylor, *Joy Ride* (New York, 1959), p. 240.

227   Arnold Schönberg. Salka Viertel, *The Kindness of Strangers* (New York, 1969), pp. 207-8.

229   *"Spare tire."* Marx, p. 86.

229   Rosabelle later married Stanley Bergerman, who became a Universal executive, but it is likely she always pined for Thalberg, and she visited his burial vault each year with an offering of flowers.

229   Thalberg's wedding. For accounts of the wedding, see *Los Angeles Herald,* September 30, 1927; *Screenland,* January 1928; *New York Daily Mirror,* September 15, 1936.

230   *"Why the hell am I killing myself..."* Thomas, p. 236.

230   *"Reports that I am leaving..."* *New York Times,* October 14, 1932.

231   *When it ended, Schenck had conceded...* Thomas, p. 237.

231   *"He wanted as much as L.B...."* Quoted in Marx, p. 164.

231   *That evening he suffered a heart attack. New York Times,* January 9, 1933; *New York Sun,* February 20, 1933.

232   *"The greatest producer..."* Memo to Louis B. Mayer, quoted in Marx, p. 249 fn.

232   *"I felt an air of suspicion..."* Letter dated February 23, 1936, in Crowther, p. 168.

232   *"Please come to see me..."* *Ibid.,* p. 170.

233   *"He found increasing resistance..."* Selznick, *A Private View,* p. 190.

233   New rumors circulated. *New York Times,* March 28, 1933.

233   *"Single centralized production head..."* Memo from David Selznick to Nicholas Schenck, May 16, 1933, in *Memo From: David Selznick,* ed. Rudy Behlmer (New York, 1972), p. 94.

233   *"Idealism is profitable."* *Los Angeles Times,* August 19, 1933.

234   *Thalberg chose not to exhaust himself...* As for Thalberg's working with the Marx Brothers, there were those who felt that his sense of refinement tamed their chaos. In one critic's words, "they became more genial, more considerate, more positive" in the films they made at MGM. [Robert Sklar, *Movie-Made America* (New York, 1975), p. 184.]

234   Thalberg's illness. See *New York Evening Journal,* September 15, 1936; *Variety,* September 16, 1936; *New York Evening Post,* September 14, 1936. Also scrapbooks, New York Public Library of the Performing Arts at Lincoln Center, MWEZ 2844.

234   *"I'm not getting the right treatment."* Marx, p. 312.

235   Thalberg's death. *New York Daily Mirror,* September 15, 1936; *New York Evening Journal,* September 15, 1936.

235   Thalberg's funeral. *New York Times,* September 17, 1936; *Variety,* September 23, 1936; *New York American,* September 17, 1936; *New York*

Herald Tribune, September 17, 1936.

235   *"I came to California..."* *Variety*, September 23, 1936, dateline September 18, 1936.

236   *"What a hell of a hole..."* "Crazy Sunday," in F. Scott Fitzgerald, *Babylon Revisited and Other Stories* (New York, 1960), p. 248.

7: HOW THEY LIVED

237   *"The rich and vulgar..."* Walter Blumenthal—Walter Lippmann, March 3, 1922, quoted in Ronald Steel, *Walter Lippmann and the American Century* (New York, 1980), p. 192.

237   *"We were sitting at a long table..."* Eugene Zukor, interviewed by author.

238   *"Mostly of railroad presidents..."* Stanton Griffis, *Lying in State* (New York, 1952), p. 84.

238   *"The headwaiters and captains..."* *New York Evening Journal*, June 17, 1936.

239   Lasky's life-style. Jesse Lasky with Don Weldon, *I Blow My Own Horn* (Garden City, NY, 1957), pp. 235–36.

239   *"Of course he lost it."* Betty Lasky, interviewed by author.

239   *"It changed everything."* BL.

240   *"They represented what we wanted to be."* EZ.

240   *"I knew we were in for trouble..."* Paul Wurtzel, interviewed by author.

241   Schenck's life-style. *U.S. v. Schenck*, FRC C-107, 439–440, pp. 286, 550, 915, 955, 982, 2543, 2569.

241   *"I don't keep any women."* PM, April 2, 1941.

241   *"You could even see the physical change..."* Philip Dunne, interviewed by author.

242   *"My childhood was so terrible..."* BL.

242   Lasky and Korda. Jesse Lasky, Jr., interview in Walter Wagner, *You Must Remember This* (New York, 1975), p. 153; Michael Korda, *Charmed Lives* (New York, 1979), pp. 233–40.

243   *"You're not emotionally equipped..."* PW.

244   *"When we got back to the beach house..."* Edith Mayer Goetz, interviewed by author.

244   When Mayer advised Selznick... Irene Selznick, *A Private View* (New York, 1983), p. 133.

244   *"I just wanted to be married quietly."* EMG.

245   *"My father often talked..."* Danny Selznick, interviewed by author.

245   *"Possessive is just barely touching it."* Angela Fox Dunn, interviewed by author.

246   *"Creatures of a drive..."* Jack Warner, Jr., interviewed by author.

246   *"I was absorbed in company business..."* Lasky and Weldon, p. 234.

246   *"Amour in Hollywood..."* Ben Hecht interview, Columbia Oral History Collection, p. 760.

246   *"Miss Sidney's health came first..."* Quoted in *Variety*, September 12, 1933.

246   *"She was still a teenager."* Budd Schulberg, "King Cohn," *Life* magazine, March 3, 1967.

247   Cohn and Calvet. Corinne Calvet, *Has Corinne Been a Good Girl?* (New York, 1983), pp. 4–9.

247   *"A lot of the girls he went with..."* Jonie Taps, interviewed by author.

247   Desperately wanted a son. Shelley Winters, *Shelley Also Known as Shirley* (New York, 1980), p. 123.

248   Studio shot 1,200 feet. Bob Thomas, *King Cohn* (New York, 1967), pp. 183–84.

248   *"Bird in a gilded cage."* WG.

248   *"The more things I gave my wife..."* Lasky and Weldon, p. 234.

249   *"After she was married for about fifteen years..."* William Schaefer, interviewed by author.

249   *Sol Wurtzel and his wife...* PW.

249   *"Hollywood was a company town..."* Ella Winter, *And Not to Yield* (New York, 1963), p. 233.

249   *"Even my doctor..."* George Oppenheimer, *The View from the 60s* (New York, 1966), p. 104.

250   *One visiting potentate...* Pandro Berman, interviewed by author.

250   Hollywood Four Hundred. Mary Pickford, quoted in Wagner, p. 13.

250   *"I marveled at this new world..."* Eddie Cantor, *My Life Is in Your Hands* (New York, 1928), p. 271.

251   *"The food was good..."* Mary Astor, *A Life on Film* (New York, 1971), p. 66.

251   *"We attended swimming parties..."* Jesse Lasky, Jr., *Whatever Happened to Hollywood?* (New York, 1975), p. 288.

251   *"When we really threw a party...* Jesse Lasky with Don Weldon, *I Blow My Own Horn* (Garden City, NY, 1957), p. 234.

251   *"Only one immovable house rule."* JW, Jr.

252   *"They were usually very dirty."* Maurice Rapf, interviewed by author.

252   *"I went to Mayer's house one night..."* Milton Sperling, interviewed by author.

253   *"Every male was automatically drawn..."* Oppenheimer, p. 130. Philip Dunne makes the same observation in *Take Two* (New York, 1980), p. 29.

253   *"He had gone into the next room..."* Edmund Wilson, *The Thirties*, ed. Leon Edel (New York, 1980), p. 128.

253   *"You know, I always hate the holidays..."* Sam Marx, interviewed by author.

254   *"Are you crazy?"* MS.

254   Budd Schulberg remembered a studio truck. Budd Schulberg, *Some Faces in the Crowd* (New York, 1953), pp. 131–41.

254   *"Society consisted of the top executives..."* Oppenheimer, pp. 130–31.

254   *"They came and went."* JW, Jr.

254   *"Physically thrown out of Louis B. Mayer's house..."* JW, Jr.

255   *"They would hire all the guys..."* PW.

255   Cohn luring the Warners. JW, Jr.; MS.

255   *"They called each other names."* EZ.

256   *"Our house is invaded by vermin..."* EZ.

257   *"The two questions most asked..."* Korda, p. 156.

258   Jews seldom drank. None of the Hollywood Jews was a big drinker. Even Harry Cohn was practically abstinent, taking just a few drinks a year. This, however, was not uncommon among the Jewish population generally. See Charles R. Steiner, *Alcohol and the Jews* (Glencoe, IL, 1958). Steiner cites several reasons for this—that Jews feared increased anti-Semitism if they exhibited inebriation, for example, and that drinking is incompatible with the goal-orientedness of most Jews (pp. 5–6 and p. 13 respectively).

258   Al Lichtman giving stake. PB.

258   *"The mark of a man's position..."* Korda, pp. 156–57.

258   *"Fellows, I've got to get to work."* SM.

258   *"Whatever the house cost..."* JW, Jr.

259   *"It took the fine edge of happiness . . ."* Selznick, pp. 168–69.

259   *"Provoked, nursed, and kept alive . . ."* Rosten, p. 39.

259   *What clinched the case . . .* New York Daily News, April 26, 1941.

260   *Schenck nevertheless offered him . . .* U.S. v Schenck, FRC-107, 439–40, vol. 1, p. 501.

260   *The Wertheimers knocked down a wall.* Ibid., p. 469. The year was 1935.

260   *He broke the wrist himself.* PW.

260   *The Clover had an air of intrigue.* Allen Rivkin, writer, interviewed by author.

261   Nick Schenck garnisheed Thau's salary. SM.

261   *"Everyone that knew Joe Schenck . . ."* U.S. v Joe Schenck, FRC-107, 439–40, vol. 1, pp. 227–29.

261   Schulberg put Mankiewicz under contract. AR.

261   *"Synonymous with thoughts of carefree days . . ."* U.S. v Schenck, FRC-107, 439–40, exhibit 109.

261   *"The huge barroom was loaded . . ."* William Wellman, A Short Time for Insanity (New York, 1974), p. 184.

262   *"As dead as a cock . . ."* Harold Corbin, quoted in New York Herald Tribune, March 18, 1941.

262   The end of Agua Caliente. U.S. v Schenck, FRC-107, 439–440, vol. 1, pp. 558, 567, 601.

262   *"There used to be a kind of floating Jewish population . . ."* PB.

262   *"The Jews had taken over the worship of horses . . ."* F. Scott Fitzgerald, The Last Tycoon (New York, 1941), p. 90.

263   Bridle Path Association. Max Vorspan and Lloyd Gartner, History of the Jews of Los Angeles (Philadelphia, 1970) p. 153.

263   Mayer's morning horseback ride. Crowther, p. 127; Selznick, p. 43.

263   *"Hillcrest with furlong markers."* JW, Jr.; see also LeRoy, pp. 116–17.

263   *Mayer had actually come to horse racing . . .* Crowther, pp. 214, 246–47.

264   Neil McCarthy. EMG.

264   *"It was a kind of classy thing . . ."* DS.

264   Man o' War. Samuel D. Riddle, quoted in Crowther, p. 249. Mayer himself disputed that he had ever made the offer, claiming instead that he had said he *would* have offered $1 million for a horse *like* Man o' War. See Humphrey S. Finney with Raleigh Burroughs, Fair Exchange: Recollections of a Life with Horses (New York, 1974), p. 50.

264   *"As he had his own specially developed relationship . . ."* DS.

265   *"What do you think I'm going to do?"* SM.

8: RABBI TO THE STARS

266   *"Consider this."* Aben Kandel, Rabbi Burns (New York, 1931), p. 256.

266   Rescheduling the Friday-night fights. Richard Z. Grinnberg, "People's Ambassador to the Movies," Jewish Tribune, January 6, 1928, p. 20.

267   W. C. Fields. Rabbi Edgar Magnin, interviewed by author.

267   *"The most important Jew in Los Angeles."* Philip Dunne, interviewed by author.

267   *"I really was the rabbi."* EM.

267   *His father would sneak into the temple . . .* Joan Saunders Wixen, "65 Years in Pulpit," Modern Maturity, December 1980–January 1981, p. 57.

267   *He always wore a silk hat . . .* Rabbi Edgar F. Magnin, "Leader and Person-

ality," interviewed by Malca Chall, Regional Oral History Office, the Bancroft Library, University of California (Berkeley, CA, 1975), p. 14.

268   *"I don't know why I didn't start to be a writer..."* Ibid., p. 25.

268   *"A Russian Jew or a descendent..."* Ibid., p. 28.

268   *He composed a parable about geese...* Ibid., p. 33.

268   *"I used to go to temple..."* Ibid., p. 30–31.

268   *"Nine turns of the crank..."* Ibid., p. 37; and EM.

269   *"Got down to the people's level."* Ibid., p. 35.

269   *Back in 1862...* For a more extensive history of the synagogue, see Marco R. Newmark, "Wilshire Boulevard Temple." Unpublished, 1947, in American Jewish Archives on the Cincinnati campus of the Hebrew Union College.

269   *"Anybody who can make that subject interesting..."* EM.

270   *"The Stuff Dreams Are Made Of."* Lawrence Goldmark, "The History of the Wilshire Boulevard Temple, 1900–1920," p. 17. Unpublished in American Jewish Archives on the Cincinnati campus of the Hebrew Union College.

270   *"He wasn't that scholarly."* EM.

270   *"I always had my eye on New York."* EM.

270   *The Jewish community Magnin entered...* Max Vorspan and Lloyd Gartner, *History of the Jews of Los Angeles* (Philadelphia, 1970), pp. 109 and 114. "Ties with the Old Country were weaker, and the milieu which existed in New York and Philadelphia and Chicago, not to mention smaller cities as well, hardly came into being in Los Angeles."

270   *"Just the other day we noticed several Russian Jewish immigrants..."* B'nai B'rith Messenger, March 31, 1905, quoted in Vorspan and Gartner, p. 110. Additional warnings were issued on April 30 and June 18.

270   Concordia Club. *Ibid.*, p. 153.

271   *"Where do the Jews live?"* Kandel, p. 15.

271   *"Marry the ugly girls..."* EM.

271   *"Those that you met were aggressive..."* Lester Roth, interviewed by author.

272   Loeb & Loeb. For more on the Loebs, see Norton Stern, "Report of an Interview with Edwin J. Loeb," January 28, 1967, and "Report of an Interview with Joseph P. Loeb," January 25, 1967, unpublished, Western Jewish History Center of the Judah L. Manges Memorial Museum, Berkeley, CA.

272   *"I was working in the library..."* Martin Gang, attorney, interviewed by author.

272   *"It was a terrible thing for me..."* Betty Lasky, interviewed by author.

272   *"Mr. Mayer, they don't accept them."* Hedda Hopper and James Brough, *The Whole Truth and Nothing But* (Garden City, NY, 1963), p. 93.

273   *"The commandant says it's the best school..."* Michael Korda, *Charmed Lives* (New York, 1979), p. 160.

273   *"The only family that I ever saw there..."* BL.

273   *"The old man handed me a paper..."* Anonymous, quoted in Otto Friedrich, *City of Nets* (New York, 1986), p. 48.

273   *It happened when Joseph Loeb...* Stern, p. 3.

274   Hillcrest. George Thompson, "The First Fifty Years of Hillcrest," *Hillcrest Fairway*, October/November 1970, pp. 1, 11–12. Archives, Jewish Community Library, Jewish Federation Council of Los Angeles.

274   *"The aristocrats and Jewish bigshots..."* Magnin interview, Chall, p. 77.

274   *To stave off default...* Thompson, pp. 1 and 11.

275   *"I saw your name on the door..."* Milton Sperling, interviewed by author.

275   *"In his shirt-sleeves."* Danny Selznick, interviewed by author.

276   *"It was known as a very elite place..."* Robert Blumofe, interviewed by author.

276   *"Jewish people have to change a lot..."* Magnin interview, Chall, p. 206.

277   *"What was so beautiful about that damned shtetl?"* *Ibid.*, p. 230.

277   *"Jew-controlled..."* "Jewish Control of the American Theater," *Dearborn Independent*, January 1, 1921, p. 8. This was the first in a series of articles Ford ran on Jews and the film industry.

277   *"It is not that producers of Semitic origin..."* "The Jewish Aspect of the 'Movie' Problem," *Dearborn Independent*, February 12, 1921, p. 8.

277   *"No foreign bunch..."* Reverend William A. Sunday, *Lord's Day Leader*, January/February 1921, p. 19.

278   *"Seduction of hundreds of thoughtless girls..."* Reverend Wilbur Fisk Crafts, head of the International Reform Bureau, quoted in *The New York Times*, December 28, 1920. Crafts, a Washington lobbyist who once compared the passage of federal Sabbath laws to Columbus's discovery of America and the Pilgrims' landing at Plymouth Rock, spent the last two decades of his life proselytizing against movies. Twice, once in 1914 and again in 1916, he had pressured the House Education Committee into reporting federal censorship bills. Though he raised the issue of Jewish control of the movies, in fairness he was more likely roused against the Jews through his opposition to the movies than the other way around.

278   *"If these slanderers..."* *New York Times*, December 12, 1920.

278   *"I am a Jew..."* "A Jew Speaks to the Jews of Hollywood," *The Christian Century*, August 19, 1931, p. 1036.

278   *Dreiser blamed the Jews.* Hy Kraft interview, William Wiener Oral History Library at the American Jewish Committee, pp. 87–89.

278   *"The movies are solidly Jewish."* Quoted in Friedrich, p. 252.

278   *"Do you notice how noisy it is..."* Lauren Bacall, *Lauren Bacall By Myself* (New York, 1978), p. 124.

279   *"Through the years I had heard..."* Dore Schary, *Heyday* (Boston, 1979), p. 125.

279   *"Out of the hands of these Eastern European Jews."* Gloria Swanson, *Swanson on Swanson* (New York, 1980), pp. 148 and 150.

279   *"If he was a rabbi..."* Jack Warner, Jr., interviewed by author.

279   *When RKO production head...* Bosley Crowther, *Hollywood Rajah* (New York, 1960), p. 260.

280   *Reverse discrimination.* MS and Maurice Rapf, interviewed by author.

280   *"The right rabbi in the right temple..."* Budd Schulberg, *Moving Pictures: Memories of a Holywood Prince* (New York, 1981), p. 232.

280   *"Edgar would fit into any group."* Grinnberg, p. 20.

280   *"A democratic person."* Magnin, Chall, p. 19.

280   *"How do you know so much about business?"* *Ibid.*, p. 194.

281   *"A real shul."* Schulberg, p. 192.

281   *"Human interests throbbing freely..."* Grinnberg, p. 20.

281   *"I don't care about religion."* EM.

281   *"The tables and desks would be piled..."* Sam Marx, interviewed by author.

281   *"He loved me."* EM.

281   *"Louis, I want to have lunch..."* EM.

282   *"Do you want to go to MGM?"* EM.

282   *"Like a peacock..."* Schulberg, p. 236.
282   *"I had the voice..."* Magnin interview, Chall, pp. 105 and 117.
282   *"Third-rate poetry..." Ibid.,* p. 100.
283   *"The pulpit is a work of art..." Ibid.,* p. 127.
283   Jewish equivalent of Episcopalians. MS.
283   *"I wanted the proportions..."* Magnin interview, Chall, p. 85.
284   *"It was the first time I'd heard of any reference..."* Quoted in Friedrich, p. 357.
284   *"You let one of them in..."* DS.
284   Puffing on a large cigar. Ruth Nussbaum, wife of Rabbi Max Nussbaum, interviewed by author.
284   *"They were going down the aisle..."* PW.
284   Coming to the studio on Yom Kippur. Dona Holloway, Cohn's executive secretary, interviewed by author.
284   *"Today is Erav Yom Kippur."* Michael Blankfort, interviewed by author.
285   *Adolph Zukor enrolled his children...* Eugene Zukor, interviewed by author.
285   *"Very Catholic prone."* Edith Mayer Goetz, interviewed by author.
285   *"Louis admired power..."* EM.
285   *"He was* the *cardinal..."* LR.
286   *"Very tender with the Catholics."* PD.
286   Identified with the pope. DS.
286   *"Why isn't it Jewish?"* William Graf, Cohn's administrative assistant, interviewed by author.
286   Christian Science. See John J. Appel, "Christian Science and the Jews," *Jewish Social Studies* 1969, vol. XXXI, pp. 100–21. "Their 'conversion' if that is what it is," writes Appel, "is not flight from Judaism so much as partial withdrawal stopping short of complete 'crossing over'" (p. 117).
287   *"My father used to argue with my mother..."* JW, Jr.
287   *"If it weren't for his religious reading..."* Jesse Lasky, Jr., *Whatever Happened to Hollywood?* (New York, 1975), p. 329.
287   Cosmic painting. BL.
288   *"The worst illiterate Jew was still a Jew..."* MB.
288   Philanthropy originated in guilt. Ben Hecht, *A Child of the Century* (New York, 1954), p. 538.
289   *"When we were all assembled..."* Alvah Bessie, *Inquisition in Eden* (New York, 1965), p. 64.
289   *"All he had to say..."* JW, Jr.
289   *"If they wanted big contributions..."* SM.
289   *At one fund-raiser, Hal Wallis...* William Schaefer, Jack Warner's administrative assistant, interviewed by author.
290   *Ben Hecht didn't find his men...* Hecht, pp. 544 and 539.
290   Hecht and Selznick. *Ibid.,* pp. 539–45.
291   *"I'm your rabbi, not Dear Abby."* Magnin interview, Chall, p. 115.
291   *"Its whole mental and spiritual climate..."* Samuel Spewack interview, Columbia University Oral History Collection, p. 10.
292   *"In achieving a state of sin..."* Dunne, p. 21.
292   *"Don't you know there's a lady here?"* WG.
292   *Harry Warner might tell...* WS.
292   *"If you have the right values..."* Selznick, p. 68.
292   *"Fuck."* EMG.
293   *"Fire him. He's a crook."* WG.

293   *"If a thing worked, it was moral."* JW, Jr.

293   *"A group in the motion picture industry..."* Mendel Silberberg to Maurice Wertheim, May 29, 1942, American Jewish Committee Archives.

294   *"If you weren't my partner..."* Arthur Groman, partner of Mitchell, Silberberg & Knupp, interviewed by author.

295   *"There were more judges..."* Joseph Roos, one-time organizer on the Jewish Community Relations Council, interviewed by author.

295   *"Mendel Silberberg wasn't aware that he was Jewish..."* JR.

296   *"He was the accepted Jew..."* JR.

297   *"The most valuable piece of manpower..."* Memorandum from N[ate] B. Spingold to the members of the Public Relations Group of the American Jewish Committee, July 10, 1944, AJC Archives, Silberberg file (42–61). See also Paul Jacobs, *Is Curly Jewish?* (New York, 1965), pp. 159–61, for more on the proliferation of Jewish agencies in Los Angeles.

297   *"Now that was our most important client..."* AG.

298   *"Silberberg was the peacemaker."* Robert Cohn, interviewed by author.

298   *"Mendel was not a 'yes-man.'"* AG.

298   *"They are all so deeply engrossed..."* Letter from chairman, Committee on Public Relations, AJC, to Silberberg, November 25, 1942; letter from Silberberg to attorney David Rosenblum, February 3, 1943, AJC Archives, Silberberg file (42–61).

299   *"Most satisfactory results..."* Minutes, Domestic Public Relations Committee, October 30, 1944, AJC, MDW file, Public Relations Committee, 1943–45.

299   *"Dick understood perfectly..."* Background memo for meeting with Hollywood group on AJC relation to movie industry, October 11–12, 1947, AJC, HMPP file.

299   Making the victim black. Eric A. Goldman, "The Fight to Bring the Subject of Anti-Semitism to the Screen," *Davka*, Fall 1975, p. 24. According to Goldman, Warner Brothers threatened not to exhibit the film in its theaters, though the threat turned out to be idle.

299   Crossfire *had tested poorly...* Schary, p. 156.

299   Silberberg rose to its defense. Background memo for meeting with Hollywood group, AJC, HMPP file.

300   Jewish identity on screen. For two extensive surveys on the portrayal of Jews in films, see Patricia Erens, *The Jew in American Cinema* (Bloomington, IN, 1984); and Lester D. Friedman, *Hollywood's Image of the Jew* (New York, 1982).

300   *"Jews are for killing..."* Unattributed quote in Tom Tugend, "The Hollywood Jews," *Davka*, Fall 1975, p. 5.

300   *"This show is by Jews..."* Producer Max Gordon, quoting Richard Rodgers in Garson Kanin, *Hollywood* (New York, 1974), p. 373.

300   *"I don't believe this."* WG.

300   *"Ruffle the goyim."* MB.

300   *"Rabbis don't look dramatic."* EM.

300   *"Our impression was simply..."* Ring Lardner, Jr., interviewed by author.

301   *"When he first called me into conference..."* RL, Jr.

301   *"With acting there was definitely the feeling..."* MR.

301   *"What kind of a name is Garfield?"* Larry Swindell, *Body and Soul: The Story of John Garfield* (New York, 1975), p. 111. "Look, kid," said the executive. "The people are gonna find out you're a Jew sooner or later, but better later. If you stick and they like you, they won't mind. But if we say

right off you're a Jew, they ain't gonna like you."

302   *"One of the unhappiest men..."* Hy Kraft interview, Columbia Oral History Collection, p. 120.

302   *"The screen was Judenrein."* Martin Gang, interviewed by author.

302   *"We left it to Mendel Silberberg..."* JR.

302   *"Hollywood was a huge, untapped source..."* Leo Rosten, interviewed by author.

303   *"In some cases, such pictures should be taken out of production..."* Memorandum on community relations program with the motion picture industry, March 1947, NCRAC, AJC Archives, MM/Films—Movies/Hollywood Project/Committees/NCRAC file.

303   *For two days the sides traded...* JR.

303   John Stone. *Jewish News,* June 13, 1958.

303   *"They'd give us the scripts."* MG.

304   Picking nits. See "Report on John Stone's Work," AJC Archives, AJC-HMPP file.

304   *"Jewish group is trying to censor..."* Minutes of Motion Picture Committee, November 15, 1948, AJC Archives, AJC-HMPP file.

304   *"We must keep our hands on Hollywood..."* Memo from Robert Disraeli to George J. Heston, regarding status of Hollywood Project, December 27, 1950, AJC Archives, AJC-HMPP file.

305   Byzantine rapprochement. JR; memo from Robert Disraeli to David Danzig, AJC, October 21, 1953; letter from Dore Schary to John Slawson of AJC, November 14, 1952; letter from I. B. Benjamin, William Gordon, and Walter Hilborn of AJC to Schary, December 12, 1952; letter from Schary to Jacob Blaustein of AJC, January 14, 1953; draft letter from AJC and ADL to Schary, January 27, 1953; letter from Bernard Trager of AJC to Schary, March 27, 1953; letter from Mendel Silberberg to Blaustein, Bernard Trager, and Henry Edward Schultz of the AJC, September 18, 1953; letter from Blaustein to Silberberg, September 18, 1953.

305   *"When he was young in Berlin..."* RN.

306   *The temple had been founded...* Max Nussbaum, "Jews in the Motion Picture Industry—How Jewish Are They?" *The Reconstructionist,* November 28, 1952, p. 27; see also Lewis Barth, "The History of Temple Israel of Hollywood, 1926–1931," unpublished term paper, UCLA, 1959, in American Jewish Archives at the Hebrew Union College, Cincinnati; Dorothy Corwin, wife of Sherrill Corwin, theater chain owner and activist in Temple Israel, interviewed by author.

306   *"Jewish members of the industry could affiliate..."* Nussbaum, p. 27.

306   *"Car dealer sort."* LR.

306   *"Most reactionary man..."* MS.

306   *"Cardinal Magnin."* MB.

306   *Rabbi Burns.* Kandel, pp. 7, 35, 292.

307   *"We had a desire to do good..."* Quoted in Barth, p. 4.

307   Isadore Isaacson. DC; Barth, p. 6.

307   *One evening in 1938...* Tape recording of Max Nussbaum, Temple Israel.

308   *"He was an intense Jew."* JR.

308   *"When Nussbaum came here he was very young..."* Walter Kohner, agent, interviewed by author.

308   *"I wouldn't blame you for being jealous."* Magnin interview, Chall, p. 121.

309   Enjoyed the Hollywood connection. As with Magnin, so too for Nussbaum, this led to a kind of advocacy of Hollywood. In the November 28,

1952, issue of *The Reconstructionist*, a Jewish periodical, Nussbaum, as spiritual leader of the Hollywood Jews, wrote an article commending them: "There is, I believe, a Jewish consciousness in the hearts of most of these men which guides their obligations, both to our Jewish group and to the community at large. I know of instances where some of these oft maligned producers went out of their way to acquire a book or a script to be filmed, either in order to enhance the position of the Jewish community, or to stress a fundamental principle of liberty or justice on the American scene" (p. 28).

309 *After one benefit...*" DC.

309 Decorated by Fox Pictures. PW. Wilshire was the synagogue of MGM (Mayer and Thalberg), Universal (the Laemmles), and Warner Brothers (Jack and Harry); Temple Israel the synagogue of Fox (Wurtzel and Stone) and Columbia (Sam and Irving Briskin, and Sam Bischoff).

309 *"This is your life!"* RN.

9: REFUGEES AND BRITISH ACTORS

311 *"Refugees and British Actors."* Isolationist Senator Gerald Nye in a speech said Hollywood "swarms with refugees... [and] with British actors." Senator Gerald P. Nye, "War Propaganda," *Vital Speeches of the Day*, September 15, 1941, p. 721.

311 *"I sort of went back to the twenties..."* U.S. Congress, House Un-American Activities Committee, *Hearings on Communist Infiltration of the Hollywood Motion Picture Industry*, part 3, 1953, pp. 1457–58.

311 *"Utopia is the opiate..."* Quoted in Allen Guttman, "The Conversions of the Jews," in *The Ghetto and Beyond*, ed. Peter Isaac Rose (New York, 1969), p. 443.

312 *"He has barely got started..."* Upton Sinclair, *I, Governor of California* (Los Angeles, 1934), p. 2, quoted in Lewis A. Fretz, "Upton Sinclair: The Don Quixote of American Reform," Ph.D. diss., Stanford University, 1970, p. 157

312 He was thought to be running ahead. Arthur Schlesinger, *The Politics of Upheaval* (Boston, 1960), pp. 118–19.

312 *"A quiet, slight figure..."* *New York Times*, September 9, 1934, quoted in Leon Harris, *Upton Sinclair: American Rebel* (New York, 1975), p. 371.

312 *"Keep that Bolshevik away..."* Sam Marx, interviewed by author.

312 *"I was present, but was not called..."* Letter from Sinclair to Lewis Browne in Upton Sinclair, *My Life in Letters* (Columbia, MO, 1960), p. 265.

312 *"He's had his fill of politics."* Letter from Craig Sinclair to Mrs. John Kling, n.d., in Harris, p. 270.

312 *"I don't think I'm egotistical..."* Upton Sinclair, "The Movies and Political Propaganda," in *The Movies on Trial*, ed. William J. Perlman (New York, 1936), p. 189.

313 *"Humble and obedient..."* Upton Sinclair interview, Columbia University Oral History Collection, vol. 2. no. 502, p. 213.

313 *"Who knew the smell of money..."* Upton Sinclair, *The Autobiography of Upton Sinclair* (New York, 1962), pp. 274–75.

313 *"And what happened then?"* Sinclair, *Autobiography*, pp. 275–76. As a postscript, Mrs. Fox sent Sinclair a handwritten note after receiving a copy: "[A]s Mr. Fox has been quite ill these past weeks I have thought of nothing

else as I have never ceased blaming myself for the strain put upon him in living all those agonies over again in connection with the writing of the book. You can imagine it is difficult to write you in my depressed state of mind." Still, Mrs. Fox added, "In looking over the contract I see Mr. Fox has reserved for himself the screen and dramatic rights and I doubt very much that he would be interested in parting with either of these rights." July 28, 1933, Sinclair Manuscripts, Manuscript Department, Lilly Library, Indiana University, Bloomington, Indiana.

314 False stories. James Lambert Harte, *This Is Upton Sinclair* (Emmaus, PA, 1938), p. 53.

314 *"Not as yet." New York Herald Tribune*, October 6, 1934.

314 Newsreels. *New York Times*, November 4, 1934, quoted in Sinclair, "The Movies and Political Propaganda," p. 193.

314 *A popular black Los Angeles minister...* Schlesinger, pp. 118–19.

314 *The industry raised nearly half a million dollars...* Schlesinger, pp. 118–19. An anonymous California official estimated that $10 million was spent to defeat Sinclair. Charles W. Van Devander, *The Big Bosses* (New York, 1944), p. 297.

314 *"This campaign against Upton Sinclair has been and is dynamite." Ibid.*, p. 194.

315 *"I made those shorts."* Kyle Crichton, *Total Recoil* (Garden City, NY, 1960), pp. 245–46.

315 Jews and the Republican party. Lawrence H. Fuchs, *The Political Behavior of American Jews* (Glencoe, IL, 1956), p. 51. Fuchs also cites the antagonism between Eastern European Jews and Irish Catholics, who controlled the Democratic party in many urban centers.

315 *"All the people I knew were Republicans."* Adolph Zukor interview, William Wiener Oral History Library, American Jewish Committee, p. 33.

315 *"Least likely to be tolerant..."* Edgar Litt, "Ethnic Status and Political Perspectives," *Midwest Journal of Political Science*, August 1961, cited in Charles S. Liebman, *The Ambivalent Jew* (Philadelphia, 1973), p. 146.

316 Salaries. *New York Times*, July 1, 1940; untitled clipping dated October 27, 1938, in Zukor file at the New York Public Library of the Performing Arts at Lincoln Center.

316 *"When anyone important..."* Lester Roth, interviewed by author.

316 *"He was so at home there."* Edith Mayer Goetz, interviewed by author.

317 *Mayer "seemed often at the head..."* "Louis B. Mayer a National Figure," *Variety*, June 21, 1932.

317 Talk that Mayer would himself be a candidate. Henry F. Pringle, "Profiles," *The New Yorker*, March 28, 1936, p. 27. LR.

317 *"The country is in chaos."* Jack Warner with Dean Jennings, *My First Hundred Years in Hollywood* (New York, 1965), pp. 207–8.

317 *When Roosevelt carried the state... New York Herald Tribune*, August 10, 1932; *New York Sun*, January 26, 1933.

317 *"I think he enjoyed having me around..."* Warner with Jennings, p. 223.

318 Reward him with an ambassadorship. *Ibid.*, p. 224.

318 *"For what I did..."* William Schaefer, Warner's executive assistant, interviewed by author.

318 *"The New Deal, as Harry sees it..."* "Warner Brothers," *Fortune* magazine, December 1937, p. 212.

319 *In the summer of 1934, just before Sinclair's campaign...* Maurice Rapf, interviewed by author.

320   Brief career of Sergei Einsenstein. Yon Barna, *Eisenstein* (Boston, 1973), pp. 154–55.

321   Motion Picture Academy. For a brief history of the Academy, see Richard Shale, *Academy Awards: An Unger Reference Index* (New York, 1982), pp. 5–25.

321   *"Don't worry, L. B."* Samuel Marx, *Mayer and Thalberg: The Make-Believe Saints* (New York, 1975), pp. 258–59.

322   *"Created more communists..."*Quoted in Nancy Lynn Schwartz, *The Hollywood Writers' Wars* (New York, 1982), p. 10.

322   *"Your only competition is idiots."* Quoted in Otto Friedrich, *City of Nets* (New York, 1986), p. 90.

322   *"My father read the* Forward." Milton Sperling, interviewed by author.

323   *Young Jews with a gift*... Malcolm Goldstein, *The Political Stage* (New York, 1974). Goldstein cites the *aesthetic* ties between the young political playwrights and the Russian theater. The experiments of the Russian stage had extra political appeal to young men trying to create not only new worlds, but a new theater. (See p. 12.)

323   *"There were a number of people..."* Dore Schary interview, Columbia University Oral History Collection, p. 13. Schary uses the word "entity," but it seems clear that he meant "integrity."

323   Deliberately hired progressives. Alvah Bessie, *Inquisition in Eden* (New York, 1965), p. 65.

323   *"I loved the hills..."* Jerome Chodorov interview, William Wiener Oral History Library, American Jewish Committee, p. 23.

323   *"Its overpowering pleasantness."* Harold Clurman, *The Fervent Years* (New York, 1945), pp. 178 and 200–201.

324   *"You had to punch the clock."* MS.

324   *"We had a six-day week."* Billy Wilder, interviewed by author.

324   *"I want to profit by these two experiences..."* Letter to daughter, July 1937, in *The Letters of F. Scott Fitzgerald*, ed. Andrew Turnbull (New York, 1963), p. 17.

324   *"These people are more impressed..." Ibid.*, letter to Tom Carey, Jr., June 9, 1939, p. 585.

325   *"I've got America's best writer..."* Quoted in Joseph Blotner, *Faulkner* (New York, 1974), p. 1134.

325   *"The higher the class of talent..."* Ben Hecht, *Charlie: The Improbable Life and Times of Charles MacArthur* (New York, 1957), pp. 157–58.

325   *"My writer."* Dunne, p. 42.

325   *"They were afraid."* Michael Blankfort, interviewed by author.

325   *"At a Hollywood party, there would be forty or fifty celebrities..."* Ben Hecht interview, Columbia University Oral History Collection, pp. 753–54.

326   *"Jews are the writers..."* Josh Greenfeld, interviewed by author.

326   *"Don't you think it's a shame..."* Liam O' Flaherty, *Hollywood Cemetery* (London, 1935), pp. 148–49.

326   *"The main topic of conversation..."* MB.

326   *"Nobody would live in Hollywood..."* Quoted in Murry C. Faulkner, *The Faulkners of Mississippi: A Memoir* (Baton Rouge, 1967), pp. 195–97 in Blotner, p. 964.

326   *"There was no art to the film."* Hecht interview, Columbia University Oral History Collection, p. 713.

326   Foreign films. Jerome Chodorov interview, William Wiener Oral History Library, AJC, p. 49.

326   *"The heroes are the great corruptionists..."* Letter to Gerald Murphy, September 14, 1940, Turnbull, p. 429.

326   *"You didn't live through the Depression."* Jerome Chodorov interview, Wiener Oral History Library, p. 35.

327   *"I began to realize why..."* Letter dated 1942 in Dalton Trumbo, *Additional Dialogue*, ed. Helen Manfull (New York, 1970), p. 24.

327   *"Cliff is furious at me..."* Ella Winter, *And Not to Yield* (New York, 1963), pp. 223–24.

327   *"I feel that I need to sin..."* Clurman, p. 170.

327   *"It started with much fewer people..."* PD.

327   *"Self-contained community of self-centered people..."* Bessie, p. 48.

327   *"Are we history..."* Quoted in Stefan Kanfer, *A Journal of the Plague Years* (New York, 1973), p. 37.

328   *"We're up to our necks in politics..."* Mary McCall, Jr., *Screen Guild Magazine*, February 1937, quoted in John Cogley, *Report on Blacklisting Volume 1* (The Fund for the Republic, 1956), p. 26.

328   *"There is hardly a tea party..."* Ella Winter, "Hollywood Wakes Up," *The New Republic*, January 12, 1938, p. 276.

328   *"Probably 70 percent..."* PD.

328   *"Congealed with a kind of horror."* Quoted in Thomas H. Arthur, "The Political Career of an Actor: Melvyn Douglas and the New Deal," Ph.D. diss., Indiana University, 1973, p. 36.

328   The Anti-Nazi League. Larry Ceplair and Steven Englund, *The Inquisition in Hollywood: Politics in the Film Community, 1930–1960* (Garden City, NY, 1980), p. 107. This encyclopedic book provides the fullest account of political Hollywood.

329   V. J. Jerome. United States Congress (82:1), House Committee on Un-American Activities, part 1, March 8, 1951, pp. 56–57.

329   *Jerome was doctrinaire...* Jerome was also something of an innocent. Imprisoned in the fifties for violation of the Smith Act—conspiring to overthrow the government—Jerome was playing a game of doubles Ping-Pong against a man arrested for murdering a federal agent and another in for robbing a bank. As Lillian Hellman heard it from Jerome's partner, Dashiell Hammett, "Jerome insisted the possible murderer had called a bad shot when it was really good. Hammett suggested that maybe Jerome shouldn't expect honesty from criminals. Jerome had held up the game to explain to Dash the socialist necessity to believe in the reform of all men, the duty to show them the honest way. When they resumed the game with their impatient partners, all seemed to go better until about the tenth shot, when Jerome shouted across the table that the murderer had cheated again and that he was shocked. The murderer threw his bat across the table and advanced on Jerome with a knife. Hammett said, 'Mr. Jerome wishes to apologize.'

Jerome said, 'I do not wish to apologize. You should be ashamed of yourself for cheating a jailed comrade. You must learn—'

As the knife was thrown, Hammett pushed Jerome to the floor and held on to the murderer with repeated apologies that hinted Jerome wasn't all there in the head." Lillian Hellman, *Scoundrel Time* (New York, 1976), p. 88.

329   *He spoke often and easily...* United States Congress, HUAC, part 4 (1951), Martin Berkeley testimony, p. 1581.

329   *"Agitprop drama was better..."* Quoted in Schwartz, p. 44.

329   *"The status they achieved..."* Cogley, Volume 1, p. 34.

330   *"The slogans, the sweeping formulae..."* Murray Kempton, *Part of Our Time* (New York, 1955), p. 197; *"It is not accidental..."* Letter to Sam Sillen, 1946, in Helen Manfull, p. 41.

330   *Estimates ranged as high...* Ceplair and Englund, pp. 65–66. These are rough estimates based on the HUAC investigations and the memories of Party members.

330   *In America, the Party was a group...* Nathan Glazer, *The Social Basis of American Communism* (New York, 1961), pp. 130–31. Glazer writes, "The party was so heavily middle class in large part because it was so heavily Jewish."

331   *One leading Communist estimated...* Arthur Liebman, *Jews and the Left* (New York, 1979), pp. 59–60.

331   *"There were a lot of liberals like me..."* Quoted in Schwartz, p. 82.

331   *Jewish percentage of the Communist party.* Jack Stachel, *The Communist* (April 1929), p. 183, quoted in Glazer, p. 220 fn; RL, Jr.

331   *Role of Jews "was discussed..."* RL.

331   John Howard Lawson. Dos Passos, who accompanied Lawson on the voyage over, described him as "an extraordinarily diverting fellow, recently out of Williams, wth bright brown eyes, untidy hair and a great beak of a nose that made you think of Cyrano de Bergerac. There was a lot of the Gascon in him at that. He was a voluble and comical talker. He had drastic ideas on every subject under the sun. He was never away from you for ten minutes that he didn't come back with some tale of abracadabrating adventures that had happened in the meanwhile." *The Best Times: An Informal Memoir* (New York, 1966), p. 47.

332   *"Bourgeois Hamlet."* *New Masses*, April 10, 1934, quoted in Ceplair and Englund, p. 62.

333   *"Tragic figure."* Quoted in Schwartz, p. 153.

333   *"Commitment is essential..."* John Howard Lawson, *Film: The Creative Process* (New York, 1964), pp. 123–24.

333   *"My aim is to present the Communist position..."* Quoted in Schwartz, p. 59.

333   *"She was very much of an assimilationist..."* RL, Jr.

334   *"Jewish self-hate and the striving for total assimilation..."* Lucy Davidowicz, "Book Reviews: *The Social Basis of American Communism* by Nathan Glazer, and *Writers on the Left* by Daniel Aaron," in *American Jewish Historical Quarterly*, vol. LIII, no. 2, p. 194.

334   *"He settled all questions."* United States Congress (82:1), House Committee on Un-American Activities, April 25, 1951, *Communist Infiltration of the Hollywood Motion Picture Industry*, part 2, p. 417.

334   *"Ruthless."* SR.

334   *"They had best be treated..."* Letter to daughter, dated March 15, 1940, in *The Letters of F. Scott Fitzgerald*, ed. Andrew Turnbull (New York, 1963), pp. 64–65.

334   *One writer compared him to Lenin.* MB.

335   *"I would have to get away from this..."* United States Congress (82:1), House Committee on Un-American Activities, *Hearings on Communist Infiltration of the Hollywood Motion Picture Industry*, part 3, May 23, 1951, p. 587.

335   *"I was wrong about writing."* Ibid., pp. 588–89.

335   *"The Hollywood novel."* Charles Glenn. "Novel—The Story of a Holly-

wood Heel," in *People's World*, April 2, 1941, p. 5, quoted in *Ibid.*, p. 593.

336   *"On the basis of quite lengthy discussion..."* Quoted in *Ibid.*, p. 593.

336   *"I wonder if the thing that makes Sammy..."* Budd Schulberg, *What Makes Sammy Run?* (New York, 1941), pp. 119, 211–12, 244, 249.

337   *"I blame you for this."* Quoted in Schwartz, p. 167.

338   Meeting to discuss *Sammy*. RL.

338   *Mayer asked his friend William Randolph Hearst...* Bosley Crowther, *Hollywood Rajah* (New York, 1960), p. 196.

338   *"A lot of Jews will lose their lives..."* Crichton, p. 247.

338   *Who is Hitler?* Joseph Roos, interviewed by author.

339   *"I don't know when they took the street..."* Walter Laemmle, interviewed by author.

340   *When the State Department started questioning...* Stanley Bergerman, Laemmle's son-in-law, interviewed by author.

340   *"I don't think that Hollywood should deal..."* *The Argus*, Melbourne, Australia, August 12, 1939.

340   *"Being kind of unterrifiable..."* SM.

340   Meeting at Hillcrest. Memorandum of meeting held at Hillcrest Country Club, March 13, 1934, Jewish Community Library, Los Angeles.

341   *"We met with them several times..."* Hy Kraft interview, William Wiener Oral History Library, American Jewish Committee, pp. 143–45.

341   *"Because it was known as a Jewish industry..."* MR.

341   *"It was a matter of business."* Hy Kraft interview, Wiener Oral History Library, p. 147.

342   *Warner Brothers only closed its German office...* Jack Warner with Dean Jennings, *My First Hundred Years in Hollywood* (New York, 1964), p. 249.

342   *"It was a pretty representative group..."* Martin Gang, interviewed by author. The fear was by no means limited to Hollywood Jews. "The growth of domestic anti-Semitism projected against what was happening in Europe brought out the latent insecurities of American Jewry and sharpened internal divisions." See Henry L. Feingold, *The Politics of Rescue: The Roosevelt Administration and the Holocaust, 1938–45* (New Brunswick, NJ, 1970), p. 302.

342   *"Their attitude was that Jews should not..."* Chodorov interview, Wiener Oral History Library, pp. 38–39.

343   *"Are we making it because we're Jews..."* Jack Warner, Jr., interviewed by author.

343   *Mayer warned that war...* *Variety*, September 2, 1936.

343   *Two weeks later, four hundred motion picture luminaries...* *New York American*, September 17, 1936.

343   *"This nation will remain a neutral..."* "Fireside Chat," September 3, 1939.

343   *"Personally we would like to do all in our power..."* Memo from Jack and Harry Warner to President Roosevelt, May 20, 1940, collection OF73, "Motion Pictures, 1940," Franklin D. Roosevelt Library, Hyde Park, New York.

343   Nick Schenck's offer. Memo from A. A. Berle, assistant secretary of state, to President Roosevelt, August 28, 1940, OF73, #4, "Motion Pictures, 1940," Roosevelt Library.

344   *"There is a great deal of hysteria..."* Letter from Douglas Fairbanks, Jr., to Steve Early, secretary to the president, May 27, 1940; Steve Early to

Douglas Fairbanks, Jr., June 1, 1940, OF73, #4, "Motion Pictures, 1940," Roosevelt Library.

344 *"He spoke to the gathering..."* Letter from Douglas Fairbanks, Jr., to President Roosevelt, November 19, 1940, in memo from Sumner Welles to Roosevelt, President's Secretary's file, #53, "Great Britain, Kennedy," Roosevelt Library.

344 *"As a result of Kennedy's cry..."* Hecht, *Child of the Century*, p. 520.

344 Public opinion surveys. John Morton Blum, V *Was for Victory: Politics and Culture During World War II* (New York, 1976), p. 172.

345 *"There will be no cycle of 'hate' pictures."* Letter from Will Hays to Senator Burton Wheeler, January 14, 1941, PPF 1945, "Will Hays," Roosevelt Library.

345 *"Greatest danger to this country..."* Quoted in "Propaganda or History?" *The Nation*, September 20, 1941, pp. 241–42. See also Wayne S. Coles, *American First: The Battle Against Intervention* (Madison, WI, 1953), p. 186.

345 *"Who are the men..."* Senator Gerald P. Nye, "War Propaganda," *Vital Speeches of the Day*, September 15, 1941, pp. 720–23.

345 *"I was not naming those names..."* U.S. Congress, Senate, Interstate Commerce Committee, *Hearings on Moving-Picture and Radio Propaganda*, September 9, 1941, pp. 10–11. Stefan Kanfer quotes Nye as having said, "If anti-Semitism exists in America, the Jews have themselves to blame." Stefan Kanfer, A *Journal of the Plague Years* (New York, 1973), p. 20.

346 *"The moving picture industry is a monopoly..."* Ibid., September 10, 1941, p. 73.

346 *"The best men in the industry..."* Memo from Lowell Mellett to President Roosevelt, August 27, 1941, OF73, #5, "Motion Pictures, 1941," Roosevelt Library.

346 *"When you live in a society..."* Hearings on Moving-Picture and Radio Propaganda, p. 246.

346 *"I would not produce pictures..."* Ibid., p. 326.

347 *"You can correctly charge me..."* Ibid., p. 348.

347 *"If Chaplin had made a laughable caricature..."* Time magazine, September 22, 1941, p. 13.

347 *"Pastmasters about comedy."* Motion Picture Herald, September 20, 1941, p. 16.

347 *"I have never found such a group..."* United States Congress, Senate, Special Committee for Investigation of National Defense Program, *Hearings on Investigation of the National Defense Program*, February 16, 1943, pp. 6896–97.

348 *Draped in the flag...* For a detailed study of World War II films, see Bernard F. Dick, *The Star-Spangled Screen: The American World War II Film* (Lexington, KY, 1986).

348 *"I want our films to sell America..."* New York Journal American, August 4, 1946.

348 *"We are prepared to take a loss..."* New York Times, March 24, 1946.

348 Cohn *"never expressed a feeling..."* William Graf, interviewed by author.

348 *Barney Balaban was devastated.* Judith Balaban, interviewed by author.

349 *"All they talk about is the Holocaust..."* Rabbi Edgar F. Magnin, interviewed by author.

349 *Scott admitted he got severe stomach pains...* Adrian Scott, "You Can't

Do That," speech given at the Conference on the Subject of Thought Control in the United States, quoted in Ceplair and Englund, p. 317. See chapter 8 for Jewish resistance to *Crossfire*.

349   "*It took me two hours to convince them...*" The source of this story wished to remain anonymous.

349   *To which Schary replied...* Dore Schary, *Heyday* (New York, 1979), p. 157.

350   *Mayer was ardently anti-Zionist...* EMG; *Harry Cohn was pressured...* LR; *Jack Cohn visited Israel...* Robert Cohn, interviewed by author.

350   "Those" people. Dorothy Corwin, widow of the president of the southern California region of the Union of the American Hebrew Congregations, interviewed by author.

350   "*Most of us had a feeling that we were homeless...*" Robert Blumofe, interviewed by author.

351   Origins of HUAC. Walter Goodman, *The Committee* (New York, 1968), p. 10.

351   "*Radical Jewish minority...*" *Ibid.*, p. 10.

351   "*Many of our Jewish citizens wanted Dickstein...*" Martin Dies, *The Martin Dies Story* (New York, 1963), p. 59.

351   *If the Jews had hoped to find a defender...* William Gelberman, *Martin Dies* (New York, 1944), pp. 49 and 51.

352   Openly consorted with anti-Semites. Frank Donner, *The Un-Americans* (New York, 1961), pp. 26–27.

352   *When one committee witness repeated...* Hearings of Special House Committee, pp. 3217, 3218, 4044, quoted in Gelberman, p. 108.

352   "*In the beginning, our Committee obtained...*" Dies, p. 99.

352   *His war was against Karl Marx...* Martin Dies, "More Snakes Than I Can Kill," *Liberty* magazine, February 10, 1940, p. 42.

352   A dastardly scheme. Goodman, pp. 59–61.

352   "*It was apparent that un-Americanism...*" Dies, *Martin Dies Story*, p. 158.

353   "*Not only reply to them...*" Letter from Art Arthur to Sidney Wallach, June 5, 1939, MDW, U.S. Govt., Cong. Investigation, Dies 1938–1940, American Jewish Committee Archives.

353   *HUAC seemed to enjoy widespread support.* August Raymond Ogden, *The Dies Committee* (Washington, D.C., 1943), p. 101.

353   *Producers invited Dies...* Milton Sperling, interviewed by author. "This is one theory. I have no evidence of that at all, but, you know, it makes sense in this way: it was a way to smash budding unionism in Hollywood."

353   John L. Leech. Ogden, p. 211. See also *New York Times*, July 18, 1940.

354   "*Thirty-two thousand motion picture workers...*" Quoted in Howard Suber, "The Anti-Communist Blacklist in the Hollywood Motion Picture Industry," Ph.D. diss., UCLA, 1968, pp. 18–19.

354   "*So exaggerated...*" *New York Times*, August 28, 1940.

354   "*Jimmy, I see by the papers...*" H. Allen Smith, *Lost in the Horse Latitudes* (Garden City, NY, 1944), pp. 53–54.

354   "*You should tell your Jewish friends...*" Chester Nickolas, quoted by Professor Clyde Miller in sworn affidavit, U.S. Congress, *Congressional Record*, February 19, 1946, p. A872.

355   *With its authorization about to expire...* Robert K. Carr, *The House Committee on Un-American Activities, 1945–1950* (Ithaca, NY, 1952), pp. 19–23.

355   *"If I am any judge..."* Quoted in Donner, pp. 28–29; *"Slime-mongering kike."* *Congressional Record*, February 14, 1946, p. 1240; *"That little Communist kike..."* Quoted in Walter Davenport, "Big Wind from the South," *Collier's* magazine, December 1, 1945, p. 66; *"Jewish gentleman."* *CR*, 91, pt. 8, October 24, 1945, p. 10035; *"I have no quarrel..."* *CR*, 92, pt. 2, February 24, 1946, p. 1727.

356   *"Stalin is a gentile..."* Quoted from *Labor Action*, March 13, 1944, in Irving Howe and Lewis Coser, *The American Communist Party: A Critical History (1919–1957)* (Boston, 1957), p. 433.

356   *"We don't know what information..."* Quoted in Goodman, p. 172.

356   *"One of the most dangerous plots..."* *New York Herald Tribune*, July 1, 1945, quoted in Carr, p. 56. See also *New York Times*, July 1, 1945, p. 20.

356   *"Not trying to hound legitimate producers..."* *CR*, 91, pt. 6, July 9, 1945, p. 7372.

357   *"Are they planning..."* *CR*, 91, pt. 6, July 17, 1945, p. 7649; *CR*, 91, pt. 6, July 18, 1945, p. 7736.

357   *"Communism is the most dangerous influence..."* *CR*, 91, pt. 6, July 18, 1945, p. 7737.

358   *Among the planks of its platform...* "America First Party Platform," *The Cross and the Flag*, October 1944, vol. 3, no. 6, p. 455.

358   Undermining "the influence and teachings of the Church..." *The Cross and the Flag*, September 1944, vol. 3, no. 5, p. 448.

358   *"The Rape of America by Hollywood."* Ibid., August 1945, vol. 4, no. 5, pp. 609 and 610.

359   *"We Christian Nationalists..."* Quoted in *CR*, 91, February 12, 1946, p. 1247.

359   *The line of marchers...* Fred Rinaldo, quoted in Schwartz, p. 229.

360   *They emerged with the news...* Carr, p. 57.

360   *"There is a general belief that Russian Jews..."* U.S. Congress, House Un-American Activities Committee, *Investigation of Un-American Propaganda Activities in the United States*, January 30, 1946, p. 26.

360   *Representative Landis scolded Rankin...* Memo on House Committee on Un-American Activities, April 11, 1946, AJC-HUAC, 1946–50, American Jewish Committee Archives, p. 13.

360   *"America's most raucous purveyor..."* Letter from Representatives Emanuel Celler, Hugh De Lacy, Vito Marcantonio, Ellis E. Patterson, and Charles R. Savage to HUAC in *Investigation of Un-American Propaganda*, January 30, 1946, p. 26.

360   *"Although Congressman Wood is the nominal chairman..."* Memorandum in re. Gerald L. K. Smith's appearance before the House Committee on Un-American Activities from M. Cohn to John Slawson, January 30, 1946, AJC-Smith, AJC Archives, p. 1. The AJC also assisted a campaign by other congressmen to discharge the committee, and early in March it had approached Speaker of the House Sam Rayburn to enlist his aid in challenging HUAC. (Letter from Marcus Cohen, AJC Washington representative, to Norman Levy, March 8, 1946; Irving Engel, attorney, to George Hexter, AJC staff, March 1, 1946, AJC-HUAC File, AJC Archives.)

361   *"He can get recognition and business..."* *St. Louis Post-Dispatch*, December 1, 1948, quoted in Otto Friedrich, *City of Nets* (New York, 1986), p. 299.

361   *"Pickwickian."* *Life* magazine quoted in *A Quarter Century of Un-Americana*, ed. by Charlotte Pomerance, (New York, 1963), pp. 39–40.

361   *"Those who signed the petitions..."* "Hollywood on the Griddle," *The Cross and the Flag*, vol. 5, no. 10, January 1947, p. 888.

362   *"Some people will ride..."* Told to screenwriter Nat Perrin, quoted in Schwartz, p. 63.

362   *"No concerted effort on the part of studio heads..."* CR., vol. 93, pt. II, p. A2688. This statement might be called a "which" hunt.

363   *"Nobody can tell me..."* Deposition of Lester Cole, September 10 and 11, 1948, *Cole* v. *Loew's, Inc.*, in the District Court of the United States, Southern District of California, Central Division, No. 8005-Y, pp. 137–38, quoted in Ceplair and Englund, p. 259.

363   *"The New Deal is either for the Communist Party..."* Hearings Before a Special Committee on Un-American Activities, pp. 898–99, quoted in Gelberman, p. 68.

363   *"Iron entered his soul."* Jeane Wood, quoted in Ceplair and Englund, p. 210.

364   *"Held by Americans for the American people..."* Variety, February 7, 1944.

364   *"Who were the Communists..."* Hello, Hollywood!, ed. by Allen Rivkin and Laura Kerr (Garden City, NY, 1962), p. 446.

364   *Since its formation...* Letter to Senator Robert Reynolds (D–N.C.) quoted in Variety, March 15, 1944.

365   *Robert Stripling was a southern white supremacist...* David Wesley, *Hate Groups and the Un-American Activities Committee* (New York, 1962), p. 10. Wesley quotes Albert E. Kahn, who investigated Nazi atrocities: "The myth that the American film industry was controlled by Communists and Jews was assiduously cultivated by the Nazi Propaganda Ministry. *Welt-Diest* [World Service of Goebbels's propaganda] carried lists of 'Jew-Communists' laboring in the Hollywood vineyard and Kuhn, Coughlin, and Pelley in their respective publications repeatedly echoed demands for an 'investigation' of the movie industry." Wesley believes Gerald L. K. Smith, however, was "chiefly responsible" for the HUAC investigations.

365   *"What sort of questions did they ask you?"* John Huston, *An Open Book* (New York, 1980), pp. 130–31.

366   *"They got it on you."* MS.

366   *Forty-three subpoenas...* Note: Some sources say only forty-one were issued.

366   Ten were Jewish. According to Alvah Bessie, himself one of those subpoenaed, thirteen were Jewish. Alvah Bessie, *An Inquisition in Eden* (New York, 1965), p. 191.

366   *"Anti-Semitism played a strong part."* RL, Jr.

366   *"Every executive in the business knew..."* LR.

367   *"I was rather emotional..."*; *As much contempt for communism...* Gordon Kahn, *Hollywood on Trial* (New York, 1948), pp. 19–26 (for Warner), pp. 27–30 (for Mayer). Kahn was one of the unfriendly witnesses.

368   *"Your kind don't grow on trees."* Lester Cole, *Hollywood Red: The Autobiography of Lester Cole* (Palo Alto, CA, 1981), p. 272.

369   *Meeting in high spirits...* PD.

369   *"It is unfortunate and tragic..."* U.S. Congress (80:1), HUAC, *Hearings*, October 27, 1947, p. 294; *"Next you are going to ask me..."* HUAC, *Hearings*, October 28, 1947, p. 366; *"Under this kind of censorship..."* and *"The Jew is the first one to suffer..."* Kahn, p. 98 and pp. 116–17.

370   *"I was only trying to help my country..."* JW, Jr.

370   *"When he came back to the coast..."* MS.

371   *Dunne and Silberberg met with the studio head . . .* PD.

371   *"Protect the American people . . ."* CR, vol. 93, pt. 7, November 24, 1947, p. 10792.

372   *Two days before that vote . . .* Quoted in *Variety*, March 26, 1980, p. 32.

372   *When producer Sam Goldwyn said it sounded as if they were panicking . . .* "One would like to think it [Goldwyn's objection] was a vote for freedom, but most people who knew him well, I among them, knew he always voted against any group decision." Lillian Hellman, *Scoundrel Time* (New York, 1976), p. 70.

372   *If ever they wanted to earn the respect of the American people . . .* Schary, p. 164.

373   *James Byrnes assured them . . . Ibid.*, p. 165.

374   *"I don't think the heads of movie companies . . ."* Hellman, pp. 65–66.

374   *"I didn't want to do anything."* Quoted in Suber, p. 29.

374   *Harry Cohn argued aggressively . . .* LR.

375   *"One of the prime purposes of the Un-American Activities Committee . . ."* and Slawson's response. Memoranda quoted in Victor Navasky, *Naming Names* (New York, 1980), pp. 112–13.

375   *Jewish agencies funneled affidavits . . .* Paul Jacobs, *Is Curly Jewish?* (New York, 1965), p. 198; Martin Gang, interviewed by author; David Caute, *The Great Fear* (New York, 1978), p. 505.

376   *"The CRC was a natural place . . ."* Paul Jacobs to Victor Navasky in Navasky, p. 111.

376   *The process often began with Silberberg himself.* JR; Navasky, p. 111.

376   *"Industry expert in frying producers."* Letter from Trumbo to Gang, January 22, 1949, in Manfull, p. 120.

377   Sterling Hayden. MG.

377   *"Other lawyers referred people to me."* MG.

378   *"There used to be a Japanese place . . ."* Quoted in Navasky, p. 102.

378   *"You had James O'Neill . . ."* MG.

379   *"We built up this person, Al Chamie . . ."* JR.

379   *"Why should Jews sit back . . ."* Rabbi Edgar F. Magnin, "Leader and Personality," interviewed by Malca Chall, Regional Oral History Office, Bancroft Library, University of California, Berkeley, 1975, pp. 178–79.

380   *"A professional and probably profiteering Communist baiter . . ."* Quoted in Merle Miller, *The Judges and the Judged* (Garden City, NY, 1952), p. 153. See also "Background Paper: The American Jewish League Against Communism," January 9, 1950, American Jewish League Against Communism file, AJC Archives, New York.

380   *Gerald L. K. Smith praised him . . .* Memo on Schultz, AJLAC file, AJC Archives.

380   *"This resolution was sent out by the emissaries of Moscow."* Assemblyman Chester Gannon, quoted in Robert E. Burke, *Olson's New Deal for California* (Berkeley, CA, 1953), p. 62.

381   *"Guilty of understatement . . ."* *San Francisco Chronicle*, July 1, 1945, quoted in Edward L. Barrett, Jr., *The Tenney Committee* (Ithaca, NY, 1951), p. 30.

381   *"During the nearly ten years of my chairmanship . . ."* Letter from Jack B. Tenney to constituents, April 14, 1954, in Jack Tenney file, AJC Archives.

381   *"Most Jews realize that a 'Jewish League Against Communism' . . ."* Dr. S. Andhil Fineberg, Community Service Director, AJC, interview in AJLAC file, AJC Archives.

381   *"This is a scandalous business . . ."* Letter from Eugene Lyons to Ed Lukas,

February 4, 1951; letter from Ed Lukas to Eugene Lyons, February 8, 1951, AJLAC file, AJC Archives.

382   Gallup poll showed public evenly divided. Goodman, p. 219.

383   *"Our top level executives must not make..."* Variety, May 14, 1950, quoted in Suber, p. 36.

383   *"Hey, Bolshie!"* Cole, p. 317.

383   *"Without getting into a debate with a witness..."* Letter from Marcus Cohn to Edwin Lukas, July 23, 1951, AJLAC file, AJC Archives.

384   *"I went to Twentieth Century-Fox..."* George Chasin, interviewed by author. Later Garfield was subpoenaed by HUAC and testified that he had "always hated communism.... I think it is a subversive movement and is a tyranny and is a dictatorship and is against democracy" (HUAC hearings, *Communism in Motion-Picture Industry*, p. 330). But he couldn't shake the label of subversive, and he died after a three-day binge—broken, remorseful, and alone. See Larry Swindell, *Body and Soul: The Story of John Garfield* (New York, 1975).

385   *"He ran wildly about..."* Robert Ardrey, "Hollywood: The Fall of the Frenzied Fifties," *The Reporter*, March 21, 1957, p. 30.

385   *"You just had to look at them."* Jerome Chodorov interview, Columbia Oral History Collection, pp. 69–70.

385   *"This is a mistake."* Billy Wilder, interviewed by author.

385   *"I'm suspicious of everybody."* Robert Parrish, *Growing Up in Hollywood* (New York, 1976), pp. 197–98.

385   *The Jews actually* in *Hollywood...* Y. Frank Freeman testified that on March 30 and 31, 1952, the presidents of the major companies met with representatives from the American Legion in Washington under the auspices of Eric Johnston's Motion Picture Producers Association: "My best recollection of what happened at that meeting was that Mr. Johnston demonstrated to the presidents of the companies and others that there was a great problem that had arisen in connection with adverse publicity to the motion picture industry, created over the country, and that the head of the American Legion, Mr. Wilson, had stated that he was receiving many complaints from various American Legion posts throughout the United States in reference to certain individuals that were employed in the making of motion pictures.... There was a discussion as to the adverse effect that could be felt by the pictures because of all these complaints that were coming in...." Y. Frank Freeman testimony, *Independent Productions Corporation* v. *Loew's Inc., et al.*, United States District Court, Southern District of New York, box 417, pp. 4904–5 and 4935.

386   *Zanuck remonstrated that the coercion...* PD.

386   *"I don't think it's okay."* JB.

10: THE END

387   *"Now, these aren't men who know pictures."* Budd Schulberg, *What Makes Sammy Run?* (New York, 1941), p. 265.

387   *"They're mechanical bastards."* Quoted in Bob Thomas, *King Cohn* (New York, 1967), p. 174.

387   *"Could make or break movie people..."* William Saroyan, *Sons Come & Go, Mothers Hang in Forever* (New York, 1976), pp. 136–37.

388   *"No Jew can ever cheat an Armenian."* Quoted in Bosley Crowther, *Hollywood Rajah* (New York, 1960), p. 243.

389   *"The worst calamity..."* Irene Mayer Selznick, A *Private View* (New York, 1983), p. 262.

389   *"Stay home and sit in front of the fire..."* Crowther, p. 264.

389   Discouraged her from having sexual intercourse. Danny Selznick, interviewed by author.

389   *"The Talmud says..."* Crowther, p. 257.

389   *"The most unsophisticated, strait-laced man..."* Selznick, p. 263.

389   *"I believe that he was such a moral man..."* DS. Eleanor Powell tells a story that seems to confirm this. Powell, then an MGM starlet, was asked to accompany Mayer to a dance. Mayer danced with her ("Mr. Mayer was very much the exhibitionist on the dance floor. He liked to dance on the outer edge") lecturing her throughout about the benisons of working at MGM, then asked her to go club hopping with him. But Mayer was more solicitous than amorous. John Kobal, *People Will Talk* (New York, 1985), pp. 233–36.

390   *"He has a theory that dancing..."* Henry Pringle, "Profile," *The New Yorker*, April 4, 1936, p. 26.

390   *"Doing it with my father!"* Samuel Marx, *Mayer and Thalberg: The Make-Believe Saints* (New York, 1975), p. 281.

390   *"Do you have a dentist..."* Ibid., p. 282.

391   Mayer met her at one of Schenck's parties. Crowther, p. 195.

391   *"I'm sure I would have gone to bed with him..."* Marx, p. 285.

391   *One account reported...* Crowther, p. 194. Marx's main source seems to be Miss Howard herself. Crowther's unnamed source was most likely Howard Strickling.

392   *"Caged lion."* Gary Carey, *All the Stars in Heaven* (New York, 1981), p. 185.

392   *"Neither married nor unmarried..."* Selznick, p. 263.

392   *"Louis likes slim girls..."* Hedda Hopper and James Brough, *The Whole Truth and Nothing But* (Garden City, NY, 1963), p. 221.

392   *"He felt she didn't grow..."* Edith Mayer Goetz, interviewed by author.

392   Shopping expedition. Hopper and Brough, p. 221.

392   *"Never lost his ties to Maggie."* DS.

392   *"There was something funny..."* DS.

393   *"Look out for yourself."* Mervyn LeRoy, *LeRoy: Take One* (New York, 1974), pp. 134–35.

393   *"You could never get a decision..."* Sam Marx, interviewed by the author.

394   *Schenck had met Schary...* Dore Schary interview, Columbia University Oral History Collection, pp. 36–37 and 47. The transcript reads "Joe Schenck," but it is likely he meant Nick.

394   *Schary was a first-generation American Jew...* Dore Schary, *For Special Occasions* (New York, 1962), pp. 4–6.

394   *"She writes tough..."* Dore Schary, *Heyday* (Boston, 1979), p. 56.

395   *"The most imbecilic..."* Ben Hecht interview, Columbia University Oral History Collection, pp. 716–17.

395   *"Strong, big, sure-footed, firm."* Schary, *Heyday*, p. 116.

396   *Impressed by Schary's devotion to his mother...* Crowther, p. 280.

396   *Danny Selznick had a different theory.* DS.

396   *"Simple, down-to-earth pictures..."* Lillian Ross, *Picture* (New York, 1952), p. 92.

396   *"When we heard it was Dore Schary..."* EMG.

        "He calls me and tells me..." Ross, p. 162.

397   *"You stupid kike bastard."* Schary, *Heyday*, p. 125.

397   *"I had a premonition . . ." Ibid.*, p. 179.

397   *"He'll bring you caviar . . ." Ibid.*

398   Mayer's marriage. *New York Times*, December 5, 1948.

398   *"Everything was white."* EMG.

399   *"Her paintings are life."* Ross, p. 169.

400   *"The degree of strictness!"* DS.

400   *"Suzie found her situation confusing."* Selznick, p. 358.

401   *"She was a beautiful woman."* DS.

401   *"He was looking for a fellow like me . . ."* Jonie Taps, interviewed by author.

402   *"Harry Cohn was a player with women."* JT.

402   One serious affair of the heart. JT.

404   *"I'm too tired to play games."* Thomas, p. 143. The source, evidently, was Buchman himself.

405   *Buchman would have been found in contempt . . .* Many of Victor Navasky's interviewees apparently took the same view—that Cohn was responsible. See *Naming Names* (New York, 1980), p. 305 fn.

406   *"I've had self-searching sessions . . ."* Jack Warner, Jr., interviewed by author.

406   *When Jack Jr. returned from service . . .* William Schaefer, Jack Warner's executive assistant, interviewed by author.

406   *"The trouble with Jackie . . ."* WS. Jackie himself concurred. He didn't have the temperament to do what his father had done.

407   Dandy Kim. *New York Herald Tribune*, February 26, 1960; *New York Post*, February 25, 1960.

408   *One deal to sell the company . . .* Michael Freedland, *The Warner Brothers* (New York, 1983), p. 212. Freedland conducted interviews for his book but doesn't cite the source for this particular episode.

408   *Jack did finally get his revenge.* The same story is told by JW, Jr., who heard it from Harry Warner's widow, by Milton Sperling, and by William Schaefer.

408   *"I've got the old bastard by the balls . . ."* Freedland, p. 215.

408   *"The treachery really killed Harry."* MS.

408   *"Jack Warner had just gone over to the south of France . . ."* WS.

409   Warner's auto accident. For Warner's own version of the accident, see Jack Warner with Dean Jennings, *My First Hundred Years in Hollywood* (New York, 1965), pp. 3–5.

409   *"I think I'm going to go over to see my father."* WS.

409   *He blasted the independent producer . . . New York Times*, August 28, 1961; *"How the hell did you become the head . . ." New York Times*, March 4, 1964.

410   *"From the old Warners people . . ."* WS.

411   *"How could he pick Dore Schary . . ."* DS.

411   *"What would you do . . ."* The account of this incident comes primarily from Schary, *Heyday*, pp. 231–36. He gives a slightly different version in *The Real Tinsel*, eds. Bernard Rosenberg and Harry Silverstein (New York, 1970), pp. 145 and 149.

412   *"L.B., I've been through this before . . ."* Rosenberg and Silverstein, p. 149.

412   *"At a studio and under conditions . . ." New York Times*, June 26, 1951.

412   *"Schary had become the message maker."* Pandro Berman, interviewed by author.

412   *"I know what the audience wants."* Ross, p. 170.

412   *Two days after the resignation . . .* Rosenberg and Silverstein, p. 149.

413   *"Like Knute Rockne without a football team . . ."* Quoted in Crowther, p. 316.

413   *"Once he left MGM . . ."* DS.

414   *"Idling by himself on the fringes . . ."* Daniel Fuchs, "Writing for the Movies," *Commentary*, February 1962, pp. 112–13.

414   *"I stayed with him for three weeks . . ."* DS.

414   *"Snoogie, did you turn down an offer. . . ."* EMG.

415   *As Irene told it, Goetz ignored . . .* Selznick, pp. 358–59; *Edith came to her husband's defense . . .* EMG.

415   *The final breach . . .* EMG.

416   *"He couldn't really love anybody."* EMG.

416   *"The more McCarthy yells . . ."* Haverhill Gazette, April 2, 1954.

416   *"He thought Joe McCarthy was one of the greatest men . . ."* John Huston, *An Open Book* (New York, 1980), p. 135.

417   *"I'm sorry to have to say . . ."* DS.

418   Laemmle's death. *Variety*, September 27, 1939; *New York Daily News*, September 25, 1939; *New York World Tribune*, September 25, 1939; *New York Times*, September 25, 1939.

418   *"He had a shelf this big . . ."* Joseph Roos, interviewed by author.

418   Dread of physical contact. SM.

418   *"No woman in her right mind . . ."* SM.

418   *"They formed a conspiracy to drive me out . . ."* New York Herald Tribune, November 24, 1933.

418   *"Conspiracy hallucinations."* Harley L. Clarke, Chicago utilities magnate, testifying before Senate Committee, *New York Herald Tribune*, November 25, 1933.

418   *"Mr. Fox is now not only in a position . . ."* New York Herald Tribune, October 18, 1934.

418   *"An influence for good."* New York Evening Post, October 10, 1934.

418   *He had spent over $1 million . . .* Variety, October 23, 1934.

419   *"Very slippery fellow."* H. L. Mencken to Upton Sinclair, April 4, 1933, in Upton Sinclair, *My Lifetime in Letters* (Columbia, MO, 1960), p. 320.

419   *Rather than leave his bankruptcy proceedings to chance . . .* Philadelphia Evening Public Ledger, May 21, 1941; *New York Herald Tribune*, May 21, 1941.

419   *"I started with nothing . . ."* New York Times, April 9, 1944.

419   *"He never said a word about it."* Angela Fox Dunn, interviewed by author.

419   *"Don't ever marry a gentile."* AFD.

420   *Lasky rushed over to Mayer . . .* Jesse Lasky, Jr., *Whatever Happened to Hollywood?* (New York, 1975), pp. 309–11.

420   *"There was a big rift . . ."* Betty Lasky, interviewed by author.

420   *"Religion?"* Norman Zierold, *The Moguls* (New York, 1969), p. 10.

421   *"You've got enemies . . ."* Schary, Heyday, pp. 4–5.

421   *"You see, Dore, you're strange." Ibid.*, pp. 318–19.

421   *Vogel had never liked Schary . . .* Variety, March 26, 1980, reported by Thomas M. Pryor.

422   *"I got into trouble because of you . . ."* Rosenberg and Silverstein, pp. 150 and 152; Schary, Heyday, pp. 321–22; Ross, p. 194.

422   *A month later Schenck himself was bounced . . .* New York Times, November 16, 1956.

422   *"The ruler of rulers..."* Ross, p. 15.

423   *"Mr. Schenck and the board of directors are responsible..."* United States Congress, Senate, Committee on Interstate Commerce, *Propaganda in Motion Pictures* (1942), p. 281.

423   *In his final years, he was obsessed...* PB.

423   *Back at Loew's...* Crowther, p. 319. This is the most coherent account of the aborted battle for control, and Crowther appears to have interviewed many of the principals.

423   *"He couldn't be happy without MGM."* DS.

423   *As the stay stretched into weeks...* Selznick, pp. 360–61.

424   *"In unstated collaboration, we stayed away..."* Ibid., p. 362.

424   *"He opened his eyes..."* EMG.

424   Mayer's funeral. *New York Herald Tribune,* November 1, 1957; *New York Times,* October 30, 1957; *Variety,* November 6, 1957.

425   *Cohn's fatalism deepened.* His nephew, Robert Cohn, had been told that "from that time on there was a big change in his life." Death was on his mind. (Robert Cohn, interviewed by author.)

425   *"It was a beautiful day..."* Dona Holloway, interviewed by author.

425   *"I think he always wanted to be seen at his best."* DH.

425   Incident with Irving Briskin. JT.

426   *"I certainly saw a change..."* RC.

426   *"Harry and I went to a board meeting..."* JT.

426   Cohn's death. JT; Thomas, pp. 362–63; *Variety,* March 5, 1958; Garson Kanin, *Hollywood: Stars and Starlets, Tycoons and Flesh-Peddlers, Movie-makers and Moneymakers, Frauds and Geniuses, Hopefuls and Has-Beens, Great Lovers and Sex Symbols* (New York, 1974), pp. 245–46; *New York Times,* February 28, 1958.

427   *"Men cannot be all things..."* Eulogy by Danny Kaye at Harry Cohn Memorial Services, March 2, 1958. Pamphlet.

427   *"He intrigued me..."* Max Youngstein, interviewed by author.

428   *"What am I doing?"* Adolph Zukor interview, Columbia University Oral History Collection, p. 36.

428   *In 1953, two of ten...* Ben B. Seligman, "They Came to Hollywood," *Jewish Frontier,* July 1953, p. 29.

428   *"She had a little closet..."* Eugene Zukor, interviewed by author.

429   Outlive his enemies. *Films in Review,* December 1976.

429   *"There was barely anyone around to remember..."* Quoted in Carey, p. 302.

429   *At ninety-three he still smoked...* Newark Evening News, January 7, 1966; *New York Times,* January 4, 1966.

429   *At ninety-seven he was still spending...* "Hollywood, From A to Zukor," by Aljean Harmetz, *New York Times,* February 4, 1973; *Variety,* January 10, 1973.

429   Attending movies. Eugene Zukor interview, William Wiener Oral History Library, American Jewish Committee.

429   *Paramount held a gala party...* Harmetz; *New York Times,* January 9, 1973; *Variety,* January 10, 1973; *New York Daily News,* January 12, 1973. Rabbi Edgar F. Magnin, "Leader and Personality," interviewed by Malca Chall, Regional Oral History Office, Bancroft Library, University of California, Berkeley, 1975, p. 201.

429   *"He was still going strong at 101."* EZ.

A NOTE ON SOURCES

Original documentation is the lifeblood of history, so one of the obstacles that daunts any film scholar is the dearth of primary materials, especially materials of a personal nature. Novelists, playwrights, and visual artists, political figures, military commanders, and businessmen, all live with an eye cocked toward history. Their lives are records. Not so in film and certainly not so in the American film industry of the twenties, thirties, and forties—the period before the movies became an acceptable subject for serious examination. Self-important but without a sense of their *cultural* importance, the film magnates left nothing but their movies. In the course of my research for this book, I asked a relative of Louis Mayer if any of Mayer's personal correspondence had survived. I learned that Mayer had, in fact, left a considerable personal correspondence, but that his widow and the executor of his estate, a man named Myron Fox, had decided to destroy it. The reason, they said, was that the letters were ungrammatical and full of misspellings. They reflected badly on the man.

Though the story provides a perfect example of the Hollywood Jews' tendency to aestheticize themselves and be aestheticized, even after their deaths, it also provides an example of what a film historian, at least one who attempts to pierce the veil of stereotype, is up against. Carl Laemmle's son-in-law vaguely recalled a cache of correspondence, but he couldn't remember where it had been placed. Adolph Zukor's papers are housed at the Motion Picture Academy, but they are incomplete, largely impersonal, and hardly a window on his life. Harry Warner's papers at the American Jewish Archives in Cincinnati are really a scattershot collection of speeches and clippings with very limited correspondence included.

Wherever possible, I have used original documents: from the American Jewish Archives at the Hebrew Union College in Cincinnati, the Margaret Herrick Library of the Motion Picture Academy in Beverly Hills, the Jewish Community Library in Los Angeles, the New York Public Library of the Performing Arts at Lincoln Center, and the American Jewish Committee Archives in New York. I also consulted or corresponded with literally dozens of libraries, archives, and collections, among them the Franklin D. Roosevelt Presidential Library at Hyde Park, New York; the Herbert Hoover Presidential Library at West Branch, Iowa; the John F. Kennedy Library in Boston; the Upton Sinclair Papers at Indiana University in Bloomington; the Maine Historical Society; the American Jewish Historical Society in Waltham, Massachusetts; the Western Jewish History Center of the Judah L. Manges Memorial Museum in Berkeley, California; the Department of Special Collections at the University of California at Los Angeles; and The Newberry Library in Chicago.

By default, however, I have had to rely primarily on lengthy interviews with individuals who knew the men about whom I was writing. I conducted nearly one hundred of these taped interviews throughout 1981 and 1982, usually at the home of the subject and generally lasting about two hours. Many were longer. Some of these individuals declined to speak on the record. While their comments served as valuable background, providing context and confirmation, I decided in virtually every instance not to use a quotation which I could not attribute. In addition to the interviews I conducted myself, I used dozens of other oral histories at the Columbia University Oral History Collection and the William E. Wiener Oral History Library at the American Jewish Committee.

The vast preponderance of this book is based on these interviews, on original documentation, and on a reasonably thorough—as thorough as one individual without infinite time could accomplish—reading of the relevant periodicals and newspapers of the period, especially *Motion Picture Daily, Motion Picture World, Film Daily,* and *Variety.* I also read completely the testimony given during the three congressional investigations of Hollywood—by the Senate Committee on Interstate Commerce in 1941, the Special Senate Committee Investigating the National Defense Program in 1943, and the House Committee on Un-American Activities in 1947, 1951, 1953, and 1954. Only after that did I consult previously published books, and even then I tried to use reminiscences and autobiographies, falling back on secondary sources only when there were no other sources available. Every source has its biases. I have made my choice fully realizing it necessarily inflicts the vagaries and the glosses of memory.

The bibliography that follows is highly selected. Periodical sources, interviews, oral histories, government documents, pamphlets, and other primary records are cited in the notes. The books and unpublished manuscripts on this list will, I hope, provide an industrious reader with a solid grounding in the world of the Jews, the world of Hollywood, and the point at which the two intersected.

A SELECTED BIBLIOGRAPHY

Arthur, Thomas H. "The Political Career of an Actor: Melvyn Douglas and the New Deal." Ph.D. diss. Bloomington, IN: Indiana University, 1973.

Astor, Mary. *A Life on Film*. New York: Delacorte Press, 1971.

Bacall, Lauren. *Lauren Bacall By Myself*. New York: Alfred A. Knopf, 1978; New York: Ballantine, 1980.

Balaban, Carrie. *Continuous Performance: The Story of A. J. Balaban*. New York: G. P. Putnam's Sons, 1942.

Barna, Yon. *Eisenstein*. Translated by Lise Hunter. Boston: Little, Brown, 1973.

Barrett, Edward L., Jr. *The Tenney Committee*. Ithaca, NY: Cornell University Press, 1951.

Barth, Lewis. "The History of Temple Israel of Hollywood, 1926–1931." Unpublished research paper. Cincinnati, OH: American Jewish Archives, 1959.

Baxter, John. *Hollywood in the Thirties*. New York: Paperback Library, 1968.

Behlmer, Rudy, selected, edited, and annotated by. *Inside Warner Brothers (1935–1951)*. New York: Viking Press, 1985.

Berlin, Isaiah. *Against the Current: Essays in the History of Ideas*. Edited by Harry Hardy. New York: Viking Press, 1979.

Bessie, Alvah. *Inquisition in Eden*. New York: Macmillan Co., 1965.

Blotner, Joseph. *Faulkner: A Biography*, 2 vols. New York: Random House, 1974.

Brady, William. *Showman*. New York: E. P. Dutton, 1937.

Brownlow, Kevin. *The Parade's Gone By...* New York: Alfred A. Knopf; New York: Ballantine, 1968.

Cagney, James. *Cagney By Cagney*. New York: Doubleday & Co., 1976; New York: Pocket Books, 1977.

Cahan, Abraham. *The Rise of David Levinsky*. New York: Harper & Bros., 1917.

Capra, Frank. *The Name Above the Title*. New York: Macmillan Co., 1971.

Carey, Gary. *All the Stars in Heaven: Louis B. Mayer's MGM*. New York: E. P. Dutton, 1981.

Carr, Gary. *The Left Side of Paradise: The Screenwriting of John Howard Lawson*. Ann Arbor, MI: University of Michigan Press, 1984.

Carr, Robert K. *The House Committee on Un-American Activities, 1945–1950*. Ithaca, NY: Cornell University Press, 1952.

Carringer, Robert L., ed. *The Jazz Singer*. Madison, WI: University of Wisconsin Press, 1979.

Caute, David. *The Great Fear: The Anti-Communist Purge Under Truman and Eisenhower*. New York: Simon & Schuster, 1978.

Ceplair, Larry, & Stephen Englund. *The Inquisition in Hollywood: Politics in the Film Community, 1930–1960*. Garden City, NY: Doubleday, 1980.

Clurman, Harold. *The Fervent Years: The Story of the Group Theatre and the Thirties*. New York: Hill & Wang, 1957.

Cogan, Sara G. *The Jews of Los Angeles, 1849–1945: An Annotated Bibliography*. Berkeley, CA: Western Jewish History Center, 1980.

Cogley, John. *Report on Blacklisting*, 2 vols. The Fund for the Republic, 1956.

Cole, Lester. *Hollywood Red: The Autobiography of Lester Cole*. Palo Alto, CA: Ramparts Press, 1981.

Crichton, Kyle. *Total Recoil*. Garden City, NY: Doubleday & Co., 1960.

Crowther, Bosley. *The Lion's Share: The Story of an Entertainment Empire*. New York: E. P. Dutton, 1957.

———. *Hollywood Rajah: The Life and Times of Louis B. Mayer*. New York: Holt, Rinehart, & Winston, 1960.

Dana, Julian. *A. P. Giannini: Giant in the West*. Englewood Cliffs, NJ: Prentice-Hall, 1947.

Davis, Bette. *The Lonely Life*. New York: G. P. Putnam's Sons, 1962.

Davis, Sammy, Jr, with Jane and Burt Boyar. *Yes, I Can*. New York: Farrar, Straus & Giroux, 1965; New York: Pocket Books, 1966.

De Mille, Cecil B. *Autobiography*. Edited by Donald Hayne. Englewood Cliffs, NJ: Prentice-Hall, 1959.

deMille, William. *Hollywood Saga*. New York: E. P. Dutton, 1939.

Dies, Martin. *The Martin Dies Story*. New York: Bookmailer, 1963.

Dietz, Howard. *Dancing in the Dark*. New York: Quadrangle Press, 1974.

Dmytryk, Edward. *It's a Hell of a Life but Not a Bad Living*. New York: Times Books, 1978.

Donner, Frank. *The Un-Americans*. New York: Ballantine, 1961.

Drinkwater, John. *The Life and Adventures of Carl Laemmle*. New York: G. P. Putnam's Sons, 1931.

Dunne, Philip. *Take Two: A Life in Movies and Politics*. New York: McGraw-Hill, 1980.

Eames, John Douglas. *The MGM Story*. New York: Crown, 1979.

Edmonds, I. G. *Big U: Universal in the Silent Days*. South Brunswick, NJ: A. S. Barnes, 1977.

Ephron, Henry. *We Thought We Could Do Anything: The Life of Screenwriters Phoebe and Henry Ephron*. New York: W. W. Norton & Co., 1977.

Erens, Patricia. *The Jew in American Cinema*. Bloomington, IN: Indiana University Press, 1984.

Farber, Stephen, & Marc Green. *Hollywood Dynasties*. New York: G. P. Putnam's Sons, 1984.

Finney, Humphrey S, with Raleigh Burroughs. *Fair Exchange: Recollections of a Life with Horses*. New York: Charles Scribner's Sons, 1974.

Fitzgerald, F. Scott. *The Stories of F. Scott Fitzgerald*. New York: Charles Scribner's Sons, 1951.

———. *The Last Tycoon*. New York: Charles Scribner's Sons, 1941.

———. *The Letters of F. Scott Fitzgerald*. Edited by Andrew Turnbull. New York: Charles Scribner's Sons, 1963.

Freedland, Michael. *The Warner Brothers*. New York: St. Martin's Press, 1983.

French, Philip. *The Movie Moguls*. London: Weidenfeld and Nicholson, 1969.

Fretz, Lewis A. "Upton Sinclair: The Don Quixote of American Reform." Ph.D. diss. Stanford University, 1970.

Friedman, Lester D. *Hollywood's Image of the Jew*. New York: Ungar, 1982.

Friedrich, Otto. *City of Nets: A Portrait of Hollywood in the 1940's*. New York: Harper & Row, 1986.

Frohman, Daniel D. *Daniel Frohman Presents*. New York: Kendall & Sharp, 1935.

Fuchs, Lawrence H. *The Political Behavior of American Jews*. Glencoe, IL: The Free Press, 1956.

Gelberman, William. *Martin Dies*. New York: John Day, 1944.

Gill, Brendan, & Derry Moore. *The Dream Come True: Great Houses of Los Angeles*. New York: Lippincott & Crowell, 1980.

Glazer, Nathan. *The Social Basis of American Communism*. New York: Harcourt, Brace and World, 1961.

Goldmark, Lawrence. "The History of the Wilshire Boulevard Temple, 1900–1920." Unpublished research paper. Cincinnati, OH: American Jewish Archives, 1967.

Goldstein, Malcolm. *The Political Stage: American Drama and Theater in the Great Depression.* New York: Oxford University Press, 1974.

Goodman, Ezra. *The Fifty Year Decline and Fall of Hollywood.* New York: Simon & Schuster, 1961.

Goodman, Walter. *The Committee: The Extraordinary Career of the House Committee on Un-American Activities.* New York: Farrar, Straus & Giroux, 1968.

Grau, Robert. *The Theatre of Science.* New York, 1914; reprint, New York: B. Blom, 1969.

Griffis, Stanton. *Lying in State.* Garden City, NY: Doubleday & Co., 1952.

Hampton, Benjamin. *History of the American Film Industry: From Its Beginnings to 1931.* New York: Covici-Friede, 1931; reprint, New York: Dover Publications, 1970.

Harris, Leon. *Upton Sinclair: American Rebel.* New York: Thomas Y. Crowell Co., 1975.

Hecht, Ben. *Charlie: The Improbable Life and Times of Charles MacArthur.* New York: Harper & Bros., 1957.

———. *A Child of the Century.* New York: Simon & Schuster, 1954.

Hellman, Lillian. *Scoundrel Time.* Boston: Little, Brown, 1976; New York: Bantam, 1977.

Higham, Charles. *Warner Brothers.* New York: Charles Scribner's Sons, 1975.

Higham, Charles, & Joel Greenberg. *Hollywood in the Forties.* New York: Paperback Library, 1968.

Hirschhorn, Clive. *The Universal Story.* New York: Crown, 1983.

———. *The Warner Brothers Story.* New York: Crown, 1979.

Hopper, Hedda, & James Brough. *The Whole Truth and Nothing But.* Garden City, NY: Doubleday & Co., 1963; Pyramid, 1963.

Howe, Irving, with Kenneth Libo. *World of Our Fathers.* New York: Simon & Schuster, 1976.

Howe, Irving, & Lewis Coser. *The American Communist Party: A Critical History (1919–1957).* Boston: Beacon Press, 1957.

Huston, John. *An Open Book.* New York: Alfred A. Knopf, 1980.

Irwin, Will. *The House That Shadows Built.* Garden City, NY: Doubleday & Co., 1928.

Jacobs, Lewis. *The Rise of the American Film.* New York: Teachers College Press, 1939.

Jacobs, Paul. *Is Curly Jewish?* New York: Atheneum, 1965.

Jessel, George. *So Help Me.* New York: Random House, 1943.

Jews in America. The editors of *Fortune* magazine. New York: Random House, 1936.

Jolson, Harry, as told to Alban Emley. *Mistah Jolson.* Hollywood: House-Warven, 1951.

Jowett, Garth. *Film: The Democratic Art.* Boston: Little, Brown, 1976.

Kahn, Gordon. *Hollywood on Trial: The Story of the Ten Who Were Indicted.* New York: Boni & Gaer, 1948.

Kandel, Aben. *Rabbi Burns.* New York: Covici-Friede, 1931.

Kanfer, Stefan. *A Journal of the Plague Years.* New York: Atheneum, 1973.

Kanin, Garson. *Hollywood: Stars and Starlets, Tycoons and Flesh-Peddlers, Moviemakers and Moneymakers, Frauds and Geniuses, Hopefuls and Has-Beens, Great Lovers and Sex Symbols.* New York: Viking Press, 1974.

Kempton, Murray. *Part of Our Time: Some Monuments and Ruins of the Thirties.* New York: Simon & Schuster, 1955.

Kennedy, Joseph P., ed. *The Story of the Films.* Chicago: A. W. Shaw Company, 1927; reprint, New York: Jerome S. Ozer, 1971.

Kiell, Norman, ed. *The Psychodynamics of American Jewish Life.* New York: Twayne Publishers, 1967.

Kobal, John, ed. *People Will Talk.* New York: Alfred A. Knopf, 1986.

Kohner, Frederick. *The Magician of Sunset Boulevard.* Palos Verdes, CA: Morgan Press, 1977.

Korda, Michael. *Charmed Lives: A Family Romance.* New York: Random House, 1979.

Lambert, Gavin. *On Cukor.* New York: G. P. Putnam's Sons, 1972.

Lasky, Jesse, Jr. *Whatever Happened to Hollywood?* New York: Funk & Wagnalls, 1975.

Lasky, Jesse L., with Don Weldon. *I Blow My Own Horn.* Garden City, NY: Doubleday & Company, 1957.

Latham, Aaron. *Crazy Sundays: F. Scott Fitzgerald in Hollywood.* New York: The Viking Press, 1970.

Lawrence, Jerome. *Actor: The Life and Times of Paul Muni.* New York: G. P. Putnam's Sons, 1974.

Lawson, John Howard. *Film: The Creative Process.* New York: Hill & Wang, 1964.

LeRoy, Mervyn, as told to Dick Kleiner. *LeRoy: Take One.* New York: Hawthorn Books, 1974.

Liebman, Arthur. *Jews and the Left: Genesis and Exodus.* New York: Wiley, 1979.

Liebman, Charles S. *The Ambivalent Jew.* Philadelphia: Jewish Publication Society, 1973.

Magnin, Edgar F. "Leader and Personality." Interview conducted by Malca Chall. Berkeley, CA: Regional Oral History Office, Bancroft Library, University of California, 1975.

Mailer, Norman. *The Deer Park.* New York: G. P. Putnam's Sons, 1955; New York: Perigee, 1981.

Maland, Charles J. *Frank Capra.* Boston: Twayne Publishers, 1980.

Marion, Frances. *Off with Their Heads!* New York: The Macmillan Co., 1972.

Marx, Samuel. *Mayer and Thalberg: The Make-Believe Saints.* New York: Random House, 1975; New York: Warner Books, 1980.

McWilliams, Carey. *A Mask for Privilege: Anti-Semitism in America.* Boston: Little, Brown, 1948.

Miller, Merle. *The Judges and the Judged.* Garden City, NY: Doubleday & Co., 1952.

Navasky, Victor. *Naming Names.* New York: Viking Press, 1980.

Newmark, Marco. "Wilshire Boulevard Temple," rev. ed.; unpublished. Cincinnati, OH: American Jewish Archives, 1947.

Ogden, August Raymond. *The Dies Committee.* Washington, D.C.: The Catholic University of America Press, 1945.

Oppenheimer, George. *The View from the 60s.* New York: David McKay, 1966.

Palmer, Edwin O. *The History of Hollywood,* 2 vols. Hollywood: Arthur H. Cawston, 1937.

Parrish, Robert, *Growing Up in Hollywood.* New York: Harcourt, Brace, Jovanovich, 1976.

Perlman, William J., ed. *The Movies on Trial.* New York: The Macmillan Co., 1936.

Powdermaker, Hortense. *Hollywood: The Dream Factory.* Boston: Little, Brown, 1950.

Ramsaye, Terry. *A Million and One Nights.* New York: Simon & Schuster, 1926.

Regan, Michael. *Stars, Moguls, Magnates: The Mansions of Beverly Hills.* Los Angeles: Regan Publishing, 1966.

Rischin, Moses. *The Promised City: New York's Jews, 1870–1914.* Cambridge, MA: Harvard University Press, 1962.

Rivkin, Allen, & Laura Kerr, eds. *Hello, Hollywood!* Garden City, NY: Doubleday & Co., 1962.

Robinson, Edward G., with Leonard Spiegelgass. *All My Yesterdays: An Autobiography.* New York: Hawthorn Books, 1973.

Robinson, Edward G., Jr., with William Dufty. *My Father, My Son.* New York: Frederick Fell, 1958.

Rosenberg, Bernard, & Harry Silverstein, eds. *The Real Tinsel.* New York: Macmillan Co., 1970.

Ross, Lillian. *Picture.* New York: Avon, 1969.

Rosten, Leo C. *Hollywood: The Movie Colony, The Movie Makers.* New York: Harcourt, Brace & Co., 1941.

Saroyan, William. *Sons Come & Go, Mothers Hang in There Forever.* New York: McGraw Hill, 1976.

Schary, Dore. *For Special Occasions.* New York: Random House, 1962.

———. *Heyday.* Boston: Little, Brown, 1979.

Schickel, Richard. *D. W. Griffith: An American Life.* New York: Simon & Schuster, 1984.

Schulberg, Budd. *Moving Pictures: Memories of a Hollywood Prince.* New York: Stein and Day, 1981.

———. *What Makes Sammy Run?* New York: Random House, 1941.

Schwartz, Nancy Lynn. *The Hollywood Writers' Wars.* Completed by Sheila Schwartz. New York: Alfred A. Knopf, 1982; New York: McGraw-Hill, 1983.

Selznick, David. *Memo From: David Selznick.* Selected and edited by Rudy Behlmer. New York: Viking Press, 1972; New York: Avon, 1973.

Selznick, Irene Mayer. *A Private View.* New York: Alfred A. Knopf, 1983.

Sinclair, Upton. *The Autobiography of Upton Sinclair.* New York: Harcourt, Brace and World, 1962.

———. *Upton Sinclair Presents William Fox.* Los Angeles: by the author, 1933.

Sklar, Robert. *Movie-Made America: A Cultural History of American Movies.* New York: Random House. 1975.

Suber, Howard. "The Anti-Communist Blacklist in the Hollywood Motion Picture Industry." Ph.D. diss. UCLA, 1968.

Swanson, Gloria. *Swanson on Swanson: An Autobiography.* New York: Random House, 1980; New York: Pocket Books, 1981.

Talmadge, Margaret L. *The Talmadge Sisters.* Philadelphia: Lippincott, 1924.

Taylor, Dwight. *Joy Ride.* New York: G. P. Putnam's Sons, 1959.

Thomas, Bob. *King Cohn: The Life and Times of Harry Cohn.* New York: G. P. Putnam's Sons, 1967.

———. *Thalberg: Life and Legend.* New York: Doubleday & Co., 1969.

Torrence, Bruce T. *Hollywood: The First Hundred Years.* New York: New York Zoetrope, 1982.

Trumbo, Dalton. *Additional Dialogue: Letters of Dalton Trumbo, 1942–1962.* Edited by Helen Manfull. New York: M. Evans & Co., 1970.

Viertel, Salka. *The Kindness of Strangers.* New York: Holt, Rinehart, & Winston, 1969.

Vorspan, Max, & Lloyd Gartner. *History of the Jews in Los Angeles.* Philadelphia: Jewish Publication Society, 1970.

Wagner, Walter. *You Must Remember This.* New York: G. P. Putnam's Sons, 1975.

Wallis, Hal, with Charles Higham. *Starmaker: The Autobiography of Hal Wallis.* New York: Macmillan Co., 1980.

Warner, Jack L., with Dean Jennings. *My First Hundred Years in Hollywood*. New York: Random House, 1965.

Wellman, William. *A Short Time for Insanity: An Autobiography*. New York: Hawthorn, 1974.

Wesley, David. *Hate Groups and the Un-American Activities Committee*, 2nd ed. (revised). New York: Emergency Civil Liberties Committee, 1962.

Winter, Ella. *And Not to Yield: An Autobiography*. New York: Harcourt, Brace and World, 1963.

Winters, Shelley. *Shelley Also Known as Shirley*. New York: William Morrow & Co., 1980; New York: Ballantine, 1981.

Zierold, Norman. *The Moguls*. New York: Coward, McCann, 1969.

Zukor, Adolph, with Dale Kramer. *The Public Is Never Wrong: The Autobiography of Adolph Zukor*. New York: G. P. Putnam's Sons, 1953.

ACKNOWLEDGMENTS

This book has been the result of many years and many kindnesses. I hope, as no doubt every author does, that those who helped will regard the book itself as a form of appreciation, but that sentiment notwithstanding, I wish to extend my sincere gratitude to my agents, Elaine Markson and Geri Thoma, for their steadfastness and faith; to my editor, Barbara Grossman, for her sound judgment, her standards, her unflagging concern, and, above all, her friendship; to Danny Selznick for his interest, his assistance, and his candor; to Terry McCabe, a former student and current friend, for his poring over congressional and judicial transcripts with me; to Ted Solotaroff for his encouragement and suggestions; to the MacDowell Colony for its environment; to Helen Ritter, Ruth Rauch, and the staff of the American Jewish Committee for their perseverance; to Mary Corliss and Terry Geesken of the Museum of Modern Art Film Stills Archive for helping me select photos; to Don Bowden of Wide World Photos for doing likewise; to Ms. Hava Ben-Zvi of the Jewish Community Library in Los Angeles for the use of her archive; to Mrs. Ruth Nussbaum and Doria Steedman, daughter of Mendel Silberberg, for providing photos from their own collections; to the staffs of the Billy Rose Collection at the New York Public Library of the Performing Arts and the Margaret Herrick Library at the Academy of Motion Picture Arts and Sciences; to Donald B. Schewe, assistant director of the Franklin D. Roosevelt Library, for unearthing records; to my friend Charles Maland, professor of English and film at the University of Tennessee, for letting me use him as an occasional sounding board; to Ann Cahn for her diligence in production-editing; to June Bennett for her thoughtful design; to Kay Riley for production; to Alice Peck for performing numerous chores and providing help; to the interviewees for sharing their experiences and permitting me to use their words; to my parents; and to my wife, Christina.

The final responsibility, as always, remains the author's, but the inspiration and support came from them.

INDEX

ABOUT THE AUTHOR

Neal Gabler was co-host of the national movie preview program "Sneak Previews" on PBS and has appeared on numerous television and radio programs, including "Good Morning America" and "Entertainment Tonight." Mr. Gabler's articles and reviews have been published in the *New York Times, The Nation, American Film, Child* magazine, *Oui, Signature,* and many other magazines. He holds advanced degrees in film and American culture and has taught at the University of Michigan and at Pennsylvania State University. He was born in Chicago and lives with his wife and two daughters in Brooklyn Heights, New York.